GARDENS
ACROSS AMERICA

GARDENS ACROSS AMERICA

The American Horticultural Society's Guide
To American Public Gardens and Arboreta
Volume I: East of the Mississippi

THOMAS S. SPENCER AND JOHN J. RUSSELL

TAYLOR TRADE PUBLISHING
Lanham • *New York* • *Dallas* • *Boulder* • *Toronto* • *Oxford*

Back cover photos (top to bottom): Florida Botanical Gardens, Largo, Florida; Masonic Village
of the Grand Lodge of Free and Accepted Masons of Pennsylvania, Elizabethtown,
Pennsylvania; The Mount, Edith Wharton's Estate and Gardens, Lenox, Massachusetts

Published by Taylor Trade Publishing
An Imprint of the Rowman & Littlefield Publishing Group, Inc.
4501 Forbes Boulevard, Suite 200
Lanham, Maryland 20706

Distributed by National Book Network

Library of Congress Cataloging-in-Publication Data

Spencer, Thomas S., 1946–
    Gardens across America : the American Horticultural Society's guide to American public
gardens and arboreta / Tom Spencer and John Russell.
       p. cm.
    Includes bibliographical references and index.
    ISBN 1-58979-102-9 (pbk. : alk. paper)
    1. Gardens—United States—Guidebooks. 2. Botanical gardens—United States—
Guidebooks. 3. Arboretums—United States—Guidebooks. 4. Parks—United States—
Guidebooks. 5. United States—Guidebooks. I. Russell, John J., 1945– II. Title.
    SB466.U6S64 2005
    712'.5'0973—dc22

                                                                    2005002525

⊗™ The paper used in this publication meets the minimum requirements of
American National Standard for Information Sciences—Permanence of
Paper for Printed Library Materials, ANSI/NISO Z39.48–1992.
Manufactured in the United States of America.

CONTENTS

THE AMERICAN HORTICULTURAL SOCIETY

Founded in 1922, the non-profit American Horticultural Society (AHS) is one of the oldest member-based national gardening organizations in North America. The Society's membership includes more than 35,000 avid gardeners and horticultural professionals as well as numerous regional and national partner organizations. The AHS vision is to make America a nation of gardeners, a land of gardens.

The AHS headquarters at George Washington's River Farm in Alexandria, Virginia, is a national showcase for gardening and horticultural practices. The natural beauty of this 25-acre historic site along the Potomac River is enhanced by a blend of formal and naturalistic gardens, including woodlands, meadows, a water feature, an azalea garden, and award-winning children's gardens.

Through its national educational programs, awards, and publications, AHS connects people to gardening to help raise awareness of earth-friendly gardening practices, introduce children to plants, bring together leaders to address important national issues, and showcase the art and science of horticulture. Among these programs are

- The annual National Children and Youth Garden Symposium
- The National Awards program
- The AHS Plant-Heat Zone map
- The horticultural reference book series
- The SmartGarden™ earth-friendly gardening program
- Online gardening courses through the Horticultural Gardening Institute
- The Travel/Study program to visit inspiring gardens around the world
- The Horticultural Internship program
- The Great American Gardeners lecture and workshop series

Benefits of AHS membership include a subscription to the nationally acclaimed *The American Gardener* magazine, access to a toll-free gardener's hotline, participation in a free member seed exchange, free or discounted admission to many flower shows and botanical gardens, and much more.

If you care about gardening—whether it's your hobby, your passion, or your profession—you should be a member. It's not just what you'll learn that makes AHS membership so rewarding, it's what you share as part of a community of gardeners—past, present, and future. For more information about the American Horticultural Society, call (800) 777-7931, or visit the AHS Web site at www.ahs.org.

The AHS Mission: To open the eyes of all Americans to the vital connection between people and plants; to inspire all Americans to become responsible caretakers of the Earth; to celebrate America's diversity through the arts and sciences of horticulture; and to lead this effort by sharing the Society's unique national resources with all Americans.

FOREWORD

America's public gardens are extraordinary places. Whether small or large, whether framed by spectacular views or nestled in the fabric of the city, whether originally created as a personal garden or designed specifically for public use, each public garden is a unique expression of its region, its mission, its designers, and its caretakers.

We are so fortunate in this country to have a strong tradition of exceptional public gardens. There is no better way to experience the remarkable and varied beauty of this great land of ours—or to understand the creativity and ingenuity of its gardeners—than by visiting our public gardens.

What do public gardens offer? First and foremost, they are well-designed green spaces filled with the beauty and wonder of plants. They also offer what all good gardens offer—inspiration for the spirit and refreshment for the soul. In addition, public gardens display many design ideas that can be taken home to a personal garden or emulated in public parks, school grounds, or other municipal green spaces.

Public gardens are also important places of learning. They not only showcase a wide variety of plants suitable for home gardens in their region, but they offer opportunities to see these plants grown well using environmentally sound practices. If the public garden is also a botanic garden or arboretum, it will have collections of plants identified with informative labels and signs.

In addition, public gardens are often places of research. Public gardens test plants from different regions for adaptability. They conserve endangered plants both in the wild and in the laboratory. They evaluate the environmental effects of modern day culture, from pollution to chemical use to non-renewable resources. This research is critical to guiding the decisions and practices of home gardeners, industry leaders, and policy makers.

Many public gardens also express the character of their communities through special events and seasonal celebrations. These range from displays of spring bulbs, lilacs, and tropical flowers to chili peppers, pumpkins, and poinsettias, and from concerts and ethnic festivals to art exhibits and holiday light displays.

The America Horticultural Society believes strongly that public gardens in America are among our greatest and most underappreciated treasures. To demonstrate our support for public gardens, members of the AHS are entitled to free or discount admission to many public gardens through the AHS "Reciprocal Admissions Program." Gardens that participate in this program are indicated in this guide.

Our public gardens help to connect each one of us, no matter how old or young, to the larger world of plants and gardens. It is my hope that this book will inspire the reader to want to visit each and every one of the gardens listed. In return you will receive the precious gifts these gardens offer—peace, serenity, inspiration, and education—as well as cherished memories of visits shared with family and friends.

Katy Moss Warner
President, American Horticultural Society

EDITORS' INTRODUCTION

We believe that this book, along with its companion volume dealing with facilities west of the Mississippi, fills a need long-felt by the American garden-loving public for a comprehensive guide to public gardens and arboreta that is portable, readable, useful, attractive, and comprehensive. Our book is intended to enable the garden lover to plan more productive and enjoyable excursions by providing essential information on sites and their offerings.

It is unique in its scope, focusing on more than 735 of a total of almost 1,200 gardens and arboreta in both volumes. No other source contains detailed information on so many. We have sought to be as inclusive as possible, the thought being to permit the reader to decide not to visit a facility, which he can do only after being made aware of its existence.

Our book is "current" in that it provides complete and accurate contact data (address, telephone, facsimile, TDDY telephone, and website address) as well as information on hours and days of operation, admission fees, on-site food availability, accessibility for the disabled, parking facilities, and other such topics. It also describes the facility's collection and the facility itself, in many instances illustrating one or the other with a color photograph. These descriptions and illustrations not only help the reader to place the facility as to type, but also, along with facts about annual attendance, size, membership availability, and other factors, permit the reader to make qualitative and quantitative judgments about it. Of course, the sophisticated garden visitor knows that such a process is not without its dangers; there are hundreds of wonderful small and, sadly, sparsely attended gardens in the United States.

Finally, a few words about accuracy are in order. First, space limitations have prevented us from setting forth in as much detail as we would have liked regarding facilities and operations. For example, a garden listed as accessible to the disabled may be only partly so. Second, some attendance figures may include persons attending related facilities, such as zoos. Third, some institutions listed have not responded fully to our repeated requests for information, perhaps in a few cases resulting in publication of dated or misinterpreted information. Fourth, we have chosen to not include specific information on the scheduling and nature of temporary events and exhibits in the belief that such transitory information is most reliably gained by contacting the institution directly as close to the time of a proposed visit as possible. Finally, we have chosen not to include in the main body of the guide display and other gardens operated by commercial facilities, such as nurseries. A list of commercial facilities maintaining display gardens may be found in the Appendix.

We have made every possible effort to verify the information contained in this book, by sending each facility a questionnaire, making follow-up telephone calls, visiting websites, and checking a number of secondary sources. Nevertheless, the data in this book can be no more accurate than that which we have received (we hope no less accurate), and, therefore, when in doubt, the reader should contact the facility directly. We apologize for any inconvenience caused by errors in this book, whatever the source. We also welcome suggestions from those who use this book regarding institutions that should be added or other changes that would make future editions more useful.

John J. Russell and Thomas S. Spencer
Monkton, Maryland
May 15, 2005

HOW TO USE
THIS BOOK

We have approached questions of design and organization in this book from the point of view of the reader; ease of use and accessibility were our paramount concerns. To that end, we have tried to be consistent in format and to avoid unnecessary and annoying abbreviations as much as possible, even though to do so uses more space on the page.

The main body of the guide is organized alphabetically by state and then community. Each state listing is preceded by a map, which indicates the communities in which facilities may be found. In a few appropriate cases, we have included maps of metropolitan areas as well. The number in parentheses after a community indicates the number of facilities listed in this guide in that community; the absence of a number means that there is only one such facility listed. The maps are intended merely to indicate the approximate location of communities with gardens or arboreta, in order to assist the reader in planning excursions, not to function as a detailed road map.

Organizations are arranged alphabetically under the community in which they are located. If there is an initial "The" in an institution's name, it is ignored in determining entry order. Also, "St." is alphabetized as "Saint" and "Ft." as Fort. ("The University of Arizona Campus Arboretum" falls under U, not T. "St. John's University" sorts as "Saint John's University.)"

Within entries, information always occupies the same position. Contact information immediately follows the organization name, followed by data on admission fees, attendance, year established, availability of membership, accessibility to the disabled (a "P" means partial accessibility), and parking arrangements.

Next is information on hours of operation. The data following "Open:" are the regularly scheduled hours of operation. Following "Closed:" are the exceptions to the hours shown in "Open:", such as holidays. Please note that if an institution is regularly closed on Mondays, it will be shown as "Open: Tuesday to Saturday, XX am-XX pm"; Monday would not appear under "Closed:", as it is understood in the "Open:" section.

"Facilities:" and "Activities:" have been designed to allow the reader to skim the listings for a particular piece of information without having to read the entire text. The categories in bold type are in alphabetical order followed by specific information in parentheses when appropriate. For instance, if you wish to know which gardens in a certain city have libraries, simply look under "Facilities:" in each entry. You might find, for example, "Library (12,000 volumes; non-circulating; Tues-Wed, 11am-1pm)." Finally, there is a more detailed description of the facility, designed to give the reader a "feel" for it.

The index, in addition to the formal name of each institution, includes cross references to facilitate finding the entries of organizations for which the proper name is unknown.

We encourage users of this guide to contact us with any suggestions for improving the organization and presentation of data in future editions.

(AHS RAP)

When you see this acronym/symbol after the name of a garden, it means the garden participates in the American Horticultural Society's Reciprocal Admissions Program (RAP). Through this program, American Horticultural Society (AHS) members are eligible for free or discounted admission and many other benefits at the nearly 200 participating gardens and arboreta located throughout North America.

To learn more about the RAP and the many other benefits of membership in the American Horticultural Society, see page 4 or visit the AHS website at www.ahs.org.

ALABAMA

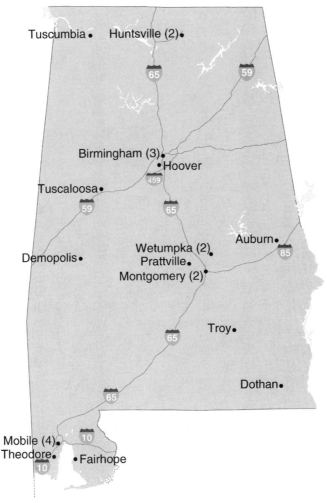

The number in the parentheses following the city name indicates the number of gardens/ arboreta in that municipality. If there is no number, one is understood. For example, in the text three listings would be found under Birmingham and one listing under Troy.

AUBURN UNIVERSITY

AUBURN UNIVERSITY—DONALD E. DAVIS ARBORETUM

241 S. College Street at Garden Drive, Auburn University, AL 36849-5407
Tel: (334) 844-5770; Fax: (334) 844-1645
Internet Address: http://www.auburn.edu
Admission: Free
Established: 1963
Membership: Y
Open: Daily, dawn-dusk.
Facilities: Grounds (13 acres); Pavilion
Activities: Self-Guided Tour (map available)

Located a few hundred yards south of the university's President's mansion, the arboretum specializes in Alabama woody plants. Under the direction of the College of Sciences and Mathematics, it contains more than 250 species of trees, shrubs, and vines. Also of possible interest are the gardens at the nearby Jule Collins Smith Museum of Fine Art.

BIRMINGHAM

BIRMINGHAM BOTANICAL GARDENS (AHS RAP)

2612 Lane Park Road, N.E., Birmingham, AL 35223
Tel: (205) 414-3950; Fax: (205) 414-3906
Internet Address: http://www.bbgardens.org/
Admission: Free
Attendance: 200,000
Established: 1962
Membership: Y
Wheelchair Accessible: P
Parking: Limited parking
Open: Daily, sunrise-sunset.
Facilities: Auditorium (400 seats); Food Services Café de France (Mon-Sat, 11am-2pm; 871-1000); Gardens (bog, fern, herb, Japanese, rhododendron, rose, vegetable, wildflower, Alabama woodland); Greenhouse (largest clear span glass greenhouse in the Southeast); Grounds (67 acres); Library (3,500 volumes; Mon-Fri, 9am-4pm); Shop Gatehouse Gift Shop (Mon-Sat, 10am-4pm, 414-3970); Temporary Exhibition Space.

Activities: Concerts; Docent Program; Education Programs (students, adults, and children); Guided Tours (groups, book 2 weeks in advance; Sunday Strolls (Sun, 3-4pm; free); Lectures; Plant Sales.

The site contains many specialty gardens including Japanese, wildflower, Alabama woodlands, rhododendron, rose, fern, herb, bog, and *Southern Living* gardens. The Dunn Formal Rose Garden is an accredited All-America Rose Selections display garden. This major American botanical garden features a twelve-month blooming schedule, that is significantly different each month.

BIRMINGHAM-SOUTHERN COLLEGE—SOUTHERN ENVIRONMENTAL CENTER—ECOSCAPE (SEC)

900 Arkadelphia Road, Birmingham, AL 35254
Tel: (205) 226-4493; Fax: (205) 226-3046
Internet Address: http://www.bsc.edu/sec
Admission: Fee, per activity: adult $1.00; child $1.00; senior $1.00.
Attendance: 18,000
Established: 1996
Membership: Y
Wheelchair Accessible: Y
Parking: Cars and busses welcome
Open: Monday to Friday, 9am-5pm; Saturday to Sunday, 1pm-5pm, by appointment only.
Best Time(s) of Year to Visit: Spring to Fall.
Facilities: Demonstration Garden (native wildflowers, medicinal plants and herbs, wetland); Gazebo; Sculpture Garden.
Activities: Guided Tours museum and gardens (reserve in advance).

A demonstration garden and outdoor environmental classroom, EcoScape teaches environmentally-friendly design and organic gardening techniques emphasizing the use of native and drought-tolerant plants. The facility has been nationally recognized for its innovative approach to environmental education.

RUFFNER MOUNTAIN NATURE CENTER

1214 81st Street South, Birmingham, AL 35206-4599
Tel: (205) 833-8264; Fax: (205) 836-3960
Internet Address: http://www.ruffnermountain.org
Admission: Fee: $2.00, family: $5.00
Attendance: 30,000
Established: 1977
Membership: Y
Wheelchair Accessible: N
Parking: Free on site
Open: Tuesday to Saturday, 9am-5pm; Sunday, 1pm-5pm.
Best Time(s) of Year to Visit: Spring (wildflowers), Fall (foliage)
Facilities: Garden (wildflower); Grounds Center (1,011 acres), Garden (1 acre); Picnic Area; Trails (11 miles); Visitor Center
Activities: Education Programs

Situated in the midst of Alabama's largest city, the nature center protects one of the largest remaining forests in the area. Among its offerings are a wildflower garden and a fern glade. The center is managed by the Ruffner Mountain Nature Coalition, Inc., a private nonprofit organization.

DEMOPOLIS

GAINESWOOD GARDENS

805 S. Cedar Avenue Demopolis, AL 36732
Tel: (334) 289-0270
Internet Address: http://www.preserveala.org
Admission: Fee: adult $5.00, child $3.00, student $4.00, senior $4.00.
Attendance: 3,500
Membership: Y
Wheelchair Accessible: P
Parking: Parking outside the fenced grounds
Open: Tuesday to Saturday, 9am-4pm
Closed: State Holidays
Best Time(s) of Year to Visit: Spring to Fall
Facilities: Architecture (Greek Revival mansion, 1843-1861); Gardens (north and south parterres; balustraded).

Considered one of America's finest examples of Greek Revival architecture, Gaineswood features original furnishings, domed ceilings, fluted columns, and ornate friezes. Operated by the Alabama Historical Commission, the site is listed on the National Register of Historic Places and is designated a National Historic Landmark. The English-influenced picturesque lawn is juxtaposed with formal balustraded gardens bordering the mansion. The landscape restoration is based on an 1860 steel engraving and family correspondence.

DOTHAN

DOTHAN AREA BOTANICAL GARDENS (AHS RAP)

5130 Headland Avenue (Houston Co. Road 105, off Route 431 North, near Landmark Park), Dothan, AL 36302
Tel: (334) 793-3224; Fax: (334) 793-5275
Internet Address: http://www.dabg.com/
Admission: Free.
Established: 1990
Membership: Y
Open: 7am-7pm
Facilities: Gardens (demonstration, display, herb, patio, rose, vegetable, xeriscape); Grounds (50 acres)
Activities: Guided Tours (by appointment)

The Dothan Area Botanical Gardens seek to preserve the spirit and beauty of the early southern garden in an environment that presents native plants in an attractive balance with traditional botanical garden elements. Completed gardens include a rose garden containing 400 different varieties of roses, a formal herb garden, and a variety of demonstration gardens.

FAIRHOPE

FAIRHOPE CITY ROSE GARDEN

1 Fairhope Avenue, Fairhope, AL 36532
Tel: (251) 928-2136
Internet Address: http://www.cofairhopw.com
Established: 1985
Open: Daily
Best Time(s) of Year to Visit: April to September

The garden is an All-America Rose Selections accredited display garden, located on Mobile Bay.

HOOVER

ALDRIDGE GARDENS (AHS RAP)

3530 Lorna Road at Rocky Ridge Ranch Road, Hoover, AL 35216
Tel: (205) 682-8019; Fax: (205) 682-8085
Internet Address: http://www.aldridgegardens.com
Admission: Free
Established: 1997
Membership: Y
Wheelchair Accessible: Y
Parking: Large lot in front of site
Open: Monday to Saturday, 8am-5pm; Sunday, 11am-5pm
Closed: New Year's Day, Thanksgiving Day, Christmas Day
Facilities: Gardens (herb, native plant, perennial, shade, wildflower); Grounds (30 acres); Shop; Special Collections (hydrangea)
Activities: Education Programs; Events Fall Festival (Oct; Holiday Festival (Dec), Hydrangea Festival (early June); Lectures; Plant Sales

Aldridge Gardens features many varieties of hydrangeas and other native plants and trees. The 30-acre botanical garden includes a seven-acre lake with a walking trail and a three-acre wildflower garden, as well as annual, perennial and herb gardens. The signature flower of Aldridge Gardens is the snowflake hydrangea, developed and propagated by noted nurseryman Eddie Aldridge. Aldridge owned the acreage before he and his wife Kay conveyed it to the city of Hoover in the mid-1990s.

HUNTSVILLE

BURRITT ON THE MOUNTAIN—A LIVING MUSEUM

3101 Burritt Drive, Monte Sano Mountain, Huntsville, AL 35801-1142
Tel: (256) 536-2882; Fax: (256) 532-1784; TDDY: (256) 532-1550
Internet Address: http://www.burritmuseum.com
Admission: Fee: adult $5.00, child(<2) free, child(2-12) $3.00, student $4.00, senior $4.00.

Attendance: 100,000
Established: 1955
Membership: Y
Wheelchair Accessible: Y
Parking: Free on-site parking
Open: April to October, Tuesday to Saturday, 9am-7pm; Sunday, noon-5pm
November to March, Tuesday to Saturday, 10am-4pm; Sunday, noon-4pm
Facilities: Architecture (mansion listed on National Register; period rooms); Grounds
(167 acres); Picnic Area; Trails; Visitor Center
Activities: Self-Guided Tours

Perched on a mountaintop with a breathtaking view of Huntsville and the Tennessee Valley, the site includes the 1936 Burritt mansion, the unusual retirement home of Dr. William Henry Burritt, with old-fashioned southern landscaping. The slopes around the mountaintop site consist of a 167-acre nature preserve traversed by a system of trails that bring hikers by a wide selection of southern wildflowers. The museum has developed a living history program centered around five nineteenth-century farmsteads complete with heirloom vegetable gardens and croplands. Historic breeds of farm animals demonstrate to visitors the important roles they played on southern farms more than one hundred years ago.

HUNTSVILLE/MADISON COUNTY BOTANICAL GARDEN (AHS RAP)

4747 Bob Wallace Avenue, Huntsville, AL 35805
Tel: (256) 830-4447; Fax: (256) 830-5314
Internet Address: http://www.hsvbg.org
Admission: Fee: adult $8.00, child $3.00, senior $6.00
Open: Memorial Day to Labor Day, Monday to Saturday, 9am-8pm; Sunday, 1pm-5pm
Other days, Monday to Saturday, 9am-5pm; Sunday, 1pm-5pm
Closed: New Year's Day, Thanksgiving Day, Christmas Day
Facilities: Gardens (aquatic, day lily, herb, native plant, rose)
Grounds (112 acres)
Activities: Guided Tours

The facility centers on an aquatic garden, but also features displays of herbs, roses, bulbs, native plants, ferns, daylilies, garden pavilions and architecture, as well as a "Lunar Greenhouse."

MOBILE

BATTLESHIP MEMORIAL PARK—ROSE GARDEN

Battleship Parkway (Route 90), Mobile, AL 36601-0065
Tel: (251) 433-2703; Fax: (251) 433-2777
Internet Address: http://www.ussalabama.com
Admission: Fee: adult $10.00, child(<6) free, child(6-11) $5.00,
senior $9.00
Attendance: 301,000
Established: 1965
Membership: N

Wheelchair Accessible: P
Parking: 500 parking spaces
Open: October to March, Daily, 8am-4pm
April to September, Daily, 8am-6pm
Closed: Christmas Day
Facilities: Gardens (rose); Grounds; Shop (432-0261)

In addition to the battleship *Alabama*, the submarine *Drum*, vintage warplanes, and other war-related memorabilia, the park contains an All-America Rose Selections accredited garden. Park operations are overseen by the USS Alabama Battleship Commission, an independent agency of the State of Alabama.

CONDE-CHARLOTTE MUSEUM HOUSE—GARDEN

104 Theatre Street, Mobile, AL 36602-3010
Tel: (251) 432-4722
Internet Address: http://www.angelfire.com/al2/CondeCharlotte
Admission: Fee: adult $5.00, child (<6) free, child (6-18) $2.00
Attendance: 2,000
Established: 1958
Membership: N
Wheelchair Accessible: N
Parking: On street; parking lot 1 block
Open: Tuesday to Saturday, 10am-4pm
Best Time(s) of Year to Visit: Spring to early Summer (peak bloom)
Facilities: Architecture (Mansion built 1822-1824); Garden (walled Spanish)
Activities: Guided Tours (group 10+, $2.00/person)

The museum house, built of brick by the French, probably pre-dates adjacent Fort Conde, which was constructed in 1720. Originally serving as a powder magazine, it was modified to become the city's first courthouse/city jail and was later converted to a residence in the 1850s. Its rooms are furnished with antiques to reflect the periods of Mobile's history under five flags: French (1702-1763), British (1763-1780), Spanish (1780-1813), American (1813-1861), the Confederacy (1861-1865), and again American. The museum is complemented by a walled Spanish garden of late eighteenth-century design. Listed on the National Register of Historic Places, the site is owned and maintained by the National Society of Colonial Dames of the State of Alabama.

MOBILE BOTANICAL GARDENS—SOUTH ALABAMA BOTANICAL AND HORTICULTURAL SOCIETY (MBG) (AHS RAP)

5151 Museum Drive, Langan Park, Mobile, AL 36689
Tel: (334) 342-0555; Fax: (334) 342-3149
Internet Address: http://www.mobilebotanicalgardens.org
Admission: Free
Established: 1970
Membership: Y
Wheelchair Accessible: P
Parking: On site, handicapped spaces available
Open: dawn-dusk.
Facilities: Gardens (camellia grove, fern glade, herb, long leaf pine forest, magnolia grove, sensory); Grounds (100 acres); Picnic Area

Activities: Guided Tours (on request); Plant Sales: MBG Market Place (Apr-Jun, Sat, 9am-11am); Plantasia (mid-Oct)

Located in the Spring Hill Community, the gardens feature Alabama and Gulf Coast plants, including native as well as exotic, azaleas, camellias, hollies, magnolias, and ferns.

RICHARDS DAR HOUSE MUSEUM

256 N. Joachim Street Mobile, AL 36603
Tel: (334) 208-7320
Internet Address: http://www.gulftel.com/asdar/richards.htm
Admission: Free
Attendance: 10,000
Membership: N
Parking: On-street parking
Open: Monday to Friday, 11am-3:30pm; Saturday, 10am-4pm;
Sunday, 1pm-4pm
Best Time(s) of Year to Visit: Spring, Fall to Christmas
Facilities: Architecture (Italianate townhouse (1860); fee for tour); Picnic Area; Shop; Walled Garden
Activities: Guided Tours (with teas and cookies, reserve in advance)

A period house-museum located in historic de Tonti Square, the Richards DAR House is listed on the National Register of Historic Places. The 1860 residence, one of Mobile's finest surviving examples of the Italianate style, features a cast iron façade depicting the four seasons and contains pre-1870 furnishings. To the north of the house a formal garden displays wide beds of camellias, azaleas, sweet olive, magnolias, and seasonal plantings. There are award-winning Christmas decorations in December.

MONTGOMERY

OLD ALABAMA TOWN

301 Columbus, Montgomery, AL 36104
Tel: (334) 240-4450; Fax: (334) 404-4519
Internet Address: http://www.OldAlabamaTown.com
Admission: Fee: adult $7.00, child $3.00
Attendance: 60,000
Established: 1969
Membership: Y
Wheelchair Accessible: P
Parking: Adjacent to site
Open: Monday to Saturday, 9am-3pm.
Closed: New Year's Eve to New Year's Day, Thanksgiving Day, Christmas Eve to Christmas Day
Best Time(s) of Year to Visit: Spring to Fall
Facilities: Architecture (50 restored historic structures); Gardens (cotton field, dye, rose, herb, vegetable); Shop
Activities: Plant Sales Herb Day (May); Self-Guided Tours

Stretching along six blocks in the heart of historic downtown Montgomery, Old Alabama Town is a historic district portraying life in central Alabama between 1820 and 1920.

The site features a variety of appropriately historical plantings. Landmarks Foundation of Montgomery, a non-profit corporation, develops and administers Old Alabama Town.

WYNTON M. BLOUNT CULTURAL PARK— SHAKESPEARE GARDENS

6055 Vaughn Road, Montgomery, AL 36116
Tel: (334) 274-0062; Fax: (334) 274-8916
Internet Address: http://www.blountculturalpark.org
Admission: Free
Established: 1999
Open: Daily, 9am-9pm
Closed: during scheduled events
Facilities: Gardens (Shakespeare, landscape design by Edwina von Gal and Company of New York); Grounds Blount Park (300 acres), Shakespeare Garden (1.3 acres); Picnic Areas
Activities: Guided Tours Gardens (groups, reserve in advance, 334-274-0062 Ext. 1)

The gardens feature plants and flowers mentioned in Shakespeare's poems and plays, including perennial herbs, annual flowers, willow arbors, shade trees, and garden shrubs, as well as a thatched-roof Pavilion and a six-tiered, 325-seat amphitheater. Intensely planted, the gardens contain 8,000 narcissus bulbs (additional bulbs include Asiatic lilies and chives), 4,000 Catlin sedges, 4,790 yellow archangels, 570 rosemary and lavender plants, a canopy of 55 trees, more than 200 ornamental shrubs, and 1,285 moneyworts used as ground cover. In addition to the Shakespeare Gardens, Blount Cultural Park is home to the Montgomery Museum of Fine Arts and the Carolyn Blount Theatre. Additional, smaller garden sites scattered along walking trails to be located throughout the park will eventually be made available to Montgomery-area garden clubs that wish to participate in the park's development. Please note: The Shakespeare Gardens serve as a venue for a variety of events from non-amplified music concerts, lectures, and theatrical productions to private activities such as weddings and receptions During scheduled events, the gardens will be closed to the public. A free brochure, providing directions and information, is available.

PRATTVILLE

HISTORIC PRATTVILLE AND GARDENS

Old Pratt Village, First Street, Prattville, AL 36068
Tel: (334) 361-0961
Internet Address: http://www.visithistoricprattville.com/
Admission: Free
Open: Daily
Facilities: Gardens (annual, butterfly/hummingbird, herb, heritage, native plant, orchard, perennial)

Located on First Street in Prattville, Old Prattvillage is a collection of structures from the 1800s. Some are standing in their original locations and others have been relocated to the site. Developed by the Autauga County Master Gardeners Association, the cottage-style gardens surrounding a nineteenth-century chapel include a butterfly and hummingbird walk as well as herb, heritage, perennial, annual, native plant, and fruit gardens.

THEODORE

BELLINGRATH GARDENS AND HOME

12401 Bellingrath Gardens Road, Theodore, AL 36582
Tel: (334) 973-2217; Fax: (334) 973-0540
Internet Address: http://www.bellingrath.org
Admission: Fee, gardens only: adult $9.00, child $5.25. Reduced fees for groups
Attendance: 175,000
Established: 1932
Open: New Year's Day to Thanksgiving Day, Daily, 8am-5pm
Day after Thanksgiving Day to New Year's Eve, Daily, 8am-9pm
Closed: Christmas Day
Best Time(s) of Year to Visit: Spring (azaleas)
Facilities: Architecture (1935 design by architect George B. Rogers); Conservatory;
Food Services Restaurant; Gallery; Gardens (azalea, oriental, rose); Grounds (65
acres); Museum Store
Activities: Films; Guided Tours (of home); Riverboat Cruise

The gardens contain over 250,000 azaleas, 90,000 bulbs, 60,000 chrysanthemums,
10,000 waterlilies, 4,000 camellias, and 2,500 roses. They also include a rose garden,
bridal garden, mermaid pool, oriental garden, and conservatory. There are significant varieties of blooming plants all year long.

TROY

TROY STATE UNIVERSITY ARBORETUM

Pell Avenue (off George Wallace Drive, east of Park Street), Troy, AL 36082
Tel: (334) 670-3938
Internet Address: http://www.troyst.edu/artsandsciences/biologicalsciences/
arboretum.htm
Admission: Free
Established: 1988
Membership: N
Wheelchair Accessible: N
Parking: Grass parking area on site
Open: Daily, sunrise-sunset
Facilities: Arboretum; Greenhouse (Mon-Fri, 8am-5pm); Grounds (75 acres);
Herbarium (14,000 specimens); Special Collections (butterfly, medicinal/herb, native
plant); Trails (5 miles)
Activities: Guided Tours (schedule in advance: (205) 670-3626 or (205) 670-3776);
Self-Guided Tours (2, ½-mile nature trails)

Located adjacent to the main campus, Troy State's Arboretum displays over 300 different species of trees, as well as many shrubs, vines, ferns, and wildflowers representative of
the flora of the Wiregrass region of Southeast Alabama in situations that mimic the natural conditions under which the species would occur. The Dr. Henry Bridges Greenhouse
houses a large collection of orchids and other tropical vegetation including some rare
South African plants. The arboretum also operates the eighteen-acre Pocosin Nature Preserve, located approximately six miles due east of the main campus.

TUSCALOOSA

UNIVERSITY OF ALABAMA AT TUSCALOOSA—ARBORETUM

4400 Arboretum Way (off Pelham-Loop Road), Tuscaloosa, AL 35487
Tel: (888) 349-1815; Fax: (205) 348-1786
Internet Address: http://bama.ua.edu/~arbor/
Admission: Free
Established: 1958
Membership: Y
Open: Daily, 8am-5pm
Closed: New Year's Day, Thanksgiving Day, Christmas Day
Facilities: Arboretum; Classrooms; Gardens (herb, native plant, wildflower);
Greenhouses; Grounds (60 acres); Picnic Area
Activities: Guided Tours (by reservation); Lectures; Plant Sales (2nd weekend in April)

Emphasizing botanical education, the arboretum specializes in native tree and plants. Settings include woodland and ornamental areas, a wildflower garden, and an experimental organic garden featuring herbs and medicinal plants.

TUSCUMBIA

IVY GREEN: BIRTHPLACE OF HELEN KELLER—GROUNDS

300 W. North Commons (2 miles off Routes 72 & 43), Tuscumbia, AL 35674
Tel: (256) 383-4066; Fax: (256) 383-4068
Internet Address: http://www.helenkellerbirthplace.org/
Admission: Fee: adult $6.00, child $2.00, student $2.00, senior $5.00
Established: 1954
Parking: Parking both inside and outside gates
Open: Monday to Saturday, 8:30am-4pm; Sunday, 1pm-4pm
Closed: Legal Holidays
Facilities: Architecture (Virginia cottage, ca. 1820); Gardens (herb); Grounds (640 acres); Shop
Activities: Events Helen Keller Festival (late June); Guided Tours (last tour 3:45pm, reserve in advance); Performances, The Miracle Worker (June—mid-July, weekends)

The birthplace of Helen Keller, Ivy Green Plantation is listed on the National Register of Historic Places. The entire estate is nestled under a cooling canopy of mature English boxwood, magnolia, mimosa, and other trees, accented by roses, honeysuckle, smilax, and an abundance of English ivy. The home and museum room are decorated with much of the original furniture of the Keller family.

WETUMPKA

JASMINE HILL GARDEN AND OUTDOOR MUSEUM

1500 S. Jasmine Hill Road, Wetumpka, AL 36106
Tel: (334) 567-6463; Fax: (334) 263-5715

Internet Address: http://www.jasminehill.org
Admission: Fee: adult $6.00, child (>4) $3.00, senior $5.50
Parking: Large parking lot with handicapped spaces
Open: Tuesday to Sunday, 9am-5pm
Monday holidays, 9am-5pm
Closed: New Year's Day, Thanksgiving Day, Christmas Day
Best Time(s) of Year to Visit: Spring
Facilities: Gardens/Collections (azaleas, camellias, cherry trees); Grounds (17 acres);
Sculpture Gardens

Gardens features traditional southern plants set against Classical art and fountains.

WILLIAM BARTRAM ARBORETUM

Fort Toulouse/Jackson Park, 2521 W. Fort Toulouse Road (off U.S. 231),
Wetumpka, AL 36093
Tel: (334) 567-3002; Fax: (334) 514-6625
Internet Address: http://www.preserveala.org
Admission: Fee: adult $5.00, child (<6) free
Attendance: 110,000
Membership: N
Wheelchair Accessible: P
Parking: Paved lot on site
Open: April to October, Daily, 6am-8pm
November to May, Daily, 8am-7pm
Best Time(s) of Year to Visit: Spring to Fall
Facilities: Arboretum; Picnic Area (in main park across from trailhead); Visitor Center
(daily, 8am-5pm)
Activities: Guided Tours (groups, schedule in advance)

This historical site contains a Native American mound, reconstructions of Forts
Toulouse and Jackson, and a restored tidewater cottage (circa 1825-30), as well as the
William Bartram Arboretum. Begun in cooperation with the Garden Club of Alabama, the
arboretum is named in honor of eighteenth-century naturalist and friend of Benjamin
Franklin, William Bartram, who visited the site in 1775. It consists a gravel trail that leads
through wildflower fields, bogs, and forests from the visitor's center to the fort and then
down to a river overlook. Shrubs and flowers are identified and picturesque ravine bridges
and rest/study glades are situated at intervals.

CONNECTICUT

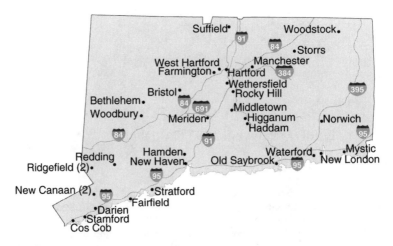

The number in the parentheses following the city name indicates the number of gardens/
arboreta in that municipality. If there is no number, one is understood. For example, in the
text two listings would be found under Ridgefield and one listing under Stamford.

BETHLEHEM

BELLAMY-FERRIDAY HOUSE AND GARDEN

9 Main Street, Bethlehem, CT 06751
Tel: (860) 266-7596
Internet Address: http://www.hartnet.org/als/alsprop.html
Admission: Fee (House & Grounds Tour): adult $5.00, child (<18) $2.00. Fee
(Grounds Self-Guided Tour): $3.00
Open: May to October, Wednesday, 11am-4pm; Friday to Sunday, 11am-4pm
Facilities: Architecture (eighteenth-century residence with additions); Garden (formal,
1915); Grounds (9 acres); Shop
Activities: Garden Walks (4th Sun in month, 3pm); Guided Tours; Plant Sales

After beginning life as a farm and spiritual sanctuary in 1744, the Bellamy-Ferriday estate evolved over two centuries into a gracious manse with manicured gardens. The house
was built by the Rev. Joseph Bellamy and was part of a working farm. In 1912, Henry Mc-
Keen Ferriday of New York acquired it as a summer home for his family, and his wife and
daughter gradually replaced farm fields with sweeping lawns, wood lots, and gardens. The
formal gardens include large collections of lilacs, old roses, peonies, perennials, herbaceous plants, and specimen trees and shrubs. The property was given to the Antiquarian
and Landmarks Society in 1990 by his daughter Miss Caroline Ferriday.

BRISTOL

THE AMERICAN CLOCK &
WATCH MUSEUM—GARDEN

100 Maple Street, Bristol, CT 06010
Tel: (860) 583-6070; Fax: (860) 583-1862
Internet Address: http://www.clockmuseum.org
Admission: Fee: adult $5.00, child (8-15) $2.00, senior $4.00.
Attendance: 5,800
Established: 1952
Membership: Y
Wheelchair Accessible: P
Parking: On site
Open: April to November, Daily, 10am-5pm
Closed: Easter, Thanksgiving Day
Best Time(s) of Year to Visit: May to September

Facilities: Architecture (residence, 1801); Garden (period, early American)
Activities: Education Programs

The museum, displaying over 1,500 clocks and watches, also offers an authentic early American garden with sundial and period flowers and herbs, tended by the Bristol Garden Club.

COS COB

MONTGOMERY PINETUM AND GARDEN EDUCATION CENTER OF GREENWICH

Bible Street, Cos Cob, CT 06807
Tel: (203) 869-9242; Fax: (203) 869-0619
Internet Address: http://www.gecgreenwich.org/
Established: 1957
Membership: Y
Wheelchair Accessible: P
Open: September to May, Weekdays, 9am-3:30pm; Saturday,
10am-3pm; Saturday, 10am-3pm
Facilities: Greenhouse; Shop (2); Trails
Activities: Education Programs; Plant Sales

A non-profit organization dedicated to developing interest and involvement in horticulture, GEC is located within the Montgomery Pinetum, a registered historic site and public park in the Cos Cob section of Greenwich. It is surrounded by a lush forest of 102 acres of wooded trails, majestic trees, and a broad variety of unusual specimen plantings and vibrant wildflowers. The Pinetum was formerly the estate of Colonel Robert Montgomery, a successful businessman and avid horticulturist. Colonel Montgomery collected rare conifers on his estate and in 1947 donated 200 specimen trees to the New York Botanical Garden, which transplanted them from the Montgomery Pinetum to the NYBG. He also founded the Fairchild Tropical Garden in Coral Gables, Florida.

DARIEN

BATES-SCOFIELD HOUSE GARDEN

45 Old Kings Highway North, Darien, CT 06820
Tel: (203) 655-9233; Fax: (203) 656-3892
Internet Address: http://www.historicaldarien.org
Admission: Fee (House Tour)
Attendance: 200
Established: 1953
Membership: Y
Wheelchair Accessible: N
Parking: Free on site
Open: Tuesday, 9am-2pm; Wednesday to Thursday, 9am-4pm;
Friday, 9am-2pm
Facilities: Architecture (New England saltbox house, ca. 736); Gardens (herb)
Activities: Guided Tours House (Wed & Thurs, 2pm-4pm; groups, reserve in advance)

The Darien Historical Society operates the Bates-Scofield Homestead, an eighteenth century house-museum with garden, resource library, and exhibition art galleries. The garden adjacent to the house, planted and maintained by the Garden Club of Darien, contains over 30 varieties of culinary, medicinal, and strewing herbs known to have been used in Connecticut in the eighteenth century and more than twenty varieties of historical roses.

FAIRFIELD

OGDEN HOUSE MUSEUM AND GARDEN

1520 Bronson Road, Fairfield, CT 06430
Tel: (203) 255-2716
Admission: Fee: adult $2.00, child $1.00
Open: mid-May to mid-October, 1pm-4pm
Best Time(s) of Year to Visit: June to October
Facilities: Architecture (eighteenth-century saltbox farmhouse); Gardens (herb, kitchen, wildflower walk)
Activities: Fall Festival (late September); Guided Tours

An eighteenth-century style kitchen garden behind the house is laid out symmetrically with raised beds. The garden features vegetables and herbs typical of those used at the time. The garden contains over 100 medicinal and culinary plants used during the eighteenth century. A bridge across the brook leads to a trail planted with native Connecticut wildflowers and shrubs. Ogden House is listed on the National Register of Historic Places.

FARMINGTON

HILL-STEAD MUSEUM

35 Mountain Road, Farmington, CT 06032
Tel: (860) 677-4787; Fax: (860) 677-0174
Internet Address: http://www.hillstead.org/
Admission: Fee: adult $9.00, child (<6) free, child (6-12) $4.00, student $7.00, senior $8.00.
Attendance: 35,000
Established: 1946
Membership: Y
Wheelchair Accessible: P
Parking: Parking available
Open: May to October, Tuesday to Sunday, 10am-5pm
November to April, Tuesday to Sunday, 11am-4pm
Closed: New Year's Day, Independence Day, Thanksgiving Day, Christmas Day
Facilities: Architecture (1901 building by Theodate Pope with McKim, Mead & White); Garden (sunken, ca. 1920 design by Beatrix Farrand); Grounds (152 acres); Library; Shop (prints, note cards, books; 677-2846); Walking Trails
Activities: Concerts; Guided Tours (groups of 10+ reserve in advance; Garden (May-Oct); Readings: Sunken Garden Poetry Festival (Jun-Aug)

A National Historic Landmark, Hill-Stead Museum is noted for its 33,000 square-foot house filled with art and antiques. Pioneering female architect Theodate Pope Riddle designed the Colonial Revival-style house in 1901 to showcase the collection of Impressionist paintings amassed by her father, Cleveland industrialist Alfred A. Pope. Mature trees, seasonal gardens, over three miles of stone walls and woodland trails accent the grounds. A centerpiece of the property is the sunken garden designed by landscape architect Beatrix Jones Farrand and today the site of a summer-long poetry festival. The octagonal garden, containing over ninety varieties of perennials, is entirely bordered by shrub yews with beds bounded by walking paths tapering toward the center.

HADDAM

WILHELMINA ANN ARNOLD BARNHART MEMORIAL GARDEN (THANKFUL ARNOLD HOUSE)

Hayden Hill Road & Walkley Hill Road, Haddam, CT 06438
Tel: (203) 345-2400
Internet Address: http://www.haddamhistory.org/
Admission: Free (garden); Fee (house tour): $4.00
Established: 1970
Parking: Free on site
Open: Daily, dawn to dusk (Garden)
Facilities: Architecture Thankful Arnold House (restored 1794 home); Gardens (1/2 acre; herbs, vegetables, and flowers)
Activities: Education Programs; Guided Tours

Garden design and plants reflect the period 1790-1820. There are fifty-seven varieties of herbs in the garden.

HAMDEN

CITY OF NEW HAVEN—PARDEE ROSE GARDEN

East Rock Park, 180 Park Road, Hamden, CT 06514
Tel: (203) 946-8142
Established: 1923
Parking: Free on street
Open: Daily, dawn-dusk
Best Time(s) of Year to Visit: June to July
Facilities: Gardens (herb, rose); Greenhouse; Grounds (2 acres); Special Collections (dogwood, crab apple, azalea, spring bulbs)
Activities: Guided Tours

With over fifty varieties of roses as well as annuals, perennials, and herbs, the Pardee Rose Garden is an All-America Rose Selections accredited display garden. In addition to the Garden, East Rock Park, New Haven's oldest park, includes walking trails and a road to the summit and Soldiers & Sailors Monument; the Giant Steps up the cliff; ranger station (946-6086) and playground at College Woods; and athletic fields.

HARTFORD

BUTLER-MCCOOK HOUSE AND GARDENS

396 Main Street, Hartford, CT 06103-9857
Tel: (860) 522-1806; Fax: (860) 249-4907
Internet Address: http://www.hartnet.org/als/alsprop.html
Admission: Fee: adult $5.00, child $2.00
Attendance: 1,000
Established: 1971
Wheelchair Accessible: P
Parking: Lot in back of museum
Open: Monday to Friday, 9am-5pm; Sunday, noon-4pm; 1st Thursday in month,
10am-8pm
Best Time(s) of Year to Visit: Summer
Facilities: Architecture (1782 homestead); Garden (nineteenth-century garden design
by Jacob Weidenmann); Grounds (one acre)
Activities: Education Programs (seasonal, family, First Thursday Programs [first
Thursday in month]; Guided Tours (Christmas Tour; Walking Tour of City second
Saturday in summer)

Hartford's oldest house, the homestead contains art, antiques, and household items from
four generations of the Butler-McCook families. Its restored Victorian garden is the only
surviving domestic commission by pioneer landscape architect Jacob Weidenmann, later
the partner of Frederick Law Olmsted. It features old roses, basswood, and bald cypress,
planted in the 1860s. The house is a property of the Antiquarian and Landmarks Society.

HIGGANUM

SUNDIAL GARDENS

Brault Hill Road Extension, Off Route 81, Higganum, CT 06441
Tel: (860) 345-4290
Internet Address: http://www.sundialgardens.com/
Admission: Fee (Spring-Fall): adult $2.00, child (<6) free, student
$2.00, senior $2.00. Free (Winter)
Established: 1976
Parking: Free on site

Sundial Gardens,
Higganum, CT.

Open: mid-June to mid-October, Saturday to Sunday, 10am-5pm
Closed: New Year's Day, Thanksgiving Day, Christmas Day
Best Time(s) of Year to Visit: June to September
Facilities: Architecture (eighteenth-century farmhouse); Food Services (tea room, open
for special events); Gardens (herb, topiary, knot); Shop Tea Chest Gift Shop (teas and
accessories)
Activities: Classes; Guided Tours (for groups by prior appointment)

Located in the Higganum section of Haddam, the Sundial consists of formal gardens
and a gift shop specializing in fine teas, tisanes, and accessories. The gardens include a
Persian-style knot garden, an eighteenh-century-style garden with geometric walkways,
and a topiary garden with boxwood, roses and ivy garlands surrounding a fountain. These
architectural gardens, or "outdoor rooms" are carefully incorporated into the landscape

around a restored eighteenth-century farmhouse. The gardens are not officially open during the winter months, but are accessible during shop hours.

MANCHESTER

WICKHAM PARK

1329 West Middle Turnpike, Manchester, CT 06040
Tel: (860) 528-0856
Admission: Fee, per vehicle: $3.00 Monday-Friday; $4.00 Saturday-Sunday
Established: 1961
Parking: On-site parking
Open: First Saturday in April to last Sunday in October, 9:30am-sunset
Best Time(s) of Year to Visit: May to September
Facilities: Aviary (8,000 square feet, pheasants, peacocks, waterfowl, raptors); Gardens (Oriental, lotus, Italian, cabin, English); Grounds (250 acres); Trails (3 miles)

Clarence H. Wickham left his estate in trust with the understanding that it be developed into a park. The park contains ten acres of gardens, sports facilities, an aviary, and a nature center.

MERIDEN

CITY OF MERIDEN—HUBBARD PARK

W. Main Street, Meriden, CT 06540
Tel: (203) 630-4259
Internet Address: http://www.cityofmeriden.org/services/parkspw/hubbard-park.asp
Admission: Free
Established: 1900
Open: April to October, Daily, 10am-5pm
Best Time(s) of Year to Visit: mid-April to early-May
Facilities: Grounds (1,800 acres); Special Collections (daffodil)
Activities: Concert Series (Summer); Events Daffodil Festival (Apr), Autumn Fest (Oct), Christmas in the Park & Silver Lights Festival (Dec), Independence Day Fireworks

Maintained by the city, the park contains over 600,000 daffodils representing sixty-one different varieties. The tract was laid out originally in consultation with the Olmsted Brothers, sons of Frederick Law Olmsted, America's foremost landscape architect. A great deal of effort has been taken to preserve and accentuate the historic nature of the park.

MIDDLETOWN

WESLEYAN UNIVERSITY—JAPANESE GARDEN (SHOYOAN TEIEN)

Mansfield Freeman Center for E. Asian Studies, 343 Washington Terrace, Middletown, CT 06459-0435

Tel: (860) 685-2330; Fax: (860) 685-2331
Internet Address: http://www.wesleyan.edu/east/mansfield/japanese_garden.htm
Established: 1995
Membership: N
Wheelchair Accessible: Y
Parking: Disabled parking and on street
Open: Academic Year, September to May
Facilities: Garden (Japanese); Grounds (design by landscape architect Steven A. Morrell)

An educational resource of the Center for East Asian Studies, the garden and its accompanying traditional Japanese room are used for a wide variety of purposes, ranging from meetings of small classes and Japanese tea ceremonies to quiet contemplation and meditation. It is a traditional dry-landscape viewing garden constructed for the appreciation of a stationary viewer on the courtyard edge.

MYSTIC

DENISON PEQUOTSEPOS NATURE CENTER (DPNC)

109 Pequotsepos Road, Mystic, CT 06355
Tel: (860) 536-1216; Fax: (860) 536-2983
Admission: Fee: adult $4.00, child (<6) free, child (6-12) $2.00.
Attendance: 20,000
Established: 1946
Open: Monday to Saturday, 9am-5pm; Sunday, 10am-4pm
Closed: New Year's Day, Easter, Thanksgiving Day, Christmas Day
Best Time(s) of Year to Visit: Spring to late Summer (wildflowers)
Facilities: Gardens (butterfly, wildflower); Grounds (125 acres, habitat management demonstration areas); Museum (natural history of southeastern Connecticut); Shop (field guides, resources for exploring natural history, locally produced items); Trails (seven miles)
Activities: Demonstrations Meet the Animals (Jun-Aug, Sat, noon); Education Programs; Guided Tours (wildflower walks, birding trips, family hikes); Self-Guided Tours (map available)

The nature preserve encompasses a diversity of habitats—pond, stream, field, and forest. More than 150 species of birds have been identified on DPNC grounds, and a wildflower garden contains many species of native plants. Additional land owned by the Denison Society and the Avalonia Land Conservancy lie adjacent to the sanctuary and are accessed by interconnecting trails. The DPNC is also the steward of the Peace Sanctuary on River Road in Mystic and the Manatuck Lane Preserve, a 207-acre private sanctuary in Stonington.

NEW CANAAN

NEW CANAAN NATURE CENTER— ARBORETUM AND GARDENS

144 Oenoke Ridge (Route 124, ¼ mile north of town center),
New Canaan, CT 06840

Tel: (203) 966-9577
Internet Address: http://www.newcanaannature.org/
Membership: Y
Open: Grounds, Daily, dawn-dusk
Buildings, Monday to Saturday, 9am-4pm
Facilities: Arboretum; Gardens (bird and butterfly; herb, culinary, dye, fragrance, gray
and silver, medicinal; native plant; wildflower); Greenhouse (4,000 square feet);
Grounds (40 acres); Shop; Trails (2 miles); Visitors Center
Activities: Education Programs

A satellite of the New York Botanical Gardens, the New Canaan Nature Center features unusual habitat diversity, including wet and dry meadows, two ponds, wet and dry woodlands, dense thickets, an old orchard, and a cattail marsh. Its arboretum, planted by Susan Dwight Bliss, former owner of the Nature Center property, includes magnificent specimens of several evergreens. Garden highlights include the Herb Garden with more than 300 varieties of plants; the Wildflower Garden, which won the 1997 Homer Lucas Landscape Award from the New England Wild Flower Society; and the Naturalists' Garden, which was designed as a "model backyard," featuring native and long-naturalized species of plants that benefit a wide range of local wildlife.

OLIVE AND GEORGE LEE MEMORIAL GARDEN

89 Chichester Road, New Canaan, CT 06840
Tel: (203) 966-6306
Admission: Free
Established: 1978
Open: dawn to dusk
Best Time(s) of Year to Visit: mid-May
Facilities: Gardens; Grounds; Special Collections (azalea, rhododendron)

Willed by George S. Lee to the New Canaan Garden Center, the gardens contain approximately 2,000 azaleas (including an extensive collection of gable hybrids) and 300 rhododendrons, as well as other flowering shrubs, perennials, and wildflowers.

NEW HAVEN

EDGERTON PARK—GREENBRIER GREENHOUSE AND CROSBY CONSERVATORY

75 Cliff Street (at Whitney Ave.), New Haven, CT 06511
Tel: (203) 946-8009
Internet Address: http://www.edgertonpark.org/
Open: Park, Daily, dawn-dusk; Greenhouse & Conservatory: Daily, 10am-5pm
Closed: Conservatory: Holidays
Facilities: Conservatory; Greenhouses; Grounds (22 acres); Library (horticultural, open Sunday afternoons)
Activities: Concerts New Haven Symphony Orchestra (Jun-Jul); Events Eli Whitney Folk Festival (weekend in Sept, 203-624-3559), Sunday in the Park: An English Country Fair (2nd Sun in Sept, 203-776-9503); Performances Shakespeare in the Park (3 weekends in Aug, 203-934-0399); Plant Sales Greenbrier Greenhouse (year-round); Self-Guided Tour (brochure available at greenhouse complex)

On the Hamden/New Haven border, the Park is a former estate that sits on property that once was owned by Eli Whitney. Designed in the first decade of the twentieth century, the estate's grounds were intended to replicate English landscape design, emphasizing the importance of open space. With facilities for walking and biking, the park features a greenhouse conservatory complex, a community garden center, and a horticulture library open on Sunday afternoons. The Greenbrier Greenhouse is maintained by a vocational program run by Easter Seals. Also maintained by the Greenbrier program, the Sarah T. Crosby Conservatory houses a collection of plants from various parts of the world and includes a rain forest exhibit as well as dry landscape. Listed on the National Register of Historic Places, the Park was restored and is maintained by the Edgerton Park Conservancy, a non-profit organization.

NEW LONDON

CONNECTICUT COLLEGE ARBORETUM

Connecticut College, Williams Street, New London, CT 06320
Tel: (203) 439-5020; Fax: (203) 439-2519
Internet Address: http://www.conncoll.edu/ccrec/greennet/arbo/welcome.html
Admission: Voluntary Contribution
Attendance: 5,000
Established: 1931
Membership: Y
Open: Daily, sunrise-sunset
Facilities: Greenhouse (1935 Lord & Burnham; 8,500 square feet); Grounds (750 acres)
Activities: Education Programs; Guided Tours (May-Oct, 1/week, free; private group tours, arrange in advance, fee); Lectures

The Arboretum encompasses approximately 750 acres of preserved open space in the city of New London and the town of Waterford in southeastern Connecticut, including the Connecticut College Campus. Major elements include the following: The Native Plant Collection is a twenty-acre site containing 288 taxa, including trees, shrubs, and woody vines indigenous to the forested region of eastern North America. The Native Plant Collection contains the Edgerton and Stengle Memorial Wildflower Gardens, a two-acre plot designed as a representative display of eastern woodland wildflowers, as well as a number of smaller collections and gardens that are of particular horticultural and aesthetic interest. A self-guided tour brochure is available in a small box on the notice board just inside the Native Plant Collection entrance on Williams Street. The Caroline Black Garden, located directly across from the college main entrance on Route 32, is distinctive among the Arboretum plant collections. It includes native and exotic species as well as some very unusual cultivars. It currently contains 187 different woody taxa. The Connecticut College Campus, currently including 223 different taxa of trees, is managed as one of the Arboretum plant collections. The greenhouse contains a tropical house with plantings in the ground, a cactus collection, and an area for botany and cell biology experiments.

NORWICH

NORWICH MEMORIAL ROSE GARDEN

Mohegan Park (off Route 32), 400 Rockwell Street at Judd Road, Norwich,
CT 06360
Tel: (860) 823-3759

Internet Address: http://www.norwichct.org
Admission: Free
Open: Daily, dawn-dusk
Best Time(s) of Year to Visit: late June to mid-July
Facilities: Garden (rose); Grounds Park (380 acre)

Situated on two acres of gently sloping parkland, the garden, accredited by All-America Rose Selections, features 2,500 rose bushes representing 120 varieties.

OLD SAYBROOK

GENERAL WILLIAM HART HOUSE

350 Main Street, Old Saybrook, CT 06475-2319
Tel: (860) 388-2622
Internet Address: http://www.oldsaybrook.com/History/
Admission: Suggested Contribution: adult $2.50, child (<12) free
Open: Memorial Day to Labor Day, Friday to Sunday, 1pm-4pm
Facilities: Architecture (1767 Georgian residence); Gardens (herb, kitchen, rose); Library (Wed, 10:30am-12:30pm, 388-2622)

The Hart House is the headquarters of the Old Saybrook Historical Society, which has recreated the Colonial gardens that adjoin the house at the side and rear. Volunteers planned and planted the area to duplicate what General Hart might have maintained — fruit trees, lilacs, a hawthorn, a quince, a black walnut, a dogwood, a tulip, and other trees native to the region. Adjacent to the kitchen are some 125 medicinal, culinary, and fragrant herbs. Beyond them, complete with sundial, stands a rose garden. Many of the herbs, flowers, and trees are clearly identified.

REDDING

HIGHSTEAD ARBORETUM

127 Lonetown Road (Route 107), Redding, CT 06875
Tel: (203) 938-8809; Fax: (203) 938-0343
Internet Address: http://www.highsteadarboretum.org
Admission: Free, donations Accepted
Attendance: 1,000
Established: 1984
Membership: Y
Wheelchair Accessible: P
Parking: On site
Open: Monday to Friday, 8am-4pm, by appointment
Best Time(s) of Year to Visit: April to July (azalea bloom), early June (mountain laurel bloom)
Facilities: Arboretum; Greenhouse; Grounds (50 acres); Herbarium (1,000 specimens); Library (900+ volumes); Special Collections (azalea, kalmia, native tree); Trails (3 miles)
Activities: Education Programs; Guided Tours Walks & Talks (in conjunction with the Garden Conservancy); Lectures; Self-Guided Tours Azalea Collection (brochure available), Kalmia Collection and Companion Plants (brochure available)

Intended as a sanctuary for the study and appreciation of the woodland habitat, Highstead Arboretum contains an unusual variety of habitats: woodland, meadow, wetland, and ledge. It features a two and a half-acre pond, swamp walk, a native tree and shrub walk, and recently planted collections of kalmia (mountain laurel, three species) and native azalea (fourteen species/three native).

RIDGEFIELD

BALLARD PARK

Main Street, Ridgefield, CT 06877
Tel: (203) 438-2755
Admission: Free
Established: 1964
Membership: N
Parking: Limited parking
Open: Daily, dawn-dusk
Best Time(s) of Year to Visit: May to October
Facilities: Children's play park; Gardens perennial; Greenhouse

The garden has been maintained by the Ridgefield Garden Club since it was deeded to the town. It contains boxwood, perennial peonies, climbing roses, asters, and many other perennials.

KEELER TAVERN MUSEUM—CASS GILBERT GARDEN

32 Main Street (Route 35), Ridgefield, CT 06877
Tel: (203) 438-5485; Fax: (203) 438-5485
Internet Address: http://www.keelertavernmuseum.org
Admission: Fee (Museum): adult $5.00, child $2.00, student $3.00, senior $3.00
Free (Gardens)
Established: 1915
Membership: Y
Wheelchair Accessible: P
Parking: Free on site, 40 spaces
Open: February to December, Daily, dawn to dusk
Best Time(s) of Year to Visit: May to October
Facilities: Architecture (early eighteenth-century tavern); Garden (perennials, unusual annuals; original design of sunken garden by architect Cass Gilbert); Garden House (design by Cass Gilbert); Shop
Activities: Concerts; Education Programs; Guided Tours (Wed, Sat & Sun, 1pm-4pm); Lectures

Listed on the National Register of Historic Places, the Keeler Tavern Museum has been a farmhouse, tavern, stagecoach stop, post office, hotel for travelers, home of noted architect Cass Gilbert, and, since 1966, a museum. It is now decorated with period furnishings and changing exhibits from the museum's collections. In 1910, Gilbert designed the garden and garden house for his wife, Julia, in the manner of Charleston gardens. Intended to be viewed and enjoyed by guests in the adjoining garden house, visitors look out at a sunken garden with brick walls, arches, and a reflecting pool with cherub fountain. Restored in 1967, the garden contains over one hundred varieties of annuals and perennials. Additionally, in the front courtyard of the museum, there is a classic herb garden containing many varieties of culinary, medicinal, and household herbs known to have been used in Connecticut during the eighteenth century. The site is maintained by the Keeler Tavern Museum Preservation Society.

ROCKY HILL

DINOSAUR STATE PARK ARBORETUM

400 West Street, Rocky Hill, CT 06067-3506
Tel: (860) 529-8423; Fax: (860) 529-8423
Internet Address: http://www.dinosaurstatepark.org
Admission: Exhibit Center Admission Fee: adult $5.00, child (<6) free, child(6-17) $2.00
Attendance: 65,000
Membership: Y
Wheelchair Accessible: Y
Parking: On site
Open: Grounds, Daily, 9am-4:30pm
Exhibit Center, Tuesday to Sunday, 9am-4:30pm
Closed: New Year's Day, Thanksgiving Day, Christmas Day
Best Time(s) of Year to Visit: Spring to Summer
Facilities: Gardens (butterfly, native plant)

Dinosaur State Park is one of the largest dinosaur track sites in North America. Flowering plants originated during the Mesozoic Era, also known as the age of reptiles. The goal of the arboretum is to grow representatives of as many of the Mesozoic Era plant families as possible in climate zone 6. Dinosaur State Park Arboretum contains more than 250 species and cultivars of conifers, as well as katsuras, ginkgoes, magnolias and other living representatives of plant families that appeared in the age of dinosaurs.

STAMFORD

BARTLETT ARBORETUM

151 Brookdale Road (off Route 137), Stamford, CT 06903-4199
Tel: (203) 322-6971; Fax: (203) 595-9168
Internet Address: http://bartlett.arboretum.uconn.edu
Admission: Voluntary Contribution
Attendance: 20,000
Established: 1965
Membership: Y
Open: Daily, 8:30am-sunset
Facilities: Arboretum; Conservatory; Gardens (All-American Selection, azalea/rhododendron, conifer, perennial, wildflower, witches broom); Greenhouse; Grounds (63 acres); Library (non-circulating, by appointment to members, 321-4827); Trails (5 miles); Visitor Center
Activities: Concerts; Education Programs; Guided Tours (selected Sundays, 1pm, free); Lectures; Plant Sales (spring)

The arboretum was begun in 1913 by Dr. Francis A. Bartlett, an eminent dendrologist, as his residence, training school, and research laboratory for his tree-care company. Over the years he assembled on the property a large number of plant specimens from all over the world. The arboretum was opened to the public for the first time in 1965, when it was purchased by the State of Connecticut to serve as the official Connecticut State Arboretum under the auspices of the state Department of Environmental Protection and managed by the University of Connecticut's Department of Plant Science. In July 2001, the university and the state Department of Environmental Protection turned the arboretum over to the City of Stamford. The Bartlett Arboretum Association, a non-profit organization, now operates the arboretum under lease from the city. The arboretum contains more than 2,000 types of annuals, perennials, wildflowers, and woody plants growing under a variety of conditions, ranging from the intensely managed perennial gardens to natural woodlands, meadows, freshwater wetlands, and a two-acre pond. Exhibits include an All-American Selections Garden, featuring the prize winners of the last five years, interplanted with other annuals and perennials; the Mehlquist Garden, displaying a unique collection of rhododendrons and azaleas of native, Japanese, Korean and European origins; a perennial border, displaying over 150 varieties of flowering perennials; a witches broom collection, consisting of dwarf conifers grown from seeds infected with witches' broom; a pollarded tree display; a conifer garden; a nut tree grove; a secluded garden; a wildflower garden; and a notable tree collection. The arboretum's greenhouse, primarily used for propagation, houses various tropical and temperate plants, including a noteworthy collection of cacti and succulents.

STORRS

UNIVERSITY OF CONNECTICUT—ECOLOGY AND EVOLUTIONARY BIOLOGY CONSERVATORY AND GARDENS

Torrey Life Science Building (rear), 75 N. Eagleville Road, Storrs, CT 06269
Tel: (860) 486-3644
Internet Address: http://florawww.eeb.uconn.edu/
Admission: Free; Voluntary contribution
Established: 1960
Membership: N
Wheelchair Accessible: P
Parking: Use North Parking Garage
Open: Monday to Friday, 8am-4pm
Closed: State Holidays
Facilities: Greenhouses (3, plus fern room; 10,400 square feet—10 zones);
Outdoor Garden
Activities: Guided Tours (reserve in advance, fee), Group Tours (weekends, fee)

The EEB Greenhouse facilities consist of a three-greenhouse range of plant collections used for teaching botany and related courses at the University of Connecticut. The collections are exceptionally diverse and feature over 3,000 species representing nearly 300 plant families. Highlights include an extensive cactus and succulent collection and large species orchid collections.

STRATFORD

BOOTHE MEMORIAL PARK AND MUSEUM—ROSE GARDEN

N. Main Street (Route 110), Stratford, CT 06615
Tel: (203) 381-2046
Internet Address: http://www.connix.com/~cs/
Admission: Free
Established: 1990
Membership: Y
Wheelchair Accessible: Y
Parking: Large lot on site
Open: Grounds: June to October, Daily, 9am-5pm
Museum: June to October, Tuesday to Friday, 11am-1pm; Saturday to Sunday,
1pm-4pm
Best Time(s) of Year to Visit: June to September
Facilities: Gardens (rose, sunken); Grounds (32 acres); Picnic Area
Activities: Guided Tours

   The former homestead of the Boothe Family (1663-1949), the site is now a park featuring historic buildings and an All-America Rose Selections accredited garden, as well as exhibits on early farming, baskets, trolleys, and carriages. The homestead is listed on the
National Register of Historic Places.

SUFFIELD

PHELPS-HATHEWAY HOUSE—GARDEN

55 South Main Street (Route 75), Suffield, CT 06078
Tel: (860) 247-8996; Fax: (860) 240-4907
Internet Address: http://www.hartnet.org/als/alsprop.html
Admission: Fee: adult $4.00, child $2.00
Attendance: 500
Membership: Y
Wheelchair Accessible: P
Open: May 15 to October 15, Wednesday, 1pm-4pm; Friday to Sunday,
1pm-4pm.
Best Time(s) of Year to Visit: Summer
Facilities: Architecture (Colonial residence, 1761 with Neo-classical-style addition,
1794); Garden (period, Colonial); Grounds
Activities: Guided Tours

   An historic house museum, the residence's north wing is one of earliest examples of
Neo-Classical design in the Connecticut River Valley. The grounds are set off from the
street with an ornate fence and a summerhouse overlooks formal flower beds, maintained
by the local garden club. The site is maintained by the Antiquarian and Landmarks Society, a non-profit organization.

WATERFORD

HARKNESS MEMORIAL STATE PARK (EOLIA)

275 Great Neck Road, Waterford, CT 06385
Tel: (203) 443-5725; Fax: (203) 443-3789
Internet Address: http://www.dep.state.ct.us/stateparks/parks/harkness.htm
Admission: Varies by season
Attendance: 250,000
Established: 1953
Membership: N
Wheelchair Accessible: P
Parking: Handicapped accessible parking
Open: Daily, 8am-sunset
Best Time(s) of Year to Visit: Spring to Fall
Facilities: Architecture Eolia (Roman Renaissance Revival-style mansion, 1906 design
by the architectural firm of Lord & Hewlett); Gardens (boxwood parterre, Italian,
oriental, rock, cutting); Greenhouses (6,000 square-foot greenhouse under
construction); Grounds (230 acres); Picnic Area

The elegant fourty-two-room summer mansion of the Harkness family was designed
by the architectural firm of Lord & Hewlett. The west garden was originally landscaped in stiff geometric style by the firm of Brett & Hall in collaboration with architect James Gambel Rogers who was also responsible for extensive interior renovations.
Subsequently (between 1918 and 1929), landscape designer Beatrix Jones Farrand redesigned the west garden and created and installed the East Garden, the Boxwood
Parterre, and the Alpine Rock Garden. The greenhouses are of historical significance,
housing the oldest surviving grapery in the state, as well as serving an important functional purpose. The estate was left to the State of Connecticut in 1950.

WEST HARTFORD

CITY OF HARTFORD—ELIZABETH PARK

915 Prospect Avenue at Asylum Avenue, West Hartford, CT 06119
Tel: (860) 242-0017
Internet Address: http://www.elizabethpark.org/
Admission: Free
Established: 1904
Membership: Y
Open: Daily, dawn-dusk
Best Time(s) of Year to Visit: early-May (tulips), August to September (dahlias), early-
June to mid-June (roses, iris, rhododendrons)
Facilities: Food Services Pond House Café (May-Sept, daily, 11am-8pm; Oct-Apr,
reduced hours); Gardens (annual, herb, perennial, rock, rose); Greenhouses (1898, Lord
& Burnham; Mon-Fri, 8am-3pm); Grounds (102 acres)
Activities: Festivals Rose Weekend (Spring); Flower Shows; Guided Tours; Workshops

Charles H. Pond willed his estate to the City of Hartford with the stipulations that it
be used as a horticultural park and that it be named for his wife. Subsequently, the

boundary between West Hartford and Hartford was moved to its present location, it resulted in the unusual situation of one of Hartford's larger parks being situated mostly beyond the city limits. Listed in the National Register of Historic Places, Elizabeth Park contains the country's oldest municipal rose garden. One of the largest rose gardens in the country, the 2½-acre oval garden contains more than 15,000 rose bushes (more than 900 varieties) in 108 beds and is an All-America Rose Selections Test Garden. Additionally, the park is home to annual, perennial, herb, and rock gardens; a collection of ornamental grasses; ponds; and more than 100 tree species. The greenhouses' permanent collection includes cacti, bird of paradise, palm trees, a banana tree, a Ponderosa Lemon tree, and much more. Listed on the National Register of Historic Places, the park is maintained by the Friends of Elizabeth Park, a non-profit organization.

WETHERSFIELD

WEBB DEANE STEVENS MUSEUM— GARDENS

Webb Deane Stevens Museum—
gardens, Wethersfield, CT.

211 Main Street at Church Street, Wethersfield, CT 06109
Tel: (860) 529-0612; Fax: (860) 571-8636
Internet Address: http://www.webb-deane-stevens.org/
Admission: Fee (3 house tour): adult $8.00; child (<5) free; child, senior $7.00.
Fee (house tour): adult $3, child (<5) $1.00
Membership: Y
Wheelchair Accessible: N
Open: May to October, Monday, 10am-4pm; Wednesday to Sunday, 10am-4pm
November to April, Saturday to Sunday, 10am-4pm
Best Time(s) of Year to Visit: Summer to Fall
Facilities: Architecture Buttolph-Williams House (residence, 1720), Isaac Stevens House (residence, 1789), Joseph Webb House (residence, 1752), Silas Deane House (residence, 1766); Gardens (Colonial Revival, 1921 design Amy Cogswell); Shop
Activities: Education Programs; Guided Tours (on the hour)

The museum offers four eighteenth-century houses containing period furnishings. Between the Webb House and its barn is a Colonial Revival Garden with plantings and arbors leading to sweeping lawns and a large stone patio. Created in 1921, the garden was extensively restored in 1999. Also located around the barn at the rear of the property are a variety of shrubs, ornamental trees, and fruit trees. Located in the Old Wethersfield Historic District, the site is owned by the Connecticut Colonial Dames.

WOODBURY

THE GLEBE HOUSE MUSEUM—GERTRUDE JEKYLL GARDEN

Hollow Road, Woodbury, CT 06798
Tel: (203) 263-2855; Fax: (203) 263-2855
Internet Address: http://www.theglebehouse.org
Admission: Fee: adult $5.00, child (<12) $2.00
Attendance: 6,000
Established: 1923

Membership: Y
Parking: Free on site
Open: April to November, Wednesday to Sunday, 1pm-4pm. December to March, by appointment
Best Time(s) of Year to Visit: June to September
Facilities: Architecture (1750 Glebe House, Birthplace of American Episcopacy); Gardens (perennial border, 1926 design by Gertrude Jekyll); Library (reference only); Shop (gardening books and accessories)
Activities: Concerts; Education Programs; Guided Tours House & Garden (by reservation, $6/person); Lectures

The Glebe House, originally built around 1750 and an important site in the history of the foundation of the Episcopal Church in America, was restored between 1923-1925 under the direction of William Henry Kent, curator of early American decorative arts at the Metropolitan Museum of Art, New York. In 1926, the famed English horticultural designer and writer Gertrude Jekyll was commissioned to plan an "old fashioned" garden to enhance the newly created museum. For reasons unknown today, the garden Miss Jekyll planned was never fully installed in the 1920's. After the rediscovery of her plan in the late 1970's the project was completed according to the original plans. Although a small garden, when compared with the some 400 more elaborate designs she executed in England and on the Continent, the Glebe House garden, Miss Jekyll's only American commission, includes 600 feet of classic English-style mixed border and foundation plantings, a planted stone terrace, and in intimate rose allée. The house and garden are listed on the National Register of Historic Places.

WOODSTOCK

HENRY C. BOWEN HOUSE-ROSELAND COTTAGE

556 Route 169 (facing Woodstock Common), Woodstock, CT 06281-2344
Tel: (860) 928-4074
Internet Address: http://www.historicnewengland.org/visit/homes/roseland.htm
Admission: Fee: adult $8.00, child (<5) free, child (5-12) $4.00, senior $7.50
Open: Memorial Day to mid-October, Friday to Sunday, noon-5pm
Facilities: Architecture (Gothic Revival-style residence, 1846); Shop
Activities: Guided Tours (noon/1pm/2pm/3pm/4pm)

Known as "Roseland Cottage," the House contains much of its original furniture and features one of New England's oldest known boxwood parterre gardens. The entire complex, including garden, garden house, ice house, and carriage barn with a private bowling alley, reflects the principles of writer and designer Andrew Jackson Downing. In his widely popular books, Downing stressed practicality along with the picturesque, and offered detailed instructions on room function, sanitation, and landscaping. A property of Historic New England (formerly the Society for the Preservation of New England Antiquities).

DELAWARE

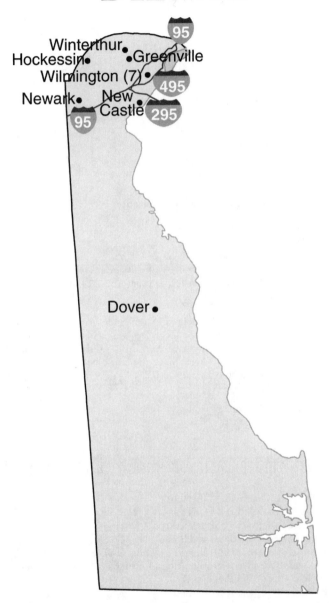

The number in the parentheses following the city name indicates the number of gardens/ arboreta in that municipality. If there is no number, one is understood. For example, in the text seven listings would be found under Wilmington and one listing under Newark.

DOVER

WOODBURN—GARDENS

151 Kings Highway, Dover, DE 19901
Tel: (302) 739-5656
Internet Address: http://www.state.de.us/woodburn.htm
Admission: Free
Parking: Free on street
Open: Daily, dawn to dusk
Closed: When governor is in residence
Facilities: Architecture (Georgian residence, 1798); Gardens
Activities: Guided Tours Grounds (Mon-Fri, 8:30am-3pm), House (Mon-Sat, 8:30am-4pm, by appointment only)

Woodburn, the official residence of Delaware's governor, was built in 1798 by Charles Hillyard, is one of the finest Middle Period Georgian houses in Delaware. The gardens of Woodburn include a formal boxwood parterre. In addition to the gardens, there is a good variety of indigenous and non-native trees. Since the house became the official gubernatorial home in 1965, it has become a tradition for each governor to make a planting on the grounds.

GREENVILLE

MOUNT CUBA CENTER FOR THE STUDY OF PIEDMONT FLORA

3120 Barley Mill Road, Greenville, DE 19807
Tel: (302) 239-4244; Fax: (302) 773-1411
Admission: Fee (by appointment only): $5.00
Open: Spring and Fall, call for dates and hours
Facilities: Gardens (formal, ca. 1930 design by Thomas W. Sears & c 1950 by Marian C. Coffin; woodland; lilac allée; water; cutting); Grounds (630 acres); Special Collection (native plants of the Piedmont)
Activities: Guided Tours (docent-led, 2 hours)

The center in a non-profit institution focusing on research and conservation of the native plants of the Piedmont and their use in landscape design. The gardens of a private estate, formerly the home of Lammot du Pont Copeland, the center is open to the public by appointment only. The plant collection is well-documented, with well over 4,000 accessions, representing over 1,800 taxa. Approximately 75 percent of the plants in the collection are of Piedmont origin.

HOCKESSIN

ASHLAND NATURE CENTER

Brackenville and Barley Mill Roads, Hockessin, DE 19707
Tel: (302) 239-2334
Internet Address: http://www.delawarenaturesociety.org/ashland.htm
Admission: Fee: adult $2.00, child (3-12) $1.00
Wheelchair Accessible: Y
Parking: Large parking lot
Open: Trails, sunrise-sunset
Visitor Center, Monday to Friday, 8:30am-4:30pm; Saturday, 9am-3pm;
Sunday, 1pm-4pm
Best Time(s) of Year to Visit: Spring to Fall
Facilities: Butterfly House (June-Sept; Mon-Fri, 2pm-4pm; Sat, 9:30am-3:30pm);
Garden (native plant); Grounds (80 acres of fields, meadows, marshes, and woodland);
Trails (4, self-guided); Visitor Center
Activities: Education Programs (year-round); Event Harvest Moon Festival (annual);
Group Tours ($3.00/person, reserve in advance); Native Plant Sale

Operated by the Delaware Nature Society, Ashland Nature Center contains meadow, marsh, pond, and forest habitats and includes a native plant garden showcasing a variety of plants that provide food and shelter for wildlife.

NEW CASTLE

THE READ HOUSE AND GARDENS

42 The Strand, New Castle, DE 19720
Tel: (302) 322-8411; Fax: (302) 322-8557
Internet Address: http://www.hsd.org/read.htm
Admission: Fee (House & Garden): adult $5.00, child (<6) free, child (6-12) $2.00,
student $4.00, senior $4.00. Garden only: $2.00
Attendance: 25,000
Membership: Y
Parking: On-street parking
Open: January to February, Saturday to Sunday, 10am-4pm; Sunday, 11am-4pm;
Monday to Friday, by appointment
March to December, Tuesday to Thursday, 11am-4pm; Friday to Saturday, 10am-
4pm; 10am-4pm
Facilities: Architecture (Federal residence, 1801, 22 rooms); Garden (1½ acres;
Victorian, 1847 design by Robert Buist of Philadelphia); Shop
Activities: Guided Tours

Built in 1801 by the son of one of a signer of the Declaration of Independence, the Read House exhibits the height of Federal grandeur. Totaling 14,000 square feet with twenty-two rooms, the mansion was the largest house in Delaware when built. The garden at Read House, designed by Robert Buist of Philadelphia, was installed in 1847. It is divided into three sections: a formal flower garden, a park filled with exotics and native favorites, and a large fruit and vegetable kitchen garden with allées of pear trees and trellised grapes set by formal boxwood hedges. Reputed to be the oldest surviving garden in the region, its restoration, begun in 1991, is ongoing. It is a property of the Historical Society of Delaware.

NEWARK

UNIVERSITY OF DELAWARE BOTANIC GARDENS (UDBG)

South College Avenue (near Townsend and Worrilow Halls), Newark, DE 19717
Tel: (302) 831-2531; Fax: (302) 831-3651
Internet Address: http://ag.udel.edu/udbg
Admission: Free
Membership: Y
Wheelchair Accessible: P
Parking: Visitor permit available in Main Office
Open: Daily, 8am-sunset
Best Time(s) of Year to Visit: Spring to Fall
Facilities: Gardens (dwarf conifer, herbaceous, meadow, native plant); Greenhouses
Activities: Guided Tours (by appointment); Plant Sale (last Sat in Apr)

The gardens include the Emily B. Clark Garden, featuring a dwarf conifer collection; the Herbaceous Garden, displaying annuals, perennials, and ornamental grasses; the Meadow Garden, a demonstration garden using a variety of plants to produce a long season of color as a colorful alternative to turf; and the Native Garden, containing a collection of plants native to the eastern United States.

WILMINGTON

BRANDYWINE PARK—JOSEPHINE GARDENS AND JASPER CRANE ROSE GARDEN

18th and Market Streets, Wilmington, DE 19802
Tel: (302) 577-7020; Fax: (302) 577-7084
Internet Address: http://www.destateparks.com/wilmsp/brandywine.htm
Established: 1885
Open: Daily, sunrise-sunset
Best Time(s) of Year to Visit: Spring (cherry tree bloom)
Facilities: Gardens (formal, rose); Grounds Brandywine Park (178 acres, designed by Frederick Law Olmsted)

Running along either side of the Brandywine River, the park contains two formal gardens dating from the 1930s. Josephine Gardens features a fountain, formal plantings, and stands of Japanese cherry trees. At its peak in the 1950s, Jasper Crane Rose Garden contained approximately 1,000 roses representing 100 varieties. The replanted garden, a project of the Friends of Wilmington Parks, offers 450 plants representing 53 varieties. Brandywine Park also includes late nineteenth-century monuments, open meadows, woodlands, ball fields, a stadium, the Brandywine Zoo, and hiking and jogging trails that are part of the Delaware "Greenway" system.

DELAWARE CENTER FOR HORTICULTURE (AHS RAP)

1810 N. Dupont Street, Wilmington, DE 19806-5308
Tel: (302) 658-6262; Fax: (302) 658-6267
Internet Address: http://www.dehort.org/
Admission: Free
Attendance: 10,000
Membership: Y
Wheelchair Accessible: P
Parking: Free on site
Open: Monday to Friday, 10am-5pm; Saturday, 10am-2pm
Best Time(s) of Year to Visit: April to October
Facilities: Gallery; Garden; Library (Mon-Fri, 9am-5pm; members have circulation
privileges)
Activities: Education Programs (focusing on the urban environment); Guided Tours;
Lectures; Temporary Exhibitions horticultural themes (in partnership with local
galleries, arts groups, and art schools); Workshops

Focus is on the urban environment. The center's major programs are greening initia-
tives, such as community gardens, public landscaping and tree programs, and education
programs. DCH maintains a demonstration garden showcasing ideas that meet
the challenges of the urban gardener. Plant selection criteria include easy commercial
availability and multi-seasonal interest. The garden features include creative adaptive
reuse of found materials such as granite curbstones, cement lampposts, and balustrades
from a local bridge. It also operates a Horticultural Hotline: (302) 658-6266.

HAGLEY MUSEUM AND LIBRARY— E. I. DU PONT RESTORED GARDEN

Route 141 & Brandywine River (north of Route 100), Wilmington, DE 19807-0630
Tel: (302) 658-2400; Fax: (302) 658-2230
Internet Address: http://hagley.lib.de.us/
Admission: Fee: adult $11.00, child (<6) free, child (6-14) $4.00, student $9.00,
senior $9.00.
Parking: Free on site
Open: March 15 to December, Daily, 9:30am-4:30pm January to March 14, Monday
to Friday, 1 tour at 1:30pm, Saturday to Sunday, 9:30am-4:30pm
Facilities: Arboretum; Gardens (period, formal French-style; hyacinths, crocuses,
daffodils); Grounds (235 acres); Library (Mon-Fri, 8:30am-4:30pm, 2nd Sat in month,
9am-4:30pm); Picnic Areas; Shop
Activities: Guided Tours (groups 15+, arrange in advance, fee varies)

Located on the site of the birthplace of the du Pont Company, this museum, depicting
home and work life in a nineteenth-century industrial community, features mills, a workers' community, gardens, and the first du Pont residence in the United States. While focusing on American economic, business, industrial, and technological history, the park-
like grounds contain ninety-four species and varieties of trees and a restored French-style
garden originally created by E. I. du Pont, an avid botanist.

NEMOURS MANSION AND GARDENS

1600 Rockland Road, Wilmington, DE 19803
Tel: (302) 651-6912

Internet Address: http://www.kidshealth.org/nf/mansion/
Admission: Fee (children <13 not admitted) $12.00
Established: 1977
Membership: N
Open: May to October, Tuesday to Saturday, Tours: 9am/11am/1pm/
3pm3pm; Sunday, Tours: 11am/1pm/3pm
Facilities: Architecture (Louis XVI-style chateau, 1910 design by Carrère and
Hastings); Gardens (formal French, formal English, cutting, parterre, English pleasure,
sunken, trial); Grounds (300 acres)
Activities: Guided Tours (reservations recommended)

Nemours, the site of the du Pont ancestral home in France, was chosen by Alfred I.
du Pont as the name for his estate north of Wilmington, Delaware. Here he created a
lovely home with landscaped gardens surrounded by natural woodlands. The mansion,
a modified Louis XVI chateau, was completed in 1910. Containing 102 rooms, the
house is furnished with fine examples of antique furniture, rare rugs, tapestries, and
outstanding works of art. The gardens, surrounded by natural woodlands, extend for
one third of a mile along the main vista from the house and offer impressive views
from many vantage points. Exquisitely landscaped with fountains, pools, and statuary,
they are held to be among the finest examples of French-style gardens in the United
States. Their overall design is credited to Alfred's son, Alfred Victor du Pont. Tours
take a minimum of two hours and include a guided tour through a series of rooms on
three floors, followed by a bus tour through the gardens. Tours conclude with a visit
to the chauffeur's garage where the family's antique cars are on view. Visitors must ar-
rive at the reception center on Rockland Road fifteen minutes prior to the tour. Visitors must be over twelve years of age.

PRESERVATION DELAWARE—GIBRALTAR GARDENS

1405 Greenhill Avenue at Pennsylvania Avenue, Wilmington, DE 19806
Tel: (302) 651-9617; Fax: (302) 651-9603
Internet Address: http://www.preservationde.org/gibraltar/estate/index.htm
Open: Monday to Friday, 9am-5pm
Facilities: Gardens (formal Italian, cypress allée); Grounds (6 acres, 1916-1923 design
by landscape architect Marian Cruger Coffin)
Activities: Guided Tours (Apr-mid June & Sept-mid Oct, Tues & Thurs, by
appointment); Self-Guided Tours

A property of Preservation Delaware, Gibraltar's formal gardens were created between
1915 and 1923 by Hugh Rodney Sharp and his wife, Isabella du Pont Sharp. Considered
to be among the finest of Marian Coffin's designs, the grounds feature large formal perennial beds, three terraced gardens, a bald cypress allée, sweeping lawns, and an Italian-style
garden pavilion. Hand-forged iron gates and railings and the Sharp's collection of statuary, urns, and fountains complete the design. The site is listed on the National Register of
Historic Places.

ROCKWOOD MANSION PARK

610 Shipley Road, Wilmington, DE 19809
Tel: (302) 761-4340; Fax: (302) 761-4345
Internet Address: http://www.co.new-castle.de.us
Admission: Free
Attendance: 108,000

Established: 1976
Membership: N
Wheelchair Accessible: P
Parking: Free on site
Open: Park, Daily, 6am-10pm
Mansion, Daily, 10am-3pm
Closed: New Year's Day, Good Friday, Easter, Independence Day, Thanksgiving Day, Christmas Eve to Christmas Day
Facilities: Architecture (mid-19th century Rural Gothic Revival residence); Food Services Butler's Pantry (self-service café, 7am-7pm); Gardens (6 acres); Grounds (72 acres, 6 landscaped); Trails (2 miles)
Activities: Concerts (summer, outdoor); Education Programs; Events Holiday Tours (Dec), Ice Cream Festival (2nd weekend in Jul); Guided Tours (on the hour); Lectures; Workshops

The estate, built by merchant banker Joseph Shipley between 1851 and 1854, includes a lush landscape with walled garden and park; conservatory filled with period flora; and Victorian mansion. The cast iron and glass conservatory is one of the earliest of its type still standing in the United States.

UNIVERSITY OF DELAWARE—WILMINGTON— GOODSTAY GARDENS

Goodstay Center, 2600 Pennsylvania Avenue, Wilmington, DE 19806
Tel: (302) 573-4450
Membership: Y
Open: Daily, dawn-dusk
Facilities: Architecture; Gardens (colonial, herb, iris, magnolia walk, peony, rose, wisteria gate, woodland); Picnic Area

Dating from about 1740, the house and garden were given in 1923 as a wedding gift from her father to artist Ellen du Pont (Meeds). In 1968, the owner, Mrs. Wheelwright, gave the property to the University of Delaware for use as a conference center. Originally planted in the early nineteenth century in the American Tudor style, with boxwood hedges bordering gravel paths, in the 1930s the garden was enhanced and enlarged by Mrs. Wheelwhisht and her landscape architect husband, Robert. Restored under the guidance of the Friends of Goodstay, the Garden features include iris, rose, peony and woodland gardens; a wisteria gate; and a magnolia walk.

WINTERTHUR

WINTERTHUR MUSEUM, GARDEN, & LIBRARY

State Route 52, Winterthur, DE 19735
Tel: (302) 888-4600; Fax: (302) 888-4880; TDDY: (302) 888-4907
Internet Address: http://www.winterthur.org/
Admission: Fee: adult $15.00, child $5.00, student $13.00, senior $13.00
Attendance: 200,000
Established: 1930
Membership: Y
Wheelchair Accessible: Y
Parking: Free on site—over 400 spaces

Open: Tuesday to Sunday, 10am-5pm
Closed: Thanksgiving Day, Christmas Day
Facilities: Auditorium (350 seats); Food Services Restaurant; Gardens (60 acres, naturalistic); Grounds (966 acres); Library (70,000 volumes); Museum (American decorative arts); Shops (2); Special Collections (azaleas, peonies, rhododendrons)
Activities: Education Programs; Films; Guided Tours; Lectures

The Winterthur Museum houses a permanent collection of more than 80,000 objects made or used in America between 1640 and 1860, including furniture, textiles, paintings, prints, silver, pewter, ceramics, glass, needlework, and brass. The museum consists of two buildings, one with 175 period rooms, and the other with three exhibition galleries. Known primarily for its great collection of American decorative arts, the museum does contain important works of fine art, including paintings by Stuart, Copley, and Peale. Inspired by the work of Gertrude Jekyll and William Robinson, Henry Francis du Pont, working with his close friend landscape architect Marian Coffin, created at Winterthur one of the world's finest naturalistic gardens. "Natural" areas include the eight-acre Azalea Woods; March Bank, the oldest surviving garden area at Winterthur featuring daffodils and other spring bulbs in a naturalistic setting; Oak Hill, featuring oaks, evergreens, deciduous azaleas, and grassy walks; the Sycamore area, a 200-year-old sycamore surrounded by summer-flowering trees and shrubs; the Winter Hazel area, featuring winterhazel and Korean rhododendrons; Magnolia Bend; and the Pinetum, one of the finest collections of confers in the east. Somewhat more formal areas include the Sundial Garden, an "April garden" of flowering shrubs arranged in concentric circles around an antique sundial; the Peony Garden; and the Reflecting Pool Garden. The last garden area to be developed was the Quarry Garden, an abandoned quarry transformed into a gigantic rock garden, planted with a rich assortment of ferns, perennial flowers, and shrubs.

DISTRICT OF COLUMBIA

Washington

Northwest (6)

Northeast (2)

National Mall (2)

The number in parentheses following the area name indicates the number of gardens/arboreta located in that area of the nation's capital.

WASHINGTON

CATHEDRAL CHURCH OF SAINT PETER AND SAINT PAUL— BISHOP'S GARDEN (NATIONAL CATHEDRAL)

Massachusetts and Wisconsin Avenues, N.W., Washington, DC 20016-5098
Tel: (202) 537-6200
Internet Address: http://www.nationalcathedral.org
Admission: Free
Open: Gardens, Daily, until dusk
Facilities: Architecture (14th-century English Gothic-style, construction begun 1907, completed 1990, Philip Hubert Frohman principal architect); Cathedral Grounds (57 acres); Gardens (30 acres); Greenhouse (Mon-Sat, 9am-5pm; Sun, 10am-5pm; 537-6263); Shops Herb Cottage
Activities: Guided Garden Tours (April-July & Sept-Oct, Wed, 10:30am; groups, reserve in advance, 244-0568); Lectures Greenhouse Lecture Series; Plant Sales Greenhouse (herbs, fruit-bearing shrubs, topiaries, and unusual annuals and perennials)

Built in the same manner as medieval churches, stone-on-stone with no structural steel, the cathedral is perhaps the world's last example of pure Gothic architecture. Over 500 feet in length, it is the sixth largest cathedral in the world and the second largest in the United States. The cathedral gardens include two perennial borders, three herb gardens (including a ninth-century herb garden of monastic and infirmary herbs), and an extensive rose garden. Emphasis is placed on those plants associated with a medieval garden. Thirty of the fifty acres that make up the cathedral close are devoted to gardens.

DUMBARTON OAKS PARK

Lovers Lane, N.W. (off R Street, east of 31st Street), Washington, DC 20007
Internet Address: http://dumbartonoakspark.org/
Admission: Free
Parking: On street, two-hour limit weekdays
Open: Daily, dawn-dusk
Facilities: Grounds (27 acres, design by Beatrix Farrand)
Activities: Guided Tours (Apr-Nov, 1st Sun in month, 1pm; (202) 426-6851)

Located to the north of the Dumbarton Oaks Research Library (see listing below) and originally part of the estate, the park was deeded to the National Park Service in 1940 as part of the transaction which included the transfer of Dumbarton Oaks house and its surrounding formal gardens to Harvard University. The park's naturalistic landscape was originally designed by Beatrix Farrand to complement the more formal gardens that surrounded the house. The park entrance is on the left side of Lovers Lane at the bottom of the hill. (Lovers Lane is on the north side of R Street between the east wall of the Estate and the west edge of Montrose Park.)

DUMBARTON OAKS RESEARCH LIBRARY AND COLLECTION

1703 32nd Street, N.W. (east of Wisconsin Avenue, between R & S Streets), Washington, DC 20007-2961
Tel: (202) 339-6410
Internet Address: http://www.doaks.org
Admission: Free (Gardens in season, $6.00)
Attendance: 38,000
Established: 1940
Parking: On street, two-hour limit weekdays
Open: Museum:, Tuesday to Sunday, 2pm-5pm
Gardens: March 15 to October, Daily, 2pm-6pm (admission fee, $5.00)
Gardens: November to March 14, Daily, 2pm-5pm (free)
Closed: Legal holidays, Christmas Eve, inclement weather (Garden)
Facilities: Architecture (19th century Federal-style house; wing, 1963 designed by Philip Johnson); Galleries; Gardens (10 acres, formal gardens); Research Library (available to accredited scholars); Shop (books, cards)
Activities: Concerts; Guided Tours (arrange in advance, 339-6409); Lectures; Permanent Exhibits

A gift of Mildred and Robert Woods Bliss to Harvard University, Dumbarton House maintains research facilities in the areas of Byzantine studies, pre-Columbian studies, and the history of landscape architecture. The collections of Byzantine and pre-Columbian art and rare books and prints relating to gardens are on exhibit. The Dumbarton Oaks Gardens, incorporating elements of traditional French, English, and Italian garden design, were created by landscape gardener Beatrix Ferrand in cooperation with her clients. Encompassing ten acres, the initial plan of formal gardens was completed between 1921 and 1941. Three principles governed the overall plan: first, that the gardens should decrease in formality as the distance from the house increases; second, that plants should be chosen for their interest in winter, as well as during their months of growth; and third, that the gardens should incorporate functional spaces including a swimming pool, tennis court (now the Pebble Garden), and an amphitheater.

HILLWOOD MUSEUM & GARDENS

4155 Linnean Avenue, N.W., Washington, DC 20008-3806
Tel: (202) 686-8500; Fax: (202) 966-7846; TDDY: (202) 363-3056
Internet Address: http://www.hillwoodmuseum.org
Admission: Reservation deposit required: adult $12.00, child (<18) $5.00, student $5.00, senior $10.00
Attendance: 40,000
Established: 1977
Membership: Y
Wheelchair Accessible: Y
Open: March to January, Tuesday to Saturday, 10am-5pm
Closed: Legal holidays
Best Time(s) of Year to Visit: April to May (azalea, rhododendron, perennials), September to November (chrysanthemum, deciduous trees)
Facilities: Architecture (Federal-style former residence of Marjorie Merriweather Post, built 1926); Food Services Café; Gardens (cutting, French parterre, Japanese,

rose); Greenhouses (orchids); Grounds (25 acres); Library (non-circulating, by appointment only); Shop
Activities: Audio Tours; Concerts; Education Programs; Guided Tours

A decorative arts museum, Hillwood contains the largest assemblage of eighteenth- and nineteenth-century Russian objects, liturgical and decorative, outside Russia. It also houses an extensive collection of eighteenth-century European, primarily French, furniture and porcelain. More than 10,000 pieces are presented in a home setting, exhibited intact and interpreted as an art collector's home. The twelve acres of formal gardens and grounds are surrounded by thirteen acres of woodland that are strategically nestled against Rock Creek Park, creating a rural ambiance. Garden highlights include a formal garden (designed by Umberto Innocenti and Richard Webel) featuring all the typical elements of an eighteenth-century French parterre garden; a circular-shaped rose garden (designed by Perry Wheeler) bounded by a pergola draped with climbing roses and boxwood hedges; and a Japanese-style garden (designed by Shogo J. Muaida) blending the traditions of Japanese architecture and garden design with the practicality of American taste. Because Marjorie Merriweather Post was in residence at Hillwood during the spring and autumn seasons when the Washington climate is most pleasant, the gardens feature plants that offer the greatest effect in spring and fall. Over 4,000 azaleas bloom in profusion through April and May, accompanied by hundreds of rhododendron, spirea, lilacs, and viburnum. The blooms of redbuds, cherries, magnolias, dogwoods, and crab apples add splashes of color above, while tulips, daffodils, forget-me-nots, primroses, and pansies sparkle below. In September through November, chrysanthemums join with the deciduous trees throughout the gardens to create a brilliant spectacle against the blaze of colors from the hardwood trees in the adjacent forest. A cutting garden provides the flowers for the mansion's interior, and the greenhouses contain a collection of over 2,000 orchids, some of which are also displayed in the mansion throughout the year. Advance tour reservations are required.

KENILWORTH PARK AND AQUATIC GARDENS

Anacostia Avenue and Douglas Street, N.E., Washington, DC 20019
Tel: (202) 426-6905; Fax: (202) 426-5991
Internet Address: http://www.nps.gov/nace/keaq/
Admission: Free
Attendance: 75,000
Established: 1882
Wheelchair Accessible: Y
Open: Daily, 7:30am-4pm
Closed: New Year's Day, Thanksgiving Day, Christmas Day
Best Time(s) of Year to Visit: late June to July
Facilities: Gardens (aquatic); Greenhouses (5); Grounds (14 acres, garden; 700 acres, park); Tidal Marsh Kenilworth Marsh (77 acres); Visitors Center
Activities: Guided Tours (call in advance)

Kenilworth Park and Aquatic Gardens is a National Park Service site under the administrative management of National Capital Parks—East. It includes Kenilworth Aquatic Gardens, Kenilworth Marsh, ball fields, and recreational facilities. Situated along the east bank of the Anacostia River, the gardens contain many varieties of water lilies and lotus and are also a great place to see birds, frogs, turtles, butterflies, and dragonflies. Begun as the hobby of Civil War veteran W. B. Shaw in 1882, the gardens operated as a commercial water garden until purchased by the federal government in 1938. The only National Park Service site devoted to the propagation and display of aquatic plants, it is included on the National Register of Historic Places. Kenilworth Marsh, the nation's capital's last tidal marsh, is a semi-natural area that borders the Aquatic Gardens on three sides. Accessed from the gardens, the marsh and the adjacent swamp forest areas can be best viewed from the river trail.

OAK HILL CEMETERY

3001 R Street, N.W. (3 blocks east of Wisconsin Ave), Washington, DC 20007
Tel: (202) 337-2835
Established: 1849
Wheelchair Accessible: N
Parking: On-street parking
Open: Monday to Friday, 10am-4pm
Best Time(s) of Year to Visit: Spring to Fall
Facilities: Architecture (Gothic Revival chapel, 1850 design by James Renwick); Grounds (25 acres)

Located in the Georgetown neighborhood of Washington, the cemetery reflects the aesthetics of the Garden Cemetery Movement.

SMITHSONIAN INSTITUTION—GARDENS AND HORTICULTURAL COLLECTIONS

National Mall, Washington, DC 20560
Tel: (202) 357-1926; Fax: (202) 786-2026
Internet Address: http://www.si.edu/gardens/
Admission: Free
Open: Memorial Day to Labor Day, Daily, 7am-9:15pm. Labor Day to Memorial Day, Daily, 7am-5:45pm
Closed: Christmas Day
Facilities: Gardens (display, fragrance)
Activities: Flower Show Orchid Exhibit; Guided Tours Butterfly Habitat Garden (early May-late Sept, Thurs, 2pm; meet at sign near garden entrance), Enid A. Haupt Garden (early May-late Sept, Wed, 1pm; meet near the Castle doors, south entrance), Heirloom & Victory Gardens (mid-Jun-late Oct, Mon, 2pm; meet at sign near flower beds at Mall entrance), Ripley Garden (early Apr-late Oct, Tues, 2pm; meet at sign between Hirshhorn and A&I Building)

The Horticultural Services Division of the Smithsonian Institution maintains a number of gardens on the grounds surrounding its facilities.

A display garden, the Enid A. Haupt Garden is constructed on the roof of the Smithsonian's underground museum complex. It covers 4½ acres and features an embroidery parterre, island garden, and fountain garden. The Island Garden, inspired by the setting for the Temple of Heaven in Beijing, reflects the collections of the Arthur M. Sackler Gallery. The Fountain Garden, reminiscent of Moorish gardens, reflects the collections of the National Museum of African Art.

Situated along the eastern border of the Arts and Industries Building, the Mary Livingston Ripley Garden, a "fragrant garden," contains more than 200 varieties of plants.

Located in front of the Arts and Industries Building to the east of the Smithsonian Castle, the Katherine Dulin Folger Rose Garden features roses, other woody plants, annuals and perennials chosen for year-round interest.

Occupying the ground between the Museum of Natural History and Washington's 9th Street Tunnel, the Butterfly Habitat Garden contains more than 100 host and nectar plants. The garden attracts a variety of butterflies by dividing the garden into five areas—one introductory and four habitats (meadow, wood's edge, urban garden, wetland).

Surrounding the National Museum of American History-Behring Center, the Heirloom Garden consists of half circles filled with annuals and perennials, most of which are open-pollinated plants handed down from generation to generation. A brochure on the plantings is available at the information desk in the museum.

Located on the terrace outside the National Museum of American History's cafeteria, the Victory Garden recreates a World War II garden from a design in a 1943 pamphlet.

Smithsonian horticultural collections include:

An orchid collection totalling 10,000 plants. Each year, running from January to Spring, the Smithsonian Institution, Horticulture Services Division, and the United States Botanic Gardens develop an orchid exhibition, which features hundreds of orchids from both collections.

The Garden Furnishings and Artifacts Collection numbering over 1,600 items.

The Archives of American Gardens containing approximately 80,000 photographic images and records documenting historic and contemporary American gardens.

TUDOR PLACE HISTORIC HOUSE AND GARDEN

1644 31st Street, N.W., Washington, DC 20007
Tel: (202) 965-0400; Fax: (202) 865-0164
Internet Address: http://www.tudorplace.org/
Admission: Suggested Contribution (House Tour): adult $6.00, child (<11) free, student $3.00, senior $5.00. Suggested Contribution (Gardens): $2.00
Membership: Y
Wheelchair Accessible: P
Parking: On street
Open: House Tours: February to December, Tuesday to Friday, 10am/11:30am/1pm/2:30pm; Saturday, 10am/11am/noon/1pm/2pm/3pm; Sunday, noon/1pm/2pm/3pm. Gardens: February to December, Monday to Saturday, 10am-4pm; Sunday, noon-4pm
Facilities: Architecture (Neo-Classical residence, 1816 design by Dr. William Thornton); Gardens; Grounds (5 acres)
Activities: Artist-Residence Program; Education Programs; Garden Tours (self-guided; group guided tour, reserve in advance); Guided Tours; Lecture Series; Temporary Exhibitions

A house of architectural distinction occupied for 180 years by six generations of a single family, Tudor Place provides a unique historical perspective on the nation's capital. The first generation of the Peter family also laid out a garden with formal parterres, sweeping lawns, and graceful trees and shrubs. Over the years, the gardens have been enriched by the changes and additions of each owner. The historic trees, the Federal period terraces, and other features are protected by the first scenic easement ever given to the U.S. Department of the Interior.

UNITED STATES BOTANIC GARDEN

The National Mall, 1st Street, S.W. (between Maryland Avenue and C Street), Washington, DC 20024
Tel: (202) 225-8333; Fax: (202) 225-1561
Internet Address: http://www.aoc.gov/pages/usbgpage.htm
Admission: Free
Attendance: 625,000

Established: 1820
Wheelchair Accessible: Y
Parking: Limited metered parking
Open: Daily, 10am-5pm
Park, Daily, dawn-dusk
Facilities: Botanical Garden; Conservatory (1933); Grounds (5 acres); Shop; Special
Collections (bromeliad, cactus and succulent, carnivorous, cycad, food and economic,
medicinal, rare and endangered, orchids)
Activities: Education Programs; Flower Shows (seasonal, 4/year); Guided Tours
(groups, reserve 3 weeks in advance); Temporary Exhibitions

Established by Congress in 1820, the United States Botanic Garden is one of the oldest botanic gardens in North America. The garden's first greenhouse was constructed in
1842; since 1849 the garden has been located at the eastern end of the Mall. Currently
maintaining approximately 26,000 plants, the garden's public facilities include the Conservatory with two acres of outside grounds and Frédéric Auguste Bartholdi Park, an outdoor display area located across Independence Avenue. Plans are under way to develop
three acres directly west of the conservatory as the National Garden. The renovated
Conservatory features plant and educational exhibits, including a reconstructed Palm
House (the central structure that rises over 80 feet to crown the Conservatory) and rooms
devoted to orchids, medicinal plants, economic plants, Jurassic plants, desert plants, a
children's garden, and seasonal displays. Bartholdi Park, named for the sculptor of its historic fountain, is a garden demonstration landscape. Each garden in the park is of a size
and scale suitable for the urban or suburban home site. The gardens illustrate design principles and display plant combinations for a variety of themes and styles. Changing seasonal display beds feature outstanding annuals and perennials. Scheduled to open in the
spring of 2004, the new National Garden will be a showcase for unusual, useful, and ornamental plants that grow well in the mid-Atlantic region. Its major features will be an environmental learning center, a rose garden, a water garden, and the Showcase Garden. The
Showcase Garden will present outstanding plants native to the mid-Atlantic region in naturalistic settings arranged along a moisture gradient. Visitors to the Botanic Garden will
continue to be welcomed in Bartholdi Park while the Conservatory and National Garden
are under construction.

UNITED STATES NATIONAL ARBORETUM (AHS RAP)

3501 New York Avenue, N.E., Washington, DC 20002-1958
Tel: (202) 245-2726; Fax: (202) 245-4575
Internet Address: http://www.usna.usda.gov/
Admission: Free
Attendance: 350,000
Established: 1927
Membership: Y
Wheelchair Accessible: Y
Parking: Ample free parking
Open: Daily, 8am-5pm
Closed: Christmas Day
Best Time(s) of Year to Visit: early Spring to May (peonies), Spring (azaleas,
dogwoods, Japanese maples), May to June (iris), June to July (day lilies, herb garden),
early Summer (rose garden), Fall (Japanese maples), Winter (conifers)
Facilities: Arboretum; Auditorium; Climatic Areas Asia (Japanese woodland, Asian
valley, Chinese valley, Korean hillside); Conservatory; Gardens (aquatic, azalea,
boxwood, conifer, dogwood, herb, holly and magnolia, Japanese, native plant,

perennial, state trees); Grounds (446 acres); Herbarium (600,000 specimens); Library (7,000 volumes, non-circulating); Museum National Bonsai and Penjing Museum (daily, 10am-3:30pm); Picnic Areas; Shop Arbor House (open daily, 10am-3pm) Activities: Classes; Films; Flower Shows; Guided Tours; Lectures; Temporary Exhibitions

Located in northeast Washington with entrances off New York Avenue and R Street, the National Arboretum is a United States Department of Agriculture research and education facility and a living museum dedicated to developing and promoting improved floral and landscape plants. Its public facilities consist of an array of display gardens, collections, and historical monuments set among native stands of eastern deciduous trees. Major collections and gardens include: The Asian Collection (13 acres), containing over 1,000 different species of wild collected and cultivated flora native to Japan, China, and Korea, are displayed in a design that allows the visitor to compare and contrast plant material. The Azalea Collection, containing over 70,000 plants of 1,900 cultivars and species, includes all five major groups of azaleas within the genus Rhododendron. The Conifer Collection is highlighted by the five-acre Gotelli Dwarf Conifer Collection, the oldest and largest (1,500 specimens) presentation of dwarf and slow growing conifers in the United States. The National Boxwood Collection (5 acres) with over 170 different species, cultivars, and accessions is recognized as one of the most comprehensive holdings of boxwood germplasm in the world. The Perennial Collections include extensive plantings of day lilies (1,000 cultivars), iris (240 varieties), and peonies. The National Bonsai and Penjing Museum with Japanese, Chinese, American, and international pavilions is the only museum in the world devoted to the art and science of bonsai and penjing. The National Herb Garden (2½ acres) consists of three beds displaying annual herbals, an intimate knot garden, ten theme gardens (first-century classical, American colonial, Native American, oriental, dye, medicinal, food flavoring, beverage, fragrance, industrial), and an antique rose garden. A demonstration garden designed by landscape architects Wolfgang Oehme and James van Sweden illustrates their New American Garden, which places emphasis on ease of maintenance and year-round interest through the use of grasses, perennials, and native plants. Other areas of note include a Japanese garden designed by Masao Knoshita, an aquatic garden, a landscaped circle in front of the Administration Building designed by Meriwether Rumrill, a landscape design by Russell Page featuring a reflecting pool and twenty-two-thirty-foot-high Corinthian columns originally designed by Benjamin Latrobe for the U.S. Capitol, and the thirty-acre National Grove of State Trees. A Visitors Guide that includes a map, descriptions of the gardens and collections, seasonal plant information, and ground rules is available in the lobby of the Administration Building.

Florida

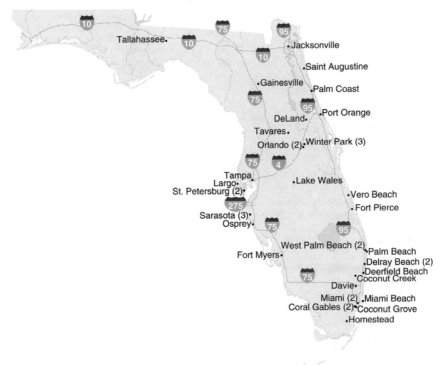

Tallahassee.

Jacksonville

.Saint Augustine

.Gainesville

.Palm Coast

DeLand.

Port Orange

Tavares.

Orlando (2).Winter Park (3)

Tampa

Largo.

.Lake Wales

St. Petersburg (2).

.Vero Beach

. Fort Pierce

Sarasota (3).

Osprey.

West Palm Beach (2)

Fort Myers.

Palm Beach

.Delray Beach (2)

.Deerfield Beach

.Coconut Creek

Davie.

Miami (2) .Miami Beach

Coral Gables (2).Coconut Grove

.Homestead

Key West (2).

The number in parentheses following the city name indicates the number of gardens/ arboreta in that municipality. If there is no number, one is understood. For example, in the text two listings would be found under Miami and one listing under Miami Beach.

COCONUT CREEK

BUTTERFLY WORLD

Tradewinds Park, 3600 West Sample Road, Coconut Creek, FL 33073
Tel: (954) 977-4400; Fax: (954) 977-4501
Internet Address: http://www.butterflyworld.com
Admission: Fee: adult $16.95, child (<4) free, child (4-12) $11.95
Attendance: 220,000
Established: 1988
Membership: Y
Wheelchair Accessible: Y
Parking: On site, 600 spaces
Open: Monday to Saturday, 9am-5pm; Sunday, 1pm-5pm
Closed: Easter, Thanksgiving Day, Christmas Day
Facilities: Aviaries (5); Butterfly House; Grounds (2.8 acres); Secret Garden; Shop;
Special Collections (Dutchman's pipe, passion vine, flowering tropical plants and trees,
water lily); Tropical Rain Forest

Butterflies, hummingbirds, and other exotic birds are displayed in aviaries and on the
grounds of Butterfly World. In addition to an interior tropical rain forest, there are extensive
outside gardens, including Lakeside Garden, English Rose Garden, and the Secret Garden.

COCONUT GROVE

NATIONAL TROPICAL BOTANICAL GARDEN—THE KAMPONG

4013 S. Douglas Road, Coconut Grove, FL 33133-6840
Tel: (305) 442-7169; Fax: (305) 442-2925
Internet Address: http://www.ntbg.org/kampong.html
Admission: Tours, by appointment: adult $10.00, child (<7) $3.00, child (>7) $5.00,
student $5.00
Membership: Y
Wheelchair Accessible: Y
Parking: Free on site, 40 spaces
Open: Monday to Friday, 7am-5pm
Best Time(s) of Year to Visit: Winter to Spring (flowering trees), Summer to Fall
(tropical fruit)
Facilities: Architecture (1892, former home of horticulturist David Fairchild, one of
the oldest buildings in Miami-Dade County on its original foundation); Grounds
(11 acres); Special Collections (aroids, bamboo, tropical fruits, flowering trees)
Activities: Guided Tours (Mon-Fri, by appointment)

Located on Biscayne Bay, the Kampong contains an extensive collection of flowering trees and tropical fruit cultivars. Listed on the National Register of Historic Places, the Kampong was originally the residence of David Fairchild, a noted collector of plants of economic/aesthetic value. Dedicated to the conservation of tropical plant diversity, the National Tropical Botanical Garden includes four gardens and three preserves in Hawaii and one in south Florida.

CORAL GABLES

FAIRCHILD TROPICAL GARDEN

10901 Old Cutler Road, Coral Gables, FL 33156-4233
Tel: (305) 667-1651; Fax: (305) 661-8953
Internet Address: http://www.ftg.org
Admission: Fee: adult $10.00, child (3-12) $5.00, senior $9.00. Contribution Day, 1st Wednesday in month; group discount
Attendance: 105,000
Established: 1937
Membership: Y
Wheelchair Accessible: Y
Open: Daily, 9:30am-4:30pm
Closed: Christmas Day
Facilities: Arboretum (10 acres); Climatic Areas (rain forest, keys coastal habitat); Conservatory (16,428 square feet); Food Services Garden Café; Grounds (83 acres); Herbarium (100,000 specimens); Library (7,000 volumes, non-circulating by appointment); Picnic Area; Shop; Special Collections (palm, cycad, flowering tree and vine, tropical fruit tree, native Florida species and tropical plant)
Activities: Education Programs (adults and children); Guided Tours (mid-Nov—April; Mon-Sat, 10:30am & 11:30am; Sun, 1:30pm); Lectures; Plant Sales Mango Festival (May), Ramble (November)

An international leader in tropical plant research, Fairchild Tropical Garden plays an important part in preserving the biodiversity of the tropical environment. The garden has assembled an outstanding collection of taxonomically arranged and well-documented tropical plants, emphasizing palms (1,500 accessions, with 193 genera and more than 500 identified species), cycads (3,700 plants, including most of the world's 200+ species) , fruit trees (450 cultivars), flowering trees, tropical vines, bamboos, arid plants, hibiscus, Bahamian plants, and mangroves. It is the headquarters of the Heliconia Society International and one of only five active repositories globally for the genus heliconia and related genera. Its collection contains more than 350 accessions of plants related to this group, including 201 accessions of heliconia, 123 of gingers, 20 marantaceae, 4 strelitziaceae, 3 lowiaceae and 8 musaceae. The conservatory features "Windows to the Tropics," a two-level display containing 1,900 species of plants that will not survive outdoors in subtropical south Florida, including rare palms and cycads, ferns, orchids, aroids, bromeliads, fruit trees, and unusual vines. The adjacent Fairchild Rain Forest is a two-acre, outdoor exhibit of tropical rain forest plants from around the world, especially plants of the American tropics. Other outside exhibits include the Montgomery Palmetum, a world-renowned display and research collection of palms from all parts of the world; the McLamore Arboretum, containing some 740 species of tropical flowering trees, a 560-foot-long vine pergola, an historic stone and wood structure supporting an array of tropical flowering vines; the Keys Coastal Habitat, marsh and mangrove primarily planted with native species from the Florida Keys that are attractive to birds; and the Lynn Fort Lummus Endangered Plant Garden, displaying a selection of endangered species of Florida and Puerto Rico from the garden's conservation collections. The Gate House Museum of Plant Exploration is an historic landmark, built in 1939 and restored in 1995. Its exhibit, In Search of Green Treasure, includes plant artifacts, photographs, text panels, and audio recordings about why plants are collected, how they are used, what scientists experience in the field, and why their work is significant. The exhibit shows the real-life experiences of men and women who, like David Fairchild, travel the globe to seek unknown plants and information about them.

UNIVERSITY OF MIAMI—JOHN C. GIFFORD ARBORETUM

University of Miami, Department of Biology, Cox Science, Coral Gables, FL 33146
Tel: (305) 284-5364; Fax: (305) 284-3973
Internet Address: http://www.bio.miami.edu/arboretum
Admission: Free
Established: 1947
Membership: Y
Parking: Parking metered weekdays; free weekends
Activities: Lecture Series (annual)

Nestled on the northwest corner of the University of Miami's Coral Gables campus is Gifford Arboretum, featuring hundreds of native trees and plants. Nearby is the Palmetum, containing a collection of rare and exotic palms.

DAVIE

FLAMINGO GARDENS (AHS RAP)

3750 S. Flamingo Road, Davie, FL 33330
Tel: (954) 473-2955; Fax: (954) 473-1738
Internet Address: http://www.flamingogardens.org/
Admission: Fee: adult $12.00, child (<4) free, child (4-11) $6.00, student $8.40, senior $9.60.
Established: 1969
Membership: Y
Open: November to May, Daily, 9:30am-5:30pm. June to October, Tuesday to Sunday, 9:30am-5:30pm.
Closed: Thanksgiving Day, Christmas Day
Facilities: Arboretum (18 champion trees); Architecture (Wray Home, on National Register of Historic Places); Aviary (Florida wading birds); Food Services; Gardens (butterfly/hummingbird, citrus, xeriscape, croton, bromeliad); Grounds (60 acres rain forest, citrus groves, wetlands); Shop; Tropical Plant House (calatheas, orchids)

The gardens showcase rare, exotic, and native plants. Visitors may tour the citrus groves and the Wray Botanical Collection.

DEERFIELD BEACH

DEERFIELD ARBORETUM

Constitution Park, 2841 W. Hillsboro Boulevard, Deerfield Beach, FL 33443
Tel: (954) 480-4494; Fax: (954) 420-5540

Internet Address: http://www.treezoo.com
Admission: Free
Established: 1995
Membership: Y
Open: Daily, dawn-dusk
Facilities: Arboretum; Butterfly Garden; Grounds (9 acres); Wetlands Demonstration Area
Activities: Guided Tours (Friday, 10am)

The arboretum contains 325 species (not including native) palms, tropical fruit trees, exotic flowering and canopy trees, bamboos, and miscellaneous exotic trees. Material is displayed in ten divisions: flowering trees, palm trees, bamboo, tropical fruit trees, native canopy trees, exotic canopy trees, butterfly garden, wetlands demonstration area, spice and herb garden, and children's garden. All specimens are identified by common name, species, and origin.

DELAND

CITY OF DELAND—SENSORY GARDEN

Bill Dreggors Park, 230 N. Stone Street, DeLand, FL 32720
Tel: (386) 734-5333
Internet Address: http://www.deland.org/Parks
Admission: Free
Established: 1995
Facilities: Gardens (butterfly, sensory); Grounds Garden (5,600 square feet),
Park (7 acres)
Activities: Self-Guided Tours (brochures available in mailbox at garden entrance)

Situated in the center of the city, the garden is designed for the visually impaired and physically challenged. The garden features plants with easily sensed characteristics such as scent, color, texture, taste, and touch and includes signs in Braille. Seven raised planters contain a variety of herbs, perennials, and annuals such as dusty miller, lamb's ear, begonias, marigolds, and petunias that can be pinched for smell and touch. In the center of these planters, a decorative water fountain provides the sounds of flowing water. Beyond the planters are other native and hardy plants and trees, textured and fragrant ground cover plants, and a butterfly garden. The garden, created by the Garden Club of DeLand, is owned and maintained by the City Parks and Recreation Department.

DELRAY BEACH

AMERICAN ORCHID SOCIETY VISITOR CENTER AND BOTANICAL GARDEN (AHS RAP)

16700 AOS Lane (off Jog Road, adjacent to Morikami Museum), Delray Beach,
FL 33446-4351
Tel: (561) 404-2000; Fax: (561) 404-2100
Internet Address: http://www.aos.org
Admission: Fee: adult $8.00, child (<12) free
Attendance: 20,000
Membership: Y

Wheelchair Accessible: Y
Parking: Free on site
Open: Tuesday to Sunday, 10am-4:30pm
Facilities: Garden (orchid); Greenhouses (2; 1 display & 1 production); Grounds
(6 acres), Garden (3½ acres, 2001 design by Connie Roy-Fisher Landscape
Architects); Shop; Visitor Center
Activities: Education Programs

In addition to thousands of orchids, the garden and greenhouse showcase more than
600 species of ornamentals and an extensive assortment of trees.

THE MORIKAMI MUSEUM AND JAPANESE GARDEN

4000 Morikami Park Road, Delray Beach, FL 33446-2305
Tel: (561) 495-0233; Fax: (561) 499-2557
Internet Address: http://www.morikami.com/
Admission: Fee: adult $9.00, child $6.00, student $3.75, senior $8.00
Attendance: 150,000
Established: 1977
Membership: Y
Wheelchair Accessible: Y
Parking: Free on site
Open: Tuesday to Sunday, 10am-5pm
Closed: New Year's Day, Easter, Independence Day, Thanksgiving Day, Christmas Day
Facilities: Bonsai Collection; Exhibition Area; Garden (Japanese); Grounds (200 acre
park); Japanese restaurant (open 11am-3pm); Library (3,000 volumes, non-circulating,
by request); Picnic Area; Theatre (225 seats)
Activities: Guided Tours (groups of 15 or more); Permanent Exhibits; Temporary
Exhibitions (5-7 per year)

The museum at the Morikami Museum and Japanese Gardens is set in a 200-acre park
of pine forests and Japanese-style gardens. The 32,000-square-foot museum itself is devoted exclusively to the living culture of Japan. It features varying exhibitions of Japanese
fine and folk art, crafts, and artifacts. A highlight of the museum is the teahouse, where
regularly-scheduled demonstrations of the Japanese tea ceremony are conducted. The
Morikami's Florida bonsai collection is among the rarest in the country, with specimens
dating to the seventeenth century and unusual tropical miniatures that bloom in season.
Surrounding it all are tranquil gardens. A near mile-long strolling path winds past cascading waterfalls, handcrafted wooden bridges and gates, stone ornaments, water vistas, and
meditative niches. The pace is slow and quiet, the progress subtle and deliberate. The
path meanders through six distinct areas, reflecting the historical development of Japanese garden philosophies, melded together by connective elements of plants, rock, and
water. In 2000, the *Journal of Japanese Gardening* ranked the Garden as one of the ten highest-quality Japanese gardens outside of Japan, out of 300 sites surveyed.

FORT MYERS

EDISON AND FORD WINTER ESTATES—
BOTANICAL GARDENS (AHS RAP)

2350 McGregor Boulevard, Fort Myers, FL 33901
Tel: (239) 334-7419
Internet Address: http://www.edison-ford-estate.com

Admission: Fee (Home & Gardens Tour): adult $15.00, child (8-12) $8.50,
family $40.00
Attendance: 250,000
Established: 1947
Parking: On site, 250 spaces, includes handicapped spaces
Open: Monday to Saturday, 9am-4pm; Sunday, noon-4pm
Closed: Thanksgiving Day, Christmas Day
Facilities: Architecture (9 historical site buildings, including Edison & Ford winter
homes); Food Services (food court); Gardens (14 acres, subtropical gardens with
imported plants used by Edison in experiments; over 1,000 species); Grounds (20
acres); Museum (20,000 square feet); Picnic Area; Shops (2, gift & garden)
Activities: Events Festival of Lights, Holiday House, Southern Living Garden Show;
Guided Tours Homes & Gardens Tour (Mon-Sat, 9am-5:30pm, last tour 4pm; Sun,
noon-5:30pm, last tour 4pm); In-Depth Botanical Tour (Thurs & Sat, 9am;
$19/person); Lectures; Plant Sales

Seminole Lodge was designed by Edison and built in sections in Fairfield, Maine, in
1885. The sections were then transported to Fort Myers by four sailing schooners and
erected in 1886. The botanical garden was originally developed for experimental purposes,
as an aid to understanding the various products and by-products of the plants, which were
used in many of Edison's scientific investigations. Later Mrs. Edison enhanced the garden
with many beautiful plants, including roses, orchids, and bromeliads. The tropical botanical garden now contains more than a thousand varieties of plants imported from all over
the world, including African sausage trees and a Banyan tree, which was a gift from Harvey
Firestone in 1925. In 1947, Mrs. Edison donated the estate to the City of Fort Myers,
which now leases it in conjunction with the Mangoes, the adjacent Henry Ford estate, to
Edison & Ford Winter Estates, Inc., a private not-for-profit corporation.

FORT PIERCE

HEATHCOTE BOTANICAL GARDENS, INC. (AHS RAP)

210 Savannah Road, Fort Pierce, FL 34982-3447
Tel: (772) 464-4672; Fax: (772) 489-2748
Internet Address: http://www.heathcotebotanicalgardens.com
Admission: Fee: adult $4.00, child (<12) free, child (6-12) $2.00
Attendance: 20,000
Established: 1985
Membership: Y
Wheelchair Accessible: Y
Open: November to April, Tuesday to Saturday, 9am-5pm; Sunday, 1pm-5pm. May to
October, Tuesday to Saturday, 9am-5pm
Closed: Legal holidays
Best Time(s) of Year to Visit: Spring
Facilities: Botanical Garden 3.5 acres; Classroom; Gardens (children's, herb,
Japanese, perennial, orchid house, bonsai, native plants); Grounds (3½ acres);
Library (150 volumes); Shop
Activities: Classes; Garden Festival; Guided Tours (reserve in advance-464-4672);
Lectures

Heathcote features flowers and foliage of the subtropics in varied gardens, including a
perennial border, palm walk, children's garden, Japanese garden, herb garden, and reflection garden. A self-guided tour is available.

GAINESVILLE

KANAPAHA BOTANICAL GARDENS

4700 S.W. 58th Drive (on SR 24 one mile west of I-75/Exit #384), Gainesville, FL 32608
Tel: (352) 372-4981; Fax: (352) 372-5892
Internet Address: http://www.kanapaha.org
Admission: Fee: adult $5.00, child (<6) free, child (6-13) $3.00
Established: 1986
Membership: Y
Wheelchair Accessible: Y
Parking: Paved parking with grass overflow on site
Open: Monday to Friday, 9am-5pm; Saturday to Sunday, 9am-dusk
Best Time(s) of Year to Visit: June to September (color)
Facilities: Arboretum (under development, 8 acres); Gardens (azalea/camellia, bamboo, butterfly, crinum, cycad, fern, herb, hummingbird, palm hammock, oriental, perennial, rock, rose, sunken, vinery, water lily, woodland); Grounds (62 acres); Nursery; Picnic Area; Shop; Special Collections (bamboo)

Developed and maintained by the North Florida Botanical Society, Inc., Kanapaha features nineteen major and minor gardens. It has a particularly extensive bamboo collection. Because of its proximity to Lake Kanapaha, the facility was named Kanapaha Botanical Gardens. "Kana-paha" is a contraction of Timucua Indian words meaning "palmetto leaves" and "house." Collectively, they refer to the thatched dwellings of the lake margin's original human inhabitants.

HOMESTEAD

MIAMI-DADE COUNTY FRUIT AND SPICE PARK

24801 S.W. 187th Avenue, Homestead, FL 33031
Tel: (305) 247-5727
Internet Address: http://www.co.miami-dade.fl.us/parks/mpattra4.htm
Admission: Free
Established: 1944
Open: Daily, 10am-5pm
Closed: New Year's Day, Thanksgiving Day, Christmas Day
Facilities: Grounds (32 acres); Shop; Special Collections (fruit, nut, spice, herb trees, and shrubs)
Activities: Guided Tours (Sat, Sun-1pm, 3pm; $1.50); Picnic Facilities; Workshops

Established by Miami-Dade Park and Recreation Department, the Fruit and Spice Park is internationally known for its more than 500 varieties of exotic and subtropical fruit, nut, spice and herb trees, and shrubs.

JACKSONVILLE

CUMMER MUSEUM OF ART & GARDENS

829 Riverside Avenue, Jacksonville, FL 32204
Tel: (904) 356-6857; Fax: (904) 353-4101

Internet Address: http://www.cummer.org
Admission: Fee: adult $6.00, child $1.00, student $3.00, senior $4.00. Free
Tuesdays, 4pm-9pm
Attendance: 110,000
Established: 1958
Membership: Y
Wheelchair Accessible: Y
Parking: Across from museum on Riverside Avenue
Open: Tuesday, 10am-9pm; Wednesday, 10am-5pm; Thursday, 10am-9pm; Friday to
Saturday, 10am-5pm; Sunday, noon-5pm
Closed: Christmas Day, New Year's Day, Thanksgiving Day, Independence Day
Facilities: Art Studios; Formal Gardens (2 acres); Galleries; Interactive Art Education
Center; Library (5,000 volumes, available by application); Shop
Activities: Children's Activities; Concerts; Guided Tours (Sun, 12:15pm); Lectures;
Permanent Exhibits; Temporary Exhibitions

The setting of the Cummer Museum is on two and one half acres of formal gardens on
the west bank of the St. Johns River. The museum has an active exhibition schedule, displaying works from its own collection and from major institutions around the country.
The first garden created by Mrs. Cummer at the residence was planted in 1903 and followed the English style. An Italian Garden designed by Ellen Biddle Shipman (1869-
1950) followed in 1931. Complementing the Cummer's English and Italian Gardens is the
North Garden. This garden was designed in 1931 by the nationally known firm of Frederick Law Olmsted. Plans are being formulated to restore the North Garden.

KEY WEST

AUDUBON HOUSE AND TROPICAL GARDENS

205 Whitehead Street, Key West, FL 33040-6522
Tel: (305) 294-2116
Internet Address: http://www.audubonhouse.com/
Admission: Fee: adult $7.50, child $2.00
Attendance: 39,000
Established: 1960
Membership: Y
Wheelchair Accessible: Y
Open: Daily, 9:30am-5pm
Facilities: Architecture (19th-century Geiger House);
Botanical Garden; Shop
Activities: Gallery Talks; Guided Tours; Lectures

The nineteenth-century home was built by Captain John H. Geiger, a harbor pilot and
master wrecker. It is believed that many of the eighteen Key West bird drawings appearing in Audubon's *Birds of America* folio were conceived in the Audubon House Garden. Orchids, bromeliads, and other tropical plants and trees abound. The herb garden and 1840-
style nursery provide an historic look at gardening, while native plants and exotics
provide an environment that is reminiscent of old Key West.

KEY WEST GARDEN CLUB—JOE ALLEN GARDEN CENTER

West Martello Tower, Atlantic Boulevard. & White Street, Key West, FL 33045
Tel: (305) 294-3210

Internet Address: http://www.keywestgardenclub.com
Admission: Free
Attendance: 12,000
Established: 1955
Membership: Y
Wheelchair Accessible: P
Parking: Parking on street
Open: Tuesday to Saturday, 9:30am-3:15pm
Facilities: Architecture (historic fort); Garden (1.5 acres); Visitor Center
Activities: Classes; Flower Shows; Guided Tours; Lectures; Plant Sales

The headquarters of the Key West Garden Club, the site contains a collection of native and exotic trees and plants, including blooming orchids, butterfly garden, water lily ponds, begonias, succulents, and ferns. Historic West Martello, a Civil War era fort, is listed on the National Register of Historic Places.

LAKE WALES

HISTORIC BOK SANCTUARY

1151 Tower Boulevard., Lake Wales, FL 33853-3412
Tel: (863) 676-9412; Fax: (863) 676-6770
Internet Address: http://www.boksanctuary.org/
Admission: Fee: adult $8.00, child (<5) free, child (5-12) $3.00.
Saturday, 8am-9am: free; group rates available
Attendance: 140,000
Established: 1929
Membership: Y
Wheelchair Accessible: P
Parking: Lot, 500 spaces, adjacent to gardens & Visitor Center
Open: Grounds, Daily, 8am-6pm
Education/Visitor Center, Daily, 9am-5pm

Historic Bok Sanctuary, Lake Wales, FL.

Facilities: Architecture Bok's Singing Tower (60-carillon), Pinewood Estate (Mediterranean Revival-style villa, early 1930s design by Charles Wait of the Olmsted firm); Food Services Carillon Café; Gardens (last admission-5pm); Grounds (250 acres, original garden design by Frederick Law Olmsted, Jr.), Pinewood Estate (8 acres, restoration by landscape architect Rudy Favretti); Shop Tower & Garden Gift Shop; Visitor Center (Daily, 9am-5pm); Wildlife Sanctuary; Trail Pine Ridge Preserve Trail (¾ mile)
Activities: Classes (adult, children); Concerts; Films; Guided Tours; Lectures; Temporary Exhibitions

Edward W. Bok, a Dutch immigrant who became a Pulitzer Prize-winning author, a respected humanitarian, and an advocate for world peace and the environment, commissioned Frederick Law Olmsted, Jr., to create "a spot of beauty second to none in the country." The original plantings included 1,000 live oaks, 10,000 azaleas, 100 sabal palms, 300 magnolias, and 500 gordonias as well as hundreds of fruiting shrubs. The visual centerpiece of the historic landscape garden is a majestic 205-foot-tall marble and coquina belltower that houses one of the world's finest carillons. Constructed of pink and gray marble from Georgia and coquina from Florida, the Singing Tower is rich in carvings depicting the flora and fauna of Florida. Carillon recitals may be heard each afternoon, with clock music throughout the day. The Sanctuary, a National Historic Landmark, is surrounded by a Longleaf Pine-Turkey Oak ecosystem and acres of citrus groves. The Pine Ridge Preserve offers a trail where visitors may enjoy the rare plants and animals of Florida's ancient sandhill ecosystem. "Window by the Pond" is a nature observatory overlooking a Florida bog. The neighboring 1930s Mediterranean Revival mansion at Pinewood Estate, also landscaped by the Olmsted Brothers firm, is open for tours. It has been restored to its original design by the nationally recognized restoration landscape architect Rudy Favretti.

LARGO

FLORIDA BOTANICAL GARDENS (AHS RAP)

Florida Botanical Gardens, Largo, FL.

Pinewood Cultural Park, 12175 125th Street North, Largo, FL 33774
Tel: (727) 582-2100;
Fax: (727) 582-2149
Internet Address: http://www.flbg.org/
Admission: No charge, donations accepted
Established: 2000
Membership: Y
Wheelchair Accessible: Y
Parking: Free on site, includes handicapped and RV parking
Open: Gardens, Daily, sunrise-sunset
Welcome Center, Monday to Saturday, 8am-5pm; Sunday, noon-4pm
Facilities: Demonstration Areas (native plant, aquatic ecosystem, compost & mulch, crepe myrtle, trial annual display); Gardens (bromeliad, cottage, day lily, ground cover, herb, heritage, hibiscus, jazz, palm, patio, rose, topiary, tropical, tropical fruit wedding); Grounds Florida Botanical Gardens (150 acres), Pinewood Cultural Park (182 acres); Shop Botanical Bounty; Visitor Center

Opened in 2000, the gardens contain a blend of Florida native plants and exotic tropicals, displayed in both natural and formal gardens. In addition to the completed gardens and demonstration area listed above, there are plans for All-American Flowering Annual, butterfly, children's, kitchen, native plant, and sensory gardens, as well as a demonstration area for home landscaping. Over eighty acres are devoted to Florida natural ecosystems, including Tupelo swamp and Pine-Palmetto forests. A program of the Pinellas county government, the gardens are a part of Pine Wood Cultural Park, which also includes Pinellas County's Heritage Village and the Gulf Coast Museum of Art.

MIAMI

CITY OF MIAMI—ICHIMURA MIAMI-JAPAN GARDEN

1101 McArthur Causeway (I-395), Watson Island (east of Biscayne Bay), Miami, FL 33130
Tel: (305) 575-5256; Fax: (305) 416-2156
Internet Address: http://www.ci.miami.fl.us/parks/pages
Admission: Fee
Established: 2004
Membership: Y
Wheelchair Accessible: P

Parking: Adjacent municipal lot, fee
Open: Garden, limited, by appointment
Watson Island, Daily, sunrise-sunset
Closed: Legal holidays
Best Time(s) of Year to Visit: November to March
Facilities: Garden (Japanese); Grounds (1 acre, design by painter, architect, and landscape architect Lester Collins Pancoast)

In the 1950s, Mr. Kiyoshi Ichimura became enamored with the City of Miami and began sending dismantled objects and materials from Tokyo along with carpenters, gardeners, and a landscape architect to design and construct what would become the "San-Ai-An Japanese Garden." The San-Ai-An was located in the heart of what is now Parrot Jungle Island, an animal theme park. The new Ichimura Miami-Japan Garden, including the sculptures given to the city by Mr. Ichimura, attempts to capture the essence of the traditional Japanese garden while utilizing subtropical and tropical plants, local materials, and building skills available in Florida. Developed and maintained by the owner of Parrot Jungle Island, the garden is open during the day for public gathering, classes, cultural exchange, and passive enjoyment. Seasonal festivals and holidays from the Japanese calendar are celebrated as garden-related events.

VIZCAYA MUSEUM AND GARDENS

3251 S. Miami Avenue, Miami, FL 33129
Tel: (305) 250-9133; Fax: (305) 285-2004; TDDY: (305) 857-6680
Admission: Fee: adult $12.00, child (6-12) $5.00. Group discounts (minimum of 20)
Attendance: 200,000
Established: 1952
Membership: Y
Wheelchair Accessible: Y
Open: Daily, 9:30am-4:30pm
Closed: Christmas Day
Facilities: Architecture (Italian Renaissance-style villa, 1916); Food Services Café; Gardens (Renaissance Italian, fountain, maze, secret, sensory); Grounds (10 acres); Library (3,700 volumes, 20,000 slides, non-circulating, by appointment); Shop
Activities: Arts Festival; Concerts; Education Programs (adults and children); Films; Gallery Talks; Guided Tours (group, by appointment); Lectures; Performances; Permanent Exhibits; Temporary Exhibitions; Traveling Exhibitions

The winter residence of industrialist James Deering, the house has thirty-four rooms of fifteenth through nineteenth-century antique furnishings and decorative arts. The grounds include over ten acres of formal gardens, fountains, grottoes, pavilions, lakes, canals, and an elaborate waterfront. The main Renaissance garden features classical statuary, architectural features, and water displays set among lawn, hedges, and sculpted trees and shrubs. There is also a variety of smaller dependent fountain, maze, secret, sensory, and theatre gardens. A property of Miami-Dade Parks and Recreation Department, Vizcaya has been designated a National Historic Landmark.

MIAMI BEACH

MIAMI BEACH BOTANICAL GARDEN

2000 Convention Center Drive (across from MBCC Hall D),
Miami Beach, FL 33139

Tel: (305) 673-7256; Fax: (305) 535-8053
Internet Address: http://ci.miami-beach.fl.us/newcity/depts/rcpa/
botanical_garden/garden
Admission: Free
Membership: Y
Open: Daily, 9am-5pm
Facilities: Auditorium (100 seats); Conservatory; Gardens (balcony, bromeliad, herb,
Japanese, kitchen, native plant, orchid, tropical, xeriscape); Grounds (4½ acres); Shop
(gardening accessories, gifts, artwork, books); Special Collections (bromeliad, orchid,
sub-tropical palm)
Activities: Education Programs; Events Herb Festival (Fall), Palm Festival (March);
Guided Tours Lincoln Road Botanical Walking Tour (Oct 15-Jun 14, Thurs-11am &
Sat-1:30pm; Jun 15-Oct 14, call for evening tour); Performances, Arts in the Garden

Located in South Beach, the garden contains a display of over 150 species of bromeliads,
the Arthur Laufferberger Memorial Orchidaria housing over 300 specimens of tropical and
subtropical orchids, a rich collection of subtropical palms, a small Japanese garden featuring
a lotus pond, and a diverse array of other interesting flora. The garden is managed by the
Miami Beach Garden Conservancy, under contract with the City of Miami Beach.

ORLANDO

HARRY P. LEU GARDENS (AHS RAP)

1920 N. Forest Avenue, Orlando, FL 32803-1537
Tel: (407) 246-2620; Fax: (407) 246-2849
Internet Address: http://www.leugardens.org
Admission: Fee: adult $5.00, child (K-12) $1.00
Attendance: 130,000
Established: 1961
Membership: Y
Wheelchair Accessible: Y
Parking: Free on site, 200 spaces
Open: Daily, 9am-5pm
Closed: Christmas Day
Best Time(s) of Year to Visit: November to March (camellia), mid-April to late April
(rose), Spring to Fall (tropical plants), October to November (rose)
Facilities: Architecture (Farm House Museum-1880's); Classrooms (4); Gardens
(bamboo, bog, butterfly, day lily, herb, home demonstration, native, palm, ravine,
rose, vegetable, white); Grounds (50 acres); Herbarium; Lecture Hall; Library (non-
circulating, 2,500 volumes, 25+ periodicals); Meeting Room; Shop; Special
Collections (bamboo, banana, bog, camellia, cycad, flowering trees, ginger, palm, rose)
Activities: Concerts (20+ annually); Education Programs (adults and children); Gardening
Festival (fall); Guided Tours Gardens (on request), House (10am-3:30pm, every 30
minutes); Lectures (200+ annually); Plant Sales Spring Plant Sale (mid-March weekend);
Workshops (30+ plant societies & environmental groups hold annual workshops)

The restored late nineteenth-century home and its varied small gardens shaded by mature
oaks provide a sense of a more leisurely time. The gardens boast the largest formal rose garden in Florida (1,500 plants) and the largest outdoor camellia collection in eastern North
America (over 500 selections). The Kitchen Garden includes a vegetable garden, herb collection, and butterfly garden. The Tropical Stream Garden includes bananas (the largest
collection of any public garden in the United States), bamboo, gingers, tropical flowering

trees, and hibiscus. The new Home Demonstration Garden features three acres of "idea gardens" including bird, shade, bog, evening, and perennial gardens; ornamental grasses; and a garden with raised beds and planters built for all abilities.

UNIVERSITY OF CENTRAL FLORIDA—THE ARBORETUM

4000 Central Florida Avenue, Orlando, FL 32816-2368
Tel: (407) 823-3146
Internet Address: http://pegasus.cc.ucf.edu/~arbor/
Admission: Free
Established: 1983
Open: Daily, sunrise-sunset
Facilities: Arboretum; Garden (bromeliad, cycad, fern, magnolia, palm, rose, vine arbor); Greenhouse (1,250 square feet, 1927); Grounds (80 acres); Picnic Area
Activities: Guided Tours (arrange in advance)

Located on the east-central periphery of campus, the arboretum contains more than 600 species of flora in variety of communities including cypress dome, long leaf pine, oak hammock, pond, pine, and scrub oak. The Stockard Conservatory Greenhouse contains exotic and tropical plants that cannot grow outdoors, and is bordered by a small rose garden. A comprehensive self-guiding tour booklet is available for loan from the UCF Library.

OSPREY

HISTORIC SPANISH POINT/GULF COAST HERITAGE ASSOCIATION, INC.

Historic Spanish Point. Gulf Coast Heritage Association, Inc., Osprey, FL. J. B. McCourtney photograph.

Visitor Center, 337 N. Tamiami Trail, Osprey, FL 34229
Tel: (941) 966-5214;
Fax: (941) 966-1355
Admission: Fee: adult $7.00, child (6-12) $3.00. Free Week in September
Attendance: 30,000
Membership: Y
Wheelchair Accessible: Y
Parking: On site, includes handicapped parking.
Open: Monday to Saturday, 9am-5pm; Sunday, noon-5pm
Closed: New Year's Day, Easter, Thanksgiving Day, Christmas Day
Facilities: Architecture (restored 19th-century homestead, citrus packing house, chapel); Gardens (4, formal, ca. 1915); Grounds (33 acres); Nature Trails
Activities: Education Programs; Guided Tours (daily, call for times); Performances (living history)

Historic Spanish Point offers visitors a look into southwest Florida's environment and unique past, from prehistoric middens, through nineteenth-century agriculture, to Mrs. Potter (Bertha) Palmer's early Twentieth-century winter estate. Historic Spanish Point's rich plant life showcases over 250 native Florida species as well as non-native plants introduced by the Palmer family. Bertha Palmer was a visionary, who in 1910 began purchasing a large portion of present-day Sarasota County. The widow of Chicago magnate Potter Palmer set about planning her acreage for real estate development, cattle ranching, and citrus groves. At Spanish Point, site of her winter estate, Osprey Point, she designed elaborate gardens while also preserving the pioneer dwellings and Indian remains. Formal lawns and plantings have been restored, including the formal Sunken Garden and Pergola, Duchene Lawn (named for French landscape designer Achilles Duchene), the Fern Walk at the base of an archaic midden, and the Jungle Walk with the scenic aqueduct. The site is bordered by mangroves on its western rim (Little Sarasota Bay) and pine flatlands to the east. Here, bamboo and creeping fig combine with the vines and air plants to create an impression of serenity. Live oaks, mastics, and gumbo-limbo trees carpet the coastal hardwood hammocks. Although Mrs. Palmer died in 1918, Historic Spanish Point remained in the Palmer family until 1980, when the site was donated to Gulf Coast Heritage Association, Inc.

PALM BEACH

THE SOCIETY OF THE FOUR ARTS—GARDEN

2 Four Arts Plaza, Royal Palm Way, Palm Beach, FL 33480
Tel: (561) 655-7227; Fax: (561) 655-7233
Internet Address: http://www.fourarts.org
Admission: Fee
Established: 1938
Attendance: 35,000
Membership: Y
Wheelchair Accessible: Y
Open: Monday to Saturday, 10am-5pm; Sunday, 2pm-5pm
Facilities: Auditorium (717 seats); Gallery (gallery design by Addison Mizner, renovation 1974 by John Volk); Gardens (Chinese, herb, native plant, rock, rose, Spanish); Library (60,000 volumes, non-circulating; children's library); Reading Room; Sculpture Garden
Activities: Concerts (Dec-Mar, 1/month); Education Programs (children); Film Series (Jan-Mar, Fri); Gallery Talks (Sat of week following exhibition opening, 3pm); Lecture Series (Tues, 3pm); Temporary Exhibitions (monthly); Traveling Exhibitions

The Society of the Four Arts was founded in 1936 by a group of Palm Beach residents to meet the cultural needs of the resort community. Maintained by the Garden Club of Palm Beach, the Four Arts Gardens are demonstration gardens designed in 1938 to display the diversity of tropical plants suitable to the South Florida climate. Landscapes include a Chinese garden, a rock garden, a rose garden, and a small herb garden, using native and tropical plants.

PALM COAST

WASHINGTON OAKS STATE GARDENS

6400 N. Ocean Shore Boulevard. (2 miles south of Marineland of Route A1A),
Palm Coast, FL 32137
Tel: (904) 446-6780; Fax: (904) 446-6781

Internet Address: http://www.dep.state.fl.us/parks/District_3/WashingtonOaks/
Admission: Fee: $4.00/auto
Established: 1970
Open: Daily, 8am-sundown
Facilities: Botanical Garden; Grounds (425 acres); Picnic Area; Special Collections (azalea, camellia, rose)
Activities: Guided Tours Garden (July-Dec, Sun, 1:30pm); Workshops

Nestled between the Atlantic Ocean and Matanzas River, Washington Oaks State Gardens combine native and exotic plantings set among magnificent live oak trees. In 1936, the land was bought by Louise Powis Clark, a designer from New York, as a winter retirement home for herself and her third husband, Owen D. Young, an attorney and industrialist. Gradually acquiring the beach front property from neighbors, the Youngs were responsible for the name "Washington Oaks," as well as the design of the gardens and the house. Shortly before her death in 1965, Mrs. Young gave most of Washington Oaks to the State of Florida, specifying that the gardens be "maintained in their present form" and expanded as funds become available. The gardens are well-known for azaleas, camellias, and roses as well as many other species of native and exotic plants and flowers complimented by a beautiful natural setting. Labels identify the wide variety of plants throughout the gardens. One of the highlights at the park are the many citrus trees along the outer perimeter of the garden. Although the park is most known for the formal garden, the majority of the land remains in natural condition.

PORT ORANGE

SUGAR MILL GARDENS

950 Old Sugar Mill Road (off Herbert Street), Port Orange, FL 32119
Tel: (386) 767-1735; Fax: (386) 767-1735
Internet Address: http://www.dunlawtonsugarmillgardens.org
Admission: Free
Attendance: 7,500
Established: 1988
Membership: Y
Wheelchair Accessible: P
Parking: Parking lot across the street, 35 spaces
Open: Daily, 8am-6pm
Facilities: Garden (butterfly, fern grotto, herb, native plant); Greenhouse; Grounds (12 acres); Library (Wed & Sat)
Activities: Education Programs (monthly); Guided Tours (call for details); Plant Sales

Surrounding the ruins of a sugar mill and containing dinosaur statues from a former theme park on the site, the garden was established for the preservation of native flora and fauna and the exhibition of exotic plants including flowering trees, palms, orchids, ginger, cacti, succulents, and bromeliads. The addition of a water feature and bridge, a butterfly garden, a native plant garden, and a greenhouse have added a new dimension to the garden. Listed in the National Register of Historic Places, the site is owned by Volusia County. The gardens were developed and are maintained by Botanical Gardens of Volusia, a non-profit organization.

SAINT AUGUSTINE

THE OLDEST HOUSE—ORNAMENTAL GARDENS

14 St. Francis Street, Saint Augustine, FL 32084
Tel: (904) 824-2872
Internet Address: http://www.oldcity.com/oldhouse
Admission: Fee: adult $6.00, child (<7) free, student $4.00, senior $5.50, family $14.00
Attendance: 55,000
Established: 1918
Membership: Y
Wheelchair Accessible: P
Parking: Free on site
Open: Daily, 9am-5pm
Facilities: Gardens (native plant, colonial era plants); Shop
Activities: Education Programs; Permanent Exhibits

The oldest European house in continuous occupancy in Florida, the site includes ornamental gardens containing native and colonial era plants typical of those grown by its Spanish, British, and American occupants.

SAINT PETERSBURG

CITY OF SAINT PETERSBURG—GIZELLA KOPSICK PALM ARBORETUM

1400 19th Street, North (North Shore Drive at the foot of 10th Avenue NE),
Saint Petersburg, FL 33713
Tel: (727) 893-7335
Established: 1977
Wheelchair Accessible: Y
Parking: Adjacent to site, free
Facilities: Arboretum (palm); Grounds (2 acres)
Activities: Guided Tours (call for info)

More than 200 palms and cycads representing some 45 species from around the world are on display. Park development is supervised by the City Beautiful Commission in cooperation with the city of Saint Petersburg Parks Department.

CITY OF ST. PETERSBURG—SUNKEN GARDENS (AHS RAP)

1825 4th Street, North, Saint Petersburg, FL 33704-4397
Tel: (727) 551-3100; Fax: (727) 894-2810
Internet Address: http://www.sunkengardens.com/st.%20petersburg.htm
Admission: Fee: adult $7.00, child (3-16) $3.00, senior $5.00
Wheelchair Accessible: Y
Parking: Free on site
Open: Monday to Saturday, 10am-4:30pm; noon-4:30
Facilities: Grounds (4 acres)
Activities: Guided Tours (Wed-Sun, 10:30am & 1:30pm)

Founded in 1903 by George Turner, Sr., Sunken Gardens, home to a tropical rain for-est, is the second oldest tourist attraction in the state. In 1999, the City of Saint Peters-burg purchased Sunken Gardens from the Turner family. City parks employees have begun to restore the facility.

SARASOTA

JOHN AND MABLE RINGLING MUSEUM OF ART

5401 Bay Shore Road (south of Sarasota-Bradenton International Airport), Sarasota, FL 34243
Tel: (941) 358-3180; Fax: (941) 359-7704
Internet Address: http://www.ringling.org
Admission: Fee: adult $15.00, child (<13) free, senior $12.00
Attendance: 330,000
Established: 1928
Membership: Y
Wheelchair Accessible: Y
Parking: Free on site
Open: Daily, 10am-5:30pm
Closed: New Year's Day, Thanksgiving Day, Christmas Day
Facilities: Architecture Museum (Italian Renaissance-style, 1927-29), Ringling Mansion, "Ca' d'Zan" (Venetian Gothic-style, 1924-26); Classrooms; Food Services Banyan Café (May-Oct, daily, 11am-4pm; Nov-Apr, daily, 11am-5pm); Galleries (21); Gardens (rose); Grounds (66 acres); Library (60,000 volumes, non-circulating); Shops (2, museum and mansion); Theatre (200 seats)
Activities: Education Programs (adults and children); Gallery Talks; Guided Tours Art Gallery & Circus Museum (tour times posted daily), Cà d'Zan Private Places Premium Tour (by reservation), Cà d'Zan Regular Tour (timed tour required); Lecture Series (Sat); Traveling Exhibitions

The John and Mable Ringling Museum of Art is part of a complex which contains in addi-tion to the internationally recognized art museum, the Cà d'Zan, John and Mable Ringling's fantastic, thirty-one-room winter home; the Museum of the Circus, displaying memorabilia and artifacts from the history of the American circus and the Ringling Bros. family enterprise; a nineteenth-century Italian theatre and archives. Ringling bequeathed the estate to the peo-ple of Florida upon his death in 1936. Today, the site is under the stewardship of Florida State University. It is surrounded by sixty-six acres of parkland overlooking Sarasota Bay. Gardens include Mable Ringling's ninety-four-year-old rose garden and a secret garden. Banyan and palm trees are featured among the wide variety of native and exotic plant materials.

THE MARIE SELBY BOTANICAL GARDENS, INC. (AHS RAP)

811 S. Palm Avenue (off U.S. 41), Sarasota, FL 34236
Tel: (941) 366-5731; Fax: (941) 366-9807
Internet Address: http://www.selby.org
Admission: Fee: adult $12.00, child (6-11) $6.00
Attendance: 165,000
Established: 1973
Membership: Y
Wheelchair Accessible: Y
Parking: Free on-site parking

Open: Daily, 10am-5pm
Closed: Christmas Day
Facilities: Arboretum; Architecture Christy Payne Mansion (American Eclectic, 1935 design by A. C. Price); Auditorium (75 seats); Gardens (bamboo, banyan grove, cactus & succulent); Greenhouses (7; 20,755 square feet); Grounds (13 acres); Herbarium (82,000 specimens); Library (6,500 volumes); Other Facilities: Bromeliad Identification Center, Orchid Identification Center, Stark Botanical Research Center (711 South Palm Avenue); Shops (2; plants, books, botanical artwork, gifts); Special Collections (epiphytic plants); Tropical Display House
Activities: Arts Festival; Concerts; Education Programs (undergraduate and graduate college students); Films; Guided Tours; Lectures; Temporary Exhibitions

The Marie Selby Botanical Gardens, best known for its living collection of more than 6,000 orchids, is an open-air and under-glass museum of more than 20,000 greenhouse plants, plus thousands more in the outdoor gardens shaded by mangroves, live oaks, pine, palms, bamboo, and six giant banyan trees. Throughout the grounds are fifteen distinct garden areas, including: the Bamboo Pavilion and the tranquil Waterfall Garden; the Banyan Grove; a cactus and succulent garden; a cycad collection; the Bayfront Restoration Project, which borders the native shore plant community; and the Baywalk Sanctuary. The Tropical Display House, where exotic flora can be seen year round, and six additional greenhouses, are the heart of botanical research and plant identification, for which Selby is internationally recognized. Also on the grounds is the former Christy Payne Mansion, now the Gardens' Museum, which serves as a showcase for rotating exhibits of eighteenth, ninteenth, and tentieth century botanical illustration from the permanent collection at Selby Gardens.

SARASOTA GARDEN CLUB—GARDEN CENTER

1131 Boulevard of the Arts, Sarasota, FL 34236
Tel: (941) 955-0875
Internet Address: http://hometown.aol.com/sgcgarden/index.html
Admission: Free
Established: 1960
Membership: Y
Wheelchair Accessible: Y
Parking: On street and in science museum lot
Open: Monday to Friday, 9am-1pm
Best Time(s) of Year to Visit: October to May
Facilities: Garden (bromeliad, butterfly, hibiscus, native, and waterfall tropical); Grounds (1 acre); Meeting Room; Reception Area (150 seats)
Activities: Education Programs; Flower Shows; Plant Sales; Workshops (design & horticulture)

The garden features native and tropical plants, a butterfly garden, a pond with water lilies, wisteria, strelizia, fountains, and a waterfall in a downtown setting. There are also wild parrots, hummingbirds, and herons.

TALLAHASSEE

ALFRED B. MACLAY STATE GARDENS

3540 Thomasville Road (U.S. Highway 319) (U.S. Highway 319), Tallahassee, FL 32309

Tel: (904) 487-4556; Fax: (904) 487-8808
Internet Address: http://www.FloridaStateParks.org/Maclay
Admission: Fee (Gardens, January-April): adult $4.00, child $2.00. Fee (Gardens, May-December): $4/vehicle, up to 8 people
Attendance: 100,000
Established: 1953
Membership: Y
Wheelchair Accessible: Y
Parking: 200 spaces at Gardens entrance, 100 at Recreation area
Open: Park, Daily, 8am-sundown
Garden, Daily, 9am-5pm
Maclay House, Daily, 9am-5pm
Best Time(s) of Year to Visit: Winter to early Spring
Facilities: Architecture (Maclay House, 1909); Gardens (28 acres); Park Grounds (1,200 acres); Picnic & Recreation Area (17 acres); Shop; Special Collections (azalea, camellia, native plant); Trails (5+ miles)
Activities: Education Programs (adults and children); Guided Tours Bloom Season (Feb-Mar, Sat-Sun); Lectures

Maclay Gardens has been a Florida state park since 1953, when the property was given to the State of Florida by the family of Alfred Barmore Maclay of New York, who planned and developed the gardens on the grounds of his winter home. In designing the gardens, Mr. Maclay wanted to demonstrate that native plants and exotic plants could be used together to create a setting of scenic beauty. The gardens, featuring 150 varieties of camellias and 50 varieties of azaleas, were designed to be in bloom during the winter and early spring, the time of year that the family would be in residence. But, Maclay, concerned with landscape design, planned the garden to have good "bones" of trees and shrubs, so that it would be a place of beauty year round.

TAMPA

UNIVERSITY OF SOUTH FLORIDA BOTANICAL GARDEN (AHS RAP)

Pine and Alumni Drives, Tampa, FL 33620
Tel: (813) 974-2329
Internet Address: http://www.cas.usf.edu/envir_sci_policy/botanical/
Admission: Free
Established: 1968
Membership: Y
Parking: Free on site
Open: Monday to Friday, 9am-5pm; Saturday, 9am-4pm; Sunday, noon-4pm
Closed: Legal holidays
Facilities: Conservatory; Gardens (bromeliad, butterfly, carnivorous plant, herb, palm); Grounds; Shop; Special Collections (begonia)
Activities: Education Programs; Plant Sales (semi-annual); Workshops

Located near the southwest corner of the USF Tampa campus, the USF Botanical Garden offers a variety of gardens and habitat types through which to stroll. A trail begins at the parking area. Current collections include: fruit trees and palms from around the world, temperate forest, carnivorous plants, tropical and subtropical trees and shrubs as well as plant species found in Florida's upland habitats. A collection of rare begonias can be seen by appointment.

TAVARES

LAKE COUNTY HORTICULTURAL LEARNING CENTER— DISCOVERY GARDENS

Lake County Agriculture Center, 30205 State Road 19, Tavares, FL 32778-4262
Tel: (352) 343-4101
Internet Address: http://discoverygardens.ifas.ufl.edu/
Wheelchair Accessible: Y
Open: Monday to Saturday, 9am-4pm
Facilities: Gardens (19 themed); Grounds (3½ acres)
Activities: Guided Tours (reservations required)

The Discovery Garden is a joint effort of the Lake County Board of Commissioners, University of Florida County Extension Service, Friends of the Horticultural Learning Center, and the Master Gardener Society of Lake County. The Garden consists of twenty themed gardens: backyard, butterfly, children's, cottage, courtyard, kitchen, oriental, palm path, rose, seasonal, shade, southwest, Spanish, sub-tropical, tropical fruit, turf display, vegetable, vineyard, wetlands, xeriscape. Each garden is designed to show a different horticultural application in gentral Florida. The garden contains more than 300 different plants and is dedicated to demonstrating how home owners can achieve the landscape they want. All plants are labeled and cultural information is available upon request at the Master Gardener Plant Clinic in the main building.

VERO BEACH

MCKEE BOTANICAL GARDEN (AHS RAP)

350 U.S. Highway 1, Vero Beach, FL 32962
Tel: (772) 794-0601; Fax: (772) 794-0602
Internet Address: http://www.mckeegarden.org/
Admission: Fee: adult $6.00, child $3.50, child, student $1.00, senior $5.00
Attendance: 25,000
Membership: Y
Wheelchair Accessible: Y
Parking: Free parking
Open: Tuesday to Saturday, 10am-5pm; Sunday, noon-5pm
Facilities: Architecture (2 structures built by founder Waldo Sexton); Food Services Garden Café; Grounds (18 acres; on National Register of Historic Places); Library; Shop

This tropical botanical garden is filled with both native plants and exotic specimens unique to the growing zone. There are ponds filled with water lilies and wetland plantings, palms, and ferns.

WEST PALM BEACH

ANN NORTON SCULPTURE GARDEN (ANSG)

253 Barcelona Road, West Palm Beach, FL 33401
Tel: (561) 835-5328; Fax: (561) 835-9305

Internet Address: http://www.realpages.com/annnorton
Admission: Fee $5.00
Established: 1977
Membership: Y
Wheelchair Accessible: Y
Parking: On street
Open: October to May, Wednesday to Sunday, 11am-4pm. June to August, Friday to Sunday, 11am-4pm
Facilities: Grounds (1.7 acres); Sculpture Garden
Activities: Education Programs; Guided Tours (arrange in advance); Temporary Exhibitions; Workshops

Located near downtown West Palm Beach on the Intercoastal Waterway, the former residence and studio of sculptor Ann Weaver Norton displays more than 100 sculptures (including nine monumental brick and granite works) by the artist throughout the house, studio, and gardens. The site also offers a schedule of temporary exhibitions by recognized artists. Designed in the natural-form English style, the gardens contain over 300 species of tropical palm. The house is listed in the National Register of Historic Places.

MOUNTS BOTANICAL GARDEN (AHS RAP)

531 N. Military Trail, West Palm Beach, FL 33415-1395
Tel: (561) 233-1749; Fax: (561) 233-1723
Internet Address: http://www.mounts.org/
Admission: Free
Established: 1954
Membership: Y
Wheelchair Accessible: P
Open: Monday to Saturday, 8:30am-4:30pm; Sunday, 1pm-5pm
Closed: New Year's Day, Thanksgiving Day, Christmas Eve to Christmas Day
Facilities: Grounds (14 acres); Shop (books)
Activities: Guided Tours (Sat, 11am; Sun, 2:30; groups, by prior appointment, 233-1757); Lectures; Plant Sales; Workshops

Palm Beach County's oldest and largest public garden, Mounts Botanical Garden displays tropical and subtropical plants from around the world, including plants native to Florida, exotic trees, tropical fruit, herbs, citrus, palms, and much more. Mounts is a component of the Palm Beach County Cooperative Extension Service and affiliated with the University of Florida's Institute for Food and Agricultural Sciences.

WINTER PARK

ALBIN POLASEK MUSEUM AND SCULPTURE GARDEN (AHS RAP)

633 Osceola Avenue, Winter Park, FL 32789
Tel: (407) 647-6294; Fax: (407) 647-0410
Internet Address: http://www.polasek.org
Admission: Fee: adult $4.00, child (<12) free, student $2.00, senior $3.00
Attendance: 8,000
Membership: Y

Wheelchair Accessible: Y
Parking: Free on site; can accommodate large tour bus
Open: Wednesday to Saturday, 10am-noon; 1pm-4pm; Sunday, 1pm-4pm
Closed: July to August
Facilities: Architecture (home & studio of sculptor Albin Polasek); Galleries (2);
Grounds Sculpture Garden (3 acres)
Activities: Guided Tours; Permanent Exhibits; Rotating Exhibits

Located in the home and studio of the Czech-American sculptor Albin Polasek (1879-1965), the gardens and galleries contain many of the sculptor's works. Antiquities from his collection are on display in the salon of his home. An intimate chapel on the grounds is also open for viewing. The site is listed on the National Register of Historic Places.

CITY OF WINTER PARK—KRAFT AZALEA GARDENS

Alabama Drive (off Palmer Avenue), Winter Park, FL 32789
Tel: (407) 599-3334; Fax: (407) 599-3454
Admission: Free
Membership: N
Wheelchair Accessible: P
Parking: Limited parking along Alabama Drive, residential area
Open: Daily, sunrise-sunset
Best Time(s) of Year to Visit: January to March (azaleas)
Facilities: Grounds; Picnic Area; Trails

Located along the shores of Lake Maitland, the garden contains azaleas, tropical shrubs, and trees.

CITY OF WINTER PARK—MEAD BOTANICAL GARDEN

S. Denning Drive at Garden Drive (off Highway 17-92), Winter Park, FL 32789
Tel: (407) 599-3334; Fax: (407) 599-3454
Admission: Free
Membership: N
Wheelchair Accessible: P
Parking: On site
Open: Daily, 8am-sunset
Facilities: Grounds (55 acres); Picnic Area
Activities: Classes

Home of the Winter Park Garden Club and Friends of Mead Garden, this city park features walking trails winding among plantings of sub-tropical trees.

GEORGIA

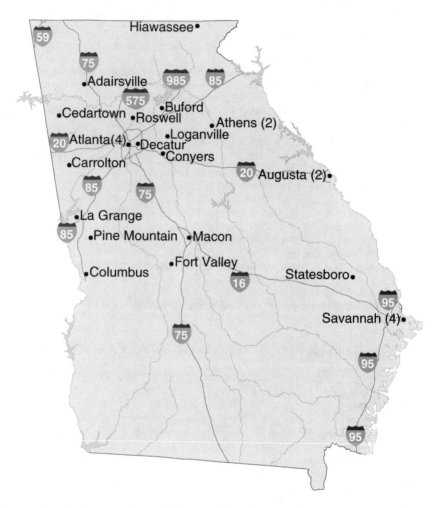

The number in the parentheses following the city name indicates the number of gardens/arboreta in that municipality. If there is no number, one is understood. For example, in the text four listings would be found under Atlanta and one listing under Decatur.

ADAIRSVILLE

BARNSLEY GARDENS

597 Barnsley Garden Road, N.W., Adairsville, GA 30103-5709
Tel: (770) 773-7480
Admission: Fee, day visitors: adult $10.00, child (<12) $5.00, senior $8.00
Facilities: Gardens; Mountain Bike Track; Museum; Shop (plants)

Godfrey Barnsley, an expatriate Englishman married to a Savannah woman, built Woodlands in the late 1830s. In designing the gardens surrounding the home, Barnsley and his caretaker John Connolly were strongly influenced by Andrew Jackson Downing's "*A Treatise on the Theory and Practice of Landscape Gardening.*" While the house is derelict, the gardens that surround Woodlands have been restored and include 150 varieties of roses, a bog garden, and an Oriental garden.

ATHENS

THE GARDEN CLUB OF GEORGIA, INC.—FOUNDERS MEMORIAL GARDEN (FOUNDERS GARDEN)

325 S. Lumpkin Street, Athens, GA 30602
Tel: (706) 542-4776
Internet Address: http://www.uga.edu/gardenclub/Founder.html
Admission: Voluntary contribution
Established: 1946
Open: Monday to Friday, 9am-4pm
Facilities: Architecture (Federal-style brick house, 1857); Formal Gardens; Grounds (2½ acres)
Activities: Guided Tours

Completed in 1946, the garden was designed by Dean Hubert B. Owens, his staff, and students of the University of Georgia's Landscape Architecture Department. It consists of a formal boxwood garden, two courtyards, a retrace, a perennial garden, and an arboretum. The garden not only serves as a museum of landscape design but also as a natural laboratory for botany, forestry, and related disciplines. The nineteenth-century brick house served as the headquarters of the club between 1961-1998; its new headquarters building is adjacent to the State Botanical Gardens. Founded in 1891, the Ladies Garden Club was the first garden club organized in America.

THE STATE BOTANICAL GARDEN OF GEORGIA (AHS RAP)

2450 S. Milledge Avenue
(1 mile from South Athens Perimeter),
Athens, GA 30605-1624
Tel: (706) 542-1244;
Fax: (706) 542-3091
Internet Address: http://www.uga.edu/botgarden
Admission: Voluntary contribution
Attendance: 150,000
Established: 1968
Membership: Y
Wheelchair Accessible: Y
Open: Grounds: October to March, Daily, 8am-
6pm. Grounds: April to September, Daily, 8am-
8pm. Visitors Center, Monday to Saturday, 9am-
4:30pm; Sunday, 11:30am-4:30pm

The State Botanical Gardens of Georgia, Athens, GA. Alice Hand Callaway Visitor Center and Conservatory.

Closed: New Year's Eve to New Year's Day, M. L. King Day, Independence Day, Thanksgiving Day, Christmas Eve to Christmas Day
Best Time(s) of Year to Visit: Spring (Shade Garden), Summer (Annual/Perennial Garden), Summer to Frost (Dahlia Garden), Fall (Natural Areas)
Facilities: Auditorium (125 seats); Classrooms; Food Services Garden Room Café (Tues-Sun, lunch; snacks, reservations 542-6359); Gardens (annual/perennial, herb, heritage, international, physic, native plants, rose, shade, trial); Greenhouses; Grounds (313 acres); Nature Trails; Visitors Center/Conservatory
Activities: Concerts; Guided Tours; Lectures; Temporary Exhibitions; Workshops

The State Botanical Garden of Georgia is a preserve set aside by the University of Georgia for the study and enjoyment of plants and nature. The garden is a "living laboratory" serving teaching, research, and public service missions for the university and the citizens of Georgia. The garden contains a wide variety of natural physiographic features and includes plant communities and habitats common to the Georgia Piedmont. A number of specialty gardens and collections presently exist and others will be added as the master plan is implemented. Serving as the focal point for the garden, the Visitor Center contains offices and classrooms, a small theater, gift shop, cafeteria, atrium, and three-story conservatory. The conservatory features a permanent collection representing beneficial plants of the tropics—plants from which beverages, foods, spices, medicines, fibers, building materials, and industrial products are derived. The adjacent International Garden portrays the interrelationship between people and plants within its borders. Eleven botanical and horticultural collections depict the geographic origin of plants, plant hunters who sought them, and the forces that drove the plant hunters. Other gardens include the Heritage Garden displaying plants of historic and socioeconomic interest to Georgia; an official All-America Rose Garden featuring a wide variety of roses including all major classes; the Native Flora Garden containing over 300 species; an annual/perennial garden including special theme collections such as plants that attract hummingbirds and butterflies, a traditional perennial border and an All-American Selections display garden; a dahlia garden; a trial garden planted with a collection of shrubs and trees; a rhododendron collection; a native azalea collection; a shade garden; and a ground cover collection. Five miles of color-coded nature trails extend into the far reaches of the Garden along the Middle Oconee River and into the upland plateau areas of hardwood foreStreet The headquarters of the Garden Club of Georgia is located at the State Botanical Garden.

ATLANTA

ATLANTA BOTANICAL GARDEN (AHS RAP)

1345 Piedmont Avenue, N.E. (Piedmont Park at the Prado), Atlanta, GA 30309
Tel: (404) 876-5859; Fax: (404) 876-7472
Internet Address: http://www.atlantabotanicalgarden.org/
Admission: Fee: adult $12.00, child (<3) free, student $7.00, senior $9.00. Free:
Thursday after 3pm
Attendance: 150,000
Established: 1976
Membership: Y
Wheelchair Accessible: Y
Parking: Free on site, but limited
Open: April to September, Tuesday to Sunday, 9am-7pm
October to March, Tuesday to Sunday, 9am-5pm
Closed: New Year's Day, Thanksgiving Day, Christmas Day
Best Time(s) of Year to Visit: Spring (rock garden), Fall, November to February (upper
woodlands-camellias)
Facilities: Arboretum Storza Woods (15-acre hardwood forest); Classroom;
Conservatory; Gardens (15 acres; children's, conifer, fragrance, herb, Japanese,
perennial, rock, rose, vegetable, vine, wildflower); Grounds (30 acres); Library (3,224
volumes, non-circulating); Shop; Special Collections (orchids palms, succulents, fruit
trees, native trees); Visitors Center; Workshop
Activities: Education Programs (adults and children); Exhibit Tropical Orchids:
Splendor Under Glass (annual, 1st Sun in December-April); Films; Guided Tours;
Lectures; Permanent Exhibits; Plant Shows

The outdoor display gardens at the Atlanta Botanical Garden include cultivated plants
environmentally suited to the southeastern United States along with woodlands. Plants
are chosen to illustrate certain botanical, horticultural, architectural, or ecological principles, and many displays are designed with special reference to the urban environment.
Highlights of the gardens include the carnivorous plant bog in the Children's Garden; the
Dwarf Conifer Garden featuring more than 200 varieties, including a large collection of
Japanese cedar (cryptomeria japonica) cultivars, the upper woodland of Storza Woods,
devoted to shade gardens and containing the camellia collection; the Container Gardens;
the Herb Garden; the Perennial Garden; the Rock Garden; the Rose Garden; and the
Vine Arbor. The Dorothy Chapman Fuqua Conservatory houses over 6,000 tropical and
desert plants, including 2,000 orchids (rotated into the conservatory from support greenhouses as they bloom) and an extensive collection of Old World succulents. Permanent
displays focus on plant diversity, ecological principles, conservation and adaptations to
specific environments with an emphasis on education. Priority is given to plants that are
sensitive, rare, threatened, or endangered.

ATLANTA HISTORY CENTER GARDENS

130 W. Paces Ferry Road, N.W., Atlanta, GA 30305-1366
Tel: (404) 814-4000; Fax: (404) 814-4186; TDDY: (404) 814-4000
Internet Address: http://www.atlantahistorycenter.com/
Admission: Fee: adult $12.00, child $7.00, student $10.00, senior $10.00.
Group discounts

Attendance: 165,000
Established: 1926
Membership: Y
Wheelchair Accessible: Y
Open: Monday to Saturday, 10am-5:30pm; Sunday, noon-5:30pm. Memorial Day, noon-5:30pm; Independence Day, noon-5:30pm; Veterans' Day, noon-5:30pm; New Year's Eve, noon-5:30pm
Closed: New Year's Day, Thanksgiving Day, Christmas Eve to Christmas Day
Facilities: Architecture Swan House (Italian/English Classical-style residence, 1928 design by architect Philip Trammell Shutze), Tullie Smith Farm (ca. 1845); Food Services Coca-Cola Café; Gardens; Grounds (33 acres); Museum Atlanta History Museum (30,000 square feet); Shop
Activities: Education Programs (adults and children); Guided Tours Swan House (Mon-Sat, 11am-4pm; Sun, 1pm-4pm;, Tullie Smith Farm (Mon-Sat, 11:15am-4pm; Sun, 1:15pm-4pm); Lectures; Permanent Exhibits; Temporary Exhibitions; Workshops

The center consists of two historic homes, a museum, research archives, and thirty-three acres of period gardens. Atlanta residents Edward and Emily Inman traveled widely in Europe, collecting both ideas and antiques. In 1926, they employed local architect Philip Trammell Shutze to design a classically-styled mansion and its accompanying grounds and formal gardens. Acquired by the Atlanta Historical Society in 1966 and now on the National Register of Historic Places, the design of the house echoes English country manors of centuries past, while the surrounding fountains and elegant gardens have a distinctly Italian flavor. The ten-acre Swan Woods Trail provides a link between the formal elegance of Swan House and the rural lifestyle of Tullie Smith Farm. It also provides an opportunity to explore the ecological succession in the Georgia Piedmont through signage explaining the surrounding environment and providing ecological information. A plantation-plain house built in the 1840s by the Robert Smith family, the Tullie Smith House is also listed on the National Register of Historic Places. Originally located east of Atlanta, outside the city limits, the house with detached kitchen and related outbuildings were moved to the Atlanta History Center beginning in 1969. While nineteenth-century yeoman farmers had little time or inclination to maintain formal gardens, the traditional vegetable, herb, and flower gardens on the site are composed of plants typical to a period Piedmont plantation. Other center gardens include: The Mary Howard Gilbert Memorial Quarry Garden, a three-acre former rock quarry now devoted to the study of plants native to pre-settlement Georgia, including trillium, ferns, and magnolias; the Frank A. Smith Rhododendron Garden, a contemporary shade garden design devoted to two of Atlanta's most beautiful plants, rhododendron and azalea; and the Cherry Sims Asian-American Garden, comparing the evolution of Asian plants with those of the southeastern United States and featuring extensive collections of Japanese maples, hydrangeas, Satsuki azaleas, and ferns.

THE CARTER PRESIDENTIAL CENTER—GARDENS

453 Freedom Parkway, Atlanta, GA 30307
Tel: (404) 331-3900; Fax: (404) 420-5100
Internet Address: http://www.cartercenter.org
Admission: Free
Wheelchair Accessible: P
Parking: Free on site
Open: April to October, Daily, 6am-9pm. New Year's Day to March, Daily, 7am-7pm
Best Time(s) of Year to Visit: Spring, Fall
Facilities: Gardens (cherry orchard, Japanese, rose, wildflower meadow); Grounds (35 acres)
Activities: Self-Guided Tour (a gardens brochure is available)

Located in a wooded park just five minutes from downtown Atlanta, the Carter Presidential Center's grounds include formal gardens, a wild flower meadow, a cherry orchard, and waterfalls tucked between two small lakes. Visitors may stroll through the Rose Garden, which is home to forty varieties, including the coral Rosalyn rose, or view the serene Japanese Garden, designed by master gardener Nakane Kinsaku.

FERNBANK MUSEUM OF NATURAL HISTORY— ROBERT L. STATON MEMORIAL ROSE GARDEN

767 Clifton Road, Atlanta, GA 30307-1221
Tel: (404) 378-4311; Fax: (404) 370-1336
Internet Address: http://fsc.fernbank.edu/
Admission: Free
Established: 1983
Parking: Free on site
Open: rose garden, Sunday to Friday, dawn-dusk
Best Time(s) of Year to Visit: Spring
Facilities: Food Services (restaurant); Forest (65 acres, Sun-Fri, 2pm-5pm; Sat, 10am-5pm); Garden (rose, 1 acre); Greenhouses Fernbank Science Center (2—Lord and Burnham ca 1920; open Sun, 1pm-5pm,); Shop

One of only three gardens in the United States to have both All-America Rose Selections (AARS) and American Rose Society (ARS) test roses, the garden contains approximately 1,300 roses. Other Fernbank Science Center facilities of horticultural interest are the greenhouses (1256 Briarcliff Road) containing the center's collections of tropical and succulent plants; and Fernbank Forest (156 Heaton Park Drive, located behind the main Science Center building), a tract of relatively undisturbed mature mixed hardwood foreStreet

AUGUSTA

GEORGE WALTON HOME—MEADOW GARDEN

1320 Independence Drive (at 13th Street and Walton Way), Augusta,
GA 30901-1038
Tel: (706) 724-4174
Admission: Fee: adult $4.00, child (<5) free, child (K-12) $1.00, student $3.00, senior $3.50
Membership: N
Wheelchair Accessible: P
Open: Monday to Friday, 10am-4pm; Saturday to Sunday, by appointment
Closed: Legal Holidays
Best Time(s) of Year to Visit: Spring to Summer
Facilities: Architecture (1½ storey, 18th-century farm home)
Activities: Guided Tours Drop-in (daily), Group 10+ (by appointment only)

Meadow Garden, the home of George Walton (a signer of the Declaration of Independence), includes grounds landscaped with plants and herbs of the seventeenth and eighteenth century. The site is owned and operated by the Georgia State Society of the Daughters of the American Revolution.

GEORGIA GOLF HALL OF FAME BOTANICAL GARDENS (AHS RAP)

One 11th Street, Augusta, GA 30901
Tel: (706) 724-4443
Internet Address: http://www.gghf.org
Established: 1982
Membership: Y
Closed: New Year's Day, Thanksgiving Day, Christmas Day
Facilities: Gardens (arbor, aquatic, azalea, bulb, butterfly, coastal, cottage, formal, grass, oriental, rose, xeriscape); Grounds (17 acres), Gardens (8 acres)
Activities: Concerts; Education Programs

The display gardens at GGHF include a rose garden, complete with rose arbor entrances and over 800 varieties of bright miniature roses, a formal garden filled with all green and white plants and flowers, an Asian garden featuring a koi pond, moon gate and plants from the Orient, and a tropical garden complete with birds of paradise, palm and banana trees as well as statues of inductees in the Georgia Golf Hall of Fame.

BUFORD

LANIER MUSEUM OF NATURAL HISTORY—BUTTERFLY GARDEN

2601 Buford Dam Road, Buford, GA 30518
Tel: (770) 932-4460
Internet Address: http://www.gwinnettcounty.com
Admission: Fee $1.00
Attendance: 14,000
Wheelchair Accessible: P
Parking: Parking is available
Open: Tuesday to Saturday, noon-5pm
Facilities: Garden (Butterfly)

This small museum, focusing on Gwinnett County's natural environment, includes a butterfly garden.

CARROLTON

STATE UNIVERSITY OF WEST GEORGIA—ARBORETUM

1601 Maple Street, Carrolton, GA 30118
Tel: (770) 836-6576; Fax: (770) 836-6749
Admission: Free
Established: 2001
Membership: N
Wheelchair Accessible: P
Parking: Free on campus
Open: Daily, sunrise-sunset
Best Time(s) of Year to Visit: Spring to Fall
Facilities: Arboretum (native plants); Grounds University Campus (385 acres); Trails (6 miles)

Through a cooperative agreement between the Biology and Campus Landscaping departments, the university has established an arboretum for the purpose of demonstrating the rich botanical diversity of its West Georgia campus.

CEDARTOWN

POLK COUNTY HISTORICAL SOCIETY GARDENS

205 N. College Street, Cedartown, GA 30125
Tel: (770) 748-0073
Internet Address: http://polkhiStreethome.mindspring.com/
Admission: Voluntary contribution
Membership: Y
Wheelchair Accessible: N
Parking: On-street parking
Open: Wednesday, 2pm-4pm; last Sunday in month, 2pm-5pm
Best Time(s) of Year to Visit: Summer
Facilities: Architecture (former library building, 1921 design by Neel Reid)

Originally the Hawkes Children's Library, the museum building is listed on the National Register of Historic Places. Immediately behind the museum, a formal garden is built around the fountain that stood for many years on the old courthouse grounds. Inserted in the wall is the grillwork of the clock from the old courthouse.

COLUMBUS

THE COLUMBUS MUSEUM

1251 Wynnton Road, Columbus, GA 31906
Tel: (706) 649-0713; Fax: (706) 649-1070
Internet Address: http://www.columbusmuseum.com
Admission: Free
Attendance: 91,000
Established: 1953
Membership: Y
Wheelchair Accessible: Y
Parking: Free on site
Open: Tuesday to Saturday, 10am-5pm; Sunday, 1pm-5pm; Thursday, 10am-8pm
Closed: Legal Holidays
Facilities: Architecture (Italianate Tuscan-style residence, early 20th century); Auditorium (298 seats); Children's' Discovery Gallery ("Transformations"); Classrooms (2); Galleries (17; 30,000 square feet); Grounds (landscaped garden, design by firm of Frederick Law Olmsted); Library (non-circulating); Shop; Theater (50 seats)
Activities: Education Programs (adults and children); Films; Gallery Talks; Guided Tours; Permanent Exhibits; Temporary Exhibitions; Traveling Exhibitions

The Columbus Museum focuses on American art and regional history. It features changing art exhibitions, almost 300 years of American fine and decorative art in fifteen galleries. There are also two galleries devoted to permanent exhibitions Chattahoochee Legacy, focusing on regional history, and Transformations, a hands-on discovery gallery.

Originally a private residence, the museum's landscaped garden was designed by the firm of Frederick Law Olmsted.

CONYERS

LEWIS VAUGHN BOTANICAL GARDEN

Main Street (adjacent to the Pavilion), Conyers, GA 30012
Tel: (770) 602-2606
Internet Address: http://www.conyersga.com
Admission: Free
Established: 1994
Membership: N
Wheelchair Accessible: Y
Open: Daily, 7am-6pm
Best Time(s) of Year to Visit: Spring to Fall
Facilities: Goldfish pond; Grounds (1½ acres); Special Collections (native plants of the Georgia Piedmont region)

The garden highlights plants native or indigenous to the Piedmont region of Georgia. A water feature, employing the city's original granite water tower built in 1900, narrates and interprets the hydrological cycle of the region.

DECATUR

GEORGIA PERIMETER COLLEGE—BOTANICAL GARDEN

Wildflower Center, South Campus, 3251 Panthersville Road, Decatur, GA 30034
Tel: (404) 244-5001
Internet Address: http://www.gpc.peachnet.edu/~ddonald/botgard/george3.htm
Admission: Free
Parking: Free on site
Facilities: Gardens 4 acres
Activities: Guided Tours; Plant Sales

The garden contains one of the largest collections of native plants in the southeaStreet There are over four thousand species of native, rare, and endangered indigenous plants, including bog plants, native trees, shrubs, vines, ferns, and perennials.

FORT VALLEY

MASSEE LANE GARDENS—HOME OF THE AMERICAN CAMELLIA SOCIETY (AHS RAP)

100 Massee Lane, Fort Valley, GA 31030
Tel: (478) 967-2358; Fax: (478) 967-2083
Internet Address: http://www.camellias-acs.com

Admission: Fee: adult $5.00, child (<12) free. AAA discounts
Established: 1945
Open: Tuesday to Saturday, 10:30am-4:30pm; Sunday, 1pm-4:30pm
Facilities: Auditorium; Gardens (camellia, environmental, Japanese, rose);
Greenhouse; Grounds (24 acres); Museum and Gallery (porcelain collection); Shop;
Special Collections (camellia, native plant); Visitor Center

Massee Lane had its beginnings as the private garden of David C. Strother in the 1930s. Mr. Strother donated the land to the American Camellia Society for its headquarters in 1966. The nine-acre Camellia Garden contains more than a thousand varieties of camellias, plus sasanquas, fragrant tea olives, Lady Banksia roses, and delightfully scented daphne odoras. The T. J. Smith Memorial Greenhouse houses the present collection of some 200 camellia plants grown under glass in an attractive landscaped setting. The Camellia Garden is supplemented by a Japanese garden and a rose garden with over 150 roses. A fifteen–acre environmental garden featuring native plants in seven ecological niches is under development.

HIAWASSEE

FRED HAMILTON RHODODENDRON GARDEN

Georgia Mountain Fair Grounds, U.S. Route 76 West, Hiawassee, GA 30546
Tel: (706) 896-4191
Internet Address: http://www.georgia-mountain-fair.com/hamgar.html
Admission: Free
Open: Daily, 8am-7pm
Best Time(s) of Year to Visit: late April to mid-May (rhododendron bloom)
Facilities: Trail (1 mile)
Activities: Festival Blue Grass & Rhododendron Festival (annual, early May)
Located along the shore of Lake Chatuge within the Georgia Mountain Fairgrounds, the Hamilton Rhododendron Garden contains more than 3,000 plants representing over 400 varieties, including, in addition to rhododendrons, dogwoods, tulip magnolias, native azaleas, lady slippers, and trillium. Fred Hamilton developed the yellow azalea, the only domestic yellow azalea in existence, which he named after his wife, Hazel.

LAGRANGE

HILLS AND DALES ESTATE

1916 Hills and Dales Drive, LaGrange, GA 30241
Tel: (706) 882-3464
Internet Address: http://www.hillsanddalesestate.org
Admission: Fee: adult $10.00, child (<6) free, child (7-18) $6.00, student $6.00, senior $10.00. $8.00 each for groups over 15
Attendance: 20,000
Established: 1998
Membership: Y
Wheelchair Accessible: P
Parking: Parking for cars and buses

Open: March to August, Tuesday to Saturday, 10am-6pm. September to February, Tuesday to Saturday, 10am-5pm
Closed: New Year's Day, Thanksgiving Day, Christmas Day
Facilities: Architecture (Italian-style residence, 1916 design by architect J. Neel Reid of Hentz, Reid & Adler); Gardens (Italian Renaissance & Baroque, boxwood terraces); Greenhouse; Grounds (35 acres), Gardens (5 acres); Visitor Center (6,000 square feet)

Hills and Dales Estate includes the historic Ferrell Gardens, the Fuller E. Callaway family home, and the surrounding outbuildings and landscape. The continuity of the original landscape from the mid-nineteenth century is one of the most exceptional aspects of the gardens. Ferrell Gardens, originally called "The Terraces," was begun in 1841 by Sarah Coleman Ferrell who expanded a small formal garden begun in 1832 by her mother. Between 1841 and 1903 Sarah Ferrell developed what became one of the most widely acclaimed gardens in the southeastern region of the United States. Mrs. Ferrell's formal boxwood garden covered a series of six terraces—formerly cotton fields—running east to west, with steps and retaining walls made of native stone. The stone was quarried on land owned by the Ferrell's and the garden walls were built by slave masons. The boxwoods used in the gardens were largely rooted by Mrs. Ferrell while other exotic ornamentals were ordered from nurseries across the region. After Judge Blount Ferrell's death in 1908, garden maintenance was interrupted until the property was purchased by Fuller E. Callaway and Ida Cason Callaway in 1911. Shortly after purchasing the historic property in 1911, Fuller E. Callaway commissioned the noted architectural firm of Hentz, Reid, & Adler of Atlanta to the design a new home to be built on the site of the old Ferrell homestead. Completed in 1916, the Italian villa-style residence, complementing Sarah Ferrell's existing four-acre terraced boxwood garden, is widely regarded as one of Neel Reid's finest works. Ida Cason Callaway kept and loved the boxwood paths and beds and added other highlights to the garden, nurturing it until her death in 1936. Beginning in 1936, Fuller E. Callaway, Jr. and his wife, Alice, took over the care of the house and garden giving them the same loving attention until Alice Hand Callaway's passing in 1998. In 1998, according to the wishes of Fuller E. Callaway, Jr. and Alice Hand Callaway, the estate was bequeathed to Fuller E. Callaway Foundation. The property, now known as Hills and Dales Estate, was opened to the public in October of 2004 upon the completion of the Visitor Center.

LOGANVILLE

VINES BOTANICAL GARDENS

3500 Oak Grove Road, Loganville, GA 30249
Tel: (770) 466-7532
Internet Address: http://www.vinesbotanicalgardens.com/
Admission: Fee: adult $5.00, child (<5) free, child (5-12) $4.00, senior $4.00
Wheelchair Accessible: Y
Parking: Free on site
Open: Tuesday to Sunday, 10am-5pm
Facilities: Architecture (Manor House-18,000 square feet); Food Services Manor House Restaurant; Gardens (culinary herb, hardy tropical ornamental grass, oriental, rose, seasonal color beds, white, winter); Grounds (24 acres); Shop Arbor Gift Shop
Activities: Education Programs; Guided Tours (arrange two weeks in advance)

Originally a private estate, Vines features curving pathways through gardens, a lake graced by fountains and swans, and a manor house overlooking the gardens. The numerous gardens include an extensive collection of heirloom roses, an oriental garden focusing on harmonious combinations of leaf textures and flower color with exotic and native plants, a white garden, the Brook Garden with waterfalls, seasonal color beds, and antique European statuary and architectural elements.

MACON

MACON STATE COLLEGE—BOTANICAL GARDEN

100 College Station Drive, Macon, GA 31206-5144
Tel: (912) 471-2780
Admission: Free
Open: Daily
Facilities: Grounds Campus (167 acres)

Initially planted in 1967 under the direction of Clay Adamson, horticulturist, the Macon State College campus presently contains an unusual diversity of flora. Beginning in 1999, the college has been working to convert its entire campus into a recognizable botanic garden.

PINE MOUNTAIN

CALLAWAY GARDENS

U.S. Highway 27, Pine Mountain, GA 31822
Tel: (800) 225-5292; Fax: (706) 663-5068
Internet Address: http://www.callawaygardens.com/
Attendance: 525,000
Established: 1952
Membership: Y
Open: 9am-6pm.
Facilities: Butterfly Conservatory; Classrooms; Food Services (5 restaurants); Gardens; Greenhouses; Grounds (14,000 acres, 2,500 acres cultivated); Shop; Special Collections (azalea, holly, native plant, rhododendron); Theatre; Trails
Activities: Arts Festival; Concerts; Education Programs (adults, graduate/undergraduate students, and children); Films; Guided Tours; Lectures

A year-round resort, Callaway Gardens is located at the southern end of the Appalachian Mountains. Its walking trails, seven-mile Discovery Bicycle Trail, and five-mile Scenic Drive feature particularly extensive collections of hollies (400 varieties) and azaleas (over 700 varieties), as well as magnolias, crab apples, dogwoods, mountain laurels, oak-leaf hydrangeas, and sourwoods. The John A. Sibley Horticultural Center, a garden/greenhouse, contains five acres of native and exotic plants within a tropical conservatory, rock wall garden, sculpture garden, fern grotto, floral conservatory, and outdoor garden. Mr. Cason's Vegetable Garden, the southern filming site of the PBS television series, The Victory Garden, consists of 7.5 acres of demonstration gardens including areas for vegetables, fruits, herbs, flowers, All-American Trials, and a composting area. The Cecil Day Butterfly Center, the largest glass-enclosed tropical butterfly conservatory in North America, houses more than 1,000 free-flying butterflies, representing more than 50 different species, in a tropical rain forest environment.

ROSWELL

CHATTAHOOCHEE NATURE CENTER—GARDENS

9135 Willeo Road, Roswell, GA 30075-4723
Tel: (770) 992-2055; Fax: (770) 552-0926
Internet Address: http://www.chattnaturecenter.com/
Admission: Fee: adult $3.00, child (<3) free, child (3-12) $2.00, senior $2.00
Attendance: 100,000
Established: 1976
Membership: Y
Wheelchair Accessible: P
Parking: On site
Open: September to August, Monday to Saturday, 9am-5pm; Sunday, noon-5pm
Closed: New Year's Day, Thanksgiving Day, Christmas Day
Facilities: Gardens (bog, butterfly, sandhills, wildflower); Greenhouse (only open by appointment, 992-2055 x229); Grounds (127 acres)
Activities: Education Programs; Plant Sales

The nature center's gardens exhibit vegetation from a wide range of Georgia habitats, including coastal bogs, sandhills of central Georgia, and mature woodlands of the Piedmont. The Bonnie Baker Butterfly Garden employs a large selection of both native and non-native plants to attract butterflies and feed caterpillars.

SAVANNAH

CHATHAM COUNTY GARDEN CENTER AND BOTANICAL GARDENS

1388 Eisenhower Drive (at Sallie Mood Drive), Savannah, GA 31406-3902
Tel: (912) 355-3883
Internet Address: http://www..ChathamCountyBotanicalGardens.org
Admission: Suggested Contribution: adult $3.00, child $1.00
Attendance: 5,000
Established: 1991
Membership: Y
Wheelchair Accessible: Y
Parking: Paved parking with spaces for disabled
Open: gardens, 9:30am-4:30pm
farmhouse, Weekdays, 10am-2pm
Facilities: Amphitheater; Arboretum (mixed hardwoods, pines, sweetgum, nature trails); Gardens (herb, perennial, rose, shade, vegetable, camelias, azalea, seasonal gardens, shade garden); Grounds (10 acres); Visitor Center (restored farmhouse, ca.1840)
Activities: Education Programs (workshops, flower arranging); Guided Tours ($3/person); Lectures

Located on the Southside, the site contains more than 900 varieties of trees, shrubs, and flowering plants. Exhibits include roses, perennials, herbs and vegetables, a shade garden, separate gardens devoted to flowering plants that bloom during the different seasons of the year, a small pond, and a nature walk. The gardens are a project of the Savannah Area Council of Garden Clubs in conjunction with Chatham County.

THE ISAIAH DAVENPORT HOUSE MUSEUM—GARDEN

324 E. State Street and Habersham, Savannah, GA 31401
Tel: (912) 236-8097; Fax: (912) 233-7938
Internet Address: http://www.davenportsavga.com
Admission: Fee: adult $7.00, child (<6) free, child (6-18) $3.50
Attendance: 40,000
Established: 1963
Parking: Metered on street
Open: Tour Hours, Monday to Saturday, 10am-4pm; Sunday, 1pm-4pm
Closed: New Year's Eve to New Year's Day, Street Patrick's Day, Easter, Independence
Day, Thanksgiving Day, Christmas Eve to Christmas Day
Facilities: Architecture (historic Federal-style home, 1820); Gardens (English, formal,
herb); Grounds (1 acre); Shop
Activities: Education Programs; Evening Tours (Dec 26-30); Events October Living
History (yellow fever); Guided Tours

An historic house museum, the Isaiah Davenport House is furnished as it would have
been shortly after its construction in the 1820s. The grounds include a courtyard garden.

OWENS-THOMAS HOUSE MUSEUM—GARDENS

124 Abercorn (Ogelthorpe Square, between State & York Streets), Savannah, GA 31401
Tel: (912) 233-9743; Fax: (912) 233-0102
Internet Address: http://www.telfair.org
Admission: Fee: adult $8.00, child (6-12) $2.00, student $7.00
Attendance: 60,000
Established: 1954
Membership: Y
Wheelchair Accessible: P
Parking: Metered on street
Open: Tuesday to Saturday, 10am-5pm; Monday, 12pm-5pm; Sunday, 1pm-5pm,
Spring, Fall
Facilities: Architecture (1819 residence, design by William Jay); Gardens (period,
Regency-style); Grounds (1954, designed by Clermont Lee)

The gardens, though modern, are designed in traditional Regency-style to match the
style of the house.

UNIVERSITY OF GEORGIA COLLEGE OF AGRICULTURAL
AND ENVIRONMENTAL SCIENCES—BAMBOO FARM AND
COASTAL GARDENS

2 Canebrake Road (intersection of Route 17 & Canebrake Road), Savannah, GA
31419
Tel: (912) 921-5460; Fax: (912) 921-5890
Internet Address: http://pubs.caes.uga.edu/caespubs/horticulture/coastalgarden/coastalga
Admission: Free
Membership: Y
Open: Monday to Friday, 9am-4pm
Facilities: Gardens (cottage, day lily, xeriscape); Grounds (52 acres); Special
Collections (bamboo, day lilies, ornamental grasses, crape myrtles, ornamental vines)

Activities: Plant Sale; Education Programs; Events (Annual Fall Festival; Spring Gardening Festival)

Located in southwestern Savannah, the Bamboo Farm is part of the University of Georgia's College of Agricultural and Environmental Sciences. It houses a number of plant collections, gardens, demonstration projects, and research plots. The Bamboo Farm is perhaps best known for its collection of more than 140 varieties of shade and sun-loving bamboo, reputed to be the largest collection of bamboo in North America. Collections of ornamental grasses, magnolia (sixteen varieties), crape myrtles, ornamental vines, day lilies (600 varieties), and butterfly plants are also exhibited. The site also offers two display gardens: the Cottage Garden, a trial garden where old and new varieties of perennials, annuals, and bulbs are evaluated for their adaptability to the southeastern coastal climate and soil, and the Xeriscape Garden, demonstrating the principles of water-wise landscaping. In 1998, the Southeastern Palm and Exotic Plant Society (SEPEPS) began assembling a palm collection at the Bamboo Farm.

STATESBORO

GEORGIA SOUTHERN BOTANICAL GARDEN (AHS RAP)

1505 Bland Avenue, Statesboro, GA 30460
Tel: (912) 871-1149; Fax: (912) 871-1777
Internet Address: http://welcome.georgiasouthern.edu/garden
Admission: Free
Established: 1990
Membership: Y
Wheelchair Accessible: Y
Open: Garden, Daily, 9am-dusk
Visitor Center, Tuesday to Saturday, 10am-4pm
Visitor Center, Sunday, 1pm-4pm
Best Time(s) of Year to Visit: early Spring, early Fall
Facilities: Grounds (11acres); Shop (gifts); Visitor Center Bland Cottage (farmhouse with outbuildings)
Activities: Events; Guided Tours; Plant Sales; Self-Guided Tours

Centered on a southern farmstead, Georgia Southern Botanical Gardens offers visitors a unique view of the cultural and natural heritage of the southeastern coastal plain. The site, located in the middle of Statesboro, includes an arboretum, woodland walking trails, a heritage garden, a rose arbor, a camellia garden, a native plant landscape demonstration garden, a native azalea collection, and a bog garden. The Bland Barns and other farmstead buildings are considered important aspects of the carden, serving to connect visitors to the rural heritage of southeastern Georgia.

ILLINOIS

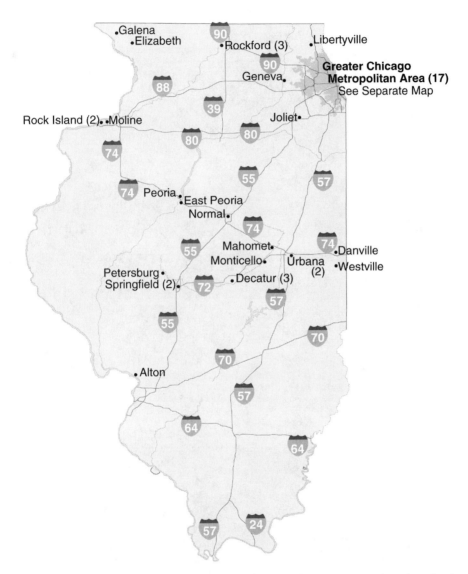

The number in the parentheses following the city name indicates the number of gardens/ arboreta in that municipality. If there is no number, one is understood. For example, in the text three listings would be found under Decatur and one listing under Westville. Cities within the greater Chicago metropolitan area will be found on the map on the next page.

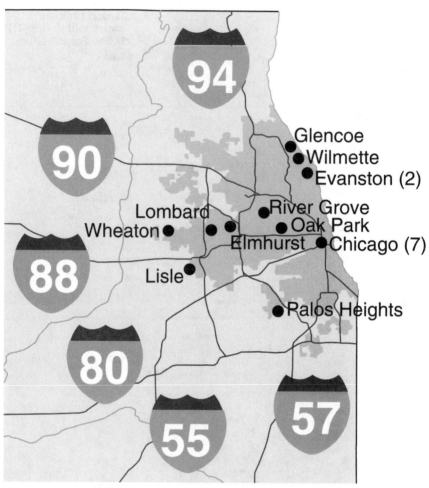

Greater Chicago metropolitan area (including Chicago, Elmhurst, Evanston, Glencoe, Lisle, Lombard, Oak Park, Palos Heights, Wheaton, and Wilmette).

ALTON

CITY OF ALTON—NAN ELLIOTT MEMORIAL ROSE GARDEN

Gordon F. Moore Community Park, 4550 College Avenue (Route 140), Alton, IL 62002
Tel: (618) 463-3580
Admission: Free
Established: 1982
Facilities: Gardens (oriental, rose); Grounds Garden (1 acre), Park (700 acres)

Accredited by All-America Rose Selections, the garden offers more than 1,800 roses. The park also offers an oriental-style garden and the Nature Institute Prairie Trail, a ¼-mile, self-guided trail giving access to the largest prairie grass restoration area in Illinois.

CHICAGO

CHICAGO PARK DISTRICT— GARFIELD PARK CONSERVATORY AND GARDENS (AHS RAP)

Chicago Park District—
Lincoln Park Conservatory and
Gardens, Chicago, IL

300 N. Central Park Avenue, Chicago, IL 60624-1996
Tel: (773) 746-5100; Fax: (773) 638-1777
Internet Address: http://www.garfield-conservatory.org
Admission: Free
Attendance: 400,000
Established: 1874
Membership: Y
Wheelchair Accessible: Y
Parking: Free lot, just south of Conservatory
Open: Daily, 9am-5pm
Facilities: Conservatory (1908, built by landscape architect Jens Jensen; 4.5 acres, inside and out); Food Services: The Flower Cart Café; Gardens (aquatic, demonstration, sensory); Grounds Garfield Park (185 acres, 1869 design by architect William Le Baron Jenney, design modified by Jens Jensen and Oscar Dubuis); Library (350 volumes); Nature Center; Park Museum; Shops: The Gift Cart (Sat-Sun, 10am-4:30pm); Special Collections (aroid, cactus, fern, palm, tropical plant)
Activities: Classes and Workshops (638-1766 ext 6); Flower Shows (5/year; Azalea, Spring, Summer, Chrysanthemum, Holiday); Guided Tours (groups, reserve in advance, 638-1766 ext 14 or kakre@garfieldpark.org); Lectures; Permanent Exhibits; Temporary Exhibitions

The oldest of the three great original Westside parks (Humboldt, Garfield, Douglas), the first forty-acre segment of Garfield Park (originally known as Central Park) was formally opened to the public in 1874. In 1905, Jens Jensen, now known as the dean of Prairie-style landscape architecture, was appointed as the superintendent of the West Park System where he experimented with design ideas and improvements to the deteriorated and unfinished sections of Garfield Park. His most notable work in Garfield Park can be seen in the formal flower garden south of Madison Street where he combined Prairie-style elements with traditional formal elements and in the conservatory. One of the largest gardens under glass in the world, the conservatory occupies approximately 4.5 acres inside and out, including cold frames and propagating houses. Inside the conservatory is organized as a series of naturalistic landscapes under glass (Aroid House, Children's Garden, Desert House, Fern Room, Monet Garden, Palm House, Show House, Warm House). Outside there are a sensory garden and demonstration gardens focusing on the urban environment. The site also offers the Garfield Market, an historic building and rustic grounds, offering twelve unique shops, a garden center, an outdoor café, and a farmers market on Sundays. Farther south in the park the Chicago Park District maintains an annual garden at the corner of Jackson and Independence Boulevards. Both Garfield Park and its conservatory are listed on the National Register of Historic Places.

CHICAGO PARK DISTRICT—GRANT PARK GARDENS

Michigan Avenue to Lake Michigan (from Randolph Street to Roosevelt Road), Chicago, IL 60601
Tel: (312) 742-7648
Internet Address: http://www.chicagoparkdistrict.com
Admission: Free
Open: Daily, 7am-11pm
Facilities: Gardens (formal, annual); Grounds Grant Park (303 acres, 1907 landscape plans by Olmsted Brothers, altered by Edward H. Bennett between 1915 & 1930)

Known as Chicago's "front yard," Grant Park contains numerous formal gardens as wells as mature trees, shrubs and lawns. There are both annual and perennial beds surrounding the park's focal point, the Clarence Buckingham Memorial Fountain (off of Columbus Drive, between Balbo Avenue and Jackson Boulevard). Additional annual plantings include: Cancer Survivors Garden (Upper Randolph Street, just east of Daley Bicentennial Park Fieldhouse), Congress Median/Congress Triangle Gardens (Congress Parkway between Columbus Drive and Michigan Avenue), Logan Monument Garden (Balbo Avenue and Michigan Avenue), Patrillo Bandshell Garden (Columbus Drive and Jackson Boulevard), North & South Court of Presidents Gardens (Columbus Drive and Congress Parkway), Spirit of Music Garden (Balbo Avenue and Michigan Avenue), and the Museum Campus Welcome Garden (Roosevelt Road and Michigan Avenue).

CHICAGO PARK DISTRICT-JACKSON PARK—OSAKA GARDEN

57th Street and Lake Shore Drive (behind the Museum of Science and Industry), Chicago, IL 60637
Tel: (312) 747-2474; Fax: (312) 742-5349
Internet Address: http://www.chicagoparkdistrict.com
Admission: Free
Established: 1893
Open: Daily, 6am-11pm
Best Time(s) of Year to Visit: Spring
Facilities: Food Services (teahouse); Garden (Japanese)
Activities: Events Osaka Garden Festival (fall)

Located at the north end of Wooded Island in historic Grant Park, Osaka Garden is a Japanese stroll garden filled with traditional Japanese horticulture and landscaping featuring a pavilion, tea house, Shinto gate, lily pond, lagoons, and running water. The seeds of the garden were planted in 1893, when the Japanese government presented Chicago with the Phoenix Pavilion (Ho-o-den) for the World's Columbian Exhibition. In the mid-1930s, the Chicago Park District established a garden on the site to complement the Ho-o-den and a new teahouse. In 1993 the garden was named to honor the Chicago-Osaka sister cities relationship. Owned and managed by the Chicago Park District, the garden receives support from the Friends of the Parks, the Osaka Committee of the Chicago Sister Cities Program, the City of Osaka Japan, and other cultural organizations.

CHICAGO PARK DISTRICT—JACKSON PARK PERENNIAL GARDEN

59th Street and Cornell Drive, Chicago, IL 60637
Tel: (312) 742-7529
Admission: Free
Established: 1937
Membership: N
Wheelchair Accessible: P
Parking: On street
Open: Daily, 7am-11pm
Facilities: Gardens (perennial); Grounds Garden (1 acre), Park (500 acres)

Located across the street from the Museum of Science and Industry, the Jackson Park Perennial Garden features many shade-tolerant plants. Jackson Park contains stately trees, reflecting ponds, acres of grass, and an eighteen-hole golf course.

CHICAGO PARK DISTRICT—LINCOLN PARK CONSERVATORY AND GARDENS

2931 N. Stockton Drive, Chicago, IL 60614-4700
Tel: (312) 742-7736; Fax: (312) 742-5619
Admission: Free
Attendance: 501,000
Established: 1892
Membership: Y
Wheelchair Accessible: Y
Parking: Parking at Stockton and Fullerton—$8.00
Open: Daily, 9am-5pm
Facilities: Conservatory (palm house, fern room, orchid room); Gardens (formal, conifer); Greenhouses; Grounds Conservatory
(3 acres), Lincoln Park (1,208 acres)
Activities: Flower Shows (6/year); Guided Tours; Lectures; Permanent Exhibits; Temporary Exhibitions

Lincoln Park, extending from North Avenue all the way to Ardmore Avenue at the north end of Lake Shore Drive, contains the Lincoln Park Conservatory as well as the oldest free public zoo in America. Adjacent to the Lincoln Park Zoo, the conservatory consists of several rooms: the Palm House, the Fernery, and the Show House. The Show House is the site of seasonal displays, including an azalea and camellia show in February, a spring flower show from February to May, a summer flower show, a chrysanthemum show in November, and a Christmas show in December. Behind the main conservatory are multi-roomed greenhouses used by the staff for propagation. Outside the conservatory on the west, south, and east sides is a conifer garden showcasing conifers with a host of shrubs, perennials, and annuals and a Shakespeare Garden, featuring flowers and plants mentioned in the Bard's works. Other perennial gardens in Lincoln Park include Grandmother's Garden (corner of Stockton Drive and Webster Avenue) established in the 1880s featuring perennials, annuals, and shrubs and the Historical Society Garden (off North Avenue and Clark Street). Annual plantings may be found in the Lincoln Park Great Garden (west of Lincoln Park Zoo, off Stockton Drive) and at the Benjamin Franklin Statue (corner of Stockton Drive and North Avenue), the Hamilton Statue (corner of Stockton Drive and Fullerton Avenue), North Avenue Triangle (west of Lake Shore Drive), and the Rowing Lagoon (west of Lake Shore Drive and north of North Avenue at south end of lagoon).

CHICAGO PARK DISTRICT—MARQUETTE PARK TRIAL GARDEN

6734 S. Kedzie Avenue (along circular drive through park), Chicago, IL 60629
Tel: (312) 747-6469
Admission: Free
Attendance: 50,000
Membership: N
Wheelchair Accessible: P
Parking: On street and lot
Open: Daily, 7am-11pm
Best Time(s) of Year to Visit: May to October
Facilities: Gardens (annual, perennial); Grounds Marquette Park (323 acres).

Situated along the park's circular drive, the Trial Gardens include both perennial and annual plantings.

CHICAGO PARK DISTRICT—WASHINGTON PARK ARBORETUM

Bounded by East 51st Street, Ellsworth Drive, East 55th Street & South M. L. King Drive, Chicago, IL 60637
Tel: (312) 742-7529; TDDY: (312) 747-2001
Internet Address: http://www.chicagoparkdistrict.com
Admission: Free
Open: Daily, 7am-11pm
Best Time(s) of Year to Visit: March to early April (Cornelian Cherry bloom), Spring (flowering trees), Fall (color)
Facilities: Arboretum; Grounds Washington Park (1,000 acres, original 1871 landscape design by Frederick Law Olmsted and Calvert Vaux)
Activities: Education Programs ((312) 742-5039); Guided Tours (groups, schedule in advance, (312) 742-5275, free)

The arboretum in Washington Park, containing more than forty-five varieties of trees, is a special collection of trees that are among the oldest and most unusual found in Chicago's parks. The mature lindens, hickories, and sycamores have witnessed the dynamic history of Chicago, Washington Park, and the surrounding communities and the Burr Oaks were likely present in 1871 when Olmsted designed the park. A collaboration of the Morton Arboretum and the Chicago Park District, the arboretum in Washington Park is the first of an intended series of arboreta to be developed in select city parks. The Chicago Park District also maintains two annual gardens in Washington Park near the arboretum at East 55th Place and M. L. King Drive and farther away at 740 East 65th Place.

DANVILLE

KENNEKUK COUNTY PARK—HERB GARDEN

22296-A Henning Road, Danville, IL 61834
Tel: (217) 442-1691; Fax: (217) 442-1695
Internet Address: http://www.vccd.org/herbs.html
Admission: Free
Attendance: 5,000
Established: 1993
Membership: Y
Wheelchair Accessible: P
Parking: Paved parking lot within 100 feet
Open: Mid-January to mid-March, Daily, 7am-4:30pm. Mid-March to September, Daily, 6am-11pm. October 1 to Standard Time, Daily, 5am-11pm. Standard Time to Thanksgiving Day, Daily, 5am-8pm. Thanksgiving Day to mid-January, Daily, 5am-4:30pm
Best Time(s) of Year to Visit: July to October
Facilities: Architecture Bunker Hill Historic Area (collection of 19th- and early 20th-century buildings); Garden (herb, raised beds); Grounds Kennekuk County Park (3,000 acres)
Activities: Interpretive Programs; Plant Sale–Herb Garden Open House (Aug or Sept)

With geometrically shaped raised beds and brick walkways, the herb garden is a focal point of color at the Bunker Hill Historic Area. Annual flowers are mixed with the herbs to form colorful borders. Some of the most common herbs grown are basil (many types), lemon grass, borage, chives, tansy, nasturtium, oregano, thyme, and sage. A variety of peppers is also grown. The flowers, such as stattice and silver king, are dried and sold. The Herb Garden is located in the Bunker Hill Historic Area, consisting of three restored buildings: Vermilion Chapel, Neff Grocery, and Red Oak School, a one-room school. Buildings are staffed by volunteers on weekends from Memorial Day through October.

DECATUR

ANNA BETHEL FISHER ROCK GARDEN

Nelson Park, Nelson Park Boulevard & Lake Shore Drive, Decatur, IL 62521
Tel: (217) 422-5911
Internet Address: http://www.decatur-parks.org
Admission: Free
Established: 1927
Membership: Y
Wheelchair Accessible: Y
Parking: Free lot on site
Open: April to October, Daily, 7:30am-dusk
Best Time(s) of Year to Visit: April to May
Facilities: Garden (rock)

Originally called the Sunken Garden, it was built on the site of an old sand pit once located within Nelson Park adjacent to Lake Decatur. Completely renovated in 1992, the prize-winning restoration features a variety of flowering plants nestled among boulders and outcrops beneath a canopy of cypress trees.

FAIRVIEW PARK ROSE GARDEN

West Eldorado & Oakcrest Avenue, Decatur, IL 62521
Tel: (217) 422-5911
Internet Address: http://www.decatur-parks.org
Admission: Free
Established: 1959 Membership: N
Facilities: Garden (rose)

Containing 800 roses representing twenty-five different varieties, the garden is designed as an array of beds radiating out from a central location. Each bed contains its own rose variety and each row its own color scheme.

SCOVILL PARK—ORIENTAL GARDENS

71 S. Country Club Road, Decatur,
IL 62521
Tel: (217) 421-7435
Internet Address: http://www.decatur-parks.org
Admission: Free
Established: 1948
Membership: N
Wheelchair Accessible: Y
Parking: Adjacent lot
Open: April to November, Daily, 7:30am-dusk
Facilities: Gardens (oriental, annual); Park (62 acres); Picnic Area; Zoo

Scovill Park—Oriental
Gardens, Decatur, IL.

Originally a part of the Scovill family estate, the garden contains many pieces of oriental sculpture, the Scovill House Oriental Pavilion, a sod bridge, and a waterfall that flows through a boulder-strewn creek into a pond. Adjacent to the Oriental Gardens, the Scovill Gazebo Gardens features rows of annual flower beds encircling a large gazebo.

EAST PEORIA

ILLINOIS CENTRAL COLLEGE—HORTICULTURE LAND LABORATORY AND ARBORETUM

One College Drive, East Peoria, IL 61635-0001
Tel: (309) 694-5415
Internet Address: http://www.icc.edu/horticulture/tour.asp
Admission: Free
Attendance: 3,000
Established: 1980
Membership: N
Wheelchair Accessible: P
Parking: Paved parking lot—60 spaces
Open: dawn-dusk
Best Time(s) of Year to Visit: May, June to September, October

Facilities: Arboretum (3 acres; hostas, dwarf conifers); Gardens (flower, perennial, vegetable, demonstration); Greenhouses (5,000 square feet); Grounds (7 acres) Activities: Demonstrations; Education Programs; Events Landscape & Garden Day (1st Sat after Labor Day); Workshops

Constructed exclusively by ICC horticulture students and staff, the arboretum contains a wide variety of trees, shrubs, vines, and perennials that are hardy to central Illinois. Gardens include All-American Selections of flowers and vegetables (over 200 varieties of annuals are showcased each summer), the Cooperative Extension Demonstration and Evaluation Plot, raised planters, lath structure, and, still under development, a water garden with seventy-five-foot stream, which will highlight dwarf conifers in the area surrounding it. Featured plant collections encompass crab apples, birches, oaks, arborvitae, hydrangeas, and extensive shade perennial beds boasting over 300 varieties of hosta.

ELIZABETH

TIMBER RIDGE GARDENS

201 S. Elizabeth-Scales Mound, Elizabeth, IL 61028
Tel: (815) 858-3740
Admission: Free
Attendance: 5,000
Established: 1993
Membership: N
Wheelchair Accessible: P
Parking: Park along lane
Open: May to October, 10am-5pm
Facilities: Gardens (15 acres; hostas (900 varieties), perennials, grasses, trees, shrubs)

This perennial nursery features landscaped display gardens and an arboretum containing over 3000 varieties of ornamental and native perennials, grasses, specimen trees, and shrubs.

ELMHURST

CITY OF ELMHURST—WILDER PARK CONSERVATORY AND GARDENS

225 Prospect (near Church Street), Elmhurst, IL 60126
Tel: (630) 993-8900; Fax: (630) 993-8913
Internet Address: http://www.epd.org/conserv.htm
Established: 1923
Open: Daily, 9am-4pm (9pm during flower shows)
Facilities: Conservatory (2,000 square feet, 1926,); Gardens (herb, perennial); Greenhouses (2 greenhouses & a growing house); Grounds Wilder Park (17.3 acres). Activities: Exhibit Environmental for Kids (February); Flower Shows Fall (November); Holiday (December), Spring (Easter)

Located in the southwest corner of Wilder Park is an elaborate series of glass buildings. Known as the conservatory, it is actually a conservatory, two greenhouses, and a growing house. Surrounding gardens include an award-winning, 8,800-square-foot herb garden containing over 50 varieties of culinary, medicinal, and fragrant herbs.

EVANSTON

MERRICK PARK ROSE GARDEN

Oak Avenue and Lake Avenue (southeast corner), Evanston, IL 60203
Tel: (847) 866-2910
Internet Address: http://www.cityofevanston.org/parks/
Admission: Free
Established: 1951
Best Time(s) of Year to Visit: June to October
Facilities: Garden (rose)

The garden contains over 2,000 roses representing over 200 varieties and an historic fountain.

NORTHWESTERN UNIVERSITY—SHAKESPEARE GARDEN

1967 Sheridan Road, Evanston, IL 60201-2924
Tel: (708) 491-4000
Established: 1920
Best Time(s) of Year to Visit: May to August
Facilities: Garden (Elizabethan plantings in Tudor-style garden, 1915 design by landscape architect Jens Jensen); Grounds (7,000 square feet)

Located on the north end of the Evanston campus at the east end of Garrett Place (just north of the Howes Chapel), the Shakespeare Garden is listed on the National Register of Historic Places. It includes eight flower beds filled with nearly 100 species of flowers, herbs, and vegetables. Among the fifty plants that can be planted in the garden are rosemary, lavender, thyme, hyssop, rue, lemon balm, columbine, sweetbrier (eglantine), oxeye daisy, (Japanese) anemone, daffodil, pansy, poppy, nasturtium, and marigolds. Parsley, holly, ivy, mint, and peonies are also allowed. Summer annuals vary from year to year. The garden is maintained by the Evanston Garden Club.

GALENA

LINMAR GARDENS

504 S. Prospect, Galena, IL 61036
Tel: (815) 777-1177
Admission: Fee: adult $4.00, child $2.00
Attendance: 2,000
Established: 1985
Membership: N
Wheelchair Accessible: Y
Open: June to October, 10am-4pm; 1pm-4pm.
Best Time(s) of Year to Visit: June to October.
Facilities: Gardens (rock, sunken); Grounds (3½ acres—waterfall, hostas, viburnums, conifers, grasses, day lilies)

Situated among limestone outcrops on a hillside overlooking Galena, the gardens include a sunken garden in the ruins of one of the first African-American churches in Illinois. Plantings include conifers, day lilies, grasses, hostas, viburnums, and other perennials and annuals.

GENEVA

FABYAN VILLA AND JAPANESE GARDENS

Fabyan Forest Preserve, 1925 Batavia Avenue (Routes 31 and 25), Geneva, IL 60134
Tel: (708) 232-4811
Admission: Voluntary contribution
Attendance: 5,000
Established: 1941
Membership: Y
Open: Villa: mid-May to mid-October, Wednesday, 1pm-4pm; Saturday to Sunday,
1pm-4:30pm; Holidays, 1pm-4:30pm. Garden: Memorial Day to Labor Day, Sunday,
1pm-4pm
Facilities: Architecture (Colonel George Fabyan home, 1907, redesigned by Frank
Lloyd Wright); Exhibition Area; Forest Preserve; Garden (Japanese, 1915 design by
Taro Otuska, a Japanese landscape architect); Grounds (235 acres)
Activities: Guided Tours; Lectures

In the early 1900s, George and Nelle Fabyan bought a small farmhouse and ten acres
south of Geneva. They developed this farm into a fabulous estate of nearly 600 acres with
a model farm, large greenhouses, nineteenth-century windmill, Japanese Garden, and
many other ornamental gardens. In the 1940s, the Forest Preserve District of Kane
County purchased 235 acres of the estate on the east and west banks of the Fox River.
The Villa is maintained as a museum containing part of Fabyan's collection of natural and
oriental artifacts. Below the Villa lies the Japanese Garden (restored in 1971 and 1994)
with plant-ings, pool, bridges, and restored structures.

GLENCOE

CHICAGO BOTANIC GARDENS (AHS RAP)

1000 Lake Cook Road, Glencoe, IL 60022
Tel: (847) 835-5440; Fax: (847) 835-4484; TDDY: (847) 835-0790
Internet Address: http://www.chicago-botanic.org/
Admission: Voluntary contribution
Attendance: 900,000
Established: 1972
Membership: Y
Wheelchair Accessible: Y
Parking: On site, $10/auto, $16/commercial van, $36/commercial bus
Open: Daily, 8am-sunset
Closed: Christmas Day
Best Time(s) of Year to Visit: Spring (bulbs & flowering trees), June (rose garden),
Fall (prairie)
Facilities: Auditorium (200 seats); Classrooms (6); Education Center; Exhibit Hall;
Food Services Restaurants (3; 8am-4:30pm, hours extended Apr-Oct); Gardens
(annual, aquatic, bulb, children's, dwarf conifer, enabling, endangered, English walled,
English oak meadow, fruit/vegetable, heritage, Japanese, landscape, native plant,
perennial, rose, sensory, sun & shade evaluation, waterfall); Greenhouses; Grounds (385
acres); Herbarium; Library (25,000 volumes, 4,500 rare books, 2,556 periodical titles;
Mon-Sat, 9am-4pm; members have borrowing privileges); Museum of Floral Arts; Picnic
Area; Shop (specialty gift & seasonal items, books, clothing, garden antiques)

Activities: Art Exhibits; Demonstrations; Education Programs (adults, graduate/undergraduate students and children); Events (seasonal); Flower Shows; Guided Tours; Lectures; Plant Sales (seasonal); Tram Tours; Workshops

Visitors to the Chicago Botanic Gardens may walk amidst tall grass on a midwestern prairie and minutes later enjoy the refined pleasures of a Japanese garden. These experiences and many more unfold in a "living museum" containing over 2.2 million plants representing more than 9,000 species. Twenty-three gardens showcase the best plants for the Midwest in a wide variety of settings. Gardens include a variety of water gardens; an enabling garden and a sensory garden for people of differing abilities; an English-walled garden with six garden "rooms" demonstrating English gardening styles; the Heritage Garden, a tribute to the history of the scientific study and display of plants; a native plant garden, offering ideas for using native Illinois plants in home landscaping; shade and sun evaluation gardens; rock, herb, and perennial landscape gardens; an English Oak meadow, a Japanese garden, the Sansho-en (Garden of Three Islands); on All-America Rose Selections test garden; and a bonsai exhibit (May-October). Greenhouses offer unusual plants from around the world in a landscape under glass supplemented by seasonal displays. Additionally, three native habitat areas feature native and endangered flora of Illinois. In each of the four seasons, visitors can explore the 385 acres of islands, lakes, and woodlands and learn about the splendor and fragility of our living environment. A program of the Chicago Horticultural Society, the Chicago Botanic Garden is owned by the Forest Preserve District of Cook County.

JOLIET

BIRD HAVEN GREENHOUSE AND CONSERVATORY

Pilcher Park, 225 N. Gougar Road, Joliet, IL 60432
Tel: (815) 741-7278; Fax: (815) 722-5317
Internet Address: http://www.jolietpark.org/birdhaven.html
Admission: No charge, donations accepted
Parking: Parking for 200 cars
Open: Greenhouse, Daily, 8am-4:30pm. Outside Gardens: June to October.
Facilities: Gardens; Greenhouse (Lord & Burnham, early 1900s); Grounds Greenhouse & Gardens (3 acres), Pilcher Park (660 acres); Horticultural Center
Activities: Education Programs; Flower Shows; Plant Sales (poinsettia)

The Bird Haven Greenhouse & Conservatory was constructed in the early 1900s. An Italian Renaissance-style facility, it was designed by the firm of Lord and Burnham. Surrounded by outside seasonal gardens, the greenhouse contains a tropical house, a cacti and succulent collection (some of which was donated by the Smithsonian in 1923), and floral shows with seasonal motifs, for example, poinsettias in the winter, tulips and daffodils in the spring, and mums in the fall. The Greenhouse also offers field trips on leaf identification, desert environments, hummingbird migration, and other topics.

LIBERTYVILLE

CITY OF LIBERTYVILLE—LYNN J. ARTHUR ROSE GARDEN

Cook Memorial Park, Libertyville, IL 60048
Tel: (708) 362-2025
Admission: Free
Established: 1952

Membership: N
Wheelchair Accessible: Y
Parking: Free on-street parking and two nearby lots
Open: always open
Facilities: Architecture Cook Mansion (Victorian residence, 1878); Garden (rose); Grounds (1.7 acres)
Activities: Concerts (summer)

Created by the Men's Garden Club, the garden is accredited by All-America Rose Selections and is maintained by the Gardeners of Central Lake County.

LISLE

THE MORTON ARBORETUM (AHS RAP)

4100 Illinois Route 53 (west of Interstate 355 and north of I-88.), Lisle, IL 60532-1293
Tel: (630) 719-2400; Fax: (630) 719-2433
Internet Address: http://www.mortonarb.org/
Admission: Fee: adult $5.00, child (0-2) free, child (3-12) $2.00, senior $4.00.
Wednesday: adult $3.00, youth (3-12) $1.00, senior $2.00
Attendance: 325,000
Established: 1922
Membership: Y
Wheelchair Accessible: Y
Parking: Fee: Wednesday, $3/auto, $10/van, $25/bus
Open: Central Daylight Time, Daily, 7am-7pm. Central Standard Time, Daily, 7am-5pm.
Best Time(s) of Year to Visit: Spring (daffodils & crab apples), Summer (prairie & gardens), Fall (colors), Winter (landscapes)
Facilities: Climatic Areas (Appalachians; central, northeast, west Asia; Balkans; China; Europe; northern Illinois; Japan; Korea; Ozarks; eastern U.S. wetlands); Education Center (auditorium and classrooms, Mon-Fri, 9am-4:30pm; Morton Family Exhibit); Food Services Ginko Room & Restaurant (daily, 9am-5pm); Gardens (bulb & perennial, children's, dwarf woody plants, four seasons, fragrance, ground cover, hedge, maze, native, reading, wild); Grounds (1,700 acres; natural areas 900 acres, including 100-acre tall grass prairie); Herbarium (165,00 specimens); Library Sterling Morton Library (30,000 volumes, non-circulating; Tues-Fri, 9am-5pm; Sat, 10am-4pm); Picnic Area (near Visitor Center); Roads (9 miles); Shop: the Arboretum Store (daily, 9am-5pm); Special Collections (beech, buckeye, crab apple, elm family, linden, magnolia, maple, pine family); Trails (14 miles); Visitor Center (daily, 9am-5pm)
Activities: Education Programs (adults, graduate students and children); Guided Tours (Wed & Sat-Sun, walking tours;, Group (reserve in advance, 630-719-2466), Tram (Nov-Mar, Wed & Sat-Sun, weather permitting); Lectures; Plant Sale; Temporary Exhibitions

Specializing in the display and study of trees, shrubs, and vines, the Arboretum was established on his Thornhill estate by Mr. Joy Morton, owner of the Morton Salt Company and son of W. Sterling Morton, the founder of Arbor Day. Dr. Charles Sprague Sargent, who had directed the Arnold Arboretum for fifty years, visited the arboretum several times and was a significant influence in its formation. Gardens and landscapes, containing more than 40,000 plants representing 3,300 different varieties from around the world, are found throughout the arboretum. The plants are grouped into themed collections, which helps in their interpretation and evaluation. Each accessioned plant in the collections has a label bearing its name, location, and date of inclusion into the collection. Major geographically defined woody plant collections include: China (more than 770 plants, nearly 300 species), northern Illinois (160 species), central and west Asia, eastern United States wetlands, Appalachian highlands (120 species), and Japan. The leading taxonomic collections include: elms (200 trees) and pine (700 coniferous trees and shrubs, 150 varieties). Gardens include: Hedge Garden (a two-acre formal garden, containing thirty sheared hedges and twenty-eight unsheared natural hedges), Ground Cover Garden (woody and herbaceous ground cover plants arranged for sun, partial shade, and shade), Dwarf Woody Plants (small shrubs and dwarf conifers), Four Seasons Garden (small-scale woody and herbaceous plants recommended for home landscaping in the Chicago region and selected for winter color, bark texture, flowers, fruit, and other multi-seasonal attractions), Fragrance Garden (trees, shrubs, vines, perennials, and annuals possessing fragrant leaves or flowers, including many hardy roses and lilacs), Joy Path Gardens (bulb and perennial plants displayed against a backdrop of flowering trees and shrubs), Wild Garden (woody and herbaceous plants native to the upper Midwest), and May T. Watts Reading Garden (plants associated with events and personalities in the history of botanical exploration and horticulture). A four-acre Children's Garden and a ½-acre Maze Garden opened in 2005. The arboretum's natural areas, accessible by road and trail, include oak and maple woodlands, wetlands, lakes, and a 100-acre planted tallgrass prairie (Schulenberg Prairie) begun in 1962, one of the first such plantings in the nation. The Prairie Visitor Station and Big Rock Visitor Station offer interpretive panels and trailheads, introducing visitors to surrounding landscape.

LOMBARD

LILACIA PARK

Corner of Park & Parkside Avenues, Lombard, IL 60148
Tel: (708) 627-1281; Fax: (708) 627-1286
Internet Address: http://www.lombardparks.com
Admission: Fee (during festival non-residents): adult $2.00, child (11<) free, child, senior $1.00.
Attendance: 16,000
Established: 1927
Wheelchair Accessible: Y
Open: Daily, 9am-9pm
Best Time(s) of Year to Visit: early May
Facilities: Botanical Garden; Country Store; Garden (lilac, 1929 design by landscape architect Jens Jensen; tulip); Grounds (8½ acres); Information Center (coach house, 1888); Picnic Area
Activities: Concert Series; Festival Lilac Time (1st two weeks in May); Guided Historical Tours (during Lilac Time); Seminars (lilac planting and care)

In 1927, Colonel William R. Plum bequeathed his home and adjacent lilac gardens to the town as a park and library site. Designed by famed landscape architect Jens Jensen, Lilacia Park contains approximately 1,000 lilacs representing over 100 varieties and 20,000 tulips. The annual Lilac Time Festival is a village-wide tradition that dates back to the late 1920s and attracts visitors from throughout the Midwest and beyond. A brochure *Lilac Time in Lombard* is available. The park is managed by the Lombard Park District.

MAHOMET

LAKE OF THE WOODS PARK—MABERY GELVIN BOTANICAL GARDENS

508 N. Route 47, Mahomet, IL 61853
Tel: (217) 586-6852

Internet Address: http://www.ccfpd.org/gardens.htm
Open: 8am-closing time posted
Facilities: Gardens (display, enabling); Greenhouse; Grounds (600 acres, park)

Mabery Gelvin Botanical Gardens includes an All-American Selections display garden featuring plants and vegetables and an enabling garden focusing on design and techniques that make gardening accessible to those with special needs.

MOLINE

BUTTERWORTH CENTER AND DEERE-WIMAN HOUSE—GARDENS

Deere-Wiman House: 817 11th Avenue, Butterworth Center: 1105 8th Street, Moline, IL 61265
Tel: (309) 765-7935; Fax: (309) 748-9867
Internet Address: http://www.butterworthcenter.com
Admission: Voluntary contribution
Attendance: 55,000
Membership: N
Wheelchair Accessible: P
Parking: Parking lots on 8th Street and on 11th Avenue
Open: Houses: September to June, Monday to Friday, 8:30am-4:30pm. Houses: July to August, Monday to Friday, 8:30am-4:30pm; Saturday to Sunday, 1pm-4pm. Gardens, Daily, dawn-dusk
Closed: Holidays
Best Time(s) of Year to Visit: May to July
Facilities: Architecture Butterworth Home (1892, 25,000 square feet), Deere-Wiman House (1872, 15,000 square feet); Gardens; Grounds Butterworth Center (2 acres), Deere-Wiman House (7 acres)
Activities: Guided Tours Butterworth Center (July-Aug, Sun, 1-4pm, on hour; other times by appointment), Deere-Wiman House (July-Aug, Sun, 1pm-4pm on the hour; other times by appointment)

The Deere-Wiman House was the residence of Charles Deere, son of agricultural machinery manufacturer John Deere; the Butterworth Center (formerly Hillcrest), now a civic and education center, was built as wedding gift for his daughter Katherine Butterworth. Both houses feature formal gardens, begun in 1910, containing a wide variety of flowers and plants.

MONTICELLO

UNIVERSITY OF ILLINOIS AT URBANA-CHAMPAIGN— ROBERT ALLERTON PARK

515 Old Timber Road, Monticello, IL 61856
Tel: (217) 244-1035; Fax: (217) 244-9982
Internet Address: http://www.conted.ceps.uiuc.edu/RAPCC/allerton.html
Admission: Free
Attendance: 100,000
Closed: Christmas Day

Best Time(s) of Year to Visit: mid-March to early May (wildflowers), May (bulbs, peonies), Summer (lilies, annuals)
Facilities: Architecture (inspired by the English country manor, 1900 design by architect John J. Borie); Grounds (1,500 acres); Sculpture Gardens; Trails (20 miles)

Robert Henry Allerton donated his private estate, "The Farms" to the University of Illinois in 1946. The property, located just outside of Monticello, Illinois, consists of a manor house and fifteen hundred acres of upland and lowland forests, restored prairie, and landscaped gardens along the Sangamon River. A major attraction of the park is its extensive use of landscape architecture. Formal gardens with decorative art objects are blended skillfully into areas left in their natural state and monumental sculpture sites are designed to accentuate the museum-quality art while preserving the integrity of the woodland areas. The manor, outbuildings, and initial gardens were designed by architect John J. Borie. After Borie went to live in England, Robert Allerton continued to develop the park as his own designer, creating the series of formal gardens that culminated in the amphitheater of the Sunken Garden. Subsequent additions and reconstructions to the park were made by Allerton working in conjunction with his adopted son, John Gregg Allerton. In 1971, 1,000 acres of the lowland and southern forests were declared a National Natural Landmark. Robert and John Gregg Allerton's Hawaii residence is also listed; see National Tropical Botanical Garden—Allerton Garden.

NORMAL

ILLINOIS STATE UNIVERSITY—FELL ARBORETUM

ISU Campus, College Avenue, Normal, IL 61790
Tel: (309) 438-2085; Fax: (309) 438-2089
Internet Address: http://www.ilstu.edu/depts/arboretum
Admission: Free
Attendance: 20,000
Established: 1995
Membership: N
Wheelchair Accessible: Y
Parking: Campus-wide
Open: Daily, 24 hours
Best Time(s) of Year to Visit: early May, mid-October
Facilities: Arboretum; Grounds campus (350 acres)
Activities: Plant Sale (spring); Self-Guided Tour (brochure available)

The Fell Arboretum is a curated collection of trees, shrubs, and plants integrated with the art and architecture of the Illinois State campus. The arboretum consists of nearly 4,000 tree representing of 80 varieties.

OAK PARK

THE OAK PARK CONSERVATORY

615 Garfield Street at East Avenue, Oak Park, IL 60304
Tel: (708) 386-4700
Admission: Suggested contribution: adult $1.00, child $0.50

Attendance: 19,000
Established: 1929
Membership: Y
Wheelchair Accessible: Y
Open: Monday, 2pm-4pm; Tuesday to Sunday, 10am-4pm.
Holidays, 10am-3pm
Facilities: Classrooms; Conservatory (8,000 square feet); Gardens (Herb, Prairie);
Library (by request)
Activities: Education Programs (adults, undergraduate college students and children);
Films; Flower Shows (Feb, Mar, Nov, Dec); Guided Tours (groups 10+, by
appointment); Lectures; Permanent Exhibits; Plant Clinics (Mon, 2pm-4pm);
Temporary Exhibitions; Workshops

Exhibits at the conservatory include desert, tropical, and sub-tropical plants as well as
native prairie. The Park District of Oak Park has begun the construction of the Oak Park
Conservatory Urban Horticulture Education and Resource Center adjacent to the old
conservatory.

PALOS HEIGHTS

LAKE KATHERINE NATURE PRESERVE

7402 Lake Katherine Drive (at Route 83 and 75th Avenue),
Palos Heights, IL 60463
Tel: (708) 361-1873; Fax: (708) 361-2978
Internet Address: http://www.palosheights.org/lake/indexlk.html
Admission: No charge, donations accepted
Attendance: 115,000
Established: 1990
Membership: Y
Wheelchair Accessible: Y
Parking: Plentiful parking
Open: Daily, dawn-dusk
Facilities: Arboretum; Gardens (woodland wildflower, butterfly, heritage vegetable,
herb, conifer, butterfly); Grounds (136 acres); Nature Center (Mon-Fri, 9am-5pm;
Sat-Sun, 9am-4pm);
Trail (3.5 miles)
Activities: Events Monarch Butterfly Festival (Sept)

The preserve is one of several nature centers in the Illinois and Michigan Canal National
Heritage Corridor. It includes the Children's Forest, containing a wide variety of trees
planted by children and their parents; a woodland wildflower garden; a regional native plant
display; an arboretum; a one-mile walking and jogging trail around the twenty-acre lake; a
pier; and observation decks. In addition, the preserve features the largest waterfall in Cook
County.

PEORIA

GEORGE L. LUTHY MEMORIAL BOTANICAL GARDEN (AHS RAP)

2218 N. Prospect Road, Glen Oak Park, Peoria, IL 61603-2126
Tel: (309) 686-3362; Fax: (309) 685-6240

Internet Address: http://www.peoriaparks.org/luthy/luthymain.html
Admission: Voluntary contribution
Attendance: 130,000
Established: 1975
Membership: Y
Wheelchair Accessible: Y
Parking: On site, ample
Open: Conservatory: September to May, Daily, 10am-5pm. Conservatory: June to
August, Monday to Thursday, 10am-5pm; Friday to Saturday, 10am-8pm; Sunday,
noon-5pm. Grounds: Daily, 8:30am-dusk.
Closed: New Year's Day, Thanksgiving Day, Christmas Day. Closes at 3pm on some
holidays.
Best Time(s) of Year to Visit: May to October (outdoor gardens)
Facilities: Classrooms; Conservatory (5,000 square feet); Gardens (children's, crab
apple cove, flowering shrub, herb, rose, viburnum, wildlife, woodland); Grounds
Gardens (5 acres); Rental Gallery; Shop Trellis Gift Shop (items relating to
horticulture, gardening, outdoor living, home décor)
Activities: Classes; Concerts (jazz, call for dates and time); Education Programs (adults
and children, by appointment); Events Old-fashioned Sunday (1st Sun in Jun;, Rhapsody
in Bloom (usually last weekend in June); Flower Shows Bonsai (spring); Chrysanthemum
(late fall), Lily (spring), Orchid (early spring), Poinsettia (Nov-Jan); Guided Tours (by
appointment); Permanent Exhibits; Plant Sales; Temporary Exhibitions

The Luthy Botanical Garden traces its roots back to 1896 when the Palm House was
opened as the first structure within Oscar Dubuis' grand design for the first Peoria Park System. The current conservatory and gardens were opened in 1951. The conservatory displays
a permanent tropical collection as well as offering seasonal flower shows. Surrounding the
conservatory are eleven theme gardens, including a formal All-America Rose Selections display garden, a cottage garden, an herb garden, an all-season garden, a crab apple grove, a
children's garden, a woodland garden, a wildlife garden, a flowering shrub garden, a viburnum collection, and the Wilson Garden, a memorial to pioneer plant explorer Ernest "Chinese" Wilson, who introduced to the western garden many of our favorite plants.

PETERSBURG

STARHILL FOREST ARBORETUM

Route 1, Petersburg, IL 62675-9736
Tel: (217) 632-3685
Admission: Free
Attendance: 100
Established: 1976
Membership: N
Wheelchair Accessible: Y
Parking: Limited parking; cars only
Open: by appointment
Best Time(s) of Year to Visit: Spring to Fall
Facilities: Arboretum; Botanical Garden; Greenhouses; Grounds (48 acres-herb and
perennial landscapes, native prairie garden); Library (2,000 volumes, non-circulating)
Activities: Guided Tours (by appointment); Lectures

The arboretum contains approximately 600 accessioned woody taxa, including the North
American Plant Preservation Council North American reference collection for Quercus.

RIVER GROVE

TRITON COLLEGE—BOTANICAL GARDEN

2000 5th Avenue (north of Robert M. Collins Center), River Grove,
IL 60171
Tel: (708) 456-0300 *Ext:* 3785
Internet Address: http://www.triton.edu
Admission: Free
Wheelchair Accessible: P
Parking: Free parking
Open: Daily, sunrise to sunset
Best Time(s) of Year to Visit: Summer to Fall
Facilities: Gardens (formal, vegetable); Greenhouse; Grounds (3.5 acres);
Nursery; Shop (Summer, Mon, 9am-3pm)

Planted and maintained by horticulture students and faculty, the Botanical Gardens
offer thousands of annuals and hundreds of marigolds, petunias, and begonias, an organic
vegetable garden, and a nursery. The Triton Botanical Gardens are part of the Cook
County Forest Preserve and operated in cooperation with Triton's Horticulture Program.

ROCK ISLAND

LONGVIEW PARK CONSERVATORY

1300 17th Street at 18th Avenue, Rock Island, IL 61201
Tel: (309) 788-7275
Internet Address: http://www.rigov.org/citydepartments/parks/parkinfo.html
Open: Conservatory, Monday to Friday, 9am-3:30pm; Saturday to Sunday,
noon-3:30pm
Best Time(s) of Year to Visit: June to October (flowers and landscaped beds)
Facilities: Conservatory; Gardens; Greenhouses; Grounds park (39 acres)

Longview Park includes a conservatory, greenhouse, and annual flower gardens.

QUAD CITY BOTANICAL CENTER (AHS RAP)

2525 4th Avenue, Rock Island, IL 61201-8003
Tel: (309) 794-0991; Fax: (309) 794-1572
Internet Address: http://www.qcgardens.com/
Admission: Fee: adult $3.50, child (7-12) $1.00, senior $3.00
Established: 1998
Membership: Y
Parking: Free on site
Open: Monday to Saturday, 10am-5pm; Sunday, noon-5pm
Closed: New Year's Day, Thanksgiving Day, Christmas Day
Facilities: Conservatory Sun Garden Conservatory (6,444 square feet); Gardens
(children's, physically challenged, conifer); Grounds; Shop
Activities: Art Shows Art in the Garden; Flower Shows; Guided Tours (groups, reserve
in advance); Lecture & Luncheon Series

Situated next to the Mississippi River in downtown Rock Island, the Quad City Botanical Center offers the Scott County Regional Authority Conifer Garden containing over forty rare and unusual conifers and a variety of theme gardens as well as the award-winning Sun Garden Conservatory featuring exotic tropical flowers, fourteen-foot waterfall, and reflecting pool.

ROCKFORD

ANDERSON GARDENS (AHS RAP)

318 Spring Creek Road, Rockford, IL 61107
Tel: (815) 229-9390; Fax: (815) 229-9391
Internet Address: http://www.andersongardens.org/
Admission: Fee: adult $5.00, child (<4) free, student $3.00, senior $4.00
Established: 1978
Membership: Y
Wheelchair Accessible: P
Open: Monday to Friday, 10am-5pm; Saturday, 10am-4pm; Sunday, noon-4pm
Facilities: Gardens (Japanese, 1978 design by landscape architect Hoichi Kurisu); Grounds (12 acres); Shop Blue Iris Gifts (Japanese merchandise, 815-997-1197); Visitor Center

Originally designed as a private garden, in 1998 the facility became a non-profit corporation (qualifying as a public charity as a supporting organization of the Rockford Rotary Charitable Association) and opened to the public on a regular basis. It features an authentic pond-strolling garden, tea house, stone lanterns, and waterfalls, along with a contemporary garden with a strong Japanese influence. In 2000, the *Journal of Japanese Gardening* ranked the garden as one of the ten highest-quality Japanese gardens outside of Japan out of 300 sites surveyed.

KLEHM ARBORETUM & BOTANICAL GARDEN (AHS RAP)

2701 Clifton Avenue, Rockford, IL 61102-3537
Tel: (866) 419-0782; Fax: (815) 965-5914
Internet Address: http://www.klehm.org/
Admission: Fee$2.00. Free on Monday
Attendance: 65,000
Established: 1989
Membership: Y
Wheelchair Accessible: Y
Parking: Three hundred parking spaces
Open: Labor Day to Memorial Day, Daily, 9am-4pm. Memorial Day to Labor Day, Daily, 9am-8pm.
Closed: New Year's Day, Thanksgiving Day, Christmas Eve, Christmas Day
Facilities: Arboretum; Botanical Education Center; Gardens (children's, demonstration, fountain); Grounds (155 acres; 1.5 mile paved pathway); Library; Shop; Special Collections (evergreens)
Activities: Classes; Guided Tours (reserve in advance, $2/person); Self-Guided Tours

Originally established in 1910 as a commercial nursery, today Klehm Arboretum and Botanical Garden is a partnership between the Winnebago County Forest Preserve and Klehm Arboretum & Botanic Garden, Inc. The arboretum features many species that do not normally thrive in northern Illinois as well as a vigorous evergreen collection.

SINNISSIPPI GREENHOUSE AND GARDENS

1300 North 2nd Street, Rockford, IL 61107-3086
Tel: (815) 987-8800; Fax: (815) 969-4066; TDDY: (815) 963-3323
Internet Address: http://www.rockfordparkdistrict.org/parks_sinnissippi.htm
Admission: No charge, donations accepted
Established: 1909
Membership: N
Wheelchair Accessible: Y
Parking: On site
Open: April to November, Daily, 9am-4pm. December to March, Tuesday to Friday,
9am-4pm; Saturday to Sunday, 10am-2pm.
Facilities: Greenhouse (7:30am-3:45pm); Music shell; Park (124 acres); Rose Gardens
Activities: Flower Shows Fall Mum Show (November), Holiday Poinsettia (December),
Spring (late Feb)

The first park purchased by the Rockford Park District, Sinnissippi Park includes formal
gardens on the east bank of the Rock River with greenhouse, award-winning sunken rose
gardens (seventy-three varieties of roses), a floral clock, a shade perennial garden, an annual garden, and a small lagoon. The greenhouse contains changing floral displays complemented by waterfalls and an aviary. In the fall, over 4,000 brilliantly colored chrysanthemums fill the greenhouse, shortly followed by poinsettias.

SPRINGFIELD

LINCOLN MEMORIAL GARDEN AND NATURE CENTER

2301 E. Lake Drive, Springfield, IL 62707-8908
Tel: (217) 529-1111; Fax: (217) 529-1503
Internet Address: http://www.lmgnc.com/
Admission: Voluntary contribution
Attendance: 50,000
Established: 1936
Membership: Y
Wheelchair Accessible: Y
Open: Grounds: daily, sunrise-sunset
Closed: Easter, Independence Day, Thanksgiving Day, Christmas Week
Best Time(s) of Year to Visit: April to May, October
Facilities: Arboretum; Garden (original 63-acre garden, 1936 design by Jens Jensen;
modern garden 112 acres); Nature Center (Tues-Sat, 10am-4pm; Sunday, 1pm-4pm);
Shop
Activities: Education Programs (adults, graduate/undergraduate students and children;
weekends); Guided Tours (seasonal); Lectures; Temporary Exhibitions

A joint project of the City of Springfield and the Garden Clubs of Illinois, the site was
designed on the mid-1930s by Jens Jensen, a leader of the prairie school of landscape architecture and one of the state's earliest conservationists. Jensen's basic plan for the garden is that of a series of interconnected paths bordered by various arrangements of native
plants resulting in a mosaic of mature upland woods interspersed with prairie openings.
This pattern of lanes is held together by eight council rings, circular benches of stone designed as a means of fostering friendly gatherings within the garden. All the plants found
at the garden are native to the three states in which Lincoln lived: Kentucky, Indiana, and

Illinois. The oaks, maples, and hickories as well as the prairie grasses and forbs would have been known by Lincoln, and reflect the landscape of his time. Since 1952, the Abraham Lincoln Memorial Garden Foundation, a not-for-profit organization, has been responsible for the development, maintenance, and operation of the garden. The garden was listed on the National Register of Historic Places in 1992.

WASHINGTON PARK BOTANICAL GARDEN (AHS RAP)

1740 W. Fayette Avenue (corner of Fayette Avenue & Chatham Road),
Springfield, IL 62704
Tel: (217) 753-6228; Fax: (217) 546-0257
Internet Address: http://www.SpringfieldParks.org/Garden
Admission: Voluntary contribution
Attendance: 108,000
Established: 1972
Membership: Y
Wheelchair Accessible: Y
Parking: Free on site
Open: Conservatory, Monday to Friday, noon-4pm; Saturday to Sunday, noon-5pm.
Closed: Thanksgiving Day, Christmas Eve to Christmas Day
Facilities: Conservatory; Gardens (cactus, monocot, peony, perennial, rock, rose, shade); Greenhouses (9,000 square feet); Grounds Horticultural Attractions (20 acres); Library (162 volumes); Shop
Activities: Education Programs (adults and children); Events Rain Forest Festival; Flower Shows (Easter, Christmas, orchid, Japanese bonsai); Guided Tours (by appointment); Lectures

The Botanical Gardens offer a domed conservatory filled with 150 species of tropical plants from Africa, Asia, and South America; a 2,500-square foot exhibit hall set aside for seasonal floral displays; and a bonsai display house. Surrounding the conservatory are an All-America Rose Selection formal garden containing over 3,500 roses; the Betty Mood Smith Rockery, a "New American Garden" blending traditional rock garden plants, herbaceous perennials, and flowering trees/shrubs with landscape roses and culinary herbs; and the Roman Cultural Garden, a formal garden employing the Ionic columns salvaged from Springfield's historic Lincoln Library as well as a perennial border, a peony collection and monocot, hardy cactus, and shade gardens.

URBANA

UNIVERSITY OF ILLINOIS AT URBANA-CHAMPAIGN—ARBORETUM

South Campus, 2000 S. Lincoln Avenue (near Florida Avenue), Urbana, IL 61802
Tel: (217) 333-7579
Internet Address: http://www.arboretum.uiuc.edu/
Admission: Free
Membership: Y
Parking: On street, near arboretum entrance
Open: Daily, sunrise to sunset
Facilities: Arboretum; Gardens; Grounds (160 acres)
Activities: Guided Tours (schedule in advance)

A work in progress, when completed, the arboretum will offer a variety of gardens, collections, and habitats on 160 acres of the university's south campus. Completed areas include: the three-acre Hartley Garden, offering hundreds of different flowering annuals and bedding plants; the University of Illinois All-American Selections Trial Garden; a demonstration garden featuring plants and design ideas in six specialized areas including borders, ornamentals, vegetables, and children's projects; and Japan House and Tea Garden. Future plans for the arboretum include adding other theme gardens; woody plants, arranged in a park-like setting; and woodland, savanna, and wet-prairie ecosystems.

UNIVERSITY OF ILLINOIS—
PLANT BIOLOGY GREENHOUSE

1201 S. Dorner Drive (off Pennsylvania), Urbana, IL 61801
Tel: (217) 333-7857
Internet Address: http://www.life.uiuc.edu/plantbio/greenhouse
Admission: No charge, donations accepted
Attendance: 10,000
Wheelchair Accessible: N
Parking: Metered on street and in parking lots
Open: Monday to Friday, 8:30am-4:30pm
Best Time(s) of Year to Visit: late June (butterfly garden)
Facilities: Conservatory (1,500 square feet); Gardens (desert, tropical, carnivorous);
Greenhouses
Activities: Education Programs; Guided Tours (groups <25, arrange 3 weeks in advance)

The Conservatory and Plant Collection Greenhouses contain over 1,500 plants. The conservatory houses over 200 species and 60 families of plants from tropical areas around the world. Located directly off the conservatory, the Plant Collection Greenhouses have individual rooms displaying ferns, orchids, bromeliads, cacti and succulents, sub-tropical and tropical, and aquatic and carnivorous plants. Outdoors, sheltered between the Plant Collection Greenhouses and the next range of greenhouses, are carnivorous plant, tropical, and desert gardens.

WESTVILLE

FOREST GLEN PRESERVE

20301 East 900 North Road (County Highway 5, 7 miles east of Westville),
Westville, IL 61883
Tel: (217) 662-2142; Fax: (217) 662-2146
Internet Address: http://www.vccd.org
Admission: Free
Attendance: 150,000
Established: 1968
Membership: N
Wheelchair Accessible: P
Parking: On site, multiple parking areas
Open: Mid-March to Daylight Savings Time, Daily, 8am-8pm. Daylight Savings Time to Memorial Day, Daily, 8am-10pm. Memorial Day to Labor Day, Daily, 8am-11pm. Labor Day to Standard Time, Daily, 8am-10pm. Standard Time to Thanksgiving Day, Daily, 8am-8pm. Thanksgiving Day to mid-March, Daily, 8am-4:30pm

Best Time(s) of Year to Visit: Summer to Fall
Facilities: Arboretum; Architecture (reproduction pioneer homestead); Grounds
Arboretum (40 acres), Preserve (1,800 acres); Special Collections (oaks, pine, ash,
willow, viburnum, crab apple, larch)
Activities: Education Programs; Plant & Tree Sale (Arbor Day); Self-Guided Tours
(arboretum guide available, $3)

   The preserve consists of beech, maple, and oak-hickory forest types. There are four
registered Illinois nature preserves within the park (Duffin Woods, 200 acres; Forest Glen
Seep, 11 acres; Howard's Hollow Seep, 30 acres), and Doris L. Westfall Prairie (40 acres).
There is also a twenty-two acre savanna restoration area. Focusing on Illinois native trees,
the Michael G. Reddy Arboretum contains specimen plantings of over 650 different
species of trees and shrubs. The preserve serves as the Illinois state headquarters for the
Illinois Native Plant Society and the Illinois Walnut Council. Also of possible interest, the
reproduction pioneer homestead at the site includes a kitchen herb garden. The preserve
is maintained by the Vermilion County Conservation District.

WHEATON

CANTIGNY

1 South 151 Winfield Road, Wheaton, IL 60187
Tel: (630) 668-5161; Fax: (630) 260-8260
Internet Address: http://www.cantignypark.com
Attendance: 200,000
Established: 1967
Parking: Pay on site, $7/auto; $70/bus
Open: Museums: February, Friday to Sunday, 10am-4pm; March to December,
Tuesday to Sunday. Grounds: February, Friday to Sunday, 9am-sunset; March to
December, Tuesday to Sunday, 9am-sunset
Best Time(s) of Year to Visit: early Spring (Douglas Fir Garden), late Fall (Green Garden)
Facilities: Food Services: Fareways Restaurant, Tack Room Café (lunch, light snacks);
Gardens (23; 1967 design by landscape architect Franz Lipp; dryland, formal, grape
arbor, green, rock, rose, walled); Golf Courses (2; 27-hole championship & 9-hole youth;
reservations, 630-668-8463); Greenhouse; Grounds gardens (15 acres), park (500 acres);
Museum: First Division Museum, McCormick Mansion Museum (beaux-arts-style
residence, 1896 design by Charles A. Coolidge, 1936-38 renovated and expanded by
Willis Irvin); Nature Trails (2½ miles); Picnic Area (50 tables); Shop (souvenirs, gifts,
greenhouse flowers); Special Collections (alder/birch, ash/dogwood, beech, columnar tree,
euonymus, flowering and silver shrubs, larch, linden); Visitors Center
Activities: Classes Gardening (reserve in advance, 668-5161); Concerts (Memorial
Day-Labor Day, Sunday); Education Programs (Gardening, (630) 668-5161); Lectures.

   Left by Colonel Robert R. McCormick, editor and publisher of the *Chicago Tribune*, "for
the recreation, instruction and welfare of the people of the state of Illinois," the grounds
include the McCormick Museum, numerous gardens, the First Division Museum, and two
golf courses. The manicured gardens include numerous formal designs, a rose collection; a
green garden, emphasizing foliage texture in hues of gray and green; rock and dryland
gardens, featuring low-maintenance plants that require little moisture; the Douglas Fir
Garden, containing a wide variety of flowering trees and shrubs; the Alder-Birch Collection with its dense understory of hostas, ferns, and bergenias; the Burr Oak Garden,
which serves as a testing and display area for annuals and perennials; and the Idea Garden, demonstrating unique gardening projects for adults and children.

WILMETTE

BAHA'I HOUSE OF WORSHIP GARDENS

100 Linden Avenue, Wilmette, IL 60091-2879
Tel: (847) 853-2396
Internet Address: http://www.us.bahai.org/how/index.html
Admission: Free
Attendance: 200,000
Established: 1953
Membership: N
Wheelchair Accessible: Y
Parking: Parking at Linden Avenue Entrance
Open: May to September, Daily, 10am-10pm
October to April, Daily, 10am-5pm
Activities: Guided Tours (every Sunday at 1:45)

Baha'i House of Worship
Gardens, Wilmette, IL.

Surrounded by fountains and gardens and listed in the National Register of Historic Places, the Baha'i House of Worship is a landmark on the lakeshore north of Chicago.

INDIANA

The number in the parentheses following the city name indicates the number of gardens/arboreta in that municipality. If there is no number, one is understood. For example, in the text three listings would be found under Indianapolis and one listing under Terre Haute.

BLOOMINGTON

INDIANA UNIVERSITY—ARBORETUM AND JORDAN HALL GREENHOUSE

Arboretum: E. 10th Street (next to Main Library), Greenhouse: E. 3rd Street (near Hawthorne Street), Bloomington, IN 47401
Tel: (812) 855-7717; Fax: (812) 855-6705
Admission: Free
Open: Greenhouse, Monday to Friday, 8am-4pm; Saturday to Sunday, 9am-3pm
Arboretum, Daily, sunrise-sunset
Facilities: Greenhouse; Grounds Arboretum
Activities: Guided Tours Greenhouse (groups, by appointment)

Located between the main library and the School of Health, Physical Education, and Recreation, the Arboretum is home to more than 450 trees and shrubs as well as hundreds of varieties of plants. Jordan Hall Greenhouse, located next to the I. U. Biology Department building, contains a variety of unusual indigenous and exotic plants.

INDIANA UNIVERSITY—HILLTOP GARDEN AND NATURE CENTER

2301 E. 10th Street, Bloomington, IN 47405
Tel: (812) 855-2799; Fax: (812) 855-3998
Internet Address: http://www.indiana.edu/~hilltop
Admission: Free
Established: 1948
Membership: Y
Wheelchair Accessible: Y
Parking: Limited parking
Open: Monday to Friday, 1pm-5pm
Facilities: Gardens (daffodil, dwarf iris, peony, prairie, youth, herb, wildlife habitat); Greenhouses; Grounds (5 acres); Library
Activities: Education Programs; Films; Guided Tours; Lectures

Hilltop is a program of the Department of Recreation and Park Administration at Indiana University. It is a teaching garden-nature center offering classes and workshops to all age groups, a summer youth garden program, and a laboratory for University students to work with younger gardeners. Hilltop's collections include perennials and woody herbaceous plants.

INDIANA UNIVERSITY—WYLIE HOUSE MUSEUM

307 East 2nd Street (at Lincoln Street), Bloomington, IN 47401
Tel: (812) 855-6224
Internet Address: http://www.indiana.edu/~libwylie
Admission: Free
Attendance: 2,000
Wheelchair Accessible: P
Parking: Parking on street and behind museum
Open: March to November, Tuesday to Saturday, 10am-2pm
Closed: Legal holidays
Best Time(s) of Year to Visit: May to October
Facilities: Architecture (Federal/Georgian brick residence, 1835); Garden (heirloom)
Activities: Education Programs; Guided Tours (by appointment); Seeds from heirloom plants for sale

The home of Indiana University's first president, Wylie House is an historic house museum recreating and interpreting the Wylie home of the 1840s. The house contains early-to mid-nineteenth century American furnishings, including many Wylie family artifacts. The gardens feature heirloom flowers, vegetables, and herbs.

OLIVER WINERY—GARDENS

8024 N. State Road 37, Bloomington, IN 47404
Tel: (812) 876-5800; Fax: (812) 876-9309
Internet Address: http://www.oliverwinery.com/index.html
Admission: Free
Established: 1972
Membership: N
Wheelchair Accessible: P
Parking: Ample parking provided
Open: Monday to Saturday, 10am-6pm; Sunday, noon-6pm
Closed: New Year's Day, Thanksgiving Day, Christmas Day, Election Days
Facilities: Gardens; Picnic Area; Sculpture Garden; Shop (gourmet cheese, fresh bread, wine-related gifts)
Activities: Education Programs; Tours of wine-making facility

Indiana's oldest and largest winery, Oliver Winery is set in fifteen acres of grounds, which include woodland, gardens, a pond surrounded by native grasses, a waterfall, wildflowers, and limestone sculptures. The Gardens boast hundreds of varieties of perennials, annuals, bulbs and shrubs, both familiar and unusual. The emphasis is on plants and trees native to Indiana.

COLUMBUS

IRWIN GARDENS

608 5th Street (next to Bartholomew County. Public Library), Columbus, IN 47201
Tel: (812) 376-3331
Admission: Free
Established: 1910
Membership: N

Wheelchair Accessible: P
Parking: Parking on street
Open: May to November, Saturday to Sunday, 8am-4pm
Best Time(s) of Year to Visit: Summer
Facilities: Garden (herb, Roman); Grounds (½ acre—wisteria, bulbs, begonias, petunias, lythrum, asters)

A private garden in downtown Columbus, it is open to the public on weekends throughout the season. Its formal flower, shrub, and herb gardens are modeled after an early garden in Pompeii.

FORT WAYNE

FOELLINGER-FREIMANN BOTANICAL CONSERVATORY (AHS RAP)

1100 S. Calhoun Street, Fort Wayne, IN 46802-3007
Tel: (260) 427-6440; Fax: (260) 427-6450
Internet Address: http://www.botanicalconservatory.org/
Admission: Fee: adult $4.00, child (<3) free, child (3-17) $2.00, student $2.00, senior $4.00
Attendance: 72,000
Established: 1983
Membership: Y
Wheelchair Accessible: Y
Parking: Parking garage (fee) or metered on street
Open: Monday to Saturday, 10am-5pm; Sunday, noon-4pm
Closed: New Year's Day, Labor Day, Christmas Day
Facilities: Conservatory; Grounds (4.7 acres); Shop Tulip Tree (botanically inspired gifts, cards, clothing)
Activities: Guided Tours group (Mon-Sat, 10am-5pm; Sun, noon-4pm)

The Foellinger-Freimann Botanical Conservatory features three glass-enclosed greenhouses: the Showcase Garden, offering seasonal displays; the Tropical Garden, where orchids and palms thrive in the shadows of a cascading waterfall; and the Desert Garden, a quiet oasis with over seventy-two different cacti. The Foellinger-Freimann Botanical Conservatory is owned and operated by the Fort Wayne Parks and Recreation Department.

INDIANAPOLIS

GARFIELD PARK—CONSERVATORY AND SUNKEN GARDEN

2450 Shelby Street, Indianapolis, IN 46203-4235
Tel: (317) 327-7184
Admission: Fee (Conservatory): adult $2.00, child $1.00, senior $1.50
Open: Conservatory: Sept to May, 10am-5pm; June to August, 10am-6pm
Facilities: Conservatory; Grounds Garfield Park (122½ acres); Special Collections (bromeliad)

The conservatory presents tropical plants in a natural setting, an Amazon River region rain forest complete with a large collection of bromeliads and other epiphytes as well as seasonal floral displays.

INDIANAPOLIS MUSEUM OF ART (IMA)

4000 Michigan Road, Indianapolis, IN 46208
Tel: (317) 920-2660; Fax: (317) 931-1978
Internet Address: http://www.ima-art.org
Admission: Fee for museum admission
Attendance: 220,000
Established: 1883
Membership: Y
Wheelchair Accessible: Y
Parking: Free on site
Open: Tuesday to Wednesday, 10am-5pm; Thursday, 10am-8:30pm; Friday to
Saturday, 10am-5pm; Sunday, noon-5pm
Closed: Major holidays
Facilities: Auditorium (250 seats); Exhibit Pavilions (4—Hulman, Krannert, Clowes
and Lilly); Food Services Café (Tues-Sat, 11:30am-2pm), Garden on the Green
Restaurant (Tues-Sun, 11am-1:45pm, reservations recommended); Formal Gardens;
Greenhouse (Tues-Sat, 9am-5pm; Sun, noon-5pm; Tel: 920-2652); Library (32,000
volumes); Rental Gallery; Shop
Activities: Arts Festival; Concerts; Education Programs (adults and children—
horticultural); Films; Gallery Talks; Guided Tours (Tues-Sun, noon & 2pm; also
Thurs, 7pm); Lectures; Permanent Exhibits; Temporary Exhibitions; Traveling
Exhibitions; Workshops

At the Indianapolis Museum of Art visitors can see permanent and changing exhibitions ranging from ancient artifacts to works by contemporary artists. Galleries in four art
pavilions feature paintings, sculpture, textiles, decorative arts, prints, and drawings. The
museum's setting includes fifty acres of gardens and grounds. In addition to the gardens
surrounding the museum buildings, the grounds at IMA include the twenty-six-acre Oldfields estate. The Oldfields grounds were designed by the Olmsted Brothers firm and include the Ravine Garden, a dramatic one-acre hillside garden considered a masterwork of
garden design; the Wood Formal Garden; a formal Allée; border gardens; a greenhouse
and vegetable gardens. The expanded Madeline F. Elder Greenhouse functions as both a
display space housing an extensive orchid collection and retail garden shop offering a
wide assortment of perennials, annuals, herbs, orchids, house plants, and garden accessories. A one hundred-acre art and nature park is in development.

INDIANAPOLIS ZOOLOGICAL SOCIETY—
WHITE RIVER GARDENS

1200 W. Washington Street (adjacent to the Indianapolis
Zoo), Indianapolis, IN 46222
Tel: (317) 630-2001; Fax: (317) 630-5153
Internet Address: http://www.whiterivergardens.com
Admission: Fee (Spring-Fall): adult $7.00, child (<2) free,
child (2-12) $6.00, senior $6.00. Fee (Winter): Adult:
$5.00; Youth & Senior: $4.00
Attendance: 200,000
Established: 1999
Membership: Y
Wheelchair Accessible: Y
Parking: On site, $5.00
Open: January to mid-March, Wednesday to Sunday, 9am-4pm. Mid-March to late-
April, Monday to Thursday, 9am-4pm; Friday to Sunday, 9am-5pm. Late-April to

Indianapolis Zoological
Society—White River Gar-
dens, Indianapolis, IN. Knot
Gardens. Rich Clark photograph.

October, Monday to Thursday, 9am-5pm; Friday to Sunday, 9am-6pm. November, Wednesday to Sunday, 9am-4pm. December, Daily, noon-9pm.
Closed: New Year's Eve to New Year's Day, Thanksgiving Day, Christmas Eve to Christmas Day
Best Time(s) of Year to Visit: April to September
Facilities: Conservatory (5,000 square feet); Food Services Flora Café (counter service, sandwiches & snacks, 10am-3pm); Gardens (knot, shade, sun, water, wedding & design); Grounds (3.3 acres); Resource Center; Shop
Activities: Flower Shows Hilbert Conservatory (winter/orchids, spring-summer/butterflies, fall/bonsai, Dec/poinsettias & trains)

White River Gardens, the sister institution to the Indianapolis Zoo, is located adjacent to the White River levee that flanks the east side of the zoo and extends south to Washington Street and north to the main zoo entrance. The zoo and the gardens share the same main entrance at 1200 West Washington Street and the same parking lot. The gardens include a glass-enclosed conservatory; a design garden with eleven themed garden plantings; shade and sun gardens; a water garden; and a wedding garden for ceremonies and receptions. While White River Gardens retains many elements of the traditional garden, the designers intended to present them in a new contemporary manner. It is really more of an "idea" garden, where visitors can see and experience innovative garden displays and gather information in order to duplicate some of the ideas at home. The gardens contain over 1,000 varieties of plants. If habitat gardening is of interest, allow time to visit the neighboring Indianapolis Zoo, accredited by the American Association of Museums as a habitat botanical garden.

LAFAYETTE

JERRY E. CLEGG BOTANICAL GARDEN (CLEGG GARDEN)

1782 N 400 E, Lafayette, IN 47905-8857
Tel: (765) 423-1325
Admission: No charge, donations accepted
Attendance: 4,000
Established: 1965
Membership: Y
Parking: Free on site
Open: Daily, dawn-dusk
Best Time(s) of Year to Visit: March to October
Facilities: Grounds (16 acres, savanna, gravel hill prairie); Special Collections (wildflowers, oak)
Activities: Guided Tours (schedule in advance, 423-1325)

The site features self-guided nature trails, oak savanna and gravel hill prairie restoration, native woodland, and prairie wildflowers during season.

MICHIGAN CITY

BARKER CIVIC CENTER GARDEN

631 Washington Street at 7th Street, Michigan City, IN 46360
Tel: (219) 873-1520; Fax: (219) 873-1520
Internet Address: http://www.emichigancity.com/cityhall/

departments/barkermansion/missio
Admission: Fee: adult $4.00, child (<17) $2.00
Attendance: 12,000
Established: 1900
Wheelchair Accessible: Y
Parking: On street
Open: June to October, Daily, 10am-3pm. November to May, Monday to Friday, 10am-3pm
Closed: Legal holidays
Best Time(s) of Year to Visit: June to September, Christmas season
Facilities: Architecture (English manor house-style, 1905 design by Chicago architect Frederick Perkins); Gardens (English, Italian, rose, sunken)
Activities: Education Programs; Garden Teas (summer); Guided Tours Mansion (Mon-Fri, 10am/11:30am/1pm)

The home of industrialist, John H. Barker, the site was given to Michigan City in 1968 by Catherine Barker Hickox as a memorial to her father. The building is listed on the National Register of Historic Places. Outside, an elaborate sunken garden includes teahouse, pergola, sculptures, and sundial.

MUNCIE

MINNETRISTA CULTURAL CENTER AND OAKHURST GARDENS

1200 N. Minnetrista Parkway (between North Walnut Street & Wheeling Avenue), Muncie, IN 47303-2925
Tel: (765) 282-4848; Fax: (765) 741-5110
Internet Address: http://www.mccoak.org/about.htm
Admission: Fee: adult $7.00, child $4.00, student $4.00, senior $6.00
Open: Monday to Friday, 9am-5:30pm; Saturday, 9am-8pm; Sunday, 11am-5:30pm
Closed: New Year's Day, Easter, Christmas Day
Facilities: Galleries (3); Gardens (formal, native plant, rose); Grounds (35 acres, 6 acres formal gardens); Shop
Activities: Concerts (summer); Education Programs; Guided Tours; Temporary Exhibitions

Minnetrista Cultural Center and Oakhurst Gardens was conceived as a center for life-long learning. It features nationally-touring science exhibits in addition to a variety of exhibitions showcasing the art and history of east central Indiana. Oakhurst is the refurbished turn-of-the-century home of the late George and Frances Ball and their daughter Elisabeth, who majored in botany at Vassar College. The site contains nine formal gardens featuring native plantings and beautiful woods. There is also a children's garden at Minnetrista comprised of thirty-one theme gardens.

NASHVILLE

T. C. STEELE STATE HISTORIC SITE—GARDENS

4220 T.C. Steele Road (1 mile south of Belmont off State Road 46), Nashville, IN 47448

Tel: (812) 988-2785; Fax: (812) 988-8457
Internet Address: http://www.tcsteele.org
Admission: Suggested contribution
Established: 1945
Membership: Y
Wheelchair Accessible: P
Open: Spring to late Autumn, Tuesday to Saturday, 9am-5pm; Sunday, 1pm-5pm
Closed: Legal holidays
Facilities: Architecture House of the Singing Winds (1907, summer home of artist
T.C. Steele, large studio, other historic buildings); Gardens; Grounds (211 acres)
Activities: Guided Tours House & Studio; Permanent Exhibits; Temporary Exhibitions

   In 1907, Indiana impressionist artist Theodore Clement Steele and his second wife,
Selma Neubacher Steele, purchased 211 acres in Brown County and began construction of their home, which they named the House of the Singing Winds. They built a
large studio (where today changing exhibits display paintings done throughout Steele's
life) to accommodate Steele's work and landscaped the surrounding hillsides to enhance the beauty of their property. Selma Steele created several acres of gardens
around the home that display a festival of flowers from spring to autumn. The site also
includes four hiking trails, the Dewar Log Cabin, and the ninety-two-acre Selma
Steele Nature Preserve.

NEW HARMONY

NEW HARMONY STATE HISTORIC SITE—
LABYRINTH AND GARDEN

506½ Main Street, Hew Harmony, IN 47631
Tel: (812) 682-4488
Fax: (812) 682-4313
Internet Address: http://www-lib.iupui.edu/kade/newharmony/home.html
Admission: Fee.
Membership: Y Wheelchair Accessible: P
Open: March to December, Daily, 10am-4pm. January to February, call for hours.
Closed: Easter, Thanksgiving Day, Christmas Eve to Christmas Day
Facilities: Architecture Athenæum/Visitor Center (1979, design by architect Richard
Meier), David Lenz House (residence, ca.1820); Gardens (Harmonist garden, labyrinth)
Activities: Guided Tours (tours originate at the Athenæum/Visitor Center)

   New Harmony is the site of two of America's earliest utopian communities. The first,
Harmonie on the Wabash (1814-1824), was founded by the Harmony Society, a group
of Separatists from the German Lutheran Church. In 1825, when the Harmonists
moved back to Pennsylvania, Robert Owen, Welsh-born industrialist and social
philosopher, bought their Indiana town and the surrounding lands for his communitar-
ian experiment. The town was largely self-sufficient. There were 2,000 acres of highly
cultivated land, including a fifteen-acre vineyard and a thrity-five-acre orchard of
choice apple and pear tress. Four large brick dwellings, a steam engine, two large gra-
naries, wool and cotton factories, a threshing machine, a five-acre vegetable garden,
and more than 126 family dwelling houses were carefully cataloged by the Harmonists
in a final inventory of the town that was prepared prior to its sale to Robert Owen.
Today, the town contains twelve early nineteenth-century buildings and twenty from
mid-nineteenth century, a museum, a library, a gallery, and a theater. The Lenz garden

is a partial reconstruction of a Harmonist garden, which would have been larger than this with dirt paths and would have included flowers, vegetables, fruit trees, and herbs. Most plants in the garden are marked with small signs. The present day Labyrinth, located on Route 69 on the south side of town, was reconstructed between 1939-1941 on the site adjacent to the original Labyrinth. It is planted in accordance with a Harmony Society plan in concentric circles of privet hedge leading to a stone temple in the center. The New Harmony State Historic Site is a part of the unified program of the University of Southern Indiana and the Indiana State Museums and Historic Sites.

RICHMOND

CITY OF RICHMOND—GLEN MILLER PARK GARDENS

2500 E. Main Street (U.S. Route 40 East), Richmond, IN 47374
Tel: (765) 983-7275
Internet Address: http://www.waynenet.org/nonprofit/rosegarden.htm
Admission: Free
Established: 1985
Membership: N
Wheelchair Accessible: Y
Parking: Paved parking lot
Open: Daily, 7am-11pm
Best Time(s) of Year to Visit: early June, September
Facilities: Grounds Park (195 acres)
Activities: Guided Tours (call 765-962-2142)

Glen Miller Park contains three rose gardens, testimony to Richmond's position as a center of the cut rose industry. An All-America Rose Selections Garden contains over 1,600 rose bushes (110 varieties), as well as annuals, perennials, evergreens, and ornamental trees. The E. G. Hill Memorial Rose Garden offers more than seventeen varieties of roses. Situated between the AARS and Hill Gardens is the newest addition to the gardens, the Richmond-Friendship Garden. Reflecting German design and featuring many German roses, it commemorates the city's friendship with the German City of Zweibruken.

HAYES ARBORETUM

801 Elks Road, Richmond, IN 47374-2526
Tel: (317) 962-3745; Fax: (317) 966-1931
Internet Address: http://www.hayesarboretum.org
Admission: Free
Attendance: 80,000
Established: 1959
Membership: Y
Wheelchair Accessible: Y
Parking: Parking is available
Open: April to December, Tuesday to Saturday, 9am-5pm
January to March, Tuesday to Saturday, 9am-5pm
Best Time(s) of Year to Visit: May to October
Facilities: Arboretum (466 acres); Auditorium (100 seats); Classrooms; Grounds (355 acres); Library (non-circulating); Nature Center; Reading Room; Shop; Special Collections (native wild plants)
Activities: Guided Tours; Permanent Exhibits; Temporary Exhibitions

The arboretum is a repository for wild plants indigenous to the Whitewater Drainage Basin in Indiana.

SOUTH BEND

CITY OF SOUTH BEND—POTAWATOMI PARK CONSERVATORIES AND GREENHOUSES

2105 Mishawaka Avenue, South Bend, IN 46615-1624
Tel: (219) 235-9442
Internet Address: http://www.sbpark.org/conservatory/conservatory.html
Admission: Fee: adult $1.00, child (<5) free
Open: Monday to Friday, 9am-3:30pm; Saturday to Sunday, 11am-3:30pm
Facilities: Greenhouses; Special Collections (cactus)
Activities: Flower Shows (3/year; Spring, Chrysanthemum, Winter); Guided Tours (arrange in advance)

The Potawatomi Greenhouses were begun in the 1920 as a production facility to provide municipal parks and facilities with flowers and plants. The addition of the Ella Morris and Muessel-Ellison Botanical Conservatories in 1963 and 1967 provided a more people-friendly area for the enjoyment of tropical plants and flower shows. The completion of the Arizona Desert Dome in 1973, expanded offerings to include many types of cacti, succulents, and other desert flora, including century plants and a large monkey puzzle tree.

COPSHAHOLM HOUSE MUSEUM AND HISTORIC OLIVER GARDENS

Northern Indiana Center for History, 808 W. Washington, South Bend, I N 46601-1439
Tel: (219) 235-9664; Fax: (219) 235-9059
Internet Address: http://www.centerforhistory.org/cops.html
Admission: Fee: adult $8.00, child $5.00, student $5.00, senior $6.50
Attendance: 25,000
Established: 1990
Membership: Y
Wheelchair Accessible: N
Open: mid-February to early January, Tuesday to Saturday, 10am-5pm; Sunday, noon-5pm.
Closed: Legal holidays
Facilities: Architecture (Romanesque Queen Anne residence, 1895-96 design by New York architect Charles Alonzo Rich.); Exhibition Area; Gallery; Gardens (Italian, rose; 1907 design by Alice Neale); Grounds (2.5 acres); Shop
Activities: Arts Festival; Classes; Guided Tours (last tour begins 4pm); Lectures; Workshops

The former residence of J. D. Oliver, president of the Oliver Chilled Plow Works, is surrounded by landscaped gardens, including a garden tea house, formal Italianate garden, rose garden, pergola, tennis lawn, and fountain. With the assistance of photographs, plant orders, correspondence, and Neale's blueprints, the gardens are being restored to look as they did in 1915. Lilies, peonies, lilacs, tulips, daffodils, dogwood, irises, and lilies-of-the-valley are some of the flowers and bushes that bloom in the gardens. Copshaholm and its gardens are listed on the National Register of Historic Places.

TERRE HAUTE

CITY OF TERRE HAUTE—CLARK-LANDSBAUM DEMING PARK HOLLY ARBORETUM

500 S. Fruitridge Avenue (at Poplar Street), Terre Haute, IN 47807
Tel: (812) 877-1087
Internet Address: http://www.thcityparks.com/
Admission: Free
Established: 1992
Membership: N
Wheelchair Accessible: N
Parking: Pull-off parking areas close to arboretum
Open: Daily, dawn-dusk
Best Time(s) of Year to Visit: late October to early November
Facilities: Arboretum; Grounds (8 acres); Special Collections (holly)
Activities: Guided Tours (schedule in advance)

Designated an Official Holly Arboretum by the Holly Society of America, the collection includes approximately 300 hollies representing 9 species and over 170 cultivars. The arboretum is particularly attractive in the fall when the plants are heavy with their berries, variously colored in shades of red, orange, yellow, white, and black. The arboretum was developed and is maintained by the Terre Haute Park Department in partnership with the Friends of the Arboretum, a not-for-profit organization.

VALPARAISO

TALTREE ARBORETUM AND GARDENS (AHS RAP)

450 West 100 North, Valparaiso, IN 46385
Tel: (219) 462-0025; Fax: (219) 462-0848
Internet Address: http://www.taltree.org
Admission: Fee $3.00
Membership: Y
Wheelchair Accessible: P
Parking: On site paved lot
Open: April to October, Daily, 5:30am-8pm CDT
November to March, Daily, 8am-5pm CST
Best Time(s) of Year to Visit: April to October
Facilities: Arboretum; Gardens (native plant); Grounds (300 acres); Trails (4)
Activities: Concerts (outdoor); Education Programs; Guided Tours ($3/person)

Situated on the rolling hills of the Valparaiso Moraine between Lake Michigan sand dunes to the north and the broad Kankakee plain and river to the south, Taltree is a 300-acre reserve of restored oak savanna, woodlands, wetlands, prairie, woody plant collections, and display gardens. While currently containing a significant oak savanna, woodland, and wetland exhibits, Taltree will also include exhibits of oak ecosystems from around the world in the future.

WARSAW

WARSAW BIBLICAL GARDENS

Corner of E. Canal Street & SR15N (adjacent to Municipal Park on Center Lake),
Warsaw, IN 46580
Tel: (219) 267-6419
Internet Address: http://www.warsawbiblicalgardens.org/
Open: April 15 to October 15, Daily, dawn-dusk
Best Time(s) of Year to Visit: April (bulb display), mid-May to June (highest color),
September to early October (meadow displays and grasses)
Facilities: Garden (biblical); Grounds (¾ acre)
Activities: Guided Tours (May-Sept, arrange in advance, $2/person)

One of the largest botanical gardens of biblical plants in the United States, the garden contains over 100 plants that are named in the Bible. Plants are arranged in a variety of theme areas: forest, brook, meadow, desert, crop and herb gardens; the grape arbor; and the gathering site.

WEST LAFAYETTE

PURDUE UNIVERSITY—HORTICULTURE GARDENS

Marstellar Street & Agricultural Mall (adjacent to the Horticulture Building), West
Lafayette, IN 47907
Tel: (765) 494-1296; Fax: (765) 494-0391
Established: 1982
Facilities: Festival Purdue University Garden Day (annual open house); Gardens (1/2 acre)
Activities: Guided Tours; Self-Guided Tours

Collections encompass nearly 200 species of perennial flowers and foliage plants. Special collections include peonies, day lilies, hosta, spring-flowering bulbs, and ornamental grasses. Self-guided tour brochures are available.

KENTUCKY

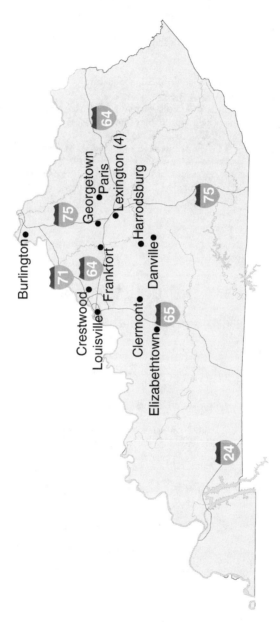

The number in the parentheses following the city name indicates the number of gardens/arboreta in that municipality. If there is no number, one is understood. For example, in the text four listings would be found under Lexington and one listing under Paris.

BURLINGTON

BOONE COUNTY ARBORETUM

Central Park, 6028 Camp Ernst Road, Burlington, KY 41005
Tel: (859) 334-4599; Fax: (859) 334-2127
Internet Address: http://www.bcarboretum.org/
Admission: Free
Established: 1999
Open: Daily, dawn-dusk
Facilities: Arboretum; Gardens (butterfly, children's, native plant, perennial, research, rose, wetland); Grounds Central Park (125 acres); Trails (2 miles)
Activities: Guided Tours (hosted by the Boone County Cooperative Extension Service, (859) 586-6101)

The arboretum currently contains more than 800 trees, including redbuds, dogwoods, magnolias, evergreens, and crab apples and over 1,500 shrubs.

CLERMONT

BERNHEIM ARBORETUM AND RESEARCH FOREST (AHS RAP)

State Highway 245, Clermont, KY 40110
Tel: (502) 955-8512; Fax: (502) 955-4039
Internet Address: http://www.bernheim.org/
Admission: Fee (Sat-Sun): $5.00/vehicle. Free (Mon-Fri)
Attendance: 250,000
Established: 1929
Membership: Y
Wheelchair Accessible: Y
Parking: 35 lots on site, approximately 1,000 spaces
Open: Daily, 7am-sunset
Closed: New Year's Day, Christmas Day
Facilities: Amphitheater; Arboretum (1935 design by Frederick Law Olmsted firm); Arboretum Center; Gardens (aquatic, perennial); Greenhouses; Grounds Arboretum (250 acres), Research Forest (14,000 acres); Library (325 volumes); Nursery; Picnic Areas; Special Collections (crab apple, conifer, dogwood, holly, magnolia, maple, oak, Kentucky native trees and shrubs); Trails (50 miles); Visitor Center
Activities: Education Programs; Guided Tours (groups, schedule in advance); Walking Lectures; Workshops

The Official Arboretum of Kentucky, Bernheim is one of the largest protected natural areas in the state. It includes a nationally recognized arboretum and a research foreStreet The arboretum contains a diverse collection of predominantly woody plants that includes some 6,000 accessioned plants displayed in a landscape setting on 250 acres. The arboretum contains special collections, including one of the largest collections of American holly (over 185 varieties) in North America; cultivated gardens; four lakes; natural forest areas; and created habitats, including a prairie, bluegrass savanna, and cypress-tupelo swamp. The 14,000-acre research forest is managed for the protection of Kentucky native plants, animals, and natural communities. Almost twenty-two square miles in size, Bernheim's forested areas include six different forest types and one grassland community. Isaac W. Bernheim (the founder of I.W. Harper brand distillery) established Bernheim Arboretum and Research Forest in 1929. The arboretum opened to the public in 1950. In keeping with I.W. Bernheim's position as a patron of the arts, pieces of significant sculpture can be found throughout the arboretum, including works by George Gray Bernard, Paul Fields, Thomas Busch, Meg White, and Karl Ceisluk.

CRESTWOOD

YEW DELL GARDENS (AHS RAP)

5800 N. Camden Lane, Crestwood, KY 40014
Tel: (502) 241-4788; Fax: (502) 241-8338
Internet Address: http://www.yewdellgardens.org
Admission: by appointment
Established: 2002
Parking: Gravel lot on site
Admission: Suggested contribution: $5.00
Open: By appointment only.
Facilities: Arboretum; Gardens (English walled, hosta, secret, serpentine);
Greenhouses (sunken, bermed, built in 1940s); Grounds (50 acres), Arboretum (8 acres); Lath House; Special Collections (European beech, dogwood, holly, hydrangea, magnolia, redbud, viburnum)
Activities: Guided Tours (by appointment); Plant Sale/Auction (Jun)

Begun as a home and nursery by Theodore Klein, an internationally known and respected nurseryman and plant expert, Yew Dell has a long family history, which began in 1940 when Klein, along with his wife, Martha Lee, purchased the twenty-three-acre farm. Over the nearly sixty years that Theodore Klein planned, planted, and tended the grounds of Yew Dell, he developed an extensive and widely varied collection of mostly woody plants and garden styles. Upon Klein's death in 1998, a board of community volunteers raised the funds to purchase the property, and then began long-term planning to restore Yew Dell Gardens and share its treasures with the public. Noteworthy collections in the arboretum include European beech, magnolia, viburnum, conifer, dogwood, redbud, hydrangea, witch hazel, and holly. The site also offers two "secret gardens," displaying dwarf and alpine plants; the Serpentine Garden, an aesthetic display of the conifer collection; two formal gardens with topiary, statuary, and clipped yew hedges; a holly allée; and an orchard. Yew Dell's primary missions are ornamental horticuluture; education; new plant development, testing, and display; and research. Yew Dell has been accepted as a partnership garden of the Garden Conservancy.

DANVILLE

MCDOWELL HOUSE, APOTHECARY AND GARDENS

125 South 2nd Street, Danville, KY 40422
Tel: (859) 236-2804; Fax: (859) 236-2804
Internet Address: http://www.mcdowellhouse.org
Admission: Fee: adult $5.00, child (<13) $1.00, child (13-20) $2.00, senior $3.00
Established: 1939
Parking: On street or across street—Constitution Square Park
Open: November to February, Tuesday to Saturday, 10am-noon & 1pm-4pm; Sunday, 2pm-4pm. March to October, Monday to Saturday, 10am-noon & 1pm-4pm; Sunday, 2pm-4pm
Closed: New Year's Day, Easter, Thanksgiving Day, Christmas Day
Facilities: Architecture (early Georgian two-story residence & office); Gardens (medicinal herb, wildflower); Grounds (¼ acre); Shop
Activities: Guided Tours

At this location in 1809, Ephraim McDowell performed the world's first successful abdominal surgery, removing a 22½ pound ovarian cyStreet Designated a National Historic Landmark, the site contains McDowell's home, medical office, apothecary shop, period furnishings and equipment, medicinal herb gardens, and a wildflower garden.

ELIZABETHTOWN

BROWN-PUSEY HOUSE—CUNNINGHAM GARDEN

128 N. Main Street, Elizabethtown, KY 42701
Tel: (270) 765-2515
Admission: Free
Membership: Y
Wheelchair Accessible: P
Parking: Municipal parking available
Open: Monday to Saturday, 10am-4pm
Facilities: Architecture (Federal-style residence, 1825); Garden; Grounds
Activities: Guided Tours (by appointment)

Formerly a boarding house, the house was donated to the community and now serves as a local history museum and genealogical library. The grounds contain a landscaped garden designed by Chicago landscape architect Chance Hill. The site is listed on the National Register of Historic Places.

FRANKFORT

LIBERTY HALL HISTORIC SITE—GARDENS

218 Wilkinson Street, Frankfort, KY 40601
Tel: (888) 516-5101

Internet Address: http://www.libertyhall.org/
Admission: Fee (Houses): adult $5.00, student $2.00, senior $4.00. Free (Gardens)
Established: 1937
Membership: N
Wheelchair Accessible: P
Parking: On-street parking
Open: mid-March to mid-December, Tuesday to Sunday
Best Time(s) of Year to Visit: May to September
Facilities: Architecture Liberty Hall (residence, 1796), Orland Brown House
(residence, 1835); Garden (Colonial Revival-style); Grounds (3 acres)
Activities: Guided Tours (Tues-Sat, 10:30am/noon/1:30pm/3pm; Sun, 1:30pm & 3pm)

Liberty Hall (1796) and the Orlando Brown House (1835), both filled with late eighteenth and early nineteenth-century decorative arts, are open as museum houses. A formal boxwood perennial garden surrounds the houses and stretches down to the Kentucky River. Rather than being a reproduction of the original garden at Liberty Hall, today's version reflects the garden as it evolved through four generations of Brown family ownership. The garden contains both historic and modern plants while honoring the spirit and structural context recorded in the garden plans and documents of the Brown family.

GEORGETOWN

GEORGETOWN COLLEGE—SCOTT COUNTY NATIVE PLANTS ARBORETUM

Corner of Main Street & Memorial Drive, Georgetown, KY 40324
Tel: (502) 863-7063; Fax: (502) 868-0157
Internet Address: http://spider.georgetowncollege.edu/arbor/
Admission: Free
Established: 1995
Membership: N
Wheelchair Accessible: Y
Parking: Parking lot
Open: dawn-dusk
Facilities: Arboretum; Garden (butterfly, hummingbird, perennial, prairie, woodland); Grounds (¼ acre)

Located on the Georgetown College Campus, the arboretum is a joint project of the City of Georgetown, Scott County, and Georgetown College. It is planted mainly with native trees, shrubs, and plants. Several different habitats are represented, including Kentucky River Palisades and Bluegrass Savannah. Native plants are displayed in more formal arrangements in the gardens facing Main Street.

HARRODSBURG

SHAKER VILLAGE OF PLEASANT HILL—GARDENS

3501 Lexington Road, Harrodsburg, KY 40330
Tel: (800) 734-5611
Internet Address: http://www.shakervillageky.org

Admission: Fee: adult $10.50, child (6-11) $4.00, child (12-17) $6.00
Membership: Y
Open: April to October, Daily, 10am-5pm. November to March, Daily, 10am-4:30pm
Closed: Christmas Eve to Christmas Day
Facilities: Architecture (33 19th-century Shaker structures); Food Services
(restaurant); Gardens (period, 19th-century; herb, vegetable); Grounds (2,800 acres);
Shops (crafts)
Activities: Demonstrations; Guided Tours; Self-Guided Tours

Designated a National Historic Landmark, the village is a living history museum that
presents America's largest and most completely restored Shaker community. Exhibits include an operating nineteenth-century farm, herb and vegetable gardens, as well as a variety of traditional Shaker craft workshops.

LEXINGTON

ASHLAND-THE HENRY CLAY ESTATE—GARDENS

120 Sycamore Road, Lexington, KY 40502
Tel: (859) 266-8581; Fax: (859) 268-7266
Internet Address: http://www.henryclay.org/
Admission: Fee: adult $7.00, child (<6) free, child (6-12) $3.00,
student $3.00
Attendance: 16,000
Established: 1950
Membership: Y
Wheelchair Accessible: P
Parking: On site paved lot and bus parking
Open: January, by appointment only; March, Tuesday to Saturday, 10am-4pm;
Sunday, 1pm-4pm; April to October, Monday to
Saturday, 10am-4pm; Sunday, 1pm-4pm; November to
December, Tuesday to Saturday, 10am-4pm; Sunday,
1pm-4pm
Closed: Legal Holidays, New Year's Eve to New Year's Day,
Christmas Eve to Christmas Day
Facilities: Architecture (1857 mansion, several nineteenth-century outbuildings); Food
Services Ginko Tree Café (Apr-Oct, daily,
11am-3pm); Gardens (formal parterre, peony); Grounds (17 acres); Shop
Activities: Guided Tours mansion (on the hour, last tour 4pm)

Statesman Henry Clay purchased the land and began construction of his home in 1806.
Little is known about the original gardens on the estate, although a garden was started
shortly after the family moved to Ashland. After Henry Clay's death in 1852, his son
James B. Clay purchased the estate in 1856. The original home was demolished due to in-
ferior brick strength. The mansion was rebuilt on the original foundation in 1857. In
1950, Ashland was opened to the public and the Garden Club of Lexington was invited
by the Henry Clay Memorial Foundation to establish and maintain a garden at Ashland.
Henry Fletcher Kenney of Cincinnati was chosen to design a new garden and work began
in the spring of 1951 on a one-half-acre, six-parterre garden based upon formal garden
plans of the eighteenth century, rather than reproducing the less formal style of Henry
Clay's era. A second garden, containing many Saunders hybrid peonies, is located to the
rear of the main garden.

LEXINGTON CEMETERY

833 W. Main Street (Leestown Road), Lexington, KY 40508-2094
Tel: (859) 255-5522; Fax: (859) 258-2774
Internet Address: http://www.lexcem.org/
Admission: Free
Established: 1849
Membership: N
Wheelchair Accessible: Y
Open: Daily, 8am-5pm
Best Time(s) of Year to Visit: March to September
Facilities: Arboretum; Garden (formal); Greenhouse (3);
Grounds (170 acres)
Activities: Self-Guided Tours (History map & children's map available)

Chartered in 1848 by the Kentucky General Assembly to establish a rural, or garden, cemetery, the Lexington Cemetery Company created more than a pleasant cemetery. From the initial application of the theories of prominent British landscape architect John C. Louden by the first general manager to the establishment of the formal garden in 1963, emphasis has been placed on landscape design and horticulture. The site contains more than 200 species of trees, flower gardens, and three lakes. The variety of gardens includes a sunken garden and flower garden that covers almost three acres. The cemetery is listed in the National Register of Historic Places. A brochure is available at the cemetery office.

MARY TODD LINCOLN HOUSE—BEULA C. NUNN GARDEN

578 W. Main Street, Lexington, KY 40501
Tel: (859) 233-9999; Fax: (859) 252-2269
Internet Address: http://www.mtlhouse.org
Admission: Free (Garden); Fee (House): adult $7.00, child (<6) free, child (6-12) $4.00
Established: 1996
Membership: Y
Wheelchair Accessible: P
Parking: Free lot on site
Open: March 15 to November, Monday to Saturday, 10am-4pm
Facilities: Architecture (Georgian residence, 1803-1806);
Gardens (period; herb, perennial); Grounds (1 acre); Shop
Activities: Guided Tours (last tour 3:15pm)

Originally constructed as an inn, the house was the childhood home of Mary Todd, Abraham Lincoln's future wife. Located in the heart of downtown Lexington, the grounds include enclosed gardens containing trees, plants, herbs, and shrubs that represent what may have been in the gardens at the Todd home in the early nineteenth century. The gardens are cared for by the Lexington Soil Mates Garden Club and the Bluegrass Herb Guild.

UNIVERSITY OF KENTUCKY/LEXINGTON FAYETTE URBAN COUNTY GOVERNMENT ARBORETUM (UK/LFUCG ARBORETUM)

500 Alumni Drive (near Commonwealth Stadium), Lexington, KY 40503
Tel: (859) 257-6955; Fax: (859) 257-6955
Internet Address: http://www.uky.edu/Arboretum

Admission: Free
Attendance: 100,000
Established: 1991
Membership: Y
Parking: Parking area with handicapped spaces
Open: Gardens, Daily, dawn-dusk; Visitor Center, Weekdays, 8:30am-4pm
Best Time(s) of Year to Visit: April to September
Facilities: Gardens (rose, fruit/nut, ground cover, herb, home demonstration, perennial, trial, vegetable); Grounds (100 acres); Special Collections (perennial, woody plant); Trail Walk Across Kentucky (2 miles)
Activities: Concerts; Education Programs; Events (Shakespeare Festival, birdhouse exhibit, art exhibits); Guided Tours (with advance notice)

Located on the campus of the University of Kentucky, the Arboretum has been designated the "Official State Botanical Garden for the Commonwealth of Kentucky." There are three major permanent exhibits. The Home Demonstration Garden displays combinations of plants and landscape structures to show how plants can be used in the residential landscape. It consists of a variety of smaller gardens, including vegetable and herb gardens, home fruit and nut gardens, beds for evaluating flowering annuals, perennials, and demonstrations of ground covers and woody plants for landscape use. The new rose garden is home to over 1,200 varieties. The "Walk Across Kentucky" offers a glimpse of the distinct vegetation found in each of Kentucky's seven regional landscapes: Bluegrass, Knobs, Appalachian Plateaus, Cumberland Mountains, Mississippian Plateaus and Outer Nashville Basin (Pennyroyal), Shawnee Hills, Mississippian Embayment, and Alluvial Basin (Jackson Purchase). The arboretum is a joint project of the University of Kentucky and the Lexington-Fayette urban county government.

LOUISVILLE

LOCUST GROVE HISTORIC HOME MUSEUM—GARDENS

561 Blankenbaker Lane (off River Road), Louisville, KY 40207
Tel: (502) 897-9845; Fax: (502) 897-0103
Internet Address: http://www.locustgrove.org/
Admission: Fee: adult $6.00, child (6-12) $3.00, senior $5.00
Attendance: 25,000
Established: 1964
Parking: Paved parking lot
Open: Monday to Saturday, 10am-4:30pm; Sunday, 1:30pm-4:30pm
Closed: New Year's Eve afternoon to New Year's Day, Easter, Derby Day, Thanksgiving Day, Christmas Eve to Christmas Day
Best Time(s) of Year to Visit: April to Fall
Facilities: Architecture (Georgian residence, ca. 1790—National historic Landmark); Gardens (period; cutting, formal, herb); Grounds (55 acres)
Activities: Education Programs; Guided Tours

Located up river from Louisville, Locust Grove includes in addition to the late eighteenth-century residence several reconstructed supporting farm buildings, formal quadrant gardens, cutting gardens, and a herb garden. Designated a National Historic Landmark, Locust Grove is owned by Historic Locust Grove, a non-profit organization.

PARIS

GARDEN CLUB OF KENTUCKY—
NANNINE CLAY WALLIS ARBORETUM

616 Pleasant Street (Route 165 and U.S. Route 68 Exit), Paris, KY 40361
Tel: (859) 987-6158
Internet Address: http://www.gardenclubky.org
Admission: Free
Open: Monday to Saturday, 10am-6pm; Sunday, noon-6pm
Facilities: Grounds (4½ acres)

Located in downtown Paris, the Wallis House is the former home of the founder of the Garden Club of Kentucky and now serves as the club's state headquarters and education facility. With some trees dating back to the mid-1850s, the Wallis Arboretum is considered one of the finest old-tree collections in central Kentucky. It contains about seventy varieties of trees (including many varieties of flowering dogwoods), numerous flowering plants, a rose garden, and a fish pool.

MAINE

Stillwater •Orono
Hermon• •Bangor

Lubec•

•Waterville

•Ellsworth

•Bar Harbor (2)
•Northeast Harbor

•South Paris •Augusta

•Camden

• Wiscasset

Freeport• •Boothbay

Gorham• /•Portland (4)

•South Berwick

•Kittery

The number in the parentheses following the city name indicates the number of gardens/ arboreta in that municipality. If there is no number, one is understood. For example, in the text four listings would be found under Portland and one listing under Freeport.

AUGUSTA

PINE TREE STATE ARBORETUM (PTSA)

153 Hospital Street, Augusta, ME 04332
Tel: (207) 621-0031; Fax: (207) 621-8245
Internet Address: http://www.pinetreestatearboretum.org
Admission: Free
Attendance: 10,000
Established: 1982
Membership: Y
Wheelchair Accessible: P
Parking: On site, 50 spaces
Open: Daily, dawn-dusk
Best Time(s) of Year to Visit: late May to early June, October, February
(groomed ski trails)
Facilities: Arboretum; Education Center Johnson Outdoor Education Center (plus 11
outdoor classrooms); Gardens (historical, native plant, perennial); Grounds (220
acres); Special Collections (day lily, hosta, heirloom apples, American chestnut,
ornamental and flowering trees); Trails (5 miles)
Activities: Guided Tours (available on request, $35 for 1 hour); Self-Guided Tour
(brochure available)

The arboretum contains over 200 species of trees and shrubs and a hosta garden. Other
plantings include azaleas, green ashes, lilacs, heirloom apples, American chestnuts, and
rhododendrons.

BANGOR

MOUNT HOPE CEMETERY

1048 State Street, Bangor, ME 04402
Tel: (207) 945-6589; Fax: (207) 990-1810
Internet Address: http://www.mthopebgr.com
Admission: Free
Established: 1834
Open: Winter, daily, dawn-4:30pm; Summer, daily, dawn-7:30pm
Facilities: Grounds (264 acres, 1834 design by local architect Charles G. Bryant)

Located on the north bank of Penobscot River, the site consists of two distinct areas, a private burial ground and a horticultural park open to the general public for educational and recreational purposes. In the summer, the Bangor Museum and Center for History (942-5766) conducts guided tours. Created in 1834 and incorporated in 1858, it is the second oldest garden cemetery in the United States and is listed in the National Register of Historic Places. (Mount Auburn Cemetery in Cambridge, Massachusetts is the oldest.)

BAR HARBOR

COLLEGE OF THE ATLANTIC—BEATRIX FARRAND GARDEN

105 Eden Street (Route 3), Bar Harbor, ME 04609
Tel: (207) 288-5015; Fax: (207) 288-4126
Internet Address: http://www.coa.edu/campustour/landscape/
farrand.html
Facilities: Garden (original, 1929 design by Beatrix Farrand; restoration,
1984 Patrick Chassé)

Two years after purchasing and extensively remodeling Guy's Cliff on Eden Street, Mrs. James Byrne of New York City asked landscape gardener Beatrix Farrand to design a rose garden here. The garden, completed in 1929, featured a geometric parterre designed to display Mrs. Byrne's rose collection. College of the Atlantic acquired the property in 1970, and after Guy's Cliff burned down in 1983, the stone walls and terraces remained. With funding provided by the Garden Club of Mount Desert and Mr. and Mrs. David Rockefeller, landscape architect Patrick Chassé developed a restoration plan for the Farrand Garden. While not a literal restoration, the footprint of the garden remains the same; the transposition is in the materials.

WILD GARDENS OF ACADIA

Acadia National Park, Mount Desert Island, Sieur de Monts Spring (off Route 3),
Bar Harbor, ME 04609
Tel: (207) 288-3338
Admission: free
Established: 1961
Open: Daily, dawn-dusk
Facilities: Garden (native plant); Grounds (¾ acre)
Activities: Self-Guided Tour (brochure available)

A joint project of the Bar Harbor Garden Club and Acadia National Park, the gardens feature over 400 native plant species. Plants are labeled and displayed in sections representing twelve different habitats found in the park: beach, bird thicket, bog, brookside/damp thicket, coniferous woods, heath, marsh, meadow, mixed woods, mountain, pond, and roadside. The work of maintaining, identifying, planting, and labeling is carried out by volunteers from nearby Mount Desert Island communities and garden clubs. The National Park supplies labels and signs, maintains the water system, and sponsors a college student who works fulltime in the summer.

BOOTHBAY

COASTAL MAINE BOTANICAL GARDENS (AHS RAP)

Barters Island Road (1 mile from intersection with Corey Lane), Boothbay, ME 04537
Tel: (207) 633-4333; Fax: (207) 633-2366
Internet Address: http://www.mainegardens.org
Admission: free
Established: 1996
Open: Grounds, daily, dawn-dusk; Office, Monday to Friday, 8:30am-4:30pm
Facilities: Garden (fern, native plant, wetlands); Grounds (128 acres); Office
(downtown in Old Fire Station near Civil War Monument on Route 27)

Located along the tidal shoreline of the Back River, two miles of walks, trails, and drives offer access to gardens and natural areas, including forest canopy, ferns, flowering plants, rock outcroppings, pond life, and tidal shoreline.

CAMDEN

MERRYSPRING HORTICULTURAL NATURE PARK AND LEARNING CENTER

Conway Road, Camden, ME 04843
Tel: (207) 236-2239; Fax: (207) 230-0663
Internet Address: http://www.merryspring.org
Admission: Free
Attendance: 10,000
Established: 1974
Membership: Y
Wheelchair Accessible: P
Parking: Free on site
Open: Daily, dawn-dusk
Best Time(s) of Year to Visit: early July (rose), August (annual border)
Facilities: Arboretum Kitty Todd Arboretum (native species); Gardens (annual border, children's, heather, herb, perennial, raised bed, rock, rose, winter color, woodland); Greenhouse; Grounds Arboretum (10 acres), Park (66 acres); Library; Special Collections (hosta); Trails (4+ miles); Visitor Center
Activities: Education Programs; Guided Tours; Plant Sales

Founded by Mary Ellen Ross, a local horticulturist who had attained national recognition through her mail-order plant business, Merry Gardens, privately-owned Merryspring rests mostly on an elevated knoll underlain by limestone, with the surrounding land falling away to the north, west, and south, affording some excellent views from the park to the surrounding countryside. The center of the park comprises several large meadows, which hearken to the days when Merryspring was a sheep farm. Many different plant collections have been established at Merryspring through the years, and gardens now include a 250-foot-long annual border, a perennial border, a heather garden, a herb garden, a rose garden, a hosta collection, and the Birds and Bees/Winter Color Garden. The Kitty Todd Arboretum offers labeled specimens of more than seventy native tree and shrub species. A brochure available at the Ross Center shows the location of all the labeled plants. Other small memorial plantings, an informal wildflower collection, and occasional specimen trees or shrubs round out the offerings. Many of the varieties seen growing in the gardens can be purchased from the small nursery/greenhouse complex.

ELLSWORTH

WOODLAWN MUSEUM—GARDENS

Surry Road (Route 172), Ellsworth, ME 04605
Tel: (207) 667-8671
Internet Address: http://www.woodlawnmuseum.com
Admission: Public Park: Free; House: Fee: adult $7.50, child (<5) free
Attendance: 3,000
Established: 1928
Membership: Y
Wheelchair Accessible: Y
Parking: On site
Open: Public Park, daily, sunrise-sunset. May, Tuesday to Sunday, 1pm-4pm; June to September, Tuesday to Saturday, 10am-5pm; Sunday, 1pm-4pm; October, Tuesday to Sunday, 1pm-4pm
Best Time(s) of Year to Visit: Summer
Facilities: Architecture (brick residence, 1824-1828); Garden (formal, orchard); Grounds (180 acres); Picnic Area; Shop; Trails (4 miles)
Activities: Concerts (noon); Guided Tours (House, June-Oct, Mon-Sat, 10am, last tour begins 4:30pm); Teas (Wednesday)

Built between 1824 and 1828 by Colonel John Black, this stately brick house is largely Federal in design, but has Greek Revival details. Woodlawn was bequeathed to the Hancock County Trustees of Public Reservations in 1928 by George Nixon Black, Jr., grandson of Colonel Black. It has been open to the public as both a historic home and a public park since 1930. The home remains much as the family left it. Originally laid out in 1903, the formal gardens at Woodlawn are much newer than the house. Located between the house and carriage barn, the gardens feature a clipped lilac hedge enclosing the tea lawn and formal garden. In the late 1920s and 1930s, Beatrix Farrand, a nationally renowned landscape architect, was a consultant on the restoration of the grounds. Mrs. Farrand recommended the replanting of the horse chestnut trees to the tomb avenue and was instrumental in bringing back the stately hemlocks that still grace the property today.

FREEPORT

STONE HOUSE CONFERENCE CENTER

The Stone House, 642 Wolf Neck Road, Freeport, ME 04032
Tel: (207) 865-3428; Fax: (207) 865-3429
Internet Address: http://www.usm.maine.edu/stonehouse
Admission: Free
Membership: N
Open: Daily, dawn-dusk

Facilities: Architecture Stone House (residence, 1917 design by John Calvin Stevens); Demonstration Garden; Gardens; Grounds; Picnic Area

The grounds of the Stone House feature red oak, white birch, numerous conifers, red raspberry and blackberry canes, and colorful gardens, including a nationally-renowned heather garden and a rhododendron display garden. Adjoining the conference center, Wolfe's Neck Woods State Park provides the opportunity for self-guided nature walks in varied ecosystems, including climax white pine and hemlock forests, a salt marsh estuary, and the rocky shorelines on Casco Bay and the Harraseeket River.

GORHAM

UNIVERSITY OF SOUTHERN MAINE—ARBORETUM

37 College Avenue, Gorham, ME 04038
Tel: (207) 780-5226; Fax: (207) 780-5251
Internet Address: http://www.usm.maine.edu/arboretum/index.htm
Admission: Free
Established: 2002
Membership: N
Wheelchair Accessible: P
Parking: In student lots or at meters in front of Corthell Hall
Open: Daily, dawn-dusk
Best Time(s) of Year to Visit: Spring to Fall
Facilities: Arboretum; Grounds Campus (100 acres)
Activities: Guided Tours (arrange in advance); Self-Guided Tours (brochure available in 106 Bailey Hall, Mon-Fri, 8:30am-4:30pm)

Designated an arboretum by the American Association of Botanical Gardens and Arboreta, the USM campus contains over eighty-five tree species as well as various perennial gardens. A tree index and map is available on the arboretum's internet site.

HERMON

ECOTAT GARDENS AND ARBORETUM

Route 2 & Annis Road, Hermon, ME 04402-6300
Tel: (207) 848-3700; Fax: (207) 848-3316
Admission: Free
Established: 1995
Facilities: Arboretum; Garden; Grounds (91 acres); Library (gardening & birding)

Formerly a private residence, Ecotat Land Trust offers gardens with 56 flower beds containing more than 1,500 perennials and woodlands with more than 140 species of trees.

KITTERY

CELIA THAXTER'S GARDEN

Shoals Marine Laboratory, Appledore Island, Isles of Shoals, Kittery, ME 03908
Tel: (607) 254-2900; Fax: (607) 255-0742
Internet Address: http://www.sml.cornell.edu
Admission: by reservation only, $36.50
Attendance: 300
Membership: N
Wheelchair Accessible: N
Parking: At ferry, Barker Wharf on Market Street, Portsmouth, NH
Open: July to August, Wednesday, Ferry departs Portsmouth, NH 9:25am
Best Time(s) of Year to Visit: early July
Facilities: Garden (historic); Picnic Area; Special Collections (19th-century annuals)
Activities: Education Programs (adult education courses); Guided Tours (reserve in advance, (607) 255-3717)

Operating under the College of Agriculture and Life Sciences at Cornell University (Ithaca, NY) and in cooperation with the University of New Hampshire in Durham, the Shoals Marine Laboratory (SML) is active in the summer on ninety-five-acre Appledore Island, Isles of Shoals in the Gulf of Maine. A century ago, Appledore Island was the center of summer life for artists, writers, and musicians. Poet Celia Thaxter (1835-1894), daughter of a local lighthouse keeper, designed a special garden for the fertile terrace that sloped from her cottage porch toward the sea. Her garden became the island's centerpiece, nearly as famous as her parlor, where were assembled many of the literary and artistic greats of nineteenth-century New England, including Emerson, Twain, Lowell, and Jewett. In the last year of her life, she published perhaps her handsomest book, *An Island Garden*, with illustrations by the early American impressionist Childe Hassam. In it, Celia named and located all the plants of her garden of 1893. After her death, the island's population slowly diminished and by 1914 her garden was derelict. In the 1970s, the Shoals Marine Laboratory with the help of garden clubs and many volunteers recreated Celia's garden exactly in its original position. Due to SML's mission and Appledore Island's fragile nature, access to the island is controlled. The Isles of Shoals Steamship Company will allow only individuals approved by the SML office to board the ferry to Star Island. The ISSC ferry departs from Portsmouth, New Hampshire, at 9:25am, and returns at 4:15pm. SML's R/V Kingsbury shuttles visitors between Star Island's dock and Appledore Island. For those interested in a more in-depth exploration of Celia's Garden, SML offers an adult education course "A Garden is a Sea of Flowers."

LUBEC

COTTAGE GARDEN

934 North Lubec Road (4½ miles from North Lubec turnoff), Lubec, ME 04652
Tel: (207) 733-2902
Admission: Free
Open: June to AuguStreet daily, dawn-dusk.

Facilities: Gardens (alpine, riparian, herb, perennial); Grounds
(2 acres); Museum Shoreline Nature Center; Shop (art, handcrafts)

The Cottage Garden features seven gardens full of old-fashioned roses, delphinium, hollyhocks, perennials, and herbs on two wooded acres surrounding a Greek Revival Cape house. Bordered by orchards, the gardens include a herb garden, stream-side damp garden, alpine collection, and perennial beds.

NORTHEAST HARBOR

ASTICOU TERRACES—THUYA GARDENS

Peabody Drive, Northeast Harbor, ME 04662
Tel: (207) 276-5130
Admission: Voluntary contribution, $2.00
Open: Mid-June to September, daily, 9am-5pm
Facilities: Architecture Thuya Lodge (Maine summer cottage home of Boston landscape architect Joseph Henry Curtis); Gardens (English); Grounds Gardens (1½ acres, design by Charles Savage, 1988 redesign Patrick Chassé), Park (200 acres); Library; Special Collections (perennial)

Set on the slope of Eliot Mountain, the site contains over 200 acres of woodland trails and terraced gardens. Named for the area's abundant white cedars (Thuya Occidentalis), Thuya Lodge, the summer residence of Boston landscape architect Joseph Henry Curtis, is the centerpiece of the park. On his death the site was left to the town. Thuya Garden is an English-style, semi-formal perennial garden containing a variety of native and exotic perennials, including many from Beatrix Farrand's Bar Harbor home. As renovated by Patrick Chassé, the garden now displays over 110 varieties of perennials, representing 60 genera, set against a backdrop of granite outcrops and alpine woods.

ORONO

UNIVERSITY OF MAINE—LYLE E. LITTLEFIELD ORNAMENTALS TRIAL GARDEN

Rangeley Road (adjacent to University of Maine Credit Union),
Orono, ME 04469
Tel: (207) 581-2948; Tel: (207) 581-29998
Internet Address: http://www.ume.maine.edu/~nfa/lhc/little.htm
Open: Daily, sunrise-sunset
Facilities: Gardens, Grounds Facility(14 acres), Gardens (7acres)
Activities: Guided Tours (group, begins end of May, by appointment, 581-3112)

One of the nation's premier research facilities for hardy plants, the Littlefield Garden houses the Horticulture Program's permanent collection of over 2,500 woody and herbaceous ornamentals. Major focus collections include: crab apples (210 varieties), lilacs (180 varieties), rhododendrons (150 varieties), and magnolias (35 varieties). Hollies, woody and herbaceous vines, day lilies, hostas, and early spring bulbs are also well represented.

PORTLAND

CITY OF PORTLAND—LONGFELLOW ARBORETUM

Payson Park (off Baxter Boulevard), Portland, ME 04103
Tel: (207) 874-8793; Fax: (207) 756-8390
Internet Address: http://www.ci.portland.me.us
Admission: Free
Established: 1976
Wheelchair Accessible: P
Parking: On street
Open: Daily, 6:30am-sunset
Best Time(s) of Year to Visit: June to October
Facilities: Arboretum; Grounds (3 acres)
Activities: Self-Guided Tour (brochure available)

Located on the western side of Payson Park adjacent to a small tidal marsh, the arbore-
tum features forty species of non-native trees not commonly grown in this area of New
England. The arboretum is a joint effort of the Longfellow Garden Club and the City of
Portland Parks and Recreation Department.

CITY OF PORTLAND ROSE CIRCLE

Deering Oaks Park, State Street and High Street Extended, Portland, ME 04101
Tel: (207) 756-8275; Fax: (207) 756-8279; TDDY: (207) 756-8936
Internet Address: http://www.ci.portland.me.us
Best Time(s) of Year to Visit: late July to early August
Facilities: Garden (rose); Grounds Park (51 acres, 1871 design by William Goodwin)

The garden contains over 600 species of hybrid tea roses. Deering Oaks Park is listed
on the National Register of Historic Places.

MAINE HISTORICAL SOCIETY—LONGFELLOW GARDEN

487 Congress Street, Portland, ME 04101
Tel: (207) 774-1822; Fax: (207) 775-4301
Internet Address: http://www.mainehistory.org
Admission: Free
Established: 1901
Wheelchair Accessible: P
Parking: On street and in local parking garages
Open: May to October, Daily, 10am-4pm
Best Time(s) of Year to Visit: late Summer
Facilities: Architecture (adjacent residence of General Peleg Wadsworth, 1785);
Garden (Colonial Revival)
Activities: Guided Tours House (reserve in advance)

Located behind the Wadsworth-Longfellow House, the secluded garden is an oasis of
green and quiet in the heart of downtown Portland. Beautifully landscaped, it is open to
the public during seasonal weather. For an admission fee, guided tours are available of
the restored Wadsworth-Longfellow House, childhood home of the poet Henry

Wadsworth Longfellow. Maine Historical Society facilities consist of the Wadsworth-Longfellow House, the Maine Historical Society Museum and Research Library, and the Longfellow Garden.

THE TATE HOUSE MUSEUM—GARDEN

1270 Westbrook Street, Portland, ME 04102
Tel: (207) 774-9781
Internet Address: http://www.tatehouse.org/
Admission: Fee: adult $7.00, child (<6) free, child (<12) $2.00, senior $5.00
Established: 1931
Membership: N
Parking: Parking on street and in lot
Open: June 15 to September, Tuesday to Sunday, 10am-4pm; Sunday, 1pm-4pm; October, Friday to Saturday, 10am-4pm; Sunday, 1pm-4pm
Closed: Independence Day
Best Time(s) of Year to Visit: June 25 to September 15
Facilities: Architecture (residence, ca. 1755); Garden (Colonial herb); Grounds (native plants); Shop
Activities: Events Garden Days (mid-June—mid-Sept, Wed, 10am-4pm; 774-6177); Guided Tours (house; garden, Wed)

Built by the Senior Mast Agent for the British Royal Navy, Tate House includes a colonial herb garden containing more than eighty varieties of herbs. A property of the National Society of the Colonial Dames of America in the State of Maine, the site was designated a National Historic Landmark in 1972. The house tour includes an explanation of the uses of the herbs placed in the rooms.

SOUTH BERWICK

HAMILTON HOUSE

40 Vaughan's Lane (off Route 236), South Berwick, ME 03908
Tel: (207) 384-2454
Internet Address: http://www.historicnewengland.org/visit/homes/hamilton.htm
Admission: Fee (house tour): adult $8.00, child $4.00, student $4.00, senior $4.00
Established: 1949
Wheelchair Accessible: P
Parking: Parking available—unpaved
Open: House: June to October 15, Wednesday to Sunday, noon-4pm; Grounds: all year, dawn-dusk.
Facilities: Architecture (Georgian residence, 1785); Garden (formal, Victorian); Grounds (33 acres)
Activities: Concert Series (summer); Guided Tours House (11am, noon, 1pm, 2pm, 3pm, 4pm)

Overlooking the Salmon Falls River, the house is restored to reflect its appearance as an turn-of-the-century summer residence. The grounds include the remnants of an extraordinary early twentieth-century garden, which is well documented in photographs. The site is a property of Historic New England (formerly the Society for the Preservation of New England Antiquities).

SOUTH PARIS

THE MCLAUGHLIN FOUNDATION—
BERNARD MCLAUGHLIN GARDEN

97 Main Street (junction Grand Trunk Railroad & Route 26), South Paris, ME 04281
Tel: (207) 743-8820; Fax: (207) 743-3977
Internet Address: http://www.mclaughlingarden.org
Admission: Free
Established: 1996
Open: Garden: May to October, daily, 9am-5pm; Horticultural Center, daily
Facilities: Food Services (tea/lunch room); Garden (lilac, lily, iris, hosta, native wildflowers); Grounds (3 acres); Shop
Activities: Guided Tours; Lectures; Workshops

Bernard McLaughlin began the garden in 1936, while working in a South Paris grocery store, and gardened in his spare time until retiring in 1967. From that point until his death, McLaughlin devoted his full energies to the garden, which features lilacs, lilies, irises, hostas, and native wildflowers. After his death in 1996, the McLaughlin Foundation was organized to preserve the home, garden, and grounds and to preserve its fifty-year "open door" visiting tradition.

STILLWATER

ROGERS FARM—DEMONSTRATION GARDEN

Rogers Farm, Stillwater Avenue and Bennoch Road, Stillwater, ME 04489
Tel: (207) 942-7396
Internet Address: http://www.umaine.edu/mafes/farms/rogers.htm
Admission: Free
Established: 1947
Open: Summer, daily
Facilities: All American Selections Display Garden; Demonstration Garden (annual flowers, vegetables, herbs, white garden, children's garden, small fruits); Grounds Demonstration Garden (1 acres), Farm (100 acres)
Activities: Field Days; Guided Tours; Self-guided Tours

Operated by the University of Maine, Rogers Farm is home to the Penobscot County Master Gardener Demonstration Garden. The site has extensive plantings of annual flowers, vegetables, and herbs. Plantings include a white garden, a children's garden, a perennial border, small fruits, and an All-American Selections Display Garden. There are also trials of geraniums and New Guinea impatiens from Ball Seed Company and Maine's only trials of plants from Blooms of Bressingham (English perennials) and Proven Winners.

WATERVILLE

COLBY COLLEGE—PERKINS ARBORETUM AND BIRD SANCTUARY

Mayflower Hill Drive, Waterville, ME 04901
Tel: (207) 872-3000

Admission: Free
Wheelchair Accessible: N
Parking: Campus parking lots nearby
Best Time(s) of Year to Visit: Spring to Fall
Facilities: Grounds College Campus (714 acres), Perkins Arboretum (128 acres);
Nature Trail

Colby's entire campus is designated as a State Wildlife Management Area. The Perkins Arboretum consists of 128 acres of relatively undisturbed plant and animal habitat. The area has three trails maintained for walking and nature study.

WISCASSET

NICKELS-SORTWELL HOUSE GARDEN

12 Main Street at Federal Street (junction Routes 1 & 218), Wiscasset, ME 04578
Tel: (207) 882-6218
Internet Address: http://spnea.org/visit/homes/nickels.htm
Admission: Fee-$5.00
Attendance: 1,800
Parking: Behind shops on Main Street
Open: June to October 15, Friday to Sunday, 11am-5pm
Facilities: Architecture (Federal-style residence, 1807); Gardens (period)
Activities: Guided Tours House (Wed-Sun, 11am/noon/1pm/2pm/3pm/ 4pm)

Built in 1807 by Captain William Nickels, a ship owner and trader, the house was transformed into a hotel around 1830. Toward the end of the century, when the Maine coast had become fashionable as a summer resort, Alvin Sortwell purchased the building as a summer residence. Sortwell and his daughter, Frances, a leader in the local preservation movement, refurbished it in the Colonial Revival manner. The grounds, landscaped in 1926 with period gardens and an elaborate classical fence, are being restored. The site, listed on the National Register of Historic Places, is a property of Historic New England. The adjacent sunken garden, donated by Frances Sortwell to the Town of Wiscasset, was created in the foundation of a former hotel that burned to the ground in 1900.

MARYLAND

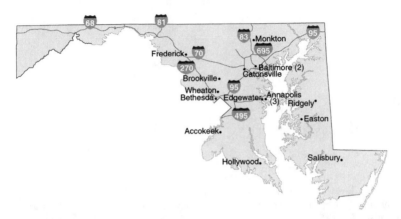

The number in the parentheses following the city name indicates the number of gardens/ arboreta in that municipality. If there is no number, one is understood. For example, in the text three listings would be found under Annapolis and one listing under Edgewater.

ACCOKEEK

ACCOKEEK FOUNDATION—GARDENS AND ARBORETA

3400 Bryan Point Road, Accokeek, MD 20607
Tel: (301) 283-2113; Fax: (301) 283-2049
Internet Address: http://www.accokeek.org
Admission: Fee: adult $2.00, child $.50, family $5.00
Established: 1957
Membership: Y
Parking: Free at Visitor Center
Open: Tuesday to Sunday, 10am-4pm
Closed: Legal holidays
Facilities: Arboretum; Exhibition Area Ecosystem Farm, National Colonial Farm
Museum; Grounds (200 acres); Visitor Center
Activities: Guided Tours (Sat-Sun, 1pm)

The foundation's two primary projects, located in Piscataway Park along the Potomac River at the southern tip of Maryland's Prince George's County, are the National Colonial Farm and the Ecosystem Farm. The National Colonial Farm is a living history museum portraying middle-class rural life in 1775. The site features period buildings, gardens, and heritage animal breeds. The extensive garden features eighteenth-century varieties of herbs, flowers, and vegetables, and is the source for much of the farm's heirloom seed stock. Historic varieties of field crops such as Orinoco tobacco, Virginia Gourdseed corn, and Red May wheat are cultivated on a seasonal basis. The modern-day organic Ecosystem Farm demonstrates that by adapting farming practices to the natural constraints of the environment, it is possible to produce a sustainable harvest of vegetables in an ecologically sound manner. The hillside facing Mount Vernon features the Accokeek Foundation Native Tree Arboretum, containing 108 trees and shrubs representing 85 species documented by the early European settlers of the Chesapeake Bay region.

ANNAPOLIS

CHARLES CARROLL HOUSE OF ANNAPOLIS—GARDENS

107 Duke of Gloucester Street, Annapolis, MD 21401-2504
Tel: (410) 269-1737; Fax: (410) 269-1746
Admission: Fee: adult $5.00, child (<12) free, child (12-17) $2.00, senior $4.00
Attendance: 2,000
Membership: Y

Wheelchair Accessible: Y
Open: March to December, Friday, noon-4pm; Saturday, 10am-2pm; Sunday, noon-4pm
Closed: Easter, Thanksgiving Day, Christmas Eve to Christmas Day
Facilities: Architecture (birthplace of Charles Carroll, 1722); Gardens (period, eighteenth-century); Library; Shop
Activities: Education Programs (adults and children); Guided Tours (groups, by appointment); Lectures; Temporary Exhibitions

The house features a largely-intact, formal eighteenth-century garden. Research has demonstrated the garden was laid out in the form of a 3-4-5 right triangle in order to control sight lines from the house, as well as the view of the far shore of the creek on which the house is situated.

HELEN AVALYNNE TAWES GARDEN

Tawes State Office Building, Sachs Drive (off Taylor Avenue), Annapolis, MD 21401
Tel: (410) 260-8189; TDDY: (410) 974-2609
Internet Address: http://www.dnr.state.md.us/publiclands/tawesgarden.html
Admission: Voluntary contribution
Open: Daily, dawn-dusk
Facilities: Food Services cafeteria (Mon-Fri, 7:30am-3pm);
Grounds (5 acres); Shop (Mon-Fri, 9am-3pm)
Activities: Concerts; Education Programs; Guided Tours
(by reservation); Plant Sales; Self-Guided Tours

Named in honor of Mrs. J. Millard Tawes, a former first lady of Maryland, the garden features examples of the state's varying natural environments, including a western Maryland forest, a streamside environment, and an Eastern Shore peninsula. There are also raised sensory and fragrance beds and many cultivated plantings. A booklet for self-guided tours is available.

WILLIAM PACA HOUSE AND GARDEN

186 Prince George Street, Annapolis, MD 21401-1718
Tel: (800) 603-4020; Fax: (410) 267-6189
Internet Address: http://www.annapolis.org/paca.htm
Admission: Fee (House & Garden Tour): adult $8.00, child $5.00, senior $7.00, family $25.00; Fee (House only): $4.00; Fee
(Garden only): $4.00
Attendance: 255,000
Established: 1973
Membership: Y
Wheelchair Accessible: N
Parking: Use city garages or on-street parking
Open: January to March, Friday to Saturday, 10am-4pm;
Sunday, noon-4pm; Monday, 10am-4pm; April to December, Monday to Saturday, 10am-5pm; Sunday, noon-5pm;
November to December, Monday to Saturday, 10am-4pm;
Sunday, noon-4pm
Facilities: Architecture (Georgian residence, 1763-1765); Garden (historic, eighteenth-century garden); Grounds (2 acres); Shop
Activities: Guided Tours

The five-part Georgian residence was built as a town home for William Paca, a wealthy young planter who was a signer of the Declaration of Independence. The recreated eighteenth-century garden behind Paca House, features five landscaped terraces with plantings appropriate to the era of William Paca's residency. The garden opened to the public in 1973; the house has been open to the public since 1976. A National Historic Landmark, the site is a property of the Historic Annapolis Foundation.

BALTIMORE

BALTIMORE CITY CONSERVATORY AND BOTANIC GARDEN

Druid Hill Park, Gwyns Falls Parkway and McCulloh Street, Baltimore, MD 21217
Tel: (410) 396-0180
Internet Address: http://www.ci.baltimore.md.us/government/
recnparks/conservatory.html
Admission: Free
Attendance: 5,000
Open: Gardens, Thursday to Sunday, 10am-3pm; Conservatory & Greenhouse, temporarily closed for renovation
Closed: Legal holidays
Facilities: Conservatory (Victorian Palm House, 1888);
Gardens; Greenhouses (3); Grounds Druid Hill Park (674 acres), Gardens (1½ acres)
Activities: Events Chrysanthemum Display (Fall), Holiday Poinsettia Display (Dec), Spring Flower Display

Located just inside Druid Hill Park, the conservatory houses a collection of tropical plants. Other greenhouses contain plants associated with the desert, Mediterranean, and tropical climates.

CYLBURN ARBORETUM

4915 Greenspring Avenue, Baltimore, MD 21209
Tel: (410) 367-2217; Fax: (410) 367-7112
Internet Address: http://www.cylburnassociation.org
Admission: Free
Established: 1954
Membership: Y
Parking: Free on site
Open: Grounds, daily, dawn-dusk; Mansion, Monday to Friday, 7:30am-3:30pm; Museums, Tuesday & Thursday, 1pm-3pm.
Facilities: Architecture (Italianate residence, begun 1863, completed 1888); Gardens (butterfly, children's, dahlia, day lily, demonstration, formal, memorial, rose, sensory, shade, vegetable); Greenhouses (production, not open to public); Grounds (207 acres); Herbarium; Library (horticultural reference); Museums (2; Bird & Nature); Trails (2½ miles)
Activities: Education Programs (children & adult); Guided Tours (by appointment, 410-396-7839); Lectures; Plant Sales

Baltimore businessman Jesse Tyson began the mansion as a private summer residence in 1863. In 1954, the Baltimore City Board of Recreation and Parks founded the Cylburn

Wildflower Preserve and Garden Center on the site (later renamed the Cylburn Arboretum Association). Surrounding the Victorian mansion are spacious lawns, an extensive collection of trees and shrubs based loosely on the original Tyson estate plantings, and a wide variety of gardens. Gardens include a restored Victorian formal garden; a sensory garden with waist-high beds allowing the physically challenged to touch and smell the plants; a children's garden; an All-American Selections garden, growing test annuals and display favorites; low-maintenance and urban backyard demonstration gardens; a vegetable garden; heritage and miniature rose gardens; a butterfly garden; and several memorial gardens. Trees include collections of Japanese maples, hollies, conifers, Maryland oaks, beeches, tree peonies, maples, and magnolias. Trails wind through the woodlands, where native plants and wildflowers may be seen. Cylburn is maintained by the Cylburn Arboretum Association in partnership with the Baltimore City Department of Recreation and Parks, Division of Horticulture.

SHERWOOD GARDENS

Greenway & Stratford Road (east of St. Paul Street), Baltimore,
MD 21218
Tel: (410) 323-7982
Admission: Free
Parking: Free on site
Open: daily, dawn-dusk
Best Time(s) of Year to Visit: Mid-April to May (tulips)
Facilities: Gardens (6¼ acres)

Bounded by Highfield, Stratford, Greenway, and Underwood, Sherwood Gardens is known for its spectacular display of more than 70,000 tulips in late April and May. Other plantings include azaleas, English boxwoods, flowering cherries, dogwoods, magnolias, and wisteria. Owned by the Guilford Association, Inc., the park is maintained with assistance from Baltimore City Recreation and Parks Department.

BETHESDA

MCCRILLIS GARDENS AND GALLERY

6910 Greentree Road, Bethesda, MD 20817
Tel: (301) 962-1401
Internet Address: http://www.mc-mncppc.org/parks/brookside/mccrilli.htm
Admission: Free
Established: 1978
Parking: Limited on-street parking
Open: Daily, 10am-sunset
Facilities: Galleries (changing exhibitions, 365-1657); Gardens (shade); Grounds (5 acres); Special Collections (rhododendron, viburnum)

A premier shade garden, McCrillis Gardens features azaleas, rhododendrons, and other blooming and non-blooming ornamental trees and shrubs, bulbs, ground covers, and shade-loving perennials. McCrillis Gardens was donated to the Maryland-National Capital Park and Planning Commission in 1978 by its owners, William and Virginia McCrillis. It is managed by Brookside Gardens (see separate listing under Wheaton, Maryland).

BROOKEVILLE

BRIGHTON DAM AZALEA GARDENS

Brighton Dam Road, Brookeville, MD 20833
Tel: (301) 774-9124
Admission: Free
Established: 1950
Parking: Lot at Brighton Dam Visitor Center
Open: Daily, 8am-8pm
Best Time(s) of Year to Visit: late May to mid-June (azalea bloom)
Facilities: Gardens; Grounds (5½ acres); Picnic Area;
Special Collections (azalea)

Overlooking the Triadelphia Reservoir, the gardens contain over 22,000 azaleas and other plants. Adjoining Patuxent River State Park, the site is owned by the Washington Suburban Sanitary Commission.

CATONSVILLE

CATONSVILLE HISTORICAL SOCIETY—KNOT GARDEN

Townsend House, 1824 Frederick Road, Catonsville, MD 21228-5503
Tel: (410) 744-3034
Internet Address: http://www.catonsvillehistory.org/knotgarden.html
Admission: Fee (House) $2.00, family $5.00; Free (Gardens)
Attendance: 500
Membership: Y
Wheelchair Accessible: Y
Parking: On site and on street
Open: Grounds, daily, 9am-3pm; House: first three Sundays in month, 2pm-4pm, or by appointment
Facilities: Garden (knot); Nature Walk

The grounds of the society's headquarters, Townsend House and Pullen Museum, feature many trees, shrubs, and plantings, including a knot garden developed in cooperation with the Catonsville Garden Club. Townsend House, designed with an eighteenth-century floor plan, includes a variety of antiques from the eighteenth and nineteenth centuries as well as the society's collections.

EASTON

HISTORICAL SOCIETY OF TALBOT COUNTY GARDENS

25 S. Washington Street, Easton, MD 21601
Tel: (410) 822-0773; Fax: (410) 822-7911

Internet Address: http://www.hstc.org/
Admission: Free
Open: Tuesday to Friday, 11am-3pm; Saturday, 10am-4pm
Best Time(s) of Year to Visit: May to October
Facilities: Architecture (3 historic houses); Gardens (historic, Federal-style);
Historical Museum
Activities: Guided Tours Houses ($5)

The award-winning Federal-style gardens of the Historical Society, designed in the 1960s, feature over 100 English boxwoods, a terrace shade garden, and perennials known to have been used in eighteenth-century Maryland. They may be entered through the museum, or through any of the property gates. The gardens, which are main-tained by the Talbot County Garden Club, provide a peaceful oasis in the middle of Easton.

EDGEWATER

HISTORIC LONDON TOWN AND GARDENS

839 Londontown Road, Edgewater, MD 21037-2120
Tel: (410) 222-1919; Fax: (410) 222-1918
Internet Address: http://www.historiclondontown.com
Admission: Fee (House & Garden): adult $7.00, child (<7) free, child (7-12) $3.00, senior $5.00; Fee (Garden only): $4.00
Attendance: 21,000
Established: 1971
Membership: Y
Wheelchair Accessible: P
Parking: Free on site
Open: Tuesday to Friday, 9am-4pm; Saturday, 10am-4pm; Sunday, noon-4pm
Closed: Legal holidays
Best Time(s) of Year to Visit: Spring
Facilities: Architecture (Georgian house, ca. 1760); Gardens (woodland, eighteenth century kitchen, eighteenth century medicinal); Grounds (23 acres; garden 8 acres); Museum; Special Collections (holly, hosta, viburnum, wildflower)
Activities: Concerts; Education Programs (children & adult); Events Needlework Show; Flower Shows (daffodil); Guided Tours House (mid-March-Dec, hourly; Jan—mid-March, by appointment); Lectures; Plant Sales; Temporary Exhibitions

London Town Publick House is a striking Georgian building, furnished as it might have appeared as the home and tavern for the keeper of the ferry that ran between Londontown and Annapolis in the late eighteenth century. Also on the site is the Lord Mayor's Tenement, an authentic reconstruction of a ca. 1700 house. There are eight acres of Tidewater woodland gardens with many native and exotic species as well as eighteenth-century kitchen and medicinal garden collections. The site is listed on the National Register of Historic Places.

FREDERICK

SCHIFFERSTADT ARCHITECTURAL MUSEUM—GARDENS

1110 Rosemont Avenue, Frederick, MD 21701
Tel: (301) 668-6058; Fax: (301) 668-4807
Internet Address: http://www.frederickcountylandmarksfoundation.org
Admission: Suggested contribution (tour) $3.00
Membership: Y
Wheelchair Accessible: N
Parking: Parking on street
Open: April to mid-December, Wednesday to Friday, 10am-4pm; Saturday to Sunday, noon-4pm
Facilities: Architecture (German colonial residence, 1756); Gardens (heritage garden (herbs and vegetables) and orchard); Shop
Activities: Education Programs; Events Oktoberfest (October)

Schifferstadt is reputed to be America's finest example of German colonial architecture and the oldest extant house in Frederick. The grounds include flowerbeds, a fenced foursquare garden, and an apple orchard. The raised beds feature herbs and include eighteenth-century varieties of vegetables and small fruits.

HOLLYWOOD

SOTTERLEY PLANTATION—GARDENS

44300 Sotterley Lane, Hollywood, MD 20636
Tel: (800) 681-0850; Fax: (301) 373-8474
Internet Address: http://www.sotterley.org
Admission: Fee: adult $7.00, child (<6) free, child (6-16) $5.00, senior $6.00; Ground fee—$2.00
Established: 1717
Membership: Y
Wheelchair Accessible: P
Open: Tuesday to Saturday, 10am-4pm; noon-4pm
Facilities: Architecture (Tidewater manor house, ca. 1710; outbuildings; slave cabin, ca. 1830); Gardens (Colonial Revival, ca. 1910; children's, herb, vegetable); Grounds (100 acres with trails)
Activities: Education Programs; Guided Tours House (May-Oct; Sat, 10am-4pm; Sun, 1pm-4pm); Self-Guided Walking Tour

Overlooking the Patuxent River, Sotterley Plantation was originally a tobacco plantation and a colonial port of entry. The Colonial Revival garden design of four large squares bordered by boxwood hedges and grass walkways was laid out in 1910 and continues to be the basic guide for the efforts of Sotterley's volunteer Garden Guild. The southwest square is a croquet and play lawn, the southeast square (originally designated for larger crops and fruit trees) is now also in lawn with a few of the original fruit trees, the two southern squares (originally kitchen, herb, and cutting gardens) contain a cutting garden, nursery beds, and a children's garden. In addition to the four garden squares, there are ten separate flowerbeds on the east end of the garden. The property has been designated a National Historic Landmark by the Department of the Interior.

MONKTON

LADEW TOPIARY GARDENS

3535 Jarrettsville Pike, Monkton, MD 21111
Tel: (410) 557-9466 Fax: (410) 557-7763
Internet Address: http://www.ladewgardens.com/
Admission: Fee: adult $10.00, child $2.00, student $8.00,
senior $8.00
Attendance: 35,000
Established: 1977
Membership: Y
Wheelchair Accessible: P
Open: Mid-April to October, Monday to Friday, 10am-4pm; Saturday to Sunday,
10:30-5pm
Facilities: Auditorium (50 seats); Exhibition Area; Food Services Café; Gardens (15
themed; apple orchard, berry, cottage, herb, oriental iris, pink, portico, yellow, red,
rose, terrace, Victorian, water lily, white, wild); Grounds (22 acres); House Museum
(Tour, additional $2 fee); Picnic Grounds; Shop
Activities: Concert Series; Group Tours (by arrangement); Guided Tours House
(additional $2.00/person); Horticultural Lecture Series

The house and gardens were developed as a private estate between 1929 and 1976 by Harvey S. Ladew. There are a variety of themed gardens surrounding a central bowl, terraces and allée, and outlined by tall sculptured hedges. However, its crowning glory is the twenty-two-acre topiary garden, where shrubs are shaped as a pyramid, staircase, birds and animals, and even a fox hunt with dogs and a hunter on horseback. The restored and enlarged late eighteenth-century house, decorated in a mixture of styles, may be toured. Run by a private foundation, both the house and gardens are listed in the National Register of Historic Places.

RIDGELY

THE ADKINS ARBORETUM

12610 Eveland Road, Ridgely, MD 21660
Tel: (410) 634-2847; Fax: (410) 634-2878
Internet Address: http://www.adkinsarboretum.org/
Attendance: 14,000
Established: 1980
Membership: Y
Parking: Parking adjacent to Visitor's Center
Open: Daily, 9am-5pm
Visitor Center: April to October, Monday to Saturday, 9am-5pm; Sunday, 11am-3pm
Facilities: Arboretum; Camp Sites; Gardens (native garden and preserve); Grounds
(400 acres; 4 miles of paths); Library; Shop; Trails (4 miles); Visitor Center (9am-
5pm, Mon-Sat; 11am-3pm, Sun (April-Oct))
Activities: Art Exhibits; Education Programs; Guided Tours (garden); Lectures; Workshops

Adkins Arboretum features more than four miles of interpretive paths along meandering streams, meadows, and bottomland forest. The arboretum offers year-round programs in ecology, horticulture, and natural history for adults and children.

SALISBURY

SALISBURY UNIVERSITY ARBORETUM

1101 Camden Avenue, Salisbury, MD 21801
Tel: (410) 543-6323; Fax: (410) 543-6188
Internet Address: http://www.salisbury.edu/arboretum
Admission: Free
Wheelchair Accessible: Y
Open: Daily
Facilities: Arboretum (Perdue Courtyard, pergola, sculpture, water features); Grounds, Campus (147 acres); Special Collections, (magnolia, cedrus, lagerstomia, taxodium, tilia)
Activities: Guided Tours, Large Groups (upon request; Mon-Fri, 7am-3:30pm)

An integral part of the university campus, the arboretum has identified and tracks the growth of over 750 plant species. The campus landscape is continuously being developed, as both indigenous and exotic plant species are added yearly. A directory of arboretum plantings, including photos and detailed descriptions, is available on the internet website.

WHEATON

BROOKSIDE GARDENS

Wheaton Regional Park, 1800 Glenallan Avenue, Wheaton, MD 20902
Tel: (301) 962-1400; Fax: (310) 949-0571; TDDY: (301) 949-8231
Internet Address: http://www.mc-mncppc.org/parks/brookside/
Admission: Voluntary contribution
Attendance: 180,000
Established: 1969
Membership: Y
Wheelchair Accessible: Y
Open: Conservatories, Daily, 10am-5pm; Grounds, Daily, sunrise-sunset
Closed: Christmas Day
Facilities: Conservatories (2; open 10am-5pm); Gardens (aquatic, azalea, formal, fragrance, Japanese, rock, rose, trial, viburnum, winter, yew); Grounds (50 acres); Library (3,300 volumes, non-circulating; open, Mon-Fri, 10am-3pm); Shop; Visitor Center (9am-5pm)
Activities: Education Programs (adults and children); Flower Shows Fall (Oct-Nov), Holiday (Dec), Summer (May-Sept), Winter/Spring (Jan-May); Guided Tours (groups 10+, schedule 2 weeks in advance, 962-1407); Lectures

Brookside Gardens is a public display garden located within Wheaton Regional Park. Included in the gardens are several distinct areas; an azalea garden, an All-America Rose Selections display garden, a yew garden, a formal garden, a fragrance garden, a Japanese-style garden, and a trial garden. The garden also features two conservatories containing a large collection of tropical plants including banana, giant bird of paradise, and mimosa as well as year-round seasonal displays. The gardens are under the aegis of the Maryland-National Capital Park and Planning Commission. McCrillis Gardens and Gallery (see separate listing), a five-acre shade garden in Bethesda, Maryland, is managed by Brook-side Gardens.

MASSACHUSETTS

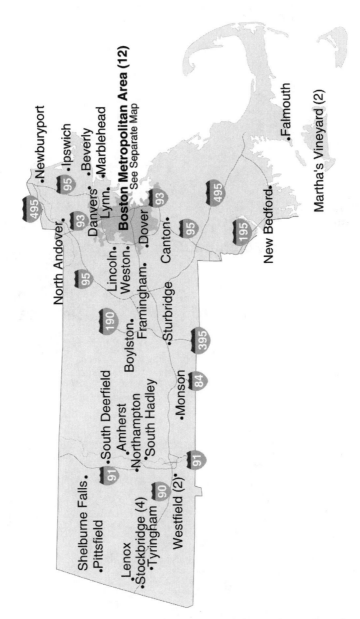

The number in the parentheses following the city name indicates the number of gardens/ arboreta in that municipality. If there is no number, one is understood. For example, in the text four listings would be found under Stockbridge and one listing under Lenox. Cities within the greater Boston metropolitan area will be found on the map on the next page.

GREATER BOSTON
METROPOLITAN AREA

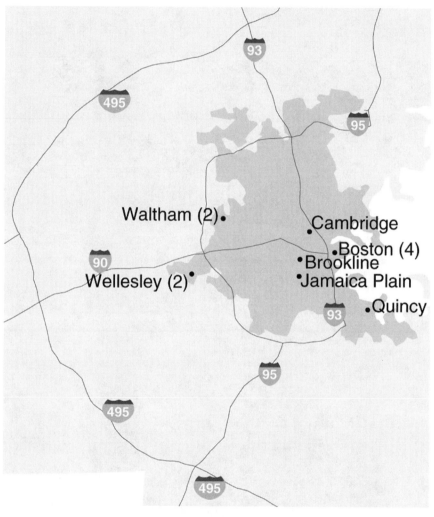

Greater Boston metropolitan area (including Boston, Brookline, Cambridge, Jamaica Plain, Quincy, Waltham, and Wellesley).

AMHERST

UNIVERSITY OF MASSACHUSETTS—DURFEE CONSERVATORY AND WAUGH ARBORETUM

Department of Plant and Soil Sciences, French Hall, Amherst, MA 01003
Tel: (413) 545-5234
Admission: Free
Established: 1867
Membership: N
Wheelchair Accessible: Y
Open: Conservatory, Monday to Friday, 8:30am-4:30pm; Saturday to Sunday,
by appointment
Facilities: Arboretum; Conservatory; Greenhouses (4)
Activities: Guided Tours (arrange in advance)

Located adjacent to French Hall, the conservatory, which dates back to the mid-1800s, features a small rain forest and a Victorian collection modeled after Kew Gardens. Associated gardens include an All-American Selections Display Garden. Additionally, the entire campus has been designated the Waugh Arboretum, including thousands of unusual specimens of trees and shrubs and outlying areas of forest and wetlands.

BEVERLY

THE SEDGWICK GARDENS AT LONG HILL

572 Essex Street (Route 22), Beverly, MA 01915
Tel: (978) 921-1944; Fax: (978) 921-1948
Internet Address: http://www.thetrustees.org/
Admission: No charge, donations accepted
Established: 1979
Wheelchair Accessible: P
Parking: Free on site
Open: Gardens, daily, sunrise-sunset; House, Monday to Friday, by appointment only
Facilities: Architecture (antebellum-style house, 1921); Gardens
(5 acres); Grounds (114 acres); Library Sedgwick Garden Library (extensive collection
of horticultural periodicals, books; Mon-Fri, 9am-5pm); Trails (2 miles)
Activities: Guided Tours Groups (arrange in advance, $5/person), Gardens (seasonal)

Originally, Long Hill was the summer home of Ellery Sedgwick, editor of the *Atlantic Monthly*, and his wife Mabel Cabot Sedgwick, author of *The Garden Month by Month*. The estate house, built in 1921, is a copy of the Isaac Ball House in Charleston, South Carolina. It contains original woodwork from the Ball House, which Mr. Sedgwick purchased after that house had been abandoned. The gardens were first designed and planted by Mrs. Sedgwick. After her death in 1937, Mr. Sedgwick's second wife, the former Marjorie Russell of England, a distinguished gardener and propagator of rare plants, added many plants to the gardens, including unusual species and varieties of trees and shrubs, many introduced by the Arnold Arboretum. The gardens, containing over 400 species of plants, are laid out in a series of separate garden areas surrounding the house, each distinct in its own way and accented by a tremendous diversity of garden ornaments, structures, and statuary. They are especially noted for their extensive plantings of spring bulbs, azaleas, rhododendrons, and tree peonies. These areas are flanked on all sides by over 100 acres of woodland as well as an apple orchard and meadow. An interpretive brochure and map is available for free on-site. Long Hill is now the headquarters of a non-profit conservation organization, the Trustees of Reservations.

BOSTON

BOSTON PUBLIC GARDEN

Bounded by Arlington, Beacon, Boylston & Charles Streets, Boston,
MA 02201
Tel: (617) 635-7381; Fax: (617) 635-7255
Internet Address: http://www.ci.boston.ma.us/parks/
Admission: Free
Established: 1837
Membership: Y
Wheelchair Accessible: Y
Parking: Underground public garage enter from Charles Street
Open: Daily, dawn-10pm
Facilities: Grounds (24 acres)
Activities: Swan Boats

Situated adjacent to the Boston Common, the Boston Public Garden was the nation's first botanical garden, founded in 1837. Though nothing remains of the original garden, the site continues to be "a green and flowering oasis in the heart of a great metropolis." Today, it contains plantings chosen for their ornamental excellence and botanical diversity as well as approximately 125 different kinds of trees.

FENWAY PARK—JAMES P. KELLEHER ROSE GARDEN

Back Bay Fens, Park Drive, Boston, MA 02118
Tel: (617) 635-4505
Admission: Free
Parking: On street
Open: Daily, 7:30am-dusk
Facilities: Grounds (1931 design by landscape architect Arthur Shurcliff)

Located in the Back Bay Fens across from the Museum of Fine Arts, the Kelleher Rose Garden was designed by landscape architect Arthur Shurcliff. An All-America Rose Selections display garden, it offers over 800 roses representing over 100 varieties bordered by yew hedges. The Emerald Necklace Conservancy, in conjunction with the Boston Parks

Department, began a renewal effort in 2003. Also of possible interest, the oldest remaining wartime "Victory Garden" (1941) is found within the Back Bay Fens. Planted by citizens, it is a well-loved and tended community garden containing approximately 300 plots of flowers and vegetables.

ISABELLA STEWART GARDNER MUSEUM

280 The Fenway, Boston, MA 02115
Tel: (617) 566-1401; Fax: (617) 566-7653
Internet Address: http://www.gardnermuseum.org
Admission: Fee: adult $10.00, child (<18) free,
student $5.00, senior $7.00.
New Year's Day: Free
Attendance: 180,000
Established: 1900
Membership: Y
Wheelchair Accessible: Y
Parking: Metered on street and nearby commercial garage
Open: Tuesday to Sunday, 11am-5pm; Monday holidays, call for hours.
Closed: Thanksgiving Day, Christmas Day
Facilities: Architecture (15th-century Venetian inspired palace, 1901); Food Services
Café (Tues-Fri, 11:30am-4pm; Sat-Sun, 11am-4pm); Galleries; Library (by
appointment only); Shop
Activities: Concerts (late Sept-early May, Sat-Sun, 1:30pm); Guided Tours (Fri,
2:30pm); Lecture Series

Isabella Stewart Gardner Museum, Boston, MA.

The Isabella Stewart Gardner Museum, designed in the style of a fifteenth-century Venetian palace, combines architecture, paintings, sculpture, decorative arts, and the color and fragrance of a flowering interior courtyard to create a unique atmosphere and experience. Bearing the name of its creator, Isabella Stewart Gardner, the museum is the only private art collection in which the building and collection are the creation of one individual. Construction of the museum began in 1899 and was completed by 1901 after which Isabella Gardner undertook the task of arranging her collection within the museum walls before finally opening its doors to the public in 1903. The collection of paintings, sculpture, furniture, textiles, tapestries, lace, ceramics, metal work, prints, drawings, rare books, photographs, and correspondence is displayed in galleries on three floors, each room overlooking a central courtyard that is filled with changing flowers, plants, and trees, complemented by marble sculptures and a Roman mosaic tile floor.

MUSEUM OF FINE ARTS BOSTON—
TENSHIN-EN (JAPANESE GARDEN)

465 Huntington Avenue, Boston, MA 02115
Tel: (617) 267-9300
Internet Address: http://www.mfa.org
Admission: Free
Attendance: 1,000,000
Membership: Y
Wheelchair Accessible: Y
Parking: On site, outdoor surface lot & 472 space garage
Open: May to September, Daily, 10am-4pm
Facilities: Garden (Japanese, design by Kinsaku Nakane and Julie Moir Messervy)

The Tenshin-en (Garden of the Heart of Heaven) brings together elements and traditions drawn from Japan, the MFA, and New England in a seventeenth-century Japanese style. Over seventy species of plants, both Japanese and American, give color and texture to the garden. Cherries, Japanese maples, and pine evoke the changing seasons. Azaleas of many colors and varieties provide continuous bloom from spring to summer. Stone lanterns are used to light paths and highlight special areas of the garden design. Taken together, all the elements of the garden create a new interpretation of an ancient art form. In 2000, the *Journal of Japanese Gardening* ranked the garden as one of the ten highest-quality Japanese gardens outside of Japan, out of 300 sites surveyed.

BOYLSTON

TOWER HILL BOTANIC GARDEN—WORCESTER COUNTY HORTICULTURAL SOCIETY (AHS RAP)

11 French Drive, Boylston, MA 01505
Tel: (508) 869-6111; Fax: (508) 869-0314
Internet Address: http://www.towerhillbg.org
Admission: Fee: adult $8.00, child (<6) free, child (6-18) $5.00, senior $5.00; Free: May-August, Wednesday evenings, 5pm-8pm
Attendance: 30,000
Established: 1986
Membership: Y
Wheelchair Accessible: Y
Open: September to April, Tuesday to Sunday, 10am-5pm; May to August, Tuesday, 10am-5pm; Wednesday, 10am-8pm; Thursday to Sunday, 10am-5pm; Holiday Mondays, 10am-5pm
Closed: New Year's Day, Thanksgiving Day, Christmas Day
Facilities: Arboretum; Food Services TWIGS Café (May-Oct, 10am-4pm); Gardens (apple orchard, cottage, lawn, secret, systematic, wildlife); Grounds (132 acres); Library (7,000 volumes); Orangerie (4,000 square feet); Picnic Area; Shop; Trails
Activities: Education Programs New England School of Gardening; Flower Shows; Guided Tours (May-Oct, Sun, 2pm); Lectures; Plant Sales; Temporary Exhibitions; Workshops (adults and children)

Tower Hill offers a variety of distinctive gardens, meadows, and woodland trails, with a seasonal display of over 95,000 flowering bulbs. The Entry Court and Entry Garden present a mix of unusual annuals, ground covers, shrubs, and trees. The green expanse of the Lawn Garden is bordered by 350 species and varieties of trees and shrubs, underplanted with easy-care perennials, such as peonies, day lilies, Siberian iris, and a variety of ground covers. To the south of the Lawn Garden, the Secret Garden features a fountain with garden pool, statuary, a wide variety of grasses, and perennials and annuals selected for their fragrance. In the Systematic Garden, plant families are arranged according to their evolutionary sequence, from ancient to modern. Complementing the historic farmhouse on the site are a cottage garden composed of annuals, perennials, and woody plants; a vegetable garden featuring unusual vegetable and annuals; and an orchard displaying 238 trees of 119 pre-twentieth century apple varieties. Situated in a protected spot below the main gardens, the Wildlife Garden features singing birds, colorful butterflies, and flying bats in their natural habitat. In the Orangerie, four large palms provide a canopy, beneath which is found a selection of citrus trees and an understory composed of shrubs, perennials, annuals, and bulbs chosen for their natural winter bloom or other winter attributes. The Worcester County Horticultural Society, which operates Tower Hill Botanic Garden as its headquarters, has adopted an ambitious development plan scheduled to be fully complete in 2040.

BROOKLINE

FREDERICK LAW OLMSTED NATIONAL HISTORIC SITE (FAIRSTED)

99 Warren Street at Dudley Street, Brookline, MA 02445
Tel: (617) 566-1689; Fax: (617) 232-4073
Internet Address: http://www.nps.gov/frla
Admission: Free
Attendance: 6,870
Wheelchair Accessible: P
Parking: On site, handicapped space available
Open: Daily, 10am-4:30pm
Closed: New Year's Day, Thanksgiving Day, Christmas Day
Facilities: Architecture (residence); Grounds (7 acres); Shop (books)
Activities: Education Programs; Guided Tours Design Office (10:30am-3:30pm on the
½ hour); Fairsted residential landscape (may be available in season); House, Office, &
Grounds (Fri-Sun, 10am-4:30pm)

Frederick Law Olmsted (1822-1903) is recognized as the founder of American landscape
architecture and the nation's foremost park maker. Olmsted moved his home to suburban
Boston in 1883 and established at Fairsted, the world's first full-scale professional office for
the practice of landscape design. Managed by the National Park Service, the restored
Fairsted historic landscape and century-old design office remain virtually unchanged from
the days when the Olmsted firm's activity was at its height. Housed within the office complex are nearly 1,000,000 original design records detailing work on many of America's
most treasured landscapes including the U. S. Capitol and White House Grounds; Great
Smoky Mountains and Acadia National Parks; Yosemite Valley; New York's Central Park;
and whole park systems in cities such as Seattle, Boston, and Louisville. First-floor exhibits
explore the history and innovations of Frederick Law Olmsted and his firm through a study
of some of the thousands of Olmsted designed landscapes. A park brochure, a guide to the
Olmsted Archives, a walking guide to the Fairsted residential landscape, and brochure information on nearby national parks and historic designed landscapes (including Boston's
"Emerald Necklace" parks) are available. Fairsted has been designated a National Historic
Landmark and is listed in the National Register of Historic Places.

CAMBRIDGE

MOUNT AUBURN CEMETERY

580 Mount Auburn Street (near Cambridge/Watertown town line), Cambridge, MA
02138-5529
Tel: (617) 547-7105; Fax: (617) 876-4405
Internet Address: http://www.mountauburn.org/
Established: 1831
Open: October to April, Daily, 8am-5pm; May to September, Daily, 8am-7pm
Facilities: Grounds (175 acres); Roads and Paths (10 miles)
Activities: Guided Tours General (offered by Friends of Mount Auburn, recorded
schedule (617) 547-7105, x821), Groups (arrange in advance)

Founded in 1831 by the Massachusetts Horticultural Society, Mount Auburn was the
first landscaped cemetery in America and was influential in the creation of America's public

parks. Still an active cemetery, it contains over 5,500 trees and woody plants representing nearly 700 species and varieties as well as thousands of bulbs and summer annuals. The landscaping reflects a variety of different styles ranging from Victorian-era plantings to contemporary gardens, from natural woodlands to formal ornamental gardens, and from sweeping vistas through majestic trees to small enclosed spaces. A map and brochure are available at the entrance gate; walking and driving tour audio tapes are also available for rental or purchase. Because of its importance as one of the country's most significant designed landscapes, the cemetery has been designated a National Historic Landmark.

CANTON

ELEANOR CABOT BRADLEY ESTATE

2468B Washington Street (Route 138), Canton, MA 02021
Tel: (781) 821-2977; Fax: (781) 821-4027
Internet Address: http://www.thetrustees.org/
Admission: Free
Established: 1991
Membership: Y
Wheelchair Accessible: P
Parking: Free on site
Open: Daily, sunrise-sunset
Facilities: Architecture (manor house, 1902 by Charles Platt); Gardens (cutting, formal Italianate, orchard); Greenhouses; Grounds (90 acres); Trails (woodland, 2 miles)

Situated in the shadow of Great Blue Hill, the Eleanor Cabot Bradley Estate Reservation includes formal gardens and estate outbuilding complexes as well as agricultural fields and a woodland trail system. The formal, brick lattice-walled Italianate garden was designed in concert with the main house. With entrances and paths on axis with the house and at right angles to one another, perennial, bulb, and annual plantings have been composed within a series of brick-edged parterres around a tapis vert or green carpet of grass. Surrounding the formal garden, and embracing the edges of the garden wall, are naturalistic plantings of rhododendron, dogwood, and azalea that provide a dramatic contrast to the formality and structure of the garden. Within easy walking distance of the main house and formal garden is the working part of the estate including walled cutting garden, small orchard, greenhouses, sunken camellia house, and assorted outbuildings. Fifteen acres of open field and pasture help preserve the property's agricultural heritage and reflect landscape patterns of the early nineteenth century. In the woodlands are pockets of specimen plantings, which may be accessed by cart paths and foot trails. An interpretive trail map is available on site. A property of the Trustees of Reservations, the organization's Southeast Regional Office is headquartered on the second floor of the main house.

DANVERS

GLEN MAGNA FARMS AND ESTATE—GARDENS

Endicott Park (off Ingersoll Street), Danvers, MA 01923
Tel: (978) 774-9165
Admission: Fee (by appointment): adult $5.00

Open: by appointment
Facilities: Architecture Glen Magna (original residence, 1790; Georgian Revival, 1890s), Derby Summer House (Federal-style garden house 1794, design by Samuel McIntire); Gardens (formal, orchard, rose); Grounds Endicott Park (165 acres), Glen Magna (11 acres)
Activities: Guided Tours Garden ($5/person)

Glen Magna mansion and grounds, owned by the Danvers Historical Society, are surrounded by town-owned Endicott Park. The formal gardens, designed by Frederick Law Olmsted and Joseph Chamberlin, contain many of their original and now rare flower and plant species. Of particular interest is the Derby Summer House, or Tea House, on the Glen Magna grounds. This ornate Federal-style garden house was moved here in 1901. The two-and-a-half story structure is decorated with pilasters, swags, and Grecian urns, and is topped with carvings of a farmer and a milkmaid. An arched door leads to a walled rose garden designed by Herbert Browne. The park contains a combination of developed and natural landscapes comprised of woodlands, orchards, wetlands, and fields.

DOVER

PETERS RESERVATION

Farm Road, Dover, MA 02030
Tel: (508) 785-0339
Internet Address: http://www.thetrustees.org/
Admission: Free
Established: 1988
Membership: Y
Open: Daily, sunrise-sunset
Facilities: Grounds (97 acres, plantings were laid out by landscape architect Fletcher Steele); Picnic Area; Trails (2½ miles)

The site is dominated by an oak and hickory forest woodland, whose trails and understory plantings including a large, massed planting of Dexter hybrid rhododendrons, were laid out by landscape architect Fletcher Steele. A plantation of red pines lines much of the reservation's frontage on the Charles River. Named for the family who purchased the property as a family retreat in 1917, the site is a property of the Trustees of Reservations, the nation's oldest private, statewide conservation and preservation organization.

FALMOUTH

FALMOUTH HISTORICAL SOCIETY—
MUSEUMS ON THE GREEN-GARDENS

55 & 65 Palmer Avenue (Route 28 on the Village Green), Falmouth, MA 02541
Tel: (508) 548-4857; Fax: (508) 540-0968
Internet Address: http://www.falmouthhistoricalsociety.org/
Admission: Fee: adult $5.00, child (<12) free
Membership: Y
Wheelchair Accessible: P

Parking: Parking at 55 and 65 Palmer Avenue
Open: Museums: late June to late September, Tuesday to Saturday, 10am-4pm;
Museums: late September to October, Saturday to Sunday, 10am-4pm
Best Time(s) of Year to Visit: Summer to Fall
Facilities: Architecture Conant House (1724, half-cape), Hallett Barn
(2002 reconstructed, hand-pegged "side-drive" barn), Julia Wood House
(Federal residence, 1790); Gardens (period; Colonial, herb, Memorial Park);
Grounds (2 acres)
Activities: Guided Tours Historic Houses

Situated on the grounds of the Julia Wood House and Conant House (both Falmouth Historical Society properties) are a recreated colonial boxwood garden, an
herb garden, and memorial park. The gardens are maintained by the Falmouth Garden
Club.

FRAMINGHAM

NEW ENGLAND WILD FLOWER SOCIETY—GARDEN IN THE WOODS

180 Hemenway Road, Framingham, MA 01701-2699
Tel: (508) 877-7630; Fax: (508) 877-3658; TDDY: (508) 877-6553
Internet Address: http://www.newfs.org/garden.htm
Admission: Fee: adult $7.00, child $3.00, student $5.00, senior $5.00
Attendance: 40,000
Established: 1930
Membership: Y
Wheelchair Accessible: Y
Parking: Free on site
Open: April 15 to June 15, Daily, 9am-7pm; June 16 to October, Tuesday to Sunday,
9am-5pm
Best Time(s) of Year to Visit: May to August
Facilities: Garden (native plant); Grounds (45 acres); Herbarium; Library The
Lawrence Newcomb Library (3,000 volumes & 25,000 botanical images; open
Tues-Fri, 9am-4pm); Shop (plants, books, garden equipment); Trails;
Visitors Center
Activities: Education Programs (adults and children, largest native plant program in
America); Garden Tours (adults; Mon-Sat, 10am; Sun, 2pm); Guided Tours Groups
(by reservation); Lectures; Nature Walks (children); Plant Sales

The headquarters of the New England Wild Flower Society, the Garden in the Woods
displays more than 1,500 varieties of native plants. Of special interest is the unique New
England Garden of Rare and Endangered Plants, the first comprehensive collection of
New England's rare plant species. Displaying 200 rare and endangered species in an intimate setting, this two-acre garden contains more rare New England plant species than
most people would encounter in the wild in a lifetime. The Garden in the Woods is accredited by the American Association of Museums. Established in 1900, the New England
Wild Flower Society is America's oldest conservation organization and unique among
such organizations in having its own botanic garden.

IPSWICH

JOHN WHIPPLE HOUSE—GARDEN

1 south Village Green, Ipswich, MA 01938-2321
Tel: (508) 356-2811
Internet Address: http://www.ipswichma.com/ihs/
Admission: Fee $7.00, child (6-12) $3.00
Open: May 15 to October 15, Wednesday to Saturday, 10am-4pm; Sunday, 1pm-4pm
Facilities: Architecture (residence, prior to 1650 with large addition in 1670); Garden
(historic, Colonial)
Activities: Guided Tours (last tour 3pm; groups 15+ reserve in advance)

Home to the first six generations of the Whipple family, the house contains furnishings
and decorative arts from the period of the Massachusetts Bay Colony. In front of the
house is a colonial-style garden designed originally by landscape architect Arthur Shurcliff of Colonial Williamsburg fame. It was replanted about 1960 by well-known garden
scholar Ann Leighton, (a.k.a. Isadore Smith), as an authentic seventeenth century-style
housewife's garden. The site is a property of the Ipswich Historical Society.

JAMAICA PLAIN

ARNOLD ARBORETUM OF HARVARD UNIVERSITY (AHS RAP)

125 Arborway, Jamaica Plain, MA 02130-3519
Tel: (617) 524-1718; Fax: (617) 524-1418
Internet Address: http://arboretum.harvard.edu/
Admission: Voluntary contribution
Attendance: 250,000
Established: 1872
Membership: Y
Wheelchair Accessible: Y
Parking: Parking available along arboretum perimeter
Open: Grounds, daily, sunrise-sunset; Hunnewell Building, Monday to Friday, 9am-
4pm; Saturday, 10am-4pm; Sunday, noon-4pm
Best Time(s) of Year to Visit: Spring to Fall
Closed: Legal holidays
Facilities: Arboretum (1878-1892 design by Charles Sprague Sargent & Frederick Law
Olmsted); Grounds (265 acres); Herbarium (1.5 million specimens); Library (100,000
volumes, access to recognized scholars/verified students); Special Collections (bonsai,
beech, crab apple, honeysuckle, lilac, magnolia, oak, rhododendron,); Visitors Center
Hunnewell Building
Activities: Education Programs (adults, undergraduate/graduate students, and
children); Guided Tours (seasonally); Lectures; Lilac Sunday (May); Permanent
Exhibits; Plant Sale (September); Temporary Exhibitions

Located in the Jamaica Plain section of Boston, the Arnold Arboretum manages a collection of hardy trees, shrubs, and vines and associated herbarium and library collections.

The grounds were planned and designed by the arboretum's first director, Charles Sprague Sargent, in collaboration with the landscape architect Frederick Law Olmsted as part of Boston's Emerald Necklace park system. Olmsted laid out the path and roadway system and designated areas within the arboretum for specific groups of plants. Early on, Sargent made a decision to arrange the plant collections by family and genus, following the then generally accepted classification system of Bentham and Hooker. The arboretum continues to maintain its living collections in the naturalistic style originally established by Sargent and Olmsted. The living collections consist of over 15,000 individual plants representing over 4,400 botanical and horticultural taxa with particular emphasis on the woody species of North America and eastern Asia. Highlights include lilacs (over 300 plants representing about 185 different varieties) and the bonsai collection as well as especially comprehensive representations of beech, honeysuckle, magnolia, crab apple, oak, rhododendron, and lilac. The arboretum is an allied institution within the central administration of Harvard University.

LENOX

THE MOUNT—EDITH WHARTON'S ESTATE AND GARDENS

2 Plunkett Street (off Route 7), Lenox, MA 01240
Tel: (413) 637-1899; Fax: (413) 637-0619
Internet Address: http://www.edithwharton.org
Admission: Fee: adult $16.00, child (<12) free, student $8.00
Attendance: 25,000
Membership: Y
Wheelchair Accessible: Y
Parking: Ample parking free on site
Open: May to October, daily, 9am-5pm
Facilities: Architecture (17th-century English manor-style residence, 1902 design by New York architect Francis L.V. Hoppin); Food Services Terrace Café (sandwiches, salads & desserts; mid-June-Labor Day, daily, 11am-4pm); Gardens (formal, English, French, Italian); Grounds Garden (3 acres); Shop (books)
Activities: Guided Tours (hourly); Lecture Series Civilized Living (summer, Thurs); Women of Achievement (summer, Mon); Self-Guided Tours

The Mount—Edith Wharton's estate and gardens, Lenox, MA.

One of America's greatest authors, Edith Wharton wrote over forty books in forty years including such best-selling novels as *The Age of Innocence*, *Ethan Frome*, and *The House of Mirth*, and authoritative works on architecture, interior design, and gardens. Like Thomas Jefferson's Monticello, the Mount is an autobiographical house that reflects the life and work of its remarkable creator, and today is recognized as an icon of American architecture and garden design. Wharton constructed the forty-two-room Mount as a writer's retreat in 1902, at the height of the Gilded Age. Conceived and executed between 1903 and 1907, the gardens are an extremely significant component of the estate; they reflect the classical design principles of balance, symmetry, and suitability discussed in her 1904 book, *Italian Villas and Their Gardens*, written while she was living at the Mount. The three acres of formal gardens are designed as architectural compositions, divided into rooms, and planned in concert with the house and the surrounding natural landscape. The three acres of formal gardens include a "lime walk" of linden trees, a sunken Italian walled garden and a rock garden with two flights of grass steps. Other professionals contributed advice on plants and construction, but Wharton planned and planted her own flower gardens. Her niece, famous landscape gardener Beatrix Farrand, laid out the entrance drive and the kitchen garden, but made no known subsequent plans. Writing about her gardens in a letter to Morton Fullerton in 1911, she declared, "The Place is really beautiful . . . I was amazed at the success of my [efforts]. Decidedly, I'm a better landscape gardener than novelist, and this place, every line of which is my own work, far surpasses *The House of Mirth*." Since 1999, more than $2.5 million has been invested in restoring the original gardens and more than 2,000 historically accurate plantings are in place. The Mount has been designated a National Historic Landmark and is also listed on the National and the State Registers of Historic Places.

LINCOLN

CODMAN ESTATE (THE GRANGE)—GARDENS

Codman Road, Lincoln, MA 01773
Tel: (781) 259-8843; Fax: (781) 227-2904
Internet Address: http://www.historicnewengland.org/visit/homes/codman.htm
Admission: Fee (house tour): adult $5.00, child $2.50, senior $4.50
Established: 1969
Membership: Y
Wheelchair Accessible: N
Open: June to October 15, Saturday, 11am-5pm.
Facilities: Architecture (Georgian Mansion, c. 1740); Gardens (formal Italian, English cutting garden); Landscaped Grounds (15 acres)
Activities: Guided Tours (11am, noon, 1pm, 2pm, 3pm, & 4pm; groups reserve in advance); Lectures

Overlooking a prospect of farm and pleasure grounds, this gentleman's country seat was inhabited by five generations of the Codman family. The interiors, richly furnished with portraits, memorabilia, and art works collected in Europe, preserve the decorative schemes of every era, including those of noted interior designer Ogden Codman, Jr. The grounds feature a hidden Italianate garden, ca. 1900, with perennial beds, statuary, and a reflecting pool filled with water lilies as well as an English cottage garden, ca. 1930. The site is a property of Historic New England (formerly the Society for the Preservation of New England Antiquities).

LYNN

CITY OF LYNN—LYNN WOODS RESERVATION

106 Penny Brook Road at Great Woods Road, Lynn, MA 01905-1037
Tel: (781) 593-7773; Fax: (781) 477-7143
Internet Address: http://www.ci.lynn.ma.us/Public_Documents/
LynnMA_DPW/lynnwoods
Admission: Free
Established: 1881
Open: Daily, sunrise-sunset

Facilities: Amphitheater; Gardens (native plant, rose); Grounds Reserve (2,200 acres), Rose Garden (3 acres); Trails (30 miles)

The second largest municipal park in the United States, the site includes a rose garden. Originally planted in the 1920s and restored in 1994, the Rose Garden is elegantly landscaped with rose bushes, perennials, and a variety of trees.

MARBLEHEAD

JEREMIAH LEE MANSION—GARDENS

161 Washington Street, Marblehead, MA 01945
Tel: (781) 631-1069; Fax: (781) 631-0917
Internet Address: http://marbleheadmuseum.org/
Admission: Fee: adult $5.00, child free, student $4.50, senior $4.50
Established: 1930
Wheelchair Accessible: P
Parking: On-street parking
Open: June to October, Tuesday to Saturday, 10am-4pm
Facilities: Architecture (Georgian residence, 1768); Gardens (period; herb, perennial, sundial)
Activities: Guided Tours (June-Oct, Tues-Sat, 10am-4pm)

The eighteenth-century-style gardens, including a perennial border, a sundial garden, a lower woodland garden, and an herb garden, have been designed and cared for by the Marblehead Garden Club. The house, built by wealthy shipowner and patriot Colonel Jeremiah Lee, was one of the most opulent of its day. It is furnished with period antiques. Preserved by the Marblehead Historical Society, the site is listed on the National Register of Historic Places.

MARTHA'S VINEYARD

MYTOI JAPANESE GARDEN

Dike Bridge Road, Chappaquiddick Island, Martha's Vineyard,
MA 02539
Tel: (508) 627-7689; Fax: (508) 627-3659
Internet Address: http://www.thetrustees.org/
Established: 1976
Parking: Free on site
Open: Daily, 24 hours
Facilities: Garden (Japanese, restoration design by landscape architect Julie Messervy); Grounds (14 acres); Picnic Area

Mytoi, a small, Japanese-style garden and pine forest, contains native and exotic plants and trees in a peaceful setting on a small pond with a meandering stream. There is no staff on site, but a visitor brochure is available at a dispenser in the parking lot. The site is a property of the Trustees of Reservations, the nation's oldest private, statewide conservation and preservation organization.

POLLY HILL ARBORETUM (AHS RAP)

809 State Road, West Tisbury, MA 02575
Tel: (508) 683-9426; Fax: (508) 696-0481
Internet Address: http://www.pollyhillarboretum.org/
Admission: Suggested contribution: adult $5.00, child (<13) free
Established: 1996
Parking: Free on site
Open: Memorial Day to Columbus Day, Thursday to Tuesday, 7am-7pm; Columbus
Day to Memorial Day, Thursday to Tuesday, sunrise-sunset.
Best Time(s) of Year to Visit: Spring (dogwood, rhododendron, viburnum), late Spring
to early Summer (stewartia), Fall (foliage), Winter (conifer, holly)
Facilities: Arboretum; Architecture (farmhouse, 1670; far barn, 1750); Grounds
Cultivated (20 acres), Woodland (40 acres); Special Collections (azalea); Visitor
Center (Memorial Day-Sept, Thurs-Tues, 9:30am-4pm; Oct-Memorial Day, Sat-Sun,
9:30am-4pm)
Activities: Classes; Education Programs; Guided Tours (Jun, Fri-Sun, 10am & 2pm;
Jul-Aug, Thurs-Tues, 10am & 2pm; Sept, Thurs-Tues, 2pm; Oct, Sat-Sun, 2pm;
groups, reserve in advance); Workshops

Crisscrossed by old stone walls surrounding open, wildflower-filled meadows and charac-
terized by vernacular Vineyard architecture, the arboretum has twenty acres under cultivation
while preserving an additional forty acres as native woodland. Arboretum highlights include a
dogwood allée, a pleached hornbeam arbor, and Polly's Play Pen, a fenced area containing
many of Polly Hill's plant introductions, including the famous North Tisbury azaleas and a
wide variety of other rare and interesting species. Begun in 1958 by horticulturist Polly Hill,
the arboretum was established as a not-for-profit institution in 1996. Its primary goals are to
determine those plants that can be successfully cultivated on Martha's Vineyard, to develop
and introduce outstanding plants of ornamental merit to American horticulture, and to serve
as a sanctuary for plants that are threatened by extinction in their native habitats.

MONSON

NORCROSS WILDLIFE SANCTUARY (TUPPER HILL)

30 Peck Road, Monson, MA 01057
Tel: (413) 267-9654
Internet Address: http://www.norcrossws.org
Admission: Free
Established: 1939
Open: June to December, Monday to Saturday, 9am-4pm; January to May, Tuesday to
Saturday, 9am-4pm
Closed: Legal holidays
Facilities: Gardens (herb, native plant, rose); Greenhouse; Grounds (4,000 acres);
Museums (2 natural history); Picnic Area; Trails
(3 miles); Visitor Center
Activities: Education Programs (Sept-Jun, Tues-Fri, 10am, reservation required, Jan-Mar,
Sat, 10am, reservation required); Guided Tours (Apr-Oct)

Devoted to the preservation and propagation of rare and endangered plants native to
the Appalachian range from the Carolinas through the Maritimes, the sanctuary offers

naturalistic and informal gardens featuring a wide variety of plants, varying terrain, and moisture conditions; an herb garden with culinary, fragrance, medicinal, household and dye beds; and a rose garden.

NEW BEDFORD

THE ROTCH-JONES-DUFF HOUSE AND GARDEN MUSEUM, INC. (R-J-D)

396 County Street, New Bedford, MA 02740
Tel: (508) 997-1401; Fax: (508) 997-6846
Internet Address: http://www.rjdmuseum.org
Admission: Fee: adult $5.00, child (<13) $2.00, student $4.00, senior $4.00
Attendance: 10,000
Established: 1984
Membership: Y
Wheelchair Accessible: Y
Open: January to May, Tuesday to Saturday, 10am-4pm; Sunday, noon-4pm; June to December, Monday to Saturday, 10am-4pm; Sunday, noon-4pm
Closed: Major holidays
Best Time(s) of Year to Visit: June to September
Facilities: Architecture (Greek Revival mansion, 1834 design attributed to Richard Upjohn); Gardens (historic, boxwood/rose parterre, cutting, wildflower walk); Grounds (city block)
Activities: Concerts (summer, Friday evenings); Education Programs (adults); Guided Tours (groups 15+, reserve in advance, $5.00/person); Lectures (spring & fall); Temporary Exhibitions (4/year)

Built for Quaker whaling merchant William Rotch, Jr., between 1834-1981, three prominent families owned this twenty-eight-room Greek Revival mansion and formal gardens. The site chronicles 150 years of economic, social, and domestic life in New Bedford. The museum collections include many original furnishings, art, and decor of the Rotch, Jones, and Duff families as well as a New Bedford glass collection. The grounds encompass a full city block of gardens including a wildflower walk, a formal boxwood rose parterre garden, a cutting garden, a boxwood specimen garden, and an historic wood lattice pergola.

NEWBURYPORT

MAUDSLAY STATE PARK (MAUDSLAY)

Curzon Mill Road (off Ferry Road), Newburyport, MA 01950
Tel: (978) 465-7223; Fax: (978) 463-6958
Internet Address: http://www.state.ma.us/dem/parks/maud.htm
Admission: Free
Attendance: 130,000
Established: 1985
Membership: Y
Wheelchair Accessible: P
Parking: 400 spaces on site, $2/auto
Open: Daily, dawn-dusk

Best Time(s) of Year to Visit: May to June (Azalea/Rhododendron Bloom), September to October
Facilities: Gardens (roses, orchids, vegetables, Italian, azaleas, dogwoods); Grounds (480 acres, original design by Charles Sprague Sargeant and Martha Brooks Hutcheson)
Activities: Education Programs May-Sept; Guided Walks May-Sept; Lectures by request; seasonal

Situated along the Merrimack and Artichoke rivers, the property was once the Moseley family country retreat. The houses are gone, but the grounds feature nineteenth-century gardens and plantings of ornamental trees and hybrid azaleas and rhododendrons, rolling meadows, towering pines, and one of the largest naturally-occurring stands of mountain laurel (forty acres) in Massachusetts.

NORTH ANDOVER

STEVENS-COOLIDGE PLACE—GARDENS

139 Andover Street (Route 133), North Andover, MA 01845
Tel: (978) 682-3580; Fax: (978) 682-2143
Internet Address: http://www.thetrustees.org/
Admission: Fee (House): adult $5.00, child (<16) $2.00, student $2.00; Free: Gardens
Attendance: 2,000
Established: 1962
Membership: Y
Wheelchair Accessible: Y
Parking: Free, east side of Chestnut Street, across from house
Open: Gardens, Daily, sunrise-sunset; House: Mother's Day to June, Sunday, 1pm-5pm; House: July to August, Wednesday, 2pm-4pm; Sunday, 1pm-5pm; House: September to Columbus Day, Sunday, 1pm-5pm
Best Time(s) of Year to Visit: July to September
Facilities: Architecture (Colonial Revival-style residence; early 19th-century house, remodeled by preservation architect Joseph Everett Chandler); Gardens (perennial, French-style potager, walled rose); Greenhouse; Grounds (91 acres; formal gardens [most designed by Joseph Chandler], pastures and woodlands)
Activities: Guided Tours Garden (groups 15+, $5/person), House; Lectures; Performances; Plant Sale (May)

The summer home (also known as Ashdale Farm) of author and diplomat John Gardner Coolidge, the house is filled with Chinese porcelains, early American furniture, oriental rugs, and cut glass. Five landscaped acres feature a perennial garden, a formal walled rose garden, a French-style potager garden, spacious lawns, specimen trees, and a serpentine brick wall copied from Thomas Jefferson's wall at the University of Virginia. An interpretive brochure with map is available for free on-site. Listed on the National Register of Historic Places, the site is a property of the Trustees of Reservations, the nation's oldest private, statewide conservation and preservation organization.

NORTHAMPTON

THE BOTANIC GARDEN OF SMITH COLLEGE (AHS RAP)

Lyman Conservatory, College Lane, Northampton, MA 01063
Tel: (413) 585-2740; Fax: (413) 585-2744

Internet Address: http://www.smith.edu/garden
Admission: Voluntary contribution
Attendance: 100,000
Established: 1895
Membership: Y
Wheelchair Accessible: Y
Parking: Limited in front of Conservatory and on Elm Street
Open: Lyman Conservatory, Daily, 8:30am-4pm
Best Time(s) of Year to Visit: March-June to Sept-Nov.
Facilities: Arboretum Campus (127 acres); Gardens (herb, Japanese, rock, rose,
perennial, systematics); Greenhouses
Lyman Conservatory (12,000 square feet, earliest 1895 by Lord and Burnham);
Grounds Campus (150 acres, original 1893
design F.L. Olmsted & Co., landscape architects (Brookline, MA)); Herbarium Burton
Hall (60,000 specimens)
Activities: Arboretum (open dawn to dusk); Education Programs (undergraduate
college students); Flower Shows Lyman Conservatory (Spring Bulb, early March; Fall
Chrysanthemum, early November); Guided Tours (groups, schedule in advance; audio
tours available); Permanent Exhibits; Temporary Exhibitions (in Church Exhibition
Gallery)

The entire campus of Smith College was planned over one hundred years ago as a
botanic garden and arboretum, designed by the landscape architecture firm of Frederick
Law Olmsted. Today, the Botanic Garden encompasses the 125-contiguous-acre college
campus; the Lyman Conservatory, with 12,000 square feet under glass; and a variety of
specialty gardens, which contain over 7,000 labeled and mapped plants.

PITTSFIELD

HANCOCK SHAKER VILLAGE—FARM AND GARDENS (HSV)

Route 20, Pittsfield, MA 01202
Tel: (800) 817-1137; Fax: (413) 447-9357
Internet Address: http://www.hancockshakervillage.org
Admission: Fee(late May-late Oct): adult $15.00, child (<18)-free; Fee (late Oct-late
May): adult $12.50
Parking: Free on site
Open: Late May to late October, Daily, 9:30am-5pm; late October to late May,
Daily, 10am-3pm
Closed: Thanksgiving Day
Facilities: Architecture (Shaker village 1790-1960, 21 original buildings); Food
Services (seasonal café); Gardens (field crops, herb, heirloom vegetable, seed saving);
Picnic Area; Shop Museum Shop (a variety of garden accessories); Special Collections
(19th-century medicinal herbs, rare heirloom vegetables and seeds); Visitor Center
Activities: Demonstrations; Education Programs; Guided Tours (Mon following
Columbus Day to Fri before Memorial Day, call for times); Lectures; Self-Guided
Tours (Memorial Day weekend to weekend following Columbus Day)

Farming was at the heart of all Shaker communities and their interest in agricultural
experimentation and technology made their farms models of efficiency and innovation.
Heirloom vegetable gardens are planted and tended using documented techniques from
the 1843 Shaker *Gardener's Manual.* The varieties of vegetables chosen are based on
Shaker seed lists from the 1800s and many are rare and difficult to find today. The vil-

lage's specimen herb garden contains over 140 of the more than 300 types of plants listed in the Shaker's 1873 *Druggist's Handbook of Pure Botanic Preparations*. HSV has one of the largest Shaker medicinal herb gardens.

QUINCY

ADAMS NATIONAL HISTORIC PARK—GARDENS

135 Adams Street, Quincy, MA 02169
Tel: (617) 770-1175
Internet Address: http://www.nps.gov/adam/
Admission: Fee: adult $2.00, child (<16) free
Attendance: 1,000,000
Established: 1946
Membership: N
Parking: On-street parking available
Open: Historic Homes: mid-April to mid-November, Daily, 9am-5pm; Visitor Center mid-April to mid-November, Daily, 9am-5pm; Visitor Center: mid-November to mid-April, Tuesday to Friday, 10am-4pm
Facilities: Architecture (3 historic residences and other structures); Gardens Old House (formal, orchard); Grounds (11 acres); Visitors Center (Presidents Place Galleria, 1250 Hancock Street)
Activities: Guided Tours (9:45am, 11:15am, noon, 12:45pm, 2:15pm, & 3pm); Lecture Series (last week of June)

Managed by the National Park Service, the site consists of eleven historic structures and a cultural landscape totaling almost forteen acres. The main historic features include the John Adams Birthplace (133 Franklin Street), the John Quincy Adams Birthplace (141 Franklin Street); and the "Old House" (135 Adams Street), home to four generations of the Adams family; and the United First Parish Church, where both presidents and the first ladies are entombed in the Adams family crypt. A formal garden and apple orchard surrounds "Old House." The homes can only be seen on a guided tour; tickets and tour registration may be accomplished at the visitor center.

SHELBURNE FALLS

BRIDGE OF FLOWERS

75 Bridge Street, Shelburne Falls, MA 01370
Tel: (413) 625-2544
Internet Address: http://www.shelburnefalls.com/
Admission: Free
Attendance: 24,000
Established: 1929
Parking: On-street parking and nearby lot (on Water Street)
Open: April to October, dawn to dusk
Facilities: Architecture (trolley bridge, 1908)

Since 1929, the Shelburne Falls Women's Club has annually transformed this former 400-foot trolley bridge spanning the Deerfield River into a bridge of flowers. Over 500 varieties of plantings assure beautiful flowers from April tulips through fall chrysanthemums.

SOUTH DEERFIELD

MAGIC WINGS BUTTERFLY CONSERVATORY AND GARDENS

281 Greenfield Street (Routes 5 & 10), South Deerfield, MA 01373
Tel: (413) 665-2805; Fax: (413) 665-4062
Internet Address: http://magicwings.net/
Admission: Fee: adult $7.50, child (<3) free, child (3-17) $4.50, student $4.50, senior $6.50; Fee (Wednesdays): Senior, $5.00
Attendance: 200,000
Established: 2000
Membership: Y
Wheelchair Accessible: N
Parking: On site
Open: Summer, daily, 9am-6pm; Winter, daily, 9am-5pm.
Closed: Thanksgiving Day, Christmas Day
Facilities: Conservatory (8,000 square feet); Food Services Flying Rainbows Café; Gallery; Garden (1 ½ acre, butterfly); Grounds (5 ½ acres); Shops (gift & garden)
Activities: Guided Tours

Magic Wings Butterfly Conservatory and Gardens consists of a conservatory housing native and tropical butterflies and moths from around the world and an outdoor garden area planted with native flowers and trees.

SOUTH HADLEY

MOUNT HOLYOKE COLLEGE BOTANIC GARDEN

50 College Street, South Hadley, MA 01075-6440
Tel: (413) 538-2116; Fax: (413) 538-2144
Internet Address: http://www.mtholyoke.edu/acad/resources/green.shtml
Admission: Free
Wheelchair Accessible: Y
Open: Talcott Greenhouse, Monday to Friday, 9am-4pm; Saturday to Sunday, 1pm-4pm; Arboretum and Gardens, sunrise-sunset
Facilities: Arboretum Campus (250 acres); Gardens (perennial, rock, shade); Greenhouse Talcott Greenhouse (6,500 square feet, constructed 1897-98)
Activities: Flower Show Annual Spring Flower Show (March); Lectures

The Mount Holyoke College Botanic Garden includes the Talcott Greenhouse complex, a solar greenhouse, a 250-acre collection of living woody and herbaceous plants on the college campus, and 550 acres of relatively undisturbed natural communities. The main campus is an arboretum with a diverse collection of trees and shrubs. Individual specialty gardens on campus include the 1904 Garden, containing mostly sun-loving herbaceous perennials; a rock garden, featuring alpine and rock garden plants as well as a small frog pond and shade garden; a rhododendron garden with many plantings of shade-loving woodland perennials, including many interesting species from temperate eastern Asia; the Chapel Garden employing trees, shrubs, and herbaceous perennials in the college colors of blue and white color scheme; courtyard gardens at the Ciruti Center for Foreign Languages, and Mount Holyoke College's conference facilities at the Willits-Hallowell Center. The Talcott Greenhouse complex, including its renovated Victorian glass house, is used for teaching, research, ornamental display, and plant propagation. About two-thirds of the complex is devoted to the permanent collection, which includes orchids, cacti and succulents, ferns, begonias, bromeliads, and aquatic plants as well as other tropical and sub-tropical plants.

STOCKBRIDGE

BERKSHIRE BOTANICAL GARDEN (AHS RAP)

Intersection of Routes 102 & 183, Stockbridge, MA 01262
Tel: (413) 298-3926; Fax: (413) 298-4897
Internet Address: http://www.berkshirebotanical.org/
Admission: Fee: adult $7.00, child (<12) free, student $5.00, senior $5.00
Attendance: 10,000
Established: 1934
Membership: Y
Wheelchair Accessible: P
Parking: Free on site
Open: May to October, daily, 10am-5pm
Best Time(s) of Year to Visit: mid-May to mid-September
Facilities: Gardens (cottage, herb, perennial, primrose meadow, native border, rock, rose, shade, ornamental vegetable, pond & wetland); Grounds (15 acres); Library (1,000 volumes, by appointment); Meeting Hall (150 seats); Shop (garden gear, books, ornaments, herb products); Solar Greenhouse; Special Collections (day lily, herbs)
Activities: Education Programs (adults and children); Events Fete des Fleurs (Gala) (mid-July), Flower Show (early August), Harvest Festival (1st weekend in October), Holiday Marketplace (early December); Guided Tours (groups, by appointment); Lectures; Plant Sale (May); Seasonal Exhibits; Workshops

The Berkshire Botanical Garden features eight acres of woodlands and eight acres of informal country gardens composed of plants that thrive in the Berkshires. Among its plantings are old fashioned rose, cottage, day lily, perennial, rock, herb, and vegetable gardens as well as a primrose meadow and a woodland pond garden.

CHESTERWOOD ESTATE

4 Williamsville Road off Route 183, Glendale Section, Stockbridge, MA 01262
Tel: (413) 298-3579; Fax: (413) 298-3973; TDDY: (413) 298-3579
Internet Address: http://www.chesterwood.net/
Admission: Fee: adult $10.00, child $5.00, student $7.00, senior $9.50, family $25.00
Attendance: 35,000
Established: 1955
Membership: Y
Wheelchair Accessible: Y
Parking: Free on site
Open: May to October, Daily, 10am-5pm
Facilities: Architecture (summer residence and studio of Daniel Chester French); Gallery; Garden; Grounds (120 acres); Library (use by scholars and researchers by appointment); Shop
Activities: Art Classes; Education Programs (students K-12); Gallery Talks; Guided Tours; Landscape Lectures; Lectures; Permanent Exhibits; Temporary Exhibitions

Chesterwood was the summer home of sculptor Daniel Chester French. The residence and studio at Chesterwood were designed by Henry Bacon, while French himself laid out the gardens and woodland walks. The property was donated in 1969 to the National Trust for Historic Preservation. Visitors can view French's studio, the Colonial Revival residence, and exhibits in the Barn Gallery. Chesterwood houses over 500 pieces of sculpture by French.

MISSION HOUSE

19 Main Street (at Sergeant Street), Stockbridge, MA 01262
Tel: (413) 298-3239; Fax: (413) 298-5239
Internet Address: http://www.thetrustees.org/
Admission: Fee: adult $6.00, child (6-12) $2.50
Established: 1948
Wheelchair Accessible: P
Parking: On street
Open: Memorial Day to Columbus Day, Daily, 10am-5pm
Facilities: Architecture (house, 1739); Garden (historic, Colonial Revival-style, 1928-1933 design by landscape architect Fletcher Steele); Grounds (½ acre)
Activities: Guided Tours (groups, by appointment, House and Garden (daily, 10am-5pm, last tour departs 4pm, free)

Built in 1739 by John Sergeant, a Yale graduate who had previously established a mission to the Mohican Indians, Mission House features gardens and a small museum on Native American history in South Berkshire County. The house was restored in 1928 by Mabel Choate and moved from nearby Prospect Hill to its current location. Colonial Revival gardens and related outbuildings were designed between 1928-1933 by noted landscape architect, Fletcher Steele. A free visitor brochure with map is available. Designated a National Historic Landmark, the site is a property of the Trustees of Reservations, whose Western Regional Office is located in the barn behind Mission House.

NAUMKEAG HOUSE AND GARDENS

5 Prospect Hill Road, Stockbridge, MA 01262
Tel: (413) 298-3239; Fax: (413) 298-5239
Internet Address: http://www.thetrustees.org/
Admission: Fee: adult $9.00, child (6-12) $3.00
Attendance: 13,000
Established: 1959
Membership: Y
Wheelchair Accessible: P
Parking: Free on site
Open: Memorial Day to Columbus Day, Daily, 10am-5pm
Facilities: Architecture (shingle-style 44-room Victorian mansion, 1885 design by Stanford White of McKim, Mead, and White); Formal Gardens (16, 8 acres, 1886 design by Nathan Barrett and 1926-1958 design by Fletcher Steele—including the famous Blue Steps); Grounds (46 acres); Shop
Activities: Festival Farm Day (Sat of Labor Day Weekend), Summer Garden Party (July); Guided Tours

An historic house museum, Naumkeag was the summer residence of lawyer and former Ambassador to Great Britain Joseph Choate. His family summered here until 1958. The rooms contain the Choate family's collections of Chinese export porcelain, antique furniture, elegant rugs, and tapestries. The formal gardens are considered among the most beautiful in America and came to fruition over the course of thirty years, initially under the direction of Nathan Barrett and later under landscape architect Fletcher Steele who worked along with Choate's daughter Mabel. A guided house and landscape tour map is included with paid admission. Listed on the National Register of Historic Places, the site is a property of the Trustees of Reservations, the nation's oldest private, statewide conservation and preservation organization.

STURBRIDGE

OLD STURBRIDGE VILLAGE—GARDENS (OSV)

1 Old Sturbridge Village Road (Route 20), Sturbridge, MA 01566
Tel: (800) 733-1830; TDDY: (508) 347-5387
Internet Address: http://www.osv.org/
Admission: Fee: adult $20.00, child (3-17) $5.00, senior $18.00; Free second-day visits within 10 days
Attendance: 350,000
Established: 1946
Membership: Y
Wheelchair Accessible: Y
Parking: Free on site
Open: January to March, Wednesday to Sunday, 9:30am-4pm; April to October, Daily, 9:30am-5pm; November to December, Daily, 9:30am-4pm
Closed: Christmas Day
Facilities: Architecture (assembled 1830's village); Food Services (several restaurants); Gardens (historic, vegetable, flower, herb)
Activities: Education Programs; Self-guided tours

A living history museum, Sturbridge Village portrays the daily work activities and community celebrations of a rural early nineteenth-century New England town. The vegetable and flower gardens at the village exhibit plant types, gardening practices, and garden styles of the 1830s. These are based on extensive research by staff members using historic sources such as letters, diaries, reminiscences, seed and nursery catalogs, and garden advice books. At the Freeman Farm, Fenno House, and Bixby House, garden layouts, cultivation practices, and vegetable varieties follow common practice in rural gardens of the 1830s. At the Parsonage, the minister's kitchen garden follows an advice book and demonstrates a more scientific and experimental approach. The flower gardens show a variety of plants and garden styles. Formal gardens at the Towne House and Fitch House contrast with modest dooryard gardens at the Parsonage and the Fenno House. The museum also maintains an extensive herb garden in the formal exhibit area where over 400 plants grow in terraced beds. Each plant is labeled and has documented nineteenth-century household, culinary, and/or medicinal uses.

TYRINGHAM

ASHINTULLY GARDENS

Sodem Road, Tyringham, MA 01264
Tel: (413) 298-3239; Fax: (413) 298-5239
Internet Address: http://www.thetrustees.org/

Admission: Free
Established: 1996
Parking: Roadside
Open: Mid-June to mid-September, Wednesday, 1pm-5pm; Saturday, 1pm-5pm
Facilities: Gardens; Grounds (120 acres); Trail (woodland, 1 ½ miles)
Activities: Guided Tours (groups 15+, schedule in advance $5/person); Self-guided
Tours (map available)

Ashintully (Gaelic meaning "on the brow of the hill") was the name given to the original 1,000-acre estate assembled in the early twentieth century by Egyptologist and two-
time state representative, Robb de Peyster Tytus. On a hill overlooking the southern end
of Tryingham Valley, Tytus built, between 1910-1912, a white, Georgian-style mansion,
which came to be known as the Marble Palace. In 1937, John McLennan (Jr.), son of
Tytus's widow by second marriage, acquired the estate, where he had spent all his childhood summers. In 1952, the Marble Palace was destroyed by fire. Only the front terrace,
foundation, and four Doric columns remain today. John McLennan, an accomplished
composer of contemporary music, created, over the course of thirty years, Ashintully
Gardens. The gardens blend several natural features—a rushing stream, native deciduous
trees, a large knoll, and rising flanking meadows—into an ordered arrangement with both
formal and informal beauty. Garden features include the Fountain Pond, Pine Park, Rams
Head Terrace, Bowling Green, Regency Bridge, and Trellis Triptych. Urns, columns, and
statuary ornament the garden, while footbridges, footpaths, stone stairs, and grassy terraces connect various parts of it. In 1997, Ashintully Gardens received the H. Hollis Hunnewell Medal, established in 1870 by the Massachusetts Horticultural Society to recog-
nize gardens of country residences embellished with rare and desirable ornamental trees
and shrubs. The Garden Conservancy, a national organization working to save outstanding American gardens, has recognized Ashintully Gardens as a garden worthy of conservation in perpetuity. No staff is resident on site, however, a free garden map is available.
All visitors are requested to respect the privacy of Katharine McLennan, who lives in the
farmhouse next to the gardens.

WALTHAM

GORE PLACE

52 Gore Street (off Main Street, Route 20), Waltham, MA 02453-6866
Tel: (617) 894-2798; Fax: (617) 894-2798
Internet Address: http://www.goreplace.org
Admission: Fee (House Tour): adult $9.00, child (5-12) $5.00, student $7.00,
senior $7.00
Attendance: 60,000
Established: 1935
Membership: Y
Wheelchair Accessible: P
Parking: Free parking
Open: April 15 to November 15, Thursday to Monday, 11am-4pm; November 16 to
April 14, call to arrange tour
Facilities: Architecture (Federal mansion, 1806; Carriage House, 1793; Farmer's
Cottage, 1835); Gardens; Grounds (45 acres, small farm with early breeds of sheep,
goats, and poultry); Shop (Mon-Fri, 9am-4pm)
Activities: Education Programs; House Tours (last tour departs 3pm)

Gore Place was built as the summer home for Christopher and Rebecca Gore of Boston. The Gores were a sophisticated couple, possessing excellent literary tastes and social graces. Among the guests entertained by the Gores were the Marquis de Lafayette, James Monroe, and Daniel Webster. Today the house is furnished with fine art and antiques of the eighteenth and early nineteenth centuries. The gardens and grounds surrounding Gore Place reflect European influence. Having resided between 1796 and 1804 in England, the Gores must have been aware of the work of Sir Humphrey Repton, an English landscape architect, then at the height of his popularity. Repton advocated broad lawns, open fields, ponds, clumps of trees, and inconspicuous gardens; he would not tolerate formal gardens or abundant shrubbery. The Gores incorporated many of Repton's ideas. Shaded walks radiated from the house and another skirted the grounds. A road lined with trees still approaches the house from the west. Owned and operated since 1935 by the Gore Place Society, the estate is designated a National Historic Landmark.

THE LYMAN ESTATE—THE VALE (THE VALE)

185 Lyman Street, Waltham, MA 02154-5645
Tel: (617) 891-4882 *Ext:* 244
Internet Address: http://spnea.org/visit/land/mass.htm
Admission: No charge, donations accepted
Attendance: 8,000
Wheelchair Accessible: N
Parking: Parking for all types of vehicles
Open: Grounds, daily, 9am-5pm; Greenhouses, Monday to Saturday, 9:30am-4pm; Mansion, by appointment for group tours
Facilities: Architecture (Federal estate, 1793 design by Salem architect Samuel McIntire); Greenhouses (historic, 1804-1930); Grounds (37 acres).
Activities: Guided Tours Greenhouses (arrange with horticulturist); Plant Sales Greenhouses; Workshops.

One of the finest examples of a Federal period country estate in America, The Vale was the Lyman family's summer residence for over 150 years. Designated a National Historic Landmark, the mansion, greenhouse complex, and thirty-seven acres of land are owned and maintained by Historic New England (formerly the Society for the Preservation of New England Antiquities). The greenhouses are a reminder of the fascination with horticulture prevalent among wealthy nineteenth-century Bostonians. Typical of structures that adorned landed estates in the nineteenth and early twentieth centuries, they shelter grapevines planted in 1870, 100-year-old camellia trees, and other exotic plants. Visitors may purchase plants propagated from the collection. The grounds contain a number of specimen trees, a 600-foot peach wall, and late nineteenth-century rhododendrons and azaleas introduced by the Lyman family.

WELLESLEY

MASSACHUSETTS HORTICULTURAL SOCIETY— ELM BANK RESERVATION (AHS RAP)

900 Washington Street (Route 16,, 1 mile west past Wellesley College), Wellesley, MA 02482-5725
Tel: (617) 933-4929; Fax: (617) 933-4901; TDDY: (781) 235-5655
Internet Address: http://www.masshort.org/

Established: 1829
Membership: Y
Open: Daily, 8am-dusk
Facilities: Gardens (display, Italianate, trial); Greenhouses (2); Grounds (182 acres, 36 acres leased to MHS); Horticultural Education Center
Activities: Classes; Demonstrations; Education Programs; Lectures; Plant Clinic; Workshops

Located in a portion of the Metropolitan District Commission's Elm Bank Reservation, the society's horticultural and education center includes open fields and meadows, streams and pools, wooded areas, and formal gardens as well as serving as a hub for horticultural activity and information. Its gardens include a restored 1926 Italianate Garden; a trial garden, offering a place for professionals and home gardeners to view and compare hundreds of plant cultivars grown and displayed under uniform conditions; display gardens; and a tree nursery specializing in disease tolerant American elms. The site's two greenhouses are used for propagating and growing plants used at Elm Bank and at the society's annual New England Spring Flower Show. Elm Bank's history as a private residence begins in the seventeenth century with its gardens having been designed and improved by the Olmsted Brothers, landscape architects, in 1907. The entire site is listed on the National Register of Historic Places.

WELLESLEY COLLEGE—BOTANIC GARDENS

106 Central Street
Adjacent to Science Center (off College Road), Wellesley, MA 02481-8203
Tel: (781) 283-3094 Fax: (781) 283-3624
Internet Address: http://www.wellesley.edu/FOH/greenhouse/home/home.html
Admission: Free
Parking: Gray Lot next to Science Center
Open: Greenhouses, daily, 8:30am-4pm; Visitor Center, Mon-Fri 10am-4pm and most weekends.
Facilities: Arboretum; Gardens (woody plants, rhododendron, azalea); Greenhouses (15; 7,700 square feet); Grounds (22 acres)
Activities: Guided Tours (groups, arrange in advance)

Home to a diverse and valuable living collection that serves both the academic and public communities, the gardens include the Alexandra Botanical Garden, Hunnewell Arboretum, and Margaret C. Ferguson Greenhouses. This outdoor/indoor teaching facility is a twenty-two-acre tract that contains a wide variety of trees, shrubs, and plants. The botanical gardens contain over 500 species of woody plants in 53 families. The collection of specimen trees and shrubs include mature American white and English oaks, lindens, tulip trees, bald cypress, and Chinese golden larch as well as different species and cultivars of azaleas, lilacs, viburnums, hollies, weeping cherries, and rhododendrons, providing spectacular flowering in the spring and range of color in the autumn. The Margaret C. Ferguson Greenhouses house 1,000 kinds of plants. Its permanent collection emphasizes the diversity and adaptations of desert plants, orchids, and ferns and includes large numbers of sub-tropical, temperate, and aquatic plants.

WESTFIELD

GRANDMOTHER'S GARDEN

Chauncey Allen Park, Smith Avenue (off Route 20), Westfield, MA 01085
Tel: (413) 562-2022

Internet Address: http://community.masslive.com/cc/GrandmothersGarden
Admission: Free
Membership: Y
Wheelchair Accessible: Y
Parking: Handicapped parking lot adjacent to garden
Open: Daily
Best Time(s) of Year to Visit: Late April to October
Facilities: Garden (Colonial Revival); Grounds Garden (½ acre), Park (6 acres, currently undergoing restoration)
Activities: Guided Tours (docent-led, call in advance)

In 1929, the city of Westfield received a gift of land from Albert Steiger, on which it created an award-winning garden designed in the Colonial Revival style. The park is now maintained by Friends of Grandmothers' Garden, a volunteer organization dedicated to preserving the garden and park for the educational and recreational interests of all of its visitors.

STANLEY PARK

400 Western Avenue, Westfield, MA 01085-2560
Tel: (413) 568-9312; Fax: (413) 568-9548
Internet Address: http://www.stanleypark.org/welcome.htm
Admission: No charge, donations accepted
Attendance: 350,000
Established: 1949
Membership: Y
Wheelchair Accessible: P
Parking: Free on site
Open: Daily, 8am-sunset
Best Time(s) of Year to Visit: Early May (wildflowers), mid-May to early June (rhododendron, Japanese garden)
Facilities: Arboretum (5 acres); Carillon Tower (concerts, May-Oct, 1st Sun in month, 3pm-4pm); Gardens (bog, herb, Japanese, rhododendron, rose, wildflower); Grounds; Library; Picnic Area

The gardens at Stanley Park include an All-America Rose Selections test garden, containing over 50 varieties of roses and 2,500 rose bushes; the Evelyn B. Rose Garden, displaying roses chosen for their hardiness and carefree maintenance in the New England climate; the American Wildflower Society Display Garden, featuring indigenous shade-tolerant New England wildflowers; a rhododendron garden with hundreds of rare varieties, sponsored by the Massachusetts chapter of the American Rhododendron Society; a Japanese garden with tea house surrounded by plantings of alpine conifers, rhododendron, azaleas, and flowering deciduous shrubs; an herb garden containing numerous varieties of fragrant, culinary, and medicinal herbs as well as large old-fashioned formal perennial gardens and colorful annual plantings; and a wetlands garden. The park's arboretum features a collection of trees and shrubs on a five-acre site embellished with a thirty-foot fountain.

WESTON

CASE ESTATES OF THE ARNOLD ARBORETUM

135 Wellesley Street, Weston, MA 02193
Tel: (617) 524-1718

Internet Address: http://www.arboretum.harvard.edu
Admission: Free
Established: 1944
Open: Daily, 9am-sunset
Facilities: Gardens (rhododendron, perennial, ground cover plots); Grounds (75 acres); Special Collections (day lily, hosta, iris, native american plants, peony, rhododendron)
Activities: Annual Plant Sale (fall); Education Programs; Guided Tours (by appointment)

Developed by Marion Case between 1909 and 1942 to "provide summer employment and practical education for local youth," the estates now serve as a nursery and experimental station for Harvard University's Arnold Arboretum. The Rhododendron Display Garden is one of two display gardens maintained by the Massachusetts chapter of the American Rhododendron Society.

MICHIGAN

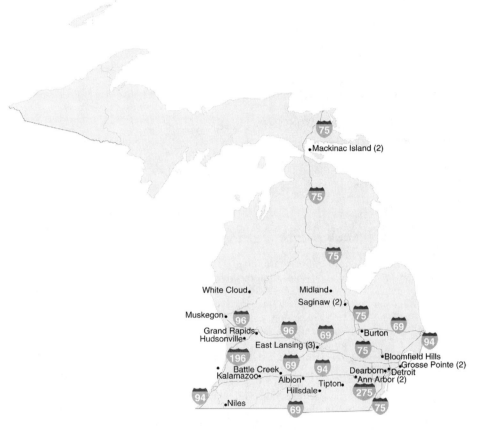

Mackinac Island (2)

White Cloud
Midland
Saginaw (2)

Muskegon
Grand Rapids
Hudsonville
East Lansing (3)
Burton

Battle Creek
Kalamazoo
Albion
Tipton
Dearborn Detroit
Ann Arbor (2)
Bloomfield Hills
Grosse Pointe (2)

Hillsdale

Niles

The number in the parentheses following the city name indicates the number of gardens/arboreta in that municipality. If there is no number, one is understood. For example, in the text two listings would be found under Ann Arbor and one listing under Detroit.

ALBION

ALBION COLLEGE—WHITEHOUSE NATURE CENTER

Hannah Street (¼ mile SE of college campus), Albion, MI 49224
Tel: (517) 629-0582
Internet Address: http://www.albion.edu/naturecenter/
Admission: Free
Attendance: 15,000
Established: 1972 Membership: N
Wheelchair Accessible: P
Parking: Parking lot at Interpretive Building
Open: Grounds, Daily, dawn-dusk; Interpretive Building, Monday to Friday, 9am-4:30pm; Saturday to Sunday, 10:30am-4:30pm
Closed: Legal holidays, academic holidays
Best Time(s) of Year to Visit: Spring, Fall
Facilities: Arboretum (native plants and trees); Gardens (wildflower); Grounds (135 acres); Trails (6, self-guided)
Activities: Education Programs; Guided Tours (arrange in advance); Self-guided Tours

Situated along the north branch of the Kalamazoo River, the nature center contains over 400 plant species and an herbarium in the interpretive building. Features include the Adele D. Whitehouse Wildflower Garden, the Stowell Arboretum of Michigan trees and shrubs, twenty-five acres of oak-hickory and flood-plain forest, a tall-grass prairie and spring, and a habitat improvement area including ponds.

ANN ARBOR

UNIVERSITY OF MICHIGAN—MATTHAEI BOTANICAL GARDENS (AHS RAP)

1800 N. Dixboro Road, Ann Arbor, MI 48105-9741
Tel: (313) 998-7061; Fax: (313) 998-6205; TDDY: (313) 998-7061
Internet Address: http://www.lsa.umich.edu/mbg/
Admission: Fee (Conservatory): adult $5.00, student $2.00
Free (Grounds & Conservatory): Mon, 10am-1pm
Attendance: 60,000
Established: 1961
Membership: Y

Wheelchair Accessible: P
Parking: Free on site.
Open: Grounds, Daily, 8am-sunset
Conservatory, Daily, 10am-4:30pm
Closed: New Year's Day, Thanksgiving Day, Christmas Eve to Christmas Day
Best Time(s) of Year to Visit: July to August (herb garden), June to October (perennial garden)
Facilities: Auditorium; Classrooms; Climatic Areas (New World plants); Conservatory; Gardens (experimental, herb, knot, rose, woodland wildflower); Greenhouses; Grounds (350 acres); Herbarium; Library; Nature Trails (5); Shop (10am-4:30pm); Special Collections (orchids, wildflowers)
Activities: Classes; Education Programs (adult); Flower Sales; Flower Shows; Guided Tours (by prior arrangement); Lectures

Situated along Fleming Creek, the Matthaei Botanical Gardens include themed gardens, four nature trails, mature woodlands, wetlands, several ponds, and a tall grass prairie. The Gateway Garden features more than 6,000 annuals, perennials, trees, and shrubs derived from plants native to North, Central, and South America. The Herb Knot Garden showcases four of the traditional uses for herbs: cooking, medicinal, fragrance, and everlasting (dried ornamental). The Perennial and Rose Garden, a symmetrical formal garden in an English tradition, displays roses and perennials (including more than 120 varieties of cultivars) in long, straight beds bordered by hedges of hedge maple and yew. The Woodland Wildflower Garden contains more than 100 species, including Michigan's native wildflowers, woody plants, and ferns as well as European and Asian exotics and Appalachian species that have been hardy enough to naturalize in the southern Michigan woods. There are also shade and rock gardens as well as a reconstructed prairie, featuring field flowers and big bluestem grass and a constructed wetland area. The conservatory, containing more than 1,200 unusual and exotic plants from around the world, is divided into three "houses," designed to exhibit the tremendous diversity of the plant world: tropical, warm-temperate, and arid.

UNIVERSITY OF MICHIGAN—NICHOLS ARBORETUM

1610 Washington Heights, Ann Arbor, MI 48104-1700
Tel: (734) 998-9540
Internet Address: http://www.umich.edu/~wwwarb/
Admission: Voluntary contribution
Attendance: 100,000
Established: 1907
Membership: Y
Wheelchair Accessible: Y
Parking: Park in city or UM Hospital structures
Open: Daily, sunrise-sunset
Facilities: Arboretum (1906 design by O.C. Simonds; 64 species of trees); Environmental Education Center; Grounds (123 acres); Special Collections (lilac, peony)
Activities: Guided Tours (3rd Sun in month, 2pm, groups arrange in advance; $1.00 per person)

Nestled in the hills adjacent to the University of Michigan's Central Campus, the arboretum's design celebrates the dramatic topography; long views are framed by the arboretum's collection of Michigan native plants and plants from around the world. Features include historic peony (800 plants) and lilac collections and a restored prairie. The James D. Reader, Jr. Urban Environmental Education Center at the Burnham House features seasonal exhibits, provides information, and is the base for tours and classes.

BATTLE CREEK

CITY OF BATTLE CREEK—LEILA ARBORETUM (AHS RAP)

928 W. Michigan Avenue (at 20th Street), Battle Creek, MI 49017-2176
Tel: (616) 969-0270; Fax: (616) 969-0616
Internet Address: http://www.LeilaArboretumSociety.org
Admission: No charge/donations accepted
Open: Daily, sunrise-sunset
Facilities: Garden (children's); Grounds (71 acres); Picnic Area

The arboretum contains more than 3,000 exotic and native of trees as well as other Michigan shrubs and plants, including shade and rhododendron gardens.

BLOOMFIELD HILLS

CRANBROOK GARDENS

380 N. Lone Pine Road, Bloomfield Hills, MI 48303-0801
Tel: (810) 645-3149; Fax: (810) 645-3151
Internet Address: http://www.cranbrook.edu/
Admission: Fee (Gardens): adult $6.00, child (<5) free, student $5.00, senior $5.00
Established: 1971
Membership: Y Wheelchair Accessible: P
Open: Gardens: May to August, Monday to Saturday, 10am-5pm; Sunday, 11am-5pm; September, daily, 11am-3pm; October, Saturday to Sunday, 11am-3pm
Best Time(s) of Year to Visit: Spring to Summer
Facilities: Architecture Cranbrook House (Arts and Crafts-style home, 1908 design by Albert Kahn), Saarinen House (1930, design by Eliel Saarinen); Gardens (herb, oriental, perennial, rock, sunken, wildflower); Greenhouse; Grounds Cranbrook Education Community (325 acres), Cranbrook Gardens (40 acres, design by O.C. Simonds); Statuary (sculpture and fountains)
Activities: Concerts; Films; Guided Tours Cranbrook Gardens (June-Sept; call for reservation 248-645-3147), Cranbrook House (June- Sept, reservation required), Saarinen House & Garden (May-Oct, Tues -Sun); Plant Sales Greenhouse (Mon, 10am-2pm)

Cranbrook had its beginnings in 1904, when George Gough Booth, publisher of the *Detroit News*, and his wife, Ellen Warren Scripps Booth, bought a large farm in the rolling countryside of Bloomfield Hills. Taking up residence in 1907, the Booths gradually transformed their farm estate into a cultural and educational complex, including an academy of art, art museum, science and natural history museum, schools, and other affiliated cultural and educational programs. A superb integration of architectural and landscape design elements, the Cranbrook Educational Community (major components designed and built 1926-1943) represents a unique masterpiece in the history of American architecture. Designated a National Historic Landmark, it embodies the belief shared by its founder, George G. Booth, and its principal architect, Eliel Saarinen, that art should permeate every aspect of life. Cranbrook House and Gardens are situated on 40 acres within the 325 acres of the Cranbrook complex. Its beautiful English-style landscape has been designated an arboretum with over 300 species of native and exotic trees and shrubs and includes formal, bog, herb, oriental, and wildflower gardens.

BURTON

FOR-MAR NATURE PRESERVE AND ARBORETUM

2142 N. Genesee Road, Burton, MI 48509-1209
Tel: (810) 789-8567
Internet Address: http://www.geneseecountyparks.org
Admission: Free
Attendance: 20,000
Established: 1970
Wheelchair Accessible: Y
Parking: Paved lot with handicapped accessibility
Open: Grounds, daily, 8am-sunset
Facilities: Arboretum; Garden Memorial Garden (in arboretum); Grounds Arboretum (120 acres), Nature Preserve (260 acres); Shop The Nutshell (nature and science oriented gifts); Visitor Center (daily, 8am-5pm)
Activities: Education Programs; Guided Tours Nature Hikes (by reservation)

A facility of Genesee County Parks and Recreation Commission, 120 acres of the land are maintained as an arboretum and the rest is kept as nearly as possible in its natural state. The visitor center, consisting of a nature center and a horticultural center, houses the Corydon Foote Bird Collection (600 specimens) as well as an extensive collection of the native flora and fauna.

DEARBORN

HENRY FORD ESTATE: FAIR LANE—GARDENS

4901 Evergreen Road, Dearborn, MI 48128
Tel: (313) 593-5590
Internet Address: http://www.henryfordestate.org
Admission: Fee (outdoors only) $2.00
Attendance: 100,000
Established: 1916
Membership: N
Wheelchair Accessible: P
Parking: Lot adjacent to estate
Open: Grounds, mid-June to Labor Day, daily; Estate Tours, April to December, Monday-Saturday, 10am-3pm (on the hour, except noon); Sunday, 1pm-4:30pm (every half hour); January to March, Monday to Friday, 1:30pm (on the hour, except noon); Sunday, 1pm-4:30pm (every half hour)
Facilities: Architecture (residence, 1914-16); Food Services Estate Restaurant (Mon-Fri, 11am-2pm, (313) 436-9196); Gardens (5 acres); Grounds (72 acres); Shop (gifts reflecting Clara & Henry Ford's interests)
Activities: Guided Tours Estate, Grounds (groups, May-Sept, schedule in advance); Self-guided Tour Grounds

Designated a National Historic Landmark, the Henry Ford Estate is the former home of automaker Henry Ford and his wife Clara. In addition to the residence and its power-house, the 1,300-acre estate, whose grounds were designed by noted landscape architect Jens Jensen, includes a summer house, man-made lake, staff cottages, gatehouse, pony barn, skating house, greenhouse, root cellar, vegetable garden, thousand-plant peony garden, ten thousand plant rose garden, a "Santa's Workshop" for Christmas celebrations, maple sugar shack, working farm for the Ford grandchildren built to their scale, agricultural research facilities, and five hundred birdhouses to satisfy Mr. Ford's interest in ornithology. The Fords lived at the estate from 1915 until their deaths in 1947 and 1950. In 1957, the Ford Motor Company donated the residence, powerhouse, 210 acres, and $6.5 million to the University of Michigan for the creation of the Dearborn campus. At present five acres of gardens and grounds have been renewed and restored.

DETROIT

ANNA SCRIPPS WHITCOMB CONSERVATORY AND GARDENS (BELLE ISLE GREENHOUSE) (AHS RAP)

Belle Isle Park, Conservatory Drive, Detroit, MI 48207
Tel: (313) 852-4075; Fax: (313) 852-4074
Internet Address: http://www.bibsociety.org
Admission: Free
Attendance: 88,000
Established: 1904
Membership: Y
Wheelchair Accessible: Y
Parking: Free parking
Open: Daily, 10am-5pm
Facilities: Conservatory (1904 design by Albert Kahn, >1 acre); Display Rooms; Gardens (formal, perennial, water lily); Grounds (10 acres, design by Frederick Law Olmsted); Special Collections (orchids, cacti, succulents, ferns, tropicals, large palms)
Activities: Flower Shows (seasonal); Guided Tours Groups (with advance notice); Lectures; Permanent Exhibits

Covering more than one acre and featuring an eighty-five-foot-high dome, the conservatory is divided into five distinct sections. The dome provides 100,600 cubic feet of space for large palms and other tropical trees. The south wing features tropical plants of economic importance (bananas, oranges, coffee, sugar cane, etc.), as well as one of the largest municipally-owned orchid collections in the nation. The north wing contains ferns, cacti, and succulents. The show house on the east side of the dome presents continuous displays of blooming plants during the six major flower seasons of the year. Water, heritage rose, perennial, and annual gardens flank the conservatory. The Belle Isle Botanical Society (BIBS), a non-profit organization, assists the gardening efforts by the City of Detroit Recreation Department on Belle Isle and provides educational programs for the public.

EAST LANSING

MICHIGAN STATE UNIVERSITY—BOTANY GREENHOUSE

Farm Lane, North Campus, East Lansing, MI 48824-1312
Tel: (517) 355-0229
Admission: Free
Parking: Metered on East and West Circle Drives

Open: Monday to Friday, 8am-5pm; Saturday to Sunday, 10am-2pm
Closed: Academic holidays
Best Time(s) of Year to Visit: February to April (Orchids), March to May (Cacti),
March to October (Butterflies)
Facilities: Greenhouses; Special Collections (cactus, orchid)
Activities: Guided Tours (reserve 2 weeks in advance; $1/adult, $.50/student, $15
minimum); Self-Guided Tours

Specifically designed for self-guided exploration, the Botany Greenhouse features a
wide range of diverse plant habitats, including a desert room, sub-tropical house, and rain
forest exhibit. Highlights include the orchid collection and butterfly house.

MICHIGAN STATE UNIVERSITY HORTICULTURE
GARDENS (AHS RAP)

South Campus, Bogue Street (next to Plant & Soil Sciences Building),
East Lansing, MI 48823
Tel: (517) 353-3770; Fax: (517) 353-0890
Internet Address: http://www.hrt.msu.edu/gardens
Admission: Free
Established: 1991
Membership: Y
Wheelchair Accessible: Y
Parking: Pay lot on site
Open: May to October, daily, dawn-dusk
Best Time(s) of Year to Visit: April to November
Facilities: Arboretum; Butterfly House; Gardens (annual, children's, conifer, fragrance,
fruit, herb, Japanese, native plant, perennial, maze, rose, sunken, topiary, vegetable);
Greenhouses; Grounds (10 acres); Visitor Center (May-Sept, 10am-8pm)
Activities: Guided Tours (June-Sept, reserve 2 weeks in advance, $3/adult, $2/child-
minimum $30); Self-guided Tours

The MSU Horticulture Gardens consists of three distinct units: the Horticultural
Demonstration Gardens, the Clarence E. Lewis Landscape Arboretum, and the 4-H Children's Garden. Planned to meet the teaching needs of the Department of Horticulture,
the Horticultural Demonstration Gardens contain over 35,000 annuals and a wide range
of perennials in six different gardens and a wide variety of woody ornamental trees and
shrubs hardy to mid-Michigan. Highlights include a two-acre All-American Selections
display and trial garden showcasing over 1,000 different cultivars in a formal setting; a
perennial garden displaying hundreds of different flowering perennials, bulbs, and ornamental grasses in eleven island beds; and an All-America Rose Selections trial garden offering over 700 hybrid teas, grandifloras, floribundas, and miniatures. Located at the site
of the old campus nursery on the grounds of the MSU Horticulture Gardens and conceived as a collection of landscapes, the Clarence E. Lewis Landscape Arboretum is an instructional arboretum for students interested in landscape development. Many remaining
specimen trees lend a mature characteristic to the arboretum. At the entrance, dwarf and
exotic evergreens, herbaceous ground covers, rhododendrons, and many flowering trees
from the permanent collection are featured. To the west are a variety of landscape
demonstration gardens and informal plantings. Highlights include a Japanese garden illustrating the hill and pond, dry landscape, and the stroll garden styles; a native plant garden
containing plants native to the eastern United States that are adaptable to Michigan gardens; a conifer garden; a vegetable garden demonstrating innovative horticultural techniques; a herb knot garden; and Michigan fruit display gardens. Also located within the

MSU Horticulture Gardens, the 4-H Children's Garden is a project of the Michigan State University Extension. The garden features over sixty individual theme areas designed specifically for children. The Clarence E. Lewis Landscape Arboretum and the Michigan 4-H Children's Garden, located in the Horticultural Demonstration Gardens, are listed separately.

MICHIGAN STATE UNIVERSITY—W. J. BEAL BOTANICAL GARDENS (AHS RAP)

MSU Campus, West Circle Drive, East Lansing, MI 48824-1047
Tel: (517) 355-9582; Fax: (517) 432-1090
Internet Address: http://www.cpp.msu.edu/beal/
Admission: Free
Established: 1873
Open: Daily, 24 hours
Facilities: Arboretum; Gardens (fragrance, herb, water); Greenhouses; Grounds (5+ acres); Special Collections (threatened and endangered native Michigan species, aquatic, wetland)
Activities: Guided Tours

Established in 1873 by Professor William James Beal, the botanical gardens is the oldest continuously operated university botanical garden of its kind in the United States. This beautiful display garden, containing over 5,000 different varieties of plants, is an outdoor laboratory for their study and appreciation. The collection is displayed in five major assemblies. To the east of the crosswalk the systematic collection is displayed in forty beds. The next fifty beds are devoted to economic plants with separate beds devoted to specific categories of plant products or usefulness. The forest communities collection, consisting of trees and shrubs of Michigan and the eastern United States underplanted with many wildflowers, is situated on the slopes that surround the garden. The ornamental plants collection displays spring flowering shrubs and bulbs, useful groundcovers, and medium-sized trees in designed compositions that demonstrate landscape design principles. The endangered and threatened species exhibit features selected Michigan native plants whose remaining populations are protected by the Endangered Species Act. The Beal Botanical Garden is administered by the MSU Division of Campus Park and Planning.

GRAND RAPIDS

FREDERIK MEIJER GARDENS (AHS RAP)

1000 E. Beltline NE, Grand Rapids, MI 49525
Tel: (616) 957-1580; Fax: (616) 957-5792
Internet Address: http://www.meijergardens.org/
Admission: Fee: adult $10.00, child (<5) free, child (5-13) $6.00, student $8.00, senior $8.00
Established: 1995
Membership: Y
Wheelchair Accessible: Y
Open: Monday to Saturday, 9am-5pm; Sunday, noon-5pm
Closed: New Year's Day, Thanksgiving Day, Christmas Day
Facilities: Conservatory (15,000 square feet); Food Services Taste of the Gardens Café (reservations 977-7691); Gardens (display, native plant, orchid, perennial,

tropical, wetland); Grounds (125 acres); Library (Mon-Fri, 9am-5pm; Sat-Sun, 1pm-3pm; 975-3144); Sculpture Park; Shop DeVos Family Gift Shop (glass, jewelry, pottery, garden sculpture), Keeler Gift Shop (house plants, garden tools, garden supplies, handmade pots, art); Tram (May-Oct, 9am-4pm; narrated tours)
Activities: Education Programs; Guided Tours (groups 20+, reserve in advance, 975-3171); Self-guided Tours; Temporary Art Exhibitions; Temporary Exhibitions Butterflies Are Blooming (early Spring), Christmas Around the World (Thanksgiving, New Years Day)

Owned and operated by the West Michigan Horticultural Society, Frederik Meijer Gardens feature a tropical conservatory, outdoor gardens, nature trails, and over 100 sculptures by renowned artists, including Butterfield, Calder, Fredericks, and Liberman. Standing five stories high, the Lena Meijer Conservatory is the largest glass conservatory in Michigan. It houses tropical plants from around the world, including a changing display from the gardens' collection of over 2,000 orchids. In early spring, the conservatory is the focal point for the "Butterflies Are Blooming" exhibit, when hundreds of butterflies are released in the largest temporary butterfly exhibit in the United States. Other inside exhibits include the Earl and Donalee Holton Victorian Garden Parlor, featuring plants that were popular during the Victorian era; an arid garden, housing both Old and New World xeriphytic plants; and the Grace Jarecki Seasonal Display Greenhouse. Outdoor exhibits include an English perennial and bulb garden, designed by Penelope Hobhouse; a New American Garden, designed by landscape designer James Van Sweden and featuring large drifts of perennials and grasses that have four-season appeal and require little maintenance; a woodland shade garden; and woodland and wetland habitats.

GROSSE POINTE FARMS

GROSSE POINTE GARDEN CENTER (THE MOORINGS)

Grosse Point War Memorial, 32 Lake Shore Drive,
Grosse Pointe Farms, MI 48236-3784
Tel: (313) 881-4594
Admission: Free (Gardens)
Established: 1949
Membership: Y
Wheelchair Accessible: Y
Parking: On site
Open: Grounds, Monday to Saturday, 9am-dusk
Office, Tuesday to Thursday, 9am-3pm
Best Time(s) of Year to Visit: June to September
Facilities: Architecture (Italian Renaissance-style residence, 1910 design by Charles A. Platt); Grounds (1919 design by landscape architect Ellen Biddle Shipman)
Activities: Garden Tours; Lectures

The offices of the Grosse Pointe Garden Center are housed in the Grosse Pointe War Memorial (GPWM) overlooking Lake St. Clair. Originally the home of Russell A. Alger, Jr., one of the founders of the Packard Motor Company, the property serves as a community center for educational and charitable purposes. While there have been a number of major additions to the structure, the essentials of Ellen Shipman's original design for the grounds are still apparent. The Garden Center maintains Trial Gardens featuring annual, perennial, herb, and rose beds. The Grosse Pointe War Memorial is also the site of the "Seeds to Grow On," a program in which children three years of age and up tend the Grace Adams Harrison Children's Garden.

GROSSE POINTE SHORES

EDSEL & ELEANOR FORD HOUSE

1100 Lake Shore Road, Grosse Pointe Shores, MI 48236
Tel: (313) 884-4222; Fax: (313) 884-5977
Internet Address: http://www.fordhouse.org
Admission: Fee: adult $7.00, child $5.00, senior $6.00; Grounds only—$3.00
Attendance: 50,000
Established: 1978
Wheelchair Accessible: Y
Parking: Free on site
Open: January to March, Tuesday to Sunday, noon-4pm; April to December, Tuesday to Saturday, 10am-4pm; Sunday, noon-4pm
Closed: New Year's Day, Thanksgiving Day, Christmas Day, last two weeks of Jan.
Facilities: Architecture (designed by Albert Kahn); Exhibition Area (2,500 square feet); Food Services (Tea Room); Gardens; Grounds (87 acres, designed by Jens Jensen); Shop
Activities: Children's Programs; Guided Tours (groups 15+, reserve in advance); Lectures; Traveling Exhibitions

The Edsel & Eleanor Ford House is a sixty-room Cotswold-style mansion designed by Albert Kahn and completed in 1929. Furnished with English antiques, the house also contains an art collection. The Danish-born landscape architect Jens Jensen was commissioned to provide the home with suitable landscaping. Known as the master of the naturalistic approach, Jensen designed few formal gardens. His landscape design sought to engage all five human senses—the sight of many colors and shapes, the sound of water running, the smell of flowers in bloom, the taste of berries, and the feeling of being surrounded by nature.

HILLSDALE

HILLSDALE COLLEGE—SLAYTON ARBORETUM (AHS RAP)

201 Hillsdale Street, Hillsdale, MI 49242
Tel: (517) 437-7341
Internet Address: http://www.hillsdale.edu/academics/bio/Grigore/Arboretum.html
Established: 1892
Open: Daily
Facilities: Arboretum; Gardens (water); Grounds (40 acres); Special Collections (crab apple, lilac)

The arboretum features over 1,100 plant species as well as examples of landscape design and horticultural principles.

HUDSONVILLE

OTTAWA COUNTY—HAGER HARDWOODS PARK AND ARBORETUM

28th Avenue at Bauer Road, Hudsonville, MI 49426
Tel: (616) 738-4810

Internet Address: http://www.co.ottawa.mi.us/parks/hager.html
Admission: Free
Best Time(s) of Year to Visit: April to May (wildflowers)
Facilities: Arboretum; Grounds Arboretum (40 acres), Park (108 acres); Picnic Area;
Trails; Visitor Center

The park contains a visitor center, exhibit hall, trails, the Lumberman's Museum, and an arboretum.

KALAMAZOO

KALAMAZOO NATURE CENTER—ARBORETUM AND GARDEN

7000 N. Westnedge Avenue, Kalamazoo, MI 49009
Tel: (269) 381-1574; Fax: (269) 381-2557
Internet Address: http://www.naturecenter.org/
Admission: Fee: adult $5.50, child (<4) free, child (4-13) $3.50, senior $4.00; Group discounts
Established: 1960
Membership: Y
Attendance: 208,000
Parking: Paved lot on site
Open: Monday to Saturday, 9am-5pm; Sunday, 1pm-5pm
Closed: New Year's Day, Thanksgiving Day, Christmas Eve to Christmas Day
Facilities: Architecture Pioneer Log Cabin, 1858 Homestead; Arboretum (11 acres);
Conservatory; Garden (hummingbird/butterfly); Grounds (1,000 acres); Interpretive
Center (designed by architect Alden B. Dow); Picnic Area; Trails (11, some suitable
for x-c skiing)
Activities: Education Programs

The Kalamazoo Nature Center is headquartered in an interpretive center featuring state-of-the-art interactive exhibits, including a three-story atrium housing a tropical forest. Situated on rolling hills, the center's ground contain a variety of habitats, including mature beech-maple forests, wetlands, and prairies. The arboretum features many specimens of native and exotic trees and shrubs as well as the Hummingbird-Butterfly Garden, which blooms from June through October with a variety of native plants attractive to hummingbirds and butterflies.

MACKINAC ISLAND

GRAND HOTEL

Mackinac Island, MI 49757
Tel: (906) 847-3331; Fax: (906) 847-3259
Internet Address: http://www.grandhotel.com/
Established: 1887
Wheelchair Accessible: P
Open: May to October, Daily, dawn-dusk
Facilities: Architecture (summer hotel, 1887 design by architect George D. Mason);
Gardens (English cottage, labyrinth, rose, lilac, perennial, topiary, wildflower,

woodland); Greenhouses; Grounds (200 acres with 50 acres of formal gardens); Special Collections (lilac, tulip, geranium)

Reputed the world's largest summer hotel since its opening in 1887, the Grand Hotel is designated a National Historic Landmark. The famous 700 foot-long front veranda houses 2,500 geraniums in 260 planting boxes with seven tons of potting soil. Its landscaped grounds contain both numerous gardens and wooded sections. Over one ton of bulbs are planted in the fall, including 25,000 tulips and 15,000 daffodils. More than 125,000 annual bedding plants are used to create the many gardens on Grand Hotel grounds.

MACKINAC ISLAND STATE PARK—MARQUETTE PARK

Main Street (across from State Park Visitor Center), Mackinac Island, MI 49757
Tel: (231) 847-3328
Internet Address: http://mackinacparks.com/
Admission: Free
Established: 1909
Wheelchair Accessible: P
Parking: Automobiles are not permitted on the island
Best Time(s) of Year to Visit: May (lilac), October
Facilities: Garden (lilac); Grounds (10 acres)
Activities: Festival Lilac Festival (June)

Located below Fort Mackinac (est.1780), Marquette Park was the site of the commandant's house, and was used as the soldiers' garden from 1810 to 1895. The lilac display garden in the park contains 260 lilac bushes representing 65 named varieties. The park also features beautiful views of the harbor, the bluff, and the fort.

MIDLAND

DOW GARDENS

Eastman Avenue and W. Street Andrews, Midland, MI 48640
Tel: (800) 362-4874; Fax: (517) 631-0675
Internet Address: http://www.dowgardens.org/
Admission: Fee: adult $5.00, child (<6) free, child (6-17) $1.00
Attendance: 275,000
Established: 1899
Wheelchair Accessible: P
Open: Daily, 9am-1 hour before sunset
Closed: New Year's Eve to New Year's Day, Thanksgiving Day, Christmas Eve to Christmas Day
Facilities: Arboretum; Architecture (Herbert Henry Dow house [not open to public]); Classroom; Conservatory; Gardens (children's, herb, maze, perennial, rock, rose, sensory, test, wildflower); Grounds (110 acres); Library (2,000 books, 50 journals, non-circulating); Reading Room; Shop Crab Apple Shop (plants, plant related items, books, gardening tools); Special Collections (crab apple, juniper, pine, rhododendron)
Activities: Perennial Exchange; Arts Festival; Concerts; Education Programs (adults, undergraduate college students and children); Festival Butterflies in Bloom (mid-March-mid-April); Guided Tours Dow Homestead Tour (approximately 1/month;, Gardens (groups, reserve 2 weeks in advance); Lectures

Started in 1899 by Herbert Dow, founder of the Dow Chemical Company, the Dow Gardens are now managed by the Herbert H. and Grace A. Dow Foundation. The gardens, featuring plants that are hardy in mid-Michigan, contain more than 1,700 varieties of trees, shrubs, herbaceous perennials, and flowers. Plantings of crab apples, pines, junipers, rhododendrons, and other ericaceous plants are interspersed among numerous flower displays. Attractions include a conservatory herb garden, native wildflowers, a perennial border, a rose garden (containing most of the All-American Rose Selections), a sensory trail, a rose garden, and a test bedding plant area (300 species and/or cultivars).

MUSKEGON

MONET GARDEN OF MUSKEGON

5th & Clay Streets, Muskegon, MI 49442
Tel: (231) 724-6361; Fax: (231) 724-4409
Internet Address: http://www.muskegonmastergardeners.org/monet1.htm
Admission: Free
Established: 2002
Membership: Y
Facilities: Garden

Located in the historic district of downtown Muskegon, the design of this pocket park was inspired by Monet's Garden in Giverny, France. The garden is a project of the Muskegon County Chapter of the Michigan Master Gardener Association in conjunction with the City of Muskegon and the Community Foundation for Muskegon County.

NILES

FERNWOOD BOTANIC GARDEN AND NATURE PRESERVE (AHS RAP)

13988 Range Line Road, Niles, MI 49120-9042
Tel: (269) 695-6491; Fax: (269) 695-6688
Internet Address: http://www.fernwoodbotanical.org
Admission: Fee: adult $5.00, child (<6) free, child (6-13) $2.00, student $3.00, senior $4.00
Attendance: 40,000
Established: 1964
Membership: Y
Wheelchair Accessible: P
Parking: Lot outside Visitor Center, free with admission
Open: Winter, Tuesday to Saturday, 10am-5pm; Sunday, noon-5pm; Spring to Fall, Tuesday to Saturday, 10am-6pm; Sunday, 10am-6pm
Closed: Easter Sunday, Thanksgiving Weekend, Christmas Day to New Year's Day
Best Time(s) of Year to Visit: April to May (wildflowers), June to October
Facilities: Arboretum; Conservatory (1,000 square feet; Tues-Sat, 10am-6pm; Sun, noon-6pm); Food Services (café; sandwiches, soups, desserts; noon-3pm); Gardens (children's, fern, ornamental grass, herb/sensory, hosta, Japanese, native plant, perennial, rock, shade, wildflower); Greenhouse (for propagation, not open to public); Grounds Arboretum (40 acres), Gardens (8 acres), Nature Preserve (50 acres), Prairie

(5 acres); Library (circulating for members); Nature Center (Tues-Fri, 10am-5pm; Sat, 10am-6pm; Sun, noon-6pm); Shop (hand-crafted items, books, educational toys, garden- and nature-related items); Trails (3 miles)
Activities: Concerts; Education Programs (adults and children); Events Christmas Lights (3 weekends before Christmas); Guided Tours (by appointment); Lectures; Temporary Exhibitions, Clark Gallery (art with emphasis on the natural world); Workshops

Fernwood is a special place that connects people with plants and nature. Completely surrounded by forest, eight acres of gardens are tucked in a scenic valley along the historic St. Joseph River. Miles of trails allow visitors to explore the gardens, arboretum, forest preserve, and restored tallgrass prairie. The nature center offers an expansive wildlife viewing area, where visitors may see and hear a wide variety of birds and other animals via picture windows and microphones. The conservatory features tropical ferns and other plants from around the world. The visitor center offers a café, gift shop, and art gallery.

SAGINAW

CITY OF SAGINAW—SAGINAW-TOKUSHIMA FRIENDSHIP GARDEN

Japanese Cultural Center, 527 Ezra Rust Drive at Washington Avenue,
Saginaw, MI 48601-2861
Tel: (989) 759-1648; Fax: (989) 759-1618
Internet Address: http://www.saginaw-mi.com/
Parking: (517) 776-1480
Open: Teahouse, Tuesday to Saturday, 10am-4pm; Garden: April to November, daily
Facilities: Gardens (Japanese, rose); Tea House
Activities: Classes (bonsai, calligraphy, ikebana, origami, tea ceremony); Festival Tea Ceremony (2nd Sat in month); Guided Tours (on request, noon-3:30pm)

The Japanese Cultural Center, consisting of the tea house and garden, was established as a symbol of friendship and cultural exchange with Saginaw's Sister City, Tokushima, Japan. The tea house is of authentic design and crafted in keeping with traditional Japanese architecture.

SAGINAW ART MUSEUM

1126 N. Michigan Avenue, Saginaw, MI 48602
Tel: (517) 754-2491; Fax: (517) 754-9387
Internet Address: http://www.saginawartmuseum.org
Admission: Voluntary contribution
Attendance: 14,000
Established: 1947
Membership: Y
Wheelchair Accessible: Y
Parking: Free on site
Open: Tuesday to Saturday, 10am-5pm; Sunday, 1pm-5pm
Closed: Legal holidays
Facilities: Architecture (Colonial Revival residence, 1904 design by Charles Adams Platt); Galleries (7, one is hands-on); Gardens (formal, wild); Grounds (landscaped by Charles Adams Platt); Library (2,000 volumes); Studio and Classrooms

Activities: Education Programs (adults and children); Gallery Talks; Guided Tours; Lectures; Temporary Exhibitions; Workshops

Housed in a National Register Georgian Revival mansion designed by Charles Adams Platt for lumberman Clark Lombard Ring, the Saginaw Art Museum has an active exhibition schedule. It annually presents over twenty art exhibitions, including two regional juried art competitions, traveling shows of statewide and national importance, and exposure to the art of Asian, African-American, and Hispanic cultures. The building is surrounded by formal and wild gardens, also of Platt design and restored to their Ring-era appearance.

TIPTON

MICHIGAN STATE UNIVERSITY—
HIDDEN LAKE GARDENS (AHS RAP)

6280 W. Munger Road (State Route 50), Tipton, MI 49287
Tel: (517) 431-2060; Fax: (517) 431-9148
Internet Address: http://www.cpp.msu.edu/hlg/
Admission: Fee $3.00; Fee: November to March: $2.00/person
Attendance: 61,000
Established: 1926
Open: April to October, Daily, 8am-dusk; November to March,
Daily, 8am-4pm
Closed: New Year's Day, Thanksgiving Day, Christmas Day
Best Time(s) of Year to Visit: Spring (azaleas, rhododendron, wildflowers), Fall (foliage)
Facilities: Auditorium (80 seats); Classrooms; Conservatory; Garden; Grounds (755 acres); Library (1,800 volumes, non-circulating); Nature Center; Picnic Area; Shop; Special Collections (dwarf and rare conifers); Trails (5 miles)
Activities: Education Programs (adults); Guided Tours (by reservation); Lectures; Permanent Exhibits; Plant Sales

Set among the knolls and valleys formed by ice age glaciers, Hidden Lakes Gardens offers over 2,500 species of trees, shrubs, and plants. Outdoors, plant collections, including azaleas and rhododendrons, birches, crab apples, hostas, lilacs, magnolias, maples, ornamental shrubs, and an outstanding collection of dwarf and rare conifers are displayed in both natural and developed landscapes. There are also plantings of spring bulbs, annuals, and perennials as well as an All-American Selections display garden. A conservatory features indoor plants including bamboo, banana, cactus, camphor, cocoa, coffee, fig, palm, sisal, sugar cane, tapioca, vanilla, and many useful ornamentals. Bonsai are a seasonal attraction. Hidden Lake Gardens is owned by Michigan State University and administered by the Division of Campus Park & Planning.

WHITE CLOUD

HURON/MANISTEE NATIONAL FORESTS—
LODA LAKE WILDFLOWER SANCTUARY

Felch Avenue & Five Mile Road (off State Route 37), White Cloud, MI 49304
Tel: (231) 745-4631
Internet Address: http://www.fs.fed.us/r9/hmnf

Admission: Fee: $3.00/vehicle
Attendance: 1,500
Established: 1938
Wheelchair Accessible: P
Parking: On site
Best Time(s) of Year to Visit: March to June
Facilities: Grounds (72 acres); Picnic Area; Trail (1 ½ miles)
Activities: Self-guided Tour Botany Tour (brochure available on site)

The preserve contains over 150 different species of native plants, wildflowers, trees, and vegetation. Support for the sanctuary is provided by the Federated Garden Club of Michigan. A detailed brochure on the Sanctuary and its diverse flora is available from the Ranger District Office at 650 N. Michigan Avenue, Baldwin, MI 49304.

MISSISSIPPI

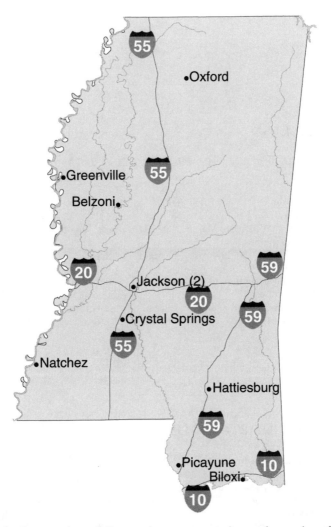

The number in parentheses following the city name indicates the number of gardens/arboreta in that municipality. If there is no number, one is understood. For example, in the text two listings would be found under Jackson and one listing under Crystal Springs.

BELLZONI

WISTER GARDENS

500 Henry Road (Route 7, just north of Belzoni), Belzoni, MS 39038
Tel: (662) 247-3025
Admission: Free
Open: Daily, 9am-5pm
Closed: Legal holidays
Best Time(s) of Year to Visit: late March to April (azaleas), June to July (day lilies), July to September (crape myrtles)
Facilities: Gardens (azalea, day lily, rose); Grounds (14 acres)

The gardens contain thousands of azaleas of many varieties lining pathways, wooded areas, and drives. Also providing spring color are a variety of fruit trees, such as pear, peach, plum, apple, apricot, and nectarine. Other collections include day lilies; hundreds of roses, both scattered throughout the site and featured in two designated rose gardens; and crape myrtles.

BILOXI

BEAUVOIR: THE JEFFERSON DAVIS HOME AND PRESIDENTIAL LIBRARY—GARDENS

2244 Beach Boulevard (Route 90), Biloxi, MS 39531
Tel: (800) 570-3818; Fax: (228) 388-7082
Internet Address: http://www.beauvoir.org
Admission: Fee: adult $7.50, child $4.50, senior $6.75
Attendance: 85,000
Membership: Y
Wheelchair Accessible: Y
Parking: Gravel parking lot, approximately 120 spaces
Open: Spring to Summer, daily, 9am-5pm; Fall to Winter, daily, 9am-4pm
Closed: Thanksgiving Day, Christmas Eve to Christmas Day
Best Time(s) of Year to Visit: April to May, October to November
Facilities: Architecture Beauvoir (antebellum residence, 1852); Gardens; Grounds (52 acres)
Activities: Education Programs; Guided Tours (daily), Groups (reserve in advance)

The last home of Jefferson Davis, president of the Confederate States of America as well as United States senator and secretary of war, Beauvoir was constructed in 1853. The restored house and out buildings, furnished mostly with original Davis pieces, are surrounded by landscaped grounds, a bayhead swamp, and ancient forest. The grounds are being developed into a botanical garden, Gulf Coast Botanical Gardens at Beauvoir, to enhance the historic buildings and to restore wildlife and migratory bird habitats. Owned and operated by the Mississippi Division, United Sons of Confederate Veterans, Inc., the site is listed on the National Register of Historic Places and is designated a National Historic Landmark.

CRYSTAL SPRINGS

MISSISSIPPI STATE UNIVERSITY—TRUCK CROPS EXPERIMENT STATION DEMONSTRATION GARDENS

Highway 51 South (25 miles south of Jackson), Crystal Springs,
MS 39059
Tel: (601) 892-3731; Fax: (601) 892-2056
Internet Address: http://www.msstate.edu/dept/cmrec/truckcrops.htm
Admission: Free
Attendance: 9,000
Established: 1938
Membership: N
Wheelchair Accessible: P
Parking: Free on site
Open: Monday to Friday, 9am-2pm
Best Time(s) of Year to Visit: October (during FF&G Fest)
Facilities: Gardens (flower, herb, vegetable); Greenhouses (9); Grounds
Demonstration Gardens (3 acres), Station (175 acres)
Activities: Events Fall Flower & Garden Fest (mid-October); Plant Sales

The site contains plantings of several varieties of over forty species of vegetables as well as an extensive herb garden, an annual flower garden, and a corn maze. Exhibits include an All-America Selections display garden, a Mississippi Medallion Winners garden, ornamental grasses, a Latino garden, an African garden, a shade garden, climbing vegetables/flowers, compost demonstration, and butterfly gardening.

GREENVILLE

WASHINGTON COUNTY COURTHOUSE ARBORETUM

900 Washington Avenue, Greenville, MS 38703
Tel: (662) 332-1595
Admission: Free
Established: 1978
Membership: N
Parking: Courthouse parking lot and on street
Facilities: Arboretum (native trees)

The courthouse grounds contain an arboretum featuring indigenous trees. Labels identify each of the twenty-six different species, a project of the Greenville Council of Garden Clubs.

HATTIESBURG

UNIVERSITY OF SOUTHERN MISSISSIPPI—ROSE GARDEN

Hardy Street Entrance, Hattiesburg, MS 39406
Tel: (601) 266-4491
Established: 1973

Situated on the campus front lawn, this All-America Rose Selections accredited garden features 750 hybrid tea and grandiflora patented rose bushes. Semi-circular in design, the garden consists of thirty-two separate beds, each with its own unique rose hybrid. An additional 500 roses are scattered in plantings throughout the campus. The Hattiesburg Area Rose Society provides development assistance.

JACKSON

CITY OF JACKSON—MYNELLE GARDENS

4736 Clinton Boulevard, Jackson, MS 39209-2406
Tel: (601) 960-1894; Fax: (601) 922-5759
Admission: Fee: adult $4.00, child (4-12) $1.00
Attendance: 12,392
Established: 1958
Membership: Y
Wheelchair Accessible: Y
Parking: Paved parking
Open: March to October, Monday to Saturday, 9am-5:15pm; November to February, Monday to Saturday, 8am-4:15pm
Facilities: Gardens (azalea, camellia, day lily, oriental, white)

The gardens, the work of Mynelle Westbrook Haywood and now a city park, include an azalea trail, an All-American Selection garden, a camellia trail, an oriental island, a white lawn (Wedding Lawn), and a Hemerocallis Society display garden.

MISSISSIPPI AGRICULTURE AND FORESTRY MUSEUM—ROSE GARDEN

1150 Lakeland Drive, Jackson, MS 39216
Tel: (800) 844-8687; Fax: (601) 982-4292
Internet Address: http://www.mdac.state.ms.us/Library/BBC/
AgMuseum/AgForMuseum.html
Admission: Fee: adult $4.00, child (3-5) $.50, student $2.00, senior $3.00
Established: 1985
Parking: Across the bridge at Smith Wills Stadium lot
Open: Monday to Saturday, 9am-5pm
Best Time(s) of Year to Visit: April to May
Facilities: Garden (rose); Grounds (¾-1 acre)

The complex of museum buildings includes an All-America Rose Selections accredited rose garden.

NATCHEZ

ROSALIE MANSION—GARDENS

100 Orleans Street at Canal Street, Natchez, MS 39120-3452
Tel: (601) 445-4555
Internet Address: http://www.rosalie.net
Admission: Fee: adult $6.00, student $3.00
Established: 1938
Open: Daily, 9am-5pm
Facilities: Architecture (Federal-style residence, 1820); Gardens (annual, fernery, herb, perennial, rose, vegetable, water); Grounds (10 acres), Formal Gardens (4 acres, 1985 design by landscape architect Ron Griffin)
Activities: Guided Tours (9:30am-4:30pm, $6/person), Garden Tours (arrange in advance)

Overlooking the Mississippi River, Rosalie's grounds include classical planting beds and gardens featuring many southern heritage plants, a fernery, a water garden, an herb garden, a vegetable garden, and educational plantings of cotton and indigo. Owned and operated by the Mississippi State Society Daughters of the American Revolution (MSS-DAR), the site is listed on the National Register of Historic Places.

OXFORD

UNIVERSITY OF MISSISSIPPI—ROWAN OAK

Old Taylor Road, Oxford, MS 38655
Tel: (601) 234-3284
Internet Address: http://www.mcsr.olemiss.edu/~egjbp/faulkner/rowanoak.html
Admission: Voluntary contribution
Attendance: 70,000
Membership: N
Wheelchair Accessible: P
Parking: 15 parking spaces
Open: Daily, dawn to dusk
Facilities: Architecture (antebellum Greek Revival residence; fee or tour); Gardens (formal, rose, scuppernong arbor); Grounds (20 acres)

The home of author William Faulkner, the landscaped grounds include a concentric circle garden surrounded by cedars and featuring raised brick beds, a rose garden, and a scuppernong arbor.

PICAYUNE

MISSISSIPPI STATE UNIVERSITY—
THE CROSBY ARBORETUM (AHS RAP)

Interpretive Center, 370 Ridge Road, Picayune, MS 39466
Tel: (601) 799-2311 Ext: 22; Fax: (601) 799-2372

Internet Address: http://msstate.edu/dept/crec/camain.html
Admission: Fee: adult $4.00, child (<12) $2.00
Attendance: 7,000
Established: 1980
Membership: Y
Wheelchair Accessible: Y
Parking: Parking available at visitors' entrance
Open: Wednesday to Sunday, 9am-5pm
Closed: Thanksgiving Day, Christmas Eve to New Year's Day
Best Time(s) of Year to Visit: Spring to Summer
Facilities: Arboretum; Architecture Pinecote Pavilion (1986, design by architect
Euine Fay Jones); Grounds (8 sites; 1,000 acres), Interpretive Center (104 acres);
Nature Paths; Shop
Activities: Education Programs (adults and children); Films; Guided Tours (by
appointment; groups only); Lectures; Native Plant Sales

Situated in the Pearl River Drainage Basin, Crosby Arboretum consists of the interpretive center and seven natural areas, totaling more than 1,500 acres and supporting more than 700 species of native trees, shrubs, grasses, and wildflowers. Activities are coordinated from the interpretive center with Pinecote Pavilion serving as the hub, a starting point for tours, a place for exhibits and performances, and a setting for social gatherings. The natural areas were selected to portray a diversity of vegetation types, including beech-magnolia woodland; hillside bog; low, non-alluvial, hardwood swamp; longleaf pint forest; bottomland hardwood; flat savanna; deadwater stream; and sandy areas. Tours of the natural areas are regularly scheduled as part of the arboretum program schedule. Established in 1980 as a memorial to south Mississippi timber pioneer L. O. Crosby, the arboretum was donated to Mississippi State University by the Crosby Foundation in 1997.

NEW HAMPSHIRE

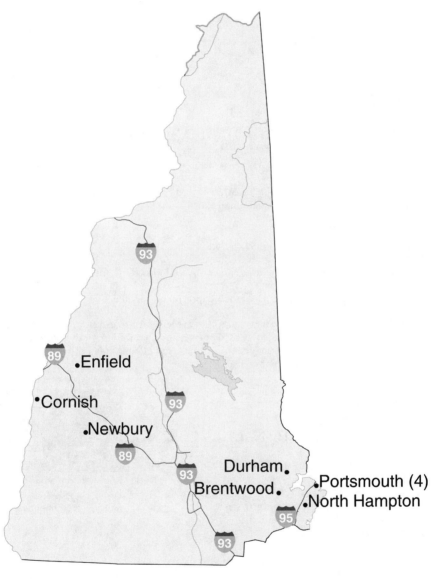

The number in the parentheses following the city name indicates the number of gardens/ arboreta in that municipality. If there is no number, one is understood. For example, in the text four listings would be found under Portsmouth and one listing under Cornish.

BRENTWOOD

ROCKINGHAM COUNTY BOTANICAL GARDEN (AHS RAP)

113B North Road 1 (off Route 101, across from the County Nursing Home),
Brentwood, NH 03833-6623
Tel: (603) 679-5616; Fax: (603) 679-8070
Internet Address: http://rockinghambotanical.org
Admission: Free
Membership: Y
Open: April to mid-October, Thursday, 9am-noon
Best Time(s) of Year to Visit: June to August
Facilities: Gardens (butterfly, children's, day lily, herb, labyrinth, perennial,
vegetable); Grounds (10 acres)
Activities: Demonstrations; Events Garden Expo (June); Guided Tours

Located on a portion of the county farm, the gardens feature exhibits and demonstrations on vegetable gardening, perennials, lawn care, and composting. In the early stage of its development, the garden is a project of the University of New Hampshire Cooperative Extension Master Gardeners program.

CORNISH

SAINT-GAUDENS NATIONAL HISTORIC SITE

139 Saint-Gaudens Road (off Route 12A), Cornish, NH
03745
Tel: (603) 675-2175; Fax: (603) 675-2701
Internet Address: http://www.nps.gov/saga
Admission: Fee: adult $5.00, child free
Attendance: 35,000
Established: 1964
Wheelchair Accessible: P
Parking: Free on site
Open: Late May to October, Daily, 9am-4:30pm

Saint-Gaudens National
Historic Site, Cornish, NH.
Jeffrey Nintzel photograph.

Facilities: Architecture (Federal-style home c. 1800 & sculptor's studios); Galleries (2 with
sculpture of Augustus Saint-Gaudens, 1 with contemporary art); Gardens (Italian-style
terraced perennial gardens with sculpture); Grounds (150 acres); Library (2,000 volumes)
Activities: Concerts (Jul-Aug, Sun, 2pm); Education Programs (on request); Gallery
Talks; Guided Tours (daily); Temporary Exhibitions (3-4 contemporary artists during
season)

A unit of the National Park Service, the site features the home, gardens, and studios of Augustus Saint-Gaudens (1848-1907), one of America's greatest sculptors. During his life in Cornish, Saint-Gaudens landscaped the grounds with gardens and outdoor spaces connected by walkways, terraces and steps, and partitioned by extensive hedges. Several original trees remain, a grove of white birch trees planted before 1894 and a New Hampshire state champion honey locust tree. The terraced perennial gardens reflect a style popular in the first decades of this century: Italian in inspiration, but personal in planting details, which emphasize aesthetic effect rather than botanical interest. Sculpture, pools and fountains adorn the grounds. A popular feature is a 350-foot double allée of native white birch trees. The hills of Cornish were the site of one of the earliest artists' colonies in the United States. Also making their home in the area were landscape architect Charles Platt, garden designer Ellen Biddle Shipman, and garden writer Rose Standish Nichols.

DURHAM

UNIVERSITY OF NEW HAMPSHIRE— JESSE HEPLER LILAC ARBORETUM

Plant Biology Department, Nesmith Hall, Durham, NH 03824-3597
Tel: (603) 862-3222; Fax: (603) 862-2621
Admission: Free
Established: 1941
Open: Monday to Friday, 9am-4:30pm
Closed: Legal holidays
Facilities: Arboretum; Special Collections (lilac)
Activities: Guided Tours (by appointment)

The arboretum is devoted to New Hampshire's state flower, the lilac.

ENFIELD

ENFIELD SHAKER MUSEUM—GARDENS

24 Caleb Dyer Lane, Enfield, NH 03748
Tel: (603) 632-4346; Fax: (603) 632-4346
Internet Address: http://www.shakermuseum.org/
Admission: Fee: adult $7.00, child (<10) free, child (10-17) $3.00, student $5.00, senior $6.00
Attendance: 10,000
Established: 1986
Membership: Y
Wheelchair Accessible: N
Parking: Free on site
Open: Memorial Day to Halloween, Monday to Saturday, 10am-5pm; Sunday, noon-5pm; Halloween to Memorial Day, Saturday, 10am-4pm; Sunday, noon-4pm
Best Time(s) of Year to Visit: Summer
Facilities: Architecture (9 historic structures); Gardens (herb, flowers); Grounds (28 acres); Shop
Activities: Classes; Demonstrations; Education Programs; Temporary Exhibitions; Workshops

The site is a living history museum dedicated to interpreting and preserving the complex history of the Enfield, NH, Shaker village. Founded in 1793, the village was the ninth of eighteen Shaker communities to be established in this country and at its height consisted of more than 200 buildings (including the Great Stone Dwelling, the largest Shaker dwelling ever built) on 3,000 acres of land. The last eight Shaker's left in 1923. The extensive garden, begun in 1987, displays the various herbs, shrubs, roses, and flowers that the Shakers grew and used during the time they lived in Enfield. The Shakers valued flowers and herbs only for their functional purposes, never as decoration. Containing over 100 varieties of plants, the garden is divided into areas by type (shrub, everlastings, roses) or application (dyes, culinary, fragrance, medicinal).

NEWBURY

THE FELLS, JOHN HAY NATIONAL WILDLIFE REFUGE

Route 103A, Newbury, NH 03255
Tel: (603) 763-4789
Internet Address: http://www.thefells.org/
Admission: Fee (weekends & holidays): adult $5.00, child (<6) free, child (6-15) $2.00; Fee (weekdays & off-season): $4.00
Membership: Y
Parking: Free parking lot at entrance
Open: Grounds, daily, dawn-dusk
Best Time(s) of Year to Visit: June to August
Facilities: Architecture (Hay residence, 1891, colonial revival); Art Gallery; Gardens (perennial, rock, rose terrace, woodland); Grounds (62 acres); Shop; Trail; Visitor's Center
Activities: Guided Tours House (Memorial Day-Columbus Day, weekends & holidays); Plant Sales (daily in season)

Situated on the shores of Lake Sunapee, the Fells was the summer residence of American statesman and author John Hay. The grounds offer a blend of formal and naturalistic gardens, including a nationally-important rock garden, a rose terrace trial planting of hardy roses and unusual annuals, a perennial border, and a shade garden. The restoration of the gardens is a project of the Garden Conservancy.

NORTH HAMPTON

FULLER GARDENS

10 Willow Avenue, North Hampton, NH 03862-2228
Tel: (603) 964-5414; Fax: (603) 964-8901
Internet Address: http://www.fullergardens.org/
Admission: Fee: adult $6.00, child (<12) $2.00, student $4.00, senior $5.00
Attendance: 10,000
Membership: Y
Open: Mid-May to mid-October, Daily, 10am-5:30pm
Best Time(s) of Year to Visit: May (tulips, Japanese Garden), July to October (annuals, perennials, roses)

Facilities: Conservatory; Gardens (Colonial revival-style; hosta, Japanese, rose); Grounds Gardens (2½ acres, portions designed by Leon H. Zach of Olmsted Brothers, Boston, MA and landscape architect Arthur A. Shurcliff)
Activities: Education Programs; Horticultural Events

Formerly the summer home of Massachusetts governor Alvan T. Fuller, Fuller Gardens represent one of the last working formal estate gardens of the early twentieth century. Although the house no longer stands, the gardens, complemented by statuary and fountains, remain. Highlights include an All-America Rose Selections display garden containing over 2,000 roses; a Japanese garden liberally planted with azaleas, rhododendrons, and wisteria; a hosta display garden; a wildflower walk; colorful perennial borders and annual beds enclosed by sculpted hedges; and a conservatory filled with exotic tropical and desert plants. The gardens are maintained by the Fuller Foundation of New Hampshire.

PORTSMOUTH

CITY OF PORTSMOUTH—PRESCOTT PARK

105 Marcy Street (along the Piscataqua River, between State & Mechanic Streets), Portsmouth, NH 03801-4616
Tel: (603) 431-8748; Fax: (603) 427-1539
Internet Address: http://www.cityofportsmouth.com/prescottpark/
Admission: Free
Facilities: Gardens; Grounds (10 acres)
Activities: Arts Festival; Concerts; Performances

Located across from Strawbery Banke Museum at the edge of the Piscataqua River, Prescott Park features extensive flower gardens, including a trial garden with over 500 flower varieties, a rose garden, and a flower wall as well as tree-lined walkways, fountains, and lawn.

MOFFATT-LADD HOUSE—GARDENS

154 Market Street, Portsmouth, NH 03801-3730
Tel: (603) 436-8221; Fax: (603) 431-9063
Admission: Fee (House & Garden): $6.00; Fee (Garden only): $2.00
Established: 1911
Parking: Parking garage, 1 block away
Open: Mid-June to mid-October, Monday to Saturday, 11am-5pm; Sunday, 1pm-5pm
Facilities: Architecture (Georgian residence, 1763); Garden (late 19th century)
Activities: Garden Walks; Guided Tours

This three-story mansion, one of New England's finest examples of Georgian architecture, was the residence of William Whipple, a signer of the Declaration of Independence. The site includes a perennial garden laid out in the late nineteenth century by the last full-time resident of the house, Alexander Hamilton Ladd. It features a 300-foot axis path flanked by formal gardens leading from the house up four terraces to a wrought-iron gate at the rear boundary of the property. Highlights include an English damask rose planted in 1768 and a horse chestnut tree planted by William Whipple in 1776. Owned and operated by the National Society of the Colonial Dames of America in the State of New Hampshire, the site is designated a National Historic Landmark.

RUNDLET-MAY HOUSE—GARDENS

364 Middle Street, Portsmouth, NH 03801
Tel: (603) 436-3205
Internet Address: http://www.historicnewengland.org/visit/homes/rundlet.htm
Admission: Fee $6.00
Open: June to October 15, 1st Saturday in month
Facilities: Architecture (Federal-style residence, 1807); Grounds (2 acres)
Activities: Guided Tours (11am, noon, 1pm, 2pm, 3pm, 4pm)

The house was constructed by James Rundlet, a merchant who derived his wealth from the textile trade. Constructed on a terraced rise above the street, the house and grounds were laid out according to traditional precepts and Rundlet's predisposition for organization. Formal terraces, garden beds, a spiral trellis, and extensive fruit orchards were clearly delineated by fences, a geometric system of paths, and rows of shrubs. The landscaping is largely unchanged since Rundlet's site plan of 1812. Additional trees were planted to screen out the traffic on Middle Street. The orchard fell into disuse, and some open areas became overgrown. But the family was conservative and introduced remarkably few permanent changes. A property of Historic New England (formerly the Society for the Preservation of New England Antiquities), both the original designs for house and grounds and subsequent additions are recorded in detail in HNE's archives.

STRAWBERRY BANKE MUSEUM—GARDENS

Marcy Street on the Waterfront, 454 Court Street, Portsmouth, NH 03801-4603
Tel: (603) 433-1100; Fax: (603) 433-1115
Internet Address: http://www.strawberybanke.org/
Admission: Fee: adult $15.00, child (<5) free, child (5-17) $10.00, senior $14.00, family $28.00; reduced fees in winter.
Established: 1965
Open: May to October, Daily, 10am-5pm; Sunday, noon-5pm; November to April, Wednesday to Saturday, 10am-2pm; Sunday, noon-2pm
Closed: January
Facilities: Architecture (30 buildings); Food Services (Café); Gardens (historic); Grounds (10 acres); Picnic Area; Shop Dunaway Museum Shop; Visitor Center
Activities: Education Programs; Guided Tours

A living history museum, Strawberry Banke Museum offers a glimpse into the everyday lives of the people of Portsmouth over nearly four centuries. The site includes furnished historic houses; costumed role-players going about their daily lives and celebrating holiday traditions; and award-winning period gardens. Spanning the entire history of the area, gardens include: Sherburne Garden, a recreated early eighteenth-century vegetable and herb garden; Rider-Wood Yard, a utilitarian urban yard of the 1830s, including shed, fences, and heirloom plant varieties based on archaeological and documentary evidence; a mid-nineteenth-century orchard planted with antique varieties of fruit trees; Goodwin Garden, a mid- to late-nineteenth-century garden recreated from the original landscape plan and planted with showy exotic American and foreign plants mentioned in the detailed diary of Sarah Goodwin; Aldrich Garden (ca. 1908), a Colonial Revival garden planted with flowers mentioned in Thomas Bailey Aldrich's poetry; Victory Garden (ca. 1944), recreation of a victory garden planted with varieties advertised in the intensely patriotic garden seed catalogues of the era; and Herb Garden, a modern exhibit garden displaying herbs used for medicine, dye, housekeeping, and cooking in eighteenth- and nineteenth-century New England. The museum approaches the landscape as not merely ornamental or accidental conglomeration, but as a document for understanding the attitudes, values, resources, and forces which shaped the lives of those who lived here. For example, the Colonial Revival Garden reveals as much, if not more, about its early twentieth-century creators as it does about their idealized eighteenth-century forebears. The site is listed on the national Register of Historic Places.

NEW JERSEY

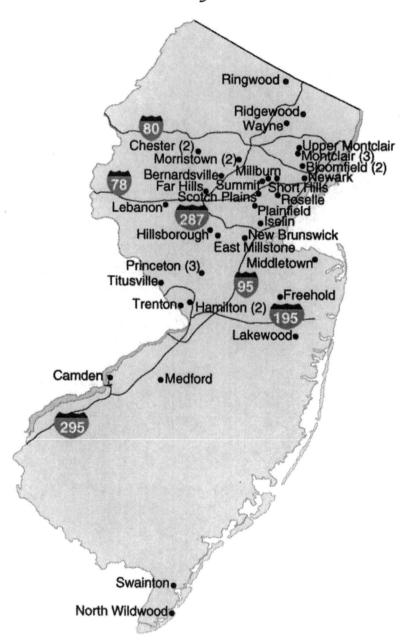

Ringwood •

Ridgewood •
Wayne •

80

Chester (2) •
Morristown (2) •
Bernardsville • Millburn
Far Hills • Summit •
Scotch Plains •
Lebanon •

78

• Upper Montclair
• Montclair (3)
• Bloomfield (2)
• Newark
• Short Hills
• Roselle
• Plainfield
• Iselin

287

Hillsborough • • New Brunswick
East Millstone

Princeton (3) •
Titusville •

95

Middletown •

• Freehold

Trenton • • Hamilton (2)

195

Lakewood •

Camden • • Medford

295

Swainton •

North Wildwood •

The number in the parentheses following the city name indicates the number of gardens/ arboreta in that municipality. If there is no number, one is understood. For example, in the text three listings would be found under Princeton and one listing under Trenton.

BERNARDSVILLE

CROSS ESTATE GARDENS

Old Jockey Hollow Road, Bernardsville, NJ 07924
Tel: (973) 539-2016
Admission: Fee $4.00
Established: 1987
Membership: Y
Parking: Small parking area adjacent to gardens.
Open: Daily, dawn-dusk
Best Time(s) of Year to Visit: Spring
Facilities: Gardens (formal walled gardens, vine-covered pergola, mountain laurel allée)

Cross Estate features an early twentieth-century formal garden containing a variety of exotic plants. There are shade gardens planted with ferns, shrubs, and perennials, a native plant area with sun- and shade-loving plants, ornamental grasses, and exceptional shrubs, hollies, and trees. The gardens are on the grounds of the Morristown National Historic Park.

BLOOMFIELD

ESSEX COUNTY—BROOKDALE PARK ROSE GARDEN

Division Street & Wildwood Avenue, Bloomfield, NJ 07003
Tel: (973) 783-9595
Established: 1959
Open: Daily, 8am-dusk
Best Time(s) of Year to Visit: May to September
Facilities: Grounds Brookdale Park (121 acres; 1928-1930 design Olmsted Brothers)

Located in Brookdale Park, an Essex County Park lying within the municipalities of Bloomfield and Monclair, the rose garden features over 750 roses representing over 100 species donated by the North Jersey Rose Society.

OAKESIDE BLOOMFIELD CULTURAL CENTER

240 Belleville Avenue, Bloomfield, NJ 07003
Tel: (973) 429-0960; Fax: (973) 429-0697
Established: 1980
Membership: Y

Wheelchair Accessible: Y
Open: Monday to Friday, 9am-3pm
Best Time(s) of Year to Visit: Spring, Summer
Facilities: Architecture (Colonial Revival-style residence, 1895); Gardens (kitchen, rose, terrace, water); Grounds (3 acres); Solarium

Oakeside was the home of the Oakes family, owners of the local textile factory and prominent citizens of Bloomfield. The house, a turn-of-the-century Colonial Revival-style residence with formally landscaped gardens and grounds, serves as a backdrop for numerous cultural events. The house and gardens are being restored with assistance from the New Jersey Historic Trust. The garden restoration is meant to return the beds to the way they were during World War I and the 1920s, when the Oakes family lived in the house, and the plot was intensely cultivated. Plans call for the conversion of the Carriage House into a horticultural learning center, expanding the interpretation possibilities for the gardens on the site. Oakeside is listed on the State and National Registers of Historic Places.

CAMDEN

CAMDEN CHILDREN'S GARDEN

3 Riverside Drive, Camden, NJ 08103
Tel: (856) 365-8733; Fax: (856) 365-9750
Internet Address: http://www.camdenchildrensgarden.org
Admission: Fee: adult $5.00, child $3.00
Established: 2000
Open: April 16 to September 15, Monday to Friday, 9:30am-5:30pm; Saturday to Sunday, 10am-5pm ; September 16 to April 15, Monday to Friday, 9:30am-4:30pm; Saturday to Sunday, 10am-5pm
Closed: New Year's Day, Thanksgiving Day, Christmas Day
Facilities: Gardens (themed children's; topiary, herb, rock, maze, native plant, picnic, dinosaur, cityscape); Grounds (4 acres; designed by Venturi, Scott, Brown)
Activities: Education Programs (on site and distance)

A project of the Camden City Garden Club, the gardens are located across the Delaware River from Philadelphia and adjacent to the New Jersey State Aquarium on the Camden waterfront. Providing horticultural experiences for creative and imaginative play, the gardens include railroad, dinosaur, picnic, tree house, and storybook gardens as well as a maze and carousel. Indoor exhibits include the Philadelphia Eagles Four Seasons Butterfly House and Education Centre and the "Plaza de Aibonito, Puerto Rico!" greenhouse exhibit.

CHESTER

BAMBOO BROOK OUTDOOR EDUCATION CENTER

170 Longview Road, Chester, NJ 07930
Tel: (800) 852-7899
Internet Address: http://parks.morris.nj.us/parks/bbrookmain.htm
Admission: Free
Parking: On site
Open: Daily, dawn-dusk
Facilities: Arboretum; Garden; Grounds (100 acres); Trails

Adjacent to Willowwood Arboretum, the center was formerly the home of William and Martha Brookes Hutcheson from 1911 to 1959. The grounds contain fields, woodlands and a formal garden designed by Mrs. Hutcheson, one of the first women to be trained as a landscape architect in the United States (MIT, 1901). Plantings include mature specimens of such trees as the Japanese Scholar Tree (sophora japonica) and American hophornbean (ostrya virginiana) as well as many native plants. Water features and a white cedar allée are some of the attractions that make wandering through the garden a delight. In addition to the formal areas, there are trails that wind through the fields and along the brook. The center is a unit of the Morris County Park Commission.

WILLOWWOOD ARBORETUM

300 Longview Road, Chester, NJ 07930
Tel: (201) 326-7600
Internet Address: http://parks.morris.nj.us/parks/wwmain.htm
Admission: Free
Wheelchair Accessible: P
Parking: Free on site
Open: Daily, 8am-dusk
Closed: New Year's Day, Thanksgiving Day, Christmas Day
Facilities: Arboretum; Architecture (residence, ca. 1792); Gardens; Grounds (130 acres); Special Collections (cherry, conifer, holly, lilac, magnolia, maple, oak, willow); Trails; Visitor Center
Activities: Self-guided Tours (map available in parking lot)

Willowwood Arboretum contains approximately 3,500 varieties of native and exotic plants, some of which date from the original plantings of Henry and Robert Tubbs, who purchased the site in 1908. In addition to the naturally landscaped arboretum, two small formal gardens flank the original residence. The arboretum is a unit of the Morris County Park Commission.

EAST MILLSTONE

COLONIAL PARK ARBORETUM AND GARDENS

156 Mettler's Road, East Millstone, NJ 08873-9802
Tel: (732) 873-2459; Fax: (732) 873-3896; TDDY: (732) 873-0327
Internet Address: http://www.park.co.somerset.nj.us/
Admission: Free; Rose Garden: $1.00 donation requested
Established: 1970
Wheelchair Accessible: Y
Parking: Free on site
Open: Garden: Memorial Day to Labor Day, Daily, 10am-8pm; Garden: Labor Day to October, Daily, 10am-4:30pm; Arboretum, Daily, dawn-dusk.
Best Time(s) of Year to Visit: May to early June, early October
Facilities: Arboretum; Gardens (bridal, herb, perennial, rose, sensory/fragrance); Grounds Arboretum (144 acres), Garden (5 acres), Park (568 acres); Picnic Area; Visitor Center
Activities: Guided Tours (groups by reservation in advance)

A wide variety of horticultural displays are found in Colonial Park. The arboretum exhibits labeled specimens of flowering trees, evergreens, shade trees, and flowering shrubs that grow well in central New Jersey. Located near parking lot F, the van der Goot Rose Garden, features formal plantings of more than 3,000 roses of 325 varieties. Named after Somerset County's first horticulturist, it is an accredited All-America Rose Selections display garden. Just beyond the Rose Garden are the Fragrance and Sensory Garden, a circular garden, designed to be of special interest to visitors who are visually or physically impaired, with raised beds of scented flowers, fragrant leaves, and plants with unusual textures, and the Perennial Garden, a selection of flowering bulbs, perennials, annuals, and flowering trees and shrubs planted in beds surrounding a gazebo. The park is a unit of the Somerset County Park Commission.

FAR HILLS

LEONARD J. BUCK GARDENS

Somerset County Park Commission, 11 Layton Road, Far Hills, NJ 07931
Tel: (908) 234-2677; Fax: (908) 234-9409
Internet Address: http://www.park.co.somerset.nj.us/
Admission: Suggested contribution: adult $3.00, child $1.00, senior $1.00
Attendance: 11,000
Membership: N
Wheelchair Accessible: P
Parking: Visitor Center & adjacent overflow lot
Open: April to November, Monday to Friday, 10am-4pm; Saturday, 10am-5pm; Sunday, noon-5pm; December to March, Monday to Friday, 10am-4pm.
Closed: Legal holidays
Best Time(s) of Year to Visit: Spring, Fall (foliage)
Facilities: Gardens (rock, meadow, pond, stream, woodland); Grounds Gardens (13 acres), Park (33 acres)
Activities: Guided Tours (groups by advance reservation); Workshops

Located in Far Hills, Buck Gardens is one of the premier rock gardens in the United States. Designed to be ecologically correct and not recognizable as being man-made, it features planted rock outcroppings, woodland trails lined with wildflowers, stream and lakeside plantings as well as displays of azaleas, ferns, heaths, and heathers. The garden is a unit of the Somerset County Park Commission.

FREEHOLD

HOLMDEL ARBORETUM

Holmdel Park, 85 S. Holmdel Road, Freehold, NJ 07733-2129
Tel: (732) 842-4000
Internet Address: http://www.manasquan.com/parks/holmdel.htm
Admission: Free
Wheelchair Accessible: P
Open: Daily, 8am-dusk
Best Time(s) of Year to Visit: Late April to June
Facilities: Arboretum; Grounds Park (347 acres); Picnic Area; Special Collections (dwarf conifer)
Activities: Guided Tours (schedule in advance)

Containing over 800 varieties of flowering trees, ornamentals, shrubs, and plant collections, the arboretum includes the Jane Kluis Memorial Dwarf Conifer Garden and the Alvarez Synoptic Garden. Holmdel Park is also the site of historic Longstreet Farm, a living history farm where employees dressed in period costume re-create Monmouth County's turn-of-the-century agricultural lifestyle. Holmdel Park is a unit of the Monmouth County Parks System.

HAMILTON

KUSER FARM MANSION—GARDENS

Entrances: 390 New Kirk Avenue & Kuser Road at Ferrante Lane, Hamilton, NJ 08610
Tel: (609) 890-3630; Fax: (609) 890-3632
Internet Address: http://www.hamiltonnj.com
Admission: No charge, donations accepted
Attendance: 28,000
Established: 1977
Wheelchair Accessible: P
Parking: Parking lot available at both entrances
Open: Gardens, Daily, dawn-dusk.
Mansion: February to April, Saturday to Sunday, 11am-3pm; May to November, Thursday to Sunday, 11am-3pm
Best Time(s) of Year to Visit: Summer (Garden)
Facilities: Architecture (Queen Anne-style 1892 residence, 22 rooms); Gardens; Grounds (22 acres); Picnic Area
Activities: Concerts(Summer); Education Programs; Guided Tours Mansion (Feb-Apr, Sat-Sun, last full tour 2pm; May-Nov, Thurs-Sun, last full tour 2pm; Jun-Aug, additional Sunday evening tours, 5pm/6pm/7pm); Events Winter Wonderland (Victorian Christmas Holiday Open House with 42 decorated trees and 150 poinsettias), Self-guided Tours Grounds (map available at mansion)

The farm was the former summer home of the Kusers, manufacturers of the Walter Car and the Mercer Car and originators of the Fox Film Corporation in 1915. Surrounding the mansion are natural environs punctuated with a formal garden, flowerbeds, a gazebo, tennis courts, lawn bowling courts, a lovely fountain, and park benches.

SAYEN PARK BOTANICAL GARDEN (SAYEN GARDENS)

155 Hughes Drive (at Mercer Street), Hamilton Township, NJ 08690
Tel: (609) 890-3543; Fax: (609) 581-4122
Internet Address: http://www.hamiltonnj.com/development/dev_parks.html
Admission: No charge, donations accepted
Attendance: 15,000
Established: 1991
Membership: Y
Wheelchair Accessible: Y
Parking: Parking available
Open: Daily, dawn-dusk
Best Time(s) of Year to Visit: Spring
Facilities: Architecture (historic Arts and Crafts home); Gardens; Grounds (27 acres—ericaceous plants, koi pond)
Activities: Events Azalea Festival (Mother's Day)

The garden features thousands of rhododendron and azaleas, daffodils and perennial displays, including rare and exotic plants from all over the world.

HILLSBOROUGH

DUKE FARMS (DUKE FARMS)

80 Route 206 South, Hillsborough, NJ 08844
Tel: (908) 722-3700
Internet Address: http://www.dukefarms.org
Admission: Guided Tour (reserve in advance): adult $10.00, child (6-12) $5.00, senior $8.00
Attendance: 40,000
Established: 1964
Membership: N
Wheelchair Accessible: N
Parking: Paved parking lot
Open: Mid-April to mid-November, Wednesday to Sunday, 9:30-3:30 (Park Tour); September to May, Wednesday to Sunday, 10:40-3:00 (Greenhouse Tour)
Closed: Legal holidays
Facilities: Climatic Areas (American desert, semi-tropical, tropical rain forest); Gardens (Chinese, English: knot, herbaceous border, rock, succulent, topiary, French parterre, Italian courtyard, Indo-Persian, Japanese, south Atlantic Coast Colonial); Greenhouses
Activities: Guided Tours bus tour of 700-acre estate (reserve in advance)

Built in 1893, Duke Farms was the estate of James B. Duke, one of the most successful entrepreneurs at the turn of the twentieth century. The Park Tour explores the 700-acre estate, featuring lakes, lawns, woods, meadows, waterfalls, ornamental fountains, and bridges, which became a showplace of American ingenuity and success. The greenhouse displays are a breathtaking collection of gardens from diverse cultures and regions of the world, designed by Doris Duke. Italian, English, Colonial, Chinese, Japanese, and Indo-Persian designs are juxtaposed with desert, semi-tropical, and jungle environments. The gardens are exquisitely maintained and presented at their peak, all under an acre of glass.

ISELIN

WOODBRIDGE GARDEN CLUB—GARDEN FOR THE BLIND (GARDEN FOR THE BLIND)

1081 Green Street, Iselin, NJ 08830
Tel: (732) 283-1200
Admission: Free
Established: 1974
Parking: Small parking lot
Open: Daily, dawn-dusk
Best Time(s) of Year to Visit: Spring to Summer
Facilities: Garden (annual, rose, rock, sensory, spring, summer)

Divided into summer, primrose, rose, spring, rock & annuals section, the garden also contains a "Circle of the Senses," featuring plantings at waist level accompanied by Braille signs.

LAKEWOOD

GEORGIAN COURT UNIVERSITY—SISTER MARY GRACE BURNS ARBORETUM

900 Lakewood Avenue, Lakewood, NJ 08701-2697
Tel: (732) 987-2373; Fax: (732) 987-2021
Internet Address: http://www.georgian.edu
Admission: Free
Established: 1989
Membership: N
Wheelchair Accessible: P
Parking: Free on site
Open: Daily, 8am-dusk
Best Time(s) of Year to Visit: April to May (Japanese & Sunken Gardens), mid-May to September (Formal & Italian Garden)
Facilities: Arboretum; Architecture (Georgian-style residence, 1896 design by Bruce Price); Gardens (formal, Italian, Japanese, sunken); Greenhouse (300 square feet); Grounds Campus (150 acres)

The Georgian Court University campus is the former winter home of George Jay Gould, and has been designated a National Historic Landmark. Major elements of the arboretum are the estate's four original gardens and the newer Founders Grove. As well as designing the buildings of the estate, architect Bruce Price designed three of the four major gardens: the Classic or Italian Garden, the Sunken Garden or Lagoon, and the Formal Garden. The fourth, a Japanese Garden, was designed by Takeo Shiota. In addition to a large number of exotic plant species, the arboretum features a collection of native plants found in the New Jersey Pine Barrens. The college greenhouse, featuring geraniums, succulents, ferns, orchids, insectivorous plants, and bromeliads, is also open to the public.

LEBANON

HUNTERDON COUNTY ARBORETUM

1020 Route 31, Lebanon, NJ 08833
Tel: (908) 782-1158
Admission: Free
Parking: Free on site
Open: Daily, dawn-dusk
Facilities: Gardens (butterfly/hummingbird, herb, moon, native plant, rock); Greenhouse; Grounds (73 acres); Picnic Area; Trails

Once a commercial nursery, the arboretum contains distinctive trees, shrubs, and native and exotic plant material, including approximately 26,000 square feet of themed display gardens. The Edmund Laport Greenhouse features a colorful assortment of house and garden plants that are grown on site and used for demonstration purposes. An additional thirty-two undeveloped acres, named after the former property owner, J. C. Furnas, features a mixed hardwood community that serves as a haven for a wide variety of birds and animal life. The arboretum is maintained by the Hunterdon County Park System.

MEDFORD

LEWIS W. BARTON ARBORETUM AT MEDFORD LEAS RETIREMENT COMMUNITY

State Highway 70 (¼ mile east of Medford Circle), Medford, NJ 08055
Tel: (609) 654-3000
Internet Address: http://www.medfordleas.org/arbor.htm
Admission: Free
Established: 1981
Membership: N
Wheelchair Accessible: P
Parking: Park at Nature Center
Open: Daily, 9am-5pm
Best Time(s) of Year to Visit: Spring
Facilities: Arboretum; Food Services Coffee Shop (10:45am-1:45pm); Gardens (courtyard, herb, rhododendron, terrace); Greenhouses (2); Pinetum; Special Collections (chestnut, conifer, crab apple, holly, viburnum)
Activities: Guided Tours (arrange in advance, 654-3007)

Located on the edge of the New Jersey Pine Barrens, the landscaped grounds, courtyard and patio gardens, wildflower meadows, recreational areas, wetlands and natural woodlands of the Medford Leas Retirement Community constitute the Lewis W. Barton Arboretum. The arboretum was created and is maintained with the advice and technical assistance of the staff of the Morris Arboretum of the University of Pennsylvania. It is affiliated with Greater Philadelphia Gardens, a consortium of public gardens in the Delaware Valley. Horticultural sites include terrace and herb gardens, thirty-six courtyard gardens, a greenhouse, the Maldeis Rhododendron Garden, and many others. A natural area of flood plain forest occupies approximately one-third of the grounds. Visitors should check in at the reception desk in the Community Building, where maps and brochures for self-guided walks through the courtyards and along various trails in the pinetum, meadow, and woodlands are available.

MIDDLETOWN

MONMOUTH COUNTY PARKS—DEEP CUT GARDENS

352 Red Hill Road, Middletown, NJ 07748-2410
Tel: (732) 671-6050
Internet Address: http://www.monmouthcountyparks.com/parks/deepcut.html
Admission: Free
Established: 1977
Wheelchair Accessible: P
Open: Daily, dawn-dusk
Facilities: Gardens (butterfly/hummingbird, meadow, perennial, rock, shade, vegetable); Greenhouse; Grounds (52 acres; 1935 design by Theodore Stout); Horticultural Center; Library Elvin McDonald Horticultural Library (3,000 volumes; Mon-Fri, 9am-4pm)
Activities: Classes; Events Deep Cut Gardens Festival (spring)

Dedicated to the home gardener, Deep Cut Gardens is planned as a living catalogue of cultivated and native plants. Highlights include a butterfly and hummingbird garden, lily pond, shade garden, azalea and rhododendron walk, rockery, meadow walk vegetable gardens, display greenhouse, and dried flower production field. A new rose garden is planned for the spring of 2005. The gardens are a unit of the Monmouth County Park system.

MILLBURN

TOWNSHIP OF MILLBURN—WALLBRIDGE ROSE GARDEN

Taylor Park (1 block S of Main Street & Millburn Avenue), Millburn, NJ 07041
Tel: (973) 564-7058
Admission: Free
Established: 1980
Membership: N
Wheelchair Accessible: Y
Parking: Metered on street
Open: June to frost, daily, dawn-dusk
Best Time(s) of Year to Visit: June to July
Facilities: Gardens (rose)

Containing 188 rose plants, the garden is arranged in concentric rings in four triangular beds with a gazebo in the center. The peripheral plantings consist of Korean boxwood, sorrel trees, holly, mahonia, and rhododendron. The garden is maintained jointly by the Township of Milburn and the Short Hills Garden Club.

MONTCLAIR

THE GARDEN CLUB OF MONTCLAIR—AVIS CAMPBELL GARDENS

60 South Fullerton Avenue (behind the United Way Building), Montclair, NJ 07042
Tel: (973) 746-9614
Internet Address: http://www.gardenclubofmontclair.tripod.com
Admission: Free
Established: 1952
Wheelchair Accessible: Y
Parking: Parking lot at rear of garden
Open: Daily, dawn-dusk
Best Time(s) of Year to Visit: Spring to Fall
Facilities: Gardens (English-style walled, herb, rose; shrubs); Grounds (1/4 acre)
Activities: Guided Tours

Maintained by volunteers from the Garden Club of Montclair, the gardens include a formal, English-style walled garden with a central fountain, a rose garden, and an herb garden.

CRANE HOUSE GARDENS

110 Orange Road, Montclair, NJ 07042-2133
Tel: (973) 744-1796
Internet Address: http://www.montclairhistorical.org
Admission: Free
Established: 1965

Membership: Y
Wheelchair Accessible: P
Parking: On-street parking
Open: Friday to Saturday, 1pm-4pm (House); Sunday, 2pm-5pm; dawn-dusk (Gardens)
Best Time(s) of Year to Visit: Spring to Fall
Facilities: Architecture (1796 residence, furnished with period pieces; eighteenth-century kitchen); Gardens (herb, eighteenth-century pleasure)
Activities: Guided Tours House (groups, arrange in advance)

A property of the Montclair Historical Society, the house features gardens as well as period furnishings, a schoolroom, an early American kitchen, and a country store.

VAN VLECK HOUSE & GARDENS (AHS RAP)

21 Van Vleck Street (off North Mountain Avenue), Montclair, NJ 07042
Tel: (973) 744-0837; Fax: (973) 746-1082
Internet Address: http://www.vanvleck.org/
Admission: Suggested contribution $3.00
Attendance: 4,000
Membership: Y
Parking: Limited on-site parking
Open: May, daily, 10am-5pm; June to August, Monday to Wednesday, 10am-5pm; Thursday, 10am-dusk; Friday to Sunday, 10am-5pm; September to October, daily, 10am-5pm
Best Time(s) of Year to Visit: May (wisteria, blueberry), mid-May to June (azalea, magnolia, rhododendron)
Facilities: Architecture (Mediterranean-style villa, 1916 design by Joseph Van Vleck, Jr.); Gardens (formal); Greenhouses; Grounds (6 acres); Special Collections (broad-leaved evergreens, azalea, rhododendron)
Activities: Education Programs (botanical illustration classes); Guided Tours (May; other times by appointment)

A preservation project of the Garden Conservancy, the Van Vleck House and Gardens is dedicated to preserving for public enrichment the spirit and beauty of this late nineteenth- and early twentieth-century site. The gardens, the product of the efforts of three generations of the family, feature a collection of azaleas, rhododendrons, and other broad-leaved evergreens.

MORRIS TOWNSHIP

THE GEORGE G. FRELINGHUYSEN ARBORETUM (AHS RAP)

53 E. Hanover Avenue, Morris Township, NJ 07962-1295
Tel: (201) 326-7600; Fax: (201) 644-2726
Internet Address: http://parks.morris.nj.us/asp/parks/park_results.asp
Admission: Voluntary contribution
Attendance: 50,000
Established: 1970
Membership: Y
Wheelchair Accessible: Y

Open: Grounds, daily, 9am-dusk; Education Center, daily, 9am-4:30pm
Closed: New Year's Day, Thanksgiving Day, Christmas Day
Facilities: Architecture (located on grounds of Whippany Farm Residence, 1891);
Auditorium (200 seats); Classrooms (2); Education Center; Gardens (formal rose, lilac,
perennial, wildflower); Grounds (127 acres); Library (2,500 volumes, by
appointment); Nature Conservation Center
Activities: Arts Festival; Concerts (summer); Education Programs (adult,
undergraduate and children); Films; Gallery Talks; Guided Tours (groups reserve in
advance); Lectures; Temporary Exhibitions; Traveling Exhibitions; Workshops

Surrounding a magnificent Colonial Revival mansion, the arboretum contains woodlands, meadows, gardens, and distinctive collections of trees and shrubs. Also located in
the arboretum are the Joseph F. Haggerty Education Center and Home Demonstration
Gardens. Self-guiding trail booklets are available at the reception desk. The Frelinghuysen
Arboretum is a unit of the Morris County Parks Commission.

MORRISTOWN

ACORN HALL—GARDENS

68 Morris Avenue, Morristown, NJ 07960-4212
Tel: (973) 267-3465
Internet Address: http://www.acornhall.org
Admission: Fee (Museum): adult $5.00, student $2.00, senior $4.00
Established: 1971
Parking: Next door at the Governor Morris Hotel
Open: Monday, 10am-4pm; Thursday, 10am-4pm; Sunday, 1:30pm-4pm
Closed: Legal holidays
Best Time(s) of Year to Visit: Spring to Summer
Facilities: Architecture (Italianate Victorian residence, 1853); Gardens; Library
(Victorian research); Shop
Activities: Guided Tours Groups (by appointment), Museum (Thurs, 11am-3pm; Sun,
1:30pm-4pm)

Acorn Hall derives its name from one of the largest and oldest red oak trees in New Jersey located on its grounds. The mansion retains 95 percent of its original furnishings, plus
other examples of Victoriana, including costumes, furnishings, and "made in Morristown"
pieces. The landscaped Victorian gardens, featuring nineteenth century flowers and
shrubs, were designed and are maintained by the Home Garden Club of Morristown. The
site is the headquarters of the Morris County Historical Society.

NEW BRUNSWICK

RUTGERS UNIVERSITY—THE RUTGERS GARDENS

112 Ryders Lane at U.S. Route #1, New Brunswick, NJ 08901
Tel: (908) 932-8451; Fax: (908) 932-7060
Internet Address: http://www.cook.rutgers.edu/%7erugardens/
Admission: Voluntary contribution
Attendance: 50,000

Established: 1935
Open: May to September, Daily, 8:30am-dusk; October to April, Daily, 8:30am-4:30pm
Facilities: Gardens; Grounds (50 acres)
Activities: Education Programs (undergraduate college students, youth and children); Festival Fall Foliage Festival (October); Guided Tours; Plant Sales Spring Flower Fair (Mother's Day Weekend)

The gardens contain a wide variety of plant collections arranged in a series of gardens, including a display garden, gardens for sun and shade, and an All-American Selections display garden. Collections include azaleas/rhododendrons, dogwoods, evergreens, hollies, shrubs, small trees, and shade trees. The gardens adjoin Frank G. Helyar Woods, a virgin forest that can be toured via its marked trails, Weston's Mill Pond, and the Log Cabin & Pavilion.

NEWARK

ESSEX COUNTY—BRANCH BROOK PARK

Park Avenue and Lake Street (off Heller Parkway), Newark, NJ 07109
Tel: (973) 268-3500; Fax: (973) 481-5302
Internet Address: http://www.newark1.com/branchbrook
Established: 1895
Open: Daily, dawn-dusk
Best Time(s) of Year to Visit: late April (cherry blossoms)
Facilities: Grounds (360 acres, 1900 revision of original design by Olmsted Brothers landscape architectural firm); Special Collections (flowering cherry trees)
Activities: Events Cherry Blossom Festival (Apr)

The first county park to be opened for public use in the United States, Branch Brook Park is listed on both the New Jersey and the National Registers of Historic Places. The park was originally intended to remain in its natural state, a gently rolling terrain of open meadowland with small patches of woodland, but today it is used largely for athletic activities. Branch Brook is especially known for its annual cherry blossom festival, reputed to be the largest such display in the world. The site contains more than 2,200 ornamental cherry trees of four different species.

NORTH WILDWOOD

HEREFORD LIGHTHOUSE GARDENS

1st & Central Avenues, Village of Anglesea, North Wildwood, NJ 08260
Tel: (609) 522-4520
Admission: Fee (lighthouse): adult $4.00, child (<12) $1.00;
Free (gardens)
Attendance: 40,000
Established: 1986
Membership: N

Hereford Lighthouse Gardens, North Wildwood, NJ.

Wheelchair Accessible: P
Parking: Small off street lot and on street parking
Open: Gardens: daily, dawn-dusk; Lighthouse: mid-May to mid-October, daily, 9am-5pm; Lighthouse: mid-October to mid-May, daily, 10am-4pm
Best Time(s) of Year to Visit: June to July
Facilities: Architecture (Swiss Gothic-style lighthouse, 1874); Garden (cottage; herb, scent, shade, winter); Grounds (1½ acres)
Activities: Guided Tours (groups 10+); Self-guided Tour; Temporary Exhibitions

A functioning lighthouse and a living history museum, the Hereford Inlet Lighthouse is listed in the National Register of Historic Places. The lighthouse gardens are planned in the "cottage" style, intended to mimic the unplanned, rustic look of the peasant gardens of early England. Plantings are placed thickly with many different varieties, heights, shapes, and colors. The gardens contain approximately 200 varieties of plants, including cottage garden favorites hollyhocks, nicotiana, nasturtium, snapdragons, and foxgloves. Garden features such as arbors, fences, birdbaths, urns and clay pots are almost as important as flowers in this style. The site is under the stewardship of the City of North Wildwood.

PLAINFIELD

UNION COUNTY—SHAKESPEARE GARDEN AT CEDAR BROOK PARK

Pemberton Avenue & Randolph Road, Plainfield, NJ 07060
Tel: (908) 527-4900; Fax: (908) 527-4901
Internet Address: http://www.plainfield.com/bardgard/index.htm
Admission: Free
Established: 1927
Parking: Lot near garden, 20 vehicles & along Park Drive
Open: Daily, dawn-dusk
Best Time(s) of Year to Visit: June to August
Facilities: Garden (Shakespeare, 1927 design by Olmsted Brothers of Boston); Grounds

Located in Cedar Brook Park, one of Union County's system of public parks and recreation spaces, the garden consists of two beds, each one hundred feet long, plus seventeen other flower beds. In addition to plants mentioned in Shakespeare's work, the garden includes rock garden plants, herbs, and a rose bed featuring old-fashioned roses, and a rustic arbor shaded by woodbine and bordered by wild thyme and eglantine. Among the trees on the site are holly, English hawthorn, mulberry, and yew clipped in topiary style. The Shakespeare Garden is maintained by the Plainfield Garden Club, with the assistance of the Union County Parks Department.

PRINCETON

PRINCETON UNIVERSITY—PROSPECT GARDEN

Prospect House (near Art Museum), Princeton, NJ 08544
Tel: (609) 258-3603; Fax: (609) 258-1273
Internet Address: http://facilities.princeton.edu/prospect/

Open: Daily, dawn-dusk
Facilities: Architecture (Italianate-style residence, 1849 design by architect John Notman); Garden

One of the few university buildings not originally part of the campus, Prospect House was built as a private residence in 1849, served as the official residence of Princeton University's president from 1879 to 1968, and now houses the university's Faculty Club. Planting on the grounds, including the Cedar of Lebanon, hawthorn, and yew that stand near the tower on the west side, began shortly after the house was completed. The flower garden at the rear of Prospect was laid out in approximately its present form by Mrs. Woodrow Wilson after her husband had the iron fence erected around the garden's perimeter. Mrs. Wilson also supervised the planting of the evergreens, predominantly Canadian hemlock, that serve as a backdrop for the flower garden. The flowers are changed at regular intervals throughout the growing season. Additionally, the Princeton campus offers an extensive collection of mature specimen trees.

ROCKINGHAM STATE HISTORIC SITE—GARDENS

Route 603 (along the Delaware & Raritan Canal), Princeton, NJ 08540
Tel: (609) 683-7132
Internet Address: http://www.rockingham.net
Admission: Free
Attendance: 6,000
Membership: Y
Wheelchair Accessible: P
Parking: Lot to north of house
Open: Wednesday to Sunday, call for hours
Best Time(s) of Year to Visit: June to October
Facilities: Garden (period, 18th-century kitchen); Grounds (11 Acres); trail (canal path)
Activities: Guided Tours <10 (on a drop-in basis), group 10+ (on request)

Believed to be the second oldest house in the Millstone River Valley, dating somewhere between 1702 and 1710, Rockingham served as George Washington's last wartime headquarters in 1783. The house contains a collection of authentic eighteenth-century furniture. The house was moved to a new site in 2000. In front of the house is a recreated eighteenth-century kitchen garden, containing seventy-five varieties of vegetables, herbs, and flowers arranged in sixteen raised beds. The property is a New Jersey State Historic Site under the Department of Parks and Forestry, DEP.

TOWNSHIP OF PRINCETON—MARQUAND PARK

Lovers Lane (between Mercer Street & Route 206), Princeton, NJ 08540
Tel: (609) 497-7616; Fax: (609) 688-2040
Internet Address: http://www.princetontwp.org/marquand.html
Admission: Free
Established: 1957
Open: Daily, dawn-dusk
Best Time(s) of Year to Visit: Mid-May
Facilities: Arboretum; Grounds (17 acres); Picnic Area

Marquand Park offers woodlands, forest glades, and open parkland. The arboretum contains over 200 species of domestic and exotic and shrubs; eleven of which are the largest of their kind in the state of New Jersey. A map near the parking lot shows the location of tree specimens throughout the park. Maps detailing all specimen trees are available at Bainbridge House, the Princeton Historical Society headquarters on Nassau Street.

RIDGEWOOD

THE JAMES ROSE CENTER FOR LANDSCAPE ARCHITECTURAL RESEARCH AND DESIGN

506 E. Ridgewood Avenue (at Southern Parkway), Ridgewood, NJ 07450
Tel: (201) 446-6017; Fax: (201) 444-8085
Internet Address: http://www.jamesrosecenter.org
Admission: Fee $8.00
Open: Mid-April to October, 1st & 3rd Sat in month, 10am-4pm
Facilities: Gardens
Activities: Education Programs; Guided Tours Group (by appointment); Lecture Series; Self-guided Tours

Between 1953, when James C. Rose began constructing the house and garden, and 1991, when he died, the site was his residence. Rose was one of the founders of the modernist movement in American landscape design. More than a house and garden, it was Rose's living laboratory for the exploration and expression of his then radical ideas about the concept of home and garden. The Center provides classes, internships, scholarships, and research opportunities as well as a place to study and retreat.

RINGWOOD

NEW JERSEY STATE BOTANICAL GARDENS AT SKYLANDS MANOR

Ringwood State Park, Morris Road, Ringwood, NJ 07456
Tel: (201) 962-9534; Fax: (201) 962-1553
Internet Address: http://www.njskylandsgarden.org/
Admission: Fee (for Manor House tours): adult $5.00, child $2.00, senior $4.00
Attendance: 7,000
Established: 1966
Membership: Y
Wheelchair Accessible: N
Parking: On site (parking fee Memorial Day-Labor Day)
Open: Gardens, daily, 8am-8pm
Closed: State holidays
Best Time(s) of Year to Visit: May (crab apple blossoms)
Facilities: Architecture (45-room Tudor-style Manor House, 1922 design by John Russell Pope); Exhibition Area (1,200 square feet apart from museum); Gardens (formal, 1922 design by Vitale & Geiffert); Grounds Gardens (96 acres), Meadows & Woodland (1,000 acres); Library (600 volumes); Pinetum; Shop; Special Collections (azalea. crab apple. lilac, rhododendron. Wildflower)
Activities: Guided Tours Manor House (Mar-Dec, 1st Sun in month); Holiday Open House; Lectures; Plant Sale; Workshops

The New Jersey State Botanical Garden, part of the Ringwood State Park System, offers an elegant Tudor-style manor house, formal and naturalized gardens, and woodland paths. The garden is the culmination of the efforts of two owners of the estate, Francis Lynde Stetson from 1891 to 1922 and Clarence McKenzie Lewis from 1922 to 1966, when Skylands was acquired by the state. In 1984, the central ninety-six acres surrounding the manor house was designated the state's official botanical garden. The garden contains an extensive variety of plants, evergreens, and deciduous trees and shrubs in specialty areas. Of particular interest are the crab apple allée (a ?-mile-long, double row of 166 trees marking the border between the formal landscape and the naturalized eastern side of the estate); the terraced gardens, the extensive lilac collection (400 varieties representing 8 species), and the perennial and annual gardens. Skylands is listed on both the State and National Registers of Historic Places.

ROSELLE

UNION COUNTY—WARINANCO PARK GARDENS

St. Georges Avenue, Roselle, NJ 07203
Tel: (908) 245-2288; Fax: (908) 527-4901
Admission: Free
Established: 1926
Membership: N
Wheelchair Accessible: Y
Parking: Large lot at Chatfield Garden & roadside at Azalea Garden
Open: Daily, sunrise-sunset
Best Time(s) of Year to Visit: April to early June (azalea), mid-April to May (tulip), Summer (annuals)
Facilities: Gardens (azalea, bulb & annual)

Each spring, the Henry S. Chatfield Memorial Garden, located in Warinanco Park, features 14,200 tulips imported from Holland planted in 21 beds. As spring fades into summer, over 9,300 annual flowers, ranging from marigolds and zinnias to ageratum and celosia, dominate the garden. Additionally the Caxton Brown Memorial Azalea Garden, containing hundreds of plants in many dozens of manicured beds, is located just north of the Warinanco Park Administration Building.

SCOTCH PLAINS

TOWNSHIP OF SCOTCH PLAINS—OSBORN CANNONBALL HOUSE MUSEUM

1840 Front Street, Scotch Plains, NJ 07076
Tel: (908) 322-6700
Admission: Free
Established: 1926
Membership: N
Wheelchair Accessible: Y
Parking: Free, behind museum in parking lot by Town Hall
Open: Garden, daily, 24 hours; Museum, March to December, 1st Sun in month, 2pm-4pm and by appointment
Best Time(s) of Year to Visit: June (annuals)

Facilities: Architecture (salt-box-style farmhouse, ca. 1760); Gardens (period, flower, herb)
Activities: Guided Tours (Mar-Dec, 1st Sun in month)

Owned by the township of Scotch Plains, the historic house museum is surrounded by a colonial-style flower and herb garden. Completed in 1979, the design consists of brick paths forming a hexagonal walkway around dwarf boxwoods, yews, and annuals; roses and a fence form a barrier to the village green. The herb garden contains such plantings as lovage, sage, chives, parsley, and lamb's ear. A rear garden surrounds an old concave stone, now a bird bath, with lavender, germander, lady's mantle, marjoram, and creeping thyme. A grape arbor with an old privy adds to the Colonial theme.

SHORT HILLS

CORA HARTSHORN ARBORETUM AND BIRD SANCTUARY

324 Forest Drive South, Short Hills, NJ 07078-2308
Tel: (201) 376-3587
Internet Address: http://www.hartshornarboretum.com/
Admission: Free
Established: 1960
Membership: Y
Open: Stone House: Monday, 9am-3pm; Tuesday to Thursday, 9am-4:30pm; Friday, 9am-3pm; Saturday, 9:30am-11:30am; Grounds: daily, dawn-dusk.
Closed: Stone House: State holidays, school vacations
Best Time(s) of Year to Visit: April to May (wildflowers), October to November (autumn foliage)
Facilities: Classrooms; Grounds (16½ acres); Nature Conservation Center Stone House Museum; Shop; Trails
Activities: Concerts; Education Programs (adults and children); Films; Guided Tours (on request; groups, arrange in advance); Lectures; Workshops

The arboretum contains 45 varieties of trees and 150 species of native wildflowers and common flowers. A trail map may be found on Stone House door.

SUMMIT

REEVES-REED ARBORETUM

165 Hobart Avenue, Summit, NJ 07901-2908
Tel: (908) 273-8787; Fax: (908) 273-6869
Internet Address: http://www.reeves-reedarboretum.org/
Admission: Voluntary contribution
Attendance: 23,000
Established: 1974
Membership: Y
Wheelchair Accessible: Y
Parking: On site, 40 spaces
Open: Grounds, daily, dawn-dusk
Best Time(s) of Year to Visit: April (daffodils)

Facilities: Arboretum; Architecture Wisner House (Colonial revival residence, 1889 design the New York architecture firm of Babb, Cook and Willard); Education Center; Gardens (azalea, daffodil bowl, day lily border, herb, lilac, perennial border, rock-pool, rose); Greenhouse; Grounds (12½ acres, 1889 design by Calvert Vaux, 1924 design by Ellen Biddle Shipman, 1925 design by Carl F. Pilat), woodland (6 acres); Library (700 volumes); Shop: The Garden Shop (books, nature-related home accessories; Mon-Sat, 10am-4pm); Trails
Activities: Concerts; Education Programs (adults and children); Guided Tours; Lectures; Plant Sales; Readings; Workshops

The arboretum is noted for its gardens that represent design trends by several promi-nent landscape architects of the late nineteenth and twentieth centuries. The original landscape plan was executed by Calvert Vaux in 1889, shortly after John Horner Wisner and his wife Isobel purchased the property and contracted to have a colonial revival-style shingle house constructed on the rise between two glacial kettles. In 1924, the next own-ers, Richard and Susie Graham Reeves, commissioned New York landscape architect Ellen Biddle Shipman to devise a garden scheme. While Shipman's plan was not fully adopted as drafted, the restored Gretchen Keller azalea garden was suggested by her designs. However, Shipman's concept of a series of garden rooms was retained in the 1924-1925 designs of landscape architect Carl F. Pilat. Among the Pilat-inspired restored gardens are the Susie Graham Reeves Rose Garden, containing over 150 varieties of roses and the Richard, Graham, and Susan Reeves Rock Garden. Other highlights include an herb gar-den, a lilac garden, a serpentine perennial border, a day lily border, and a winter interest garden. In addition to the more formal gardens, the arboretum features numerous native trees that are typical of eastern deciduous low wetlands and dry uplands forests, clusters of daffodils, a wildflower trail, and a wildlife habitat. The property is now owned by the City of Summit and is listed on the National and State Registers of Historic Places.

SWAINTON

LEAMING'S RUN GARDENS AND COLONIAL FARM

1845 Shore Road (Route 9 North), Swainton, NJ 08210
Tel: (609) 465-5871
Internet Address: http://www.leamingsrungardens.com
Admission: Fee: adult $7.00, child (<7) free, child (7-18) $4.00; Annual Ticket: $15.00
Established: 1977
Wheelchair Accessible: Y
Parking: Free parking
Open: May 15 to October 20, Daily, 9:30am-5pm
Best Time(s) of Year to Visit: July, August to September
Facilities: Gardens (27 theme gardens); Shop Cooperage Gift Shop (May 15- Oct. 30, 10am-5pm; dried flowers, wreaths)

The largest annual garden in the nation, Leaming's Run Gardens features acres of flow-ers, ferns, lawns and ponds. The gardens were designed and created by Jack and Emily April and their children over an approximate five-year period. Themed gardens include yellow, blue and white, English cottage, blue and red, red and white, orange, sweetheart (pink and purple), reflection, celosia, dried flower, down Jersey, hibiscus, shades of rose, pink, and serpentine. The Colonial Farm is a replica of a New Jersey whaler's 1695 home-stead. A vegetable garden, laced with herbs, as well as tobacco and cotton, grow outside the one-room furnished log cabin.

TITUSVILLE

GEORGE WASHINGTON MEMORIAL ARBORETUM

Washington Crossing State Park, 355 Washington Crossing-Pennington Road,
Titusville, NJ 08560-1517
Tel: (609) 737-0623; Fax: (609) 737-0627
Internet Address: http://www.nj.com/outdoors/parks/washington.html
Admission: Free
Membership: N
Wheelchair Accessible: P
Parking: On site; summer, $5.00/car, fall-spring; free
Open: Nature Center, Wednesday to Saturday, 9am-4pm; Sunday, noon-4pm
Facilities: Arboretum; Grounds Arboretum (140 acres), Washington Crossing State
Park (841 acres); Nature Center (737-0639); Picnic Area; Visitor Center (737-9404)
Activities: Education Programs

Established to commemorate Washington's crossing of the Delaware in December 1776,
the park offers a variety of historic sites, natural habitats, and exhibits. It supports an interesting assortment of plants, including mixed hardwoods, red cedar forests, plant-ings of
eastern white pine, Japanese larch, Norway spruce, and red pine. A splendid variety of
spring and summer wildflowers can be found throughout the park, including the spring
avens, a rare woodland herb of the rose family. Located in the northwest portion of the
park, the Washington Crossing Natural Area contains mature mixed oak-hardwood forest,
young woodlands, and successional fields. A nature center offers exhibits and displays, and
schedules a wide range of environmental educational activities for families and groups. Additionally, the Johnson Ferry House, an eighteenth-century gambrel roof farmhouse and
tavern, includes an eighteenth-century kitchen garden and an orchard of period fruit trees.

TRENTON

1719 WILLIAM TRENT HOUSE

15 Market Street, Trenton, NJ 08611
Tel: (609) 989-3027
Internet Address: http://www.williamtrenthouse.org
Admission: Fee: adult $2.50, child (<13) $1.00, student $2.00, senior $2.00
Attendance: 18,000
Established: 1939
Wheelchair Accessible: P
Parking: Free in adjacent lot
Open: Daily, 12:30pm-4pm
Closed: Legal holidays
Best Time(s) of Year to Visit: Spring, Summer
Facilities: Architecture (Georgian residence, 1719); Gardens (period; Colonial era
kitchen garden); Grounds (2 acres)
Activities: Education Programs; Guided Tours (groups, by appointment)

The oldest building in Trenton and an important example of early Georgian domestic architecture, the house contains an extensive collection of late seventeenth- and eighteenth-
century furniture. A restored Colonial-era kitchen garden is located in the dooryard.

UPPER MONTCLAIR

PRESBY MEMORIAL IRIS GARDENS (AHS RAP)

Mountainside Park, 474 Upper Montclair Avenue, Upper Montclair, NJ 07043-1201
Tel: (973) 783-5974; Fax: (973) 783-3833
Internet Address: http://presbyiris.tripod.com
Admission: Free
Attendance: 6,000
Established: 1927
Membership: Y
Wheelchair Accessible: Y
Parking: On street
Open: Daily, dawn-dusk
Best Time(s) of Year to Visit: Mid-May to early-June
Facilities: Gardens (iris); Shop (iris and garden-related items)
Activities: Guided Tours (May 15-June 6, daily, 10am-8pm, by appointment, small fee)

Established to honor Frank H. Presby, one of the country's leading horticulturists and a founder of the American Iris Society, Presby features a collection of approximately 6 species and over 2,000 varieties of iris, some dating back to the 1500s. The gardens are listed in the National Register of Historic Places.

WAYNE

DEY MANSION GARDENS

199 Totowa Road, Wayne, NJ 07470
Tel: (973) 696-1776
Admission: Fee-$1.00
Parking: Free on site
Open: Wednesday to Friday, 1pm-4pm; Saturday to Sunday, 10am-noon & 1pm-4pm
Facilities: Architecture (Georgian residence, ca. 1740-1750); Gardens (colonial revival, herb, vegetable); Grounds (2 acres); Picnic Area
Activities: Guided Tours House (groups, by appointment)

Constructed between 1740-1750 by Dirck Dey, a Dutch-born planter, the mansion is an amalgam of Dutch and English influences. For three months in 1780, Washington used a wing as his headquarters. The gardens on the site include a formal Colonial Revival garden, herb, and vegetable gardens. The site is managed by the Passaic County Department of Parks and Recreation.

NEW YORK

The number in the parentheses following the city name indicates the number of gardens/arboreta in that municipality. If there is no number, one is understood. For example, in the text seven listings would be found under Rochester and one listing under Syracuse. Cities within the greater New York metropolitan area and on Long Island will be found on the map on the next page.

GREATER NEW YORK METROPOLITAN AREAS & LONG ISLAND

Greater New York metropolitan area and Long Island (including the New York City boroughs of Bronx, Brooklyn, Manhattan, Staten island, and Queens [Flushing and Long Island City]), and the Long Island municipalities of Bridgehampton, East Hampton, Farmingdale, Great River, Lattingtown, Mill Neck, Old Westbury, Roslyn Harbor, Oyster Bay, Sagaponack, and Southhampton).

ALEXANDRIA BAY

BOLDT CASTLE—FORMAL GARDENS

Heart Island, Alexandria Bay, NY 13607
Tel: (800) 847-5263
Internet Address: http://www.boldtcastle.com
Admission: Fee: adult $5.25, child (6-12) $3.00
Attendance: 15,000
Established: 1977
Wheelchair Accessible: Y

Boldt Castle—formal gardens, Alexandria Bay, NY.

Open: Mid-May to June, daily, 10am-6:30pm; July to August, daily, 10am-7:30pm;
September to mid-October, daily, 10am-6:30pm
Facilities: Architecture (Rhenish-style castle & dependencies, 1900-04); Food Services;
Gardens; Grounds (5 acres); Picnic Area; Shop
Activities: Self-guided Tours

At the turn-of-the-century, George C. Boldt, proprietor of the Waldorf Astoria Hotel
in New York City, set out to build a Rhineland castle as a family retreat on Heart Island
in Alexandria Bay. On the death of his wife in 1904, he abandoned the project. When the
Thousand Islands Bridge Authority acquired the property in 1977, it began restoration efforts and opened the site to the public. Accessible by water taxi, tour boat, and private
boat, the grounds include an All-American Selections display garden.

AMENIA

WETHERSFIELD ESTATE AND GARDENS

Pugsley Hill Road (off County Route 86), Amenia, NY 12501
Tel: (845) 373-8037
Admission: No charge, donations accepted
Attendance: 2,000
Membership: N
Wheelchair Accessible: P
Parking: Parking in lot
Open: Gardens: June to September, Wednesday, noon-5pm; Friday to Saturday,
noon-5pm; House & Stables, by appointment
Best Time(s) of Year to Visit: June to September
Facilities: Architecture (Georgian residence, carriage house—artworks, carriages);
Gardens 10 acres (formal, statuary)
Activities: Guided Tours House & Carriage House (by appointment)

Home of investor and philanthropist Chauncey Stillman (1907-1989), the grounds feature a formal, classical Italian-style garden surrounding a Georgian-style brick house built in 1940. The gardens were created over a twenty-five-year period by landscape architects Bryan J. Lynch and Evelyn Poehler.

ANNANDALE-ON-HUDSON

MONTGOMERY PLACE

River Road (Route 103) (3 miles north of Kingston/Rhinecliff Bridge), Annandale-on-Hudson, NY 12504
Tel: (845) 758-5461; Fax: (845) 758-0545
Internet Address: http://www.hudsonvalley.org/web/mont-main.html
Admission: Fee: adult $7.00, child $4.00, student $4.00, senior $6.00
Attendance: 28,000
Membership: Y
Wheelchair Accessible: Y
Parking: Free on site
Open: April to October, Monday, 10am-5pm; Wednesday to Sunday, 10am-5pm; November, Saturday to Sunday, 10am-5pm; December, Saturday to Sunday, noon-5pm (1st 2 weekends)
Facilities: Architecture (Federal-style residence, 1804; additions design by Alexander Jackson Davis); Garden Shop; Greenhouse (1920's); Grounds (434 acres, design influenced by Andrew Jackson Downing); Picnic Area
Activities: Education Programs; Events Antique Car Show (mid-July), Harvest Fair (mid-Oct), Hudson Valley Wine & Food Festival (mid-June); Guided Tours House, Twilight Garden Walks; Workshops

Andrew Jackson Downing, the nation's premier landscape architect, described the mansion's setting as "nowhere surpassed in America in point of location, natural beauty, or landscape gardening charms." He also considered Montgomery Place a quintessential country seat, worthy of publication and emulation. "If we have not sooner spoken at large of Montgomery Place, second as it is to no seat in America, for its combination of attractions, it is rather that we were silent like a devout gazer at the marvelous beauty of Apollos from excesses of enjoyment, than from not deeply feeling all its varied mysteries of pleasure ground, and lawns, wood and water." Today, Montgomery Place offers a restored classical revival mansion, formal gardens, woods, and walking trails with views of Hudson River and Catskill Mountains. The site is operated by the non-profit preservation organization, Historic Hudson Valley of Tarrytown.

BINGHAMTON

CORNELL COOPERATIVE EXTENSION OF BROOME COUNTY— CUTLER BOTANIC GARDENS

840 Upper Front Street (at Interstate 81, Exit 5), Binghamton, NY 13905-1500
Tel: (607) 772-8953; Fax: (607) 723-5951
Internet Address: http://www.cce.cornell.edu/broome

Admission: Voluntary contribution
Attendance: 40,000
Established: 1979
Membership: Y
Wheelchair Accessible: Y
Parking: Free on site, 200 autos, plus handicapped
parking spaces
Open: June to October, daily, daylight hours
Facilities: Garden; Greenhouse; Grounds (3½ acres)
Activities: Classes (summer and fall); Guided Tours (schedule in advance); Lectures

Situated on land given to Cornell Cooperative Extension by Miss Frances Curler, the garden is a center for teaching horticulture amd environmental issues. Displays include a perennial garden, designed to demonstrate the importance of form, color, and texture in plants; the Heritage Garden, modeled after a French potager; annual gardens, an All-American Selections Display Garden, a rose garden and rose border, a heath and heather garden, a rock garden, an herb garden, an ornamental grass garden, a native plant garden, collections of trees and shrubs, and a composting demonstration site. Cutler Botanic Gardens offers on-site opportunities for learning about new plant materials and gardening techniques. Supported solely by private contributions, the garden is administered by the Cornell Cooperative Extension of Broome County and maintained by master gardener volunteers.

ROSS PARK ZOO AND GARDENS (AHS RAP)

60 Morgan Road, Binghamton, NY 13903
Tel: (607) 724-5461
Internet Address: http://www.rossparkzoo.com/gardens.htm
Admission: Fee: adult $5.00, child (<3) free, child (3-11) $3.50; Fee (April-November, Sunday, 10am-noon): $3.00/person
Wheelchair Accessible: Y
Open: January to March, Selected Weekends, call for hours; April to October, Daily, 10am-5pm; November to December, Call for hours
Facilities: Gardens (butterfly, hosta, iris, ornamental grass, shade, sun, water); Grounds Zoo (60 acres); Picnic Area

The Ross Park Zoo is not only a zoological facility but a botanical park as well. Some of the gardens of interest include a hosta garden, a butterfly garden, an ornamental grass garden, an iris garden, and a memorial garden.

BRIDGEHAMPTON

BRIDGE GARDENS TRUST

36 Mitchell Lane, Bridgehampton, NY 11932
Tel: (631) 537-7440; Fax: (631) 537-3667
Internet Address: http://www.bridgegardens.org/
Admission: Fee $15.00
Attendance: 1,500
Established: 1988
Membership: Y

Wheelchair Accessible: P
Parking: Free on Mitchell Lane
Open: Memorial Day to September, Wednesday, 2pm-4:30pm; Saturday, 2pm-4:30pm.
Facilities: Gardens (herb, knot, lavender parterre, lilac walk, perennial, Renaissance, rose, topiary, water, woodland); Grounds (5 acres)
Activities: Guided Tours (groups 10+, schedule in advance); Lecture Series

Bridge Gardens was begun in 1988 by Jim Kilpatrick and Harry Neyens, who designed and installed the gardens over the ensuing ten years. Among the more prominent features is the large, meticulously-trimmed knot garden surrounded by beds of culinary, medicinal, ornamental, and textile and dyeing herbs and the collection of 800 antique and modern roses. Bridge Gardens also contains animal topiaries, lavender parterres, perennial borders, a water garden, woodland paths, and specimen shrubs and trees. The Bridge Gardens Trust was created in 1997 to maintain and preserve the gardens.

BUFFALO

BUFFALO AND ERIE COUNTY BOTANICAL GARDENS (AHS RAP)

Buffalo and Erie County Botanical Gardens, Buffalo, NY.

2655 South Park Avenue (South Park Avenue entrance to South Park), Buffalo, NY 14218-1526
Tel: (716) 696-3555;
Fax: (716) 828-0091
Internet Address: http://www.buffalogardens.com/
Admission: Voluntary contribution
Attendance: 120,000
Established: 1900
Membership: Y
Wheelchair Accessible: Y
Open: Monday to Tuesday, 9am-4pm; Wednesday, 9am-6pm; Thursday to Friday, 9am-4pm; Saturday to Sunday, 9am-5pm
Closed: Christmas Day
Facilities: Conservatory (1897-99 design and 1930 re-design by Lord & Burnham Co.; 11 greenhouses); Gardens (3 acres, shrub garden, display bed); Greenhouses (17); Grounds (11? acres), South Park (163 acres, 1888 landscape design by Frederick Law Olmsted); Special Collections (cycad, palm, orchids, ivy, begonias)
Activities: Education Programs; Flower Shows Spring Bulb, Fall Chrysanthemum (Nov), Winter Poinsettia (Dec); Guided Tours (groups, reserve in advance, 50¢/person, 827-1584); Plant Sales; Temporary Exhibitions; Workshops

Located at the entrance to Frederick Law Olmsted's 104-year-old Victorian South Park, the conservatory building, at one time the nation's largest municipally owned conservatory, is listed on the National Register of Historic Places. The plants inside are arranged in classic Victorian style with similar plants from throughout the world grouped together. Although there are some temperate plants on exhibit, most of the plants are native to tropical or arid regions of the world. Collections on exhibit include bananas, begonias, bromeliads, cycads, desert plants, ferns, edible fruits, herbs, orchids, and palms, along with the largest collection of ivy species and cultivars in the world. Additionally, two large greenhouses offer three seasonal flower shows. Large outdoor beds are filled with flowering plants and All-American flowering annuals in summer.

CITY OF BUFFALO—JAPANESE GARDEN ON MIRROR LAKE

Delaware Park, Elmwood Avenue, Buffalo, NY 14222-1001
Tel: (716) 851-5801
Internet Address: http://members.localnet.com/~shujir/garden/
Facilities: Gardens (Japanese); Grounds Delaware Park (350 acres, 1870 design by Frederick Law Olmsted), Japanese Garden (6 acres, original design 1971/restoration 1995)

Buffalo boasts the first park system in America (1870), originally designed by landscape architect Frederick Law Olmsted and now listed on the National Register of Historic Places. Centrally located in the northern part of the city, Delaware Park is the keystone of the city's Olmsted Parks System. It contains a prominent water feature, Hoyt Lake; a large meadow of about 120 acres; and significant wooded areas. The Japanese Garden at Mirror Lake, occupying six acres at the western end of the park adjacent to the Buffalo and Erie County Historical Society Museum, is a later addition. A cooperative effort of Buffalo and its sister city, Kanazawa, Japan, it originally contained over 1,000 plantings, nearly 20 globe-type lights, and 3 small islands connected to the mainland by bridges. After a period of neglect, the city of Buffalo, in partnership with the Japanese Group of Buffalo, the Buffalo-Kanazawa Sister City Committee, and Buffalo Olmsted Parks Conservancy, has initiated a program for the redevelopment and enhancement of the site.

JOAN AND VICTOR FUZAK MEMORIAL ROSE GARDEN

Erie Basin Marina, 329 Erie Street, Buffalo, NY 14202
Tel: (716) 842-4141
Facilities: Gardens (annual, rose)

Located in the Erie Basin Marina in downtown Buffalo, the garden is an official All-America Rose Selections test garden, featuring test roses and previous All-America winning roses. Also of possible interest, the New Millennium Garden, located at the entrance to the marina, highlights annual flower introductions, including new arrivals from California, Japan, Germany, and Denmark.

CANANDAIGUA

SONNENBERG GARDENS (AHS RAP)

151 Charlotte Street (Route 21), Canandaigua, NY 14424
Tel: (716) 394-4922; Fax: (716) 394-2192
Internet Address: http://www.sonnenberg.org
Admission: Fee: adult $8.50, child (<12) free, senior $7.50; Group discounts
Attendance: 96,000
Established: 1970
Membership: Y
Wheelchair Accessible: Y

Open: May, daily, 9:30am-4:00pm; Memorial Day to Labor Day, daily, 9:30am-5:30pm; after Labor Day to mid-October, 9:30am-4:00pm
Facilities: Arboretum; Architecture (1887, 40-room Richardson Romanesque mansion); Conservatory (1903 & 1915, Lord & Burnham); Gardens (formal; blue & white, butterfly, Italian, Japanese, moonlight, old-fashioned, pansy, perennial, reflecting pond, rock, rose); Grounds (50 acres); Shop Lavender and Old Lace Gift Shop
Activities: Concerts; Education Programs (adults and children); Events Orchid & Bulb Show (Apr), Rose Week (Jun), Haunted Gardens (Oct), Festival of Lights (Nov-Dec); Flower Shows; Guided Tours (May-Sept, Fri, 1pm; Sat-Sun & Holidays, 10am & 1pm); Lecture Series Bag Lunch Series (selected Wednesdays); Plant Sale (May, Mother's Day Weekend); Temporary Exhibitions; Workshops

Formerly the summer home of Canandaigua benefactors Frederick Ferris and Mary Clark Thompson, this Victorian mansion and gardens is located at the north end of Canandaigua Lake. The conservatory is considered one of the most important residential greenhouse complexes in the United States, and includes a domed Palm House and several other display houses featuring orchids, begonias, and other tropical plants. Exterior gardens include a rose garden, containing over 4,000 rose bushes from the former Jackson & Perkins Rose Gardens in Newark, New York; the Sub Rosa, a secret garden with white marble statuary set off by rich green lawn, boxwood, and evergreens; a formal Italian Garden, consisting of four sunken parterres displaying a modified fleur-de-lis pattern bordered by trimmed yews and planted with approximately 15,000 annuals; an Old-Fashioned Garden, planted with perennials and colorful annuals and featuring over a quarter mile of low boxwood hedge forming a quincunx pattern; and a reflecting pond.

CLINTON

HAMILTON COLLEGE—ROOT GLEN GARDENS

College Hill Road, Clinton, NY 13323
Tel: (315) 859-4011
Internet Address:
http://www.hamilton.edu/applications/campus_tour/frame.html?DEP=Histor
Admission: Free
Established: 1870
Parking: 3 lots on campus, more spaces available on weekends.
Open: Daily, sunrise-sunset
Best Time(s) of Year to Visit: May to June
Facilities: Gardens (peony, woodland); Grounds (7½ acres)

Situated behind the Elihu Root House, the Root Glen is a wooded garden and ravine separating Hamilton's north and south campuses and named for the family that originally founded the gardens in 1850. It contains sixty-five species of trees, including the national champion Norway Spruce, many kinds of shrubs, and scores of varieties of flowers, including the Saunders peonies, which were hybridized by Hamilton professor A. P. Saunders and are considered to be among the world's finest peonies. Elihu Root, an 1864 Hamilton graduate who served his country as secretary of state and secretary of war and was a recipient of the Nobel Peace Prize, created a garden for his daughter, Edith Root Grant, east of the Glen's Hemlock Enclosure. This area, now known as the Grant Garden, was renovated in 1996 as a display garden for as many of the remaining Saunders tree peonies as can be recovered.

COBLESKILL

STATE UNIVERSITY OF NEW YORK AT COBLESKILL—ARBORETUM AND GROUNDS

College of Agriculture and Technology, Cobleskill, NY 12043
Tel: (518) 255-5246
Internet Address: http://www.cobleskill.edu
Facilities: Greenhouses (13); Grounds Arboretum (10 acres), Campus (750 acres), Landscaped Grounds (90 acres), Nursery (2 acres); Shop Anything Grows (garden items)

The college campus, including an arboretum and extensively landscaped grounds, is maintained by students, faculty, and staff. The arboretum offers unique specimens, conifers, rhododendrons, and a wildflower area.

COLD SPRING

STONECROP GARDENS

Route 301 (between Route 9 & Taconic Parkway), Cold Spring, NY 10516
Tel: (914) 265-2000
Admission: Fee: $5.00
Open: By appointment
Facilities: Conservatory (2,000 square feet); Gardens (alpine, enclosed English flower, grass, gravel, Himalayan slope, perennial, rock ledge, water, woodland); Grounds Display Gardens (12 acres), Fields & Woodland (50 acres); Special Collections (dwarf bulbs)

Stonecrop Gardens, home of Frank and Ann Cabot (founders of the Garden Conservancy) since 1958, opened to the public in 1992. The site offers a wide variety of garden environments (including woodland and water gardens, a grass garden, raised alpine stone beds, a cliff rock garden, perennial beds, and an enclosed English-style flower garden with a vegetable parterre), a conservatory, a display alpine house, and a pit house. Plans are being developed for a school of practical horticulture for professionals, and short courses and seminars for amateur gardeners. While there is a limited number of Open Days scheduled during the year, admission to the gardens is generally by appointment only.

CONSTABLEVILLE

CONSTABLE HALL—GARDEN

John Street & Summit Avenue (Route 26), Constableville, NY 13325
Tel: (315) 397-2323
Internet Address: http://www.rhennis.com/hall/
Admission: Fee: adult $3.00, child $1.50
Attendance: 2,000
Parking: Ample on site
Open: Memorial Day to October 15, Tuesday to Saturday, 10am-4pm; Sunday, 1pm-4pm

Best Time(s) of Year to Visit: Summer
Facilities: Architecture (Federal limestone residence, 1810-19); Garden (historic);
Grounds (17 acres)
Activities: Guided Tours

Situated on the banks of the Sugar River, Constable Hall was home to five generations of the Constable family from 1819 until the sale of the estate for restoration as an historic house museum in 1947. The grounds include formal gardens in the pattern of the Cross of St. Andrew with plants believed to be seedlings from original 1810 plantings. Owned and operated by the Constable Hall Association, the site is listed on the National Register of Historic Places.

CROSS RIVER

WARD POUND RIDGE RESERVATION—MEYER ARBORETUM AND LUQUER-MARBLE MEMORIAL WILD FLOWER GARDEN

Routes 35 & 121, Cross River, NY 10518
Tel: (914) 864-7322
Admission: Parking/entrance fee: $8/vehicle
Attendance: 10,820
Established: 1925
Membership: Y
Wheelchair Accessible: P
Open: Daily, 8am-dusk
Facilities: Arboretum; Grounds Reservation (4,700 acres), Wildflower Garden (½ acre);
Picnic Area; Trailside Museum (Tues-Sun, 9am-4pm)
Activities: Public Programs (weekends, various natural history topics)

The largest park in the Westchester County Park System, Ward Pound Ridge Reservation contains the Meyer Arboretum and the Luquer-Marble Memorial Wild Flower Garden. Wooded areas include evergreen plantations; oak, hickory, and maple forests; and wooded wetlands. A trailside museum houses exhibits featuring the natural and human history of the park. The Wildflower Garden, located near the museum, contains over 100 kinds of wildflowers.

EAST HAMPTON

LONGHOUSE RESERVE

133 Hands Creek Road, East Hampton, NY 11937
Tel: (631) 329-3568; Fax: (631) 329-4299
Internet Address: http://www.longhouse.org
Admission: Fee: adult $10.00, child (<12) free, senior $8.00
Attendance: 7,000
Established: 1991
Membership: Y
Wheelchair Accessible: P
Parking: Free on site

Open: May to September, Wednesday, 2pm-5pm; Saturday, 2pm-5pm
Facilities: Architecture (residence, 1986 design by architect Charles Forberg); Gallery; Gardens; Grounds (16 acres); Shop
Activities: Temporary Exhibitions

Textile designer, author, and collector Jack Lenor Larsen created LongHouse Reserve to encourage creativity in gardening, in collecting, and everyday living with art. Both the house, inspired by the famous Japanese shrine at Ise, and the gardens, featuring broad selections of species and cultivars, approach the physical dimension as an expressive art form. The gardens also contain permanent and long-term installations by such artists as Augustus Saint-Gaudens, Dale Chihuly, Roy Lichtenstein, Willem de Kooning, and Buckminster Fuller.

ELIZABETHTOWN

ADIRONDACK HISTORY CENTER MUSEUM— COLONIAL GARDEN

7950 Court Street, Elizabethtown, NY 12932
Tel: (518) 873-6466
Internet Address: http://www.adkhistorycenter.org
Admission: Fee (for Museum): adult $3.50, child (<13) $1.50, senior $2.50; Gardens—no fee
Attendance: 6,000
Wheelchair Accessible: P
Parking: Parking on Hand Avenue
Open: Memorial Day to Columbus Day, Monday to Saturday, 9am-5pm; Sunday, 1pm-5pm
Facilities: Gardens (Colonial)

Adjacent to the old school that houses the Adirondack History Center Museum, the Essex County Adirondack Garden Club has created a formal Colonial Garden. The garden is composed of three elements: a lawn; a symmetrical center garden containing beds of annuals, features, and perennial borders; and a secret garden.

ELLICOTTVILLE

CORNELL COOPERATIVE EXTENSION OF CATTARAUGUS COUNTY—NANNEN ARBORETUM AND LOWE HERB GARDENS

28 Parkside Drive, Ellicottville, NY 14731-9707
Tel: (716) 699-2377; Fax: (716) 699-5701
Internet Address: http://www.cce.cornell.edu/~Allegany-Cattaraugus/arb/weddings.htm
Established: 1976
Facilities: Gardens (Biblical, children's, culinary, early American, fragrance, herb, industrial, Native American, oriental); Grounds (8 acres)

The arboretum contains over 250 trees, shrubs, and perennials in a natural setting. It also includes an herb garden, a Japanese stone meditation garden, and a pond with fish.

ESPERANCE

GEORGE LANDIS ARBORETUM (AHS RAP)

Lape Road, Esperance, NY 12206
Tel: (518) 875-6935; Fax: (518) 875-6394
Internet Address: http://www.landisarboretum.org
Admission: Voluntary contribution
Attendance: 8,000
Established: 1951
Membership: Y
Parking: On site, gravel parking area
Open: Daily, dawn-dusk
Best Time(s) of Year to Visit: April to October
Facilities: Gardens (perennial); Greenhouse; Grounds
(200 acres; formal collection 40 acres); Original Homestead; Shop (May-Dec,
gardening- and nature-related items);
Trails (6 miles); Visitors Center
Activities: Concerts; Education Programs (adults);
Guided Tours); Lectures; Plant Sales (spring and fall)

Located on a nineteenth-century farm, the formal collection consists of plantings of trees, shrubs, and herbaceous perennials from around the world. Collections include perennial gardens, rhododendrons and azaleas, beeches, oaks, lilacs, clematis, and dwarf conifers. The remainder of the property consists of natural areas, woodlands, and open fields reminiscent of the former farm on the site. Trails help guide people through the formal collections and natural areas. Visitor guides and maps are available in the visitor shed.

FARMINGDALE

FARMINGDALE STATE UNIVERSITY OF NEW YORK— ORNAMENTAL HORTICULTURE TEACHING GARDENS

Route 110, Farmingdale, NY 11735
Tel: (631) 420-2113; Fax: (631) 420-2766
Internet Address: http://www.farmingdale.edu/Horticulture
Admission: Free
Established: 1916
Membership: N
Wheelchair Accessible: P
Parking: On site
Open: Spring to Fall, Monday to Saturday, 9am-4:30pm
Best Time(s) of Year to Visit: Mid-April to mid-October
Facilities: Conservatory (Lord and Burnham, 30' × 30', ca.1898); Gardens (annual, beech hedge, dwarf conifer, ornamental grass, herb, perennial, rose, spring, rockery, tropical); Grounds Gardens (4+ acres)

Evolving under the tutelage of past and present horticulture faculty, the teaching gardens have been developed from a 1930s formal garden with a pool, a flagstone terrace, and thick yew hedges into a series of theme gardens, or 'garden rooms' oriented around a center axial walkway. The unique tropical garden is the subject of a book by the curator, Dr. Richard Iversen *The Exotic Garden: Designing with Tropical Plants in Almost Any Climate* (Taunton Press, 1999).

GARRISON

BOSCOBEL RESTORATION, INC.

1601 Route 9D, Garrison, NY 10524
Tel: (845) 265-3638; Fax: (845) 265-4405
Internet Address: http://www.boscobel.org
Admission: Fee: adult $10.00, child (<6) free, child, senior $9.00
Attendance: 38,097
Established: 1955
Membership: Y
Parking: On site, paved
Open: April to October, Monday, 9:30am-5pm; Wednesday to Sunday, 9:30am-5pm; November to December, Monday, 9:30am-4pm; Wednesday to Sunday, 9:30am-4pm. Closed: Thanksgiving Day, Christmas Day
Facilities: Architecture Carriage House Reception Center (museum shop and orientation exhibition), Dyckman Family Home (Federal-style residence, 1804-1808); Gardens (herb, rose); Grounds (45 acres); Orangerie; Picnic Area; Shop (books, gifts); Woodland Trail
Activities: Guided Tours (45 minutes long; Apr-Oct, last tour 4:15pm; Nov-Dec, last tour 3:15pm), Candlelight Tours (Dec); Performances Hudson Valley Shakespeare Festival (summer)

Boscobel is an important example of Federal domestic architecture, carefully restored and furnished with period decorative arts. In addition to New York Federal-style furniture by Phyfe, Allison, and Lannuier, china, silver, crystal, and lighting fixtures, there are paintings by Benjamin West and John Watson, as well as English prints. Originally located about fifteen miles south of its present site in Montrose, Boscobel was almost destroyed in the 1950s when it was declared excess by the federal government and sold at auction to a demolition contractor for the sum of $35. It was dismantled, moved to its present site, fully restored, and opened to the public in 1961. Boscobel's grounds include rose and herb gardens as well as hundreds of tulips, lilacs, and dogwoods.

MANITOGA: THE RUSSEL WRIGHT DESIGN CENTER

Route 9D (2 miles south of Route 403 intersection), Garrison, NY 10524
Tel: (845) 424-3812; Fax: (845) 424-4043
Internet Address: http://www.russelwrightcenter.org
Admission: Suggested contribution (hiking)
Established: 1975
Membership: Y
Wheelchair Accessible: P
Parking: On site
Open: Grounds (April to October): Monday to Friday, 9am-4pm; Saturday to Sunday, 10am-6pm; Grounds (November to March): Monday to Friday, 9am-4pm
Facilities: Architecture Home and Studio (open only by advance reservation); Gardens (woodland); Grounds (75 acres); Picnic Area; Shop (books, RW designs); Trails (4+ miles)

Activities: Education Programs summer Nature & Design Camp; Guided Tours House and Landscape (Apr-Oct, daily, 11am, reservation requested, fee); Plant Sales (Native Plant); Self-guided Hikes; Seminars

The home of pioneer industrial designer Russel Wright, Manitoga is an essay in an aesthetic harmony with nature. Structures were designed to blend into a seemingly natural landscape that is actually a carefully designed backdrop of native trees, ferns, mosses, and wildflowers. Manitoga is listed on the National Register of Historic Places and is a National Trust for Historic Preservation Historic Artists' Homes and Studios Site.

GREAT RIVER

BAYARD CUTTING ARBORETUM STATE PARK

Montauk Highway (Route 27A), Great River, NY 11739
Tel: (631) 581-1002; Fax: (631) 581-1031
Admission: Fee, $6.00/car
Attendance: 120,000
Established: 1952
Wheelchair Accessible: Y
Open: Tuesday to Sunday, 10am-sunset
Facilities: Auditorium (130 seats); Botanical Garden; Food Services Cafe; Grounds (designed by the Olmsted landscape architectural firm); Nature Conservation Center
Activities: Arts Festival; Concerts; Education Programs (adults and children); Guided Tours; Lectures

Bordering the Connetquot River and the state park of the same name, Cutting Arboretum offers the most extensive collection of fir, spruce, pine, cypress, hemlock, yew, and other lesser known conifers to be found on Long Island. There are also extensive plantings of dwarf evergreens, rhododendrons, azaleas, hollies, and oaks. Wildflowers and daffodils are featured in many native woodland locations. The arboretum offers a choice of five charted paths. Formerly the estate of William Bayard Cutting, the house contains magnificent fireplaces, woodworkings, stained glass windows, and a small natural history museum featuring an extensive collection of mounted birds.

HEMPSTEAD

HOFSTRA UNIVERSITY ARBORETUM

Hofstra University Campus, Hempstead Turnpike, Hempstead, NY 11549-1010
Tel: (516) 463-5924; Fax: (516) 463-5302
Internet Address: http://www.hofstra.edu/COM/Arbor/index_Arbor.cfm
Admission: Free
Attendance: 150,000
Established: 1985
Membership: Y
Wheelchair Accessible: Y
Parking: On campus, all stalls except those noted
Open: Daily, 24 hours

Best Time(s) of Year to Visit: Mid-April to mid-May, September to October
Facilities: Arboretum; Grounds Campus (240 acres)

Designated an arboretum, the Hofstra campus contain more than 11,000 evergreen and deciduous trees representing 625 species and varieties. The campus also offers plantings of annuals, perennials, and bulbs, particularly tulips with beds containing over 250,000 bulbs. The arboretum is a registered member of the American Association of Botanical Gardens and Arboreta.

HYDE PARK

FRANKLIN D. ROOSEVELT NATIONAL HISTORIC SITE GROUNDS

4097 Albany Post Road (Route 9), Hyde Park, NY 12538
Tel: (845) 229-9115; Fax: (845) 229-0739
Internet Address: http://www.nps.gov/hofr
Admission: Fee (Home Tour & Museum): adult $14.00, child (<17) free; Grounds: Free
Attendance: 107,000
Membership: N
Wheelchair Accessible: Y
Parking: Main lot on site
Open: Grounds, Daily, 8am-dusk; House & Museum,
Daily, 9am-5pm
Closed: New Year's Day, Thanksgiving Day, Christmas Day
Facilities: Architecture (birthplace and home of Franklin Delano Roosevelt); Gardens (rose); Grounds (290 acres, 33 acres in original bequest); Visitor Center
Activities: Concerts; Guided Tours, House; Lectures Evening Program (summer)

The site includes Springwood (the furnished home of FDR), rose garden and grave site, ice house, and stables, as well as the FDR Presidential Museum and Library. Both Franklin and Eleanor Roosevelt are buried in the hemlock walled rose garden. Additionally, Roosevelt planted many varieties of trees on the grounds, eventually turning large sections of the estate into an experimental forestry station. There is a network of hiking and walking trails that lead from the house down to the river. The site is administered by the National Park Service, U.S. Department of the Interior.

ROOSEVELT-VANDERBILT NATIONAL HISTORIC SITES— THE BEATRIX FARRAND GARDEN AT BELLEFIELD

4097 Albany Post Road (Route 9) (just north of the F.D.R. Home & Library), Hyde Park, NY 12538
Tel: (845) 229-9115; Fax: (845) 229-0739
Admission: Free
Established: 1912
Membership: Y
Wheelchair Accessible: P
Parking: Main parking lot on the F.D. Roosevelt site
Open: Daily, dawn-dusk
Facilities: Gardens (enclosed formal, wild); Grounds (1912 design by Beatrix Farrand)

A unit of the Roosevelt-Vanderbilt National Historic Sites, the enclosed formal garden and surrounding wild garden of this Hudson River estate were designed by Beatrix Farrand in 1912. It is thought to be one of the earliest surviving examples of her residential estate work.

VANDERBILT MANSION NATIONAL HISTORIC SITE

4097 Albany Post Road (Route 9) (just north of the Roosevelt Home & Library), Hyde Park, NY 12538
Tel: (845) 229-9115; Fax: (845) 229-0739
Internet Address: http://www.nps.gov/vama
Admission: Fee (House Tour): adult $8.00, child (<17) free; Grounds: Free
Attendance: 329,000
Established: 1940
Membership: Y
Wheelchair Accessible: Y
Parking: Main parking lot at the Vanderbilt Mansion
Open: Monday, 9am-5pm; Thursday to Sunday, 9am-5pm
Closed: New Year's Day, Thanksgiving Day, Christmas Day
Facilities: Architecture (Beaux Arts mansion, 1896-99 designed by McKim, Mead & White); Garden (formal Italianate, 1903 design by James Greenleaf); Grounds Estate (240 acres), Italian Garden (3 acres); Shop; Visitor Center
Activities: Guided Tours

With its breathtaking views of the Hudson River and distant Catskill Mountains, three generations of owners had made improvements to the estate's grounds prior to its purchase by Frederick W. Vanderbilt. Under Frederick Vanderbilt's stewardship beginning in 1895, the pavilion, mansion, gate houses, coach house, and powerhouse were built. Beginning in 1903, Vanderbilt, who was an avid gardener himself, established an Italian-style, terrace garden containing many varieties of roses, annuals and perennials. After his death in 1938, the gardens were not maintained and soon fell into ruin. In 1940, the estate was acquired by the National Park Service. The gardens have been partially restored with the assistance of the Frederick W. Vanderbilt Garden Association. The perennial garden has been completed with over 3,500 plants and over 6,500 annuals are planted on two levels. The rose garden contains approximately 1,400 roses. The grounds also contain an extensive collection of native and exotic specimen trees.

ITHACA

CORNELL PLANTATIONS (AHS RAP)

One Plantations Road (off Route 366), Ithaca, NY 14850-2799
Tel: (607) 255-2400; Fax: (607) 255-2404
Internet Address: http://www.plantations.cornell.edu/
Admission: Free
Attendance: 150,000
Established: 1944
Membership: Y
Wheelchair Accessible: Y
Parking: Paved parking next to gift shop
Open: Daily, sunrise-sunset

Best Time(s) of Year to Visit: May to September
Facilities: Arboretum (maples, oaks, conifers, dogwoods, urban trees); Garden (14 themed gardens, including major herb garden); Grounds Arboretum (150 acres), Botanical Garden (50 acres), Natural Areas (3,400 acres—all habitats found in central New York); Library (500 volumes); Shop (gifts and books for nature lovers and gardeners)
Activities: Concerts; Education Programs; Guided Tours (groups, schedule in advance, $3/person, 255-2406; late June-early Sept, Saturday, 11am, free); Lectures

Cornell Plantations, a museum of living plants, consists of a botanical garden, arboretum, and natural areas. Its primary facilities are located on 200 park-like acres adjacent to Cornell's central campus. The Botanical Garden contains fourteen theme gardens. Located on the botanical garden site surrounding the Plantations Headquarters Building are the Decorative Arts Flower Garden, featuring ten familiar plants (sunflower, carnation, rose, poppy, peony, iris, lily, chrysanthemum, daisy, and tulip); the Groundcover Garden, displaying flowering herbaceous ground covers suitable for use in small-scale plantings in shade, sun, or slope; the Herb Garden, featuring over 500 varieties of plants used for flavor, fiber, or medicine, or valued for their spiritual and cultural associations; the Heritage Vegetable Garden, focusing on the changing role of vegetables in the American diet over time; the International Crop and Weed Garden, presenting commercially grown crops and competitive weeds; the Peony and Sun Perennial Garden, containing over ninety peony cultivars complemented by recently introduced perennials; the rhododendron and woodland perennial garden, planted with hundreds of rhododendrons and azaleas; the Rock Garden, containing alpine plants and perennials, bulbs, and miniature shrubs; and the Winter Garden, exhibiting plants chosen for their colorful winter bark, unusual growth habits, winter fruit, or evergreen foliage. The extensive Wildflower Garden, a natural setting emphasizing native plants, is located between the Botanical Garden site and the arboretum. Two botanical gardens are located in the adjacent arboretum: the Flowering Shrub and Ornamental Grass Garden, presenting shrubs, grasses, and low-maintenance perennials arranged in curvilinear beds as well as a day lily collection; and the Woodland Streamside Garden, a hemlock-shaded garden bordering a small stream. Located elsewhere on the Cornell University campus, but considered part of the Botanical Garden, are the Deans Garden (behind Warren Hall), a teaching garden displaying a diverse array of herbaceous and woody plants, many of which are rarely cultivated in the Ithaca area; and the Poisonous Plants Garden (behind the Veterinary School Library), offering an encyclopedic display of plants toxic to livestock and humans. The F. R. Newman Arboretum, specializing in trees and shrubs native to New York State, contains extensive collections of chestnut, conifer, flowering crab apple, maple, oak, trees suited for urban environments, and walnut. The Plantations also manages 2,900 acres of diverse natural areas—bogs, fens, gorges, glens, meadows, and woodlands located on, or near, campus and elsewhere in Tomkins County. Cornell is considered one of the most beautiful of American college campuses; other gardens of interest on the campus include the Daisy Farrand Secret (or White) Garden, the Ruth Uris Rock Garden, the perennial borders, and solarium at the Andrew Dickson White House; Miss Minn's Flower Garden next to the Plant Science Building on Tower Road; the Mary Rockwell Azalea Garden near Mallot Hall on Tower Road; the Willard Straight Rock Garden; and Sage Chapel's courtyards and gardens. Field guides to the botanical gardens, arboretum, and natural areas are available.

CORNELL UNIVERSITY—LIBERTY HYDE BAILEY HORTORIUM

462 Main Library, Cornell University, Ithaca, NY 14853
Tel: (607) 255-2131; Fax: (607) 255-7979
Internet Address: http://www.plantbio.cornell.edu/Hortorium/

Admission: Free
Established: 1935
Parking: Parking available nearby
Open: Conservatory, Monday to Friday, 8am-4pm
Closed: Legal holidays
Facilities: Conservatory (1930-31, Lord & Burnham, 5,000 square feet, 255-4541); Herbarium (over 821,000 specimens); Library (30,000 volumes; Mon-Fri, 9am-4pm; 255-7781); Nursery & Seed Catalogue Collection (over 131,000 catalogues)
Activities: Education Programs (undergraduate and graduate college students); Guided Tours Conservatory (on request); Lectures; Self-guided Tours (change monthly)

A botanical and horticultural museum, the Bailey Hortorium includes the herbarium, library, conservatory, and a unique Nursery and Seed Catalogue Collection. The conservatory, located on Tower Road adjacent to the Plant Science building, is divided into two sections containing 117 families and over 550 species of plants. The Palm House houses palms, cycads, ferns, bromeliads, legumes, and various aroids. The Ornamental Section contains a variety of collections including begonia, cacti, euphorbia, gesneriads, grasses, orchids, peperomia, and a wide array of temperate ornamentals.

KATONAH

CARAMOOR CENTER FOR MUSIC AND THE ARTS, INC.

149 Girdle Ridge Road (off Route 22), Katonah, NY 10536
Tel: (914) 232-5035; Fax: (914) 232-5521
Internet Address: http://www.caramoor.org
Admission: Fee: adult $7.00, child (<17) free
Attendance: 60,000
Established: 1946
Membership: Y
Wheelchair Accessible: Y
Parking: Free on site
Open: Museum: May to October, Wednesday to Sunday, 1pm-4pm (last tour at 3pm); December to May, Tuesday to Friday, by appointment
Closed: January to February
Best Time(s) of Year to Visit: Summer
Facilities: Architecture (Mediterranean-style palazzo, 19291939); Auditorium; Gardens (butterfly, cutting, sensory, Spanish courtyard, sunken, tapestry hedge); Grounds (90 acres); Picnic Facilities and Snack Bar; Sculpture Garden; Shop; Theatres (2 outdoor, 1 indoor recital hall)
Activities: Concerts Indoors (fall & spring, also Wednesday morning recitals); Festival Outdoors (annual, summer, International Music Festival); Guided Tours (museum and garden); Lectures; Teas; Wine Tastings

Caramoor is the site of an international music festival each summer and numerous concerts and recitals during the rest of the year. Its heart is the House Museum, built in the style of a Mediterranean palazzo by Lucie Bigelow Dodge Rosen and Walter Tower Rosen, Caramoor's founders. Completed in 1939, the house was constructed to accommodate their collection of Eastern, Medieval, and Renaissance art and artifacts, one of the last important private art collections that remains intact. The center offers a variety of formal and production gardens. The Sense Circle, designed around a fountain and dovecote, is planted with a variety of highly scented and brightly colored plants, some of which are edible, along with those with interesting texture and sound-producing possibility. The Butterfly Garden, adjacent to the Brunelleschi-inspired Italian Pavilion, consists of the Lion's Head fountain surrounded by plants chosen to encourage all stages of butterfly development. The Sunken Garden consists of perennial borders surrounding four box-lined center beds planted with annuals as well as antique containers and statuary. A curved bed of peonies and iris complements the Tapestry Hedge, an extensive collection of many different species of evergreens. The Spanish Courtyard, one of the chief concert sites at Caramoor, employs a vibrant Mediterranean color scheme in four triangular gardens, various antique containers, and the base of the center Florentine marble fountain. Finally, the Cutting Garden, consisting of a series of eight raised beds, is used for cut flower production for arrangements that are placed in the rooms of the House Museum.

JOHN JAY HOMESTEAD STATE HISTORIC SITE

400 Jay Street (NYS Route 22) (2 miles south of Route 35 intersection),
Katonah, NY 10536
Tel: (914) 232-5651; Fax: (914) 232-8085
Internet Address: http://www.nysparks.state.ny.us/hist/
Admission: Fee: adult $7.00, child (<5) free, child, senior $5.00
Attendance: 50,000
Established: 1958
Membership: Y
Wheelchair Accessible: P
Parking: Free on site, lot at end of entrance drive
Open: House: April to November, Tuesday to Saturday, 10am-4pm; Sunday, 11am-4pm; Grounds, open all year
Best Time(s) of Year to Visit: early May (lilac hedge bloom)
Facilities: Architecture (Federal-style residence); Gardens (formal); Grounds (64 acres); Trails
Activities: Guided Tours House (on the hour, last tour 4pm, groups reserve in advance)

American jurist and statesman John Jay retired to this farm in 1801, after a lifetime of public service. The homestead contains furnishings and paintings of the seventeenth, eighteenth, and nineteenth centuries. The grounds include lawns, landscape plantings, meadows, and nineteenth- and twentieth-century farm outbuildings.

LASDON PARK AND ARBORETUM

2610 Amawalk Road (Route 35), Katonah, NY 10536
Tel: (914) 232-9147; Fax: (914) 864-7266
Internet Address: http://www.westchestergov.com/parks
Admission: No charge, donations accepted
Attendance: 25,000
Established: 1991
Parking: Parking lot on site
Open: Daily, 8am-4pm
Closed: New Year's Day, Thanksgiving Day, Christmas Day
Best Time(s) of Year to Visit: Spring to Fall
Facilities: Arboretum; Gardens (azalea, Chinese, display, fragrance, perennial); Grounds Nature Sanctuary (20 acres), Park (234 acres, 32 acres within deer fence);

Library (by appointment); Shop (plants, gifts; open seasonally, Fri-Sun, noon-4pm); Special Collections (conifer, flowering trees, lilac, pinetum); Visitor Center Activities: Concerts (classical and jazz series); Education Programs; Events (Azalea Festival); Plant Sales (spring); Workshops

Originally part of seventeenth-century Cortlandt Manor, this former estate features many species of tree and shrubs set in woodlands, meadows, and formal gardens. The arboretum consists of woodlands, open grass meadows, and formal gardens and tree, shrub, and flower specimens from all over the world. Highlights include the William & Mildred Lasdon Memorial Garden, a one-acre garden offering a fragrance garden and formal boxwood garden surrounded by a synoptic planting featuring specimen shrubs from A to Z; and azalea garden, a historic tree trail, magnolia grove, American chestnut tree grove, and sixty varieties of dogwood. Lasdon is also home to the Chinese Culture Garden and Friendship Pavilion, a four-acre Chinese garden and pavilion symbolizing the bond between Westchester County and its sister city Jingzhou in the People's Republic of China. Plantings in the garden include kousa dogwood, a bamboo grove, dawn redwood, weeping willow, Chinese pine, and ginko. The park also contains four memorials honoring Westchester veterans. The site is managed by the Westchester County Department of Parks, Recreation and Conservation.

LATTINGTOWN

BAILEY ARBORETUM

Bayville Road and Feeks Lane, Lattingtown, NY 11542
Tel: (516) 571-8020
Internet Address: http://www.co.nassau.ny.us/parkmuse.html#Bailey
Admission: Fee $3.00
Established: 1968
Wheelchair Accessible: Y
Open: Mid-April to mid-November, Tuesday to Sunday, 9:30am-4pm
Facilities: Arboretum; Gardens (iris, perennial, rock, rose, sensory); Grounds (42 acres); Nature Trail

Formerly the summer estate of Mr. and Mrs. Frank Bailey, the estate became a Nassau County Park in 1968. From 1912 to the time of their deaths the Baileys assembled more than 600 varieties of flora including exotic trees such as dwarf Nikko fir of Japan, blue atlas cedar from North Africa, and dawn sequoia of China as well as mature native giant tulip, oaks, and maples. Special garden variety collections include perennials and ground covers for shaded areas. It also has an iris garden, a rose garden, a rock garden, a handicap-accessible sensory garden, and a perennial garden with 500 labeled varieties.

MILL NECK

JOHN P. HUMES JAPANESE STROLL GARDEN

Dogwood Lane (off Chicken Valley Road, 1 mile from Planting Fields Arboretum), Mill Neck, NY 11765
Tel: (516) 676-4486
Internet Address: http://www.locustvalley.com/
japanese%20stroll%20garden.html

Admission: Fee $5.00
Established: 1960
Open: April to late October, Saturday to Sunday, 11:30am-4:30pm
Facilities: Garden (Japanese); Grounds (4 acres)
Activities: Concerts; Demonstrations Tea Ceremony; Guided Tours Gardens & Tea
Ceremony (specified Saturdays, 10am, reservation required, $10/person); Plant Sales;
Temporary Exhibitions (seasonal; bonsai, ikebana, koi, water gardening)

Begun in 1960 upon the return of Ambassador and Mrs. Humes from Japan, this Japanese garden is situated on a steeply sloping site of deeply wooded land adjacent to a wild life sanctuary. A traditional Japanese stroll garden, the design creates a sense of entrance and progression, using the sloping terrain, pond, waterfall, moss terraces, and stepping stones to represent mountain streams flowing to the ocean. After Ambassador Humes' death, the garden was opened to the public. Subsequently, the Garden Conservancy assumed responsibility for the management of the garden and overseeing its long-term preservation.

MILLBROOK

INNISFREE GARDEN

Tyrrel Road (off Route 44, 1¾ miles east of Taconic Parkway), Millbrook, NY 12545
Tel: (914) 677-8000
Internet Address: http://www.innisfreegarden.org/
Admission: Fee (Sat, Sun & legal holidays): adult $4.00, child (<4) free; Fee (Wed-Fri):
Adult, $3.00
Established: 1960
Parking: Free on site
Open: May to late October, Wednesday to Friday, 10am-4pm; Saturday to Sunday,
11am-5pm; Legal Holidays, 11am-5pm
Facilities: Grounds (150 acres); Picnic Area

Innisfree was established in 1930 as the private garden of Walter Beck and his wife, Marion, heiress to a Minnesota mining fortune. Over the next quarter century, Beck, in collaboration with landscape architect Lester Collins, developed the garden employing Asian-inspired design principals. Using a forty-acre lake as the garden's focal point, streams, waterfalls, terraces, retaining walls, rocks, and plants are placed not only to define areas but also to establish tension or motion. After Beck's death, the naturalized gardens and woodland surrounding a picturesque lake were opened to the public.

INSTITUTE OF ECOSYSTEM STUDIES—MARY FLAGLER CARY ARBORETUM (AHS RAP)

Gifford House Visitor & Education Center, 181 Sharon Turnpike (Route 44A),
Millbrook, NY 12545
Tel: (845) 677-5359; Fax: (845) 577-6455
Internet Address: http://www.ecostudies.org
Admission: Free (visitor permits required)
Established: 1971
Open: April to September, Monday to Saturday, 9am-6pm; Sunday, 1pm-6pm;
October to March, Monday to Saturday, 9am-4pm; Sunday, 1pm-4pm
Closed: Legal Holidays

Facilities: Arboretum; Gardens (fern glen, perennial); Greenhouses (14,718 square feet, Mon-Sat, 9am-3:30pm, Sun, 1pm-3:30pm;); Grounds (1,924 acres); Shop IES Ecology Shop (gifts, plants); Trails; Visitor Center Gifford House (1817)
Activities: Education Programs; Plant Sales; Self-guided Tours

With a scientific staff of twenty-six and twenty-seven buildings, the Institute of Ecosystem Studies (IES) is one of the largest centers of ecological research in North America. Formerly under the aegis of the New York Botanical Garden, IES became an independent entity in 1993, managing the arboretum as a site for long-term research and public education. Public exhibits include display gardens and greenhouse facilities. Designed by former arboretum horticulturist, Robert Hebb and past senior vice president of horticulture at the New York Botanical Garden, Carlton B. Lees, the Gifford Garden is home to over 850 different species of plants and is reputed to be one of the largest collections of herbaceous perennials in any public garden in the northeastern United States. Collections are grouped to illustrate a theme or design concept. Settings include a sunken garden; a small water garden, containing both native and exotic plants; a rose garden, featuring winterhardy roses for growing in northern gardens; and a xeriscape bed, displaying over 170 different species of low-water-use plants. Adjacent to the Perennial Garden is the Deer Browse Demonstration Garden, where popular woody ornamental plants are evaluated for their resistance to deer browsing. A part of the Institute's Native Plant Program, the two-acre Fern Glen features native ferns and wildflowers. Over 1,000 species of plants, including begonia, orchid, peperomia, fern, cactus/succulent, citrus, and scented geranium, are on display throughout the seven units of the greenhouse.

MUMFORD

GENESEE COUNTRY VILLAGE AND MUSEUM— GARDENS (AHS RAP)

1410 Flint Hill Road, Mumford, NY 14511-0310
Tel: (585) 538-6822; Fax: (585) 538-2887
Internet Address: http://www.gcv.org/
Admission: General admission: adult $12.95, child (<4) free, child (4-16) $7.50, student $9.95, senior $9.95
Established: 1976
Membership: Y
Parking: Parking lots on site.
Open: Village (May to Jun): Tuesday to Friday, 10am-4pm; Saturday to Sunday, 10am-5pm, (Jul to Labor Day): Tuesday to Sunday, 10am-5pm, (Labor Day to Oct): Tuesday to Friday, 10am-4pm; Saturday to Sunday, 10am-5pm; Nature Center (January to Apr): Tuesday to Sunday, 10am-4pm, (May to Jun): Tuesday to Friday, 10am-4pm; Saturday to Sunday, 10am-5pm, (Jul to Labor Day): Tuesday to Sunday, 10am-5pm, (Day after Labor Day to Oct): Tuesday to Friday, 10am-4pm; Saturday to Sunday, 10am-5pm, (Nov to Dec): Saturday to Sunday, 10am-5pm
Facilities: Architecture (68 19th-century buildings); Gallery Gallery of Wildlife Art; Gardens (historic; berry, cottage, dye, formal, herb, heirloom vegetable, orchard, Shaker, Victorian); Grounds Nature Center (175 acres); Nature Center (woodland, trails); Shops (3; country store, book shop, gift shop)
Activities: Classes; Education Programs (adults & children)

New York State's largest living history museum, Genesee Village contains sixty-eight nineteenth-century buildings, restored to original condition and furnished with period antiques. The site is staffed with "villagers" in period dress who tell you about 1800s Genesee River Valley life and present live demonstrations of crafts and tasks of the nineteenth century, such as blacksmithing, cooking, and spinning. The thirteen gardens in the village, each designed as part of the historical environment of a particular building, trace the evolution of gardening of a 100-year span from sustenance through decoration. In addition to a variety of heirloom vegetable gardens and orchards, specialty working gardens include the Foster Tufts Garden, featuring berries and grapes harvested for jellies, jams, and sweets created in the village kitchens; the Amherst-Humphrey Dye Garden, containing plants used to dye yarn made by village spinners; MacArthur House Garden, a vegetable and flower garden typical of that of the average homeowner; and the Shaker Gardens. Renowned for their botanical and seed gardens, Shaker Seed packets were sold in many stores well into the twentieth century. Among the decorative gardens are the MacKay Homestead Garden, a dooryard garden, recalling the English cottage garden tradition, with rectangular beds of mixed perennials and annuals bounded by boxwood borders; the Livingston-Backus House Formal Garden, featuring classical-style rectangular boxwood bordered beds whose contents are based upon documented early nineteenth century examples found in the Genesee Country; and the Octagon House Picturesque Garden, composed of curvilinear beds and brick paths whose design is derived from plans appearing in Andrew Jackson Downing's "Cottage Residence" in 1842. Other plantings in the village include an extensive collection of trees and shrubs that demonstrate the evolution of local horticulture from the early nineteenth century to its end. The large array of fruit crops includes apples, pears, plums, quince, grapes, gooseberries, and currants. Also located at the site, the Genesee Country Nature Center contains 175 acres featuring five miles of hiking trails through woodlands, wetlands, and meadows.

NEW PALTZ

MOHONK MOUNTAIN HOUSE

1000 Mountain Rest Road, New Paltz, NY 12561-2814
Tel: (845) 255-2152
Internet Address: http://www.mohonk.com/
Established: 1869
Wheelchair Accessible: P
Parking: Valet parking with meal or overnight reservation
Open: Daily, dawn-dusk.
Facilities: Architecture (Victorian resort hotel, constructed between 1869 and 1901); Gardens (formal; annual, herb, lilac, maze, peony, perennial borders, rose); Greenhouse (plants, unique gifts, and indoor gardening supplies); Grounds Gardens (15 acres), Hotel property (2,200 acres); Shop Mohonk Flower Shop Activities: Guided Tours (garden walks); Lectures; Self-Guided Tours (garden paths and nature trails); Theme Programs Garden Dreams (winter), Garden Holiday (end of summer season)

A National Historic Landmark, Mohonk Mountain House is a nineteenth-century grand resort hotel with 251 guest rooms, 6 guest cottages, 3 spacious dining rooms, 150 working fireplaces, 200 balconies, a half-dozen parlors, and 3 inviting porches lined with rockers. Famous for large masses of summer flowering annuals and magnificent vistas and views, the grounds feature gardens, landscaping, and 128 summerhouses (gazebos), a greenhouse, picnic areas, a museum, stables, sports facilities, and an observation point known as Sky Top Tower. The gardens are notable for their mixture of Victorian picturesque and naturalistic styles. There are specimen trees, springtime daffodils, beds of peonies, and seventy-eight beds of annual, perennial, and topical flowers. The property is surrounded by the 6,400-acre Mohonk Preserve.

NEW YORK CITY—BRONX

THE NEW YORK BOTANICAL GARDEN (AHS RAP)

200th Street and Southern Boulevard (off Kazimiroff Boulevard), Bronx, NY 10458-5126
Tel: (718) 817-8700; Fax: (718) 220-6504
Internet Address: http://www.nybg.org/
Admission: Fee (includes all facilities): adult $13.00, child (<2) free, child (2-12) $5.00, student $11.00, senior $11.00; Free (Grounds only): Wed, all day & Sat, 10-noon
Attendance: 455,000
Established: 1891
Membership: Y
Wheelchair Accessible: Y
Open: April to October, Tuesday to Sunday, 10am-6pm; November to March, Tuesday to Sunday, 10am-4pm; Holiday Mondays, 10am-6pm
Closed: Thanksgiving Day, Christmas Day
Best Time(s) of Year to Visit: April to May (rock garden), June (rose garden), Summer (perennial garden), September (rose garden)
Facilities: Arboretum; Conservatory Enid A. Haupt Conservatory (Victorian-era glasshouse, 1899, Lord & Burnham); Food Services Garden Café; Gardens (autumn, children's, country, cutting, family, formal herb, fragrance, native plant, perennial, rock, rose, shade, vegetable, wildlife); Greenhouses; Grounds (250 acres); Herbarium (schedule visit in advance; Mon-Fri, 9 am-4:30pm; 817-8626); Library (27,000 volumes), LuEsther T. Mertz Library (1.25 million print and non-print items; Tues-Thurs, noon-6pm; Fri-Sat, noon-5pm); Reading Room; Shop Shop in the Garden (books and gardening products; Tues-Sun, 10am-6pm, 817-8073), Twombly Plant Shop (Tues-Sun, 10am-5pm, 817-8137); Special Collections Plants (annual, bulb, chrysanthemum, daffodil, day lily, fern, orchid, peony, tulip), Tree & Shrub (conifer, flowering trees and shrubs)
Activities: Concerts; Education Programs (adults, college students and children); Films; Guided Tours; Lectures; Temporary Exhibitions Conservatory; Workshops

One of the oldest and largest botanical gardens in the world, the New York Botanical Gardens is situated on some of the most beautiful natural terrain of any botanical garden in the world, with dramatic rock formations, a river and cascading waterfall, rolling hills, wetlands, woodland, and ponds. Over 18,000 plant species, varieties, and cultivars are displayed in forty-eight specialty gardens and plant collections, an eleven-room Victorian conservatory, and a forty-acre forest. Gardens include a 2? acre rock garden; a rose garden (originally designed by Beatrix Farrand), containing over 2,700 roses representing over 260 varieties; a perennial garden, featuring areas devoted to specific color schemes, seasons, and growing conditions (fall, bog, shade, hot, cool); a native plant garden, containing a diverse collection of ferns, perennials, shrubs, and trees native to the northeastern United States; a formal herb garden (designed by English landscape designer Penelope Hobhouse), displaying more than 160 different European and American herbs and other ornamental plants; and children's discovery and family gardens, offering a multitude of activities and experiences. There are also seven demonstration gardens: autumn, country, cutting, fragrance, shade, vegetable, and wildlife. The Enid A. Haupt

Conservatory, completely renovated in 1997, houses the permanent exhibit, "A World of Plants," an ecotour through tropical, sub-tropical, and desert environments as well as presenting seasonal shows.

WAVE HILL (AHS RAP)

675 West 252nd Street, Bronx, NY 10471-2899
Tel: (718) 549-3200; Fax: (718) 884-8952
Internet Address: http://www.wavehill.org/
Admission: Fee: adult $4.00, child (<6) free, student $2.00, senior $2.00;
Free: December to February, Tuesday & Saturday, 9am-noon
Attendance: 110,000
Established: 1965
Membership: Y
Parking: Free on site, limited
Open: April 15 to May 31, Tuesday to Sunday, 9am-5:30pm; June to July, Tuesday, 9am-5:30pm; Wednesday, 9am-9pm; Thursday to Sunday, 9am-5:30pm; August to October 14, Tuesday to Sunday, 9am-5:30pm; October 15 to April 14, Tuesday to Sunday, 9am-4:30pm
Closed: New Year's Day, Thanksgiving Day, Christmas Day
Best Time(s) of Year to Visit: Winter to early Spring (conservatory), late Winter to early Spring (alpine house), June (flower garden), Summer to Fall (monocot, aquatic & wild gardens), Fall (flower garden)
Facilities: Architecture (pergola); Conservatory; Food Services Wave Hill Café; Galleries (Glyndor Gallery & Wave Hill House Gallery); Gardens (alpine, aquatic, dry, flower, herb, monocot, wild); Greenhouses (Tues-Sun, 10am-noon & 1pm-4pm); Grounds Gardens (18 acres), Woodlands (10 acres); Shop (garden-related items, educational items, gifts)
Activities: Concerts; Contemporary Art Exhibitions; Education Programs (adults and children); Generated @ Wave Hill (a program of outdoor, site-related art); Guided Tours (groups, schedule in advance); Horticulture Programs; World Music & Dancing

Located in the northwest Bronx, Wave Hill consists of award-winning gardens, greenhouses, and urban woodland. Its Italianate pergola, adorned during the summer months with a multitude of colorful and unusual tender plants, affords sweeping views of the Hudson River. The conservatory's palm house contains a display of South African bulbs and other tender plants. Two other greenhouses exhibit collections of cacti and succulents and unusual tropical plants. In the Everett Alpine House, Wave Hill's collection of high-altitude and small, choice rock garden plants is arranged to be viewed from outside. Exterior gardens include the Flower Garden, a "glorified cottage garden" featuring informal combinations of both vintage and modern perennials, annuals, shrubs, and bulbs; an aquatic garden, a formal water feature, displaying a variety of tropical and hardy water plants bordered by ornamental grasses and seasonal container plants; a dry garden, housing a selection of plants from the warmer and drier regions of the world within the foundation walls former greenhouses; a wild garden exhibiting plants from throughout the world in a naturalistic setting as championed by the English writer William Robinson; a monocot garden, displaying the diversity and beauty of monocotyledonous plants such as lilies, cannas, and day lilies; the Elliptical Garden, which uses native plants in a surprisingly formal structure; and an herb garden. The woodland and meadow that wrap around the outer edges of the property are being restored with native plants. Wave Hill is operated by an independent non-profit cultural organization; the buildings and grounds are owned by the city of New York.

NEW YORK CITY—BROOKLYN

BROOKLYN BOTANIC GARDENS (AHS RAP)

1000 Washington Avenue, Brooklyn, NY 11225-1099
Tel: (718) 623-7200; Fax: (718) 857-2430
Internet Address: http://www.bbg.org/
Admission: Fee: adult $5.00, child (<16) free, student $3.00, senior $3.00; Free:
Tuesday & Saturday, 10am-noon
Attendance: 875,000
Established: 1910
Membership: Y
Wheelchair Accessible: Y
Open: April to September, Tuesday to Friday, 8am-6pm; Saturday to Sunday, 10am-
6pm; Holiday Mondays, 10am-6pm; October to March, Tuesday to Friday, 8am-
4:30pm; Saturday to Sunday, 10am-4:30pm; Holiday Mondays, 10am-4:30pm
Closed: New Year's Day, Thanksgiving Day, Christmas Day
Best Time(s) of Year to Visit: December to February (Steinhardt Conservatory,
conifers), March (Rock Garden), April to June (Japanese & Osborne Gardens), April
(cherry trees, daffodils, magnolias), May (bluebells, lilacs, rhododendrons), June (Herb
& Rose Gardens, wisteria), July (annuals, day lilies, perennials), August (lily pond),
September (Rose & Native Flora Gardens), October (fall foliage, Japanese Garden),
November (grasses, Rock Garden)
Facilities: Children's Garden & Discovery Center; Classrooms (4); Conservatory
Steinhardt Conservatory (44,000 square feet, Palm House design by McKim, Mead &
White); Food Services Terrace Café (luncheon and beverages); Gallery; Gardens
(annual, aquatic, children's, formal Italian-style, fragrance, herb, Japanese, native plant,
perennial, rock, rose, Shakespeare, systematic); Greenhouses (3 teaching); Grounds
(52 acres, general design by Olmsted Brothers); Herbarium (250,000 specimens; 623-
7318); Library Gardeners Resource Center (4,000 books & 200 serials; non-
circulating; Apr-Oct, Tues-Sat, 1:30pm-4:30pm; Nov-Mar, Tues-Fri, 1:30pm-
4:30pm), Rare Book Room (1,500 books, non-circulating, open by written application
and by appointment only), Science Library, 109 Montgomery Street (30,000 books &
150 serials, non-circulating, open to members and qualified researchers by
appointment only, 623-7302); Museum; Shop (gardening-related books and gifts);
Special Collections (bonsai, lilac, magnolia); Visitor Center
Activities: Concerts; Education Programs (adults and children); Films; Guided Tours
(groups, reserve in advance, 623-7220); Lectures; Plant Sale (early May); Seminars;
Symposia; Temporary Exhibitions (horticulture and art)

Located in the middle of one of America's largest cities, the Brooklyn Botanic Gardens
displays more than 12,000 varieties of plants from around the globe, both in exterior gardens and under glass. The Steinhardt Conservatory, a $2.5 million greenhouse complex,
houses an extensive indoor plant collection in realistic environments that simulate a range
of global habitats (aquatic, desert, tropical, Mediterranean). Exhibits include the largest
bonsai collection on public display outside of Japan (550-600 specimens with about 100
on display at any given time); "The Trail of Evolution," tracing the development of plants
from their origin to the present day; and submerged aquatic plants that may be viewed
from lower level windows as well as from the surface. Among the gardens are the Fragrance Garden, designed by Alice R. Ireys in 1955, the first garden in the country to be
designed for the blind; the Japanese Hill and Pond Garden, designed by Takeo Shiota in
1914, the first Japanese garden to be created in an American public garden and is consid-

ered one of the finest Japanese gardens outside of Japan; the Rose Garden, containing over 5,000 roses representing over 1,200 varieties, one of the largest rose gardens in the United States; the Osborne Garden, a three-acre, Italian-style formal garden; the Shakespeare Garden, an informal garden design exhibiting plants mentioned in the playwright's works; the Herb Garden, featuring a sixteenth-century Elizabethan knot design, surrounded by more than 300 kinds of medicinal, culinary, fragrant, and ornamental herbs; the Native Flora Garden, with more than two acres divided into eight geographical zones, exhibiting native plants growing within a 100-mile radius of New York City; the Rock Garden, designed early in the twentieth century, the first rock garden in an American botanic garden; the Mixed Perennial Border, a diverse collection of more than 100 kinds of herbaceous plants and summer-flowering shrubs; and an extensive lilac collection, displaying approximately 150 lilac species and cultivars. There is also a systematic garden, the Plant Family Collection, designed to display plants in the order in which they evolved on Earth.

NEW YORK CITY—MANHATTAN

THE CATHEDRAL CHURCH OF ST. JOHN THE DIVINE— BIBLICAL GARDEN

1047 Amsterdam Avenue at 112th Street, New York, NY 10025
Tel: (212) 316-7540
Internet Address: http://www.stjohndivine.org/
Parking: No public parking on grounds
Open: Cathedral, Monday to Saturday, 7am-6pm; Sunday, 7am-7pm; Grounds & Gardens, daily, daylight hours
Facilities: Architecture (begun in 1892, the cathedral is 2/3 complete); Garden (¼ acre; Biblical)
Activities: Education Programs; Guided Tours General (Tues-Sat, 11am; Sun, 1pm; $5/person; Groups 10+ (by reservation, Tues-Sat, 9am-2pm, (212) 932-7347); Workshops

The largest cathedral in the world, the Cathedral Church of St. John the Divine in New York City is the mother church of the Episcopal Diocese of New York and the seat of its bishop. Its grounds contain a Biblical Garden featuring herbs, flowering plants, trees, and shrubs mentioned in the Bible.

THE CLOISTERS

Fort Tryon Park, New York, NY 10040
Tel: (212) 923-3700; Fax: (212) 795-3640; TDDY: (212) 879-0421
Internet Address: http://www.metmuseum.org/collections/department.asp?dep=7
Admission: Suggested contribution: adult $12.00, child (>12) free, student $7.00, senior $7.00
Attendance: 235,000
Established: 1938
Membership: Y
Wheelchair Accessible: P
Parking: Free on site
Open: March to October, Tuesday to Sunday, 9:30am-5:15pm; November to February, Tuesday to Sunday, 9:30am-4:45pm

Closed: Thanksgiving Day, Christmas Day
Facilities: Architecture (1938, design by Charles Collens); Grounds (4 acres); Library
(12,000 volumes); Shop
Activities: Concerts (Dec-Apr); Education Programs (adults, graduate students and
children); Gallery Talks (Sat, noon & 2pm); Guided Tours (Tues-Fri, 3pm; Sun,
noon); Lectures; Performances; Permanent Exhibitions; Temporary Exhibitions

   Located on four acres overlooking the Hudson River in northern Manhattan's Fort
Tryon Park, the Cloisters is a branch of the Metropolitan Museum of Art devoted to the
art and architecture of medieval Europe. The building incorporates elements from five
medieval French cloisters (quadrangles enclosed by a roofed or vaulted passageway, or ar-
cade) and from other monastic sites in southern France. Three of the reconstructed cloisters feature gardens planted according to horticultural information found in medieval
treatises and poetry, garden documents and herbals, and medieval works of art, such as tapestries, stained-glass windows, and column capitals.

THE FRICK COLLECTION

1 East 70th Street, New York, NY 10021
Tel: (212) 288-0700; Fax: (212) 628-4417
Internet Address: http://www.frick.org
Admission: Fee (children <10 not admitted): adult $12.00,
student $5.00, senior $8.00
Attendance: 275,000
Established: 1935
Membership: Y
Wheelchair Accessible: Y
Parking: Commercial adjacent to site

The Frick Collection, New York,
NY. © The Frick Collection.
Richard di Liberto photograph.

Open: Tuesday to Thursday, 10am-6pm;
Friday, 10am-9pm; Saturday, 10am-6pm; Sunday, 1pm-6pm; Holidays, 1pm-6pm
Closed: New Year's Day, Independence Day, Thanksgiving Day, Christmas Eve,
Christmas Day
Facilities: Architecture (former residence of H. C. Frick, 1914 design by Thomas
Hastings); Frick Art Reference Library (200,000 volumes; photo archives, periodicals,
databases); Gardens (2); Library (3,000 volumes, in house); Sculpture Garden (garden
designed by Russell Page); Shop
Activities: Acoustiguide (free, in six languages);
Concerts; Education Programs (graduate students);
Lectures; Temporary Exhibitions

   Displayed within his former residence, the Frick Collection is composed of the former
private collection of Henry Clay Frick (1849-1919) with subsequent additions made by
purchase or received as gifts. The museum has two outdoor view gardens and one interior
garden courtyard. The elevated garden at the museum entrance on Fifth Avenue contains
three very large magnolias. The Seventieth Street garden was designed by Russell Page.

MERCHANT'S HOUSE MUSEUM—GARDEN

29 E. 4th Street (between Lafayette Street & Bowery), New York, NY 10003-7003
Tel: (212) 777-1089; Fax: (212) 777-1104
Internet Address: http://www.merchantshouse.com
Admission: Fee: adult $6.00, student $4.00, senior $4.00
Established: 1936

Membership: Y
Parking: On street or neighborhood commercial lots
Open: Monday, noon-5pm; Thursday to Friday, 1pm-5pm; Saturday to Sunday, noon-5pm
Best Time(s) of Year to Visit: May to September
Facilities: Architecture (late Federal-style residence, 1832); Grounds garden (period Victorian, 25' x 50'); Shop
Activities: Concerts; Guided Tours (Sat & Sun, on the half-hour;, group, by appointment (minimum fee $60); Lectures; Readings; Self-guided Tours weekdays; Temporary Exhibitions; Workshops

Located in historic NoHo, bordering Greenwich Village, the East Village, and SoHo, the Merchants House Museum offers New York City's only completely intact nineteenth-century family home. Home to a prosperous merchant family for almost 100 years, the interior contains original furniture, decorative arts, clothing, and personal memorabilia. Behind the house lies a late Victorian-style garden featuring granite parterres, cast-iron furniture, and lush plantings. The property is designated as a National Historic Landmark and is a member of the Historic House Trust of New York City.

NEW YORK CITY—CENTRAL PARK CONSERVATORY GARDEN

5th Avenue at 105th Street (East Side, between 104th and 106th Streets), New York, NY 10021
Tel: (800) 201-7275; TDDY: (800) 281-5722
Admission: Free
Established: 1937
Open: Daily, 8am-dusk
Facilities: Garden (formal; English, French, Italian); Grounds (6 acres)
Activities: Concerts; Guided Tours

The Conservatory Garden is Central Park's only formal garden. It takes its name from the huge glass conservatory that once stood on this same spot, built in 1898. In 1934, when maintenance of the facility had become too costly, the conservatory was demolished and replaced with the present garden, which opened to the public in 1937. The garden is actually three separate gardens, representing three distinct landscape styles—Italian, French, and English.

NEW YORK CITY—CENTRAL PARK SHAKESPEARE GARDEN

West Side (mid-Park between 79th & 80th Streets), New York, NY 10021
Tel: (800) 201-7275; TDDY: (800) 281-5722
Internet Address: http://www.centralparknyc.org/virtualpark/thegreatlawn/shakespearegard
Admission: Free
Established: 1916
Facilities: Gardens (Shakespeare); Grounds (4 acres)

Situated between the Delacorte Theater, Belvedere Castle, and Swedish Cottage, the Shakespeare Garden is an informal cottage garden containing 120 varieties of plants mentioned in Shakespeare's plays. The garden was established on the 300th anniversary of his death in 1916. However, only the trees and a few shrubs remain from the original plan. After many years of neglect, the garden was completely reconstructed in 1987.

RUSK INSTITUTE OF REHABILITATION MEDICINE— ENID A. HAUPT GLASS GARDEN

400 East 34th Street, New York, NY 10016
Tel: (212) 263-6058; Fax: (212) 263-2091
Internet Address: http://www.ruskinstitute.org/ri/rusk/rusk_ggover.jsp
Admission: Free
Attendance: 150,000
Established: 1958
Membership: Y
Wheelchair Accessible: Y
Parking: Commercial lots
Open: Monday to Tuesday, 8am-3:30pm; Wednesday to Friday, 8am-5:30pm;
Saturday to Sunday, noon-5:30pm; Holiday Mondays, noon-5:30pm
Facilities: Conservatory (1,700 square feet); Gardens (children's, perennial)
Activities: Education Programs Horticultural Therapy (adults & children), Therapeutic
Garden Design Training; Events Annual community Festival (early June; Tulip Festival
(annual); Plant Sales (spring & fall)

Originally built to offer patients at NYU Medical Center's Rusk Institute a refuge from the rigors and clinical environment of their physical rehabilitation treatment, the garden has evolved into a public botanic garden and important center for horticultural research, learning, rehabilitation, and recreation. Elements include a conservatory, featuring an aquatic garden and collections that include orchids, ferns, palms, bromeliads, succulents, caudates, insectivorous plants, and many other adaptable to New York offices and apartments; a 4,500-square-foot, perennial garden containing a diverse collection of plants chosen for their ability to withstand low light and the harsh conditions of an urban environment; the Alva and Bernard F. Gimbel Garden, a 4,800-square-foot formal garden; and the Children's PlayGarden, a 5,500 square-foot area presenting diverse tree, shrub, and plant collections selected to encourage children to explore nature's sensory richness, to provide material for environmental education lessons, and to attract a wide range of exciting wildlife and insect life. The mission of the Glass Garden is rehabilitation, respite, education, research, and out-reach.

UNITED NATIONS HEADQUARTERS—GARDENS

Rose Garden: 1st Avenue & 42nd Street, Peace Bell Garden: 1st Avenue & 46th Street,
New York, NY 10017
Tel: (212) 963-7713; Fax: (212) 963-0071
Internet Address: http://www.un.org
Facilities: Gardens (oriental, rose); Grounds UN Headquarters (18 acres)
Activities: Guided Tours UN Headquarters (daily, 9:30am-4:45pm; 963-8687)

The Rose Garden is accredited by All-America Rose Selections. The Peace Bell Garden, located outside the General Assembly building, was designed by Shinichiro Abe and Zen Associates. Centered on a bell cast from coins collected by children from sixty different countries, the garden symbolically represents the seven continents of the globe, as depicted on the United Nations flag.

NEW YORK CITY—QUEENS

QUEENS BOTANICAL GARDEN

43-50 Main Street, Flushing, NY 11355
Tel: (718) 886-3800; Fax: (718) 463-0263
Internet Address: http://www.queensbotanical.org/
Admission: Voluntary contribution
Attendance: 320,000
Established: 1946
Membership: Y
Wheelchair Accessible: Y
Parking: Parking $5 in summer
Open: April to September, Tuesday to Friday, 8am-6pm; Saturday to Sunday, 8am-7pm;
Holiday Mondays, 8am-6pm November to March, Tuesday to Sunday, 8am-4:30pm
Facilities: Arboretum; Auditorium; Gardens (All-America, backyard patio, bee, bird,
compost, craft, fragrance, herb, oak allée, rose, Victorian, woodland); Greenhouse;
Grounds (39 acres), Arboretum (21 acres), Gardens (18 acres); Herbarium; Pinetum; Shop
Activities: Concerts; Education Programs; Guided Tours; Lectures; Plant Sales Plant
Shop (April-Sept); Workshops

Located at the northeast corner of Flushing Meadows Corona Park, the Queens
Botanical Garden had its roots in "Gardens on Parade," a five-acre horticultural exhibit
at the 1939-1940 New York World's Fair. In 1946, a group of civic-minded individuals,
with the support of Parks Commissioner Robert Moses, founded the Queens Botanical
Garden Society. The garden was relocated to its present site in the early 1960s to accommodate plans for the 1964-1965 New York World's Fair. Today, the garden's emphasis is on fostering community participation and providing horticultural information
and education to amateur gardeners. Exhibits include demonstration gardens (beach,
fountain, patio, pergola, rock, wooded); teaching gardens (bird, bee, ethnic, herb,
woodland); a three-acre Victorian "Wedding" Garden; and a six-acre rose garden. Com-
mitted to growth, the recent master plan by the landscape architects Susan Wisniewski
and Jamie Crelly Purinton emphasizes a return to the native plants that would work well
as part of a sustainable landscape.

LONG ISLAND CITY

ISAMU NOGUCHI GARDEN MUSEUM

32-37 Vernon Boulevard, Long Island City, NY 11106
Tel: (718) 204-7088; Fax: (718) 278-2348
Internet Address: http://www.noguchi.org
Admission: Fee: adult $5.00, child $2.50, student $2.50, senior $2.50
Attendance: 20,000
Established: 1985
Membership: Y
Wheelchair Accessible: Y

Parking: On street
Open: Wednesday to Friday, 10am-5pm; Saturday to Sunday, 11am-6pm
Facilities: Architecture (designed by Isamu Noguchi); Galleries (13); Sculpture
Garden; Shop
Activities: Guided Tours (daily, 2pm); Video Programs

Housed in thirteen galleries within a converted factory building, and encircling a garden containing major granite and basalt sculptures, the museum displays a comprehensive collection of artwork by Isamu Noguchi. On exhibition are more than 250 works, including stone, bronze, and wood sculptures, models for public projects and gardens, elements of dance sets designed for choreographer Martha Graham, and Noguchi's well-known Akari lanterns.

NEW YORK CITY—STATEN ISLAND

ALICE AUSTEN HOUSE MUSEUM AND PARK

2 Hylan Boulevard, Staten Island, NY 10305-2002
Tel: (718) 816-4506
Internet Address: http://www.aliceausten.org
Admission: Fee: adult $2.00, child (<13) free
Attendance: 10,000
Established: 1979
Membership: Y
Wheelchair Accessible: P
Parking: On street
Open: March to December, Thursday to Sunday, noon-5pm
Facilities: Architecture (farmhouse, 1710 with Gothic Revival expansion, 1844);
Food Services (seasonal concession stand [hot dog wagon]); Shop (books, postcards,
Victoriana)
Activities: Guided Tours (groups, Tues-Sun, advance reservation, $2/person);
Temporary Exhibitions (photography)

The home of Alice Austen, a pioneer woman photographer, the cottage now serves as a museum for her work as well as mounting regular shows of the work of other nineteenth- and twentieth-century photographers. With a Victorian garden and lawns sloping down to the entrance to New York harbor, the house and grounds contain many noteworthy architectural and landscaping features. A National Historic Landmark, the house is owned by the City of New York and administered by Friends of Alice Austen House, Inc. Austen was an avid gardener and founding member of the Staten Island Garden Club. The park has been replanted according to the garden species, such as weeping mulberry and flowering quince, depicted in her photographs.

JACQUES MARCHAIS MUSEUM OF TIBETAN ART

338 Lighthouse Avenue, Staten Island, NY 10306-1217
Tel: (718) 987-3500; Fax: (718) 351-0402
Internet Address: http://www.tibetanmuseum.com/
Admission: Fee: adult $5.00, child $2.00, student $3.00, senior $3.00
Attendance: 10,000
Established: 1945

Membership: Y
Wheelchair Accessible: N
Parking: Street parking
Open: Wednesday to Sunday, 1pm-5pm
Facilities: Galleries; Library (2,000 volumes); Sculpture Garden; Shop
Activities: Education Programs (children); Guided Tours (groups, by appointment, $6/person); Lectures/Demonstrations (selected Sun, 2pm-3pm); Performances (selected Sun, 2pm-3pm); Workshops

The Jacques Marchais Museum of Tibetan Art promotes interest in the art and culture of Tibet and other Asian civilizations. Designed like a small Tibetan mountain temple, the museum building was constructed specifically to house the collections of Jacques Marchais (Mrs. Jacqueline Klauber). Terraced sculpture gardens, a lily and fish pond, and a distant view of Lower Bay add to the atmosphere of serenity and beauty.

STATEN ISLAND BOTANICAL GARDENS (AHS RAP)

Snug Harbor, 1000 Richmond Terrace, Staten Island, NY 10301
Tel: (718) 273-8200 *Ext:* 10; Fax: (718) 442-3645
Internet Address: http://www.sibg.org/
Admission: Voluntary contribution; Fee: Chinese Scholar's Garden & Secret Garden
Attendance: 300,000
Established: 1977
Membership: Y
Wheelchair Accessible: Y
Open: Grounds, dawn-dusk; Tuesday, 8am-9pm; Wednesday to Sunday, 8am-dusk; Fall to Spring, daily, 8am-dusk
Best Time(s) of Year to Visit: April to October (Perennial Garden)
Facilities: Arboretum; Food Services Café Chinoise (Tues-Fri, noon-3pm; Sat-Sun, noon-4pm); Gardens (butterfly, Chinese, herb, hornbeam allée, maze/secret, perennial, pond, potager/vegetable, rose, sensory, shade, white); Greenhouses (4,200 square feet); Grounds (83 acres), Wetlands Preserve (20 acres); Library (1,000 volumes); Reading Room; Shop (books, jewelry, home & garden accessories; Tues-Sun, 10am-5pm); Special Collections (dogwood, rhododendron, Siberian iris, tree peony)
Activities: Education Programs (adults and children); Guided Tours Chinese Scholar's Garden (Wed/Sat/Sun, on the hour, noon-4pm; $5.00; Connie Gretz's Secret Garden (Wed/Sat/Sun, on the hour, noon-4pm; $2.00); Lectures; Plant Sales

Situated on the campus of the Snug Harbor Cultural Center, Staten Island Botanical Garden includes a wide variety of formal and informal gardens, a greenhouse complex, woodlands, and wetlands. From the initial plantings of its English perennial border to its newest addition, the New York Chinese Scholar's Garden, the garden has focused on presenting gardens representative of particular periods or cultures, as well as contemporary styles. The botanical garden's Victorian accent plantings surrounding Snug Harbor's important points of interest reflect the cultural center's original nineteenth-century role as a home for retired sailors. Other exterior gardens include a large perennial border, containing over 200 cultivars; a formal heritage rose garden, showcasing the history of the cultivation of roses; a white garden, contained within a treillage and composed of plants which have either gray green foliage or pure white blossoms; an informal pond garden, exhibiting plants especially suited to marshy conditions; an herb garden, displaying concentric beds of herbs demarcated by the garden's Siberian iris collection; and the Potager Garden, a French-inspired design featuring plants and methods used in kitchen vegetable gardening. Other features include a tree plantation divided into sections devoted to a pinetum, oriental flowering trees and shrubs, and native wetland trees and shrubs; a model barn and farm, celebrating Staten Island's agricultural heritage; and a wetland preserve. In addition, the garden is home to the New York Chinese Scholar's Garden, a classical Chinese garden designed and built by Landscape Architecture Corporation of China. Traditionally associated with a house and built by a scholar or an administrator retiring from the emperor's court, a scholar's garden with its walled enclosure, covered walkways, scenic courtyards, pavilions, and reflecting ponds may be seen as an architectural interpretation of nature. Located across from the New York Chinese Scholar's Garden, the Connie Gretz's Secret Garden is specifically designed for children. A garden folly adapted from eighteenth-century French and English gardens, it features a castle complete with drawbridge and moat overlooking an intricate maze leading to a walled secret garden. The botanical garden's glasshouse presents changing seasonal displays and exhibitions of native and regional plants.

NEWTONVILLE

PRUYN HOUSE CULTURAL CENTER—GARDENS

Town of Colonie Cultural Center, 207 Niskayuna Road,
Newtonville, NY 12128-0212
Tel: (914) 783-1435; Fax: (914) 783-1437
Internet Address: http://www.colonie.org/pruyn/
Admission: No charge, donations accepted
Attendance: 14,000
Established: 1983
Membership: Y
Wheelchair Accessible: Y
Parking: Two large parking lots
Open: Monday to Friday, 9am-4:30pm; Saturday to Sunday, special events
Closed: Legal holidays
Facilities: Architecture (Federal/Greek Revival residence, 1830; period furniture); Gardens (herb, flower); Grounds (5½ acres)
Activities: Concerts (summer Wednesday evenings); Education Programs; Garden Shows; Guided Tours (Sat-Sun by appointment)

In addition to the house, the site contains ten outbuildings including an early nineteenth-century post and beam barn and a one-room schoolhouse (circa 1910). The grounds contain herb and flower gardens complete with brick walks, painted fences, and a sundial. Pruyn House is jointly managed and maintained by the Friends of Pruyn House and the Town of Colonie.

NORTH SALEM

HAMMOND MUSEUM AND JAPANESE STROLL GARDEN

Deveau Road off Route 124, North Salem, NY 10560
Tel: (914) 669-5033; Fax: (914) 669-8221
Internet Address: http://www.hammondmuseum.org
Admission: Fee: adult $5.00, child (<12) free, senior $4.00
Attendance: 10,000

Established: 1957
Membership: Y
Wheelchair Accessible: Y
Parking: Free on site
Open: Wednesday to Saturday, noon-4pm
Facilities: Exhibition Area; Food Services Silk Tree Café (Wed-Sat, noon-3pm; reservations recommended, 669-6777); Garden (Japanese-inspired, design by Natalie Hays Hammond); Grounds (3 acres); Shop
Activities: Concerts; Education Programs (adults and children); Films; Guided Tours Garden (groups, reserve in advance); Lectures; Performances; Workshops

A not-for-profit center for the humanities, the Hammond Museum & Japanese Stroll Garden was established to provide links between the Eastern and the Western artistic traditions. Adapting the basic principles and ideas of the stroll garden design, artist and author Natalie Hammond incorporated indigenous plantings with popular and rare Japanese and Chinese specimens. Elements include evergreen trees and shrubs (particularly azaleas), massed groves of cherry and plum trees, flowers (particularly iris), grasses, and moss.

OLD WESTBURY

OLD WESTBURY GARDENS

71 Old Westbury Road, Old Westbury, NY 11568-1603
Tel: (516) 333-0048; Fax: (516) 333-6807
Internet Address: http://www.oldwestburygardens.org/
Admission: Fee: adult $10.00, child (<6) free, child (6-12) $5.00, senior $8.00
Attendance: 80,000
Established: 1959
Membership: Y
Wheelchair Accessible: P
Parking: Free on site
Open: Mid-April to October, Monday, 10am-5pm; Wednesday to Sunday, 10am-5pm. November, Sunday, 10am-5pm; December 1 to December 10, Daily, 10am-5pm (holiday celebration)
Best Time(s) of Year to Visit: May to November
Facilities: Architecture (Charles II Revival-style mansion, 1906 by the English designer George A. Crawley and American architect Grosvenor Atterbury); Food Services Café in the Woods; Gardens (boxwood, cottage, demonstration, formal English, lilac walk, primrose path, rose, walled, yew walk, woodland); Grounds (160 acres), Gardens (88 acres); Picnic Area (benches, no cooking); Shop (2, gift & plant)
Activities: Concerts Chamber Music Series, Julliard Series, Outdoor Series (Wed night, Jul-Aug); Films; Guided Tours House (final tour 4pm; House & Garden (groups; reserve in advance; adult $9.00, child $4.50, senior $6.00); Lectures (Sun); Temporary Exhibitions (costume exhibits in May, Sept, & Dec); Workshops (horticultural, children's programs)

Listed on the National Register of Historic Places, Westbury House is the former home of John S. Phipps and his wife, Margarita Grace Phipps. Furnished with fine English antiques and decorative arts, the mansion's grand architecture and generous proportions are complemented by carefully planned formal gardens and landscaped grounds interspersed with woodlands, ponds, and lakes. Reputed to be one of finest English gardens in the

United States, Old Westbury Gardens offers a succession of bloom from May to November employing historic varieties, new hybrids, and experimental plants. Highlights include the Boxwood Garden, the Lilac Walk, the Walled Garden, the Rose Garden, Primrose Path, and the Cottage Garden. There are also a variety of small demonstration gardens, including a gray garden, a shade garden, a green garden, a vegetable and herb garden, and a variety of herbaceous and shrub borders. Visitor brochures are available in English, French, German, and Spanish.

OYSTER BAY

PLANTING FIELDS ARBORETUM STATE HISTORIC PARK (AHS RAP)

Planting Fields Road, Oyster Bay, NY 11771
Tel: (516) 922-7604; Fax: (516) 922-9226
Internet Address: http://www.plantingfields.org/
Attendance: 260,000
Established: 1955
Membership: Y
Wheelchair Accessible: Y
Parking: $6.00 parking fee May-Labor Day and weekends all year
Open: daily, 9am-5pm
Closed: Christmas Day
Best Time(s) of Year to Visit: January to March (camellia), May (azalea, rhododendron), June (rose)
Facilities: Architecture Coe Hall (Tudor Revival, 1918-1921 design by Walker & Gillette, New York, NY); Food Services Tea House; Gardens (dahlia, dwarf conifer, conifer trail, green, heather, Italian, rose, sunken, synoptic); Greenhouses (2 Lowell & Sargent; daily, 10am-4:30pm); Grounds (409 acres, design by Olmsted Brothers, Brookline, MA), Garden and Arboretum (160 acres), Greenhouse Ranges (40 acres), Woodland (200 acres); Herbarium (10,000 specimens); Library; Nature Trails; Play House; Special Collections (azalea, camellia, conifer, ornamental grasses, heather, hibiscus, holly, magnolia, maple, rhododendron)
Activities: Education Programs (adults, undergraduates and children); Films; Guided Tours; Lectures; Temporary Exhibitions

Situated between Oyster Bay and Locust Valley on Long Island's North Shore, Planting Fields Arboretum State Historic Park, consists of a former Gold coast estate, Coe Hall, with of over 400 acres of cultivated gardens, rolling lawns, and natural woodlands. The arboretum contains over 4,000 varieties of indoor and outdoor plantings, including magnificent trees, more than 600 different kinds of azaleas/rhododendrons and over 100 different types of evergreen holly as well as extensive camellia and hibiscus collections. Among the exterior gardens are a 5-acre synoptic garden, displaying more than 400 species of flowering shrubs and small trees alphabetically arranged by botanical name; a rose garden and arbor, containing over 680 tea, shrub, and miniature roses; and an English-style sunken heather garden, featuring low-growing heaths and heathers; a recently renovated dwarf conifer garden; a confer trail; and an azalea walk. Greenhouse exhibits include economic plants, orchids, bromeliads, cacti, begonias, and ferns as well as specific houses for the camellia and hibiscus collections. In addition, there are seasonal displays of chrysanthemum, poinsettia, hydrangea, lilies, and spring and summer annuals. Information about innovative garden techniques and new plant selections is available. Listed in the National

Register of Historic Districts, the site is administered by the Long Island Region of the New York State Office of Parks, Recreation, and Historic Preservation.

POUGHKEEPSIE

LOCUST GROVE: SAMUEL F.B. MORSE HISTORIC SITE—GARDENS

370 South Road, Poughkeepsie, NY 12601-5234
Tel: (914) 454-4500
Internet Address: http://www.morsehistoricsite.org/
Admission: Free (grounds only)
Open: Grounds, daily, 8am-dusk
Facilities: Architecture (original Georgian residence, 1830; Tuscan Villa-style changes and additions by Morse and architect Andrew Jackson Davis, early 1850s); Gardens (historic, Victorian, perennial, heirloom vegetable); Grounds (150 acres); Trails (3 miles)
Activities: Guided Tours Gardens (by appointment, 454-4500 x14)

Designated a National Historic Landmark, Locust Grove was the residence of Samuel F. B. Morse from 1847 to his death in 1872. Influenced by architect Andrew Jackson Davis, as well as landscape architect Andrew Jackson Downing, Morse created a unique combination of landscaped lawns, vistas, and architecture: a Tuscan-style villa surrounded by a picturesque, romantic nineteenth century landscape design. The grounds also reflect Morse's knowledge of painting and landscape architecture in the broad, sweeping river views as well as in the subtle detail of the geometric flower beds. At the top of the bluff, the main house is surrounded by extensive Victorian-style gardens containing shrubbery, trees, flowers, and scenic vistas. There is also an heirloom vegetable garden.

VASSAR COLLEGE—ARBORETUM, NATIVE PLANT PRESERVE AND SHAKESPEARE GARDEN

124 Raymond Avenue, Poughkeepsie, NY 12603
Tel: (845) 437-7270; Fax: (845) 473-0997
Internet Address: http://info.vassar.edu
Admission: Free
Attendance: 6,000
Established: 1861
Membership: N
Wheelchair Accessible: P
Parking: Visitor parking lot
Open: Daily, dawn-dusk
Best Time(s) of Year to Visit: April to June, September to November
Facilities: Arboretum; Gardens (native plant, Shakespeare); Greenhouse; Grounds Campus (1,000 acres)
Activities: Self-guided Tour (brochure available)

The campus, maintained as an arboretum, features over 230 species of trees; numerous gardens, including a Shakespeare Garden; and a native plant preserve containing streams, ponds, and a 700-foot boardwalk.

ROCHESTER

CITY OF ROCHESTER—MAPLEWOOD PARK ROSE GARDEN

100 Maplewood Avenue at Driving Park Avenue, Rochester, NY 14615
Tel: (716) 428-6770
Internet Address: http://www.rochestergardening.com/local/maplwood.html
Established: 1949
Open: Daily, sunrise-11pm
Best Time(s) of Year to Visit: mid-June (rose)
Facilities: Gardens (rose); Grounds Maplewood Park (158 acres, 1908 design by Frederick Law Olmsted), Rose Garden (3½ acres)
Activities: Rose Festival (mid-June); Workshops (3/year)

Situated in the center of the city above the river bank, Maplewood Park Rose Garden contains over 4,100 plants representing over 300 varieties of roses. An accredited All-America Rose Selections display garden, the Garden is maintained by the city of Rochester with the assistance of the Greater Rochester Rose Society and the Maplewood Neighborhood Association. Perennial beds complement the rose plantings.

ELLWANGER GARDEN

625 Mt. Hope Avenue (near Highland Park), Rochester, NY 14608-2204
Tel: (585) 546-7029
Internet Address: http://www.landmarksociety.org
Admission: By appointment
Established: 1867
Open: Lilac Festival, 10am-4pm; Peony Weekend, Saturday to Sunday, 10am-4pm; Other Times, by appointment
Facilities: Garden (perennial); Special Collections (lilac, peony)
Activities: Guided Tours Groups (by appointment)

An historic period landscape, this site has been continuously cultivated since 1867 by the family of one of Rochester's most prominent nurserymen and horticulturists, George Ellwanger of Mt. Hope Nurseries. This colorful perennial garden contains eighty different kinds of perennials, including noteworthy collections of peonies, roses, tulips, day lilies, hostas, iris, and trees. Ellwanger Garden is open annually during the Rochester Lilac Festival (mid- to late May) and for Peony Weekend; other times by appointment only. The site is owned and maintained by the Landmark Society of Western New York, Inc.

GEORGE EASTMAN HOUSE/INTERNATIONAL MUSEUM OF PHOTOGRAPHY AND FILM

900 East Avenue, Rochester, NY 14607-2298
Tel: (716) 271-3361; Fax: (716) 271-3970;
TDDY: (716) 271-3362
Internet Address: http://www.eastman.org
Admission: Fee: adult $8.00, child $3.00, student $5.00, senior $6.00; West and Rock Gardens—no fee
Attendance: 134,000
Established: 1947

Membership: Y
Wheelchair Accessible: Y
Parking: Free on site
Open: Tuesday to Saturday, 10am-5:00pm; Thursday, 10am-8pm; Sunday, 1pm-5:00pm.
Closed: New Year's Day, Thanksgiving Day, Christmas Day
Facilities: Architecture (colonial revival mansion, 1905 design by J. Foster Warner); Auditorium (80 seats); Food Services Tea Room (Tues-Sat, 11am-4pm; Sun, 1pm-4pm); Galleries (11); Grounds (12.5 acres; historically restored gardens); Library (44,000 volumes, Mon-Fri); Photographic Archive and Reading Room (by appointment); Seasonal Garden Store; Shop; Theatre (535 seats)
Activities: Concerts (Musicale Series, Sun, 3pm); Education Programs; Films (Tues-Sun, 8pm); Gallery Talks (Tues-Sun, 1:15pm); Guided Tours Garden (May-Oct; Tues-Sat, 11:30am & 3:30pm; Sun, 4pm), General (Tues-Sat; 10:30am and 2pm; Sun, 2pm); Traveling Exhibitions

George Eastman House International Museum of Photography and Film combines one of the world's leading collections of photography and film with stately pleasures of the landmark colonial revival mansion and gardens that George Eastman, founder of Eastman Kodak, called home from 1905 to 1932. With nearly a dozen galleries and display areas, the museum hosts a wide variety of exhibitions drawn from its own collections and from other museums. Many of the collections are on display in the galleries, including photography and technology (cameras); films are shown six times a week throughout the year. The library is open weekdays for walk-in visitors, but an appointment is necessary for access to the photography and motion picture study centers. The gardens were designed by landscape architect Alling S. DeForest. Four of his original eight gardens have been adapted and restored using historical photographs and the original plans. The terrace garden features perennials. The library garden contains bulbs, shrubs, and vines. The rock and gardens have bulbs, shrubs, and ground covers.

MONROE COUNTY ARBORETUM—DURAND-EASTMAN PARK

1200 Kings Highway North (off Lakeshore Boulevard & Kings Highway, Irondequoit), Rochester, NY 14617-3331
Tel: (585) 256-4950; Fax: (585) 428-2590
Internet Address: http://www.monroecounty.gov/org13.asp
Admission: Free
Open: Daily, sunrise-11pm
Facilities: Arboretum/Pinetum; Grounds Arboretum (63 acres), Park (965 acres); Picnic Area; Special Collections (conifer)

Located on the shores of Lake Ontario, the park was originally the estate of Dr. Henry Durand. In addition to Dr. Durand's gift to the city, George Eastman donated additional adjacent acreage. Its unique topography of steep wooded slopes, valleys, and small lakes allow the growing of plants not native to this area. The site contains a world-class pinetum and many mature plant specimens. Highlights include many spring flowering trees, dawn redwoods, moss sawara, dove or handkerchief trees, and paper bark maples. A self-guiding brochure is available at the Durand-Eastman Park office, the Highland Park Conservatory, or the Parks Administration office at 171 Reservoir Avenue. The Monroe County Arboretum consists of Durand-Eastman Park and Highland Park (see separate listing).

MONROE COUNTY ARBORETUM—HIGHLAND PARK AND LAMBERTON CONSERVATORY

Mt. Hope Avenue and S. Goodman Street (at Reservoir and Highland Avenues), Rochester, NY 14620-2728
Tel: (585) 256-4950
Internet Address: http://www.monroecounty.gov/org215
Admission: Fee (Lamberton Conservatory): $1.00; Free (Park)
Attendance: 200,000
Membership: N
Wheelchair Accessible: Y
Parking: On street
Open: Grounds, Daily, 6am-11pm; Conservatory (Nov to Apr): Daily, 10am-4pm; Conservatory (Mar to Oct): Daily, 10am-6pm; Lilac Festival, Daily, 9:30am-8pm
Closed: Christmas Day
Best Time(s) of Year to Visit: 2nd-3rd week in May (lilac), 3rd week in October
Facilities: Conservatory Lamberton Conservatory (1911, (716) 256-5878); Gardens (courtyard, pansy, rock, rose, shade, sunken); Grounds (155 acres, design by Frederick Law Olmsted); Special Collections (barberry, lilac, magnolia, Japanese maple)
Activities: Lilac Festival (May)

In 1888, nurserymen George Ellwanger and Patrick Barry endowed the Rochester community with the twenty acres of gently rolling hills that were the beginning of Highland Park. Designed by Frederick Law Olmsted and home to Rochester's Lilac Festival, the park contains a variety of floral exhibits including a lilac collection totaling over 1,200 plants representing more 500 varieties; a Japanese maple collection; 35 varieties of magnolias; a barberry collection; a rock garden with dwarf evergreens; 700 varieties of rhododendron, azaleas, mountain laurel, andromeda, horse chestnuts, spring bulbs, and wildflowers, and a large number of trees. The park also features a pansy bed of 10,000 plants designed into an oval floral "carpet" with a new pattern each year. The Lamberton Conservatory, reopened to the public after extensive renovations, features a tropical forest display under its main dome as well as seasonal floral displays. Additional climate-controlled rooms contain collections of exotic plants, desert plants, economic plants (such as banana and coffee trees), and house plants. The Monroe County Arboretum consists of Highland Park and Durand Eastman Park (see separate listing). Warner Castle, which is located within the park, is listed separately.

ROCHESTER CIVIC GARDEN CENTER—WARNER CASTLE

5 Castle Park (near corner of Reservoir & Mt. Hope Avenue), Rochester, NY 14620
Tel: (585) 473-5130; Fax: (585) 473-8136
Internet Address: http://www.rcgc.org/
Admission: Free
Attendance: 15,000
Established: 1964
Membership: Y
Open: Tuesday to Thursday, 9:30am-3:30pm; Saturday, 9:30am-12:30pm
Closed: Holiday weekends
Facilities: Architecture (gothic-revival residence, 1854); Gardens (courtyard, fern, herb, rock, rose, shade, sunken); Grounds; Library (4,000 volumes); Shop (gifts for home and garden, craft supplies)
Activities: Classes; Education Programs; Events Annual Summer Garden Tour (July); Guided Tours Garden; Lectures; Plant Sales; Temporary Art Exhibitions

Located in Highland Park, Warner Castle (a crenellated Gothic-style residence) serves as the headquarters of the Rochester Civic Garden Center, a not-for-profit horticultural education center. In addition to collecting and disseminating horticultural information, the center maintains a variety of display gardens including a sunken garden (designed by landscape architect Alling S. DeForest), a shady border, a rock garden, a courtyard garden, an iris and day lily bed, an old-fashioned rose bed, a miniature rose bed, a fern bed, and a thirteenth-century herb garden.

UNIVERSITY OF ROCHESTER—ARBORETUM

River Campus (Elmwood Avenue to the end of Wilson Boulevard), Rochester, NY 14627
Tel: (716) 273-5627
Internet Address: http://www.facilities.rochester.edu/arboretum/
Admission: Free
Established: 1999
Membership: N
Wheelchair Accessible: Y
Best Time(s) of Year to Visit: May to October
Facilities: Arboretum; Gardens (butterfly, magnolia, rose); Grounds River Campus (1923 design by Frederick Law Olmsted, Jr.); Special Collections (dogwood, lilac)
Activities: Self-guided Tour (map available from Department of Horticulture & Grounds at 612 Wilson Boulevard)

Throughout the history of the university, founded in 1850, trees have been planted, maintained, and preserved. In 1999, the university designated portions of the River Campus as the University of Rochester Arboretum. Originally the grounds of the Oak Hill Country Club, the university purchased the site in 1923 and retained Frederick Law Olmsted, Jr. as designer and consultant to the architects creating the new campus. Many varieties of trees cover the River Campus, including some planted in the 1920s. Campus plantings include rose, butterfly, magnolia, and native plant gardens as well as dogwood, lilac, hosta, and cherry collections.

ROSLYN HARBOR

NASSAU COUNTY MUSEUM OF FINE ART

1 Museum Drive, Roslyn Harbor, NY 11576
Tel: (516) 484-9338; Fax: (516) 484-0710
Internet Address: http://www.nassaumuseum.org
Admission: Fee: adult $6.00, child $4.00, student $4.00, senior $5.00
Attendance: 225,000
Established: 1989
Membership: Y
Wheelchair Accessible: Y
Parking: Free on site
Open: Tuesday to Sunday, 11am-5pm
Closed: Legal holidays
Facilities: Architecture (neo-Georgian mansion, 1900); Galleries (10); Gardens (formal, rose, azalea); Grounds Gardens, Lawns & Woods (145 acres); Sculpture Garden (45 important pieces of sculpture); Shop

Activities: Education Programs (adults, college students, and children); Gallery Talks; Guided Tours; Lectures; Temporary Exhibitions; Traveling Exhibitions

The museum presents four to five changing exhibitions annually featuring historical, modern, and contemporary art and accompanied by diverse educational programs. Additionally the museum features selections from an extensive permanent collection of work by both European and American artists, over 45 works of outdoor sculpture situated in the formal gardens and throughout the 145 acres of landscaped grounds, and 26 miniature rooms in the Tee Ridder Miniatures Museum. In 1919 "Clayton" (now the Nassau County Museum of Art) was given as a wedding gift by Henry Clay Frick to his son Childs and his bride Francis. The Georgian mansion, surrounded by 200 acres had been designed by Ogden Codman, Jr. in 1900. In 1925, Francis hired Marian Coffin to re-design the formal gardens. The gardens have been fully restored to reproduce Coffin's plan to the letter.

SAGAPONACK

THE MADOO CONSERVANCY—THE ROBERT DASH GARDENS

618 Main Street, Sagaponack, NY 11962
Tel: (516) 537-8200; Fax: (516) 537-8201
Internet Address: http://www.hamptons.com/madoo/
Admission: Fee $10.00
Established: 1993
Membership: Y
Open: May to September, Wednesday, 1pm-5pm; Saturday, 1pm-5pm
Facilities: Grounds (2 acres)
Activities: Guided Tours (groups 10+, schedule in advance)

Madoo is an artist's garden, begun in 1967 by the abstract expressionist artist Robert Dash. Still evolving, the garden focuses on the combination and shape of plants, rather than structure, as the determinant in design. Settings include a Renaissance perspective rose walk, Italianate courtyard, laburnum arbor, maze, and potager. The Madoo Conservancy was established in 1994 as an irrevocable trust for the purpose of preserving the gardens.

SARATOGA SPRINGS

YADDO (YADDO ROSE GARDENS)

Union Avenue, Saratoga Springs, NY 12866
Tel: (518) 584-0746
Admission: No charge, donations accepted
Attendance: 30,000
Membership: Y
Wheelchair Accessible: Y
Parking: Parking on grounds
Open: Daily, dawn to dusk
Facilities: Architecture (Tudor-revival mansion, 1893 design by William Halsey Wood); Gardens (rose, rock); Grounds (400 acres)
Activities: Guided Tours (groups, schedule in advance, Summer, Sat, 11am; also in Aug, Tues, 11am)

Originally developed by New York City financier and philanthropist, Spencer Trask and his wife, Kate (Katrina) Trask, Yaddo is endowed as an artists' retreat. The estate contains an extensive rose garden and a rock garden. The estate is closed to the public (excepting the gardens) to ensure privacy for the guest artists.

SCHENECTADY

CENTRAL PARK ROSE GARDEN

Central Parkway (Wright Avenue Park Entrance), Schenectady, NY 12304
Tel: (518) 382-5152
Internet Address: http://www.schenectadyrose.com
Admission: Free
Wheelchair Accessible: P
Open: Daily, dawn to dusk
Best Time(s) of Year to Visit: June to September
Facilities: Gardens (rose)

The rose garden was begun in late 1959 and by the late 1960s an adjacent Asian-inspired garden with weeping cherries, stream, bridge, and reflecting pool had been developed. At its peak in the 1970s, the garden contained approximately 7,100 roses and was designated by the All-America Rose Selection (AARS) as a display test garden. However, during the 1980s, the condition of the garden so deteriorated that it was placed on probation by AARS. While not as grand as at its height, the gardens had sufficiently recovered by 1998 to be designated an outstanding AARS test garden. The gardens are maintained by the Central Park Rose Garden Restoration Committee, which is currently working with a landscape architect to improve the rose garden.

UNION COLLEGE—JACKSON'S GARDEN

Nott Street (behind College Center, near Nott Memorial), Schenectady, NY 12308
Tel: (518) 388-6000; Fax: (518) 388-6098
Admission: Free
Established: 1830
Facilities: Gardens (formal, herb, wildflower, woodland); Grounds Jackson's Garden (8 acres)

Begun in the 1830s by Captain Isaac Jackson of the Mathematics Department, Jackson's Garden consists of eight acres of formal and informal gardens, meadow, woodland, and stream. The garden includes plants and trees that are not indigenous to this part of the county. Also of possible interest on campus are the Robison Herb Garden and Levine Wildflower Garden.

SOUTHAMPTON

THE PARRISH ART MUSEUM

25 Job's Lane, Southampton, NY 11968
Tel: (631) 283-2118 Ext: 12; Fax: (631) 283-7006
Internet Address: http://www.thehamptons.com/museum

Admission: Fee: adult $5.00, child (<18) free, student free, senior $3.00
Attendance: 34,000
Established: 1898
Membership: Y
Wheelchair Accessible: Y
Parking: Village parking
Open: Mid-June to mid-September, Monday to Tuesday, 11am-5pm; Thursday to
Saturday, 11am-5pm; Sunday, 1pm-5pm; mid-September to mid-June, Monday, 11am-
5pm; Thursday to Saturday, 11am-5pm; Sunday, 1pm-5pm
Closed: New Year's Day, Easter, Independence Day, Thanksgiving Day, Christmas Day
Facilities: Architecture (Italianate structure, 1898 designed by Grosvenor Atterbury);
Auditorium (250 seats); Galleries; Gardens; Library (5,300 volumes); Sculpture
Garden; Shop
Activities: Concerts; Education Programs (adults and children); Films; Guided Tours;
Performances; Temporary Exhibitions

Housed in an Italianate structure built in 1898, the museum features changing exhibitions
with a focus on nineteenth-, twentieth-, and twenty-first-century American art and the art
of the region. Enhancing the architectural charms of the Parrish are the peaceful, shaded
gardens that surround the museum, which contain more than 250 different trees and
shrubs from around the world. The gardens are decorated with various sculpture reproductions from the original Parrish collection.

SYRACUSE

DR. E. M. MILLS MEMORIAL ROSE GARDEN (THORNDEN PARK ROSE GARDEN)

Thornden Park, Ostrom Avenue & University Place, Syracuse, NY 13204
Tel: (315) 473-4330; Fax: (315) 428-8513
Internet Address: http://www.syracuse.ny.us/parks/parks/thornden.html
Admission: Free
Established: 1915
Wheelchair Accessible: Y
Parking: Along park road
Facilities: Gardens (rose, herb, annual/perennial); Grounds Thornden Park (76 acres)
Activities: Festival Rose Day (annual)

A municipal garden, the Dr. E. M. Mill Rose Garden in Thornden Park is maintained in
cooperation with the Syracuse Rose Society. Containing over 10,000 roses, the garden is
one of only six accredited test gardens for the All-America Rose Selections. Adjacent to
the rose garden are an annual and perennial garden with an attractive lily pond with waterfall and an herb garden.

TANNERSVILLE

MOUNTAIN TOP ARBORETUM

Route 23C, Tannersville, NY 12485
Tel: (518) 734-3592; Fax: (518) 589-3903
Internet Address: http://www.mtarbor.org
Admission: Free

Established: 1977
Membership: Y
Wheelchair Accessible: P
Parking: Parking area next to barn
Open: June to October, Daily, dawn-dusk
Best Time(s) of Year to Visit: May to September
Facilities: Arboretum; Grounds (woodland forest and plant demonstration area
[3 1/2 acres]; fields and woods [11 acres]), Arboretum (7 acres)
Activities: Classes; Education Programs; Guided Tours (arrange in advance);
Lecture Series

The arboretum displays a range of native and exotic trees and shrubs that can successfully
adapt to the rigorous climate at 2,500 feel elevation in the High Parks Region of the
Catskill Mountains. Collections include unusual conifers, oaks, maples, dogwood, hornbeam, birch, trees with interesting bark, and shrubs that prefer to grow in wet soils.

TARRYTOWN

LYNDHURST

635 S. Broadway, Tarrytown, NY 10591-6401
Tel: (914) 631-4481
Internet Address: http://www.lyndhurst.org/
Admission: Fee: adult $10.00, child (<12) free, child (12-17) $4.00, senior $9.00
Attendance: 73,000
Established: 1964
Membership: Y
Wheelchair Accessible: P
Open: Mid-April to October, Tuesday to Sunday, 10am-5pm; Holiday Mondays,
10am-5pm; November to Mid-April, Saturday to Sunday, 10:30am-3:30pm; Holiday
Mondays, 10am-4pm.
Facilities: Architecture (Gothic Revival Mansion, 1838 by Alexander Jackson Davis);
Conservatory (Lord & Burnham, 1891); Food Services Carriage House Café (May-
Oct, Wed-Sun, 11am-3pm); Grounds (67 acres); Shop (gifts and reproductions)
Activities: Guided Tours (11am, 2:30pm, 4:15pm); Self-guided Audio Tour (mid Apr-
Oct, 10:30am-3:45pm; Nov-mid Apr, 10:30am-2:30pm)

A property of the National Trust for Historic Preservation, Lyndhurst is one of the finest
examples of Gothic Revival domestic architecture in the United States. Its grounds, with
dramatic views of the Hudson River Valley, are an exceptional example of nineteenth-
century Romantic landscape design. The grounds contain extensive lawns planted with
shrubs and specimen trees, a circular rose garden, and a fernery. Lyndhurst's conservatory,
constructed in 1881 by Lord & Burnham for Jay Gould, was the nation's first steel-framed
conservatory and at that time the largest private conservatory in America.

VAILS GATE

KNOX'S HEADQUARTERS STATE HISTORIC SITE—
JANE COLDEN NATIVE PLANT SANCTUARY

289 Forge Hill Road (at intersection with Route 94 North), Vails Gate, NY 12584
Tel: (914) 561-5498

Internet Address: http://nysparks.state.ny.us/hist/
Admission: Fee: adult $3.00, child (<5) free, child (5-12) $1.00, senior $2.00
Attendance: 15,000
Established: 1968
Membership: Y
Wheelchair Accessible: P
Parking: Parking lot on site
Open: Memorial Day to Labor Day, Wednesday to Saturday, 10am-5pm; Sunday, 1pm-5pm
Facilities: Architecture John Ellison House (Georgian-style fieldstone residence, 1754); Grounds Historic Site (49 acres); Special Collections (native plants)

Named for America's first female botanist and daughter of the last Royal Lieutenant Governor of New York, the Jane Colden Native Plant Sanctuary, containing over 100 kinds of wildflowers, is located at this historic site. The sanctuary is planted and maintained by the Garden Club of Orange and Dutchess counties.

WATERTOWN

JEFFERSON COUNTY HISTORICAL SOCIETY— VICTORIAN GARDEN (PADDOCK MANSION)

228 Washington Street, Watertown, NY 13601-3301
Tel: (315) 782-3491; Fax: (315) 782-2913
Admission: Suggested contribution: adult $4.00, child (<12) free, child, senior $2.00, family $10.00
Attendance: 13,000
Established: 1886
Membership: Y
Wheelchair Accessible: P
Parking: Free on site
Open: May to November, Tuesday to Friday, 10am-5pm; Saturday, noon-5pm; December to April, Monday to Friday, 10am-5pm
Closed: Legal holidays
Best Time(s) of Year to Visit: May to October
Facilities: Garden (Victorian)
Activities: Events Jefferson County Blooms, Spring Flower Festival; Guided Tours (arrange in advance)

The society's headquarters, the Paddock Mansion, a nineteenth-century Victorian structure, features agricultural and woodworking tools, early machinery, a carriage barn, and a large Victorian garden.

WEBSTER

WEBSTER ARBORETUM

Kent Park, 1700 Schlegel Road, Webster, NY 14580
Tel: (585) 872-2911

Internet Address: http://www.websterparksandrecreation.org/arboretum.html
Established: 1990
Membership: Y
Open: Daily, dawn-dusk
Facilities: Arboretum; Gardens (day lily, herb, lilac, perennial, rose); Grounds Kent
Park (84½ acres), Webster Arboretum (32 acres); Trails
Activities: Plant Sale (May)

In addition to trees and shrubs, the arboretum includes a rose garden, a day lily garden, a
lilac garden, and a series of perennial gardens designed to attract hummingbirds and butterflies. The arboretum is a joint project of the Webster Arboretum Association and the
town of Webster Parks, Recreation and Community Services Department.

NORTH CAROLINA

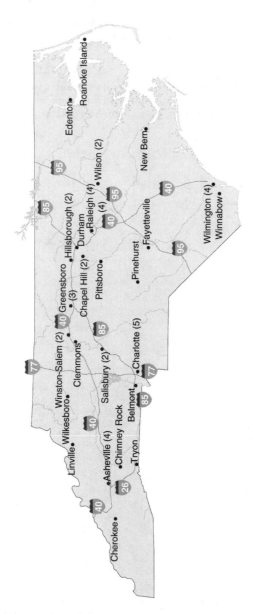

The number in the parentheses following the city name indicates the number of gardens/arboreta in that municipality. If there is no number, one is understood. For example, in the text four listings would be found under Raleigh and one listing under Durham.

ASHEVILLE

BILTMORE ESTATE

1 Approach Road, Asheville, NC 28803
Tel: (800) 543-2961
Internet Address: http://www.biltmore.com
Admission: Fee: adult $39.00, child (<6) free, child (6-16) $19.50
Attendance: 1,000,000
Established: 1930
Membership: Y
Wheelchair Accessible: Y
Parking: Parking lots with complimentary shuttles
Open: January to March, daily, 9am-4pm; April to December, daily, 8:30am-5pm
Best Time(s) of Year to Visit: May (azalea, rhododendron)
Facilities: Architecture (Biltmore House, 1895 design by Richard Morris Hunt);
Conservatory; Food Services Restaurants (4); Gardens (azalea, Italian, rose, English
walled); Greenhouses; Grounds (8,000 acres, design by Frederick Law Olmsted),
Formal Gardens (75 acres);
Pinetum; Shops (11); Special Collections (azalea, rose); Walking Trails; Winery
Activities: Concerts (Summer Concert Series, & Winery Jazz Weekends); Festival of
Flowers (spring); Guided Tours
Guided Garden Walks (offered seasonally, 800-624-1575), Specialty Tours (Behind-
the-Scenes, Rooftop, etc.);
Self-guided Tours

Biltmore Estate is a privately-owned, self-sufficient estate—a leader in historic preservation through private enterprise. The 250-room house features carvings by Karl Bitter, portraits by John Singer Sargent, and works by Dürer and Renoir, as well as sixteenth-century
Flemish tapestries. Unprecedented in scale and variety, the grounds at Biltmore range
from formal and informal gardens to parkland, woodland, and productive forest. Exterior
gardens include the formal Italian Garden, an ordered geometric arrangement of lawn,
hedge, and pools decorated with statuary, jardinières, and architectural elements; the four-
acre Elizabethan-inspired Walled Garden, featuring a succession of blooms beginning
with spring bulbs followed by plantings of annuals and perennials, a 236-foot-long grape
arbor, and espaliered fruit trees, rose of Sharon, and pyracantha; the Shrub Garden, consisting of lawn complemented by informal plantings of trees and shrubs; the Spring Garden, displaying masses of forsythia and spirea surrounded by mature white pine and hemlock underplanted with native rhododendron and holly; and the 20-acre Azalea Garden,
containing more than 1,000 native and hybrid azalea as well as rare specimens of the
Franklinia tree. The conservatory, designed by Biltmore House architect Richard Morris
Hunt, provides tender bedding plants for the gardens and flowering and foliage plants for

the Winter Garden, a glass-roofed garden room, and the rest of Biltmore House. It consists of a Palm House (palms, tree ferns, etc.), the East Wing (orchids and temperate plants), West Wing (tropicals and seasonal exhibits), and the Propagation House.

THE BOTANICAL GARDENS AT ASHEVILLE (BGA)

151 W. T. Weaver Boulevard, Asheville, NC 28804-3414
Tel: (828) 252-5190; Fax: (828) 252-1211
Internet Address: http://www.ashevillebotanicalgardens.org
Admission: Free
Attendance: 80,000
Established: 1960
Membership: Y
Wheelchair Accessible: Y
Parking: On site, 50 autos, handicapped spaces, bus spaces
Open: Visitor Center: March to December, daily, 9:30am-4pm; Grounds, daily, dawn-dusk
Facilities: Gardens (bird, bog, butterfly meadow, fern, wildflower trail); Grounds (10 acres); Herbarium; Library; Picnic Area; Shop; Trail (½ mile); Visitors Center
Activities: Concerts; Education Programs (UNC undergraduates); Festival Spring Wildflower and Bird Pilgrimage (early May); Guided Tours (special tours by arrangement); Lectures; Plant Sales (spring & fall)

The Botanical Gardens at Asheville is dedicated to the study and promotion of native plants and habitats of the southern Appalachians. Located near downtown Asheville, this ten-acre urban preserve displays collections of over 750 types of native plants, wildflowers, shrubs, and trees. The mountain climate encourages a long bloom season beginning in mid-March and extending into late fall.

THE NORTH CAROLINA ARBORETUM

100 Frederick Law Olmsted Way (off Wesley Branch Road), Asheville, NC 28806-9315
Tel: (828) 665-2492; Fax: (828) 665-2371
Internet Address: http://www.ncarboretum.org/
Admission: Free
Attendance: 250,000
Established: 1986
Membership: Y
Wheelchair Accessible: P
Parking: On site, $6.00/vehicle, Tuesday free
Open: Visitor Education Center: Monday to Saturday, 9am-5pm; Sunday, noon-5pm; Grounds (April to October): Daily, 8am-9pm; Grounds (November to March): Daily, 8am-7pm
Best Time(s) of Year to Visit: May to June (azalea)
Facilities: Food Services Savory Thyme Café (Tues-Fri, 11am-2pm); Saturday, 9am-5pm; Sun, noon-5pm); Gardens; Greenhouse (Mon-Tues, 8am-4pm; Wed, 8am-2pm; Thurs-Fri, 8am-4pm); Grounds (426 acres); Shop (handcrafts by local artists, bonsai tools, books; Tues-Sat, 10am-5pm; Sun, noon-5pm); Special Collections (azalea, bonsai, holly); Trails (10); Visitor Education Center
Activities: Demonstrations; Education Programs; Events Arbor Day Weekend Celebration (Apr), Asheville Blue Ridge Rose Society Exhibit (Jun), Asheville quilt

Competition & Exhibit (Aug), Carolina Bonsai Exhibit (Oct), Carolinas Dahlia Society Show & Harvest Festival (Sept), NC Chrysanthemum Society Annual Show (Oct), Orchid Show (late Mar/early Apr); Guided Tours (Apr-Oct, Tues-Fri), 10:30am;, Groups (schedule in advance); Workshops

Located in the eastern edge of the Bent Creek Research & Demonstration Forest, the North Carolina Arboretum offers demonstration and display gardens illustrating the great variety of native and cultivated flora, state-of-the-art greenhouses, and woodland trails. Established to help preserve and protect native azaleas, the National Native Azalea Repository presents almost every azalea species native to the United States as well as an array of cultivated varieties and hybrids, set among native ferns and wildflowers. Demonstration gardens include the Stream Garden, exploring the uses of both indigenous and non-native streamside trees, shrubs, and perennial plants in formal landscape design; the Plants of Promise Garden, presenting changing displays of award-winning landscape plants, new introductions, and superior plants derived from native flora being evaluated for residential use; and the Support Facility Perennial Border, featuring plants selected to provide continuous color throughout the season. Among other gardens on site are the Heritage Garden, showcasing plants used in the regional craft industry (such as dye making, basket making, hand paper making, and broom making); the Blue Ridge Quilt Garden, a formal garden inspired by traditional Appalachian quilt design; and the Cliff Dickinson Holly Garden, containing a wide variety of American native and non-native hollies that can be grown in this region. With more than 100 plants, the arboretum's Bonsai Collection is reputed to be one of the finest in the United States. A new bonsai display garden is scheduled to open in the spring of 2005. The Greenhouse is used to produce plants for many areas of the arboretum as well as housing rare and endangered species, tropical plants, and a bonsai collection. The arboretum is an affiliate organization of the University of North Carolina.

RICHMOND HILL INN—GARDENS

87 Richmond Hill Drive, Asheville, NC 28806
Tel: (800) 545-9238; Fax: (828) 252-8726
Internet Address: http://www.richmondhillinn.com/
Admission: Free
Attendance: 15,000
Established: 1989
Membership: N
Wheelchair Accessible: P
Parking: Paved, off-street parking
Best Time(s) of Year to Visit: April to September
Facilities: Architecture (Queen Anne-style residence, 1889); Gardens (Victorian, cottage, parterre, winter); Grounds Gardens (6 acres, 1994 design by Chip Callaway of Greensboro, North Carolina), Woodlands (40 acres)
Activities: Education Programs

Opened as an inn in 1989, Richmond Hill is set in a Victorian landscape of manicured gardens and natural areas, monuments, and several water features. The formal Parterre Garden at the Garden Pavilion was inspired by the great parterres of the Victorian age—simple, geometrically landscaped gardens with paths between the beds. The formality of the winter garden created by a manicured hedge is lost in the summer months with beds of towering perennials showing off their cool, pastel colors. The Sidney Lanier Garden centers around a monument honoring the noted poet and musician who camped on Richmond Hill in 1881 in an attempt to regain his failing health. The woodlands, featuring mature trees and native plants, are accessible by a walking trail.

BELMONT

DANIEL STOWE BOTANICAL GARDEN (AHS RAP)

6500 S. New Hope Road (Route 279, between I-85 and I-77), Belmont,
NC 28012-8788
Tel: (704) 825-4490; Fax: (704) 829-1240
Internet Address: http://www.dsbg.org/
Admission: Fee (Mon-Fri): adult $8.00, child (<4) free, child (4-12) $4.00
Attendance: 60,000
Established: 1989
Membership: Y
Wheelchair Accessible: Y
Parking: Free on site
Open: Monday to Sunday, 9am-5pm
Closed: New Year's Day, Thanksgiving Day, Christmas Day
Facilities: Gardens (canal, conifer, cottage, four season, perennial, white); Grounds
(450 acres); Shop (garden-related items, books, gifts, plants); Visitor Center (13,500
square feet); Woodland Trail
Activities: Classes; Education Programs

Located west of Charlotte, North Carolina, outside the town of Belmont at the
North Carolina/South Carolina border, the garden was begun by retired textile execu-
tive Daniel J. Stowe. Part nature preserve and part showcase for the best in southern
horticulture, the garden is in the process of implementing a forty-year master plan intended to place it among gardens with international reputations. Currently open to the
public are 110 developed acres, consisting of six themed gardens, a dozen fountains, a
visitor pavilion, and natural woodlands. The extant gardens are the Four Seasons Garden, featuring shrubs, trees, perennials, and annuals with unusual bloom times, showy
fruit, remarkable bark, evergreen foliage, and interesting growth habits; the Cottage
Garden, containing a mix of trees, perennials, and woody and herbaceous shrubs that
might have been grown in North Carolina before 1920; the Canal Garden, offering a
long row of perennial flowers and grasses anchored by fountains on either end; the
Perennial Garden, composed of four garden rooms, separated by hedges of trees and
shrubs to create a feeling of enclosure; the Conifer Garden, offering an unexpected variety of conifers showing off hues of gold, blue, purple, and green; and the West Gardens, containing two intimate courtyard gardens and a white garden. There is also a
Woodland Trail featuring plants native to the North Carolina Piedmont hardwood and
bottomland forests.

CHAPEL HILL

UNIVERSITY OF NORTH CAROLINA—
NORTH CAROLINA BOTANICAL GARDEN-
COKER ARBORETUM

Raleigh Road and Cameron Avenue (next to the Morehead
Planetarium), Chapel Hill, NC 27514
Tel: (919) 962-0522; Fax: (919) 962-3531
Admission: Free

University of North
Carolina—North Carolina
Botanical Garden—
Main visitor site, Chapel Hill,
NC. Paul Green cabin.

Established: 1903
Membership: Y
Wheelchair Accessible: Y
Parking: Metered in Planetarium parking lot
Open: Daily, dawn-dusk
Facilities: Arboretum; Grounds (5 acres)
Activities: Guided Tours (Mar-Dec, 3rd Sat in month, led by curator, free)

Located on one of the most beautiful campuses in the nation, Coker Arboretum is the oldest of the North Carolina Botanical Garden's tracts. Originally an outdoor university classroom for the study of trees, shrubs, and vines native to North Carolina, the arboretum now contains approximately 580 species, including collections of East Asian trees and shrubs, conifers, and extensive displays of daffodils and day lilies. Interpretive brochures are available in marked storage boxes at several locations on site. For information on NCBG's Main Visitor Area and other NCBG sites, see separate listing.

UNIVERSITY OF NORTH CAROLINA—NORTH CAROLINA BOTANICAL GARDEN-MAIN VISITOR SITE (NCBG)

Old Mason Farm Road (between Finley Golf Course Road & Fordham Boulevard), Chapel Hill, NC 27514
Tel: (919) 962-0522; Fax: (919) 962-3531
Internet Address: http://www.ncbg.unc.edu
Admission: Voluntary contribution
Attendance: 80,000
Established: 1952
Membership: Y
Wheelchair Accessible: Y
Parking: Lot on site
Open: Totten Center & Collections (Eastern Standard Time): Monday to Friday, 8am-5pm, Saturday, 9am-5pm, Sunday, 1pm-5pm; (Daylight Savings Time): Monday to Friday, 8am-5pm, Saturday, 9am-6pm, Sunday, 1pm-6pm
Closed: M. L. King Day, Thanksgiving Day, Christmas Day
Facilities: Administrative Building (Totten Center); Climatic Areas (piedmont, coastal pain & sandhills, mountain); Exhibition Area (carnivorous plants, horticultural therapy beds, flowering plant families); Gardens (fern, herb, native plant, wildflower); Greenhouses; Grounds (600 acres—includes several natural areas and biological reserve); Herbarium (660,000 specimens); Shop
Activities: Education Programs (adults and children); Guided Tours (Sat, 10am); Lectures (occasional); Temporary Exhibitions

The Main Visitor Site, one of three units managed by the North Carolina Botanical Garden, includes the Totten Center (which houses administrative offices, potting area, classroom, art exhibits, horticultural reference library, and gift shop) and the display gardens. NCBG collections contain representatives of the approximately 4,700 species of plants native and naturalized in North and South Carolina as well as herbs and horticultural plants from all over the world. Exhibits include the eighty-acre Piedmont Nature Trails, providing over two miles of hiking trails through Piedmont woodland; Coastal Plain and Sandhills Habitats, reproducing the wide range of ecosystems present in the eastern part of the state; Mountain Habitat Garden, featuring displays of ferns and woodland wildflowers from all the geographic regions of North Carolina that grow best in a shady location; and the Mercer Reeves Hubbard Herb Garden, presenting the theme of the dependence of human quality of life on plant diversity in a series of gardens dealing with medicinal, culinary, economic, shade, poison, evergreen, and Native American herbs. A second NCBG facility, the 367-acre Mason Farm Biological Reserve, is located east and south of the main visitor area. Containing diverse natural plant communities and protected habitats, the reserve may be accessed only by permit. (Permits are available at the Botanical Garden's Totten Center.) Adjacent to the Mason Farm Biological Preserve, the Hunt Arboretum is not open to the public. Its purpose is to protect natural areas and display a world-class collection of the woody plants of the southeastern United States. For information on NCBG's third unit, the Coker Arboretum, see separate listing.

CHARLOTTE

CHARLOTTE MUSEUM OF HISTORY—
HEZEKIAH ALEXANDER HOMESITE—GARDEN

3500 Shamrock Drive at Eastway, Charlotte, NC 28215-3214
Tel: (704) 568-1774 Ext: 115; Fax: (704) 566-1817
Internet Address: http://www.charlottemuseum.org
Admission: Fee: adult $6.00, child (<6) free, child (7-12) $3.00, student $5.00, senior $5.00; Free: Sundays
Membership: Y
Parking: Free parking in paved lot
Open: Tuesday to Saturday, 10am-5pm; Sunday, 1pm-5pm
Facilities: Architecture (residence, 1774); Gardens (herb, Native American); Grounds (7 acres)
Activities: Guided Tours (Tues-Sun, 1:15pm & 3:15pm)

The oldest structure in Charlotte and Mecklenburg County, the house was the home of Hezekiah Alexander, a signer of the Declaration of Independence. The site contains an eighteenth-century-style herb garden and Native American gardens.

HISTORIC ROSEDALE PLANTATION—GARDENS (ROSEDALE)

3427 N. Tryon Street (between 36th Street & Sugar Creek Road), Charlotte, NC 28206
Tel: (704) 335-0325; Fax: (704) 335-0384
Internet Address: http://libweb.uncc.edu/archives/crhc/rosedale.htm
Admission: Fee: adult $5.00, child free, child, student $4.00, senior $4.00
Attendance: 8,000
Established: 1987
Membership: Y
Parking: Parking—150 spaces
Open: Thursday to Sunday, 1pm-4pm
Closed: Legal holidays
Best Time(s) of Year to Visit: Spring to Fall
Facilities: Architecture (Federal-style residence, 1815); Gardens (formal English); Grounds (8 acres)
Activities: Guided Tours on the hour (groups, schedule in advance)

Designed by Mrs. Craighead Davidson, who came to Rosedale in 1918, the garden is in the English style, a long walk and crosswalk with tall evergreens at the axis and additional small crosswalks with the beds containing perennials and annuals treated as parterres. Later, she added the rose garden, again with parterres bordered with box.

MCGILL ROSE GARDEN

940 N. Davidson Street, Charlotte, NC 28206
Tel: (704) 333-6497; Fax: (704) 332-7553
Internet Address: http://www.mcgillrose.org
Membership: Y
Wheelchair Accessible: Y
Parking: On street
Open: Spring to Fall, Tuesday to Friday, 9am-4pm
Best Time(s) of Year to Visit: May to July, October
Facilities: Garden (rose); Grounds (1 1/3 acres)
Activities: Children's Activities; Classes (rose); Workshops (herb)

Begun in the 1950s by Helen and Henry McGill in the work yard of their fuel and ice company, the rose garden was opened to the public in 1967. Located on the northern edge of uptown Charlotte, the McGill Rose Garden is an All-America Rose Selections public garden featuring over 1,000 roses representing over 230 varieties and a supporting cast of annuals, perennials, and herbs. Today, the city owns the property and the Garden is managed by McGill Rose Garden, Inc., a non-profit organization.

UNIVERSITY OF NORTH CAROLINA AT CHARLOTTE— BOTANICAL GARDENS

Off University City Boulevard (Route 49), Mary Alexander & Michael Ray Craver Roads, Charlotte, NC 28223-0001
Tel: (704) 687-2364
Internet Address: http://gardens.uncc.edu
Admission: Free
Attendance: 40,000
Established: 1966
Membership: N
Wheelchair Accessible: P
Parking: Parking adjacent to greenhouse
Open: Grounds, daily, sunrise-sunset
Greenhouses, Monday to Saturday, 10am-3pm
Best Time(s) of Year to Visit: April to mid-May (Van Landingham Rhododendron Glen), January to May (Susie Harwood Ornamental Garden)
Facilities: Gardens (azalea/rhododendron, butterfly/hummingbird, dwarf conifer/rock, native plant, oriental, water, winter); Grounds Susie Harwood Ornamental Garden (3 acres), Van Landingham Rhododendron Glen (7 acres); Greenhouse (4,000 square feet; Mon-Sat, 10am-3pm—also bog garden, annuals, perennials, tropicals); herbarium (40,000 specimens); Special Collections (azalea, dwarf conifer, Japanese maple, orchid, Sarracenia pitcher plant, viburnum)
Activities: Guided Tours (by appointment, 704-687-2555)

The UNC Charlotte Botanical Gardens consists of a variety of outdoor and indoor facilities. The Van Landingham Glen, one of the largest rhododendron gardens in the southeast, contains over 3,000 hybrid rhododendrons and 1,000 species of native trees, shrubs, wildflowers, and ferns of the Carolinas. The Susie Harwood Ornamental Garden, a formal garden, displays hardy ornamental landscape plants from around the world in a semi-Oriental motif, including dwarf conifers, unusual cultivars of trees and shrubs, and an extensive winter garden. The McMillan Greenhouse complex contains plants from the world's diverse climates, including a variety of plants from the tropical rain forest as well as particularly extensive orchid and pitcher plant collections.

WING HAVEN GARDENS AND BIRD SANCTUARY (AHS RAP)

248 Ridgewood Avenue, Charlotte, NC 28209-1632
Tel: (704) 331-0664; Fax: (704) 331-9368
Internet Address: http://www.winghavengardens.com
Admission: Voluntary contribution
Attendance: 10,000
Established: 1927
Membership: Y
Wheelchair Accessible: Y
Open: Tuesday, 3pm-5pm; Wednesday, 10am-noon; Sunday, 2pm-5pm
Facilities: Gardens (fern, herb, rose, wildflower, woodland); Grounds (4 acres); Shop; Statuary
Activities: Guided Tours

   Wing Haven, a garden and bird sanctuary, combines formal gardens with wild woodlands. An antique rose garden is also on site.

CHEROKEE

CHEROKEE BOTANICAL GARDEN AND NATURE TRAIL

Route 441 (adjacent to Oconaluftee Indian Village), Cherokee, NC 28719
Tel: (828) 497-2111
Internet Address: http://www.oconalufteevillage.com
Admission: Fee: adult $13.00, child $6.00
Established: 1955
Parking: Free on site
Open: May 15 to October, 9am-5:30pm
Facilities: Architecture (Cherokee home of late 1890s); Gardens; Nature Trail (1/2 mile in length, 150 species of plants on trail)
Activities: Guided Tours

   The Cherokee arboretum, botanical gardens, and nature trail are a part of the Oconaluftee Indian Village, a replica of a Cherokee village of the mid-eighteenth century. The village features Cherokee artisans, replicas of Cherokee homes, a Council House, and Squareground. Cherokee guides escort visitors through the village explaining the various crafts, history, and lifestyle of the Cherokee. The Nature Trail leads off from the village and features arched bridges, a pond, and a Cherokee home that was moved to the area from another location. The Oconaluftee Village is sponsored by the Cherokee Historical Association.

CHIMNEY ROCK

CHIMNEY ROCK PARK

Highways 64 & 74 A, Chimney Rock, NC 28720
Tel: (828) 625-9611; Fax: (828) 277-9611
Internet Address: http://www.chimneyrockpark.com
Admission: Fee: adult $14.00, child (<4) free, child (4-12) $6.00

Attendance: 260,000
Established: 1902
Wheelchair Accessible: P
Parking: Parking in upper lot and meadows area
Open: Eastern Standard Time, daily, 8:30am-4:30pm; Daylight Savings Time, daily, 8:30am-5:30pm
Closed: New Year's Day, Thanksgiving Day, Christmas Day
Facilities: Grounds (1,000 acres); Trails (5 miles)
Activities: Guided Walks Wildflower & Bird Identification (call or visit website for details)

Situated in Hickory Nut Gorge, Chimney Rock Park is a family-owned, natural scenic attraction. Due to great variations in environmental conditions, such as topography, rocks, soils, availability of moisture, and exposure to sunlight, the park has a very diverse plant life. More than 550 species of vascular plants, including thirty-two ferns and fern allies, have been identified. A pamphlet, *The Wildflowers of Chimney Rock Park* (keyed to Newcombe's Wildflower Guide) is available for 25¢.

CLEMMONS

FORSYTH COUNTY—TANGLEWOOD PARK ARBORETUM AND ROSE GARDEN

4201 Clemmons Road (Highway 158 West), Clemmons, NC 27012
Tel: (919) 788-6312
Admission: Fee $2.00 per car
Attendance: 200,000
Established: 1951
Membership: Y
Wheelchair Accessible: P
Parking: Fifty parking spaces
Open: dawn-dusk
Best Time(s) of Year to Visit: April
Facilities: Arboretum 3.5 acres (types usable for local landscaping); Garden (AARS public rose garden); Grounds (1,152 acres)

Formerly the home of William Neal Reynolds, brother of tobacco entrepreneur R. J. Reynolds, the property with its extensive native and ornamental plantings was given to the citizens of Forsyth County for use as a public recreational park by the Reynolds family in 1951. The rose garden, in front of the manor house, contains more than 800 rosebushes, including more than 400 American Rose Society winners.

DURHAM

DUKE UNIVERSITY—SARAH P. DUKE GARDENS (AHS RAP)

418 Anderson Street, West Campus (between Campus Drive & Erwin Road), Durham, NC 27708
Tel: (919) 684-3698; Fax: (919) 684-8861
Internet Address: http://www.hr.duke.edu/dukegardens/

Admission: Free
Attendance: 300,000
Established: 1935
Membership: Y
Wheelchair Accessible: P
Open: daily, 8am-dusk
Facilities: Food Services Refreshment Cottage; Gardens (Italianate, Japanese-inspired, rock, wildflower, woodland); Grounds Culberson Arboretum (20 acres); Shop Terrace Shop (gifts, garden related items, plants; Mar-Dec; Mon-Sat, 9am-5pm; Sun, 1pm-5pm; 684-9037); Special Collections (magnolia, Japanese maple, southeastern wildflower)
Activities: Classes; Education Programs; Garden Tours; Guided Tours Free Public Tours (available most weeks; Private Docent-led Tours (available for nominal fee, schedule in advance); Trolley Tours (Mon-Fri, 8am-4:30pm, reserve in advance); Lectures; Plant Sales (spring); Workshops

Presenting the garden as fine art, Sarah P. Duke Gardens feature native flora of the southeastern United States and the closely related flora of eastern Asia in meticulously landscaped settings. The gardens consists of three major parts: the original Terraces and their immediate surroundings, the Blomquist Garden of Native Plants, and the Culberson Asiatic Arboretum. The Terraces, the gardens' historical core, is a romantic Italianate composition designed by the pioneering American landscape architect Ellen B. Shipman in the late 1930s. It features a wisteria-covered entrance Pergola, changing floral displays, a fishpond, a rock garden, and a lawn with reflecting pool. The H. L. Blomquist Garden of Native Plants, one of the finest collections of southeastern wildflowers, contains more than 900 species and varieties of plants displayed in a woodland setting dominated by mature specimens of Southern Yellow Pines. The Culberson Asiatic Arboretum, designed to illustrate the close relationship of the flora of eastern Asia with that of the eastern United States, contains about 550 species and cultivars of Asian plants, including special collections of deciduous magnolias and Japanese maples. In addition to the Asian plants themselves, the arboretum is embellished with architectural artifacts traditionally associated with the Japanese tea garden.

EDENTON

CUPOLA HOUSE AND GARDEN

106 W. Water Street, Edenton, NC 27932
Tel: (919) 482-3400
Admission: Free
Attendance: 10,000
Established: 1976
Wheelchair Accessible: Y
Parking: Limited on street & small nearby parking lots
Open: Daily, 8am-4:30pm
Closed: New Year's Day, Christmas Day
Best Time(s) of Year to Visit: March to November
Facilities: Architecture (Jacobean residence, 1758); Gardens (colonial revival, formal, vegetable); Grounds (1975 design by landscape architect Donald Parker)
Activities: Guided Tours House (by arrangement with the Edenton Visitors Center); Self-guided Tour Gardens (brochure available)

Reputed to be the best example of a Jacobean-style wooden house in the southern United States, Cupola House is designated a National Historic Landmark. The vegetable garden at the back and the formal garden in front have been restored to the late eighteenth century. The gardens are maintained by volunteers.

FAYETTEVILLE

CAPE FEAR BOTANICAL GARDEN (CFBG)

536 North Eastern Boulevard, Fayetteville, NC 28301-5100
Tel: (910) 486-0221; Fax: (910) 486-4209
Internet Address: http://www.capefearbg.org/
Admission: Fee: adult $5.00, child (<12) free; Free: 1st Saturday in month;
military—$4.00
Membership: Y
Wheelchair Accessible: Y
Open: Mid-February to mid-December, Monday to Saturday, 10am-5pm; Sunday,
noon-5pm; mid-December to mid-February, Monday to Saturday, 10am-5pm
Facilities: Architecture (farmhouse, 1886); Gardens (camellia, day lily, laurel walk, lily
pond, secret, terrace); Greenhouse; Grounds (85 acres); Herbarium; Library; Shop
Activities: Guided Tours (arrange in advance)

CFBG features a large urban forest with nature trails, a natural amphitheater, steep
ravines sheltering unusual plants, and a variety of terrain from open pine forest to lush
riverbank. Highlights include an American Hemerocallis Society display garden.

GREENSBORO

CITY OF GREENSBORO BOTANICAL GARDENS— BICENTENNIAL GARDEN

Bounded by Cornwallis, Hobbs & Holden Roads, Greensboro, NC 27410
Tel: (336) 373-2199
Internet Address: http://www.ci.greensboro.nc.us/leisure/default.htm
Admission: Free
Established: 1976
Membership: N
Wheelchair Accessible: Y
Parking: Free lot on site
Open: Daily, sunrise-sunset
Facilities: Gardens; Grounds (7½ acres); Picnic Area

Originally developed by Greensboro Beautiful in 1976 to commemorate the national
Bicentennial Celebration, the garden offers mass plantings of bulbs, annuals, and perennials as well as flowering trees and shrubs. In 1996, it was renovated to include a more formal wedding gazebo, a sensory area, and a stream water feature. The Centennial Garden
is one of three gardens constituting the City of Greensboro Botanical Gardens, a joint
venture of Greensboro Beautiful, Inc.; Guildford County Council of Garden Clubs; Guilford County Cooperative Extension; North Carolina A&T University; and the Parks and
Recreation Department of the City of Greensboro.

CITY OF GREENSBORO BOTANICAL GARDENS— THE BOG GARDEN

Hobbs Road (north of Friendly Avenue), Greensboro, NC 27405
Tel: (336) 373-2199
Internet Address: http://www.ci.greensboro.nc.us/leisure/default.htm
Admission: Free
Established: 1987
Parking: On street and at Bicentennial Gardens
Open: sunrise-sunset
Facilities: Gardens; Grounds (21 acres); Trail (½ mile)

The Bog Garden, a natural wetland, contains more than 8,000 individually-labeled trees, shrubs, bamboo, and wildflowers. In addition to natural growth, the Bog Garden contains many native plants rescued from other areas. A ½-mile boardwalk provides access to the collection. The Bog Garden is one of three gardens constituting the City of Greensboro Botanical Gardens.

CITY OF GREENSBORO BOTANICAL GARDENS— THE GREENSBORO ARBORETUM

Lindley Park (near Wendover Avenue at W. Market Street), Greensboro, NC 27405
Tel: (336) 373-2558
Internet Address: http://www.ci.greensboro.nc.us/leisure/default.htm
Admission: Free
Established: 1986
Parking: Two lots on Starmount Drive
Open: Daily, sunrise-sunset
Facilities: Arboretum; Gardens (butterfly, winter); Grounds
(17 acres, 1986 design by Robert McDuffie, Landscape Architecture and Horticulture Professor at Virginia Tech University); Trail (1+ miles)

Located within Lindley Park, the arboretum features nine permanent plant collections, garden displays, and structural features. The arboretum is one of three gardens constituting the City of Greensboro Botanical Gardens.

HILLSBOROUGH

CHATWOOD GARDEN

1900 Faucette Mill Road, Hillsborough, NC 27278
Tel: (919) 644-0791
Admission: Fee $8.00
Wheelchair Accessible: Partial
Parking: Free on site
Open: Late Spring to early Fall, Thursday, 2pm, reservation required; Saturday, 11am, reservation required
Facilities: Architecture (Federal-style residence, 1808); Gardens (perennial, rose, shade, stream, walled, Williamsburg parterre); Greenhouse; Grounds (20 acres), Gardens (6 acres)

Activities: Guided Tours (group 10+, by appointment,, Heritage Vegetable Garden (Sat, 10:15 am)

Chatwood, an 1808 Federal-style mill-tavern complex and its nationally recognized garden, is listed on the National Register of Historic Places. Most of the densely planted garden, consisting of a series of garden rooms containing about 350 varieties of old roses supplemented with annuals and perennials, was created between 1956 and 1992 by Mrs. Helen Blake Watkins, an early rose preservationist. Subsequent plantings include an English-inspired herbaceous perennial border of white, blue, and yellow plants and a Williamsburg parterre garden featuring a seasonal rotation of vegetables and flowers.

MONTROSE GARDENS

320 St. Mary's Road (next to Cameron Park School), Hillsborough, NC 27278
Tel: (919) 732-7787
Admission: Open by tour: adult $10.00, child (<6) free,
child (6-12) $5.00; Free Garden Days: 1 Spring & 1 Fall
Open: Tuesday, 10am, reservation required; Thursday, 10am, reservation required;
Saturday, 10am & 2pm, reservation required
Best Time(s) of Year to Visit: March (hellebores), April (native plants), May
(dianthus), late September to early October (sunny gardens)
Facilities: Architecture (residence, ca. 1898); Gardens (rock, scree, sunny, woodland);
Grounds (61 acres)
Activities: Classes (garden design, propagation); Guided Tours (Tues & Thurs, 10am;
Sat,10am & 2pm; by appointment)

Started in the mid-nineteenth century by North Carolina Governor William Graham and his wife Susan, the gardens were laid out by early Victorian English landscape gardener Sir Joseph Paxton. Later, the gardens became a commercial nursery specializing in hardy cyclamen and other unusual perennials. Gardens include a rock garden, scree garden, numerous sunny gardens in various color schemes, and several acres of woodland plantings with specimen trees and evergreens. Plantings include extensive collections of cyclamen, bulbs, hellebores, primulas, and epimediums. Listed on the National Register of Historic Places and a sponsored garden of the Garden Conservancy, Montrose Gardens is open for accompanied tours.

LINVILLE

GRANDFATHER MOUNTAIN

Blue Ridge Parkway, Milepost 305, Linville, NC 28646
Tel: (800) 468-7325; Fax: (828) 733-2608
Internet Address: http://www.grandfather.com/
Admission: Fee: adult $12.00, child (<4) free, child (4-12) $6.00, senior $11.00
Attendance: 250,000
Established: 1952
Wheelchair Accessible: P
Parking: Parking at Nature Museum, visitor center, and at overlooks
Open: Daily, 8am-dusk
Closed: Thanksgiving Day, Christmas Day

Facilities: Grounds (4,500 acres—animal habitats, natural history museum, hiking trails, wilderness backcountry)
Activities: Guided Tours

Grandfather Mountain, the highest peak in the Blue Ridge, is the only private park in the world designated by the United Nations as an International Biosphere Reserve. Considered the most biologically diverse mountain in eastern North America, it supports sixteen distinct ecological communities and is home to thirty-one rare and endangered plant species.

NEW BERN

TRYON PALACE HISTORIC SITES AND GARDENS

610 Pollock Street, New Bern, NC 28560
Tel: (919) 514-4900; Fax: (919) 514-4876
Internet Address: http://www.tryonpalace.org/
Admission: Fee (General Admission): adult $15.00, student $6.00; Fee: (Gardens): adult $8.00, student $3.00
Attendance: 74,000
Established: 1945
Membership: Y
Open: Monday to Saturday, 9am-5pm; Sunday, 1am-5pm
Closed: New Year's Eve to New Year's Day, Thanksgiving Day, Christmas Eve to December 26
Facilities: Architecture (Georgian residence, 1767-1770 design by English architect John Hawks); Auditorium (170 seat); Gardens Palace Gardens (colonial revival, 1955 design by landscape architect Morley Jeffers Williams), Palace Square Gardens (historic, eighteenth-century, nineteenth century, Victorian); Grounds (14 acres); Library (2,500 volumes); Shop Craft & Garden Shop (plants, garden accessories, handcrafted items), Museum Shop (books, reproductions); Visitors Center
Activities: Education Programs (adults and children); Garden Workshops; Guided Tours; Lectures; Performances

Designed by "the first professional architect to remain in America," Tryon Palace was the colonial capital of North Carolina and the residence of North Carolina's royal governor. The site offers a variety of garden styles ranging from eighteenth to the twentieth century. The Colonial Revival Palace Gardens, while not a historically accurate restoration in style or plant material, are inspired by eighteenth-century English landscape design. Palace Gardens include an eighteenth-century ornamental walled garden, containing beds of plants grown for their decorative qualities delineated by a precise geometric plan of clipped hedges; a green or knot garden, composed of yaupon holly hedges accented with Carolina cherry laurel; a formal parterre garden, derived from colonial design, but containing many more modern plants; a wilderness garden, containing native North American plants in a naturalistic setting; a variety of allées; and a kitchen garden, containing vegetables and herbs intended for household use. Additionally, surrounding the Palace Square there are several historic houses and gardens operated by Tryon Palace Historic Sites & Gardens. Palace Square gardens include Stanley House Garden, a formal eighteenth-century style "Town Garden" of brick walks edged with clipped boxwood and containing two reproduction summer houses; Hay House Garden, an example of an early nineteenth-century middle-class urban garden featuring plants of a more useful nature; Dot Tyler Garden at the Jones House, a modern design of beds and lawn employing plants cultivated during the mid-nineteenth century; Mary Kistler Stoney Flower Garden, a white picket fence-bordered garden displaying old-fashioned perennials and antique roses known to have graced New Bern gardens in the nineteenth century; Commission House Garden, a late Victorian period garden, including a variety of exotic introductions from throughout the world; and Gertrude Carraway Garden, a parterre garden with seasonal displays of modern plants mixed with more historic flowers. A free gardens booklet with a map and historical information is available at the Visitor Center.

PINEHURST

SANDHILLS COMMUNITY COLLEGE—SANDHILLS HORTICULTURAL GARDENS (AHS RAP)

3395 Airport Road, Pinehurst, NC 28374
Tel: (910) 695-3882; Fax: (910) 695-3894
Internet Address: http://normandy.sandhills.cc.nc.us/lsg/hort.html
Admission: Free
Established: 1978
Membership: Y
Wheelchair Accessible: P
Open: Daily, dawn-sunset
Best Time(s) of Year to Visit: April, Fall (hollies)
Facilities: Gardens (annual, conifer, Elizabethan, fruit and vegetable, hillside, holly, rose, wetland); Grounds (32 acres); Picnic Area; Visitor Center
Activities: Guided Tours (groups 10+, arrange at least 2 weeks in advance); Plant Sales

Established as an adjunct of the Landscape Gardening School, the Sandhills Horticultural Gardens offer an educational adventure to anyone with an interest in plants, nature, and design composition. This large site offers a variety of displays, including a rose garden, exhibiting in promenade fashion a variety of modern roses selected for their suitability to the local climate; an annual garden displaying a different theme each year; the Sir Walter Raleigh Garden, a formal English garden consisting of a holly maze, fountain courtyard, sunken garden, the ceremonial courtyard, and herb garden; a conifer garden, featuring varieties of slow-growing conifers that reflect color, form, and texture of foliage; the Ebersole Holly Garden, an arboretum certified by the Holly Society of America, containing 350 different cultivars representing 28 holly species; the Hackley Woodland Garden, consisting of an extensive collection of woodland and shade loving plants, including many varieties of azaleas, camellias, and rhododendrons; a succulent garden, demonstrating that succulents usually found in a Southwest desert setting may be grown in the Sandhills region of North Carolina; a Fruit and Vegetable Garden, consisting of an orchard of dwarf fruit trees, vegetables, and a vineyard; and the Desmond Native Wetland Trail Garden, a nature conservancy and bird sanctuary set among old poplars, pines, and plant material indigenous to wetland areas of the Sandhills.

PITTSBORO

VILLAGE OF FEARRINGTON—FEARRINGTON GARDENS

Route 15-501, Pittsboro, NC 27312
Tel: (919) 542-4000 Ext: 265; Fax: (919) 542-4020

Internet Address: http://www.fearrington.com
Admission: Free
Membership: N
Wheelchair Accessible: Y
Parking: Adequate free parking
Open: Tuesday to Sunday, 9am-4pm
Facilities: Gardens (courtyard, cutting, herb, kitchen, knot, perennial, white); Shop
The Potting Shed (display gardens, plants, garden-related items)
Activities: Guided Tours (groups, 15-30, 542-1239)

Originally a working dairy farm, the Village of Fearrington is a planned community. The Village Center, making use of many of the former farm buildings to house shops, restaurants, and an inn, is accented by Fearrington gardens. Gardens include Jenny's fragrant white garden; a perennial border; an herb garden and knot garden; an informal southern garden; and display gardens at the Potting Shed. Visitors are welcome to stroll through the gardens at any time.

RALEIGH

J. C. RAULSTON ARBORETUM AT NORTH CAROLINA STATE UNIVERSITY (JCRA)

4415 Beryl Road (near State Fair Grounds), Raleigh, NC 27695-1446
Tel: (919) 515-3132; Fax: (919) 515-7747
Internet Address: http://www.ncsu.edu/jcraulstonarboretum/
Admission: Free
Established: 1976
Membership: Y
Wheelchair Accessible: P
Parking: Free on site and along Beryl Road
Open: April to October, daily, 8am-8pm; November to March, daily, 8am-5pm
Facilities: Gardens (Japanese, perennial, water, white, wildflower, perennials, winter, southwest, paradise, rose); Grounds (8 acres); Lath House; Special Collections (barberry, boxwood, buckeye, conifers, grape holly, heavenly bamboo, holly, magnolia, maple, oak, redbud, silverbell, viburnum, wisteria)
Activities: Guided Tours (Apr-Oct, Sun, 2pm, free; groups, schedule 1 month in advance)

Containing the most diverse collection of cold hardy temperate zone plants in the southeastern United States, the arboretum is primarily a working research and teaching garden that focuses on evaluating, selecting, and displaying plants that can adapt to Piedmont North Carolina climatic conditions. Displayed in garden settings, plant collections include over 5,000 total taxa of annuals, perennials, bulbs, vines, ground covers, shrubs, and trees from over 50 different countries. Major exhibits include the Klein-Pringle White Garden, an elegant garden modeled after Sissinghurst in Kent, England; a 300-foot perennial border containing herbaceous perennials, bulbs, small shrubs, and ornamental grasses; a 300-foot mixed border; the Finley-Nottingham Rose Garden, displaying over 150 rose taxa; and a Japanese Zen garden. There are also a variety of demonstration and trial gardens, including a town house garden, a butterfly garden, a reading garden, and water gardens.

JOEL LANE MUSEUM HOUSE—GARDENS

728 W. Hargett Street at St. Mary's Street, Raleigh, NC 27605
Tel: (919) 833-3431; Fax: (919) 981-0795
Internet Address: http://www.ncneighbors.com/978
Admission: Fee: adult $3.00, child (<6) free, student $1.00, senior $1.00
Wheelchair Accessible: N
Open: March to mid-December, Tuesday to Friday, 10am-2pm; Saturday, 1pm-4pm
Facilities: Architecture (residence, ca. 1760, on National Register); Gardens (historic, formal eighteenth-century city, herb, kitchen); Grounds
Activities: Guided Tours (by appointment)

Raleigh's oldest residence, the site includes a period recreated garden, designed by Donald Parker. It is an attempt to recreate in a small urban setting elements of a colonial plantation garden, including fruit trees, a grape arbor, an herb garden, and a pleasure garden.

MORDECAI HOUSE AND GARDENS

Mordecai Historic Park, Mimosa Street & Wake Forest Road, Raleigh, NC 27604
Tel: (919) 834-4844; Fax: (919) 834-7314
Internet Address: http://capitalareapreservation.org/park.html
Admission: Fee: adult $6.00, child (<7) free, child (7-17) $2.00
Membership: Y
Wheelchair Accessible: N
Parking: Free on-site parking
Open: Tuesday to Saturday, 10am-4pm
Best Time(s) of Year to Visit: Spring to Christmas
Facilities: Architecture (Andrew Johnson's birthplace; plantation house, 1785; Greek Revival addition, 1826); Gardens (vegetable, herb, fruits, flowers)
Activities: Guided Tours (on the hour, last tour 3pm)

The site includes a recreated kitchen garden, based on first-hand descriptions, containing vegetables, fruits, herbs, and flowers that would have been grown in the mid-nineteenth century. In addition to the plantation house, two original dependency buildings survive—a storehouse and a double-door structure that possibly served as an office. The park also features a number historic structures relocated from Raleigh and the surrounding area, including the birthplace of Andrew Johnson, a small law office (circa 1810), another Raleigh office building (circa 1847), and St. Mark's Chapel, constructed in the 1840s by slaves on a Chatham County plantation. The site is maintained by Capital Area Preservation, a non-profit historic preservation organization.

RALEIGH MUNICIPAL ROSE GARDEN

301 Pogue Street (off Gardner Street), Raleigh, NC 27607
Tel: (919) 821-4579
Admission: Free
Wheelchair Accessible: Y
Open: Daily, sunrise-sunset

Located in a residential neighborhood near NC State University, the garden is an accredited All-America Rose Selections display garden, featuring 1,200 roses representing

60 different varieties. Seasonal flowers include bulbs, annuals, trees, and shrubs. An amphitheater, used for concerts and theatrical productions, is located in the garden.

ROANOKE ISLAND

FORT RALEIGH NATIONAL HISTORIC SITE— ELIZABETHAN GARDENS

1411 Highway 64/264 (adjacent to Fort Raleigh), Roanoke Island, NC 27954
Tel: (252) 473-3234
Internet Address: http://www.outerbanks.com/elizabethangardens/
Admission: Fee
Established: 1951
Open: September to May, Daily, 9am-5pm; June to Labor Day, Daily, 9am-8pm
Facilities: Gardens (herb, rose, sunken, woodland); Grounds (10 ½ acres, design by landscape architects Umberto Innocenti and Richard Webel); Orangerie

Located on the grounds of Fort Raleigh National Historic Site, Elizabethan Gardens was created by the Garden Club of North Carolina as a memorial to the first colonists. The entrance to the gardens is a Tudor-style gate house/orangerie containing antiques, paintings, and period furnishings. Gardens include a sunken garden with parterres, garden statuary, and ornaments inspired by the types of gardens that graced the English estates of the wealthy backers of the colony; the Queen's Rose Garden; and a woodland garden featuring native plants.

SALISBURY

ELIZABETH HOLMES HURLEY PARK

Lake Drive at Annandale Avenue (off I-85, Exit 76-B), Salisbury, NC 28144
Tel: (704) 638-4459
Internet Address: http://www.salisburync.gov
Admission: Free
Membership: N
Wheelchair Accessible: Y
Parking: On street
Open: Daily, sunrise-sunset
Facilities: Gardens (fragrance, holly collection, magnolia, spring bulb, and wildflower); Grounds (16 acres)

The park contains collections of hollies and magnolias, a wildflower garden, an azalea garden, and many other plantings.

WATERWORKS VISUAL ARTS CENTER (WVAC)

123 E. Liberty Street, Salisbury, NC 28144-4261
Tel: (704) 636-1882; Fax: (704) 636-1892
Internet Address: http://www.waterworks.org
Admission: Suggested contribution $2.00

Attendance: 30,000
Established: 1959
Membership: Y
Wheelchair Accessible: Y
Parking: Free on site
Open: Office, Monday to Friday, 9am-5pm; Gallery, Tuesday to Saturday, 10am-5pm
Closed: New Year's Day, Good Friday, Memorial Day, Independence Day, Labor Day, Thanksgiving Day, Christmas Eve to Christmas Day
Facilities: Galleries (4); Garden (sensory); Library (1,000 volumes)
Activities: Education Programs (adults, special populations and children); Gallery Talks; Guided Tours (upon request); Lectures

The center presents fifteen to twenty exhibitions per year in all media in four galleries. In addition, the center maintains three gardens. The Stanback, Dook, and Deal Gardens are planted to showcase the remarkable variety of nature's forms and colors year-round for the enjoyment of all who pass by. Sculptures are also featured throughout the garden areas. Designed for the visually impaired as well as the general public, the garden features plants for all four seasons labeled in Braille and English and providing scent and texture in addition to color and shape.

TRYON

PEARSON'S FALLS

Pearson's Falls Road (between Tryon and Saluda off Route 176), Tryon, NC 28782
Tel: (704) 749-3031
Admission: Fee $2.00
Attendance: 15,000
Established: 1931
Membership: N
Wheelchair Accessible: N
Parking: On site, 50 spaces
Open: March to October, Tuesday to Saturday, 10am-6pm; Sunday, noon-6pm; November to February, Wednesday to Saturday, 10am-5pm; Sunday, noon-5pm
Best Time(s) of Year to Visit: Spring to Fall
Facilities: Garden (native plant); Grounds (268 acres); Picnic Area; Trails (2).
Activities: Self-guided Tours

In addition to the ninety-foot waterfall, the site offers a native plant garden. Pearson's Falls is owned and maintained by the Tryon Garden Club. The club also maintains the Depot Garden, a village garden, in Tryon.

WILKESBORO

WILKES COMMUNITY COLLEGE GARDENS

1328 Collegiate Drive (off Route 268, ½ mile west of Route 421 intersection), Wilkesboro, NC 28697
Tel: (336) 838-6294

Internet Address: http://204.84.96.72/WCC/about_wcc/gardens.htm
Admission: Free
Facilities: Gardens (conifer, Japanese, native plant, rose, sensory, vegetable); Grounds
Campus (140 acres); Picnic Area; Visitors Center

The WCC Gardens are a diversified collection of genera and species of indigenous and ornamental plants located throughout the college campus. Highlights include the Ruth Colvard Rose Garden, containing over 600 roses; the Eddy Merle Watson Garden for the Senses, emphasizing design and plant materials suitable for the visually impaired; the Vernon and Louise Deal Native Garden, featuring a one-mile walking trail through growths of native trees and wildflowers; and the Sara Mills Japanese Garden.

WILMINGTON

AIRLIE GARDENS (AHS RAP)

300 Airlie Road at Wrightsville Beach, Wilmington, NC 28403
Tel: (910) 798-7700; Fax: (910) 256-6832
Internet Address: http://www.airliegardens.org/
Admission: Fee: adult $7.50, child $2.00, senior $7.00; Reduced admission fee for Hanover County Residents
Membership: Y
Open: Friday to Saturday, 9am-5pm; Sunday, 11am-5pm
Facilities: Gardens (post-Victorian European style); Grounds
(79 acres), Gardens (62 acres); Picnic Area
Activities: Arts Festival; Concerts; Education Programs; Self-guided Tours

Situated on Bradley Creek and bordered by salt marsh along both sides, the post-Victorian, European-style gardens feature not only extensive plantings of azaleas, spring bulbs, antique camellias, magnolias, and wisteria, but also a natural maritime forest of live oaks, pines, cedars, hollies, and wax myrtles and twelve acres of freshwater lakes. Originally a private estate begun in the early 1900s, the densely and lavishly planted gardens reached their zenith in the 1920s and 1930s, with thousands of exotics supplementing the natural coastal landscape. Since 1999, when the site was acquired by New Hanover County, the gardens have been maintained and managed by the New Hanover County Cooperative Extension Service and Arboretum. Planned and recent additions to the site include the Minnie Evans Sculpture Garden, interpreting and celebrating the unique artistic vision of this noted artist and long-time gatekeeper at Airlie Gardens; the Showcase Garden, featuring small plots landscaped by different regional nurseries, landscape companies, plant societies, and garden clubs; the Rain Garden, demonstrating the effective management and cleaning of storm water runoff through the use of water-loving native plants; a cottage garden; and a butterfly garden.

BELLAMY MANSION MUSEUM OF HISTORY AND DESIGN ARTS—GARDEN

503 Market Street at 5th Street, Wilmington, NC 28402
Tel: (910) 251-3700; Fax: (910) 763-8154
Internet Address: http://www.bellamymansion.org/
Admission: Fee: adult $7.00, child (1-4) free, child (5-12) $3.00
Attendance: 10,000

Established: 1994
Membership: Y
Wheelchair Accessible: P
Parking: Adjacent lot, 20-30 spaces
Open: Tuesday to Saturday, 10am-5pm; Sunday, 1pm-5pm
Closed: New Year's Day, Easter, Independence Day, Thanksgiving Day, Christmas Day
Best Time(s) of Year to Visit: April to May
Facilities: Architecture (Neo-Classical/Greek Revival residence, 1859 design by
architect James F. Post assisted by Rufus Bunnell); Gardens (Victorian, parterre)

Construction of the mansion was completed on the eve of the Civil War and the
Bellamy family did not take up permanent residence until the close of hostilities. The
formal landscaping of the front and sides of the house evolved between 1866-1873. By
the time the restoration of the mansion began in 1992, virtually all traces of the original formal gardens had disappeared, and most of what is known about their design is
the fruit of a two-year process of historical research and archaeological investigation.
The plan for the landscaped garden included a symmetrical series of elliptical and circular parterre (ornamental garden area) beds. A mixture of plants were chosen in order
to provide color throughout the year. The most successful plantings were hardy native
species that could withstand the region's extended hot summers under the protective
branches of mature magnolia trees. Restored in 1996, the gardens are certainly eye-
catching and quite different from our modern conception of a Victorian garden. Un-
like the front and side yards, the rear of the house was a working area, which may have
contained a fruit trees and a kitchen garden, as well as a carriage house, stables, and
servants quarters.

CITY OF WILMINGTON—GREENFIELD GARDENS

Greenfield Park, South 3rd Street (U.S. Route 421 South), Wilmington, NC 28400
Tel: (910) 341-7868
Internet Address: http://www.ci.wilmington.nc.us/prd/greenfield_park.htm
Admission: Free
Best Time(s) of Year to Visit: early Spring (azalea bloom)
Facilities: Gardens (azalea, fragrance); Grounds Gardens (20 acres), Park (158 acres
with 5 mile scenic drive); Picnic Area; Trail (4.9 miles)
Activities: Events Azalea Festival

Greenfield Park, centered on a 150-acre lake, bordered by moss-draped cypress, is a
spring showplace for azalea, dogwood, and wisteria. The gardens also contain other native trees and shrubs (camellias, live oaks, magnolias, redbud, and crepe myrtle); thousands of jonquils, daffodils, tulips; and a fragrance garden.

NEW HANOVER COUNTY EXTENSION ARBORETUM (AHS RAP)

6206 Oleander Drive (near Greenville Loop Road), Wilmington, NC 28403
Tel: (910) 452-6393; Fax: (910) 452-6398
Internet Address: http://www.arboretumnhc.org
Established: 1989
Open: Daily, 8:30am-5pm
Facilities: Arboretum; Conservatory Dr. C. E. Lewis Conservatory; Gardens (33;
aquatic, bog, children's, camellia, container, cutting, day lily, herb, hosta, iris,
Japanese, magnolia, patio, perennial, native plant, rose, salt spray, shade, vegetable);
Greenhouse George Ross Memorial Greenhouse; Grounds (6.5 acres); Shop: The

Potting Shed (gardening gifts; Mon-Fri, 10am-2pm; 452-3470); Special Collections (azalea, conifer, crepe myrtle, ground cover, ornamental grass, specimen tree)

Offering thirty-three theme gardens, the arboretum is planned, developed, maintained, and funded by area volunteers, garden clubs, corporate, and individual sponsors and members of the Arboretum Foundation. The New Hanover County Extension also maintains Airlie Gardens (see separate listing).

WILSON

CITY OF WILSON—WILSON ROSE GARDEN

1800 Herring Avenue (Route 42 East) (inside Route 301 Bypass), Wilson, NC 27894
Tel: (252) 237-4997
Internet Address: http://www.wilsonrosegarden.com
Admission: Free
Established: 1994
Membership: Y
Wheelchair Accessible: Y
Parking: Large lot at site
Open: Daily, dawn-dusk
Best Time(s) of Year to Visit: mid-May, mid-October
Facilities: Garden (rose); Grounds (1 acre); Picnic Area
Activities: Festival Sunday in the Rose Garden (3rd Sunday in May); Guided Tours (by appointment, Cyndi Lauderdale, (252) 237-4111); Self-guided Tours (visitors guide available)

Accredited by All-America Rose Selections, the garden contains more than 1,100 roses representing 174 different varieties. The garden also offers an original whirligig by folk artist Vollis Simpson, statuary, five original wrought iron arbors, a gazebo, a pergola, a lily pond, and a pecan grove/picnic area. A smaller rose garden featuring 120 plants representing 24 varieties of hybrid tea rose is located on the library grounds at 249 W. Nash Street.

WILSON COUNTY ARBORETUM AND BOTANICAL GARDEN

Wilson County Agricultural Building, 1608 Goldsboro Street, Wilson, NC 27893
Tel: (252) 237-0113
Internet Address: http://www.wilson-co.com/arboretum.html
Admission: Free
Established: 1997
Open: Daily, dawn-dusk
Facilities: Arboretum; Gardens (bird, butterfly)

Located on the grounds of the Wilson County Agricultural Building, the site demonstrates the diversity of plant material that may be used in the home landscape, displaying over 235 varieties of trees, shrubs, vines, and perennials. The garden offers a tree collection, examples of five different turf species, a hosta collection, a day lily collection, bird and butterfly gardens, and display gardens. It is sponsored by the Wilson County Master Gardeners.

WINNABOW

ORTON PLANTATION AND GARDENS

9149 Orton Road SE, Winnabow, NC 28479
Tel: (910) 371-6851; Fax: (910) 371-6871
Internet Address: http://www.ortongardens.com
Admission: Fee: adult $9.00, child (6-16) $3.00, senior $8.00
Membership: N
Wheelchair Accessible: Y
Parking: Parking on site
Open: March to November
Facilities: Architecture (residence, begun 1725; Greek Revival additions completed ca. 1910); Gardens (mid-1930s design by Robert Swann Sturtevant, MLA [Groton, MA]); Grounds Gardens (20 acres)

The gardens, begun in 1910, originally consisted of imported camellias, azaleas, banana shrubs and other ornamentals, and bulbs. The avenues of live oak trees and the terraces that overlook the old rice fields and river were also constructed at that time. In the mid-1930s the owners began enlarging the gardens to their present size. The various gardens, some formal and some natural, took advantage of the impressive oaks and other native trees, constructed lawns, water scenes, and walkways. Following this extensive enlargement the gardens were opened to the public, the admission charge helping to offset the cost of maintenance. Orton House remains a private residence and is not open, but may be viewed from the garden paths.

WINSTON-SALEM

OLD SALEM—GARDENS

924 S. Main Street, Winston-Salem, NC 27101-5335
Tel: (888) 653-7253; Fax: (336) 721-7335
Internet Address: http://www.oldsalem.org
Admission: Fee: adult $21.00, child $10.00
Attendance: 150,000
Established: 1950
Membership: Y
Wheelchair Accessible: P
Parking: On site at Visitor Center
Open: Monday to Saturday, 9am-5pm; Sunday, 12:30pm-5pm
Closed: Easter, Thanksgiving Day, Christmas Eve to Christmas Day
Best Time(s) of Year to Visit: Spring to Summer
Facilities: Food Services Old Salem Corner Deli (sandwiches, snacks), Old Salem Tavern (lunch and dinner, dinner reservations recommended), Winkler Bakery/Salem Soda Shop (baked goods/sandwiches, snacks); Gardens (historic; vegetable, herb); Shops J. Blum: Printer & Merchant (books, stationery, unique gifts), T. Bagge: Merchant (garden supplies, Old Salem exclusives)
Activities: Guided Tours Gardens, Group (contact Tour Coordinator, (800) 441-5305); Self-guided Tours Gardens (garden brochure, map & current plant list are available at the Visitor Center)

A living history museum, Old Salem is a restoration of the Moravian community that was started in 1766. Costumed interpreters describe the life and activities of this religious town, from the very beginnings through the more mature settlement of the 1840s. When Salem was a flourishing church town inhabited primarily by skilled tradesmen and their families, each lot in the community included a garden which was maintained year-round and served as the family's main source of food other than meat. The typical garden was divided into four or six "squares" separated by grass walkways. Vegetables, herbs, and flowers were grown together, with fruit trees placed around the edges or at the rear of the lot. Old Salem has one of the leading horticultural restoration programs in the country, several family gardens behind restored houses are open to the public. Thanks to the excellent record-keeping skills of the Moravians in the late 1700s and early 1800s, many of the gardens today closely resemble the year-round gardens of the original settlers. The landscaping of each lot is consistent with the period of the building on it, presenting to the visitor a wide range of plant materials.

REYNOLDA GARDENS OF WAKE FOREST UNIVERSITY (RGWFU)

100 Reynolda Village, Winston-Salem, NC 27106-5123
Tel: (336) 758-5593; Fax: (336) 758-4132
Internet Address: http://www.reynoldagardens.org
Admission: Free
Established: 1962
Membership: Y
Wheelchair Accessible: Y
Parking: At greenhouses
Open: Grounds, Daily, sunrise-sunset
Greenhouses, Monday to Saturday, 10am-4pm, closed Sat in Jan & Jul.
Best Time(s) of Year to Visit: Summer to Fall
Facilities: Auditorium (60 seat); Conservatory (erected 1912); Gardens (formal, 1917-1920, original design by landscape architect Thomas Sears; rose, blue & yellow, pink and white); Greenhouses (1913, Lord & Burnham); Grounds Fields & Woodland (125 acres), Gardens (4 acres); Nature Trails; Shop: The Garden Boutique (operated by the Garden Club Council of Winston-Salem and Forsyth County); Special Collections
Activities: Concerts; Education Programs (adults and children); Guided Tours (groups, reserve in advance, 758-3485); Lectures, Rose Care Series, Tuesday Gardening Series (Tues, 12:30pm, Greenhouse Education Wing); Plant Sales; Travel/Study Tours

Reynolda Gardens of Wake Forest University was once part of the 1,067-acre, early-twentieth-century estate of Mr. and Mrs. R. J. Reynolds. RGWFU consists of 125 acres of woodlands, wetlands, and open meadows; a four-acre formal garden; and a Lord and Burnham greenhouse. Listed on the National Register of Historic Places, the formal garden has been restored to the appearance and intent of the 1917 design created by Philadelphia landscape architect Thomas W. Sears. One half of the formal garden features themed parterre gardens, mixed borders, boxwood hedges, teahouses, pergolas, and fountain. The other half of the formal garden is used as a demonstration garden, highlighting both heirloom and modern varieties of ornamental fruits, vegetables, and flowers and current horticultural methods. An All-America Rose Selections garden is located in this area. The greenhouses supply plants for the gardens and for sale to the public. The conservatory houses collections of orchids, succulents, and ferns. The woodlands and fields are accessible by trails, which are used extensively for recreational and educational purposes.

OHIO

The number in the parentheses following the city name indicates the number of gardens/ arboreta in that municipality. If there is no number, one is understood. For example, in the text seven listings would be found under Cincinnati and one listing under Indian Hill.

AKRON

STAN HYWET HALL AND GARDENS (AHS RAP)

714 N. Portage Path, Akron, OH 44303-1399
Tel: (330) 836-5533; Fax: (330) 836-2680
Internet Address: http://www.stanhywet.org/
Admission: Fee (Mansion & Gardens): adult $12.00, child (<6) free, child (6-12) $3.00; Fee (Gardens): adult $6.00; child (6-12) $3.00
Attendance: 58,000
Established: 1957
Membership: Y
Wheelchair Accessible: Y
Open: February to March, Tuesday to Saturday, 10am-4pm; Sunday, 1pm-4pm; April to 1st week of January, Daily, 10am-4:30pm; Grounds—April to January 4, 9am-6pm. Closed: Legal holidays
Facilities: Architecture (65 room Tudor Revival mansion, 1912-15 design by Cleveland architect Charles Schneider); Auditoria (2, 260 and 200 seats); Conservatory & Greenhouses; Food Services Carriage House Café; Gardens (birch allée, cutting, walled English, Japanese, rose); Grounds (75 acres, design by Cleveland landscape architect Warren Manning); Picnic Area; Shop (souvenirs, reproductions)
Activities: Arts Festival; Concerts; Guided Tours (April-1st week of January, daily, 10am-4:30pm); Lectures; Plant Sales Garden Mart (May, plants and garden-related items)

Stan Hywet Hall (Middle English for "Stone Quarry") was built by industrialist and Goodyear co-founder F. A. Seiberling and his wife, Gertrude. The manor house is filled with treasures from around the globe. Originally an estate of more than 1,000 acres, its remaining seventy acres include landscaped grounds, a variety of gardens, and a conservatory/greenhouse complex. Its walled English garden, containing over 1,500 flowers and bulbs, was designed by Ellen Biddle Shipman. Other areas include a Japanese stroll garden, a rose garden, a cutting garden, a 550-foot-long birch allée, and less formal, naturalized plantings.

BAY VILLAGE

CAHOON MEMORIAL PARK ROSE GARDEN

Cahoon Road (1 block west of Dover Center, between Wolf and Lake Roads), Bay Village, OH 44125
Tel: (440) 871-6755
Admission: Free
Open: Daily, dawn-dusk

The garden, containing approximately 1,200 roses of 500 different varieties, is a two-time recipient of All-America Rose Selection's outstanding maintenance award.

BIRMINGHAM

SCHOEPFLE GARDEN

11106 Market Street, Birmingham, OH 44050
Tel: (440) 965-7237; Fax: (440) 965-7021
Internet Address: http://www.loraincountymetroparks.com
Admission: Free
Attendance: 70,000
Established: 1969
Wheelchair Accessible: P
Open: Standard Time, Daily, 8am-5pm; Daylight Savings Time, Daily, 8am-8pm.
Closed: New Year's Day, Christmas Day
Facilities: Arboretum; Gardens (display, perennial, annual, rose, shade); Grounds
Formal Gardens (20 acres), Natural Wooded Area (50 acres); Shop; Trails (2 miles);
Visitors Center
Activities: Guided Tours Groups (12+, reserve 4 weeks in advance)

Bordered on one side by the Vermillion River, Schoepfle Garden consists of botanical gardens and natural woodland. In addition to the many flowering shrubs, trees, and perennials, the Formal Garden and adjacent Shade Garden feature several special collections including rhododendrons, roses, cannas, hostas, topiaries, and shade plants. In contrast to the gardens, the woodland offers a natural setting with seasonal displays of indigenous trees, wildflowers, and wildlife. Mr. Otto B. Schoepfle began his garden in 1936 with major plantings, including the specimen trees, original rose garden and topiary collections occurring in the 1960s. In 1969, Mr. Schoepfle donated the site to the Lorain County Metro Parks.

CHILLICOTHE

ADENA STATE MEMORIAL—GARDENS

Box 831, Adena Road, Chillicothe, OH 45601
Tel: (740) 772-1500
Internet Address: http://www.ohiohistory.org/places/adena/
Admission: Fee: adult $6.00, child (<5) free, child (6-12) $2.00
Wheelchair Accessible: P
Open: March to Labor Day, Wednesday to Saturday, 9:30am-5pm; Sunday, noon-5pm; Holidays, noon-5pm; September to October, Saturday, 9:30am-5pm; Sunday, noon-5pm
Facilities: Architecture (Georgian stone residence 1806-1807, design by Benjamin Latrobe); Garden (historic, formal); Grounds (300 acres)
Activities: Guided Tours (schedule in advance)

Adena was the estate of Thomas Worthington, influential in the establishment of Ohio as a state in 1803 and subsequently a U.S. senator and Ohio governor. The house, one of only three extant private residences designed by Benjamin Latrobe, is complemented by restored formal gardens. More than 60 varieties of heirloom roses are among the 4,000 flowering plants in the garden. Other plantings represent the original vegetable garden, vineyard, and orchard. Adena is a property of the Ohio Historical Society.

CINCINNATI

CINCINNATI PARKS AND CIVIC GARDEN CENTER OF GREATER CINCINNATI—HAUCK BOTANIC GARDEN

2625 Reading Road at William Howard Taft Road (Civic Garden Center: 2715 Reading Road), Cincinnati, OH 45202
Tel: (513) 352-4080
Internet Address: http://www.cinci-parks.org/
Admission: Free
Parking: Free on site
Open: Daily, 6am-10pm
Best Time(s) of Year to Visit: April to May (spring bulbs & flowering trees), early Summer (annuals, day lilies), late Summer (annuals, dahlias), Fall (foliage)
Facilities: Garden Center Civic Garden Center of Greater Cincinnati (Mon-Fri, 9am-4pm); Gardens (butterfly, conifer, daffodil, dahlia, daylily, herb, hosta, rose, shade, sun, wildflower); Greenhouse; Grounds (8 acres); Special Collections (beech, daffodil, daylily, oak)

Cornelius J. Hauck, former president of the Cincinnati Park Board, transformed a residential area along Reading Road into a horticultural garden and tree sanctuary with many of the plant specimens salvaged from old estates and other areas being destroyed. His botanical garden is now a public park. A visitor to the Hauck Botanic Garden sees mostly original plantings like the naturalized bulbs that spread springtime beauty over the horticultural and wildflower gardens. Specialized gardens include the Frank Wilmot Memorial Daylily Collection, the hosta garden, the Hobson Daffodil Collection, and the All-American dahlia garden. Among the 900 varieties of trees, shrubs, and evergreens planted on the estate are especially fine beech and oak collections as well as magnolias, azaleas (both native and imported), and native trees. Several structures provide visitors a secluded place to sit and enjoy the view. While most of the park is owned and maintained by the Cincinnati Park Board, the private non-profit Civic Garden Center of Greater Cincinnati [tel: (513) 221-0981 or fax: (513) 221-0961] occupies a two-acre site within in the park. The Garden Center has developed gardens throughout the park that are maintained by staff and volunteers. Garden areas maintained by the Civic Garden Center include the Pat Kipp Memorial Shade Garden, the Morgan Bretz Memorial Garden, the Peg Macneale Memorial Daffodil Garden, the Dwarf Conifer Garden, the Hoffman Terrace, the Sun and Butterfly Garden, the Reading Road Beautification Garden, and the Herb Garden.

CINCINNATI PARKS—AULT PARK

End of Observatory Avenue (Hyde Park/Mount Lookout area), Cincinnati, OH 45208
Tel: (513) 352-4080
Internet Address: http://www.aultparkac.org/
Admission: Free
Established: 1911
Membership: Y
Parking: Free on site
Open: Daily, 6am-10pm

Facilities: Arboretum Trees for Your Yard; Gardens (design by landscape architect George Kessler; modified by landscape architect Albert D. Taylor) formal, dahlia, perennial, rose); Grounds (224 acres); Pavilion Ault Park Pavilion (Italian Renaissance-style building, 1930 design by Fechheimer & Ihorst); Picnic Areas; Special Collections (old fashioned roses); Trails
Activities: Concerts (summer); Education Programs (variety of nature programs throughout year); Events Independence Day Celebration, Summer Dance Series (3, Jun-Aug); Flower Show Cincinnati Flower Show (annual)

Ault Park contains an Italian Renaissance-style pavilion surrounded by a terrace, a cascade fountain, and formal gardens; a rose garden featuring old fashioned roses, the "Trees for Your Yard" Arboretum (dedicated in 1885), focusing on shade and ornamental trees that should do well with little care in the local climate, and a concert green.

CINCINNATI PARKS—EDEN PARK AND IRWIN KROHN CONSERVATORY

Park: Gilbert Avenue between Elsinore & Morris; Conservatory: 1501 Eden Park Drive, Cincinnati, OH 45202
Tel: (513) 352-4080; Fax: (513) 352-4096;
TDDY: (513) 352-4080
Internet Address: http://www.cinci-parks.org
Admission: Free; Fee for seasonal and special exhibitions
Attendance: 100,000
Established: 1933
Membership: Y
Wheelchair Accessible: Y
Parking: Free in back of building
Open: Daily, 10am-5pm; Easter, 7am-7pm
Best Time(s) of Year to Visit: Spring (flowering trees, daffodils)
Facilities: Cincinnati Parks Visitor Center; Conservatory Irwin M. Krohn Conservatory (1933, 421-5707); Garden; Grounds (186 acres); Library (50 volumes); Shop" Krohn Conservatory (plants, gardening accessories, gifts)
Activities: Butterfly Show Krohn Conservatory (May-Jun); Flower Shows Krohn Conservatory (6/year); Guided Tours; Holiday Show Krohn Conservatory (Sept); Lectures; Temporary Exhibitions

Located five minutes from downtown, the park is the home of the Cincinnati Art Museum, Cincinnati Art Academy, Playhouse in the Park, and Murray Seasongood Pavilion as well as the Irwin M. Krohn Conservatory. The park contains landscaped grounds punctuated with groves of trees, including the Hinkle Magnolia Garden. In the springtime, plantings of over 50,000 daffodils are in bloom. Krohn Conservatory, which is owned and operated by the park board, features more than 1,000 plant species from all over the world in simulated natural settings. Displays include the Palm House, an indoor rain forest, complete with a twenty-foot waterfall and towering trees; the Tropical House, a high humidity and warm temperature habitat containing a large variety of ferns (both terrestrial and epiphytic) and an unusual cycad, bromeliad, and begonia collection surrounding two naturalistic pools; the Orchid House, presenting selected orchids (approximately seventy-five at a time) at the height of their display from the thousands of orchids in its collection; the Desert Garden, a dry environment housing many cacti and succulents; and the Floral Display House, used for special events and seasonal floral displays. Depending on the season, portions of the conservatory's Bonsai collection may be on view in the conservatory or outside in the adjacent Elizabeth

Bakhaus Gale Memorial Garden. The Visitor Center for Cincinnati Parks is located in the lobby of Krohn Conservatory.

CINCINNATI PARKS—MOUNT AIRY FOREST ARBORETUM

5083 Colerain Avenue, Cincinnati, OH 45223-1061
Tel: (513) 541-8176; TDDY: (513) 352-4080
Internet Address: http://www.cinci-parks.org
Admission: Free
Established: 1932
Membership: N
Wheelchair Accessible: P
Parking: 33 parking spaces
Open: Arboretum, Daily, dawn-dusk
Best Time(s) of Year to Visit: Summer to Fall
Facilities: Arboretum (25 acres); Gardens (azalea, perennial, deer-hardy shrubs and perennials); Grounds (1,470 acres; hours—7am-10pm); Picnic Areas (23 areas, picnicking forbidden in arboretum); Special Collections (dwarf conifer, viburnum, magnolia, rhododendrons, lilacs); Trails (hiking, 14 miles; bridle, 16 miles)
Activities: Guided Tours (available on request); Lectures

Mt. Airy Forest had its origins in 1911, when the Cincinnati Park Board purchased 168 acres of land lying west of Colerain Avenue near the top of the Colerain hill, thus starting the first municipal reforestation project in the United States. What were once scarred, eroded, and nearly treeless ridges and slopes have become forest, including 700 acres reforested in hardwoods; 200 reforested in evergreens; 269 acres of native woodland; 170 acres of open meadows, and 20 acres of arboretum development. Located within a ten-minute drive of downtown Cincinnati, the arboretum contains more than 5,000 plants representing 800 species and varieties of deciduous trees and shrubs and evergreens, including an outstanding dwarf conifer collection surrounding a picturesque spring-fed, one-acre lake. There are a variety of naturalistic gardens and structures.

CINCINNATI ZOO AND BOTANICAL GARDEN

3400 Vine Street, Cincinnati, OH 45220
Tel: (513) 281-4700; Fax: (513) 559-7790; TDDY: (513) 559-2730
Internet Address: http://www.cincyzoo.org
Admission: Fee: adult $11.50, child (2-12) $6.00, senior $9.00
Attendance: 1,300,000
Established: 1875
Membership: Y
Wheelchair Accessible: Y
Open: Winter, Daily, 9am-5pm; Summer, Daily, 9am-6pm
Facilities: Arboretum; Climatic Areas (African veldt, Alaskan coastal, Asian & African tropical forest, China, Eastern U.S. woodlands, Japan); Gardens (butterfly, dinosaur, endangered species, hillside, native plant, oriental, winter); Special Collections (bonsai, dwarf conifers)
Activities: Guided Tours

Officially renamed the Cincinnati Zoo and Botanical Garden in 1987, the award-winning landscape includes over 2,800 varieties of trees, shrubs, tropical plants, bulbs, perennials and annuals. Many plantings are designed to represent the natural habitats of animals on exhibit, such as Jungle Trails (representing the diverse tropical forests of Asia and

Africa with over 800 kinds of plants). There are also an oriental style garden, an endangered species garden, a native plant garden, the Dinosaur Garden (displaying ancient plants including dawn redwood, cycads, and ferns), a winter garden, a bird garden (demonstrating plantings for shady areas to attract wild birds by providing food, cover, water, and nesting sites), and both indoor and outdoor butterfly gardens. The zoo's botanical center features Japanese bonsai, other seasonal displays, and demonstrations of plants.

SPRING GROVE CEMETERY AND ARBORETUM

4521 Spring Grove Avenue, Cincinnati, OH 45232-1954
Tel: (888) 853-2230
Internet Address: http://www.springgrove.org
Admission: Free
Attendance: 150,000
Established: 1845
Membership: N
Wheelchair Accessible: Y
Parking: Free on site
Open: September to April, Daily, 8am-6pm; May to August, Monday, 8am-8pm;
Tuesday to Wednesday, 8am-6pm; Thursday, 8am-8pm; Friday to Sunday, 8am-6pm
Best Time(s) of Year to Visit: Spring to Fall
Facilities: Arboretum (large specimen trees—state and national champions; 400 acres);
Architecture (several National Register Buildings); Gardens (rose, plants of the Bible);
Grounds (733 acres); Stained Glass Window Display (30 windows)
Activities: Education Programs; Guided Tours (groups 25+, schedule at least 4weeks
in advance, (513) 853-6819);
Self-guided Tour (walking tour brochure and guide to woody plants are available)

The second largest non-profit cemetery in the United States, Spring Grove features twenty State and National Champion trees as well as plantings of weeping cherry trees, rhododendrons, daffodils, roses, and lilies set among fourteen lakes and a waterfall, a ten-acre natural protected woodland, historic and contemporary architecture, sculpture, and stained glass. An All-America Selections Display Garden is also maintained on site.

TAFT MUSEUM OF ART

316 Pike Street, Cincinnati, OH 45202-4293
Tel: (513) 241-0343; Fax: (513) 241-7762
Internet Address: http://www.taftmuseum.org
Admission: Fee: adult $7.00, child free, student $5.00, senior $5.00
Attendance: 50,000
Established: 1932
Membership: Y
Wheelchair Accessible: Y
Parking: Free on site
Open: Tuesday to Wednesday, 11am-5pm; Thursday,
11am-8pm; Friday, 11am-5pm; Saturday, 10am-5pm;
Sunday, noon-5pm
Closed: New Year's Day, Thanksgiving Day, Christmas Day
Facilities: Architecture (Palladian Baum-Longworth-Taft House, 1820); Library (1,000
volume); Shop; Tea Room
Activities: Concerts; Education Programs (adults, students and children); Gallery
Talks; Guided Tours (on advance request); Lectures; Temporary Exhibitions

The Taft Museum of Art displays its permanent collection in the Federal period rooms of the Baum-Longworth-Taft House. A National Historic Landmark, the Baum-Longworth-Taft House (1820) is an excellent example of American Palladian architecture, and the room settings are enhanced by selections of early nineteenth-century New York furniture. In addition to the permanent collection, the Fifth Third Gallery and Keystone Gallery house changing special exhibitions of art throughout the year. The museum reopened in 2004 after a major renovation and expansion that includes a redesigned garden by Reed Hildebrand Landscape Architects of Boston.

CLEVELAND

CLEVELAND BOTANICAL GARDEN (AHS RAP)

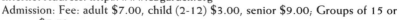

11030 East Boulevard, Cleveland, OH 44106
Tel: (216) 721-1600; Fax: (216) 721-2056
Internet Address: http://www.cbgarden.org

Cleveland Botanical Garden, Cleveland, OH.

Admission: Fee: adult $7.00, child (2-12) $3.00, senior $9.00; Groups of 15 or more—$5.50 per person.
Attendance: 100,000
Established: 1930
Membership: Y
Wheelchair Accessible: Y
Parking: On street; also garage parking, $2.00
Open: Grounds, daily, 10am-5pm
Closed: New Year's Day, Thanksgiving Day, Christmas Day
Facilities: Auditorium (325 seats); Conservatory; Gardens (herb, Japanese, rose, wildflower); Grounds (7½ acres); Library (16,000 volumes); Reading Room; Shop
Activities: Classes; Education Programs (adults and children); Lectures; Workshops

Situated close to downtown, the site contains more than 3,500 herbs, plants, and shrubs arranged in a variety of settings including formal gardens, lawn, and woodland. The herb garden, maintained by the Western Reserve Herb Society, contains approximately 3,500 plants displayed in knot, terrace, culinary, dye, fragrance, medicinal, trial, and cutting gardens. Other highlights include a Japanese garden with classic tea and zen gardens, rose garden, and a wildflower garden.

CLEVELAND CULTURAL GARDENS

Rockefeller Park, 750 East 85th Street (East Boulevard, from St. Clair to Superior), Cleveland, OH 44108
Tel: (216) 664-3534
Internet Address: http://www.universitycircle.org/members/ccgf.htm
Admission: Free
Parking: Rockefeller Park greenhouse
Open: Daily, dawn-dusk
Facilities: Gardens; Grounds Cultural Gardens (50 acres), Rockefeller Park (254 acres)
Activities: Festival One World Day (annual, Sunday closest to July 22nd); Guided Tours

The cultural gardens is a unique group of ethnic gardens running linearly through Rockefeller Park from Superior Avenue to St. Clair Avenue along Martin Luther King, Jr. Boulevard. The Shakespeare Garden was opened in 1916. Leo Weidenthal established the chain of gardens with the dedication of the Hebrew Garden in 1926; others followed from the 1930s through the 1970s. Today, gardens represent more than twenty ethnic groups, including African American, American, American Indian, British, Chinese, Czech, Estonian, Finnish, German, Greek, Hebrew, Hungarian, Irish, Italian, Lithuanian, Polish, Romanian, Russian, Slovak, Slovenian, and Ukrainian. Each cultural group designs its own plot and each garden is unique, differing in plant choices, style, and the use of art. Tour guides and booklets are available at the Rockefeller Park Greenhouse

LAKE VIEW CEMETERY

12316 Euclid Avenue, Cleveland, OH 44106-4393
Tel: (216) 421-2665; Fax: (216) 421-2415
Internet Address: http://www.lakeviewcemetery.com/
Admission: Free
Established: 1869
Open: Fall to Spring, Daily, 7:30am-5:30pm; Summer, Daily, 7:30am-dusk
Best Time(s) of Year to Visit: Spring
Facilities: Arboretum; Grounds (285 acres)
Activities: Guided Tours Trolley Tours (mid-Jun-Aug, Sunday, 1:30, $4.00/person, reserve in advance); Walking Tours (various themes, reserve in advance)

Modeled after the great garden cemeteries of Victorian England and France, Lakeview contains a variety of specimen trees, including an extensive collection of Japanese thread-leaf maples. Three acres of the site, Daffodil Hill, are planted with more than 100,000 bulbs. Five hundred of the trees and shrubs carry botanical tags.

ROCKEFELLER PARK GREENHOUSES

750 East 88th Street, Cleveland, OH 44108
Tel: (216) 664-3103
Admission: Free
Established: 1905
Membership: Y
Wheelchair Accessible: Y
Parking: Free on site
Open: Daily, 10am-4pm
Closed: Thanksgiving Day, Legal holidays
Best Time(s) of Year to Visit: December to Spring
Facilities: Gardens (herb, Japanese, peace, rose, talking, iris, vegetable); Greenhouses (show house, 1 acre—tropical, fern, cactus, orchid); Grounds (4 acres)
Activities: Self-Guided Tours

A remnant of the John D. Rockefeller estate, the greenhouse display tropicals, ferns, cacti, and orchids. Exterior gardens include the Betty Ott Talking Garden for the Blind with tape recorded descriptions of the plants as well as herb, Japanese, rose, and peace gardens.

COLUMBUS

CITY OF COLUMBUS—FRANK FETCH PARK

228 E. Beck Street (3 blocks from S. Third Street), Columbus, OH 43206
Tel: (614) 645-6640; Fax: (614) 645-3384
Internet Address: http://www.columbusparks.com/outdoors/

featured/index.html
Admission: Free
Established: 1985
Wheelchair Accessible: Y
Parking: On street
Open: Daily, 7am-11pm
Best Time(s) of Year to Visit: Spring to Summer
Facilities: Garden; Grounds (¼ acre)

In 1966, this vacant lot was converted into Beck Street Park, a neighborhood pocket park. Renamed in 1985 to honor the "Father of German Village," it is designed to resemble one of the "Social Gardens of Munich," featuring extensive landscaping, unusual trees and shrubs, flower beds, brick walls and pavement, iron fences, and decorative gaslights. The park is a joint effort of the Division of Recreation and Parks of Columbus, the Friends of Fetch Park, and the German Village Garten Club.

CITY OF COLUMBUS—PARK OF ROSES

Whetstone Park, 3923 N. High Street, Columbus, OH 43214
Tel: (614) 645-6640; Fax: (614) 645-3384
Internet Address: http://www.columbusrecparks.com/outdoors/featured/index.html
Admission: Free
Attendance: 86,000
Established: 1952
Wheelchair Accessible: Y
Parking: Lot on site
Open: Daily, 7am-11pm
Best Time(s) of Year to Visit: Spring to Fall
Facilities: Gardens (daffodil, herb, perennial, rose); Grounds Gardens (13 acres), Park (35 acres); Shop
Activities: Concerts (Summer, Sunday nights); Demonstrations; Festival Columbus Rose Festival (June); Lectures

The rose garden contains 11,000 rose bushes representing over 350 varieties. The park also contains an outstanding daffodil garden as well as herb and perennial gardens.

CITY OF COLUMBUS—SCHILLER PARK

1069 Jaeger Street, Columbus, OH 43215
Tel: (614) 645-6640; Fax: (614) 645-3384
Internet Address: http://www.columbusrecparks.com/outdoors/featured/index.html
Admission: Free
Established: 1867
Membership: Y
Parking: On street
Open: Daily, 7am-11pm
Best Time(s) of Year to Visit: May to September
Facilities: Gardens (perennial); Grounds Park (24 acres)

Bounded by Jaeger Street, City Park, Reinhard, and Deshler Avenues, Schiller Park contains perennial gardens. Gardens within the park include entrance plantings, Graces Garden and Umbrella Girl Fountain, and the Huntington Garden Promenade. Surrounding the park is German Village; a 233-acres privately funded urban restoration district with over 1,600 restored buildings and many small urban gardens. German Village is listed on the National Register of Historic Places.

CITY OF COLUMBUS—THE TOPIARY GARDEN

Old Deaf School Park, 408 E. Town Street at Washington Avenue, Columbus, OH 43215
Tel: (614) 645-6640; Fax: (614) 645-3384
Internet Address: http://www.topiarygarden.org/park.htm
Admission: Free
Membership: Y
Parking: On street
Open: Daily, 7am-11pm
Best Time(s) of Year to Visit: April to November
Facilities: Garden (topiary); Grounds (9 acres); Picnic Area; Shop Yewtopia on Town (Apr-Dec, Tues-Sat, 11am-4pm; Sun, noon-4pm; 645-0197)
Activities: Guided Tours (schedule in advance, (614) 645-0197)

The Topiary Garden recreates in sculpted evergreen shrubbery Georges Seurat's painting *A Sunday Afternoon on the Island of La Grand Jatte*. This "landscape of a painting of a landscape" consists of fifty-four topiary people, eight boats, three dogs, a monkey, a cat, and a real pond. The largest figure is twelve feet tall. A project of the Columbus Recreation and Parks Department, the concept came from artist James T. Mason who teaches sculpture at the Department's Cultural Arts Center.

FRANKLIN PARK CONSERVATORY (AHS RAP)

1777 E. Broad Street, Columbus, OH 43203-2040
Tel: (800) 214-7275; Fax: (614) 645-5921
Internet Address: http://www.fpconservatory.org
Admission: Fee: adult $6.50, child (<2) free, child (2-12) $3.50, student $5.00, senior $5.00
Established: 1895
Membership: Y
Wheelchair Accessible: Y
Parking: Free on site
Open: Tuesday, 10am-5pm; Wednesday, 10am-8pm; Thursday to Sunday, 10am-5pm; Holiday Mondays, 10am-5pm
Closed: New Year's Day, Thanksgiving Day, Christmas Day
Facilities: Climatic Areas (desert, Himalayan mountain, Pacific island, rain forest); Conservatory Palm House (historic, 1895); Food Services Shane's Café ((614) 645-5816); Gardens (community, demonstration, formal, Japanese, native plant); Greenhouses; Grounds (88 acres); Shop (gardening supplies, garden-related gifts); Special Collections (bonsai, orchid)
Activities: Education Programs; Guided Tours; Workshops

Franklin Park features the historic Victorian Palm House, state-of-the-art greenhouses, and a beautiful eighty-eight-acre urban park. The conservatory serves as the site's focal point and as a horticultural education facility with an extensive permanent plant collection and compelling exhibitions. The Palm House, built in 1859 in the style of London's Crystal Palace and listed on the National Register of Historic Places, features a diverse collection of palms, bamboo, a fountain, and gazebos as well as serving as the site for social events throughout the year. The 30,000 square feet of display greenhouses offer diverse habitats from around the world, including the Himalayan mountains, tropical rain forest, desert, and Pacific islands. Bonsai and orchid collections are also on display. The Cconservatory's outdoor park includes pastoral green spaces, mature trees, cascading waterfalls, sculptures, demonstration and community gardens, and the formal five-acre Grand Mallway.

OHIO STATE UNIVERSITY—CHADWICK ARBORETUM & LEARNING GARDENS (AHS RAP)

2001 Fyffe Court, Columbus, OH 43210
Tel: (614) 688-3479; Fax: (614) 292-3505
Internet Address: http://chadwickarboretum.osu.edu/
Admission: No charge, donations accepted
Established: 1980
Membership: Y
Wheelchair Accessible: Y
Parking: Parking—evenings and weekends free; call for daily pass
Open: dawn to dusk
Facilities: Arboretum (1,000 trees native to Ohio, representing 120 species); Gardens (annual, beech allée, dwarf conifer, labyrinth, perennial, rose); Greenhouses; Grounds (62 acres); Labyrinth; Special Collections (daffodil, day lily, hosta, native plant, native tree, willow (nation's largest collection), conifer, wildflowers, summer tropicals, perennials)
Activities: Plant Sales (spring)

Chadwick Arboretum's two major locations are the Lane Avenue Gardens and Arboretum North. The Lane Avenue Gardens include wildflower gardens featuring woody and herbaceous plants set in a variety of habitats (bog garden, sunny border, meadow, etc); a sun-loving perennial garden; an annual and perennial garden, trial gardens of annuals, a labyrinth, a dwarf and specialty conifer display (30 species), hosta (100 species and cultivars), and a beech allée. Diagonally across Lane Avenue, Arboretum North, contains approximately 120 species of native tree, a willow collection (200 species and cultivars), and extensive plantings of daffodils.

DAYTON

FIVE RIVERS METROPARKS—AULLWOOD GARDEN

900 Aullwood Road, Dayton, OH 45414
Tel: (937) 898-4006
Internet Address: http://www.metroparks.org
Admission: Free
Membership: Y
Open: March to mid-December, Tuesday to Sunday, 8am-7pm
Closed: Most school holidays
Facilities: Gardens (lilac, rock, rose, woodland); Grounds Garden (32 acres)
Activities: Guided Tours; Horticultural Displays

Adjacent to Englewood MetroPark, Aullwood Garden, a blend of woodland and meadow gardens, was begun by John and Marie Aull in 1923. The gardens, a project of the Garden Conservancy, are under the stewardship of Five Rivers MetroParks. Also of possible interest, the adjacent seventy-acre Aullwood Audubon Center and Farm offers a nature center, five mile of hiking trails through diverse habitat areas (woodland, meadow, marsh, stream, and pond), an organic garden, an herb garden, and a restored ten-acre tall-grass prairie.

FIVE RIVERS METROPARKS—COX ARBORETUM AND GARDENS (AHS RAP)

6733 Springboro Pike (Route 741), Dayton, OH 45449
Tel: (937) 434-9005; Fax: (937) 438-0601;
TDDY: (937) 275-7275
Internet Address: http://www.metroparks.org
Admission: Voluntary contribution
Attendance: 225,000
Established: 1963
Membership: Y
Wheelchair Accessible: Y
Open: Grounds, daily, 8am-dusk; Visitor Center, Monday to Friday, 8:30am-4:30pm;
Saturday to Sunday, 1pm-4pm
Closed: New Year's Day, Christmas Day
Facilities: Auditorium (100 seat); Gardens (edible, herb, Japanese, rock, rose, shrub, water, wildflower); Greenhouses (20,000 square feet); Grounds (170 acres); Library (750 volumes); Reading Room; Shop Linden Tree Gift Shop; Trails; Visitor Center
Activities: Classes; Education Programs (Children); Guided Tours; Lectures; Workshops

Cox Arboretum features specimen trees, shrubs, and other plants suitable to the local climate. The arboretum contains a variety of specialty gardens, including extensive water gardens, edible landscape garden, Japanese meditation garden, synoptic shrub garden, two herb gardens, rock garden, rose garden, and wildflower garden. Other plantings and displays include butterfly meadow, cacti/succulent, clematis arbor, cedar grove, conifer knoll, crab apple allée, ornamental grasses, hostas/ferns, and deciduous shade trees.

FIVE RIVERS METROPARKS—WEGERZYN HORTICULTURAL CENTER AND STILLWATER GARDENS

1301 E. Siebenthaler Avenue, Dayton, OH 45414-5397
Tel: (937) 277-6545
Internet Address: http://www.metroparks.org
Admission: Free
Established: 1973
Open: Horticultural Center, Monday to Friday, 9am-5pm; Grounds, daily, 8am-dusk
Closed: New Year's Day, Christmas Day
Facilities: Gardens (children's, Colonial, English, native plant, perennial, rose, Victorian); Grounds (60 acres)
Activities: Classes; Education Programs; Plant Sale May Fair (annual)

Situated on the banks of the Stillwater River, the Wegerzyn Gardens contain children's, rose, Colonial, English, and Victorian gardens with a central mall featuring a white ash allée. The formal gardens are bordered on the west by the Stillwater River and on the east by a mature lowland forest of sycamore, oak, red and silver maple, hickory, and ash accessible by a 350-foot boardwalk. The Horticultural Center offers education in horticulture and the natural sciences to all ages. Founded in 1973 as the result of a gift from Mr. Benjamin Wegerzyn and the dedicated work of area garden clubs, the Wegerzyn Center and the Stillwater Gardens are a unit of Five Rivers MetroParks.

WOODLAND CEMETERY AND ARBORETUM

118 Woodland Avenue, Dayton, OH 45409-2892
Tel: (937) 228-2581; Fax: (937) 222-7259
Internet Address: http://www.woodlandarboretum.org/
Admission: No charge, donations accepted
Established: 1841
Membership: Y
Wheelchair Accessible: P
Parking: Parking is available
Open: Daily, 8:30am-5pm
Best Time(s) of Year to Visit: Fall to Spring
Facilities: Grounds, Arboretum (230 acres)
Activities: Guided Tours (schedule in advance, 228-2581); Self-guided Tour (cassette tape, available 8am-3pm)

One of America's oldest rural garden cemeteries, Woodland occupies the highest point in the city. Its grounds, containing over 3,000 trees and flowering shrubs representing approximately 250 species, constitute one of the area's finest arboretums. Many of the specimens are labeled, and nine of Woodland's trees are designated Ohio Champions by the Ohio Forestry Association. Its Romanesque gateway, chapel and office, completed in 1889, are on the National Register of Historic Places. The chapel, has one of the finest original Tiffany windows in the country.

ELMORE

SCHEDEL FOUNDATION ARBORETUM AND GARDENS

19255 W. Portage River South Road, Elmore, OH 43416
Tel: (419) 862-3182; Fax: (419) 862-1909
Internet Address: http://www.schedel-gardens.org/
Admission: Fee $6.00
Attendance: 15,000
Established: 1963
Membership: Y
Wheelchair Accessible: Y
Parking: Free on site
Open: April 15 to October, Monday to Saturday, 10am-4pm; Sunday, noon-4pm.
Best Time(s) of Year to Visit: June to October
Facilities: Architecture (Victorian residence); Gardens (herb, iris, Japanese, oriental lily, rose, tropical, water); Greenhouse; Grounds (17 acres)
Activities: Guided Tours (groups, schedule in advance, $60 minimum, House (by appointment)

Situated on a bluff overlooking a bend in the Portage River, Schedel Gardens offers 17 acres of designed beds containing over 20,000 annuals, perennials, flowering shrubs and trees, water lilies, roses, peonies, vegetables, and fruit trees. The arboretum contains twenty-five varieties of Japanese maple, sixteen species of pine, and nearly fifty varieties of lilac as well as a wide variety of specimen trees, including a grove of dawn redwoods and a bald cypress. The Schedel Arboretum and Gardens is an operation of the Joseph J. and Marie P. Schedel Foundation.

GROVE CITY

THE GARDENS AT GANTZ FARM

2255 Home Road, Grove City, OH 43123-1867
Tel: (614) 871-6323
Internet Address: http://gardensatgantz.org
Admission: Free
Wheelchair Accessible: Y
Parking: Free lot on site
Open: Daily, dawn-dusk
Best Time(s) of Year to Visit: June to October
Facilities: Arboretum; Architecture (brick farmhouse, 1840); Garden (herb)
Activities: Education Programs; Guided Tours (call for appointment); Herb Day
(March); Plant Sales (perennial & herb, May); Self-guided Tour

A city park, the Gardens of Yesterday, Today, and Tomorrow at Gantz Farm focus on
herbs. The Garden of Yesterday is a recreation of a typical kitchen garden of an Ohio
farm in the 1840s. The Garden of Today is divided into theme gardens emphasizing the
uses made of plant products and the relationship between plants. The Garden of Tomorrow demonstrates the uses of herbs in landscaping, particularly in container gardening.
There is also a small, recently planted arboretum with labels giving the common and
botanical names of the trees.

HURON

ERIE METROPARKS—JAMES H. MCBRIDE ARBORETUM

Firelands College, BGSU, 1 University Drive (south of Route 2, off Rye Beach Road),
Huron, OH 44839
Tel: (419) 433-5560
Internet Address: http://www.eriemetroparks.org/
McBride%20Arboretum/HomeJMA.htm
Admission: Free
Attendance: 2,500
Established: 1984
Membership: N
Wheelchair Accessible: P
Parking: College parking lot
Open: Daily, 7am-dusk
Best Time(s) of Year to Visit: May (crab apple bloom)
Facilities: Arboretum; Gardens (butterfly, winter display); Grounds (50 acres); Trails
(woodland & meadow); Visitor Center
Activities: Events Mother's Day Brunch (May); Guided Tours (schedule in advance,
625-7783)

Located behind the West Building on the campus of Firelands College of Bowling Green
State University, James H. McBride Arboretum contains nearly 300 tree species in more than
20 acres of formal and ornamental plantings. A highlight of the arboretum is its extensive
collection of crab apple trees featuring over 150 trees representing more than 50 varieties.

Surrounding Parker Lake, over twenty acres of the arboretum feature formal and ornamental plantings, including winter garden beds providing color and texture to the grounds throughout the year; a butterfly garden providing sanctuary to butterflies and hummingbirds; and the Peace and Tranquility Garden, extending an invitation to pause, relax, and reflect. On the perimeter of the decorative grounds are areas dedicated to plants that are native to the Firelands. Maintained by Erie MetroParks, the site is leased from BGSU.

INDIAN HILL

STANLEY M. ROWE ARBORETUM

4600 Muchmore Road, Indian Hill, OH 45243
Tel: (513) 561-5151
Internet Address: http://rowearb@ihill.org/
Admission: No charge, donations accepted
Established: 1926
Membership: Y
Wheelchair Accessible: Y
Parking: Small paved parking lot
Open: Daily, dawn-dusk
Facilities: Grounds (10 acres; 1,200 different specimens); Special Collections (conifer, crab apple, lilac, magnolia, oak, viburnum, broadleaf evergreens, unusual deciduous)
Activities: Guided Tours (by appointment for groups)

Formerly the private estate of Stanley M. Rowe, the arboretum contains about 5,000 different types of trees and shrubs. The arboretum is particularly strong in evergreens.

KIRTLAND

HERB SOCIETY OF AMERICA—HEADQUARTERS DEMONSTRATION GARDEN (AHS RAP)

9019 Kirtland Chardon Road (adjacent to Holden Arboretum), Kirtland, OH 44094
Tel: (440) 256-0514; Fax: (440) 256-0541
Internet Address: http://www.herbsociety.org
Admission: Free
Established: 2001
Membership: Y
Open: Office, Monday to Friday, 9am-5pm
Facilities: Architecture (stone farmhouse, 1841); Garden (herb)
Activities: Demonstrations; Education Programs; Seed Exchange

The society maintains a demonstration garden at its national headquarters. The headquarters building, considered the oldest stone structure in Lake County, is listed on the National Register of Historic Places.

THE HOLDEN ARBORETUM (AHS RAP)

9500 Sperry Road, Kirtland, OH 44094-5172
Tel: (440) 946-4400; Fax: (440) 602-3857

Internet Address: http://www.holdenarb.org/
Admission: Fee: adult $4.00, child (<6) free, child (6-15) $2.00, senior $3.00; Seniors free on Tuesday.
Attendance: 100,000
Established: 1931
Membership: Y
Wheelchair Accessible: Y
Parking: Parking available
Open: April to October, 9am-5pm
Closed: November to March
Best Time(s) of Year to Visit: May to June
(Rhododendron Garden)
Facilities: Arboretum; Gardens (butterfly, lilacs, viburnums, prairie, rhododendrons, wildflowers); Grounds (3,400 acres); Library (10,000 volumes); Shop (daily, 10am-4:45pm); Special Collections (conifer, flowering crab apples, specimen trees); Visitor Center
Activities: Education Programs (adults and children); Guided Tours (schedule in advance); Lectures; Self-guided Tours

The Holden Arboretum, containing over 5,400 named plants, is dedicated to collecting woody plants of ornamental and scientific merit for northeastern Ohio. Gardens include a 20-acre main display garden, containing over 10,000 bulbs and 800 perennials as well as the arboretum's lilac, viburnum, and hedge collections; a 5-acre wildflower garden, devoted to native Ohio wildflowers and protected species; a 1-acre butterfly garden, featuring plants selected for their ability to attract butterflies and hummingbirds; and a rhododendron garden, containing over 1,200 rhododendron and 100 mountain laurel plants as well as heaths, heathers, and witch hazels. The conifer and magnolia collections (135 and 470 planting, respectively), located approximately a mile away from the Visitor Center, are also well worth a visit. The arboretum collects and displays a diversity of plants for educational and evaluation purposes in order to convey sustainable plant choices for its region.

LONDON

OHIO STATE UNIVERSITY— JAMES D. UTZINGER MEMORIAL GARDEN

Molly Caren Agricultural Center, 135 N Street (Route 38), London, OH 43140
Tel: (740) 852-3276
Internet Address: http://fsr.osu.edu/umg/history.html
Admission: Free
Established: 1991
Facilities: Gardens (butterfly, edible, ground cover, herb, native plant, ornamental grass, vegetable); Grounds Caren Ag Center (2,100 cares)
Activities: Demonstrations; Events OSU Farm Science Review (Fall, $8.00); Guided Tours Groups (schedule 2-3 weeks in advance); Lecture Series; Workshops

The grounds of the Molly Caren Agricultural Center (MCAC) are dedicated to the Farm Science Review, an annual agriculture trade show and Ohio State University's agricultural, demonstration, and research operations. Featuring plants suitable for Ohio gardens, the Utzinger Memorial Garden contains various perennial and annual displays, a vegetable garden, butterfly garden, native plant area, herb garden, deer resistant landscape, an ornamental grass collection, ground cover display, and an edible garden that includes crab apples, espalier and dwarf fruit trees, strawberries, blueberries, raspberries, a grape arbor, and vegetables. The garden is a cooperative effort of the Ohio State University Department of Horticulture and Crop Science and Ohio State University Extension Master Gardeners.

MANSFIELD

KINGWOOD CENTER (AHS RAP)

900 Park Avenue West, Mansfield, OH 44906-2999
Tel: (419) 522-0211; Fax: (419) 522-0211
Internet Address: http://www.kingwoodcenter.org
Admission: Free
Attendance: 200,000
Established: 1953
Membership: Y
Wheelchair Accessible: P
Parking: Free on site, 144 spaces plus 16 handicapped spaces
Open: Grounds (April to October): Daily, 8am-½ hour before sunset; Grounds (Nov to Mar): Daily, 8am-5pm; Greenhouse (Apr to Oct): Daily, 8am-1 hour before sunset; Greenhouse (Nov to Mar): Daily, 8am-4:30pm; Mansion (Apr to Oct): Tuesday to Saturday, 9am-5pm; Sunday, 1pm-5pm; Mansion (Nov to Mar): Tuesday to Saturday, 9am-5pm
Closed: New Year's Day, Thanksgiving Day, Christmas Day
Best Time(s) of Year to Visit: early May (tulips), June to frost (annuals)
Facilities: Gardens (annual, cutting, daylily & iris, herb, parterre, peony, perennial, rose, terrace, tulip, woodland); Greenhouse and Orangeries (6 houses, 9,000 square feet); Grounds (47 acres); Library (horticultural collection, 9,000 volumes); Special Collections (day lily, bearded iris, Siberian iris, rose)
Activities: Flower Shows (chrysanthemum, peony, daffodil, iris, lily, African violet, Fall Harvest); Guided Tours (by appointment); Lectures; Plant Sales (May 1), Greenhouse (daily); Workshops

Kingwood Hall with its spacious lawns, mature shade trees, and extensive formal, informal, and natural gardens was the residence of Charles K. King, president of the Ohio Brass Company. King died in 1952, leaving an endowment to develop and maintain the estate as a public institution, Kingwood Center. Kingwood is listed on the National Register of Historic Places.

NEWARK

THE DAWES ARBORETUM (AHS RAP)

7770 Jacksontown Road, S.E. (Route 13), Newark, OH 43056-9380
Tel: (800) 443-2937; Fax: (740) 323-4058
Internet Address: http://www.dawesarb.org
Admission: Fee (Museum): adult $2.00, child $1.00; Free (Grounds).
Attendance: 300,000
Established: 1929

Membership: Y
Wheelchair Accessible: Y
Parking: Several parking areas throughout grounds
Open: Grounds, Daily, dawn-dusk
Closed: New Year's Day, Thanksgiving Day, Christmas Day
Facilities: Auditorium (175 seats); Gardens (all seasons, azalea glen, Japanese); Grounds (1,700 acres); Library (2,000 volumes); Nature Center/Bird Watching Garden; Shop; Special Collections (bonsai, conifer, crab apple, holly, ground cover juniper, oak/beech); Visitor Center
Activities: Education Programs (adults, undergraduate students and children); Films; Guided Tours; Lectures; Temporary Exhibitions

Founded in 1929 by Beman and Bertie Dawes, the arboretum contains over 2,200 types of tress, shrubs, and woody vines displayed in gardens, collection, and natural areas. Gardens include a Japanese garden designed by Dr. Makota Nakamura, an all-seasons garden, featuring plants of year-round interest and an azalea glen. Other exhibits include the Living Legacy Apple Orchard, containing many varieties developed before 1845; Holly Hill, displaying 130 species of evergreen and deciduous holly; crab apple collection, conifer collection, including an extensive selection of dwarf conifers; ground cover juniper collection; rare tree walk; cypress swamp; and dawn redwood test site.

POWELL

COLUMBUS ZOO AND AQUARIUM—GARDENS

9990 Riverside Drive (Route 257), Powell, OH 43065
Tel: (800) 666-5397; Fax: (614) 645-3465;
TDDY: (614) 645-5362
Internet Address: http://www.columbuszoo.org
Admission: Fee: adult $9.00, child (<2) free, child (2-11) $5.00, senior $7.00
Attendance: 1,300,000
Established: 1927
Membership: Y
Wheelchair Accessible: Y
Parking: On site, $3.00
Open: Memorial Day to Labor Day, Daily, 9am-6pm; September to May, Daily, 9am-5pm
Facilities: Food Services Food Court (fast food, 270 indoor/150 outdoor seats); Grounds Site (588 acres), Zoo & Aquarium
(90 acres); Picnic Area; Shop
Activities: Education Programs Animal Shows (Memorial Day-Labor Day), Keeper Talks (daily, Memorial Day-Labor Day); Events WildLights Winter Festival (mid-Nov-Jan; Mon-Thurs, 5pm-9pm; Fri-Sat, 5pm-10pm; Sun, 5pm-9pm)

At the zoo, the botanical gardens, containing over 700 species of plant life, match the variety of the animal population. The tropical aviary houses several tropical/exotic plants, including jasmine, camphor tree, fig, and a variety of tree ferns. Much of the flora found at the zoo was planted to supplement animal diets. Whenever possible, the plants that surround an animal exhibit reflect the animal's natural habitat.

SHAKER HEIGHTS

SHAKER HEIGHTS COMMUNITY ROSE GARDEN

Woodbury Road (south of S. Woodland Road, next to Woodbury School), Shaker Heights, OH 44120
Tel: (216) 751-1995
Internet Address: http://www.shakersquare.net/roses/
Admission: Free
Open: Daily, sunrise-sunset
Best Time(s) of Year to Visit: Early June
Facilities: Garden (rose)
Activities: Self-guided Tour (information panel at the north end of garden includes map)

Located on Shaker Heights school property (between Woodbury and Onaway Schools), the garden was originally planted in 1926-1927, but fell into decline in the 1970s due to budgetary restraints. Restored between 1993 and 1998 through voluntary efforts, the garden displays approximately 1,000 rose bushes, ranging from old Damask roses to modern ever-blooming floribunda and hybrid tea roses. (Most of the roses in the current garden were planted after 1993, though there are a few plants believed to be from the original 1926-1927 planting.) The hybrid roses are organized by color and type in more than thirty beds (deep red roses in the southern-most beds, pink in the center beds, yellow and white to the north). While the Shaker Heights Schools furnish some basic support, the garden is maintained by volunteers and contributions.

STOW

CITY OF STOW—ADELL DURBIN PARK-ARBORETUM

Route 91 (south of Route 59 intersection), Stow, OH 44244
Tel: (330) 689-2759
Internet Address: http://www.stow.oh.us/page127.html
Admission: Free
Attendance: 5,000
Established: 1939
Membership: Y
Wheelchair Accessible: P
Parking: Paved lot with rest rooms, 3300 Darrow Road
Open: Daily, sunrise-sunset
Facilities: Grounds Park (34½ acres); Trails (3); Visitor Center (Harold Welch Nature Center)
Activities: Self-guided Tours

The arboretum contains 250 native and ornamental trees, shrubs, and flowers. A trail guide, keyed to tags on trees and shrubs, may be obtained from the storage box affixed to the rules sign facing the parking lot or at Stow City Hall.

STRONGSVILLE

GARDENVIEW HORTICULTURAL PARK

16711 Pearl Road (Route 42, 1½ mile south of junction with Route 82),
Strongsville, OH 44136-6048
Tel: (440) 238-6653
Internet Address: http://www.geocities.com/heartland/cottage/9303
Admission: Fee: adult $5.00, child $3.00
Established: 1949
Membership: Y
Wheelchair Accessible: N
Open: April to October, Saturday to Sunday, noon-6pm, other times by appointment
Facilities: Arboretum; Gardens (aquatic, English, perennial, shade, spring);
Greenhouse; Grounds arboretum (10 acres), gardens (6 acres); Special Collections
(crab apple; hosta; emphasis on variegated, golden and silver-leafed rare plants)
Activities: Guided Tours (groups only, schedule in advance)

Gardenview, the creation of Henry A. Ross, consists of display gardens and an arboretum. The gardens include a spring garden, featuring tulips, daffodils, azaleas, and crab apples; a shade garden, displaying early spring bulbs and hostas; perennial beds, containing day lilies, iris, peonies, and rhododendrons; and a lily pond. The arboretum offers 2,000 flowering and ornamental trees (500 varieties of crab apple) underplanted with thousands of daffodils. The garden is designated an All-America Selections Display Garden.

TOLEDO

TOLEDO BOTANICAL GARDEN (AHS RAP)

5403 Elmer Drive, Toledo, OH 43615
Tel: (419) 936-2986; Fax: (419) 936-2987
Internet Address: http://www.toledogarden.org/
Admission: Free
Attendance: 120,000
Membership: Y
Parking: Free on site, except during major events
Open: Daily, 8:30am-5:30pm
Best Time(s) of Year to Visit: May to July (peak bloom)
Facilities: Architecture (log cabin, 1837); Gardens (cottage, display, herb, kitchen,
native plant, perennial, historical pioneer, research, rose, sensory, shade, vegetable);
Grounds (60 acres); Shop: Garden Galleries (gifts, garden accessories, books; Mon-
Sat, 10am-5pm; Sun, 1pm-5pm); Special Collections (hosta, nationally recognized as
one of the largest public collections)
Activities: Arts Festival Crosby Festival of the Arts (Jun, last full weekend); Concerts
Café Concerts (Summer, Wed & Fri, noon), Jazz in the Garden (Jul-Aug, Thurs
evenings); Education Programs; Guided Tours (schedule in advance); Lectures; Plant
Sales (spring & fall)

Also home to artist studios and galleries, the gardens contain meadows, gardens, and displays of flowering trees and shrubs, such as dogwood, magnolia, forsythia, and lilacs. There are extensive perennial plantings, including the National Hosta Society display garden, an American Hemerocallis Society display garden, color garden, cottage garden, green garden, and grass collection. Other highlights include the Pioneer Garden, featuring a log cabin; a rose garden, containing 250 bushes; a shade garden, displaying shade-tolerant ferns, wildflowers, hostas, rhododendrons, and azaleas; a wildflower walk showcasing plants native to northwest Ohio; an herb garden; and a linden allée. The greenhouse houses a hydroponics project and USDA research facilities.

TOLEDO ZOOLOGICAL SOCIETY—GARDENS

2700 Broadway, Toledo, OH 43609-3121
Tel: (419) 385-4040; Fax: (419) 385-6935
Internet Address: http://www.toledozoo.org
Admission: Fee: adult $9.00, child (<2) free, child (2-11) $6.00, senior $6.00
Membership: Y
Wheelchair Accessible: Y
Parking: On site, 1,350 spaces, $5
Open: May to Labor Day, daily, 10am-5pm; Labor Day to April, daily, 10am-4pm
Closed: New Year's Day, Thanksgiving Day, Christmas Day
Facilities: Conservatory; Food Services Beastro (open air), Carnivore Café, Karamu BBQ, Timberline Bakery & Deli; Gardens (formal); Grounds (62 acres)
Activities: Events, Lights before Christmas

The Ziems Conservatory was built in 1904 and is home to a variety of tropical plants. Growing under the glass roof can be found species of bananas, palms, ferns, bromeliads, and an array of other plants from around the world. Adjacent to the conservatory are other special gardens, each with a distinct theme. The rose garden holds approximately 200 roses with varieties of hybrid teas, floribundas, grandifloras, and climbers, all flowering throughout the growing season. A butterfly garden, located near the rose garden, features plants that attract butterflies and interpretive graphics that inform visitors about these creatures. The formal garden contains an assortment of perennials, annuals, and woody plants. The zoo's horticulture staff is also responsible for the "Lights before Christmas" display, which features over 1 million lights and more than 200 animal images.

UNIVERSITY OF TOLEDO—R. A. STRANAHAN ARBORETUM

4131 Tantara Drive (near intersection of Sylvania & Whiteford), Toledo, OH 43606
Tel: (419) 841-1007
Internet Address: http://www.utoledo.edu/_campus-info/arboretum/
Admission: Free
Established: 1964
Membership: Y
Open: April to October, Monday to Friday, 9am-2pm; June to September, 10am-4pm
Facilities: Arboretum; Grounds (47 acres); Special Collections (flowering crab apple, maple)
Activities: Education Programs; Open Houses

Located within the "Oak Openings" sand dune region, Stranahan Arboretum contains more than 2,000 woody plants representing 450 varieties, including 54 species and varieties of maple and 48 species and varieties of flowering crab apple. Habitats include restored prairie, wetlands, pond, ravine (probably formed by an ancient glacial seep), and new and old growth forest.

WESTERVILLE

INNISWOOD METRO GARDENS

940 S. Hempstead Road, Westerville, OH 43081
Tel: (614) 895-6216; Fax: (614) 895-6352
Internet Address: http://www.metroparks.net/inniswood.htm
Admission: Free
Established: 1984
Wheelchair Accessible: Y
Parking: Free on site
Open: Daily, 7am-dusk
Facilities: Gardens (cutting, herb, memorial, perennial border, prairie, rock, rose, white); Grounds (122 acres), lawn & garden (14 acres), nature preserve (33 acres); Library; Special Collections (fern); Trails
Activities: Education Programs; Festival Affair of the Hort (annual); Guided Tours; Temporary Art Exhibitions (monthly); Workshops

Inniswood features landscaped grounds, a variety of gardens, and a nature preserve with hardwood forest. Totaling over 2,000 species of flowers and herbs, plantings include an extensive herb garden of non-geometric design, a rose garden displaying over 250 varieties of roses, and a perennial border as well as cutting, memorial, prairie, rock, rose, and white gardens. Once the home of Grace Innis, a pioneer of the Ohio garden club movement, Inniswood is operated and maintained by the Metropolitan Park District of Columbus and Franklin County.

WOOSTER

OHIO STATE UNIVERSITY-OHIO AGRICULTURAL RESEARCH AND DEVELOPMENT CENTER—SECREST ARBORETUM AND ROSE GARDEN

1680 Madison Avenue, Wooster, OH 44691
Tel: (330) 263-3761; Fax: (330) 202-3667
Internet Address: http://secrest.osu.edu/
Admission: Free
Membership: Y
Parking: Free on site
Open: Daily, dawn-dusk
Facilities: Arboretum; Gardens (aquatic, rhododendron, rose); Grounds Rose Garden (3 acres), Secrest Arboretum (85 acres); Visitor Center (Mon-Fri, 8am-5pm)
Activities: Education Programs; Events Autumn Discovery Day (Oct., seminars, tree sales;, Plant Discovery Day (1st Sat in May, plant sales); Guided Tours (schedule in advance, 202-3503)

The Secrest Arboretum, a part of the Ohio Agricultural Research and Development Center, is a test and display facility for trees and shrubs (2,000 varieties). Features include the Rhododendron Display Garden, a naturalized planting of azaleas and rhododendrons; flowering crab apples; native tree and shrub species; and the Ollie Diller Holly Garden. In addition, conifers, junipers, arborvitae, and forest pines are emphasized. OARDC also offers the Garden of Roses of Legend and Romance, containing over 1,200 roses representing more than 500 varieties and a demonstration water garden.

YOUNGSTOWN

MILL CREEK METROPARKS—FELLOWS RIVERSIDE GARDENS (AHS RAP)

123 McKinley Avenue, Youngstown, OH 44509
Tel: (330) 740-7116; Fax: (330) 740-7128
Internet Address: http://www.millcreekmetroparks.com
Admission: Free
Attendance: 330,000
Established: 1963
Membership: Y
Wheelchair Accessible: P
Parking: Paved lot on site
Open: Grounds, daily, dawn-dark; Education & Visitor Center, Tuesday to Sunday, 10am-5pm

A gift from Mrs. Elizabeth A. Fellows to Mill Creek MetroParks, the gardens contain labeled collections of roses, herbs, trees, conifers, rhododendrons, and perennials as well as plantings of over 50,000 spring bulbs and thousands of summer annuals. Other features include two flagstone terraces, a reflecting fountain pool, a Victorian-styled gazebo, and a climbing rose trellis. The most popular collection in the gardens is the rose collection. Four separate groups of roses are represented. Modern roses can be found in the formal rose garden where hybrid tea, floribunda, and grandiflora roses are planted around the Kidston Pavilion. Climbing roses are displayed to the west along the perennial border walk. Botanical and shrub roses are represented throughout the gardens. A collection of hybrid perpetual roses, known for their sweet scent and repeat bloom, surrounds the Victorian Gazebo. The gardens adjoins Mill Creek Park, a historic 2,600-acre natural park with over 20 miles of trails and numerous hiking trails providing access to a native hemlock gorge, rock outcrops, and three lakes.

PENNSYLVANIA

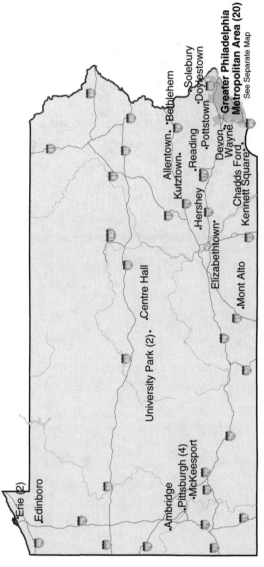

The number in the parentheses following the city name indicates the number of gardens/ arboreta in that municipality. If there is no number, one is understood. For example, in the text four listings would be found under Pittsburgh and one listing under McKeesport. Cities within the greater Philadelphia metropolitan area will be found on the map on the next page.

GREATER PHILADELPHIA METROPOLITAN AREA

Greater Philadelphia metropolitan area (including Ambler, Bryn Mawr, Fallsington, Fort Washington, Glanwyne, Haverford, Media, Morrisville, Philadelphia, Swarthmore, Upland, Villanova, and Wallingford).

ALLENTOWN

CEDAR CREST COLLEGE—WILLIAM F. CURTIS ARBORETUM

100 College Drive, Allentown, PA 18104-6196
Tel: (610) 606-4666 *Ext:* 3565; Fax: (610) 606-4616
Internet Address: http://www.cedarcrest.edu
Established: 1985
Open: Daily, dawn-dusk
Best Time(s) of Year to Visit: May to November
Facilities: Arboretum; Grounds Campus (84 acres)
Activities: Guided Tours (conducted by Biology Club); Self-guided Tours

Cedar Crest's campus, a nationally registered arboretum, contains 140 variations of trees, including many rare and unusual types. A nature trail guide is available.

AMBLER

TEMPLE UNIVERSITY AT AMBLER—LANDSCAPE ARBORETUM

580 Meeting House Road, Ambler, PA 19002
Tel: (215) 283-1292
Internet Address: http://www.temple.edu/ambler/current/camp_fac.htm
Admission: Free
Parking: Visitor Parking Lot off Meeting House Road
Open: Daily
Facilities: Arboretum; Gardens (formal, 1927 design by James Bush-Brown; ground cover, herb, perennial, native plant, dwarf ornamental); Greenhouse (6,600 square feet); Grounds Campus (187 acres)

Designated an arboretum by the American Association of Botanical Gardens and Arboreta, the Ambler campus includes formal gardens, test gardens, woodlands, fields, and nurseries. The Formal Gardens, located behind Dixon Hall, are based on the gardens of Dumbarton Oaks in Washington, DC. They include perennials, native plants, and a garden competition area. There are also a ground cover garden, an herb garden, a sustainable wetland garden, and the Fisher Garden of dwarf ornamentals.

AMBRIDGE

OLD ECONOMY VILLAGE—GARDENS

270 16th St, Ambridge, PA 15003-2298
Tel: (724) 266-4500; Fax: (724) 266-7506
Internet Address: http://www.oldeconomyvillage.org
Admission: Fee: adult $5.00, child $3.00, senior $4.50,
family $13.00
Parking: Parking lot at Visitor Center
Open: Tuesday to Saturday, 9am-5pm; Sunday, noon-5pm
Closed: New Year's Day, ML King Day, President's Day, Columbus Day,
Thanksgiving Day, Christmas Day
Best Time(s) of Year to Visit: Summer
Facilities: Architecture (17 restored buildings of nineteenth-century Christian
communal society); Gardens (period, 2); Greenhouse; Grounds (6 acres)
Activities: Guided Tours (groups, schedule in advance
266-4500 x204 or x217)

Old Economy Village was a religious utopian community constructed between 1824 and 1830. The restored buildings, grounds, library, archives, and 16,000 original artifacts are maintained as a memorial to the society's commitment to the religious discipline and economic industry. The site contains two restored gardens, the Baker House garden, a typical family garden, and the more elaborate George Rapp Garden, described by a contemporary visitor as "neatly laid out in lawns, arbors, and flower beds with an open Pavilion over the pool that held a well executed female statue holding a lyre, and a straw-roofed Grotto." The plantings in both gardens are based on contemporary descriptions and inventories. Designated a National Historic Landmark, the site is administered by the Pennsylvania Historical and Museum Commission.

BETHLEHEM

GARDEN OF SERENITY

11 W. Church Street (just west of Bethlehem Library), Bethlehem, PA 18018-0766
Internet Address:
http://www.bethlehem-pa.gov/about/sisterCities/japan.htm
Admission: Free
Wheelchair Accessible: Y
Parking: Street parking; Handicapped designations & accessiblity
Open: Daily, 24 hours
Best Time(s) of Year to Visit: Early Spring (cherry blossoms)
Facilities: Garden (Japanese, 1970 design by landscape architect Yoshinaga Sakon of
Tondabayashi, Japan); Tea House
Activities: Events Tea Ceremonies (summer, periodic)

Located on the city hall/library grounds, the Japanese garden is surrounded by flowering cherry trees, a gift of Bethlehem's Japanese sister city, Tondabayashi. The garden consists of a tea house and a small hill-and-pond style garden. A dedicated committee of the Bethlehem Garden Club maintains the garden and since 1999 has helped with its renovation.

BRYN MAWR

THE AMERICAN COLLEGE ARBORETUM

270 S. Bryn Mawr Avenue, Bryn Mawr, PA 19010
Tel: (610) 526-1229; Fax: (610) 526-1224
Internet Address: http://www.amercoll.edu/aboutus.asp
Admission: Free
Wheelchair Accessible: Y
Parking: Free on site
Open: Daily, dawn-dusk
Facilities: Arboretum; Gardens (cottage, fragrance, woodland); Grounds Campus (35 acres); Picnic Area; Special Collections (conifer, daffodil)
Activities: Education Programs (spring & fall; groups, schedule 2 weeks in advance); Self-guided Tours (brochure available)

Originally several large estates, the college campus has been designated an arboretum. A collection of 700 specimen trees forms the backdrop for a wooded stream valley, a pond, and developing gardens. The arboretum also includes plantings of annuals, perennials, and vegetables cultivated in a cottage garden and in flower beds, borders, and containers. Highlights include Daffodil Hill, featuring thousands of daffodils representing all twelve recognized daffodil divisions, and the James S. Weese Conifer Collection.

CENTRE HALL

RHONEYMEADE ARBORETUM AND SCULPTURE GARDEN

177 Rimmey Road (Route 45) (4 miles east of Boalsburg), Centre Hall, PA 16828
Tel: (814) 364-1527
Internet Address: http://www.Rhoneymeade-usa.org
Admission: Free
Attendance: 250
Established: 1989
Membership: N
Wheelchair Accessible: N
Parking: On site, grass, 14 autos
Open: April to October, Saturday to Sunday, 1st weekend in month 12:30pm-4:30pm
Best Time(s) of Year to Visit: May to September
Facilities: Arboretum; Grounds (150 acres), Plantings (6 acres); Sculpture Garden (26, marble, bronze, ceramic, wood)
Activities: Guided Tours (by appointment, fee)

Straddling a high north-south ridge in the valley between Nittany and Tussey mountains, Rhoneymeade offers a sculpture garden, arboretum, and labyrinth. Plantings include flowering and specimen trees, shrubs, perennials, and water plants.

CHADDS FORD

BRANDYWINE CONSERVANCY/BRANDYWINE RIVER MUSEUM—GARDENS

U.S. Route 1, Chadds Ford, PA 19317
Tel: (610) 388-8327; Fax: (610) 388-1197
Internet Address: http://www.brandywinemuseum.org/gardens.html
Admission: Fee: adult $8.00, child(<6) free, child, student $5.00, senior $5.00;
Free (Gardens)
Attendance: 130,000
Established: 1967
Membership: Y
Wheelchair Accessible: Y
Parking: Lot on site, ample, includes handicapped access
Open: Daily, 9:30am-4:30pm
Closed: Christmas Day
Facilities: Food Services (cafeteria-style, 80 seats; 10am-3pm, closed Mon-Tues, Jan-March); Gardens (native plant, wildflower, 1974 design by horticulturist F. M. Mooberry); Grounds; Museum (regional and American art); Shop Brandywine Museum Shop (seed); Special Collections (native plants, flowers, and shrubs)
Activities: Flower Shows Annual Bonsai Show (early June); Guided Tours wildflower gardens (schedule in advance); Plant Sales Annual Wildflower, Native Plant & Seed Sale (Mother's Day weekend)

Situated at the Brandywine River Museum, the Brandywine Conservancy's wildflower and native plant gardens are a living representation of the conservancy's mission to preserve, protect, and share American artistic, natural, and historical resources, principally of the Brandywine region. The gardens feature indigenous and some naturalized flowers, trees, and shrubs of the greater Brandywine region displayed in natural settings. Plants are selected to provide a succession of bloom from early spring through the first killing frost. Plants are located in settings akin to their natural habitats: woodland, wetland, flood plain, or meadow. The Brandywine River Museum is best known for its unparalleled collection of artworks by three generations of Wyeths and its fine collection of American illustration, still life, and landscape painting.

DEVON

JENKINS ARBORETUM

631 Berwyn-Baptist Road, Devon, PA 19333-1001
Tel: (610) 647-8870
Internet Address: http://www.jenkinsarboretum.org/jenkinshome.html
Admission: Free
Attendance: 10,000
Established: 1974
Membership: Y
Open: Daily, sunrise-sunset
Best Time(s) of Year to Visit: May (azaleas/rhododendrons)

Facilities: Arboretum; Grounds (46 acres; 1.2 miles of paved walkways); Special Collections (rhododendron)
Activities: Education Programs; Plant Sales (annual, May); Workshops

The arboretum preserves a remnant of Pennsylvania hardwood forest, including large natural stands of mountain laurel, pinxterbloom azalea, blueberry, deerberry, native wildflowers, rhododendrons, ferns, and herbs. Its genus Rhododendron collection features more than 4,000 plants representing approximately 150 different species from around the world, including evergreen and deciduous azaleas as well as small and large-leafed rhododendrons.

DOYLESTOWN

DELAWARE VALLEY COLLEGE— HENRY SCHMIEDER ARBORETUM

700 E. Butler Avenue (Route 202), Doylestown, PA 18901-2697
Tel: (215) 489-2283
Internet Address: http://www.devalcol.edu
Admission: Free
Open: Daily, dawn-dusk
Facilities: Arboretum; Gardens (annual, dwarf conifer, daylily/ornamental grass, hedge, herb); Greenhouses (30,000 square feet, open weekdays); Shop Country Market (college-grown produce and plants), Student Center (gifts); Special Collections (beech).
Activities: Education Programs (adults & children); Guided Tours (by appointment); Lectures; Plant Sales (annual, spring in conjunction with the Bucks Beautiful Garden Fair); Self-guided Tours; Workshops

Arboretum exhibits include the Gazebo Garden, offering an annual display and vine garden; the Hillman Family Garden, a part- and full-shade garden with a pink and white theme; an herb garden; a day lily and ornamental grass garden; dwarf and full-size conifer collections; a beech collection; a hedge demonstration garden, and a woodland walk. The college also operates approximately 30,000 square feet of greenhouses including the ultramodern, computerized Arthur Poley Greenhouse Complex completed in 1998. Self-guided tour literature is available at the college's security/information pavilion.

EDINBORO

GOODELL GARDENS & HOMESTEAD (AHS RAP)

221 Waterford Street, Edinboro, PA 16412-2283
Tel: (814) 734-6699
Admission: Fee: adult $3.00, child $1.50, student $2.00, senior $2.50
Established: 2004
Membership: Y
Wheelchair Accessible: Y
Parking: Gravel lot on site, 30 spaces
Open: Spring to October, Wednesday to Sunday, 11am-5pm
Best Time(s) of Year to Visit: early June (rhododendron & azalea bloom)

Facilities: Arboretum; Gardens; Grounds (78 acres); Shop
Activities: Guided Tours (schedule in advance, $2/person)

Goodell Gardens and Homestead is a non-profit organization whose purpose is to create an education-oriented botanical garden and arboretum on the Goodell family farm within the Borough of Edinboro. Its master plan calls for formal and informal gardens, walking trails, naturalistic areas, scenic overlooks, a pond, and a variety of support facilities.

ELIZABETHTOWN

MASONIC VILLAGE OF THE GRAND LODGE OF FREE AND ACCEPTED MASONS OF PENNSYLVANIA—GARDENS

1 Masonic Drive (off Highway 241), Elizabethtown,
PA 17022-2199
Tel: (717) 367-1121
Internet Address: http://www.pagrandlodge.org/villages
Admission: Free
Established: 1910
Membership: N
Wheelchair Accessible: Y
Parking: Handicapped and standard parking available
Open: Daily, 8am-noon & 12:30pm-4pm
Best Time(s) of Year to Visit: May to September
Facilities: Gardens (formal); Grounds Campus (1,400 acres), Gardens (6½ acres)
Activities: Guided Tours

Masonic Village of the Grand Lodge of Free and Accepted Masons of Pennsylvania—Gardens, Elizabethtown, PA.

The Masonic Village at Elizabethtown is a continuing care retirement community, children's home, and community service organization. The grounds include formal gardens containing rare trees, ornamental shrubs, rose beds, and arbors, complemented by a reflecting pond and large water fountain. It received the Distinguished Garden Award from the Pennsylvania Horticultural Society in 1970.

ERIE

ERIE ZOOLOGICAL PARK AND BOTANICAL GARDENS OF NORTHWESTERN PENNSYLVANIA

423 West 38th Street, Erie, PA 16508
Tel: (814) 864-4091; Fax: (814) 864-6272
Internet Address: http://www.eriezoo.org/l
Admission: Fee (Mar-Oct): adult $6.00, child(<3) free, child(3-11) $3.00, senior $5.00; Fee (Nov-Feb): adult $5; child(3-11) $2.25
Attendance: 300,000
Open: Daily, 10am-5pm
Closed: New Year's Day, Christmas Day
Facilities: Carousel; Food Services (refreshment stands); Gardens (butterfly, ornamental grasses, herb, rock); Greenhouse; Grounds (15 acres); Shop (gifts)

Featuring extensive animal and plant collections, the Erie Zoo's landscaped grounds display more than 2,500 plants representing over 600 species. Exterior exhibits include a butterfly garden with both seasonal and year-round plantings that attract adult butter-flies; the Gardens at Kiboka, containing the ornamental grass collection, ornamental trees and shrubs, and thousands of spring bulbs; an herb garden; the Julie King Memorial Garden, presenting seasonal flower displays and multi-seasonal shrubs and trees; a rock garden, incorporating hardy plants of the heath and heather family, various other orna-mental and perennial landscape plants, and seasonal flower displays. The zoo's green-house provides a tropical environment featuring exotic plants, fruits, trees, orchids, and bromeliads.

LAKE ERIE ARBORETUM AT FRONTIER PARK (LEAF) (AHS RAP)

Bounded by W. 6th Street, Bayfront Parkway & W. 6th Street, Erie, PA 16510
Tel: (814) 825-1700; Fax: (814) 825-0775
Internet Address: http://leaferie.org/
Admission: Free
Established: 1998
Membership: Y
Wheelchair Accessible: Y
Parking: Parking lot on W. 6th Street between playground and tennis courts
Best Time(s) of Year to Visit: May to October
Facilities: Arboretum 33 acres, Trails
Activities: Events Arbor Day, Leaf Fest (Sept)

   The Lake Erie Arboretum at Frontier Park contains over 225 different varieties of trees.

FALLSINGTON

HISTORIC FALLSINGTON, INC.

4 Yardley Avenue, Fallsington, PA 19054
Tel: (215) 295-6567; Fax: (215) 295-6567
Internet Address: http://www.historicfallsington.org
Admission: Fee: adult $5.00, child $2.00, student $2.00, senior $4.00; Historic Fallsington Day (2nd Sat in Oct): free
Attendance: 6,000
Established: 1953
Membership: Y
Wheelchair Accessible: P
Parking: On street and parking lot
Open: Guided Tours (May to Oct): Monday to Saturday, 10am-4pm; Sunday, noon-4pm; Office/Shop (Apr to Dec): Monday to Saturday, 9am-5pm; Sunday, noon-5pm; Office/Shop (Jan to Mar): Monday to Friday, 9am-5pm
Best Time(s) of Year to Visit: Spring to Fall
Facilities: Architecture (90 period buildings); Gardens; Shop; Special Collections (herbs)
Activities: Guided Tours (Mar-Oct, daily, reservations suggested)

   Historic Fallsington, Inc., is a private nonpprofit historic preservation organization and museum that has been conserving and sharing the 300-year-old village of Fallsing-ton since 1953. Flower, herb, and vegetable gardens surround the village, which con-sists of over 90 historic buildings from the seventeenth, eighteenth and nineteenth centuries.

FORT WASHINGTON

THE HIGHLANDS HISTORIC MANSION AND GARDEN

7001 Sheaff Lane, Fort Washington, PA 19034-2005
Tel: (215) 641-2687
Admission: Free (Grounds), Fee (House Tour): adult $4.00, student $3.00, senior $3.00.
Attendance: 10,000
Parking: Free on site
Open: Grounds, daily, 9am-4pm
Closed: New Year's Day, Memorial Day, Independence Day, Labor Day, Thanksgiving Day, Christmas Day
Best Time(s) of Year to Visit: late Spring to Fall
Facilities: Architecture (Georgian residence, 1801; 9 outbuildings including greenhouse, barn, and springhouse); Garden (2 acre, walled); Grounds (44 acres)
Activities: Guided Tours House (Mon-Fri, 1:30pm & 3pm, reservations recommended)

The Highlands Mansion and gardens encompasses a forty-four-acre historic site containing a late-eighteenth century Georgian mansion, a two-acre formal garden, and a Gothic Revival gardener's cottage. Surrounded by massive stone walls, the gardens offer an unrivaled example of early-twentieth century estate gardening with a blend of horticulture and architecture.

GLADWYNE

HENRY FOUNDATION FOR BOTANICAL RESEARCH

801 Stony Lane, Gladwyne, PA 19035
Tel: (610) 525-2037; Fax: (610) 525-4024
Admission: Voluntary contribution
Attendance: 1,200
Established: 1949
Membership: Y
Open: Monday to Friday, 10am-4pm
Facilities: Garden (rock); Grounds (50 acres); Library; Special Collections (native magnolia)
Activities: Education Programs (adults and children); Guided Tours (groups, by appointment); Lectures

Founded by Mary Gibson Henry, a respected field botanist and plantswoman, the foundation's grounds are rugged with steep slopes, boulders, and rock outcrops, providing a multitude of microclimates for plantings from a wide variety of geographical locations and climates.

HAVERFORD

HAVERFORD COLLEGE ARBORETUM

370 Lancaster Avenue, Haverford, PA 19041-1392
Tel: (610) 896-1101; Fax: (610) 896-1095

Internet Address: http://www.haverford.edu/Arboretum/home.htm
Admission: Voluntary contribution
Established: 1974
Membership: Y
Wheelchair Accessible: Y
Parking: Free visitor parking
Open: Daily, dawn-dusk
Facilities: Arboretum (mature tree specimens, perennial beds, nature trail, woodlands, duck pond); Food Services Cafeteria; Gardens (Japanese and native plants); Grounds (204 acres); Library; Special Collections (oaks, beeches, maples), Ryan Pinetum (conifers)
Activities: Films; Guided Tours (3 per year); Lectures (3 per year); Self-guided Tours (2; center campus & pinetum)

The Haverford College campus is a designated historical arboretum. Shortly after the founding of Haverford College in 1833, William Carvill, an English gardener, developed a landscape design for the new campus that featured a diverse collection of fine trees. Today, the Campus Arboretum contains over 2,000 labeled trees, including three State Champion trees, an extensive pinetum, and an Asian garden. The Campus Arboretum Association, founded in 1974, is responsible for the preservation and perpetuation of the campus.

HERSHEY

HERSHEY GARDENS (AHS RAP)

170 Hotel Road (across from Hotel Hershey), Hershey, PA 17033
Tel: (717) 534-3492; Fax: (717) 533-8289
Internet Address: http://www.hersheygardens.org
Admission: Fee: adult $7.00, child (<3) free, child (3-15) $4.00, senior $6.50
Attendance: 100,000
Established: 1936
Membership: Y
Wheelchair Accessible: Y
Parking: Free parking
Open: April to Memorial Day, daily, 9am-6pm; Memorial Day to Labor Day, Monday to Thursday, 9am-6pm; Friday to Sunday, 9am-8pm; Labor Day to October, Daily, 9am-5pm
Best Time(s) of Year to Visit: April to October
Facilities: Butterfly House (June-3rd Sat in Sept); Gardens (children's, ornamental grass, herb, Japanese, rock, rose, perennial, annual); Grounds (23 acres); Picnic Area; Shop (botanical and butterfly-related gifts); Special Collections (dwarf conifer, holly, rose, specimen tree)
Activities: Education Programs (children and youth); Guided Tours (groups, arrange in advance—chuff@hersheygardens.org)

Established as a formal rose garden in 1936, Hershey Gardens has evolved into a botanical display garden with extensive collections of specimen trees and shrubs and nationally recognized annual displays. Featured is the 3?-acre rose garden containing more than 7,000 roses of 275 different varieties and a broad range of mature specimen trees, including giant sequoia, oriental spruce, copper beech, and a collection of hollies and dwarf conifers. Several theme gardens include a Japanese garden, a garden of ornamental grasses, a children's garden, a rock garden, and an herb garden. Seasonal displays include spring flowering bulbs, annuals, and chrysanthemums. The most recent addition to the gardens is the outdoor Butterfly House, enclosing over 400 North American butterflies of twenty different varieties. Hershey Gardens is a non-profit cultural and educational organization administered by the M. S. Hershey Foundation.

KENNETT SQUARE

LONGWOOD GARDENS

U.S. Route 1, Kennett Square, PA 19348
Tel: (610) 388-1000
Internet Address: http://www.longwoodgardens.org
Admission: Fee: adult $12.00, child (<6) free, child (6-15)
$2.00, student $6.00; $4.00 off Tues adult admission, Jan—Thanksgiving
Attendance: 900,000
Established: 1906
Membership: Y
Wheelchair Accessible: Y
Parking: Free lot on site
Open: Early January to March: daily, 9am-5pm; April to May: daily, 9am-6pm;
Memorial Day to Labor Day: Monday/Wednesday/Friday, 9am-6pm,
Tuesday/Thursday, 9am-1 hour after dusk, Saturday, 9am-1 hour after dusk, Sunday,
9am-6pm; September to October: 9am-6pm; November to Thanksgiving Day: 9am-5pm; Thanksgiving Day to early January: 9am-9pm
Facilities: Architecture Pierce-du Pont house (residence, 1730, now contains
Longwood Heritage Exhibit); Carillon; Conservatory (4 acres, opens 10am); Food
Services Terrace Restaurant (400 seat); Gardens (20; formal, fountain, idea, Italian
water, rose, topiary, water); Grounds (1,050 acres); Library (20,000 volumes); Open
Air Theatre; Shop; Visitor Center
Activities: Concerts; Demonstrations; Education Programs (adults, graduate
and undergraduate students); Festivals (seasonal, 8+/year); Flower Shows;
Guided Tours (groups 15+, reserve in advance, 388-1950); Lectures;
Performances; Symposiums

Longwood Gardens, Kennett Square, PA.

Longwood Gardens, created by industrialist Pierre S. duPont (and sometimes referred to as DuPont Gardens), offers 11,000 different types of plants; spectacular fountains; extensive educational programs, including horticultural career training and internships; and 800 horticultural and performing arts events each year. The conservatory contains an orangerie; exhibition hall; estate fruit house; bonsai collection; orchid collection (7,500 plants representing 3,200 different types of orchids); Mediterranean garden; palm house; Silver Garden, featuring gray and silver-foliaged plants adapted to the dry, arid landscape of the Mediterranean and desert regions; the Cascade Garden, featuring water cascades and bromeliads; and Tropical Terrace; as well as areas devoted to acacia, roses and hibiscus, ferns, insectivorous plants, bananas, and fruits. Highlights of the twenty exterior gardens include the water "pyrotechnics" of the Main Fountain Garden, the Italian Water Garden, the 600-foot Flower Garden Walk containing 80,000 spring bulbs followed by summer annuals and perennials, fall chrysanthemums, and the five-acre Idea Garden, divided into sections showcasing eleven different plant groups and reliable plant varieties for southeastern Pennsylvania; Children's Garden; and the Topiary Garden with an analemmatic sundial.

KUTZTOWN

RODALE INSTITUTE EXPERIMENTAL FARM—DEMONSTRATION GARDEN

611 Siegfriedale Road, Kutztown, PA 19530-9320
Tel: (610) 683-1400; Fax: (610) 683-8548
Internet Address: http://www.rodaleinstitute.org/
Attendance: 25,000
Open: Grounds, daily, dawn-dusk; Bookstore (Nov to Apr): Tuesday to Saturday, 10am-4pm; Bookstore (May to Oct): Monday, 10am-2pm; Tuesday to Saturday, 10am-4pm
Closed: Legal holidays
Facilities: Bookstore (books); Gardens (children's, herb, native plant, vegetable); Grounds Farm (333 acres)
Activities: Events Rodale Institute Field Day (July); Guided Tours (groups, (610) 683-6009); Self-guided Tours (booklet available at bookstore, $4)

Dedicated to regenerative organic agriculture and gardening, the demonstration gardens include twenty-eight raised vegetable beds; an herb garden divided into culinary, dyeing, fragrance, insecticidal, medicinal and ornamental sections; a children's garden; a native plant garden; a swale (wetland); and a composting area.

MCKEESPORT

CITY OF MCKEESPORT—RENZIEHAUSEN PARK ARBORETUM AND ROSE GARDEN

1400 Pin Oak Drive (near high school and the Penn State campus),
McKeesport, PA 15132
Tel: (412) 672-1050
Admission: Free
Facilities: Arboretum; Gardens (rose); Grounds Arboretum (3 acres), Renziehausen Park (258 acres); Shop Garden Club Clubhouse

Located beside the high school and the Penn State campus, Renziehausen Park contains an arboretum and rose garden The arboretum, established in 1938 under the WPA program, was designed by Ezra C. Stiles, a noted Pittsburgh architect. The rose garden, a part of the arboretum, contains over 1,200 roses in 28 beds, plus 300 miniature roses in 3 raised beds. An All-American Rose Selection garden, it is maintained by the Garden Club of McKeesport which also has a clubhouse located on the grounds.

MEDIA

TYLER ARBORETUM (AHS RAP)

515 Painter Road (off Route 352), Media, PA 19063-4424
Tel: (610) 566-9134; Fax: (610) 891-1490

Internet Address: http://www.tylerarboretum.org/
Admission: Fee: adult $5.00, child (<3) free, child (3-15) $3.00
Attendance: 35,000
Established: 1946
Membership: Y
Wheelchair Accessible: P
Parking: On site
Open: Late March to mid-May: Monday to Wednesday, 9am-5pm; Thursday to
Saturday, 9am-6pm; Sunday, 9am-5pm. Mid-May to mid-August: Monday to
Thursday, 9am-6pm; Friday to Sunday, 9am-8pm. Mid-August to mid-September:
Monday to Thursday, 9am-6pm; Friday to Sunday, 9am-7pm. Mid-September to late-
October: Monday to Thursday, 9am-5pm; Friday to Sunday, 9am-6pm. Late-October
to late-March: Monday to Thursday, 9am-4pm; Friday to Sunday, 9am-5pm.
Closed: Thanksgiving Day, Christmas Day
Facilities: Arboretum; Architecture Lachford Hall (residence, begun in 1738); Gardens
(bird, fragrant herb, meadow maze, native woodland walk); Greenhouse; Grounds (650
acres), Pinetum (85 acres), Uncultivated (450 acres with 20 miles of trails); Shop
Bookstore (Tues-Sat, 10am-4pm; Sun, noon-4pm); Special Collections (flowering cherry,
crab apple, holly, lilac, magnolia, rhododendron & 23 historic trees); Visitor Center
Activities: Exhibitions; Lectures

Featuring mature plant collections laid out in a natural setting, Tyler Arboretum is one
of the oldest and largest arboreta in the northeastern United States. The arboretum began
as the private collection of two brothers, Jacob and Minshall Painter. In 1825, the Painters
began the systematic planting of trees and shrubs and by the 1860s, they had essentially
transformed a large portion of their estate into an arboretum containing more than 1,000
specimens. In addition to the historic Painter trees (more than twenty still survive, including several state champions), Tyler exhibits include a pinetum, featuring pines, spruces,
hemlocks, firs, cedars, false cypresses, and larches; very fine rhododendron, flowering
cherry, crab apple, holly, magnolia, and lilac collections; the Native Woodland Walk, displaying a collection of representative plants native to the eastern region of the United
States; fragrant herb, butterfly, and bird gardens; Pink Hill, a barren of serpentine stone
that is a haven for endemic wildflowers; the Meadow Maze, a curated habitat educational
exhibit, designed to teach children and adults about the relationships of animals and plants
within the context of the historical tradition of mazes; and an uncultivated natural area.

MONT ALTO

PENNSYLVANIA STATE UNIVERSITY MONT ALTO CAMPUS—
MONT ALTO ARBORETUM

One Campus Drive, Mont Alto, PA 17237
Tel: (717) 749-6061
Internet Address: http://www.ma.psu.edu
Open: Daily
Facilities: Arboretum; Trails (2)
Activities: Self-guided Tour

The arboretum was created during the inaugural year of the Pennsylvania State Forest
Academy at Mont Alto (1903). Today, the arboretum contains 35 families, 74 genera, and
191 species of trees, the majority of which were planted between 1910 and 1925, including a collection of Asiatic conifers.

MORRISVILLE

PENNSBURY MANOR

400 Pennsbury Memorial Road, Morrisville, PA 19067
Tel: (215) 946-0400; Fax: (215) 310-1011
Internet Address: http://www.pennsburymanor.org/
Admission: Fee (includes tour): adult $5.00, child (<6) free, child (6-12) $3.00, senior
$4.50, family $13.00
Attendance: 35,000
Established: 1942
Membership: Y
Wheelchair Accessible: Y
Parking: Paved lot on site
Open: Tuesday to Saturday, 9am-5pm; Sunday, noon-5pm
Best Time(s) of Year to Visit: Spring to Fall
Facilities: Architecture (recreated late 17th-century residence with outbuildings);
Gardens (formal, herb, kitchen); Grounds (43 acres)
Activities: Demonstrations; Education Programs; Guided Tours (4/day; groups,
reserve in advance); Workshops

Meticulously reconstructed on its original foundations, Pennsbury was the country home of William Penn, founder of Pennsylvania. In addition to the 1683 manor house, the site contains a worker's cottage, a smokehouse, a bake-and-brew house, an icehouse, a blacksmith shop, and stables. Farm animals and formal and kitchen gardens can also be seen. Pennsbury Manor is administered by the Pennsylvania Historical and Museum Commission in association with the Pennsbury Society.

PHILADELPHIA

AWBURY ARBORETUM

Francis Cope House, 1 Awbury Road (off Chew Avenue), Philadelphia, PA 19138-1505
Tel: (215) 849-2855; Fax: (215) 849-0213
Internet Address: http://awbury.org/
Admission: Voluntary contribution
Attendance: 10,000
Established: 1916
Membership: Y
Open: Daily, dawn-dusk
Best Time(s) of Year to Visit: Spring to Fall
Facilities: Arboretum; Architecture (stone cottage with Gothic elements, 1860; part of
National Register Historic District); Grounds (55 acres, 140 species of trees; award-
winning secret garden)
Activities: Education Programs (children); Guided Tours ($4.00 per child)

Originally purchased in 1852 by Henry Cope as a summer home, Awbury soon became a year-round home for members of the extended Cope family. Thirty Victorian and Colonial Revival houses were built between 1860 and the 1920s, forming a unique cultural landscape. (Except for the Francis Cope House, which is now the arboretum headquarters, all of the houses are privately owned.) The basic layout of the grounds, comprised mainly of open fields shaped by groups and groves of trees, ponds, and plantings in the English landscape garden tradition, was the work of one of Henry's two sons, Thomas Cope, with the advice of William Saunders, designer of the National Cemetery at the Gettysburg Battlefield and of the U.S. Capitol grounds. Concern for the preservation of this piece of open space led to the establishment of the arboretum in 1916 by members of the Cope family. Today Awbury is one of the few nineteenth-century estates where a house and its original landscaped grounds remain intact. The arboretum also maintains the Natural Resource Education Garden (located on Ardleigh Street), a community garden with fifty-nine plots and several demonstration plots.

BARTRAM'S GARDEN

54th Street & Lindbergh Boulevard, Philadelphia, PA 19143
Tel: (215) 729-5281; Fax: (215) 729-1047
Internet Address: http://www.bartramsgarden.org
Admission: Call or visit website
Attendance: 30,000
Membership: Y
Wheelchair Accessible: P
Parking: Free parking; buses welcome
Open: Grounds, daily, dawn-dusk; House: March to December, Tuesday to Sunday, noon-4pm.
Closed: Legal Holidays, Last week of year
Facilities: Architecture (eighteenth-century homestead; National Historic Landmark); Gardens (kitchen, period flower, native plant, water, wildflower meadow); Grounds (45 acres); Shop
Activities: Education Programs; Festivals; Guided Tours House, House & Gardens; Lectures; Plant Sales; Workshops

A student of Benjamin Franklin and John Logan, John Bartram bought the site in 1728, enlarged the existing stone house and started to develop with plants collected from Europe and around North America what became America's first botanical gardens. The fourteen-room house, renovated to appear the way it did in the 1700s, is furnished with eighteenth and early nineteenth century Philadelphia decorative arts and items owned and used by Bartram. The garden includes rare, unusual, and antique plant specimens. The site is designated a National Historic Landmark.

EBENEZER MAXWELL MANSION—GARDENS

200 W. Tulpehocken Street at Greene Street, Philadelphia, PA 19144-3210
Tel: (215) 438-1861
Internet Address: http://www.maxwellmansion.org
Admission: Fee: adult $5.00, child $4.00
Membership: Y
Open: Mansion: April to December, Saturday and Sunday, 1pm-4pm; Grounds, daily, dawn-dusk.
Facilities: Architecture (high Victorian Gothic villa, 1859); Gardens (period, Victorian)
Activities: Guided Tours Mansion (schedule in advance)

Located in the Tulpehocken Station Historic District in the heart of Germantown, this Victorian suburban villa contains restored period rooms reflecting life in a Philadelphia home between 1860 and 1890. The grounds, enclosed by the mansion's original iron fence, include two Victorian gardens.

GRUMBLETHORPE

5267 Germantown Avenue (at Queen Lane), Philadelphia, PA 19144-2328
Tel: (215) 843-4820
Internet Address: http://www.philalandmarks.org
Admission: Fee: adult $5.00, child free, student $4.00, senior $4.00, family $12.00
Membership: Y
Wheelchair Accessible: P
Parking: On-street parking
Open: Tuesday/Thursday, 1pm-4pm; Saturday, 1pm-4pm
Best Time(s) of Year to Visit: Spring
Facilities: Architecture (residence, 1744)

For more than 160 years Grumblethorpe was the home of the Wister family. Originally a summer residence built by John Wister, it eventually became the family's year-round residence. Today, it is restored and furnished as it might have appeared in 1744. The grounds include a recreated period garden as well as the oldest ginko tree in America. The site is managed by the Philadelphia Society for the Preservation of Landmarks.

THE HORTICULTURE CENTER

West Fairmount Park, N. Horticulture Drive & Montgomery Avenue, Philadelphia, PA 19131
Tel: (215) 685-0096; Fax: (215) 685-0103
Admission: Donation $2.50
Attendance: 15,000
Established: 1979
Wheelchair Accessible: Y
Open: May to September, Wednesday to Sunday, 9am-3pm; October to April, Monday to Friday, 9am-3pm; Saturday to Sunday, 9am-3pm
Closed: Legal holidays
Best Time(s) of Year to Visit: Spring to Summer
Facilities: Arboretum; Gardens; Greenhouses (32,000 square feet); Grounds Azalea Garden (4 acres; sculpture, fountains), Centennial Arboretum (22 acres); Meeting Room (75 seat)
Activities: Concerts; Flower Shows Philadelphia Harvest Show (annual, September, Pennsylvania Horticultural Society); Guided Tours; Lectures; Workshops

Located in West Fairmont Park, the Horticulture Center includes a landscaped arboretum with a large reflecting pool, seasonal greenhouse displays, and outdoor formal demonstration gardens. Originally the botanical garden for the 1876 Centennial Exhibition, Centennial Arboretum contains many specimen trees and shrubs, some dating from the exhibition. Home to events throughout the year, the center is managed by the Fairmount Park Commission. Shofuso: Japanese House and Garden (Pine Breeze Villa), located on the grounds of the Horticulture Center, is listed separately. Also located in Fairmount Park, the Azalea Garden features a variety of deciduous Mollis and Ghent hybrids and native azaleas complemented by plantings of companion shrubs and understory trees.

MORRIS ARBORETUM OF THE UNIVERSITY OF PENNSYLVANIA (AHS RAP)

100 Northwestern Avenue, Philadelphia, PA 19118
Tel: (215) 247-5777 Ext: 121; Fax: (215) 248-4439
Internet Address: http://www.morrisarboretum.org
Admission: Fee: adult $8.00, child (<12) $3.00, child (13-18) $6.00, student $6.00, senior $6.00
Attendance: 100,000
Established: 1933
Membership: Y
Wheelchair Accessible: Y
Parking: Free, adjacent to Visitor Center
Open: November to March, daily, 10am-4pm; April to October, Monday to Friday, 10am-4pm; Saturday to Sunday, 10am-5pm
Closed: Thanksgiving Day, Christmas Day to New Year's Day
Facilities: Education Center Widener Visitor Center; Fernery (Victorian, 1899); Food Services Café (June-Oct, daily, 11am-2:30 p.m.); Gardens (rose); Greenhouses; Grounds (166 acres); Herbarium; Library; Shop (items for gardeners, kids and plant lovers); Special Collections (maple, magnolia species, native azalea, witch hazel family, rose, holly, conifer [especially fir])
Activities: Education Programs (adults and children); Guided Tours General (Sat & Sun, 2pm, free;, Special Interest (reserve 3 weeks in advance); Lectures; Seed Exchange; Traveling Exhibitions

Listed in the National Register of Historic Places, the site of the arboretum began in 1887 as Compton, the summer home of John and Lydia Morris, brother and sister. Avid plant collectors, the Morrises laid plans for a school and laboratory at Compton devoted to horticulture and botany. Through the stewardship and vision of the Quaker family, Compton became the Morris Arboretum of the University of Pennsylvania in 1932. Designated the Official Arboretum of the Commonwealth of Pennsylvania, the Morris Arboretum contains more than 13,000 labeled plants representing over 2,500 with a primary focus on temperate species, particularly of Asia as well as North America and Europe. Plants from twenty-seven countries are set in a Victorian landscape garden of winding paths, streams, and special garden areas. A special highlight is the Dorrance H. Hamilton Fernery, the only remaining freestanding Victorian fernery in North America.

SHOFUSO: PINE BREEZE VILLA

Horticultural Center at West Fairmount Park, Belmont Avenue and Montgomery Drive, Philadelphia, PA 19103
Tel: (215) 878-5097; Fax: (215) 878-1276
Internet Address: http://www.shofuso.com
Admission: Fee (includes optional tour): adult $4.00, child (<6) free, student $3.00, senior $3.00
Attendance: 15,000
Established: 1958
Membership: Y
Wheelchair Accessible: N
Parking: On site, paved, behind facility, tour bus parking available
Open: May to October, Tuesday to Friday, 10am-4pm; Saturday to Sunday, 11am-5pm
Facilities: Architecture (Japanese shoin-zukuri (desk-centered) house, 16th-century style shoin-zukuri (desk-centered) house, built in 16th century-style, 1953 design by

Yoshimura Junzoo); Gardens (Japanese, 16th-17th century-style, design by Sano Tansai); Grounds
Activities: Demonstrations; Education Programs; Events Bonsai Exhibit and Workshop (3rd weekend in Sept), Summer Festival (June); Festivals; Guided Tours (groups 10+, schedule in advance); Lectures; Plant Sales (3rd weekend in April); Tea Ceremony (selected Sunday afternoons, or by special arrangement)

One of the most notable and unusual public gardens in Philadelphia, Shofuso House and Garden is an authentic reconstruction of a seventeenth-century shoin-zukuri house. A gift from the America-Japan Society on behalf of the people of Japan, it was originally exhibited at New York's Museum of Modern Art in 1954 and was given to Philadelphia in 1958. Sano Tansai, a sixth generation gardener of Ryoan-ji, designed the garden around the house. Designed to resemble the topography of Japan, the one-acre garden features beautifully trained trees and a large pond with several dozen koi. In 2000, the *Journal of Japanese Gardening* ranked the garden as one of the ten highest-quality Japanese gardens outside of Japan, out of 300 sites surveyed.

WYCK HISTORIC HOUSE AND GARDENS

6026 Germantown Avenue, Philadelphia, PA 19144-2191
Tel: (215) 848-1690; Fax: (215) 848-1612
Internet Address: http://www.wyck.org/
Admission: Fee: adult $5.00, student $4.00, senior $4.00, family $10.00
Attendance: 2,750
Parking: On street
Open: April to December 15, Tuesday, 1pm-4:30pm; Thursday, 1pm-4:30pm; Saturday, 1pm-4pm, or by appointment; December 16 to March, by appointment
Closed: Legal holidays
Best Time(s) of Year to Visit: May to June
Facilities: Gardens (period; herb, rose, vegetable); Grounds (2 acres)
Activities: Guided Tours

Located in the heart of Philadelphia's Historic Northwest, Wyck was home to nine generations of the same Quaker family (1689-1973). The colonial house, its interior remodeled by Philadelphia architect William Strickland in 1824, contains original family furnishings. The grounds include a nationally known garden of old roses retaining its original plan from the 1820s, herb and vegetable gardens, a park-like lawn, and original outbuildings. The home and gardens have been designated a National Historic Landmark.

PITTSBURGH

HARTWOOD

200 Hartwood Acres, Pittsburgh, PA 15238
Tel: (412) 767-9200; Fax: (412) 767-0171
Admission: Fee (House Tour): adult $5.00, child (<6) $1.00, child (6-12) $2.00, student $3.00, senior $3.00
Membership: N
Wheelchair Accessible: N
Parking: Free on site
Open: Wednesday to Saturday, 10am-3pm; Sunday, noon-4pm

Closed: Legal holidays
Best Time(s) of Year to Visit: mid-November to mid-December (Christmas decorations)
Facilities: Architecture (Tudor-style residence, 1929 design by Alfred Hopkins); Gardens (formal, design by Rose Greely); Grounds (629 acres); Sculpture (modern); Trails
Activities: Concerts; Guided Tours (on the hour, reservations required); Performances

The site consists of the Tudor mansion house housing a collection of antiques and the estate's formal gardens. Hartwood is owned and operated by the Allegheny County Parks Department.

PHIPPS CONSERVATORY AND BOTANICAL GARDENS

Schenley Park, Frank Curto Drive, Pittsburgh, PA 15213-3830
Tel: (412) 622-6914; Fax: (412) 622-7363
Internet Address: http://www.phipps.conservatory.org/
Admission: Fee: adult $6.00, child (<2) free, child (2-12) $3.00, student $4.00, senior $5.00
Attendance: 185,000
Established: 1892
Membership: Y
Wheelchair Accessible: Y
Parking: Free parking, obtain permit
Open: Tuesday to Thursday, 9am-5pm; Friday, 9am-9pm; Saturday to Sunday, 9am-5pm
Closed: Thanksgiving Day, Christmas Day
Facilities: Conservatory (1893, Lord & Burnham); Gardens (annual, aquatic, children's discovery, dwarf conifer, Japanese, medicinal herb, medieval herb, perennial, rose, semi-shade); Greenhouses; Shop
Activities: Concerts; Education Programs (adults and children); Festivals; Flower Shows (seasonal); Guided Tours general (Tues-Sat, 11am & 1pm; Sun, 1pm; free with admission), Groups (15+, schedule in advance, 622-6915 x6803); Plant Sales

A gift to the City of Pittsburgh from industrialist/philanthropist Henry Phipps, the Phipps Conservatory and Gardens is among the nation's oldest and largest Victorian glass houses, featuring 13 rooms of lush tropical plants, palms, 3,000 orchids and bromeliads, a miniature orchid collection, ferns, cacti and succulent plants, sub-tropical fruits and spice plants, a formal French knot garden, an economic plant exhibit, topiary, seasonal flower shows, and butterflies. Outdoor gardens and collections include the Outdoor Garden, a tiered garden composed of many smaller gardens including a perennial garden, a collection of dwarf conifers, a pink and white border, annual beds, a semi-shade garden, a medicinal plant garden, and a medieval herb garden; a children's discovery garden; a Japanese courtyard garden; a bonsai collection; and aquatic gardens. The site is leased by the City of Pittsburgh to Phipps Conservatory, Inc., a non-profit private organization that manages the facility.

PITTSBURGH ZOO AND AQUARIUM

1 Wild Place, Pittsburgh, PA 15206
Tel: (412) 665-3640; Fax: (412) 365-2583
Admission: Fee (Dec-Mar): adult $6.00, child $4.00, senior $5.00; Fee (Apr-Nov): adult $8.00, child $5.00, senior $7.00
Attendance: 700,000
Established: 1898
Membership: Y

Wheelchair Accessible: Y
Parking: On site, $3.50/vehicle
Open: Day after Labor Day to day before Memorial Day, daily, 9am-5pm; Memorial
Day to Labor Day, daily, 10am-6pm
Closed: Christmas Day, New Year's Day, Thanksgiving Day
Facilities: Climatic Areas (Asian forest, African savanna, tropical rain forest); Food
Services Animal Connections Café (Memorial Day-Labor Day, daily), Northern Shores
Café (daily, snacks—Memorial Day—Labor Day), Safari Plaza Restaurants (daily),
Safari Village Restaurant (Memorial Day-Labor Day, daily); Grounds (77 acres);
Shops (3)

The zoo displays over 5,000 animals representing over 400 animal species in exhibits
emphasizing naturalistic habitats, enabling animals to appear as they would in the wild.
Of particular botanical interest is the Tropical Forest Complex, a 5-acre indoor rain forest
housing more than 150 species of tropical plants as well 16 species of endangered and
threatened primates. Other exhibits include an Asian forest and an African savanna. Formerly run by the City of Pittsburgh, in 1994 the zoo became a private non-profit organization owned and operated by the Zoological Society of Pittsburgh.

RODEF SHALOM BIBLICAL BOTANICAL GARDEN

Rhodef Shalom Congregation, 4905 5th Avenue, Pittsburgh, PA 15213
Tel: (412) 621-6566; Fax: (412) 621-5475
Internet Address: http://www.biblicalgardenpittsburgh.org
Admission: Free
Attendance: 4,500
Established: 1987
Wheelchair Accessible: Y
Parking: Parking lot behind temple
Open: June to September 15, Sunday to Tuesday, 10am-2pm; Wednesday, 10am-2pm
and 7pm-9pm; Thursday, 10am-2pm; Saturday, noon-1pm
Facilities: Garden (1/3 acre, Biblical)
Activities: Education Programs (adults); Guided Tours (1st Wed in month, 12:15pm-
1pm; Groups (8-40, Sun-Thurs); Lectures (summer); Temporary Exhibitions

Located in the Oakland/Shadyside section of Pittsburgh near Carnegie Mellon University, the garden displays more than 150 varieties of plants either from ancient Israel or
with a biblical name or reference. Each year the garden features a particular theme; past
themes have included medicinal plants, plants employed in the production of textiles, and
plants used in brewing beer.

POTTSTOWN

GREEN VALLEYS ASSOCIATION—WELKINWEIR (WELKINWEIR)

1368 Prizer Road (off Route 100), Pottstown, PA 19465
Tel: (610) 469-7543; Fax: (610) 469-2218
Internet Address: http://www.greenvalleys.org/welkinweir.asp
Parking: Small gravel parking lot; larger one under construction
Open: Daily, varies by season
Best Time(s) of Year to Visit: Spring to Fall

Facilities: Gardens (azalea walk, children's); Grounds (197 acres; pinetum; barn ruins; hiking trails); Pond (water lilies)
Activities: Education Programs; Guided Tours for groups (by appointment); Plant Sales

A nature education center and the headquarters of the Green Valleys Association (GVA), a watershed protection organization, Welkinweir features both plants in natural habitats and more formal gardens surrounding the house. Everett Rodebaugh, the founder of GVA, and his wife Grace purchased the land during the Depression. They set about restoring the land by re-establishing native trees and meadows. A series of ponds was constructed in the valley. The acquisition of an entire nursery provided the beginning of formal planting around the house. A Children's Garden, containing four theme gardens (butterfly, habitat, Indian, and organic crops) was created to enhance GVA's educational programs.

READING

READING PUBLIC MUSEUM

500 Museum Road, Reading, PA 19611-1425
Tel: (610) 371-5850 *Ext:* 250; Fax: (610) 371-5632
Internet Address: http://www.readingpublicmuseum.org/
Admission: Fee (Museum): adult $7.00, child (4-17) $5.00
Attendance: 40,000
Established: 1904
Membership: Y
Wheelchair Accessible: Y
Parking: Free on site
Open: Tuesday, 11am-5pm; Wednesday, 11am-8pm; Thursday to Saturday, 11am-5pm; Sunday, noon-5pm
Closed: Christmas Day
Facilities: Auditorium (130 seat); Galleries (17, art and science); Grounds (25 acres); Library (18,000 volumes); Shop
Activities: Arboretum; Concerts; Education Programs (adults and children); Gallery Talks; Guided Tours; Lectures; Permanent Exhibits; Temporary Exhibitions; Traveling Exhibitions

Originally administered by the Reading Public School District, the museum became an independent entity in 1992 while retaining a strong commitment to its tradition of using the collection for teaching and research. The museum grounds contain hundreds of flowering trees, shrubs, and sculptures. The twenty-five acre arboretum was designed by John Nolan, a landscape architect from Harvard. Many specimens on the grounds were donated by Harvard's Arnold Arboretum.

SOLEBURY TOWNSHIP

BOWMAN'S HILL WILDFLOWER PRESERVE

1635 River Road (Routes 32 & 532) (2½ miles south of New Hope),
Solebury Township, PA 18977
Tel: (215) 862-2924; Fax: (215) 862-1846
Internet Address: http://www.bhwp.org

Admission: Free: adult $5.00, child (4-14) $2.00,
senior $3.00
Attendance: 56,000
Established: 1934
Membership: Y
Wheelchair Accessible: Y
Parking: Free on site
Open: Grounds, daily, 8:30am-sunset; Visitor Center,
daily, 9am-5pm
Facilities: Auditorium (100 seat); Grounds (100 acres);
Library (300 volume); Native Plant Nursery; Picnic Area;
Shop (nature/gardening books, gifts, seeds, live plants);
Special Collections (native plants); Trails (26)
Activities: Demonstrations; Films; Guided Tours (daily, 2pm); Lecture Series; Plant
Sales (spring & fall); Temporary Exhibitions

Located near the Delaware River in Bucks County, Bowman's Hill Wildflower Preserve
contains a botanical collection of over 1,000 species of Pennsylvania native trees and
plants set in broad array of natural and naturalistic habitats. Eastern deciduous woodland,
open meadows, and streamside habitat make up the bulk of the preserve. A pond, a bog,
and several specialized habitats illustrate other environments and the native plants that in-
habit them. Illustrated seasonal *Blooming Guides*, highlighting the flowering plants of certain
trails, are available for a small fee.

SWARTHMORE

SCOTT ARBORETUM OF SWARTHMORE COLLEGE (AHS RAP)

500 College Avenue, Swarthmore, PA 19081-1397
Tel: (610) 328-8025; Fax: (610) 328-8673
Internet Address: http://www.scottarboretum.org/
Admission: Voluntary contribution
Attendance: 30,000
Established: 1929
Membership: Y
Wheelchair Accessible: Y
Parking: Free, visitor parking lots
Open: Grounds, daily, dawn-dusk; Office: September to May, Monday to Friday,
8am-noon & 1pm-4:30pm; Office: June to August, Monday to Thursday, 8am-noon &
1pm-4:30pm; Friday, 8am-noon
Closed: Christmas Day to New Year's Day
Best Time(s) of Year to Visit: May to October
Facilities: Gardens (fragrance, perennial, rhododendron, summer bloom, texture,
winter, water); Grounds (300 acres); Library (1,000 volumes); Pinetum; Special
Collections (holly)
Activities: Education Programs (adults & children); Guided Tours General (regularly
scheduled), Groups (10+, schedule in advance); Lectures; Self-guided Tours (brochure
available); Temporary Exhibitions

The Scott Arboretum, containing over 4,000 kinds of ornamental plants, features trees,
shrubs, vines, and herbaceous plants that are hardy in the climate of eastern Pennsylvania
and are suitable for residential gardens. The arboretum maintains numerous gardens

throughout the college campus, as well as Crum Woods, a 200-acre native woodland inter-laced with walking trails. Plants have been labeled with their scientific and common names and grouped in collections to make easy and meaningful comparisons. Gardens include the Dean Bond Rose Garden containing 650 roses representing more than 200 varieties; the Rhododendron Display Garden, featuring over 300 kinds of native and exotic, evergreen and deciduous rhododendrons set under a canopy of mature trees; a fragrance garden, highlighting plants with fragrant foliage or flowers; a summer bloom border with masses of butterfly bush, summersweet, and crape myrtle, complemented by an assortment of peren-nials and annuals; a winter garden, showcasing plants that provide ornamental interest with bark, berries, and flowers from November through March; the Nason Garden, featuring plants with contrasting textures; the Cosby Courtyard, featuring containers and vines; the Teaching Garden and Entrance Garden that grace the Scott Arboretum's headquarters building; and a wide variety of other campus plantings. Other areas of interest include the James R. Frorer Holly Collection, consisting of 350 different types of hollies; a pinetum, displaying a diverse collection of pines, spruces, firs and other ornamental conifers inter-spersed with spring- and summer-flowering trees; the Scott Outdoor Amphitheater, de-signed by noted Philadelphia landscape architect Thomas W. Sears; and the Biostream, a naturalistic planting of flowering shrubs and perennials surrounding a rock-filled drainage bed demonstrating a creative and responsible use of storm water run-off.

UNIVERSITY PARK

THE PENNSYLVANIA STATE UNIVERSITY—THE ARBORETUM AT PENN STATE

Between Park Avenue & Mount Nittany Expressway. (adjacent to north end of campus), University Park, PA 16802-4300
Tel: (814) 865-9118; Fax: (814) 865-3725
Internet Address: http://www.arboretum.psu.edu
Admission: Free
Membership: N
Wheelchair Accessible: N
Parking: Bellefonte Trail: Sunset Park, end of McKee Street, about15 spaces
Open: Grounds, daily, sunrise-sunset
Best Time(s) of Year to Visit: April to October
Facilities: Arboretum (Hybrid Chestnut Plantation); Conservation Facilities Air Quality Learning & Demonstration Center (outdoor center); Grounds Planned Arboretum (395 acres, 1992 design by Sasaki and Associates, Inc.), Planned Landscape and Botanic Gardens (56-acres, 2002 design by Marshall-Tyler-Rausch); Trail Bellefonte Central Rail Trail (1.3 miles)
Activities: Guided Tours Air Quality Learning & Demonstration Center (during warmer months, arrange in advance)

The university has announced plans to develop over the next ten years a 395-acre ar-boretum on the north side of the campus. Currently, three portions of the project are available to visitors, The Air Quality Learning and Demonstration Center, an outdoor site offering display panels about air pollution formation/transportation and research gardens/plant exhibits that demonstrate the effect of ozone on sensitive plant species; the Bellefonte Central Rail Trail, a former railroad bed transformed into a pedestrian/bike trail; and the Hybrid Chestnut Plantation, a breeding program working on creating a blight-resistant variety of the American chestnut. The planned site for the arboretum at Penn State is a 395-acre tract fronting on Park Avenue and stretching back to the northwest into Big Hollow and out to the Mt. Nittany Expressway. While the majority of the grounds will be devoted to managing natural plant communities and research, the fifty-six-acre Mitchell Tract, adjacent to Park Avenue, will contain intensive landscape displays and facilities for workshops and events for the university and public alike. As a horticultural museum and showcase, the cultivated gardens and exhibits will celebrate different growing environments and demonstrate the plants that are best for growing conditions in Pennsylvania. The major elements of this site will include an Education Center; a 10,000-square-foot conservatory; pond, aquatic gardens, and fountain; a four seasons garden; a rose and fragrance garden; and a children's education center. Full directions to the arboretum and parking will be available on the website when construction is completed.

PENNSYLVANIA STATE UNIVERSITY HORTICULTURAL TRIAL GARDENS

Park Avenue & Bigler Road, University Park, PA 16801
Tel: (814) 863-2190; Fax: (814) 863-6139
Internet Address: http://hortweb.cas.psu.edu/garden/
Admission: Free
Established: 1933
Membership: Y
Parking: Free on site
Open: Daily, dawn-dusk
Best Time(s) of Year to Visit: July to August
Facilities: Arboretum (under development); Gardens (annual, medieval, perennial, vegetable, woody plant); Grounds (7 acres)
Activities: Education Programs Field Days (late July-Aug); Guided Tours (on request); Workshops

The garden includes perennial, annual, and woody plant collections and displays; a recreation of a fourteenth-century European garden and plant collection; an official All-America Selections trial garden, and a Fleuroselect display garden. The university has announced plans to develop over the next ten years a 395-acre arboretum on the north side of the campus. In conjunction with the arboretum, plans call for the relocation of the Flower Trial Gardens together with new demonstration gardens, theme gardens, a conservatory and propagation greenhouses to the Mitchell Tract off Bigler Road adjacent to Park Avenue.

UPLAND

CROZER-CHESTER MEDICAL CENTER—CROZER ARBORETUM

1 Medical Center Boulevard, Upland, PA 19018
Tel: (610) 447-2281
Facilities: Gardens Leona Gold Gardens (25 acres); Greenhouse; Grounds Medical Center Campus (68 acres)

The Crozer Arboretum contains more than 1,400 rhododendrons and a rich palette of native and exotic plants and trees.

VILLANOVA

APPLEFORD/PARSONS-BANKS ARBORETUM

770 Mount Moro Road, Villanova, PA 19085
Tel: (610) 527-4280; Fax: (610) 527-0304
Internet Address: http://www.applefordestate.com
Admission: Free
Membership: N
Wheelchair Accessible: Y
Parking: Free on site
Open: Grounds, daily, sunrise-sunset; House, by appointment
Best Time(s) of Year to Visit: Spring to Fall
Facilities: Arboretum; Architecture (Colonial Revival stone manor house, begun 1728 enlarged and renovated by Philadelphia architect R. Brognard Okie in 1920s); Gardens (formal); Greenhouse (seasonal plants & cut-flowers available for purchase); Grounds (22 acres, 1920s design by landscape architect Thomas Sears)

The harmonious blending of house, arboretum, and formal grounds is the product of a collaboration of Colonial Revival architect R. Brognard Okie and landscape architect Thomas Sears. The landscape features gardens, ponds, an island, and waterfalls.

WALLINGFORD

TAYLOR MEMORIAL ARBORETUM

10 Ridley Drive, Wallingford, PA 19086-7256
Tel: (610) 876-2649
Admission: Free
Established: 1931
Membership: N
Wheelchair Accessible: P
Parking: Parking area for four cars
Open: Daily, 9am-4pm
Closed: Legal holidays
Facilities: Arboretum; Grounds (30 acres); Special Collections (arborvitae, azalea, boxwood, dogwood, juniper, lilac, magnolia, Japanese maple, viburnum, witchhazel)

The arboretum contains unusual plant collections and wildlife habitats set among natural rock outcrops. Habitats include Anne's Grotto, a former quarry site now home to mosses, ferns, wildflowers, and azaleas; an eighteenth-century millrace, waterfall, and pond along nearby Ridley Creek; woodlands; and meadows. The arboretum currently features three Pennsylvania State Champion Trees: a giant dogwood, a needle juniper, and a lacebark elm.

WAYNE

CHANTICLEER

786 Church Road, Wayne, PA 19087-4713
Tel: (610) 687-4163; Fax: (610) 293-0149
Internet Address: http://www.chanticleergarden.org
Admission: Suggested contribution: adult $5.00, child (<16) free
Attendance: 23,000
Membership: Y
Wheelchair Accessible: Y
Parking: Free on site
Open: April to May, Wednesday to Saturday, 10am-5pm; May to August, Wednesday
to Thursday, 10am-5pm; Friday, 10am-8pm; Saturday, 10am-5pm; September to
October, Wednesday to Saturday, 10am-5pm
Facilities: Gardens (courtyard, English cutting, native wildflower, perennial, ruin,
spring bulbs, summer, vegetable, water, woodland); Grounds (351 acres)
Activities: Guided Tours Groups 10+ (Apr-Oct, Wed-Fri, 10:30am & 1:30pm,
$10/person, reserve in advance, 687-0812)

Originally the private residence of Adolph Rosengarten, Sr., head of the chemical company Rosengarten and Sons, Chanticleer became a public garden in 1993. Emphasizing
the art of horticulture, Chanticleer offers unusual and imaginative combinations of plants
in a variety of settings. Thousands of bulbs clothe the ground in spring, followed by orchards of flowering trees with native wildflowers blooming in the woods. A vegetable garden complements a cut-flower garden. Courtyards are a framework for herbaceous perennials, punctuated by containers of tropical plants. Vines grow in nooks and crannies,
trailing and twining. A "sculpture" of grains and boulders undulates while a perennial garden reaches its peak in the warmest days of summer. A woodland garden carpeted with
exotic ground covers and full of rarities precedes a water garden surrounded by grasses
and sweet-smelling herbs and a ruin garden with marble, granite, and other stone pieces
that define the ruin's spaces.

PUERTO RICO

The number in the parentheses following the city name indicates the number of gardens/
arboreta in that municipality. If there is no number, one is understood. For example, in
the text one listing would be found under San Juan.

SAN JUAN

MUSEO DE ARTE DE PUERTO RICO (MAPR)

299 De Diego Avenue, Santurce, San Juan, PR 00909
Tel: (787) 977-6277 *Ext:* 2230
Internet Address: http://www.mapr.org
Admission: Fee: adult $5.00, child $3.00
Established: 2000
Open: Tuesday, 10am-5pm; Wednesday, 10am-8pm; Thursday to Saturday, 10am-5pm; Sunday, 11am-6pm
Facilities: Amphitheater; Architecture East Wing (2000 design by designed by arquitects Otto Reyes & Luis Gutierrez), West Wing (neo-classical former municipal hospital, 1920 design by William Schimmelphening); Food Services (restaurant); Galleries; Grounds Gardens (5 acres); Shop; Theatre (400 seats)
Activities: Education Programs; Guided Tours (977-6277, x2230)

The museum collects, exhibits, and interprets Puerto Rico's artistic tradition and other art traditions from Latin America and the rest of the world. Galleries in the West Wing display the museum's permanent collection and loans of Puerto Rican art from colonial times to the present in changing exhibitions. On the fourth floor over 10,000 square feet of gallery space for temporary exhibitions surround an atrium. The garden features a variety of native Puerto Rican flora, including nearly 106,000 trees, shrubs, ground covers, and flowers. A winding trail connects the various settings of the gardens: a forest of native trees, a tropical forest, a bamboo forest, and meadows. Along the trail, sculptures by Puerto Rican artists are displayed.

RHODE ISLAND

The number in the parentheses following the city name indicates the number of gardens/ arboreta in that municipality. If there is no number, one is understood. For example, in the text one listing would be found under each Rhode Island city.

BRISTOL

BLITHEWOLD MANSION—GARDENS AND ARBORETUM (AHS RAP)

101 Ferry Road (Route 114), Bristol, RI 02809
Tel: (401) 253-2707; Fax: (401) 253-0412
Internet Address: http://www.blithewold.org/
Admission: Fee (Mansion and Grounds): adult $10.00, child (<17) free, student $8.00, senior $8.00, family $26.00
Attendance: 28,000
Established: 1976
Membership: Y
Open: Gardens, daily, 10am-5pm; House: April 15 to October 14, Wednesday to Sunday, 10am-4pm.
Facilities: Architecture (45-room English Country Manor-style mansion, ca. 1907); Gardens (bamboo grove, display, enclosed, formal, rock, rose, water); Greenhouse; Grounds (33 acres, 1896-1913 design by landscape architect John DeWolf); Library (200 volumes); Shop (Apr 15-Oct 14, Wed-Sun, 10am-4pm)
Activities: Classes; Concerts; Education Programs (adults and undergraduate students); Guided Tours (groups reserve in advance); Lectures; Plant Sales

Blithewold Mansion, Gardens and Arboretum is a landscaped historic property situated on Bristol Harbor with sweeping views overlooking Narragansett Bay. The grounds feature a primarily informal landscape with wide borders of flowers, shrubs, and trees. A sweeping 10-acre lawn stops at the water's edge and is the perfect setting for more than 1,500 trees and shrubs that grow along its borders. Specimen trees include magnolia, linden, ginkgo, black gum, metasequoia, franklinia, and sequoiadendron as well as maple, hemlock, oak, and beech. There are over 300 different kinds of woody plants in the collection, which contains both native and exotic species. Blithewold is operated and leased by Save Blithewold Inc.

KINGSTON

KINNEY AZALEA GARDENS

2391 Kingstown Road (Route 108) (near the University of Rhode Island), Kingston, RI 02881
Tel: (401) 783-2396
Admission: Free

Established: 1955
Membership: N
Wheelchair Accessible: P
Parking: On site, limited
Open: Daily, daylight hours
Best Time(s) of Year to Visit: May to June (bloom)
Facilities: Garden (azalea/rhododendron); Grounds Gardens (6 acres)

The gardens offer thousands of azaleas representing over 800 cultivars and species, many rhododendron cultivars and species, mountain laurel, and leucothoe as well as many other shrubs, trees, wildflowers, and specimen evergreens. The gardens are supported through plant sales and donations.

NEWPORT

THE PRESERVATION SOCIETY OF NEWPORT COUNTY— NEWPORT MANSION GARDENS

424 Bellevue Avenue, Newport, RI 02840
Tel: (401) 847-1000
Internet Address: http://www.newportmansions.org/
Admission: Fee—call or see website
Open: Call or see website
Facilities: Architecture Chateau-sur-Mer (original High Victorian residence, 1852; substantial remodeling in Second Empire French style, 1870s by Richard Morris Hunt), Marble House (Classical Revival residence, 1888-1892 design by Richard Morris Hunt), Rosecliff (residence modeled after the Grand Trianon, 1889-1902 design by New York architect Stanford White), The Breakers (Classical Revival residence, 1893 design by Richard Morris Hunt), The Elms (residence modeled after eighteenth-century French chateau, 1898-1901 design by Philadelphia architect Horace Trumbauer); Grounds Rosecliff (restored rose garden), The Breakers (landscape design by Ernest Bowditch), The Elms (11 acres, Classical Revival gardens and extensive plantings of specimen trees); Shops. Activities: Flower Shows Newport Flower Show (annual); Guided Tours (groups 20+, arrange at least 2 weeks in advance)

While not rivaling the grandeur of the gilded age mansions, a number of the accompanying gardens are worthy of notice. As part of the centennial of the Elms, the Preservation Society of Newport County has restored the Sunken Garden, a masterpiece of Classical Revival landscape design. The Rosecliff grounds include a formal rose garden containing approximately 200 hybrid tea roses bounded by boxwood. The Preservation Society of Newport County, a non-profit educational organization, operates eleven historic properties and landscapes (five of which are National Historic Landmarks).

PORTSMOUTH

THE PRESERVATION SOCIETY OF NEWPORT COUNTY— GREEN ANIMALS TOPIARY GARDEN

380 Cory's Lane (off Route 114), Portsmouth, RI 02871-1324
Tel: (401) 683-1267

Internet Address: http://www.newportmansions.org/connoisseurs/greenanimals.html
Admission: See website or call for fees
Open: See website or call
Facilities: Gardens (topiary, fruit, rose, vegetable); Grounds (11 acres); Picnic Area

Started by Thomas Brayton about 1880, Green Animals is the oldest and most northern topiary garden in the United States. It consists of eighty pieces of topiary sculpted from California privet, yew, and English boxwood, including twenty-one animals and birds in addition to geometric figures and ornamental designs as well as a rose arbor, espaliered fruit trees, and a vegetable garden. The house contains period furnishings and a Victorian toy collection. The site is a property of the Preservation Society of Newport County.

WESTERLY

WILCOX PARK

44 Broad Street, Westerly, RI 02891
Tel: (401) 596-2877; Fax: (401) 596-5600
Internet Address: http://www.clan.lib.ri.us/wes/index.htm
Admission: No charge, donations accepted
Attendance: 20,000
Established: 1898
Membership: Y
Wheelchair Accessible: P
Parking: Easy access from Merchants Parking Area and on street
Open: Daily, dawn-9pm
Facilities: Grounds (15 acres, designed by Warren H. Manning; arboretum); Special Collections (conifer, day lily); Statuary
Activities: Concerts; Festival Garden Market Fair; Performances (Shakespeare in the Park); Self-guided Tours (map provided)

Located on downtown Westerly, Wilcox Park contains specimen trees, conifer, and day lily collections, shrubs, display flower beds, and perennial borders as well as a koi pond, fountain, and monuments. Wilcox Park is owned and maintained by the Memorial and Library Association of Westerly.

SOUTH CAROLINA

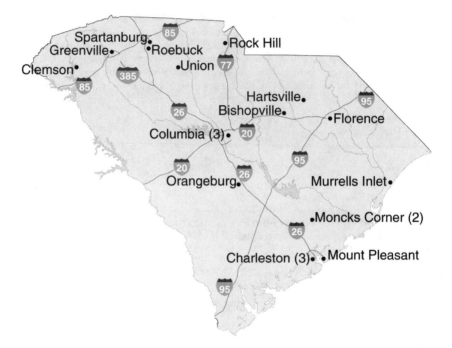

The number in the parentheses following the city name indicates the number of gardens/ arboreta in that municipality. If there is no number, one is understood. For example, in the text three listings would be found under Columbia and one listing under Orangeburg.

BISHOPVILLE

FRYAR'S TOPIARY GARDEN

145 Broad Acres Road (1 mile north of I-20, Exit 116), Bishopville, SC 29010-2819
Tel: (803) 484-5581
Internet Address: http://www.fryarstopiary.com
Open: Daily, 9am-5pm
Facilities: Garden (topiary, designed by Pearl Fryar);
Grounds (3 acres)

The garden displays trees and shrubs formed into arches, spirals, and other geometric designs.

CHARLESTON

AUDUBON SWAMP GARDEN AT MAGNOLIA PLANTATION

3550 Ashley River Road (State Route 61, 10 miles past U.S. Route 17 junction), Charleston, SC 29414
Tel: (800) 367-3517; Fax: (843) 571-5346
Internet Address: http://www.magnoliaplantation.com
Admission: Fee: adult $5.00, child (6-12) $4.00;
Group rates available.
Established: 1985
Parking: Parking on site
Open: March to October, daily, 8am-dusk (enter by 5pm); November to February, daily, restricted, call for information
Facilities: Grounds (60-acre swamp)

Accessible via boardwalks, bridges, and dikes, the cypress and tupelo swamp contains plantings of wildflowers, bog plants, and native shrubs, enhanced by plantings of exotic flora. It is also the habitat of a wide variety of wildlife, including egrets, herons, turtles, and alligators. Though located at Magnolia Plantation, the Audubon Swamp Garden is operated independently of the plantation.

MAGNOLIA PLANTATION AND GARDENS

3550 Ashley River Road (Route 61), Charleston, SC 29414-2503
Tel: (800) 367-3517; Fax: (843) 571-5346

Internet Address: http://www.magnoliaplantation.com
Admission: Museum: adult $13.00, child (6-12) $6.50;
Group rates available
Attendance: 160,000
Established: 1870
Membership: Y
Wheelchair Accessible: Y
Parking: Parking on site
Open: Daylight Savings Time, daily, 8am-5:30pm; Eastern Standard Time, daily, 8am-5pm
Facilities: Architecture (plantation house, begun 1760, moved to site after the Civil
War, subsequent additions); Gardens (50 acres; plantation-style, biblical, maze,
tropical, wildflower, herb, camellia); Grounds (500 acres); Shop; Wildlife Refuge
Activities: Arts Festival; Concerts; Guided Tours (Nature Train, Nature Boat,
house tour)

Listed in the National Register of Historic Places, the plantation house contains a collection of early American museum-quality antique furnishings. Opened to the public in
1870, Magnolia is the oldest public garden in the United States. Set in a plantation landscape of live oaks, cypress, azaleas, and Spanish moss, there are also a biblical garden, a
Barbados tropical garden, an eighteenth-century herb garden, a wildflower garden, and a
maze of large Camellia sasanquas interspersed with holly. Collections include 250 varieties of Indica azalea and 900 varieties of camellia. The plantation has been continuously
owned and operated by the Drayton family since 1676. Also located at Magnolia Plantation, the Audubon Swamp Garden is listed separately.

MIDDLETON PLACE

4300 Ashley River Road (Route 61), Charleston, SC 29414
Tel: (803) 556-6020; Fax: (803) 766-4460
Internet Address: http://www.middletonplace.org/
Admission: Fee, Gardens and Stables: adult $20.00, child (<6) free, child (6-12) $15.00
Attendance: 100,000
Established: 1974
Membership: Y
Wheelchair Accessible: Y
Open: Grounds, daily, 9am-5pm; House, Monday, 1:30pm-4:30pm; Tuesday to
Sunday, 10am-4:30pm
Closed: Thanksgiving Day, Christmas Day
Facilities: Architecture (house, ca. 1755); Food Services Restaurant (250 seats; dinner,
reservation required); Gardens (eighteenth century classic, geometric); Grounds (65
acres); Library; Shop Garden Market, Museum Shop
Activities: Concerts; Guided Tours House (on the hour and ½ hour, $10/person);
Lectures

Middleton Place is a carefully preserved eighteenth-century plantation and National
Historic Landmark, encompassing America's oldest landscaped gardens, the House Museum, and the Plantation Stableyards. The gardens reflect the elegant symmetry of seventeenth-century European design. Sculpted terraces, parterres, and reflection pools inhabited by swans are highlights of their intricate design. Rare camellias bloom in winter,
while vibrant azaleas blanket the hillside above Rice Mill Pond in the spring. The Middleton Place House Museum, built in 1755 as a gentleman's guest wing, became the family
residence after the plantation burned during the Civil War. In the Plantation Stableyards,
craftspeople including a blacksmith, potter, carpenter, and weaver, recreate the activities
of a self-sustaining Low Country plantation.

CLEMSON

CLEMSON UNIVERSITY—SOUTH CAROLINA BOTANICAL GARDEN

102 Garden Trail, Clemson, SC 29634-0174
Tel: (864) 656-3405; Fax: (864) 656-4960
Internet Address: http://virtual.clemson.edu/groups/scbg/index.htm
Admission: Free
Attendance: 110,000
Established: 1957
Membership: Y
Wheelchair Accessible: Y
Parking: Free on site
Open: Daily, dawn-dusk
Facilities: Arboretum Roland Schoenike Arboretum (70 acres); Architecture Hanover House (French Huguenot house, 1716); Discovery Center (Mon-Sat, 9am-5pm; Sun, 1pm-5pm); Garden (butterfly, camellia, ground cover, home horticulture demonstration, therapeutic horticulture, hosta, meditation, pioneer, heirloom vegetable, wildflower meadow, xeriscape); Grounds (270 acres); Picnic Area; Shop; Special Collections (dwarf conifer, magnolia, rhododendron)
Activities: Concerts; Education Programs (adult and children); Guided Tours; Lectures; Nature Walks; Plant Sales

The South Carolina Botanical Garden's offers a diversity of cultivated and natural land-scapes. The site contains twenty niche gardens, including a camellia garden; a hosta garden; an heirloom plant collection; a wildflower meadow; an arboretum, containing more than 1,000 woody plants of historic and commercial value; and a xeriscape garden. There also are two historic houses: Hanover House, an historic French Huguenot house built in 1716, with heirloom vegetables in its garden, and the Hunt Family Cabin, built in 1825.

COLUMBIA

RIVERBANKS ZOOLOGICAL PARK AND BOTANICAL GARDEN

500 Wildlife Parkway (Highway 126 & Greystone Boulevard), Columbia, SC 29210
Tel: (803) 779-8717; Fax: (803) 253-6381
Internet Address: http://www.riverbanks.org/
Admission: Fee: adult $8.75, child (<3) free, child (3-12) $6.25, student $7.50, senior $7.25
Attendance: 850,000
Established: 1974
Membership: Y
Wheelchair Accessible: Y
Parking: Free parking on-site
Open: April to August, Monday to Friday, 9am-4pm, Saturday to Sunday, 9am-5pm; September to March, Monday to Sunday, 9am-4pm
Closed: Thanksgiving Day, Christmas Day
Facilities: Food Services Restaurant; Grounds Botanical Garden (70 acres); Shop; Zoological Park
Activities: Concerts; Education Programs (adults and children); Lectures

Located on the west bank of the Saluda River across from Riverbanks Zoo, the botanical garden site offers native and exotic plant exhibits and features an American Hemerocallis Society display garden, The site contains three distinct habitats: flood plain valley, valley slopes, and uplands. The 34,000-square-foot walled garden features many smaller themed gardens and annual displays and a fine Crinum collection.

ROBERT MILLS HOUSE & PARK

1615 Blanding Street, Columbia, SC 29201
Tel: (803) 252-1770; Fax: (803) 252-7695
Internet Address: http://www.historiccolumbia.org
Admission: Fee: adult $5.00, child (<6) free, child (6-17) $3.00, student $3.00, senior $3.00
Attendance: 30,000
Established: 1961
Membership: Y
Wheelchair Accessible: P
Parking: Free parking available
Open: Tuesday to Saturday, 10am-4pm; Sunday, 1pm-5pm
Facilities: Architecture (house, 1818-1835, designed by Robert Mills); Grounds (4 acres); Gardens
Activities: Guided Tours

The antebellum city home is furnished in period pieces from the years 1835-1855. Trees, plants, and flowers surround the Mills property, but the most important feature is the Founders' Garden, situated behind the home. It replicates a nineteenth-century southern gardens, acting as an interpretation and public gathering site.

UNIVERSITY OF SOUTH CAROLINA—CAMPUS GARDENS

1100 Sumter Street, Columbia, SC 29201-3717
Tel: (803) 377-7000; Fax: (803) 576-6104
Internet Address: http://facilities.sc.edu
Admission: Free
Attendance: 30,000
Established: 1801
Membership: N
Wheelchair Accessible: P
Parking: Parking throughout campus
Open: 24 hours

The university campus contains flora traditional to a southern institution, including azaleas, camellias, roses, crepe myrtles, and other flowering shrubs, hardwoods, annuals, and here and there, palmetto palms. Listed on the National Register of Historic Places, the oldest part of the campus, the historic Horseshoe, features eleven Federal-style buildings interspersed with a variety of gardens. Other gardens on campus include the Alumni House Garden, a formal garden designed by George Baetsil, who landscaped many homes in Columbia; the A. C. Moore Garden, a wildlife garden containing a small pond surrounded by flowering shrubs, tall magnolias, and water oak; Gibbes Green, a shaded area featuring landscaped rolling lawns; and Preston Green, a newly constructed garden surrounding the president's house.

FLORENCE

CITY OF FLORENCE—HENRY TIMROD PARK (TIMROD PARK)

Spruce Street & Timrod Park Drive, Florence, SC 29501-5152
Tel: (843) 665-3253
Admission: Free
Parking: Parking areas nearby
Open: dawn-dusk
Facilities: Amphitheater; Architecture (Timrod Schoolhouse); Gardens; Grounds (18 acres)

In addition to gardens, Timrod Park contains the Florence Museum of Art, Science, and History and a one-room schoolhouse.

GREENVILLE

FURMAN UNIVERSITY—ROSE AND JAPANESE GARDENS

Campus, 3300 Poinsett Highway, Greenville, SC 29613-0001
Tel: (864) 294-3030
Internet Address: http://www.furman.edu
Admission: Free
Facilities: Gardens (Japanese, rose); Grounds Campus (750 acres)

The Furman University campus, recognized by the American Society of Landscape Architects as one of the most beautifully landscaped areas in the country, features both a rose garden (behind Duke Library) and a Japanese garden (near the Bell Tower). The Rose Garden contains 800 rose bushes, representing 21 different varieties, and by 2,000 additional plants. The Japanese Garden (Nippon Center Yagoto) includes a teahouse.

HARTSVILLE

KALMIA GARDENS OF COKER COLLEGE (AHS RAP)

1624 W. Carolina Avenue, Hartsville, SC 29550-4906
Tel: (843) 383-8145; Fax: (843) 383-8149
Internet Address: http://www.coker.edu/Kalmia/
Admission: No charge, donations accepted
Attendance: 15,000
Established: 1935
Membership: Y
Wheelchair Accessible: P
Parking: On site, gravel lot, 80 spaces
Open: Daily, dawn-dusk
Facilities: Arboretum; Architecture Hart House (farmhouse, ca. 1832); Gardens (day lily, display, herb, native plant, perennial, sensory, wetlands); Grounds (34 acres); Special Collections (camellia, day lily)
Activities: Festivals; Guided Tours; Plant Sales

Situated on a high, steep bluff overlooking Black Creek three miles from town, Kalmia Gardens was begun by May Roper Coker. The gardens, given to Coker College in 1965 (but open to the public since 1935), serve as an outdoor classroom and a public garden hosting many public programs. The site features semi-formal gardens, a sensory garden, and an American Hemerocallis Society display garden as well as an arboretum, black water swamp, pond, and forested uplands. Plantings include over 150 varieties of camellia japonica, azalea, wisteria, tea-olive, and the plentiful laurel (kalmia latifolia), from which the gardens derive their name.

MONCKS CORNER

CYPRESS GARDENS

3030 Cypress Garden Road, Moncks Corner, SC 29461-6406
Tel: (843) 553-0515; Fax: (843) 560-0644
Internet Address: http://www.cypressgardens.org
Admission: Fee: adult $9.00, child (<6) free, child (6-12) $3.00, senior $8.00
Attendance: 50,000
Established: 1932
Membership: Y
Wheelchair Accessible: P
Parking: Free on site.
Open: Daily, 9am-5pm
Closed: New Year's Day, Thanksgiving Day, Christmas Eve to Christmas Day
Best Time(s) of Year to Visit: March to early April (azaleas), June to October (wild butterflies), November to February (camellias)
Facilities: Aquarium (5,000 square feet; native fish, amphibians, & reptiles); Butterfly House (2,000 square feet, exotic plants, native butterflies, koi, & birds); Gardens (camellia, day lily, rose, swamp/woodland, wildflower, wildlife); Grounds (170 acres; 80 acres black water swamp); Meeting/Reception Facility; Picnic Area; Reptile Center (2,000 square feet, native and exotic reptiles and amphibians); Shop (gardening & nature books, nature-oriented items); Trails (4½ miles)
Activities: Concerts Breath of Spring Music Festival (1st Sat in Apr); Education Programs (reserve in advance); Halloween in the Swamp (Fri & Sat before Halloween); Guided Tours 4½ miles (daily)

Originally part of Dean Hall Plantation, Cypress Gardens is a botanical garden and wetlands preserve. The plantation's old rice reservoir is now referred to as Cypress Gardens Swamp. In 1909, the estate was purchased by B. R. Kittredge and made into a picturesque swamp garden featuring azaleas, magnolias, camellias, tea-olives, winter daphne, and bulbs. In 1996, Cypress Gardens was given to Berkeley County. The county added a butterfly house, a reptile center, an outdoor crocodile display, a fresh water aquarium, an antique rose garden, and a day lily display garden. Visitors may explore the site via garden paths, nature trails, or flat bottom boat tours.

MEPKIN ABBEY—NANCY BRYAN LUCE GARDENS

1098 Mepkin Abbey Road, Moncks Corner, SC 29461
Tel: (843) 761-8509; Fax: (843) 761-6719
Internet Address: http://www.mepkinabbey.org
Admission: Free

Membership: N
Open: Daily, daylight hours
Facilities: Gardens (designed by landscape architect Loutrell Briggs)
Activities: Guided Tours (groups over 20, reserve in advance)

Henry R. Luce, the noted publisher-philanthropist, and his wife Clare Boothe Luce purchased this former plantation in 1936. Shortly thereafter, Mrs. Luce commissioned the landscape architect Loutrell Briggs to create the Mepkin Gardens. The property was willed by the Luces to the Catholic Church and is now a Trappist monastery. The gardens were renovated in 1988 through the vision of Nancy Bryan Luce, wife of Henry Luce III. All visits originate at the Reception Center, where a small shop is also located. Midday Prayer, a ten-minute service at noon, may provide the framework for a visit to the garden.

MOUNT PLEASANT

BOONE HALL PLANTATION

U.S. Highway 17 North (9 miles north of Charleston), Mount Pleasant, SC 29464
Tel: (843) 884-4371
Internet Address: http://www.boonehallplantation.com/
Admission: Fee: adult $14.50, child (6-12) $7.00, senior $13.00
Open: April to Labor Day, Monday to Saturday, 8:30am-6:30pm; Sunday, 1pm-5pm;
September to March, Monday to Saturday, 9am-5pm;
Sunday, 1pm-4pm
Closed: Thanksgiving Day, Christmas Day
Facilities: Architecture (mid-eighteenth-century plantation house, 1935 Colonial Revival restoration); Gardens; Shop
Activities: Guided Tours

This early eighteenth-century former cotton plantation offers hundreds of varieties of camellias and azaleas, and thousands of bulbs and annuals set in formal English-style gardens with a serpentine brick wall and herringbone-patterned walks. The main house is approached through a live oak allée planted in 1743.

MURRELLS INLET

BROOKGREEN GARDENS

1931 Brookgreen Gardens Drive (US 17 between Murrells Inlet & Pawleys Island),
Murrells Inlet, SC 29576
Tel: (800) 849-1931; Fax: (843) 235-6039
Internet Address: http://www.brookgreen.org
Admission: Fee: adult $12.00, child (<13) free, child (13-18) $10.00, senior $10.00
Attendance: 185,000
Established: 1931
Membership: Y
Wheelchair Accessible: Y
Parking: Free on site

Open: Mid-August to mid-June, Daily, 9:30am-5pm; mid-June to mid-August, Monday to Tuesday, 9:30am-5pm; Wednesday to Friday, 9:30am-9pm; Saturday to Sunday, 9:30am-5pm
Closed: Christmas Day
Facilities: Architecture (4 former Colonial rice plantations); Food Services Courtyard Café, Old Kitchen, Pavilion Restaurant; Galleries (2, 1 permanent exhibit, 1 temporary exhibit); Grounds landscaped gardens (50 acres); Preserve Low Country History and Wildlife Preserve; Sculpture Garden & Court (over 500 works of American figurative sculpture); Shop (books, garden items, sculpture, educational toys); Wildlife Park (native animal habitat & domestic animals of the plantation)
Activities: Guided Tours Garden Strolls, Sculpture Focus, Botanical Focus); Preserve Programs (Creek Excursions, Trekker Excursions); Temporary Exhibitions; Wildlife Park Programs (Meet the Animals, Mother Nature's Café)

When Archer and Anna Hyatt Huntington first visited Brookgreen in 1930, their imaginations were captured by the place and its possibilities. They originally purchased Brookgreen and three adjoining plantations to serve as their winter home and a setting to display Anna's sculpture, but as their vision of a new life for Brookgreen took shape, they wanted to make it available to the public. In 1931, the Huntingtons opened Brookgreen Gardens as America's first public sculpture garden. They designated the surrounding areas of the property as a wildlife sanctuary, where local flora and fauna could thrive, and established a wildlife park where native animals could be displayed. Archer's wish was for Brookgreen to be a "quiet joining of hands between science and art." Today, the Archer and Anna Huntington Sculpture Garden displays over 500 works spanning the entire period of American sculpture from the early 1800s to the present in over fifty acres of landscaped gardens. The Low Country History and Wildlife Preserve is rich with evidence of the great rice plantations of the 1800s as well as with native plants and animals.

ORANGEBURG

CITY OF ORANGEBURG—EDISTO MEMORIAL GARDENS

Route 301 (just west of downtown Orangeburg), Orangeburg, SC 29116
Tel: (803) 533-6020; Fax: (803) 533-6027
Internet Address: http://www.orangeburg.sc.us/gardens/edisto.htm
Admission: Free
Attendance: 600,000
Membership: N
Wheelchair Accessible: Y
Parking: Ample parking
Open: Daily, dawn-dusk
Facilities: Gardens (azalea, rose, wetland); Greenhouse; Grounds (150 acres); Picnic Area
Activities: Festival Children's Garden Christmas (annual, Monday before Thanksgiving-New Year's Day, illuminated display), South Carolina Festival of Roses (annual, last weekend in Apr)

Developed in the 1920s, Edisto Gardens feature hundreds of species of roses as well as wisteria, dogwoods, azaleas, and crape myrtle. The rose gardens consist of over 50 beds, containing approximately 4,000 plants representing at least 75 varieties from miniature and grandiflora to climber. The site, one of only twenty-three official All-America Rose Selections test gardens in the United States, offers displays of past and current AARS award winners. The gardens also features a butterfly garden and a sensory garden as well as a terrace garden on the river side of the Arts Center. The adjacent Horne Wetlands Park provides the opportunity to explore the tupelo/cypress wetland that lies between the display rose garden and the north fork of the Edisto River via a series of boardwalks.

ROCK HILL

CITY OF ROCK HILL—GLENCAIRN GARDEN

Charlotte Avenue (between Edgemont Avenue & Crest Street), Rock Hill, SC 29730
Tel: (803) 329-5540
Admission: Free
Open: Daily, dawn-dusk
Best Time(s) of Year to Visit: March to mid-April (azalea)
Facilities: Gardens (azalea); Grounds (6 acres)

Located in a residential section of Rock Hill, Glencairn Garden features over 20,000 azaleas as well as daffodils, tulips, and other flowering plants, complemented by fountains, bridges, grassy areas, trees, and walking paths.

ROEBUCK

WALNUT GROVE PLANTATION

1200 Otts Shoal Road (near Route 22 & Interstate 26), Roebuck, SC 29376
Tel: (864) 576-6546; Fax: (864) 576-4058
Internet Address: http://www.spartanarts.org/history
Admission: Fee: adult $5.50, child (<6) free, child (6-18) $3.00
Attendance: 10,000
Established: 1961
Membership: Y
Wheelchair Accessible: N
Parking: Parking on site
Open: April to October, Tuesday to Saturday, 11am-5pm; Sunday, 1pm-5pm; November to March, Saturday, 11am-5pm; Sunday, 1pm-5pm
Best Time(s) of Year to Visit: May-June, October
Facilities: Gardens (herb, vegetable); Grounds (54 acres)

Located on land granted in 1763 by King George III to Charles Moore, the house contains a documented collection of antique furnishings and accessories portraying living conditions in Spartanburg County prior to 1805. The grounds include oaks and walnuts, an herb garden centered on a dipping well, vegetable gardens, a nature trail, outbuildings, and the Moore family cemetery. The site is managed by the Spartanburg County Historical Society.

SPARTANBURG

HATCHER GARDENS & WOODLAND PRESERVE

820 John B. White Sr. Boulevard, Spartanburg, SC 29300
Tel: (864) 574-7724; Fax: (864) 595-1195
Internet Address: http://www.hatchergarden.org

Admission: No charge, donations accepted
Established: 1998
Membership: Y
Wheelchair Accessible: Y
Parking: On site, paved lot, 27 spaces, including handicapped
Open: Daily, sunrise-sunset
Best Time(s) of Year to Visit: Spring
Facilities: Grounds (10 acres); Picnic Area; Trails
Activities: Self-guided Tours

The garden features a series of ponds; walking trails; plantings of annuals, perennials, and shrubs; a native woodland of mixed hardwoods; and a diverse population of wildlife.

UNION

ROSE HILL PLANTATION STATE HISTORIC SITE—GARDENS

2677 Sardis Road (8 miles south of Union, off Route 176), Union, SC 29379
Tel: (864) 427-5966; Fax: (864) 427-5966
Internet Address: http://www.travelsc.com/cgi-bin/parks/StateParkDetail.cfm?ID=43
Admission: Fee: adult $4.00, child $3.00, senior $3.25
Established: 1960
Membership: Y
Wheelchair Accessible: N
Open: Park, Thursday to Monday, 9am-6pm; House, Thursday to Monday, 1pm-4pm
Best Time(s) of Year to Visit: April to June, September to November
Facilities: Architecture (early nineteenth-century Federal-style residence); Garden (rose); Grounds (44 acres); Picnic Area; Trail (½ mile)
Activities: Guided Tours (groups, by appointment); Self-guided Tours

Former home of William H. Gist, governor at the time of secession from the Union, the house contains furnishings once owned by the Gist family. The grounds include the rose gardens, original plantation buildings, and an outstanding hardwood grove. A South Carolina State Historic Site, Roseland Plantation is listed on the National Register of Historic Places.

TENNESSEE

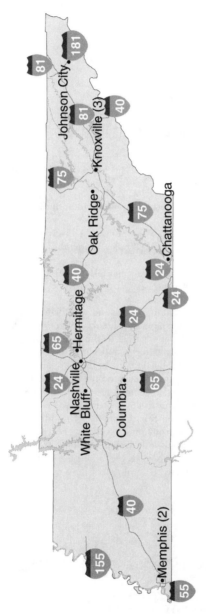

The number in the parentheses following the city name indicates the number of gardens/ arboreta in that municipality. If there is no number, one is understood. For example, in the text two listings would be found under Memphis and one listing under Chattanooga.

CHATTANOOGA

REFLECTION RIDING ARBORETUM AND BOTANICAL GARDEN (AHS RAP)

400 Garden Road, Chattanooga, TN 37419
Tel: (423) 821-1160
Internet Address: http://www.chattanooga.net/rriding/index.htm
Admission: Fee—$6.00 per car
Open: Monday to Saturday, 9am-5pm; Sunday, 1pm-5pm
Facilities: Arboretum; Driving Road (3 miles); Greenhouse; Grounds (300 acres); Trails (13 miles)
Activities: Festival Wildflower Festival (annual, mid-Apr); Guided Tours; Lectures; Plant Sales (native plants); Workshops

Consisting of meadows, mountain slopes, and woodlands situated between the western slope of Lookout Mountain and Lookout Creek, Reflection Riding features an extensive variety of trees, shrubs, and flowers native to the southeastern Appalachian region. John Chambliss, a self-educated horticulturist and landscape architect developed Reflection Riding during the 1940s. Chambliss' interest in English gardens and regional native plants fueled his vision of the Riding, and he enlisted the help of friends and horticulture experts from both America and England to complete it. Several important landscape architects provided their services in the construction of the gardens, most notably, Sylvia Hunt of Kent, England, president of the Royal Society of Landscape Architects, and Gordon Cooper, from Cleveland, Ohio, the longtime editor of *"Landscape Architecture,"* whose vision of Reflection Riding as an outdoor arboretum continues to define the purpose of the gardens. More recently, in 1982, Thomas Kane, a landscape architect from New York State, came to evaluate the Riding and to formulate a long-range plan for its preservation and future development.

COLUMBIA

JAMES K. POLK ANCESTRAL HOME—GARDENS

301 West 7th Street, Columbia, TN 38401-3132
Tel: (615) 388-2354; Fax: (615) 388-5971
Internet Address: http://www.jameskpolk.com/
Admission: Fee: adult $7.00, child (<6) free, child (6-18) $4.00, senior $6.00, family $20.00
Attendance: 10,000

Established: 1929
Membership: Y
Wheelchair Accessible: P
Parking: Free on street
Open: April to October, Monday to Saturday, 9am-5pm; Sunday, 1pm-5pm;
November to March, Monday to Saturday, 9am-4pm; Sunday, 1pm-5pm
Closed: New Year's Day, Thanksgiving Day, Christmas Eve to Christmas Day
Facilities: Architecture Polk Home (Federal-style brick residence, 1816); Gardens
(white azalea, boxwood, herb); Shop
Activities: Guided Tours

Excluding the White House, this site is the only surviving residence of the eleventh
U.S. president. In addition to the main house, other structures at the site include a detached kitchen building (reconstructed in 1946 on the original foundation) and the adjacent Sisters' House (ca. 1820), where two of the president's married sisters lived at different times. The home displays original items from James K. Polk's years in Tennessee and
Washington, D.C., including furniture, paintings, and White House china. The site's
landscaped grounds feature a formal boxwood garden, a white azalea garden, an original
Polk fountain, and an herb garden.

HERMITAGE

THE HERMITAGE: HOME OF ANDREW JACKSON—GARDENS

4580 Rachel's Lane, Hermitage, TN 37076-1344
Tel: (615) 889-2941
Internet Address: http://www.hermitage.org
Admission: Fee: adult $12.00, child (<5) free, child (6-12) $5.00, student $11.00,
senior $11.00
Open: Daily, 9am-5pm
Closed: 3rd week in January, Thanksgiving, Christmas
Facilities: Architecture (Greek Revival residence, 1834-1836); Gardens (period,
formal, vegetable); Food Services (Rachel's Garden Café), Shop, Visitor Center
Activities: Guided Tours (groups 20+, reserve in advance, 889-2941 x212)

Home of the nation's seventh president, Andrew Jackson, the Hermitage has been restored to its appearance between 1837 and 1845, the last years of Jackson's life. The mansion is unique among early presidential sites because almost all of the furnishings are original
to the home. Adjacent to the Hermitage mansion is a formal garden, originally laid out and
planted in the early 1820s as the estate was being developed. Rachel Jackson's fondness for
flowers is well documented, and following her death in 1828 the garden took on a new
meaning as a memorial to her. The garden quickly declined after the Jackson family sold the
Hermitage in 1856, but the Ladies Hermitage Association took on its restoration and maintenance soon after assuming stewardship of the property in 1889. The plantings in the garden, although not original, are species and varieties that would have been familiar to the
Jackson family and friends. The garden's overall layout and acre size remains about what it
was when the Jackson family lived here. The unusually shaped bricks edging many of the
paths and beds were made especially for this garden in the 1830s. Andrew and Rachel Jackson are buried side by side beneath the small rotunda in the garden's southeast corner, with
other members of their family at rest nearby. Also on view are small demonstration vegetable and cotton plots, designed to illustrate the plantations economic endeavors.

JOHNSON CITY

EAST TENNESSEE STATE UNIVERSITY ARBORETUM

University Parkway, Johnson City, TN 37614
Tel: (423) 439-8635; Fax: (423) 439-5958
Internet Address: http://www.etsu.edu/arboretum
Admission: Free
Established: 2000
Membership: Y
Wheelchair Accessible: Y
Open: Daily
Best Time(s) of Year to Visit: April to November
Facilities: Arboretum (college campus)
Activities: Guided Tours (arrange in advance)

Designated an arboretum by the American Association of Botanical Gardens and Arboreta in 2002, the East Tennessee State University campus is home to over 200 species of trees, some newly planted and some well over a century old. Brochures are available on request, including several self-guided walking tours and an arboretum guide that lists and maps labeled trees for each species. Brochures include guides to giant trees, selections for home landscapes, and others. The arboretum has recently planted many tree species pairs that demonstrate Asia-eastern North America disjunctive distributions.

KNOXVILLE

CRESCENT BEND: THE ARMSTRONG-LOCKETT HOUSE-W. P. TOMS MEMORIAL GARDENS

2728 Kingston Pike (Route 11/70, 500 yards west of
Route 129), Knoxville, TN 37919
Tel: (865) 637-3163; Fax: (865) 637-1709
Internet Address: http://www.korrnet.org/cresbend/
Admission: Fee
Attendance: 13,000
Established: 1977
Membership: N
Wheelchair Accessible: N
Parking: Parking for 50 cars; can accommodate motorcoaches
Open: March to December, Tuesday to Saturday, 10am-4pm; Sunday, 1pm-4pm
Closed: Legal holidays
Best Time(s) of Year to Visit: April
Facilities: Architecture (residence, 1834 -brick and stucco Federal home); Gardens
W. P. Toms Memorial Gardens (formal Italian, terraced—roses, perennials, Japanese maples, conifers, topiary, annuals); Shop

Meticulously restored, the house is furnished with eighteenth-century antique furniture, decorative arts, and an outstanding collection of English silver, circa 1640-1820. Manicured formal Italian gardens feature nine terraces and five fountains providing an open-air setting of magnolia blossoms, roses, and thousands of colorful blooming flowers.

IVAN RACHEFF HOUSE AND GARDENS

1943 Tennessee Avenue, Knoxville, TN 37921
Tel: (865) 671-2766
Admission: Free
Established: 1947
Membership: N
Wheelchair Accessible: P
Parking: Parking inside gate and on street
Open: Monday to Friday, 9am-4pm; Dogwood Arts Festival, daily, 9am-5pm
Closed: December 15 to February 1, Thanksgiving Day
Facilities: Architecture (ca. 1902; on National Register); Gardens (wildflower, fern cobble, fish pond, day lilies, teahouse, birch grove, tulips); Grounds (3 acres); Library.
Activities: Guided Tours (free; by appointment); Plant Sales (annual, spring)

Ivan Racheff bought Knoxville Iron Works, now AmeriSteel, in 1946 and started the garden in a steel junk pile. Following his death in 1970, the gardens were donated to the Tennessee Federation of Garden Clubs

UNIVERSITY OF TENNESSEE—UTIA GARDENS (UTIA GARDENS)

900 Neyland Drive (next to the UT Veterinary Teaching Hospital),
Knoxville, TN 37916
Tel: (865) 974-7324; Fax: (865) 974-1947
Internet Address: http://gardens.ag.utk.edu
Admission: Free
Established: 1983
Membership: Y
Parking: Free on site, weekend and evening in Veterinary Hospital lot
Open: Daily, 24 hours per day.
Best Time(s) of Year to Visit: Spring to Summer
Facilities: Gardens (herb, English, All-American); Grounds
(11 acres); Picnic area; Reception area
Activities: Education Programs; Guided Tours

The Department of Ornamental Horticulture & Landscape Design at the University of Tennessee at Knoxville maintains the University of Tennessee Institute of Agriculture Gardens for research as well as for the enjoyment of the public. There are over 800 trees and shrubs growing along a winding brick trail, 500 perennials, 600 annuals, and a variety of herbs. The garden also has specialty collections of hollies and dwarf conifers.

MEMPHIS

THE DIXON GALLERY AND GARDENS (AHS RAP)

4339 Park Avenue (between Getwell and Perkins), Memphis, TN 38117-4698
Tel: (901) 761-2409; Fax: (901) 682-0943
Internet Address: http://www.dixon.org
Admission: Fee: adult $5.00, child $1.00, student free,
senior $4.00
Established: 1976

Membership: Y
Wheelchair Accessible: Y
Parking: Free on site
Open: Tuesday to Saturday, 10am-5pm; Sunday, 1pm-5pm
Facilities: Architecture; Auditorium (250 seats); Gardens (English park, woodland); Grounds (17 acres); Library (3,000 volumes); Sculpture Garden; Shop
Activities: Films; Gallery Talks; Guided Tours (audio tour of gardens); Lectures; Performances; Permanent Exhibits; Temporary Exhibitions

The Dixon Gallery and Gardens, located on seventeen acres of gardens and woodlands, is the legacy of the late Margaret and Hugo Dixon. Their Georgian-style residence, which is the original building in the current gallery complex, houses the Margaret and Hugo Dixon Collection of Paintings. In 1977, one year after the museum opened to the public, a wing was added to house the growing permanent collection. In 1986, a second addition more than doubled the size of the complex. To complement and interpret its permanent collection, the Dixon maintains a diverse schedule of special exhibitions drawn from some of the finest private and public collections of art in the world. Serving as a natural foil for the beauty of the art collection, the Dixon Gardens are the creation of Hugo Dixon and his sister, Hope Crutchfield. Carefully carved out of seventeen acres of native Tennessee woodlands and landscaped in the manner of an English park, the gardens feature open vistas and a series of formal garden spaces. They also feature a two-acre Woodland Garden, a cutting garden, the Hughes pavilion, and the Stout Camellia House. Sculptures, ranging from the eighteenth-century to modern, enhance the gardens.

MEMPHIS BOTANIC GARDEN (AHS RAP)

Audubon Park, 750 Cherry Road, Memphis, TN 38117-4699
Tel: (901) 685-1566; Fax: (901) 682-1561
Internet Address: http://www.memphisbotanicgarden.com/
Admission: Fee: adult $5.00, child (3-12) $3.00, child (6-17) $2.00, student $3.00, senior $4.00
Attendance: 130,000
Established: 1964
Membership: Y
Wheelchair Accessible: Y
Open: November to February, Monday to Saturday, 9am-4:30pm; Sunday, 11am-4:30pm; March to October, Monday to Saturday, 9am-6pm; Sunday, 11am-6pm
Facilities: Arboretum; Auditorium (250 seat); Conservatory; Gallery; Gardens (butterfly, day lily, herb, iris, Japanese, native plant, rose, sensory); Grounds (96 acres); Library (1,000 volumes); Reading Room; Shop; Special Collections (day lily, southern magnolia)
Activities: Concerts; Demonstrations; Education Programs (adults, undergraduate students and children); Films; Guided Tours; Lectures; Plant Shows; Temporary Art Exhibitions

Located in Audubon Park and bounded by Southern Avenue, Park Avenue, Goodlett Road, and Perkins Road, the site encompasses lakes, woodlands, and display gardens. The garden contains twenty-four specialty gardens; highlights include the Japanese Garden of Tranquility (Seijaku-en), the Little Garden Club Sensory Garden, the Municipal Rose Garden (with more than 4,000 plants), an American Hemerocallis Society display garden, and the Tennessee Bicentennial Iris Garden. The Goldsmith Civic Garden Center, located in a building at the entrance to the botanic garden, houses tropical plants, cacti, and presents seasonal flower shows as well as offering educational programs and lectures/seminars. The Memphis Botanic Garden is owned by the City of Memphis Park Services and is managed by the Memphis Botanic Garden Foundation, Inc.

NASHVILLE

CHEEKWOOD BOTANICAL GARDEN AND MUSEUM OF ART (AHS RAP)

1200 Forrest Park Drive, Nashville, TN 37205-4242
Tel: (615) 356-8000; Fax: (615) 353-2156
Internet Address: http://www.cheekwood.org
Admission: Fee: adult $10.00, child $5.00, child (6-17) $5.00, student $5.00, senior $8.00, family $25.00; half-price after 3:00pm
Attendance: 150,000
Established: 1957
Membership: Y
Wheelchair Accessible: Y
Parking: Free on site
Open: Tuesday to Saturday, 9:30am-4:30pm; Sunday, 11am-4:30pm
Closed: New Year's Day, 2nd Sat. in June, Thanksgiving Day, Christmas Day
Facilities: Architecture (former residence, 1929 designed by Bryant Fleming); Auditorium; Food Services Pineapple Room Restaurant; Galleries; Gardens (color, day lily, dogwood trail, herb, Japanese, perennial, wildflower); Grounds (55 acres); Library (9,000 volumes); Sculpture Trail (woodland); Shop (books, gifts, Tennessee crafts)
Activities: Concerts (outdoor); Education Programs (adults and children); Films; Gallery Talks; Guided Tours (groups reserve in advance, 353-9827); Lectures; Temporary Exhibitions; Traveling Exhibitions

Once the private estate of the Leslie Cheek family of the Maxwell House coffee fortune, Cheekwood now houses an art museum and fifty-five-acres of botanical gardens. The museum showcases a prestigious collection of American art from the nineteenth and twentieth centuries, a famous collection of Worcester porcelain, European and American silver, and Asian snuff bottles. The Stallworth galleries host major traveling exhibitions. Guests at the fifty-five-acre estate continue to marvel at the historical Bryant Fleming landscape. Surrounding his design are eleven principal garden areas: the award-winning Howe Wildflower Garden, an herb study garden, the Wills Perennial Garden, the Carell Dogwood Trail, the Woodland Sculpture Trail, a color garden, a water garden, a traditional Japanese garden, and an American Hemerocallis Society display garden. The Botanic Hall features horticultural exhibits, flower shows, and the "Trees of Christmas" celebration every December. The mile-long Woodland Sculpture Trail is the only one of its kind in the United States.

OAK RIDGE

UNIVERSITY OF TENNESSEE FORESTRY EXPERIMENT STATION AND ARBORETUM

901 Kerr Hollow Road (Route 62), Oak Ridge, TN 37830-8032
Tel: (865) 483-3571; Fax: (865) 483-3572
Internet Address: http://forestry.tennessee.edu/arboretum/
Admission: Free
Attendance: 30,000
Established: 1964
Membership: Y

Parking: Free, lot accessible during visitor center hours
Open: Grounds, daily, 8am-sunset; Visitor Center
Closed: Legal holidays
Facilities: Arboretum; Climatic Areas (central China, Southern coastal plains, California forest, heath forest, Polish forest, Cumberland Gorge); Grounds (250 acres); Special Collections (azalea, conifer, crab apple, dogwood, holly, juniper, magnolia, oak, rhododendron, viburnum); Visitors Center (Mon-Fri, 8am-noon & 1pm-4:30pm)
Activities: Plant Sales (annual); Self-guided Tours (4)

This research and education facility contains over 2,500 native and exotic woody plant specimens that represent 800 species, varieties, and cultivars. It is also recognized by the Holly Society of America as an official Holly test garden. Plants are displayed both by type and by groupings known as forest association models (with associated plants found in their natural habitat). Four self-guided walking tours provide access to the plant and animal communities found in the natural areas of the arboretum. Color-coded trail markers designate the tours, and interpretive signs describe points of interest.

WHITE BLUFF

THE ARBORETUM AT INTERSTATE PACKAGING

2285 Highway 47 North, White Bluff, TN 37187
Tel: (615) 797-9000; Fax: (615) 797-5411
Admission: Free (open by appointment)
Established: 1987
Membership: N
Wheelchair Accessible: P
Open: Monday to Friday, 8:30am-4:30pm, open by appointment
Facilities: Arboretum; Grounds (22 acres)
Activities: Guided Tours (schedule in advance)

The Arboretum at Interstate Packaging consists of twenty-two landscaped acres bordering the privately-owned printing and bag-making facility. Surrounding a small lake are plantings of seventy-five different varieties of shrubs and trees, supplemented by a large number of native trees in an adjoining field. Interstate Packaging has been a member of the American Association of Botanical Gardens and Arboreta in 1987 and is also certified as an arboretum by the Tennessee Urban Forestry Council. The company's industrial activity functions with minimal environmental impact. Interstate has been the recipient of several statewide awards for environmental excellence.

VERMONT

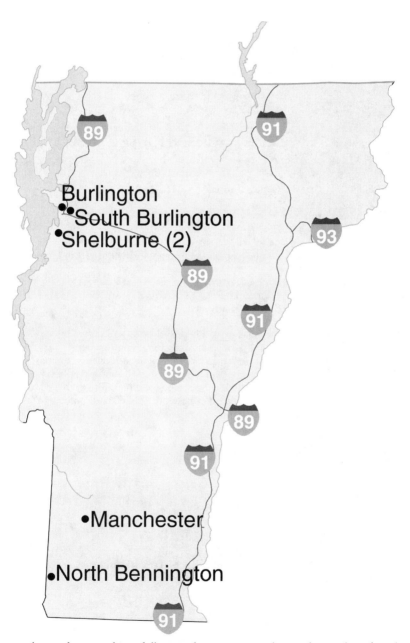

The number in the parentheses following the city name indicates the number of gardens/ arboreta in that municipality. If there is no number, one is understood. For example, in the text two listings would be found under Shelburne and one listing under Burlington.

BURLINGTON

UNIVERSITY OF VERMONT—GREENHOUSE CONSERVATORY AND HORTICULTURE CLUB GARDENS

Central Campus (off East Avenue), Burlington, VT 05405
Tel: (802) 656-0465
Internet Address: http://pss.uvm.edu/greenhouse/gh-index.htm
Admission: Free
Parking: Metered lot adjacent to site
Open: Greenhouse, Monday to Friday, 8:30am-4pm; Horticulture Club Gardens, daily
Closed: Legal holidays
Best Time(s) of Year to Visit: August (Horticulture Club Gardens)
Facilities: Gardens (nursery); Greenhouses (8,000 square feet)
Activities: Guided Tours (schedule in advance)

Located next to the water tower and attached to the Stafford Biotechnology Building, UVM's campus greenhouse. consists of eleven adjoining compartments and an outdoor nursery. Three rooms are devoted to collections of cactus, succulents, orchids, bromeliads, and ferns. The UVM Horticulture Club maintains a 150-foot-long display garden located on the south side of the Hills Building, with bulbs in the spring followed by annuals and perennials during the summer. Also on campus are a rhododendron garden and a collection of hardy vines and climbers.

MANCHESTER

HILDENE—GARDENS

Route 7A South, Manchester, VT 05254
Tel: (802) 362-1788; Fax: (802) 362-1564
Internet Address: http://www.hildene.org
Admission: Fee: adult $10.00, child (<6) free, child (6-14) $5.00
Attendance: 50,000
Established: 1905
Membership: Y
Wheelchair Accessible: P
Parking: At Visitors' Center
Open: Grounds: mid-May to October, daily, 9:30am-5:30pm; November to mid-January, Friday to Sunday, 11am-3pm
Closed: Christmas Day

Best Time(s) of Year to Visit: Mid-June to October
Facilities: Architecture (Georgian Revival-style residence, 1905); Gardens (cutting, formal, kitchen); Grounds farmland & formal gardens (412 acres, 1907 garden design by Frederick G. Todd); Trails (8½+ miles); Visitor's Center
Activities: Education Programs; Exhibits; Guided Tours Home & Formal Gardens (9:30am-3pm, every half-hour; groups reserve in advance)

Robert Todd Lincoln, the eldest son of President Abraham and Mary Todd Lincoln hired a Boston architectural firm to build this stately home on a promontory overlooking the Battenkill Valley. Mary "Peggy" Lincoln Beckwith, a great-granddaughter of Abraham Lincoln, was the last of the president's descendants to live at Hildene. In 1975, Friends of Hildene, a non-profit organization was formed to oversee, "the preservation of Hildene's open land and the restoration of those buildings that best serve the public as an educational and cultural resource and as a memorial to the Lincoln family." The interior of the home has been preserved and many of the Lincoln family's original furnishings and personal family effects are on display. Designed by Mary Lincoln as a present for her mother Mary and planted by Frederick G. Todd (an apprentice of Frederick Law Olmsted) in 1907, the formal garden at Hildene mimics a stained-glass Gothic cathedral window, the different colored flowers representing the "colored glass" and privet hedge representing the "leading" between the panes. In mid-June, over 1,000 peonies from the original planting fill the garden with color. The garden changes weekly from early spring to late fall as varieties of roses, lilies and other plantings bloom and transform the colors of the "stained glass panels." There are also cutting and kitchen gardens from which fruit, flowers, and vegetables would have been gathered for household use. Trails give access to the wooded areas of the property and provide a link to the beginnings of a working farm on the ten-acre meadow.

NORTH BENNINGTON

PARK-MCCULLOUGH HOUSE ASSOCIATION (AHS RAP)

Corner of Park and West Streets (off Route 67A), North Bennington, VT 05257
Tel: (802) 442-5441; Fax: (802) 442-5442
Internet Address: http://www.parkmccullough.org
Admission: Fee: adult $8.00, child (<12) free, child (12-17) $5.00, senior $5.00
Established: 1968
Membership: Y
Wheelchair Accessible: P
Parking: Gravel parking lot
Open: Late May to late October, daily, 10am-4pm; November to December, Saturday to Sunday, 10am-4pm
Best Time(s) of Year to Visit: Spring to Fall
Facilities: Architecture (French 2nd Empire-style "Summer Cottage," 1865 design by architects Diaper and Dudley); Garden (rose); Shop
Activities: Concert Series; Guided Tours House (10am-3pm, on the hour)

The house contains fine interior details and period furniture and décor. The grounds feature rose gardens, a playhouse, and a carriage barn, housing a collection of horse-drawn carriages, buggies, sleighs, and fire-fighting equipment. Owned and operated by the non-profit Park-McCullough House Association, the house is listed on the National Register of Historic Places.

SHELBURNE

SHELBURNE FARMS

1611 Harbor Road, Shelburne, VT 05482
Tel: (802) 985-8686
Internet Address: http://www.shelburnefarms.org/
Admission: fee: adult $6.00, child (<3) free, child (3-14) $4.00, senior $5.00
Attendance: 115,000
Established: 1972
Membership: Y
Parking: On site
Open: Buildings: mid-May to mid-October, daily, 10am-4pm; Trails, all year, daily,
10am-4pm
Facilities: Food Services Inn at Shelburne Farms (restaurant, reservations required);
Gardens; Grounds (1,400 acres); Shop Welcome Center/Farm Store (year round,
daily, 10am-5pm); Trails (8 miles)
Activities: Concerts (summer); Education Programs; Guided Tours (May 15-mid-Oct,
fee); Seminars

Situated on the shores of Lake Champlain, Shelburne Farms was created as a model
agricultural estate in 1886 by Dr. William Seward and Lila Vanderbilt Webb with architect Robert H. Robertson and landscape architect Frederick Law Olmsted. In 1972, the
property became an educational non-profit working farm, environmental education center, and National Historic Landmark. The residence, restored in 1987, is now an inn and
restaurant. The naturalistically landscaped grounds include a garden at the inn and an organic market garden.

SHELBURNE MUSEUM

U.S. Route 7, Shelburne, VT 05482
Tel: (802) 985-3346; Fax: (802) 985-2331
Internet Address: http://www.shelburnemuseum.org
Admission: fee: adult $18.00, child (<6) free, child (6-18) $9.00; Vermont residents:
½ price
Attendance: 155,000
Established: 1947
Membership: Y
Parking: Free, on site
Open: May to October, daily, 10am-5pm
Facilities: Architecture (37 structures on 45 acres); Food Services (restaurant);
Gardens (annual, herb, lilac, perennial); Grounds (45 acres, design by Umberto
Innocenti); Library (10,000 volumes); Museum Shop
Activities: Guided Tours

The museum focuses on American folk art, artifacts, and architecture. With thirty-
seven structures on fourty-five acres, the historic buildings and collections reflect the
transition from an agricultural to an industrial nation. Exhibits include three galleries of
American paintings and decorative arts, seven furnished historic houses, and a gathering
of Vermont community buildings. Gardens on the landscaped grounds include a medicinal herb garden, a culinary herb and dye plant garden, a lilac garden, and the Electra
Bostwick Memorial Garden, consisting of plantings of annuals, perennials, and roses set in

the form of an artist's palette. There are extensive collections of lilacs (400 bushes of 90 varieties) and crabapples (200 trees).

SOUTH BURLINGTON

VERMONT BOTANICAL GARDEN

Dorset & Swift Streets (across from Vermont National Golf Course),
South Burlington, VT 05403
Tel: (802) 863-5251
Internet Address: http://www.vermontgarden.org
Admission: scheduled to open in 2005
Membership: N
Wheelchair Accessible: N
Parking: Small parking lot
Facilities: Grounds planned (20-25 acres)

Not yet constructed, the Vermont Botanical Gardens will eventually occupy about twenty-two acres of the 100-acre city-owned Calkins estate. The master plan, by landscape architects Terry Boyle and Jane Sorensen, includes annual and perennial flower gardens, vegetables gardens, a rose garden, a winter garden, a children's garden, a maze, a secret garden, community gardens, a butterfly garden, an herb garden, native plant gardens, and ethnic heritage gardens. Eventually greenhouses for year-round growing, education, and display will also be incorporated. The remainder of the 100 acres will be maintained in its natural state with hiking and skiing trails planned. The gardens are a joint project staffed by volunteers from the National Gardening Association, the City of South Burlington, and other community residents and organizations. Phase 1 of the gardens is scheduled to open to the public in 2005.

VIRGINIA

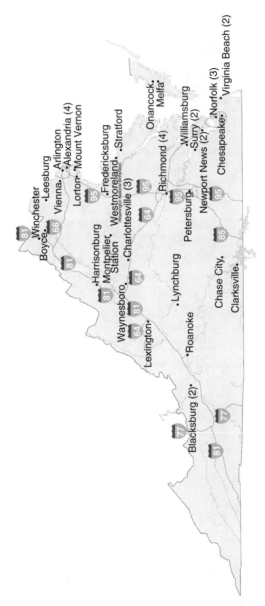

The number in the parentheses following the city name indicates the number of gardens/arboreta in that municipality. If there is no number, one is understood. For example, in the text four listings would be found under Richmond and one listing under Petersburg.

ALEXANDRIA

AMERICAN HORTICULTURAL SOCIETY AT GEORGE WASHINGTON'S RIVER FARM (RIVER FARM) (AHS RAP)

7931 East Boulevard Drive (off George Washington Parkway), Alexandria, VA 22308
Tel: (800) 777-7931; Fax: (703) 768-8700
Internet Address: http://www.ahs.org
Admission: Free
Established: 1973
Membership: Y
Parking: Free on site
Open: October to March, Monday to Friday, 9am-5pm; April to September, Monday to Friday, 9am-5pm; Saturday, 9am-1pm
Closed: Federal holidays
Best Time(s) of Year to Visit: Spring (bulb display)
Facilities: Architecture (brick estate house, begun mid-eighteenth century with many additions and remodelings down to the twentieth century); Gardens (azalea, children's, meadow, orchard, perennial border, shade, wildlife, woodland); Grounds (25 acres); Picnic Area; Shop Friends of River Farm Cottage Shop (hours vary seasonally); Visitors Center
Activities: Education Programs; Guided Tours Groups (arrange in advance); Self-guided Tours; Temporary Art Exhibitions (rotating exhibits in Estate House)

At one time the northernmost of George Washington's five farms along the south bank of the Potomac, River Farm has been the headquarters of the American Horticultural Society since 1973. The site's features include the estate house and an artful blend of naturalistic and formal garden areas. The property boasts a spectacular river view, historic trees, boxwood hedges, woodland areas, a three-acre meadow, and a children's garden. Significant and historic trees on the site include an Osage orange that was a gift from Thomas Jefferson to George Washington as well as a grove of franklinia trees, a Kentucky coffee tree, and a trifoliate orange. As the national headquarters of the AHS, River Farm provides a home base for the society's work and hosts a variety of programs attended by amateur and professional horticulturists. Following in the footsteps of George Washington, the gardens and programs at River Farm promote horticultural innovation, practical experimentation, and conservation.

CARLYLE HOUSE HISTORIC PARK

121 N. Fairfax Street (Old Town Alexandria, across from City Hall),
Alexandria, VA 22314-3229
Tel: (703) 549-2997; Fax: (703) 549-5738

Internet Address: http://www.carlylehouse.org/
Admission: Fee: adult $4.00, child (<11) free, child (11-17) $2.00
Open: April to October, Tuesday to Saturday, 10am-4:30pm; Sunday, noon-4:30pm;
November to March, Tuesday to Saturday, 10am-4pm; Sunday, noon-4pm
Facilities: Architecture (Palladian-style stone residence, 1753); Garden (period,
eighteenth-century; design by landscape architect Rudy J. Favretti; cutting); Grounds
(¾ acre); Shop (gifts and books inspired by colonial Virginia)
Activities: Education Programs; Events Garden Day (workshops, plant sales); Guided
Tours; Workshops

Built by John Carlyle, one of the founders and first landowners in Alexandria, for his first
wife Sarah, Carlyle House presents the lifestyle of an eighteenth-century Virginia family
and their servants and slaves. Designed in the eighteenth-century style with assistance from
the Garden Club of Virginia, the garden features carefully researched plant materials that
would have been available to John Carlyle during his occupancy. Brick walks, benches, boxwood parterres, and a cutting garden make the Carlyle House garden a green oasis in the
center of Old Town Alexandria. Owned and operated by the Northern Virginia Regional
Park Authority, Carlyle House is listed on the National Register of Historic Places.

GREEN SPRING GARDENS PARK AND
HORTICULTURAL CENTER (AHS RAP)

4603 Green Spring Road, Alexandria, VA 22312
Tel: (703) 642-5173
Internet Address: http://www.greenspring.org
Admission: Free
Established: 1970
Open: Daily, dawn-dusk
Facilities: Architecture (manor house, ca. 1760); Gardens Demonstration Gardens
(22; blue, children's, fruit, herb, kitchen, mixed border, rock, shade, town house,
vegetable, water-conservation, wild-flower, wildlife habitat); Greenhouse; Grounds
Manor House Gardens (5 acres, designed by Beatrix Farrand), Park (27 acres);
Horticulture Center (Mon-Sat, 9am-4:30pm; Sun, noon-4:30pm); Library; Shop: Ivy
Cupboard Shop
Activities: Classes; Community Garden Plots (annual rental); Concerts; Education
Programs; Guided Tours & Teas Manor House (Wed-Sun, noon-4pm; arrange in
advance, 941-7987); Plant Sales; Workshops

Once a plantation and finally a gentleman's country retreat, Green Spring was donated
to Fairfax County by editor and publisher Michael Straight in 1970. Straight had purchased the property in 1942 and made several modifications to the 1760 manor house
and accompanying gardens. Used primarily for entertaining, the landscape around the
Straight home features boxwood hedging, roses, and perennial borders designed by Beatrix Farrand. Since 1970, a wide variety of demonstration gardens has been developed, designed to illustrate a wide range of gardening styles as well as feature plants available to
local residents. The site is maintained by the Fairfax County Park Authority.

LEE-FENDALL HOUSE MUSEUM AND GARDEN

614 Oronoco Street (corner of N. Washington and Oronoco Streets),
Alexandria, VA 22314
Tel: (703) 548-1789; Fax: (703) 548-1789
Internet Address: http://www.LeeFendallHouse.org

Admission: Fee: adult $4.00, child (<11) free, child (11-17) $2.00
Attendance: 10,000
Membership: Y
Wheelchair Accessible: P
Parking: Small lot on site
Open: Tuesday to Saturday, 10am-4pm; Sunday, 1pm-4pm
Closed: Legal holidays
Facilities: Architecture (clapboard residence, constructed 1785, modified 1850);
Garden alexandria's Bicentennial Garden (rose)
Activities: Guided Tours (on the hour, last 3pm)

Built in 1775 by Philip Fendall on land purchased from his cousin "Light Horse" Harry Lee, father of Robert E. Lee, this gracious home was occupied by more than thirty-seven members of Virginia's Lee family between 1785 to 1903 and by John L. Lewis, president of the United Mine Workers, between 1937 and 1969. Now restored to its early Victorian elegance, the house is interpreted as a Lee family home of the 1850-1870 period. The house is furnished with a collection of Lee family heirlooms as well as period pieces produced by Alexandria furniture manufacturers. The house is complemented by its restored award-winning garden containing a mature magnolia (ca. 1861), walnut, and gingko trees; a rose garden; and boxwood paths. Lee-Fendall House is owned and operated by the Virginia Trust for Historic Preservation, a non-profit educational foundation.

ARLINGTON

BON AIR PARK—GARDENS

850 N. Lexington Street at Wilson Boulevard, Arlington, VA 22205
Tel: (703) 228-4747
Internet Address: http://www.co.arlington.va.us/prcr/scripts/parks
Open: Daily, sunrise-½ hour after sunset
Facilities: Gardens (azalea, rose, sun, shade, wildflower); Grounds Park (23½ acres)

The park features a rose garden containing 2,400 rose bushes representing 157 varieties as well as an azalea/camellia garden, ornamental tree garden, shade garden, sun garden, and a wildflower area.

BLACKSBURG

SMITHFIELD PLANTATION

1000 Smithfield Plantation Road (Virginia Tech campus), Blacksburg, VA 24060
Tel: (540) 231-3947
Internet Address: http://www.civic.bev.net/smithfield/
Admission: Fee: adult $5.00, child (<12) $2.00, student $3.00
Attendance: 5,000
Membership: Y
Wheelchair Accessible: N
Parking: Lot adjacent to site
Open: April to 1st weekend in December, Thursday to Sunday, 1pm-5pm

Facilities: Gardens (period, eighteenth-century kitchen, conjectural restoration 1984 by landscape architect Rudy J. Favretti); Grounds (12 acres)
Activities: Guided Tours (last tour 4:30pm)

Built by William Preston in 1773, Smithfield Plantation is the historic home of the Preston family, one of the founding families of Blacksburg and Montgomery County, Virginia. The house contains accoutrements and furnishings appropriate to the period when the plantation was a thriving homestead. A demonstration garden, containing flowers, herbs and small fruits, is situated between the plantation house and a reconstructed smokehouse. This garden is not an attempt to portray an authentic eighteenth-century layout, but rather to display eighteenth century plants, including food crops as well as plants used for flavoring, fragrance, healing, weaving, and dying. Smithfield Plantation, listed on the National Register of Historic Places and the Virginia Landmarks Register, is a property of the Association for the Preservation of Virginia Antiquities.

VIRGINIA POLYTECHNIC INSTITUTE—VIRGINIA TECH HORTICULTURE GARDENS (AHSRAP)

Washington Street (Virginia Tech campus), Blacksburg, VA 24061-0327
Tel: (540) 231-5970
Internet Address: http://www.hort.vt.edu/VTHG/
Admission: Free
Parking: Weekdays: visitor's pass available from Visitor's Center on Southgate, 8am-5pm
Open: Daily, dawn-dusk
Facilities: Gardens (annual, conifer, perennial, water, woody/herbaceous, xeriscape); Grounds (1 acre)
Activities: Education Programs; Guided Tours (arrange in advance, 231-5791); Plant Sale (spring)

The one-acre gardens complex is divided into four major areas of interest. The annual garden contains plants that are most showy in the summer, the perennial garden includes herbaceous plants that will survive through the winter, the xerophytic garden includes herbaceous and woody drought-tolerant species, and the wooded collection includes both woody and herbaceous species.

BOYCE

UNIVERSITY OF VIRGINIA—ORLAND E. WHITE ARBORETUM (STATE ARBORETUM OF VIRGINIA) (AHS RAP)

Blandy Experimental Farm, U.S. Route 50 (1½ miles east of Route 340), Boyce, VA 22620
Tel: (540) 837-1758; Fax: (540) 837-1523
Internet Address: http://www.virginia.edu/blandy
Admission: Free
Attendance: 25,000
Established: 1927
Membership: Y
Wheelchair Accessible: P
Open: Daily, dawn-dusk

Facilities: Amphitheater; Arboretum; Gardens (herb, native plant trail, perennial, wetlands, pond); Greenhouses (not open to public); Grounds Arboretum (170 acres—5000 woody specimens), Blandy Experimental Farm (700 acres); Herbarium (access by request only); Library; Shop (Apr-Dec; books, seeds, gardening tools, t-shirts)
Activities: Concert Series (summer); Education Programs; Guided Tours (upon advance request); Lectures; Performances

Located in the northeastern Shenandoah Valley, the White Arboretum (part of the Blandy Experimental Farm), is the state arboretum of Virginia. Its collection of over 5,000 woody plants (over 1,000 different varieties and species representing 100 genera and 50 families) includes one of the most extensive collections of boxwood in North America and more than half the world's pine species. The arboretum maintains several demonstration gardens as well as a garden of culinary and medicinal herbs near the visitor parking area. The Virginia Native Plant Trail guides visitors through a small woodlands, a large meadow, and a wetland that feature native trees, shrubs, wildflowers, and ferns.

CHARLOTTESVILLE

ASH LAWN-HIGHLAND—GARDENS

1000 James Madison Parkway, Charlottesville, VA 22902-8722
Tel: (434) 293-9539; Fax: (434) 293-8000
Internet Address: http://www.ashlawnhighland.org
Admission: Fee: adult $9.00, child (6-11) $5.00, senior $8.00
Attendance: 70,000
Membership: Y
Wheelchair Accessible: Y
Parking: On site, 200 autos
Open: April to October, daily, 9am-6pm; November to March, daily, 11am-5pm
Closed: New Year's Day, Thanksgiving Day, Christmas Day
Best Time(s) of Year to Visit: April to November
Facilities: Gardens (period, early nineteenth century; boxwood, formal, herb, kitchen); Grounds Estate (535 acres), House (4 acres)
Activities: Education Programs; Guided Tours (house, outbuildings, gardens); Performances (opera, musicals; Jul-Aug); Workshops (crafts focus)

The home of James Monroe, the fifth president of the United States, Ash Lawn-Highland is located within sight of Thomas Jefferson's Monticello. Its ornamental and utilitarian gardens represent those commonly planted in the early 1800s and include boxwood and kitchen gardens. Ashlawn-Highland is owned by the College of William and Mary.

MONTICELLO—GARDENS

931 Thomas Jefferson Parkway, Charlottesville, VA 22902
Tel: (804) 984-9800; TDDY: (804) 984-9836
Internet Address: http://www.monticello.org/
Admission: Fee: adult $13.00, child (<6) free, child (6-11) $6.00; Group rates
Parking: Free on site
Open: March to October, daily, 8am-5pm; November to February, daily, 9am-4:30pm
Closed: Christmas Day

Facilities: Arboretum The Grove (18 acres, specimen trees planted by Jefferson); Architecture (Palladian residence designed by Jefferson); Food Services Little Mountain Luncheonette (Apr-Oct, 10:30am-4pm); Gardens (flower, fruit, vegetable); Grounds (40 acres), West Lawn (1939 restoration by Alden Hopkins based on Jefferson's 1807 plan); Shop: Garden Shop at Monticello (late Mar-Oct, 9am-6pm; historic varieties of plants and seeds), Museum Shops (2 locations); Visitors Center
Activities: Education Series Saturdays in the Garden (lectures, natural history walks, workshops); Guided Tours (hourly, house, grounds, gardens, written translations of house tour available)

Home of Thomas Jefferson, third president of the United States, Monticello was described by Jefferson as his "essay on architecture." If so, it was an essay without end, subject to forty years of erasures, emendations, and corrections. Monticello's grounds were no less worthy a subject for Jefferson's inquiry. He was an avid gardener, maintaining a garden book for fifty-seven years. This wealth of documentary material unveils much about the character of early American gardens as well as the scientific and creative sensibility of Jefferson himself. The gardens at Monticello were organized as a botanic garden, an experimental laboratory of ornamental and useful plants from around the world. (Twenty-five percent of the flowers cultivated at Monticello were North American natives, and the gardens became, in part, a museum of New World botanical curiosities.) At Monticello, Jefferson cultivated over 250 vegetable varieties in his 1,000-foot-long garden terrace, 170 fruit varieties representing 31 species in the 8-acre fruit garden and approximately 105 species of herbaceous plants in the flower gardens. He designed romantic grottoes, garden temples, and ornamental groves and took visitors on rambling surveys of his favorite "pet trees." There are two elements to the Monticello flower garden: the twenty oval beds immediately around the house and the winding walk with accompanying roundabout flower border that defines the west lawn. Monticello is the only house in America included on the United Nations' World Heritage List of sites that must be protected at all costs.

UNIVERSITY OF VIRGINIA—PAVILION GARDENS

Rotunda & Lawn, Main Campus, Charlottesville, VA 22908
Tel: (804) 924-0970
Internet Address: http://www.virginia.edu/uvatours/gardens
Admission: Free
Closed: Academic holidays
Facilities: Gardens (10 gardens; reconstruction by landscape architects Alden Hopkins and Donald H. Parker); Grounds Rotunda, Lawn & Pavilions (1817 design by Thomas Jefferson)
Activities: Guided Tours (at the Rotunda entrance facing the Lawn; 10am/11am/2pm/ 3pm/4pm; 924-7969)

The University of Virginia was Thomas Jefferson's last and most public architectural experiment. Inspired by the architectural engravings of sixteenth century Italian architect Andrea Palladio, Jefferson created two parallel rows of five houses each, the Pavilions, connected by low colonnaded walkways and student rooms and joined on the north by the Rotunda. Although the garden walls were completed by 1824, Jefferson left no specific record of his intentions for the Pavilion gardens, leaving the Pavilion residents to design, plant, and maintain their own gardens. Through the years, some of the gardens were cultivated with great care, while others were used for predominantly utilitarian purposes and included smokehouses and sheds for small animals. In 1948, the Garden Club of Virginia offered to restore the Pavilion Gardens. Alden Hopkins, landscape architect for

Williamsburg, drew plans for the gardens and supervised the restoration of the West Gardens. After Hopkins's death, Donald H. Parker, his assistant, finished the work in the East Gardens. The West and the East Gardens are quite different from one another in part because there were two designers. The topography also plays a large role as the West Gardens are relatively flat while the East Gardens are terraced into the hillside. The West Gardens were dedicated in 1952 and the East Gardens in 1964. The Garden Club of Virginia continues to guide the care and maintenance of the gardens. The restored Pavilion Gardens include many of the flowers and shrubs that Jefferson grew in his gardens at Monticello as well as those recommended by eighteenth-century gardeners and writers. While professors and their families continue to reside in the pavilions, the gardens are open to the public. Other campus gardens include the arboretum at Morea (at the end of Sprigg Lane), containing a collection of hollies and many native plants and a terraced landscape of lawn, trees, and flower beds surrounding Carr's Hill, the president's residence, located on the knoll to the northwest of the Rotunda.

CHASE CITY

MACCALLUM MORE MUSEUM AND GARDEN

603 Hudgins Street, Chase City, VA 23924
Tel: (434) 372-0502; Fax: (434) 372-3483
Internet Address: http://www.mmmg.org
Admission: Fee (Museum & Garden): adult $3.50, child (<6) free, child (6-12) $2.50, senior $3.00; Fee (Gardens only): $1.00
Attendance: 2,000
Established: 1991
Membership: Y
Wheelchair Accessible: P
Parking: Along Hudgins, Walker, and Berry Sts.; 2 handicapped spaces
Open: Museum & Office, Monday to Friday, 10am-5pm; Saturday, 10am-1pm; Gardens, daily, 10am-5pm
Best Time(s) of Year to Visit: late April (dogwood, azalea, redbud bloom), May to June (rose heavy bloom), Spring to Fall (herbs, wildflowers, trees)
Facilities: Arboretum; Gardens (formal; azalea, boxwood, dogwood, herb, native plant, pink, rose, white, wildflower, wildlife habitat); Grounds (5 acres); Museum (Native American archeology, historic exhibits, revolving art exhibits); Shop: Garden Gift Shop (garden gift items, books, herbal teas, & blends); Trail (Virginia Birding and Wildlife Trail)
Activities: Concerts Spring Jazz Concert (1st Sun in May, 4pm-6pm); Education Programs (throughout the year, gardening topics); Events Archaeology Day (1st Sat in Oct, 10am-3pm), Christmas Bazaar (1st Sat in Dec, 10am-3pm; local crafts, baked goods), Herb Festival (1st Sat in Jun, 10am-3pm); Guided Tours (schedule in advance)

Lucy Morton Hudgins, wife of Edward Wren Hudgins, former Chief Justice of the Virginia Supreme Court, began MacCallum More Gardens in 1929. Their son continued to expand the gardens until his death in 1986. The organically maintained botanical garden and wildlife sanctuary feature an herb and wildflower section; an arboretum with over ninety identified and labeled species; a white memorial garden; a rose garden; a pink garden; a native wildlife habitat; and a Virginia Birding and Wildlife Trail site. Meandering paths, lined with boxwood, azalea, and dogwood, reveal imported fountains, statuary, and many eclectic works of art. The museum houses three permanent exhibits: the Arthur Robertson Exhibit displays locally collected Indian artifacts; the Thyne Institute Exhibit tells the story of an African-American boarding school established in 1876 in Chase City;

and the Mecklenburg Hotel Exhibit contains memorabilia from the hotel built in 1903 and famous for its curative waters. The museum also mounts temporary art exhibits employing a variety of media.

CHESAPEAKE

CHESAPEAKE ARBORETUM

624 Oak Grove Road, Chesapeake, VA 23320
Tel: (757) 382-7060
Internet Address: http://www.chesapeakearboretum.com
Admission: Free
Established: 1996
Membership: Y
Parking: On site, 45 cars
Open: Daily, dawn-dusk
Best Time(s) of Year to Visit: March to November
Facilities: Arboretum; Gardens (antique rose, demonstration, fragrance, vegetable); Grounds (47 acres); Trails (2½ miles); Visitor Center

With an emphasis on urban forestry, the site includes a farmhouse that serves as the arboretum's headquarters building, a forty-three-acre mature hardwood forest with many varieties of trees and plants (including oak, pine, maple, beech, dogwood, poplar, pawpaw, and gum), and a number of theme and demonstration gardens. Located on land leased from the city of Chesapeake, the arboretum is managed by a non-profit organization.

CLARKSVILLE

PRESTWOULD PLANTATION

Prestwould Drive (off Route 15), Clarksville, VA 23927
Tel: (804) 374-8672; Fax: (804) 374-3060
Admission: Fee (House): adult $8.00, child (<12) $3.00, senior $6.00; Fee (Grounds Only): $3.00
Attendance: 8,000
Membership: Y
Wheelchair Accessible: P
Parking: On site
Open: April 15 to October 31, Monday to Saturday, 12:30pm-3:30pm; Sunday, 1:30pm-3:30pm
Best Time(s) of Year to Visit: Spring, Fall
Facilities: Architecture (Georgian stone residence, 1790-1795); Gardens (period, restored using original plans)

Seat of one of the principal Cavalier families of Virginia, Prestwould was built by Sir Peyton Skipwith for himself and his second wife, Lady Jean. The house, built of stone quarried on the plantation, was laid out in 1793 and completed in 1795. When built, it was one of the largest and most complex gentry houses in Virginia. Today, the house retains an exceptional degree of it original interior and exterior detail, including three Federal-era porches and distinctly regional Georgian woodwork. It is also noted for the survival of its exquisite eighteenth-century English botanical wallpapers and a series of French scenic wallpapers from the early nineteenth century. The grounds feature a restored formal garden originally designed by Lady Jean in 1796, an octagonal summer house, a separate plantation office, loom house, smokehouses, a plantation store, a very early two-family slave house, and a slave garden. Remaining in the Skipwith family through four generations into the twentieth century, the site, now owned by the Prestwould Foundation, is designated a Virginia Historic Landmark and a National Historic Landmark.

FREDERICKSBURG

KENMORE PLANTATION AND GARDENS

1201 Washington Avenue, Fredericksburg, VA 22401-3747
Tel: (540) 373-3381; Fax: (540) 371-6066
Internet Address: http://www.kenmore.org/kenmore.html
Admission: Fee: adult $6.00, child (6-17) $3.00
Attendance: 33,000
Established: 1922
Membership: Y
Wheelchair Accessible: Y
Open: January to February, 11am-5pm; March to May, Daily, 11am-5pm; Memorial Day to Labor Day, Daily, 10am-5pm; after Labor Day to December, 11am-5pm
Closed: Thanksgiving Day, December 24 to Christmas Day, New Year's Eve, Thanksgiving Day, Christmas Eve to Christmas Day
Facilities: Architecture (Georgian manor house, 1770s; additions and alterations made by nineteenth-century owners); Gardens (period, eighteenth century; kitchen, native plant, perennial), Formal Gardens (conjectural restoration by landscape architects Charles F. Gillette and Alden Hopkins); Grounds (3 acres; Wilderness Walk (design by landscape architect Rudy J. Favretti); Museum Crowninshield Museum (eighteenth- & nineteenth-century fine & decorative arts); Shop
Activities: Education Programs; Guided Tours (every 45 minutes); Lectures

   Home of George Washington's sister Betty and her husband Colonel Fielding Lewis, the house is furnished with period antiques. Without precise archival and archaeological data, the landscape that has been created is conjectural, featuring eighteenth-century and native plant material. The front of the house consists of a tree-covered lawn; the rear of the property contains a foursquare garden edged in boxwood. The Wilderness Walk, a popular eighteenth-century landscape form, is situated in the southwest corner of the property. A garden guide with map is available to visitors free of charge. The site is owned and maintained by George Washington's Fredericksburg Foundation (formerly the Kenmore Association, Inc.), a non-profit corporation dedicated to preservation and education.

HARRISONBURG

JAMES MADISON UNIVERSITY—EDITH J. CARRIER ARBORETUM (AHS RAP)

University Boulevard, East Campus (near the Convocation Center), Harrisonburg, VA 22807
Tel: (540) 568-3194; Fax: (540) 568-6026

Internet Address: http://www.jmu.edu/arboretum
Admission: Free
Attendance: 12,000
Membership: Y
Wheelchair Accessible: P
Parking: On site
Open: Daily, dawn-dusk
Best Time(s) of Year to Visit: May to July (azalea, rhododendron)
Facilities: Amphitheater; Arboretum; Gardens (azalea/rhododendron, bog, fern, herb, native plant, perennial, rock, rose, wildflower); Grounds (125 acres)
Activities: Bulb Sale; Classes; Education Programs; Events Herb and Garden Festival; Guided Tours (arrange in advance); Lectures

With its forested slopes, lowland swale, pond and forested savanna, the arboretum provides a variety of habitats for a wide diversity of flora and fauna from a sea of daffodil blooms in the April Walk garden to winding trails through the native Oak-Hickory Forest. Exhibits include the herb garden, composed of a series of terraces organized into beds according to themes: culinary, medicinal, fragrance and ancient and medieval; the Mid-Atlantic Azalea Garden, featuring native azaleas and a number of hybrid crosses between natives; the McDonald Azalea and Rhododendron Garden, featuring more than 500 individual azaleas and rhododendrons of many varieties; a bog garden, consisting of acid-loving plants like pitcher plant, sundew, cranberry, Labrador tea, and lambkill; a rock garden, displaying numerous species that are endemic to harsh conditions found in shale deposits (including seven rare obligate heliotropes); the Viette Perennial Garden, containing eighteen varieties of day lilies, eight varieties of Siberian iris, hostas, eupatoria, and showy ornamental grasses; the Andrew Wood Memorial Garden; containing over ninety-two species of native plants and wildflowers, including pink lady slippers, Turk's cap lily, Dutchman's breeches, wild ginger, squirrel corn, and native azaleas, laurels, and rhododendrons; the Fern Valley, containing an assortment of ferns such as the New York fern, hay-scented fern, Christmas fern, ostrich fern, and marginal shield fern; a rose garden with over thirty varieties of heirloom roses; and a variety of other gardens and collections.

LEESBURG

OATLANDS PLANTATION—GARDENS (AHS RAP)

20850 Oatlands Plantation Lane (6 miles south of Leesburg off Route 15), Leesburg, VA 20175
Tel: (703) 777-3174; Fax: (703) 777-4427
Internet Address: http://www.oatlands.org/
Admission: Fee (House & Gardens): adult $10.00, child (<6) free, child (6-16) $7.00, senior $9.00; Fee (Grounds & Gardens): $7.00
Attendance: 70,000
Established: 1964
Membership: Y
Wheelchair Accessible: N
Parking: Free on site
Open: April to December, Monday to Saturday, 10am-4pm; Sunday, 1pm-4pm.
Closed: Thanksgiving Day, Christmas Eve to Christmas Day
Facilities: Architecture (Federal-style mansion, 1804); Gardens (period restoration; boxwood allée, cutting, herb, herbaceous border, rose, walled); Greenhouse (1810, 2nd oldest propagation greenhouse in the U.S.); Grounds (330 acres)
Activities: Guided Tours

Built by George Carter, great-grandson of early Virginia settler Robert "King" Carter in 1804, Oatlands forms one of the nation's most elaborate Federal estates. Donated to the National Trust for Historic Preservation in 1964, the mansion's interior reflects the taste of its most recent owners, the William Corcoran Eustises, who furnished it as a traditional English-style country house of the 1920s and 1930s. The gardens at Oatlands, considered among the nation's top historic restored gardens, feature a reflecting pool, boxwood allée leading to a Victorian period teahouse, rose garden, annual cutting garden, and a formal herb garden. They reflect the efforts of various owners over its history. The gardens were originally designed by George Carter, who constructed ingenious connecting terraces that, by sheltering the area from wind, extended the growing season to supply food for the plantation. They declined after the Civil War, but after the property changed hands in 1903, Mrs. Eustis enlarged the flower beds, extended the boxwood parterres, designed a rose garden, and added statuary and ornaments. She also was the soul behind the restoration of the four-acre walled garden. In 1920, the classical-style teahouse was built, opposing the reflecting pool and connected by the boxwood bowling allée. After suffering another period of neglect, the gardens were again renewed when the property was acquired by the National Trust, which was responsible for the addition of the formal herb garden and the restoration of the north forcing wall and the boxwood edging on the lower terraces.

LEXINGTON

BOXERWOOD GARDENS

963 Ross Road, Lexington, VA 24450
Tel: (540) 463-2697
Internet Address: http://www.boxerwood.com/
Admission: Suggested contribution $5.00
Parking: Free on site, 2 lots
Open: March 15 to November, Tuesday to Sunday, 9am-4pm
Facilities: Arboretum; Grounds (15 acres); Nature Center; Picnic Area; Special
Collections (dwarf conifer, magnolia, dogwood, rhododendron, azalea, Japanese maple).
Activities: Guided Tours (groups 8+, by appointment)

The legacy of Robert S. Munger (1911-1988), Boxerwood is an arboretum/nature center featuring native and exotic plant material in naturalistic settings. The arboretum contains approximately 2,500 labeled cultivars and 4,500 native trees and shrubs.

LORTON

GUNSTON HALL PLANTATION—GARDENS

10709 Gunston Road (Route 242, off Route 1), Lorton, VA 22079-3901
Tel: (703) 550-9220; Fax: (703) 550-9480
Internet Address: http://www.gunstonhall.org/
Admission: Fee: adult $8.00, child (<6) free, student $4.00, senior $7.00
Membership: Y
Parking: Free on site
Open: Daily, 9:30am-5pm
Closed: New Year's Day, Thanksgiving Day, Christmas Day

Facilities: Architecture (Georgian manor house, ca. 1755-60); Deerpark, pasture; Gardens (period, eighteenth century; 1954 conjectural restoration by landscape architect Alden Hopkins); Grounds (550 acres, 25 acres currently under cultivation); Library; Shop
Activities: Education Programs; Guided Tours; Special Interest Tours (groups, reserve in advance)

Located in southern Fairfax County, Gunston Hall was the home of George Mason, author of the Virginia Declaration of Rights. The one-acre formal garden situated immediately behind the mansion contains a massive central boxwood allée believed to have been planted during Mason's residence. However, the rest of this garden is in a state of transition from a Colonial Revival garden of early twentieth-century inspiration to one that based on archeological evidence will more closely approximate the garden that was laid out by George Mason in the eighteenth century. Beyond the formal garden lies a lower garden, deer park, pasture, woodland, and the Potomac River. Designated a National Historic Landmark, Gunston Hall is owned by the Commonwealth of Virginia and administered by a Board of Regents appointed from the National Society of the Colonial Dames of America.

LYNCHBURG

POINT OF HONOR—GARDENS

112 Cabell Street, Lynchburg, VA 24504
Tel: (804) 847-1459; Fax: (804) 528-0162
Internet Address: http://www.pointofhonor.org
Admission: Fee: adult $6.00, child (<6) free, child (6-16) $2.00, student $3.00, senior $5.00
Attendance: 6,000
Established: 1978
Membership: N
Wheelchair Accessible: N
Parking: Ample parking for cars and tour busses
Open: Daily, 10am-4pm
Closed: New Year's Day, Thanksgiving Day, Christmas Eve to Christmas Day
Facilities: Architecture (Federal-style residence, ca. 1815); Grounds (restoration, 1978 design by Meade Palmer and 1996 design by Rudy J. Favretti)

The home of Dr. George Cabell, Sr., friend and physician of Patrick Henry, has been carefully restored and completely furnished. The grounds contain an authentically recreated plantation kitchen, the Bertha Green Webster Carriage House, and period landscaping (including a demonstration apple orchard) sponsored by the Garden Club of Virginia. The site is administered by the Lynchburg Museum System.

MELFA

EYRE HALL—GARDEN

Route 13 (between Chariton and Eastville), Melfa, VA 23410
Tel: (757) 787-2460; Fax: (757) 787-8087
Admission: Free
Parking: On site

Open: Garden, daily; Home: Garden Week, last week of April
Facilities: Architecture (frame house 1735, enlarged 1765); Garden (walled, boxwood)

The site, a Virginia Historic Landmark, features an original boxwood garden enclosed by a wall constructed of brick brought from England as ballast in sailing ships.

MONTPELIER STATION

JAMES MADISON'S MONTPELIER

11407 Constitution Highway. (Route 20, 4 miles south of Orange),
Montpelier Station, VA 22957
Tel: (540) 672-2728; Fax: (540) 672-0411
Internet Address: http://www.montpelier.org/
Admission: Fee: adult $11.00, child (<6) free, child (6-13) $4.50, senior $8.00
Attendance: 100,000
Established: 1984
Membership: Y
Wheelchair Accessible: P
Parking: On site, with admission
Open: April to November, Daily, 9:30am-5:30pm; December to March, Daily, 9:30am-4:30pm
Closed: New Year's Eve to New Year's Day, 1st Saturday in November, Thanksgiving Day, Christmas Eve to Christmas Day
Best Time(s) of Year to Visit: April to May (gardens)
Facilities: Architecture (manor house, begun ca.1760; many subsequent changes particularly under duPont ownership beginning in 1901); Gardens (initial design by Madison's French gardener Beazee; duPont Garden design by Charles Gillette; 1992 restoration design by Rudy J. Favretti); Grounds (2,700 acres; formal gardens, pastureland, 200-acre old growth forest); Shop; Trails (2 miles); Visitor Center
Activities: Education Programs; Festival Montpelier Hunt Races (Nov, 1st Sat; steeplechase horse races); Guided Tours Behind-the-Scenes Tour (mid-Mar-Oct, daily, 11am & 3pm), General (9am-4pm), Groups 20+ (reserve two weeks in advance, 672-2728 x411), Landscape Tour (mid-Mar-Oct, Sun, 2pm), Saturday Estate Tour (mid-Mar-Oct, Sat, 2pm)

Montpelier was the life-long home of James Madison, fourth president of the United States and "Father of the Constitution." Purchased and expanded by the duPont family in 1901, the site remains famous for thoroughbred horses and the annual Montpelier Hunt Races. In 1984, the property was acquired by the National Trust for Historic Preservation and is operated as a monument to Madison. In the early nineteenth century, Madison enjoyed a garden of nearly four acres. Following the fashion of the era, the Madison garden contained a mixture of vegetables, fruit trees, flowers, and ornamental shrubs. After the widowed Dolley Madison sold Montpelier in 1844, the garden suffered a half-century of neglect under subsequent owners. The boundaries of the garden were reduced, most of the Madisons' plantings vanished over the years, and the terraces were plowed down and planted in vegetables. Following William duPont's purchase of Montpelier in 1900, his wife, Anna Rogers duPont, created a two-acre twentieth-century formal garden on the site of Madison's garden. William and Anna duPont's daughter, Marion duPont Scott made further changes and additions to the garden, including the addition of several perennial beds and the introduction of a number of unusual plants. Following Montpelier's acquisition by the National Trust for Historic Preservation, the plantings of the Montpelier formal garden were carefully identified and catalogued. Restoration, funded by the Garden Club of Virginia, is focusing on the formal garden as it may have appeared in the first decade of the twentieth century, but with the overall goal of illustrating garden design broadly typical of the early 1900s. The flowerbeds incorporate many of the perennials found in the early duPont garden, many varieties of bearded and Japanese iris, day lilies, and peonies, along with other plant materials common to the period. Much of the earlier English park-style landscape was retained by the duPonts. Exotic trees replaced the declining over-mature trees of the Madison period as these fell victim to decay or disease. Ornamental shrub beds were planted, including the double rows of boxwood along circular drive in front of the main house, as were large beds of shrubs, trees, and perennials to the sides and rear of the main house. Today Montpelier's grounds contain many mature trees including over fifty different species of evergreens and deciduous specimens. Montpelier also offers a National Natural Landmark Forest. Accessed by the Big Woods Trail, the 200 acres of trees found in the James Madison Natural Landmark Forest have been virtually undisturbed by man.

MOUNT VERNON

MOUNT VERNON—GARDENS

George Washington Memorial Parkway., Mount Vernon,
VA 22121
Tel: (703) 780-2000
Internet Address: http://www.mountvernon.org/
Admission: Fee: adult $11.00, child (<6) free, child (5-11) $5.00, senior $10.50
Attendance: 1,000,000
Established: 1858
Membership: Y
Wheelchair Accessible: P
Parking: Free, outside estate entrance
Open: March, daily, 9am-5pm; April to August, daily, 8am-5pm; September to October, daily, 9am-5pm; November to February, daily, 9am-4pm
Best Time(s) of Year to Visit: April to July
Facilities: Architecture (George Washington estate); Food Services (snack bar and restaurant located outside main gate); Gardens (kitchen, pleasure); Greenhouse (reconstruction of original eighteenth-century greenhouse complex); Grounds (500 acres, landscape design by Washington); Shops Garden Shop (books, garden themed accessories, plants, heirloom seeds); Trail Forest Trail (¼ mile)
Activities: Guided Tours Garden & Landscape (Apr-Oct, daily, 11am/1pm/3pm, start at Mansion Circle)

Mount Vernon gardens,
Mount Vernon, VA. Dean
Martin photograph.

Home of George Washington, the first president of the United States, for over 45 years, Mount Vernon has changed very little over the last 200 years. Washington carefully developed the landscape surrounding his home to create a fitting setting as a gentleman's country seat. To the east of the mansion is a wonderful view of the Potomac River and beyond the Maryland shoreline. He designed the grounds to include gardens, rolling meadows, serpentine walkways, and groves of trees. Today, the Upper Garden includes a wide variety of flowers and trees, boxwood planted in Washington's day, and a few vegetable beds. The beds have been restored to their original size, based on careful archaeological investigation, and two boxwood parterres have been recreated. The Lower Garden supplied the Mount Vernon kitchen with fresh produce, including vegetables, herbs and fruit. Farther from the house the Fruit Garden and Nursery was used by Washington to experiment with new seeds and plants before using them elsewhere on the estate and was a source for tree-ripened fruit. Adjacent to the Mount Vernon wharf on the Potomac River, the "George Washington: Pioneer Farmer Site," provides exposure to eighteenth-century farming techniques. There is also a Forest Trail illustrating the role that native flora and fauna played in an eighteenth-century plantation economy. Mount Vernon is owned and operated by the Mount Vernon Ladies' Association.

NEWPORT NEWS

CITY OF NEWPORT NEWS—HUNTINGTON PARK ROSE GARDEN (THE ROSE GARDEN)

9285 Warwick Boulevard, Newport News, VA 23607
Tel: (757) 591-4844; Fax: (757) 926-8728
Admission: Free
Established: 1970
Wheelchair Accessible: P
Parking: Parking adjacent to garden
Open: daily, dawn to dusk
Facilities: Garden 1 acre (roses—1000 bushes; 42 varieties); Grounds Huntington Park (60 acres—public beach, boat ramp, picnicking, playground)

Situated along the James River, the Huntington Park Rose Garden contains over 1,000 rose bushes. In 2002, the American Rose Society designated the City of Newport News as an "American Rose City," the only city in Virginia to receive this honor.

TEMPLE SINAI—EDWARD E. KAHN MEMORIAL BIBLICAL GARDEN

11620 Warwick Boulevard, Newport News, VA 23601-2345
Tel: (804) 596-8352
Internet Address: http://www.ujcvp.org/temple_sinai/garden.html
Admission: No charge, donations accepted
Established: 1976
Wheelchair Accessible: Y
Parking: Parking available at the Garden
Open: Daily, 9am-5pm
Facilities: Gardens (Biblical); Grounds (½ acre)
Activities: Guided Tours (arrange in advance)

The garden features almost 100 species of plants mentioned in the Old and New Testaments. Identification labels includes Hebrew name, botanical name, and common name of the plant and the scripture wherein the plant is mentioned.

NORFOLK

CHRYSLER MUSEUM OF ART—MOSES MYERS HOUSE

331 Bank Street (at Freemason Street), Norfolk, VA 23510
Tel: (757) 441-1526; Fax: (757) 333-1089
Internet Address: http://www.chrysler.org

Admission: Fee: adult $5.00, child (<12) free, student $3.00, senior $3.00
Membership: Y
Wheelchair Accessible: Y
Parking: On street
Open: January to March, Wednesday to Saturday, 1pm-5pm; April to December,
Wednesday to Saturday, 10am-5pm; Sunday, 1pm-5pm
Closed: New Year's Day, Independence Day, Thanksgiving Day, Christmas Day
Facilities: Architecture (Federal-style residence, 1792); Garden (period, 2001
restoration design by landscape architect William D. Reiley)
Activities: Guided Tours

One of two historic homes operated by the Chrysler Museum of Art, it was built by
merchant Moses Myers, one of the wealthiest men in the country. The home stayed in
the family for six generations, resulting in 75 percent of its current furnishings and artifacts having belonged to the Myers' family. The Garden Club of Virginia has undertaken
the restoration of the garden.

CHRYSLER MUSEUM OF ART—WILLOUGHBY-BAYLOR HOUSE

601 E. Freemason Street, Norfolk, VA 23501
Tel: (757) 441-1526; Fax: (757) 383-1089
Internet Address: http://www.chrysler.org
Admission: Fee: adult $5.00, child (<12) free, student $3.00, senior $3.00
Membership: Y
Wheelchair Accessible: Y
Parking: On street
Open: January to March, Wednesday to Saturday, 1pm-5pm; April to December,
Wednesday to Saturday, 10am-5pm; Sunday, 1pm-5pm
Closed: New Year's Day, Independence Day, Thanksgiving Day, Christmas Day
Facilities: Architecture (Georgian/Federal residence, 1794); Garden (period, late
eighteenth century)
Activities: Guided Tours

Located in the heart of downtown Norfolk, the Willoughby-Baylor House is one of three
historic homes operated by the Chrysler Museum. The house, furnished with authentic period pieces, depicts an upper middle-class family's lifestyle in eighteenth-century Virginia.
The grounds include a restored late eighteenth-century garden.

NORFOLK BOTANICAL GARDEN (AHS RAP)

6700 Azalea Garden Road, Norfolk, VA 23518-5337
Tel: (757) 441-5830; Fax: (757) 853-8294
Internet Address: http://www.norfolkbotanicalgarden.org
Admission: Fee: adult $6.00, child (<6) free, child (6-16) $4.00, senior $5.00
Attendance: 211,000
Established: 1938
Membership: Y
Wheelchair Accessible: Y
Open: April 14 to October 15, daily, 9am-7pm; October 16 to April 13, daily, 9am-5pm
Closed: Christmas Day
Best Time(s) of Year to Visit: May (azaleas, rhododendrons, dogwoods)
Facilities: Arboretum (flowering); Auditorium; Food Services The Azalea Room Café
(mid Mar-mid Nov, 855-3176.); Gardens (20; butterfly, camellia, Colonial herb,

desert, English border, four seasons, fragrance, healing, holly, Japanese, perennial, Italian Renaissance court, rose, sunken, woodland); Grounds (155 acres), Flowering Arboretum (17? acres); Library (1,900 volumes); Picnic Area; Shop Garden Gift Shop (Feb-Dec, daily, 9am-5pm; gifts); Special Collections (azalea, camellia, rose, rhododendron); Statuary Vista (11 heroic-sized statues of notable painters and sculptors); Visitors Center (daily, 9am-5pm)
Activities: Classes; Education Programs (adults and children); Guided Tours Boat (Mon-Fri, 11:45am-1:45, 15 minutes before the hour; Sat-Sun, 11:40am-3:45pm, 15 minutes before the hour; $3), Group (mid-Mar-Oct, daily, 10am-4pm, reserve in advance), Tram (mid-Mar-Oct, daily, 10am-4pm, on the hour, free); Lectures; Temporary Exhibitions; Workshops

The garden dates back to 1938, when 200 African-American workers sponsored by a Works Progress Administration grant cleared the dense native vegetation and planted 4,000 azaleas. Today, Norfolk Botanical Garden features major collections of azaleas, rhododendrons, camellias, hollies, dogwoods, crepe myrtles, flowering fruit trees, annuals and perennials. In the center of the site a 17½-acre arboretum displays 336 different flowering trees. Among the over twenty thematic displays are the Healing Garden, featuring medicinal plants, a gentle stream, and pools; a rose garden, containing over 4,000 rose plants representing over 250 varieties; an All-America Selections Display Garden; a two-acre butterfly garden, providing a habitat to attract and support butterflies and moths, including a swallowtail and monarch nursery, nectar garden, moonlight garden, and butterfly bush collection; a Colonial herb garden, highlighting culinary and medicinal herbs and plants within a typical American garden of the 1700s and 1800s; an English border garden, illustrating the essential elements of traditional English garden design, a fragrance garden, designed for the visually impaired and all who enjoy fragrant plants; a four seasons garden, containing more than fifty species of wildflowers and ten species of grasses; the Hofheimer Camellia Garden, containing over 450 varieties; a holly garden, displaying 121 varieties in areas devoted to English, American, and Japanese hollies; a Japanese garden, created to honor Norfolk's sister city, Kitakyushu; two perennial gardens; the Renaissance court, inspired by the classic lines of the sixteenth-century Italian landscaping; a rhododendron garden, containing over 175 varieties; and a sunken garden, featuring a small pool complemented by a variety of shade-loving and sun-tolerant plants. The six-acre Virginia Native Plant Garden recreates four historic plant habitats. A three-acre children's adventure garden will open in 2006. The Norfolk Botanical Garden, owned by the city of Norfolk, is under the operating control of the Norfolk Botanical Garden Society, a non-profit organization.

ONANCOCK

KER PLACE—GARDENS

69 Market Street, Onancock, VA 23417
Tel: (757) 787-8012
Internet Address: http://www.kerrplace.org/
Admission: Fee: adult $5.00, child (<18) $2.00
Attendance: 3,500
Membership: Y
Wheelchair Accessible: P
Parking: Free on site, 20 spaces
Open: March to December, Tuesday to Saturday, 10am-4pm
Best Time(s) of Year to Visit: May to September

Facilities: Architecture (federal residence, ca. 1799); Gardens (period, nineteenth century); Grounds (1981 restoration by the Garden Club of Virginia, design by landscape architect Rudy J. Favretti); Shop (arts, crafts, books)

Headquarters of the Eastern Shore of Virginia Historical Society, the house displays period furnishings and decorative arts. The Garden Club of Virginia undertook a restoration of the grounds in 1981. With no evidence of the appearance of the original early nineteenth-century grounds and gardens, the large trees that shaded the house were accepted as the focus of the restoration and were supplemented with a variety of specimen trees. Between the entrance gates and the front of the house large plantings of shrubs were installed in the manner of the early nineteenth century. To the rear of the house is a long walk, shaded by crepe myrtles and terminating in an arbor. Nearer the house flower borders were created, but were planted simply with day lilies and periwinkle in order to keep maintenance to a minimum and to suggest the form of a garden that might have existed. Listed on the National Register of Historic Places, Ker Place is a designated Virginia Historic Landmark.

PETERSBURG

LEE MEMORIAL PARK—WILDFLOWER SANCTUARY

1832 Johnson Road (Crater Road exit off Interstate 95), Petersburg, VA 23805
Tel: (804) 861-8490
Internet Address: http://www.pgcvirginia.org
Admission: Free
Established: 1930
Parking: Paved lot on site
Best Time(s) of Year to Visit: April to October
Facilities: Gardens (native plant); Grounds Lee Memorial Park (330 acres)

Consisting of an eighteen-acre lake surrounded by more than 300 acres of green space within the city limits of the city of Petersburg, Lee Memorial Park is a unique botanical habitat for some rare and endangered species. Listed on the National Register of Historic Places, Lee Park was the site of the only known women's conservation project accomplished by the Depression-era Works Progress Administration. Between 1935 and 1940, the project created a twenty-five acre botanical preserve containing more than 500 different species of native plants. Involving women from the Petersburg Garden Club and from Petersburg's African-American community, the work was directed by the horticulturist Donald Claiborne Holden. It also financed the establishment of a herbarium and the creation of more than 200 botanical watercolors by Bessie Niemeyer Marshall. While the sanctuary was not maintained after World War II, it is estimated that approximately 70 percent of the species from the herbarium collection are still growing in the park today. The Petersburg Garden Club and University Press of Virginia have co-published a book, *With Paintbrush and Shovel: Preserving Virginia's Wildflowers*, which showcases 222 of Marshall's botanical watercolors and the primary surviving records of the WPA project.

RICHMOND

AGECROFT HALL AND GARDENS

4305 Sulgrave Road, Richmond, VA 23221-3256
Tel: (804) 353-4241; Fax: (804) 253-2151

Internet Address: http://www.agecrofthall.com/
Admission: Fee: adult $7.00, child (<5) free, student $4.00, senior $6.00
Attendance: 20,000
Established: 1969
Membership: N
Wheelchair Accessible: P
Parking: Parking for 52 cars, three buses
Open: Tuesday to Saturday, 10am-4pm; Sunday, 12:30pm-5pm
Closed: Legal holidays
Best Time(s) of Year to Visit: April to September
Facilities: Architecture (15th-century English Tudor manor house); Gardens
Elizabethan (fragrance, knot, herb, medicinal, sunken); Grounds (designed by
landscape architect Charles Gillette); Shop
Activities: Concerts (Shakespeare Festival); Education Programs

Located in the Windsor Farms neighborhood, Agecroft Hall was actually built in Lan-
cashire, England, in the late fifteenth century. In 1925, it was purchased by Richmonder
Thomas C. Williams, Jr., who had it dismantled, crated, and shipped across the Atlantic,
and then painstakingly reassembled in Richmond. The house is furnished with authentic
pieces dating from 1485 to 1660. Agecroft's grounds reflect the order and opulence of
Elizabethan English landscaping. Gardens include a formal Elizabethan knot garden; a fragrance garden, containing Elizabethan aromatics; and a sunken garden, featuring annual
plantings.

LEWIS GINTER BOTANICAL GARDEN (AHS RAP)

1800 Lakeside Avenue, Richmond, VA 23228-4700
Tel: (804) 262-9887; Fax: (804) 262-9934
Internet Address: http://www.lewisginter.org
Admission: Fee: adult $8.00, child (3-12) $4.00, child (2-12) $4.00, senior $7.00
Attendance: 61,000
Established: 1984
Membership: Y
Wheelchair Accessible: Y
Open: Daily, 9am-5pm
Closed: New Year's Day, Thanksgiving Day, Christmas Eve, Christmas Day
Facilities: Architecture Bloemendaal House (Victorian mansion, 1884);
Conservatory/Greenhouses; Food Services Garden Café (daily, 10am-4pm), Robins
Tea House (daily, 11:30am-2:30pm); Gardens (children's, day lily, dwarf conifer,
oriental, perennial, Victorian, water, wetland, wildflower); Grounds (25 acres);
Herbarium; Library (3,500 volumes); Shop (Mon-Sat, 10am-5pm; Sun, 1pm-5pm;
gardening books, tools, stationery, containers, vases, garden ornaments, household
decorative items); Visitors Center
Activities: Arts Festival; Classes; Concerts; Education Programs (adults and children);
Flower Shows; Guided Tours; Lectures

The grounds contain the Henry M. Flagler Perennial Garden, one of the largest and
most diverse perennial gardens on the East Coast (3 acres with 770 species); the Grace
Arents Garden, an elegant Victorian-style garden restored by the Garden Club of Virginia; Asian Valley, an exotic garden setting; the Martha and Reed West Island Garden, a
wetland environment with a stunning display of pitcher plants, water irises, and lotuses; a
Children's Garden with colorful and interesting plants to attract butterflies and birds; the
Lucy Payne Minor Garden, a study garden with an extensive collection of daffodils and
day lilies (over 200 varieties, including the Stout Medal day lily collection); the Margaret

Streb Conifer Garden featuring dwarf conifers; and the Vienna Cobb Anderson Wild-flower Meadow.

MAYMONT FOUNDATION

2201 Shields Lake Drive, Richmond, VA 23220-6899
Tel: (804) 358-7166; Fax: (804) 358-9994
Internet Address: http://www.maymont.org
Admission: Suggested contribution $4.00
Attendance: 400,000
Established: 1975
Membership: Y
Wheelchair Accessible: Y
Parking: Free on site, 3 lots
Open: Grounds & Gardens, Daily, 10am-5pm; Exhibits, Tuesday to Sunday, noon-5pm
Facilities: Arboretum; Architecture (Romanesque Revival residence, 1893, design by Edgerton Rogers); Food Services Café (Tues-Sun, 11am-3pm); Gardens (butterfly, daylily, herb, English courtyard, Italian, Japanese, labyrinth, perennial, vegetable); Grounds Arboretum (100 acres); Shop; Special Collections (day lily, herb, native plant, rhododendron); Visitor Center (entrance: 2201 Shields Lake Drive, daily, 10am-5pm).
Activities: Carriage Rides (Sun, noon-4pm); Flower and Garden Show; Guided Tours Maymont House (on the hour & ½ hour); Hay Rides (Jun-Aug, Sat-Sun), 1pm-4pm); Plant Sales; Tram Rides (Tues-Sun, noon-5pm)

Originally the country estate of Major James H. and Sallie May Dooley, the gardens were developed over a period of thirty years. Upon Mrs. Dooley's death in 1925, Maymont was bequeathed to the city of Richmond. Attractions for visitors added over the years include the Nature Center, Native Virginia Wildlife Exhibits, the Children's Farm, and the Carriage Collection. At Maymont, rolling lawns in the English park style form a naturalistic backdrop connecting the major components of the landscape. Gardens include an Italian garden designed by Noland and Baskerville in 1910, incorporating balustraded terraces, geometrically shaped beds or parterres, clipped evergreens, fountains, and pergolas; a Japanese stroll garden originally created around 1911 by Muto, a master Japanese gardener, and subsequently greatly expanded; an herb garden, featuring culinary, medicinal, and olfactory herbs; an American Hemerocallis Society display garden, containing over 150 day lily cultivars; the enclosed English-inspired Carriage House Garden; a butterfly garden; and a vegetable garden. Maymont's grounds contain mature specimens of trees and shrubs not found elsewhere in Virginia, along with native species of particular size and beauty. Since 1975, Maymont has been maintained and operated by the private non-profit Maymont Foundation.

VIRGINIA HOUSE

4301 Sulgrave Road, Richmond, VA 23221-2212
Tel: (804) 353-4251
Internet Address: http://www.vahistorical.org/vh/virginia_house01.htm
Admission: Fee: adult $4.00, child $2.00, student $2.00, senior $3.00
Open: Friday to Saturday, 10am-4pm; Sunday, 12:30pm-5pm
Closed: New Year's Eve to New Year's Day, Easter Sunday, Memorial Day, Independence Day, Labor Day, Thanksgiving Day, Christmas Eve to Christmas Day
Facilities: Architecture (English Tudor-style residence, 1929); Gardens (azalea, bog, English/Italian-inspired formal, four seasons, rose, tea); Grounds (8 acres; 1927-1947 designs by landscape architect Charles F. Gillette); Picnic Area
Activities: Guided Tours (on the hour)

Situated on a hillside overlooking the James River in Richmond's fashionable West End, Virginia House was originally the home of diplomat Alexander Weddell and his wife, Virginia. Completed a few months before the stock market crash of 1929, the house is constructed from the materials of a twelfth-century English priory in a blend of three romantic English Tudor designs. Its collections reflect the romance of the American Country Place movement and include Elizabethan oak furniture, Flemish tapestries, Spanish colonial art, Oriental carpets, and fine silver and china. The formal gardens, developed in collaboration with landscape architect Charles Gillette over the twenty years following the construction of the house, are a synthesis of Italian and English gardening styles. Today, close to 1,000 types of ornamental plants thrive throughout formal and naturalistic gardens. Extensive English and American boxwood plantings lend structure and create a sense of both mystery and tranquility. Hollies, southern magnolia, and red cedar frame in distant views. Wisteria, roses, and climbing hydrangea drape balconies and garden rails. Now owned and operated by the Virginia Historical Society as a museum, the house has been preserved much as it was when the Weddells resided there.

ROANOKE

VIRGINIA WESTERN COMMUNITY COLLEGE— THE COMMUNITY ARBORETUM

3095 Colonial Avenue S.W., Roanoke, VA 24038
Tel: (540) 857-7120
Internet Address: http://www.vw.vccs.edu/arboretum
Admission: Free
Wheelchair Accessible: Y
Open: Daily, sunrise-sunset
Facilities: Arboretum; Gardens (children's, conifer, herb, perennial, rock, shade); Grounds (2 acres)
Activities: Guided Tours; Seminars; Workshops

Located adjacent to the greenhouse on South Campus, the Community Arboretum offers approximately 700 labeled plant taxa displayed in nine separate gardens and plant collections surrounding a centrally located amphitheater. Highlights include a wisteria-covered arbor, a conifer garden containing over 100 different cone-bearing trees and shrubs; a perennial garden displaying over 90 hardy herbaceous perennials in a rainbow color theme; a rock garden offering 75 different shrubs and herbaceous perennials set among rock outcrops and bordered by intersecting arcs of mortarless stone walls; a shade garden filled with 190 different low-light preferring herbaceous perennials; an herb garden; and a children's garden boasting a plant zoo (plants with animal names), a maze, and two water features.

STRATFORD

STRATFORD HALL PLANTATION—BIRTHPLACE OF ROBERT E. LEE

Route 214, Stratford, VA 22558
Tel: (804) 493-8038
Internet Address: http://www.stratfordhall.org/
Admission: Fee: adult $9.00, child (<6) free, child (6-11) $5.00, senior $8.00; Group rates
Membership: Y

Open: Daily, 9am-4:30pm
Closed: New Year's Eve to New Year's Day, Thanksgiving Day, Christmas Eve to Christmas Day
Facilities: Archeology Exhibits; Architecture (Georgian mansion, 1730-1738); Food Services (log cabin dining room; daily, 11:30am-3pm); Gardens East Garden (eighteenth-century green garden; 1930-1932 restoration by landscape architects Morley Williams & Arthur Shurcliff; 1955 by Alden Hopkins), North Vista (1 mile, numerous species of flowering trees), Slave Garden (herbs, vegetables), West Garden (eighteenth-century flower garden; annuals, perennials, bulbs); Grounds (1,670 acres); Library (by appointment; Mon-Fri, 9am-5pm); Shop (daily, 9am-5pm)
Activities: Education Programs; Guided Tours, Special (gardens, architecture, decorative arts; by appointment, $11.00/person)

The ancestral home of the Lee family of Virginia and the birthplace of Robert E. Lee, Stratford Hall is restored to its eighteenth-century grandeur. In the early 1930s, based on site archeology, the Garden Club of Virginia restored the formal East Garden in a typical eighteenth-century English style, a terraced green garden composed of irregular parterres outlined with English boxwood and enclosed by brick walls. The garden is planted with camellias, Cornelian-cherry trees, crepe myrtles, fringe trees, and golden-rain trees. To the north of the East Garden grows a small but serviceable orchard. Although archaeology indicates that the area west of the main house was historically not a garden space, this area is now devoted for educational purposes to an example of an eighteenth-century-style flower garden. This West Garden contains daffodils, roses, johnny-jumpups, and many other perennials, annuals, and bulbs in common use in the eighteenth century. Adjacent to the West Garden, enclosed within the borders of espalier-trained fruit trees, is an eighteenth-century vegetable garden and a contiguous herb garden. Also of interest, located between the Slave Quarters is a demonstration garden containing a small sampling of the varieties of herbs and vegetables grown and used by the African-American population at Stratford. The site is owned and operated by the Robert E. Lee Memorial Association, a non-profit organization.

SURRY

BACON'S CASTLE

Route 617 (just north of intersection of Routes 617 & 10), Surry, VA 23883
Tel: (757) 357-5976
Internet Address: http://www.apva.org/apva/bacon.html
Established: 1983
Open: March, Saturday, 10am-4pm; Sunday, noon-4pm; April to October, Tuesday to Saturday, 10am-4pm; Sunday, noon-4pm; November, Saturday, 10am-4pm; Sunday, noon-4pm
Closed: Independence Day
Facilities: Architecture (Jacobean house, 1665); Gardens (period, 17th-century, 1989 restoration by landscape architect Rudy J. Favretti); Grounds; Shop
Activities: Guided Tours

A rare surviving example of Jacobean architecture in the western hemisphere, Bacon's Castle was built in 1665 by a prosperous planter, Arthur Allen. Primarily of architectural interest, the house is sparsely furnished with eighteenth-century pieces and reproductions selected to interpret daily life. An archaeological investigation, jointly sponsored by the Association for the Preservation of Virginia Antiquities and the Garden Club of Virginia, revealed adjacent to the house the remains of outbuildings and three separate gardens from the seventeenth, eighteenth, and nineteenth centuries, respectively. The oldest may be the earliest of its kind found in North America. Based on these excavations the restored design consists of a rectangular grid divided into six planting beds. White sand walkways give access to the planting beds. A brick wall at the north end of the garden provides wind protection and sun-reflected warmth for the starting bed at its base. The three gardens reveal the transition in garden design and conception during three centuries at Bacon's Castle. Owned and managed by the Association for the Preservation of Virginia Antiquities, the site is designated a National Historic Landmark.

CHIPPOKES PLANTATION STATE PARK

695 Chippokes Park Road (Route 634, just off Route 10), Surry, VA 23883
Tel: (757) 294-3625
Internet Address: http://www.dcr.state.va.us/parks/chippoke.htm
Admission: Fee: adult $6.00, child $3.00
Parking: Pay on site -$2 weekdays; $3 weekends
Facilities: Architecture (Italianate mansion, 1854); Farm and Forestry Museum; Formal Gardens; Grounds (1,403 acres); Historic Working Farm; Native Woodland; Picnic Area; Shop; Trails (3.5 miles); Visitor Center
Activities: Camping; Fishing, Boating; Guided Tours Mansion (Apr-Oct, Sat-Sun)

One of the oldest working farms in the United States, Chippokes Plantation State Park is a living historical exhibit located in a rural agricultural area along the James River in Surry County. The plantation, retaining its 17th-century boundaries, offers a variety of cultivated gardens and native woodland. Azaleas, crepe myrtle, boxwood, and seasonal flowers accent the formal gardens, surrounding the mid-nineteenth-century Chippokes Mansion. The park is also home to the Chippokes Farm and Forestry Museum, a seven building complex containing a collection of more than 3,000 objects interpreting rural early American farm life. The park also includes a wide variety of traditional offerings. The Virginia Department of Conservation and Recreation operates the park in cooperation with the Chippokes Plantation Farm Foundation.

VIENNA

MEADOWLARK BOTANICAL GARDENS

9750 Meadowlark Gardens Court (off Beulah Road, between Routes 7 & 123), Vienna, VA 22182-1992
Tel: (703) 255-3631; Fax: (703) 255-2392
Internet Address: http://www.meadowlarkgardens.org
Admission: Fee (Mar-Nov): adult $4.00, child (<7) free, child (7-17) $2.00, senior $2.00
Free (Dec-Feb)
Attendance: 110,000
Established: 1980
Parking: Ample on site
Open: April to May, daily, 10am-6pm; June to August, daily, 9am-8pm; September to October, daily, 9am-7pm; November to March, daily, 10am-5pm
Closed: New Year's Day, Thanksgiving Day, Christmas Day
Best Time(s) of Year to Visit: March to June, September to October
Facilities: Atrium; Food Services (snack bar); Gardens (cancer, day lily, herb, hosta, native plant); Gazebo; Grounds 95 acres; Lakes 3; Shop; Special Collections (day lily, hosta, Potomac Valley natives); Trails (4 miles); Visitors Center
Activities: Education Programs (about 40/year); Guided Tours (by appointment); Workshops

The garden collects and displays plants from around the world with a special focus on those native to the Potomac River Valley. Surrounded by the White Garden and terrace plantings, the atrium houses flowers, fountains, and a meandering stream. Paved trails provide access to mature woods, grassy hills, open fields, and gardens. Seasonal displays of bulbs, annuals, wildflowers, and chrysanthemums dot the landscape with color, as do the permanent plantings of the flowering cherry collection, the crab apple circle, the lilac garden, the azalea woods, the hosta collection, the Stout day lily collection, the herb garden, the native conservation collections, siberian iris, peonies, and evergreens. A cancer garden displays plants from which cancer treatment medicines are derived. The site is owned and operated by the Northern Virginia Regional Park Authority.

VIRGINIA BEACH

FRANCIS LAND HOUSE HISTORIC SITE AND GARDENS

3131 Virginia Beach Boulevard, Virginia Beach, VA 23452-6923
Tel: (757) 431-4000; Fax: (757) 431-3733
Admission: Fee: adult $4.00, child (<6) free, student $2.00
Established: 1986
Parking: Free parking on-site
Open: Tuesday to Saturday, 9am-5pm; Sunday, 11am-5pm
Best Time(s) of Year to Visit: March to May
Facilities: Architecture (brick plantation house, 1800); Gardens (formal, herb, vegetable); Grounds (7 acres), Wetlands (3 acres with trail); Shop (books, coins, jewelry, pewter, toys)
Activities: Guided Tours (last tour 4:30pm)

A living history museum, the site illustrates life on a plantation in the early days of Virginia. The gardens, maintained by Virginia Beach Master Gardeners, include heirloom vegetables, herbs, and formal plantings. Also on the property is a three-acre wooded wetland area accessed by walking trail.

VIRGINIA TECH HAMPTON ROADS AGRICULTURAL RESEARCH AND EXTENSION CENTER—DEMONSTRATION GARDENS AND ARBORETUM

1444 Diamond Springs Road, Virginia Beach, VA 23455-3315
Tel: (757) 363-3900; Fax: (757) 363-3950
Internet Address: http://filebox.vt.edu/vaes/HRAREC/Projects/gardens.html
Admission: Free
Open: Grounds, daily
Office, Monday to Friday, 9am-5pm
Facilities: Arboretum (trees, shrubs); Grounds Center (107 acres); Gardens (annual, herb, perennial)
Activities: Flower Trials; Education Programs

A unit of Virginia Tech, the center conducts research on weed, insect, and disease management of ornamental plants as well as plant production and growth regulation. The demonstration gardens contain a wide array of annuals, perennials, shrubs, and trees that are being evaluated for suitability to the Hampton Roads climate and conditions.

WAYNESBORO

CITY OF WAYNESBORO—WAYNESBORO ARBORETUM

Constitution Park, Main Street & McElroy Street, Waynesboro, VA 22980
Tel: (540) 942-6735; Fax: (540) 942-6799
Internet Address: http://www.waynesboro.va.us
Admission: Free
Open: dawn-dusk
Best Time(s) of Year to Visit: Spring to Summer
Facilities: Arboretum (bulb display, shrub borders, famous and historical tree collection)

   Located in downtown Waynesboro, the arboretum contains labeled tree collections, shrub displays, bulb plantings, annual and perennial areas.

WESTMORELAND COUNTY

GEORGE WASHINGTON BIRTHPLACE
NATIONAL MONUMENT—GARDENS

Route 204 (off Route 3), Westmoreland County, VA 22443
Tel: (804) 224-1732; Fax: (804) 224-2142
Internet Address: http://www.nps.gov/gewa
Admission: Fee $4.00; Free: Washington's Birthday & Independence Day
Attendance: 25,000
Established: 1930
Membership: Y
Wheelchair Accessible: Y
Parking: Free at Visitor Center
Open: Daily, 9am-5pm
Closed: New Year's Day, Thanksgiving Day, Christmas Day
Facilities: Architecture Memorial House (Colonial Revival plantation with kitchen house and other outbuildings, 1930); Gardens (period, Colonial, herb & flower); Grounds (550 acres)
Activities: Talk (park ranger, hourly)

   Known at the time of Washington's birth as Pope's Creek Plantation (later Wakefield Plantation), the site includes a large Colonial flower and herb garden and a living history colonial farm.

WILLIAMSBURG

COLONIAL WILLIAMSBURG—GARDENS

Bounded by Boundary, Francis & Lafayette Streets,
Williamsburg, VA 23187
Tel: (757) 229-1000

Colonial Williamsburg—
Gardens, Williamsburg, VA.

Internet Address: http://www.colonialwilliamsburg.org/
Admission: Fee (1 Day Pass) $33.00, child (6-17) $16.00; Fee (Year Pass): adult
$57.00; child (6-17) $29.00
Attendance: 750,000
Membership: N
Wheelchair Accessible: Y
Parking: On site
Open: Daily, 9am-5pm
Facilities: Gardens (designs by Arthur Shurcliff and Alden Hopkins); Grounds
(Historic Area encompasses more than 300 acres, including more than 80 restored
gardens); Shop Colonial Nursery (eighteenth-century plant material in the context of a
colonial nursery)
Activities: Guided Tours

The Historic Area of Colonial Williamsburg contains numerous eighteenth-century gardens spread throughout the restored area, from the formal Anglo-Dutch gardens at the Governor's Palace to small plots behind restored houses. Each represents an effort to strike a balance between formality and natural beauty. Colonial Williamsburg also hosts seasonal
horticultural symposia. The Williamsburg Garden Symposium and the Colonial Williamsburg Holiday Symposium span a wide array of topics that change annually. Additionally, the
Colonial Nursery, an interpretive and sales site, features eighteenth-century garden plantings,
botanical histories, historically accurate plants, and reproduction gardening tools for sale.

WINCHESTER

GLEN BURNIE MUSEUM—GARDENS (AHS RAP)

801 Amherst Street, Winchester, VA 22601
Tel: (540) 662-1473; Fax: (540) 662-8756
Internet Address: http://www.glenburniemuseum.org
Admission: Fee (Museum & Gardens): adult $8.00, child (<7) free, child (7-16) $6.00,
senior $6.00; Fee (Gardens only): $5.00
Attendance: 8,000
Open: April to October, Tuesday to Saturday, 10am-4pm; Sunday, noon-4pm;
November to March, groups, by appointment
Facilities: Architecture (Georgian brick residence, 1794); Gardens (herb, oriental,
parterre, perennial, rose, vegetable, water); Grounds Gardens (6 acres)
Activities: Concert Series Glen Burnie Gardens at Night; Education Programs; Guided
Tours Garden (Fri, 10:30am), Group (schedule in advance); Performances; Self-
guided Tours

The home site of Winchester's founder, Col. James Wood, Glen Burnie offers an historic manor house furnished with fine antiques, paintings, decorative objects, and extensive formal gardens. The formal gardens surrounding the house were laid out by Julian
Wood Glass, Jr., the last of Wood's descendants to own Glen Burnie and his friend,
R. Lee Taylor. The gardens feature sculpture, fountains, and architectural follies. Also
planned for the site is the Museum of the Shenandoah Valley, scheduled to open in 2005.

VIRGIN ISLANDS

St. Croix

.Frederiksted

The number in the parentheses following the city name indicates the number of gardens/ arboreta in that municipality. If there is no number, one is understood. For example, in the text one listing would be found under Frederiksted.

ST. CROIX

FREDERIKSTED—ST. GEORGE VILLAGE BOTANICAL GARDEN OF ST. CROIX (AHS RAP)

127 Estate Street George (off Queen Mary Highway), Frederiksted, VI 00840
Tel: (340) 692-2874; Fax: (340) 692-6154
Internet Address: http://www.sgvbg.org
Admission: Fee: adult $6.00, child $3.00
Attendance: 25,000
Established: 1972
Membership: Y
Wheelchair Accessible: Y
Parking: Free parking in large lot
Open: Daily, 9am-5pm
Closed: Christmas Day
Facilities: Architecture (ruins of 18th-century sugar plantation; pre-Columbian archeological site); Gardens; Grounds
(16 acres); Herbarium; Library; Shop; Special Collections (cactus/succulent, dry growing palm, medicinal herb, native tree)
Activities: Flower Shows (Mar, July)

Located on the site of an eighteenth-century Danish sugar plantation, the gardens conserve the native plant species of St. Croix as well as threatened species of other Caribbean islands that are suited to local environmental conditions. In addition to attractive plantings, flower shows, and art exhibitions, the garden preserves the ethno-botanical history of St. Croix through living, graphic, and structural displays.

WEST VIRGINIA

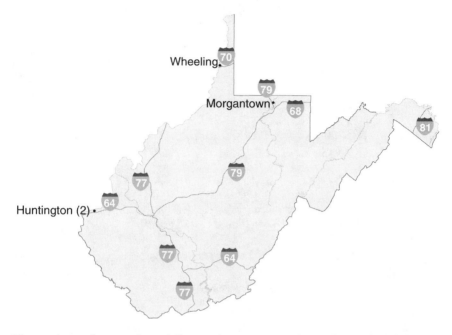

The number in the parentheses following the city name indicates the number of gardens/ arboreta in that municipality. If there is no number, one is understood. For example, in the text two listings would be found under Huntington and one listing under Wheeling.

HUNTINGTON

GREATER HUNTINGTON PARK & RECREATION DISTRICT— RITTER PARK ROSE GARDEN

1500 McCoy Road, Huntington, WV 25728
Tel: (304) 696-5954; Fax: (304) 696-5588
Internet Address: http://www.ghprd.org/
Admission: Free
Established: 1930
Membership: N
Wheelchair Accessible: P
Parking: Limited parking
Best Time(s) of Year to Visit: June to September
Facilities: Garden (rose—2 acres); Grounds Ritter Park (70 acres)

An All-American Rose Selections test garden, the site displays approximately 2,000 roses. The surrounding park offers thirty-nine species of trees.

HUNTINGTON MUSEUM OF ART, INC. (HMA)

2033 McCoy Road, Huntington, WV 25701-4999
Tel: (304) 529-2701; Fax: (304) 529-7447; TDDY: (304) 522-2243
Internet Address: http://www.hmoa.org
Admission: Free
Attendance: 65,000
Established: 1947
Membership: Y
Wheelchair Accessible: Y
Parking: Free on site
Open: Tuesday, 10am-9pm; Wednesday to Saturday, 10am-5pm; Sunday, noon-5pm
Closed: New Year's Day, Independence Day, Thanksgiving Day, Christmas Day
Facilities: Architecture (addition designed by Walter Gropius); Auditorium (270 seat); Galleries (11); Library (17,000 volumes); Nature Trail (1½ miles); Open Air Stage; Plant Conservatory (3,000 square feet); Reading Room; Sculpture Garden; Shop (regional art and crafts, jewelry, books)
Activities: Arts Festival; Concerts; Education Program (adults and children); Films; Gallery Talks; Guided Tours (groups 10+, arrange in advance); Lectures; Temporary/Traveling Exhibitions

Opened to the public in 1952, the Huntington Museum of Art is West Virginia's largest art museum. The museum collection reveals a range of artistic interests: American and European paintings, Near Eastern art, British silver, antique firearms, contemporary prints, and Appalachian folk art. Through changing exhibitions the museum shares its collection and offers a panorama of traveling exhibitions from international sources. Sculpture is displayed on the museum grounds. The Education Gallery features a participatory experience for children in an interactive environment. The museum is home to the C. Fred Edwards Conservatory, the region's only conservatory, featuring year-round displays of sub-tropical palms, shrubs, ground covers, orchids, and seasonal flowers. Fountains and sculpture enhance the atmosphere. Herb gardens, a miniature rose garden, and nature trails on fifty acres of wooded grounds provide an environment for learning and fun. Horticultural programming includes workshops and classes for children and adults as well as summer nature day camps for children.

MORGANTOWN

CORE ARBORETUM—WEST VIRGINIA UNIVERSITY

Monongahela Boulevard, Route 7, WVU Evansdale Campus, Morgantown, WV 26506
Tel: (304) 293-5201; Fax: (304) 293-6363
Internet Address: http://www.as.wvu.edu/biology/facility/arboretum.html
Admission: Free
Attendance: 25,000
Established: 1948
Membership: N
Wheelchair Accessible: P
Parking: Free on site or at adjacent WVU Coliseum
Open: Daily, dawn-dusk
Best Time(s) of Year to Visit: April to early May (wildflowers), October to early
November (fall colors)
Facilities: Amphitheater (80 seats); Arboretum (old-growth forest; wildflowers);
Grounds (91 acres); Trails (3½ miles)
Activities: Education Programs; Guided Tours Bird Walks
(Apr-May, Tues & Fri mornings), General (by appointment), Wildflower Walks (last 3
Sundays in Apr, 2pm); Lectures

Situated between Monongahela Boulevard and the Monongahela River, the arboretum contains three acres of lawn planted with specimen trees, but is composed mostly of old-growth forest on a steep hillside and the river flood plain. The approximately 200-foot drop presents a variety of natural habitats in which several hundred species of native trees, shrubs, and herbaceous plants may be seen. It is best known for its "spring ephemeral" wildflowers, including twinleaf, dwarf larkspur, wild blue phlox, Virginia bluebells, bloodroot, sessile trillium, Dutchman's breeches, and wild ginger. It is also a popular site for birding, especially during the spring migration season. The arboretum is managed by the West Virginia University Department of Biology.

WHEELING

OGLEBAY RESORT AND CONFERENCE CENTER— BISONNETTE GARDENS

Route 88 North (off Exit 2A, Route I-70), Wheeling, WV 26003
Tel: (304) 243-4000

Internet Address: http://www.oglebay-resort.com/gardens.htm
Parking: Free on site
Facilities: Gardens (herb, floral clock, formal, seasonal displays, terrace); Grounds
Bisonette Gardens (16 acres), Resort (1,650 acres); Shops Christmas in the Gardens
(holiday items & gifts), Garden Center Gift Shop (flower arranging accessories, gifts
from natural materials), Palm Room (seasonal plants, fresh flowers, herbs, hanging
baskets)
Activities: Events Festival of Lights (1 million lights, Nov-Dec); Self-guided Tours
(audio tour available)

Situated in the hills surrounding Wheeling, Bisonnette Gardens (formerly Waddington Gardens) offers changing flower displays, hanging baskets, water features, and mature trees. Seasonal displays include tulips, hyacinths, pansies, and daffodils from mid-April to early May; begonias, impatiens, petunias, fuschias, and geraniums from June to September; and chrysanthemums from mid-September through late October. Donated to the city in 1926 by Earl W. Oglebay, the facility functions as both a resort and public park. It is managed by the Wheeling Park commission.

WISCONSIN

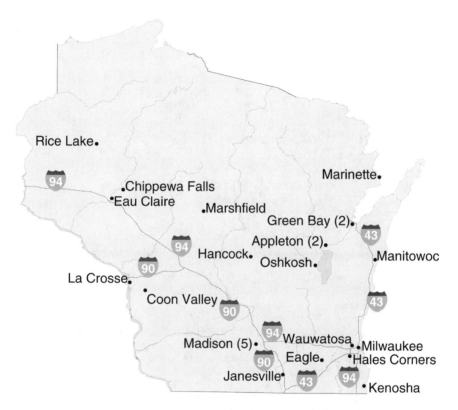

Rice Lake.

94

Marinette.

.Chippewa Falls
.Eau Claire
.Marshfield
Green Bay (2).

43

Appleton (2).
94
Hancock.
Oshkosh.
.Manitowoc

90

La Crosse.

.Coon Valley
90

43

94 Wauwatosa
Madison (5).
.Milwaukee
90
Eagle.
.Hales Corners
Janesville.
43
94
.Kenosha

The number in the parentheses following the city name indicates the number of gardens/ arboreta in that municipality. If there is no number, one is understood. For example, in the text five listings would be found under Madison and one listing under Wauwatosa.

APPLETON

CITY OF APPLETON—MEMORIAL PARK ARBORETUM AND GARDENS (THE ARB)

1313 E. Witzke Boulevard, Appleton, WI 54913-5022
Tel: (920) 993-1900; Fax: (920) 993-9492
Internet Address: http://www.the-arb.org/
Admission: No charge, donations accepted
Attendance: 100,000
Established: 1992
Membership: Y
Wheelchair Accessible: P
Parking: Plentiful parking
Open: never closed
Best Time(s) of Year to Visit: July to September
Facilities: Greenhouse (3,000 square feet [Mon-Fri, 9-5; Sat, 7-noon, May-Oct]);
Grounds (33 acres dedicated to native Wisconsin ecosystems); Visitor Center Scheig
Learning Center (designed by Taliesin Architects of Spring Green, Wisconsin)
Activities: Education Programs

The arboretum features a variety of native Wisconsin trees, shrubs, and plants. The gardens are designed to complement the arboretum and to offer changing patterns of natural beauty throughout the year.

GORDON BUBOLZ NATURE PRESERVE

4815 N. Lyndale Drive, Appleton, WI 54915
Tel: (920) 731-6041; Fax: (920) 731-9593
Internet Address: http://my.athenet.net/~bubolz/
Admission: No charge, donations accepted
Attendance: 45,000
Established: 1974
Membership: Y
Wheelchair Accessible: P
Parking: Free on site
Open: Tuesday to Friday, 8am-4:30pm; Saturday, 11am-4:30pm; Sunday, 12:30pm-4:30pm
Facilities: Garden (butterfly); Grounds (775 acres); Shop (books); Trails (8 miles);
Visitor Center (earth sheltered building)
Activities: Education Programs Maple Syrup Saturday (3rd Sat in March); Guided
Tours (group, by appointment, $2.00/person); Workshops (snowshoe building)

The preserve contains diverse habitats, including meadow, cedar swamp, forest, prairie, and pond.

CHIPPEWA FALLS

CITY OF CHIPPEWA FALLS—ROSE AND LILY GARDENS

Bridgewater Avenue & Jefferson Avenue (Route 124) (adjacent to Irvine Park),
Chippewa Falls, WI 54729
Tel: (715) 723-3890; Fax: (715) 720-6932
Facilities: Gardens (lily, rose)

Planned, planted, and maintained by volunteer efforts, the gardens are located next to
Irvine Park and across from Leinenkugel's Brewery. The rose garden contains over 500
bushes and the lily garden features more than 300 Asiatic, trumpet, and oriental lilies.

COON VALLEY

NORSKEDALEN NATURE AND HERITAGE CENTER

N455 Ophus Road, Coon Valley, WI 54623
Tel: (608) 452-3424; Fax: (608) 452-3157
Internet Address: http://www.norskedalen.org
Admission: Fee: adult $5.00, child $2.00, family$12.00
Attendance: 13,000
Established: 1977
Membership: Y
Wheelchair Accessible: P
Open: April 15 to October, Monday to Friday, 9am-4pm; Saturday, 10am-4pm;
Sunday, noon-4pm; New Year's Day to April 14, Monday to Friday, 10am-4pm;
Sunday, noon-4pm
Facilities: Arboretum; Architecture Bekkum Homestead (farmstead, ca. 1900),
Skumsrud Heritage Farm (4 nineteenth-century farmhouses, outbuildings, school);
Grounds (400 acres); Shop; Trails (5 miles); Visitor Center
Activities: Classes; Education Programs; Events; Guided Tours; Lectures; Self-guided
Tour (brochure available)

A nature and heritage center, Norskedalen includes the Helga Gundersen Arboretum.

EAGLE

WISCONSIN HISTORICAL SOCIETY— OLD WORLD WISCONSIN (OWW)

S103 W37890 Highway 67, Eagle, WI 53119
Tel: (262) 594-6300; Fax: (262) 594-6342
Internet Address: http://www.oldworldwisconsin.org

Admission: Fee: adult $14.00, child (5-12) $8.50, senior $12.80, family $39.50; Fee (June 6): $2.00.
Attendance: 80,000
Established: 1976
Membership: Y
Wheelchair Accessible: P
Parking: Free parking
Open: May to June, Monday to Friday, 10am-4pm; Saturday to Sunday, 10am-5pm; July to August, daily, 10am-5pm; September to October, Monday to Friday, 10am-4pm; Saturday to Sunday, 10am-5pm
Facilities: Architecture (65 historic buildings); Food Services Clausing Barn Restaurant; Gardens; Grounds (600 acres, gardens & working farms); Picnic Area; Shop; Visitor Center
Activities: Education Programs; Guided Tours

A living history museum focusing on immigrant farm and village life, Old World Wisconsin contains over sixty-five historic structures surrounded by fourteen heirloom gardens.

EAU CLAIRE

UNIVERSITY OF WISCONSIN-EAU CLAIRE—THE GREENHOUSES

Phillips Hall, 5th Floor, Eau Claire, WI 54702
Tel: (715) 836-3523
Internet Address: http://www.uwec.edu/biology
Admission: Fee (groups of 10-25): $10.00
Attendance: 1,000
Established: 1963
Membership: N
Wheelchair Accessible: P
Parking: Call UWEC Visitor Center
Open: Monday to Friday, 9am-3pm
Facilities: Greenhouses (3; 3,500 square feet); Herbarium
Activities: Guided Tours (arrange in advance)

One greenhouse is divided into two separate rooms housing, respectively, a tropical rain forest environment that includes many exotic and economic trees and a desert habitat with some cacti that are close to fifty years old and a twenty-five-year-old Date Palm Tree. A second greenhouse is devoted to department collections, including orchids, cacti, bromeliads (pineapple family), scented geraniums, and aquatic plants. The third greenhouse is utilized for class projects and research. The department also maintains an herbarium containing over 10,000 specimens, mostly from west-central Wisconsin.

GREEN BAY

GREEN BAY BOTANICAL GARDEN (AHS RAP)

2600 Larsen Road (behind NE Wisconsin Technical College), Green Bay, WI 54307
Tel: (920) 490-9457; Fax: (920) 490-9461

Internet Address: http://www.gbbg.org/
Admission: Fee: adult $5.00, child (<5) free, child
Membership: Y
Open: May to October, Daily, 9am-5pm; November to April, Monday to Friday,
9am-4pm
Facilities: Gardens (annual, butterfly, cottage, four seasons, herb, maze, native plant,
perennial, rose, woodland); Grounds (60 acres); Shop Trellis Gift Shop
Activities: Classes: Education Programs; Events Garden of Lights (late Nov-Dec 23;
Garden Walk (Jun); Plant Sales (Jun)

The gardens are designed to provide interest throughout the year. Displays include a
four seasons garden, woodland garden, contemporary formal rose garden, cottage garden,
new American perennial garden, and annual and herb exhibits.

UNIVERSITY OF WISCONSIN-GREEN BAY— COFRIN ARBORETUM AND CENTER FOR BIODIVERSITY (COFRIN ARBORETUM)

2420 Nicolet Drive, Green Bay, WI 54311-7001
Tel: (920) 465-4032
Internet Address: http://www.uwgb.edu/biodiversity/arboretum
Admission: Free
Attendance: 30,000
Established: 1975
Membership: N
Wheelchair Accessible: P
Parking: Three parking areas along Circle Drive
Open: 5am-11pm
Facilities: Grounds (290 acres); Trails 6 miles (through forest, grasslands, and restored
natural areas)

Encircling the campus, the arboretum preserves existing natural communities and displays examples of other habitats typical of the region. The center also includes an herbarium containing a collection of approximately 25,000 dried vascular plant specimens of
which over 90 percent are from Wisconsin and the Lenfestey Family Courtyard Gardens
(vegetables, butterfly, northern barrens, woodland, prairie, ferns).

HALES CORNERS

BOERNER BOTANICAL GARDENS

Whitnall Park, 9400 Boerner Drive, Hales Corners, WI 53130
Tel: (414) 525-5601; Fax: (414) 525-5610
Internet Address: http://www.countyparks.com/horticulture/
Admission: Fee: adult $4.00, child (6-17) $2.00, senior $3.00
Membership: Y
Wheelchair Accessible: P
Parking: On site
Open: Gardens (late Apr): If weather conditions are favorable; Gardens (May
to Oct): Daily, 8am-sunset; Gardens (early Nove) if weather conditions are
favorable

Best Time(s) of Year to Visit: June to September (rose), mid-May to early June (peonies), July (day lily)
Facilities: Arboretum; Garden House & Gift Shop (May-Dec, Mon-Sat, 10am-5pm; Sun, 10am-4pm; Oct-Apr, call for hours, 525-5653); Gardens (11; annual, bog, day lily walk, herb, peony, perennial borders, rock, rose, shrub mall, trial); Grounds Root River Parkway & Witnall Park (3,244 acres; design by landscape architect Alfred L. Boerner); Special Collections (crab apple, day lily, frisia, hosta, rose)
Activities: Education Programs (offered by Friends of Boerner Botanical Gardens); Guided Tours Garden Walks (offered by Friends of Boerner Botanical Gardens, 525-5653); Workshops (offered by Friends of Boerner Botanical Gardens)

Built on land acquired in the late 1920s, much of the original work at Boerner Park was accomplished by the Civilian Conservation Corps and later the Works Progress Administration during the Depression. Displays include an annual garden, showcasing annual plants that have done well in the controlled areas of the trial and test gardens; two perennial borders, containing many types of perennial flowers to ensure blooms from early spring through late fall; a formal rose garden, containing more than 3,000 plants representing approximately 350 varieties; an herb garden, composed of twelve beds containing over approximately 7,000 herb plants representing over 300 varieties; the Shrub Mall, inspired by English Country formal gardens and featuring tree peonies and bearded iris as well as shrubs; a woodland rock garden filled with native wildflowers and meandering trickles of water; a peony garden; a day lily walk; and a bog garden. Boerner Botanical Gardens also contains an All-America Rose Selections test garden, an All-America Selections flower display and test garden, and an All-America Selections vegetable display garden. Occupying over 1,000 acres in Whitnall Park and the adjoining Root River Parkway, the Boerner Botanical Gardens Arboretum contains an extensive collection of crab apples (1,000 trees representing approximately 250 species and varieties), a nut tree collection, over 250 lilac specimens, and displays of other reliable woody ornamental plants.

HANCOCK

HANCOCK AGRICULTURAL RESEARCH STATION—GARDENS

N3909 County Highway V (located near Interstate 39/Route 51),
Hancock, WI 54943-7547
Tel: (715) 249-5961; Fax: (715) 249-5850
Internet Address: http://www.cals.wisc.edu/research/stations/
research_stations06.html
Admission: Free
Attendance: 3,000
Membership: N
Wheelchair Accessible: P
Parking: Ample parking close to garden
Open: dawn-dusk
Best Time(s) of Year to Visit: July to September
Facilities: Gardens (flower, fruit, herb, perennial, shade, vegetable); Visitor Center.
Activities: Education Programs; Guided Tours (on request)

The A. R. Albert and Villetta Hawley-Albert Horticultural Garden showcases more than 750 varieties of fruits, flowers, and vegetables from more than two dozen seed companies. Specialty gardens include an All-America display garden, shade garden, herb garden, and grape collection.

JANESVILLE

ROTARY GARDENS, INC. (AHS RAP)

1455 Palmer Drive, Janesville, WI 53345
Tel: (608) 752-3885; Fax: (608) 752-3853
Internet Address: http://www.rotarygardens.org
Admission: Suggested contribution: adult $5.00, child $3.00
Attendance: 100,000
Established: 1989
Membership: Y
Wheelchair Accessible: Y
Parking: Free on site
Open: Grounds, daily, daylight hours; Visitors Center (January to March): Monday to Friday, 8:30am-4:30pm; Visitors Center (April): Monday to Friday, 8:30am-4:30pm; Saturday to Sunday, noon-4pm; Visitors Center (May to October): Monday to Friday, 8:30am-4:30pm; Saturday to Sunday, 10am-6pm; Visitors Center November to December: Monday to Friday, 8:30am-4:30pm; Saturday to Sunday, noon-4pm
Facilities: Arboretum; Gardens (alpine, color rooms, day lily, English cottage, fern/moss, formal French rose, hosta, formal Italian, herb, Japanese, North American perennial, prairie restoration, Scottish, shade, sunken, woodland walk); Grounds (15 acres); Shop: Cottage Garden Gifts; Visitor Center
Activities: Education Programs; Events Art in the Gardens (Nov), Bugs & Blossoms (mid-May), Harvest Fest (mid-Sept), Winter Wonderland Walk (Dec., Sat-Sun); Guided Tours (fee, $7.00/person)

Dedicated to international peace and friendship as signified by the twenty-foot sculpture at the garden entrance, Rotary Gardens feature a variety of international theme and specialty gardens. Self-described as "a community garden good enough to show the world," ground collections include over 3,000 woody plants representing 1,008 taxa, over 6,000 perennials representing 2,112 taxa, 350,000 bulbs representing 928 taxa, and 75,000 seasonal plantings representing 500 taxa.

KENOSHA

HAWTHORN HOLLOW NATURE SANCTUARY AND ARBORETUM

880 Green Bay Road (Route 31) (across from Petrifying Springs Park), Kenosha, WI 53144
Tel: (262) 552-8196
Admission: Voluntary contribution
Established: 1967
Membership: Y
Parking: Parking lot

Open: March to October, Tuesday to Sunday, 8am-5pm; December 1 to December 24, Tuesday to Sunday, 8am-4pm
Facilities: Arboretum (12 acres); Architecture (schoolhouse (1847); town hall (1859)); Gardens (perennials); Trails (2½ miles)
Activities: Guided Tours

A privately-owned nature sanctuary, the site includes an arboretum, 2½ miles of trails, historic buildings, gardens, and a prairie.

LA CROSSE

HIXON HOUSE—GARDENS

429 N. 7th Street, La Crosse, WI 54602-1272
Tel: (608) 782-1980; Fax: (608) 793-1359
Admission: Fee
Parking: On street
Open: Memorial Day to Labor Day, daily, 1pm-5pm
Facilities: Architecture (Italianate residence, 1859); Gardens (period; Victorian); Shop
Activities: Guided Tours (by guides in period costumes, last tour 4pm)

Built by lumber baron Gideon Hixon, the house contains the family's original nineteenth-century furnishings, including one of the few remaining "Turkish Nooks," and features several types of wood, many native to western Wisconsin. The grounds include restored nineteenth-century flower, shrub, and herb gardens. The site is listed on the National Register of Historic Places.

MADISON

OLBRICH BOTANICAL GARDENS (AHS RAP)

3330 Atwood Avenue at Monona Drive, Madison, WI 53704-5808
Tel: (608) 246-4550; Fax: (608) 246-4719; TDDY: (608) 267-4980
Internet Address: http://www.olbrich.org
Admission: Free (Gardens); Fee (Conservatory): adult $1.00, child (<6) free
Attendance: 250,000
Established: 1955
Membership: Y
Wheelchair Accessible: Y
Parking: Free on site
Open: Gardens (October to March): Daily, 9am-4pm; Gardens (April to September): Daily, 8am-8pm; Conservatory, Monday to Saturday, 10am-4pm; Sunday, 10am-5pm.
Closed: Thanksgiving Day, Christmas Day
Facilities: Botanical Center; Classrooms; Conservatory Bolz Tropical Conservatory (1991, 10,000 square feet, 50 feet high at center); Gardens (10; dahlia, herb, hosta, iris, perennial, rock, rose, shade, sunken, wildflower); Grounds (14 acres); Library Schumacher Library (1,000 volumes; daily, 10am-4pm; 246-5805); Shop
Activities: Classes/Workshops; Concerts; Education Program (children); Flower Shows; Guided Tours; Lectures

Located on the shore of Lake Monona, the Olbrich Botanical Gardens consist of outdoor display gardens and a tropical conservatory. Gardens include an herb garden, composed of a number of specialty gardens, including courtyard, knot, medicinal, dye, kitchen, and sensory gardens; a hosta garden, containing more than 140 hosta cultivars, an iris garden, offering more than 150 iris cultivars; a two-acre perennial garden, featuring mixed borders of colorful perennials, annuals, trees, and shrubs; a rock garden, simulating a dry, rocky mountain slope; a rose garden, containing more 650 plants representing 100 cultivars; a woodland wildflower garden, a shade garden, and a dahlia garden. The conservatory houses over 750 tropical and sub-tropical plants representing over 70 families and over 550 different species and cultivars. Olbrich Botanical Gardens is owned and operated by the city of Madison Parks Division with support from the non-profit Olbrich Botanical Society.

UNIVERSITY OF WISCONSIN-MADISON— ALLEN CENTENNIAL GARDENS

620 Babcock Drive at Observatory Drive, Madison, WI 53706
Tel: (608) 262-8406; Fax: (608) 262-4743
Internet Address: http://www.hort.wisc.edu/garden2001
Admission: Free
Established: 1989
Parking: Metered on street, very limited on weekdays
Open: Daily, dawn-dusk
Facilities: Gardens (acid, alpine, new American, arbor/vine, dwarf conifer, day lily, English, French, small fruit, ground cover, herb, hillside, iris, Italian, lawn, orchard, Japanese, rock, shade/sun, exotic shrub, terrace, vegetable, Victorian, water, wetland, woodland); Grounds (2½ acres)

Maintained by students and volunteers, the gardens serve as an outdoor classroom, offering research and training opportunities in plant identification and nomenclature as well as ecological and site management techniques. The gardens, centered around a stately Victorian gothic house listed on the National Register of Historic Places, feature an extraordinary diversity of plantings with major emphasis on herbaceous ornamental perennials, though the site also features many other plantings, including annuals and woody plants. Allen Centennial Gardens is a facility of the university's Department of Horticulture.

UNIVERSITY OF WISCONSIN-MADISON ARBORETUM

1207 Seminole Highway, Madison, WI 53711-3726
Tel: (608) 263-7888; Fax: (608) 262-5209
Internet Address: http://wiscinfo-nt.doit.wisc.edu/arboretum/
Admission: Voluntary contribution
Attendance: 650,000
Established: 1934
Membership: Y
Wheelchair Accessible: Y
Parking: Free on site
Open: Arboretum, Daily, 7am-10pm; Visitor Center (Jun to Aug):,
Monday to Friday, 9:30am-4pm; Saturday to Sunday, 11am-3pm; Visitor Center (September to May): Monday to Friday, 9:30am-4pm; Saturday to Sunday, 12:30pm-4pm

Facilities: Arboretum (forests, prairies, marshes); Classrooms (outdoor); Gardens (trees and shrubs); Greenhouses; Grounds Arboretum (1260 acres), Gardens (50 acres); Nurseries; Shop (bookstore); Visitor Center
Activities: Guided Tours

When the University of Wisconsin-Madison purchased the land where the arboretum is located, mostly during the 1930s, much of it bore little resemblance to its pre-settlement state. Instead, it had been turned into cultivated fields and pastures that had fallen into disuse. The university's arboretum committee decided to try to bring back the plants and animals that had lived on the land before its development. The arboretum is best known for this extensive collection of restored mature habitats, including prairies, oak savanna, woodlands, marshes, and ponds. In addition to these native plant and animal communities, the arboretum, like most arboreta, has traditional collections of labeled plants arranged in garden-like displays. Longenecker Gardens, located just north of the McKay Center, contains fifty acres of labeled ornamental trees and shrubs. The Viburnum Garden, just south of the intersection of Nakoma Road and Manitou Way, features more than 80 species and varieties of viburnums, and 110 species and varieties of thuja. The arboretum is a facility of the university's Department of Horticulture.

UNIVERSITY OF WISCONSIN-MADISON— BOTANY GREENHOUSE AND GARDEN

430 Lincoln Drive (adjacent to Birge Hall), Madison, WI 53706
Tel: (608) 262-2235
Internet Address: http://www.wisc.edu/botit/tour/
Admission: Free
Established: 2003
Wheelchair Accessible: Y
Open: Daily, 8am-4pm
Best Time(s) of Year to Visit: April to September
Facilities: Gardens (1.2 acres); Greenhouse (8,000 square feet)
Activities: Guided Tours (Mon/Wed, 1:30pm-3:30pm or Tues/Thurs, 9am-10:30am; 4 weeks in advance, max 15 persons)

Bounded by Chamberlain, Lathrop, and Birge Halls, the Botany Greenhouse is composed of eight rooms featuring more than 1,000 plant species displayed in distinct aquatic, desert, and tropical habitats. In addition to meeting essential teaching and research interests, the greenhouse is an aesthetic resource for students and the community. Renewed each spring, the Botanic Garden contains 400 different species from 90 different families of flowering plants displayed in taxonomic groups. The garden is the first in the world to be based on APGII Orders(Angiosperm Phylogeny Group System of Classification).

UNIVERSITY OF WISCONSIN-MADISON— D.C. SMITH GREENHOUSE

1575 Linden Drive, Madison, WI 53706
Tel: (608) 262-3844
Internet Address: http://www.hort.wisc.edu/Greenhouse/dcsmith.htm
Admission: Free
Established: 1996
Membership: N
Wheelchair Accessible: Y
Parking: Extremely limited, parking ramp 1 block away

Open: Monday to Friday, 8am-5pm
Best Time(s) of Year to Visit: Fall to Spring
Facilities: Greenhouse (10,000 square feet)
Activities: Guided Tours (arrange with manager in advance)

Consisting of ten growing bays, a high humidity propagation bay, and a 1,600 square foot conservatory, the greenhouse provides plant-growing space for the instructional needs of the departments and programs of the College of Agricultural and Life Sciences. While primarily used by students and faculty, the greenhouse also offers tours and is open to the public during regular university building hours.

MANITOWOC

WEST OF THE LAKE GARDENS

915 Memorial Drive, Manitowoc, WI 54220
Tel: (920) 684-8506
Admission: Free
Established: 1934
Membership: N
Wheelchair Accessible: P
Parking: Limited vehicle parking on site
Open: Daily, 10am-5pm
Best Time(s) of Year to Visit: mid-July
Facilities: Gardens (formal, Japanese, perennial border, rose, sunken); Grounds (6 acres)

Situated along Lake Michigan's shoreline, this formerly private estate features a rose garden, Japanese garden, sunken garden, formal garden, and more than 900 feet of herbaceous borders. The gardens are managed by the non-profit West Foundation, Inc.

MARINETTE

HARMONY ARBORETUM

½ mile S of Route 64 on County Road E, Marinette, WI 54143
Tel: (715) 732-7780; Fax: (715) 732-7532
Internet Address: http://www.uwex.edu/ces/cty/marinette/hort/mastergardener.html
Admission: Free
Membership: N
Wheelchair Accessible: Y
Parking: Free on site
Best Time(s) of Year to Visit: Mid-June to September
Facilities: Arboretum; Gardens (fruit, herb, perennial, shade, vegetable); Grounds Arboretum (417 acres), Demonstration Garden (2 acres), Prairie (17 ½ acres); Picnic Area; Trails
Activities: Demonstrations; Education Programs Master Gardeners (on site Tues evening); Events Harvest Festival (Fall); Plant Sales

Formerly a working farm, Harmony Arboretum includes a 100-acre hardwood forest, restored prairie planted with native grasses and flowers, pine plantation, winding walking trails, agricultural fields, and vegetable and flower demonstration gardens. Maintained by the Northern Lights Master Gardeners Association, the demonstration gardens include a formal herb garden with over 100 different herbs; 35 raised vegetable beds; tree fruits and grapes; perennial beds; a phenology garden; an All-American Selections winners display; a shade house; and other horticultural demonstration areas. Although the Marinette County Land and Water Conservation Division manages the site to provide wildlife habitat, recreation, and environmental education opportunities, decisions are made in consultation with the Friends of Harmony Farms, Northern Lights Master Gardeners Association, Chappee Rapids Audubon Society, and the University of Wisconsin Extension of Marinette County.

MARSHFIELD

FOXFIRE GARDENS

M220 Sugarbush Lane (3 miles N of Marshfield on County Trunk E),
Marshfield, WI 54449
Tel: (715) 387-3050
Internet Address: http://foxfiregardens.com
Admission: Free
Established: 1985
Wheelchair Accessible: P
Open: Mother's Day to September, daily, 10am-5pm
Facilities: Garden (oriental-inspired, three waterfalls, teahouse, 800 varieties of hosta);
Grounds (7 acres); Shop (hosta)
Activities: Guided Tours (10+, contact in advance, fee)

Foxfire Gardens offers landscaped gardens inspired by both eastern and western naturalistic planting philosophies. Collections include over 800 varieties of hostas.

MILWAUKEE

MITCHELL PARK HORTICULTURAL CONSERVATORY (THE DOMES)

Chicago Park District—Lincoln Park Conservatory and Gardens, Chicago, IL.

524 S. Layton Boulevard, Milwaukee, WI 53215-1295
Tel: (414) 649-9800; Fax: (414) 649-8616
Internet Address: http://www.countyparks.com/horticulture/
Admission: Fee: adult $4.50, child (<6) free, child (6-17) $3.00, senior $3.00; Group discounts available.
Attendance: 200,000
Established: 1959
Membership: Y
Wheelchair Accessible: Y
Parking: Free on site
Open: Daily, 9am-5pm
Facilities: Library (250 volume); Museum Shop; Three Domes (45,000 square feet, 1959-1967 design by architect Donald Grieb)

Activities: Classes/Workshops; Concerts; Flower Shows (5/year); Ikebana (Oct); Guided Tours; Self-Guided Tours (brochure available)

The conservatory is composed of three beehive-shaped glass domes, each having a distinct climate and exhibition program. The Arid Dome features an extensive collection of succulents and water conserving trees, shrubs, and bulbs displayed in naturalistic settings. Plants are grouped by geographic region and include collections from Madagascar, southern Africa, eastern Africa, the Canary Islands, South America, and North America. The Tropical Dome houses a rain forest containing over 1,200 species of both economic and ornamental tropical plants as well as birds and iguanas. The Show Dome offers changing exhibits based on historical, cultural, or aesthetic themes. Shows typically run for six to fourteen weeks with successive replantings of displays during longer events.

OSHKOSH

THE PAINE ART CENTER AND ARBORETUM

1410 Algoma Boulevard (intersection of Highways. 21 and 110),
Oshkosh, WI 54901-7708
Tel: (920) 235-6903; Fax: (920) 235-6303
Internet Address: http://Focol.org/~paineart
Admission: Fee: adult $6.00, child (5-12) $3.00, student $4.00, senior $5.00, family $15.00; Garden admission free October—April
Attendance: 36,000
Established: 1947
Membership: Y
Wheelchair Accessible: Y
Parking: On street or in lot at corner of Congress and Elmwood
Open: Labor Day to Memorial Day, Tuesday to Friday, 11am-4pm; Saturday to Sunday, 11am-4pm; Memorial Day to Labor Day, Tuesday to Thursday, 11am-4pm; Friday, 11am-7pm; Saturday to Sunday, 11am-4pm
Closed: Legal holidays
Facilities: Arboretum; Architecture (Tudor Revival house, 1920 design by Bryant Fleming); Classrooms/Studios; Gardens (formal English, native plant, rose); Library (5,000 volumes, art and horticultural research); Museum Store; Reading Room; Sales Gallery; Sculpture Garden
Activities: Concerts; Docent Program; Education Program (adults and children); Films; Guided Tours (reserve two weeks in advance); Lectures; Temporary/Traveling Exhibitions

Designed as a residence for Oshkosh lumber baron Nathan Paine, but never occupied, the building and its contents were donated as an art center. In the main gallery on the first floor, the museum exhibits works from its permanent collection as well as frequently changing temporary exhibitions. Three other galleries, displaying specialized collections, are located on the upper and lower levels. The gardens draw upon the heritage of English landscape design and gardening with the Formal Garden emulating the Pond Garden at Hampton Court, England. The newly planted Rose Garden boasts over 100 varieties of roses reflected in a shimmering pool. Plantings include both native Wisconsin plants and trees and non-native specimens. The center hosts horticultural lectures, demonstrations, and classes throughout the year as well as Arbor Day festivities and semiannual plant sales.

RICE LAKE

UNIVERSITY OF WISCONSIN-BARRON COUNTY—
JAPANESE FRIENDSHIP GARDEN (YUUJOU NIWA)

1800 College Drive (adjacent to the library), Rice Lake, WI 54868-2497
Tel: (715) 234-8176 *Ext:* 5423
Admission: Free
Established: 1998
Membership: Y
Wheelchair Accessible: N
Parking: On campus, in summer free
Open: Daily, 24 hours
Best Time(s) of Year to Visit: May to September
Facilities: Garden (Japanese); Grounds (1,400 square feet)
Activities: Guided Tours (schedule in advance, jrankin@uwc.edu); Self-guided Tour
(brochure available at site)

In commemoration of ten years as sister cities, Miharu, Japan, sent three master gardeners to Rice Lake to help build a Japanese garden. Located on the campus of the University
of Wisconsin-Barron County, the garden contains over 200 plants and trees in a naturalistic setting surrounded by a bamboo fence. The garden is maintained by the Rice Lake International Friendship Association.

WAUWATOSA

WAUWATOSA HISTORICAL SOCIETY—KNEELAND-WALKER
HOUSE AND VICTORIAN GARDENS

7406 Hillcrest Drive, Wauwatosa, WI 53213-2226
Tel: (414) 774-8672; Fax: (414) 774-3064
Internet Address: http://www.wauwatosahistoricalsociety.org/
Admission: No charge, donations accepted
Established: 1987
Membership: Y
Parking: On-street parking
Facilities: Architecture (Queen Ann residence); Gardens
(period; Victorian); Grounds (1½ acres)

Headquarters of the Wauwatosa Historical Society, the property features native plants,
cultivated stock, and annuals and perennials of special significance to the region and, with
its profusion of annuals, in the spirit of a Victorian garden.

APPENDIX
COMMERCIAL NURSERIES
WITH DISPLAY GARDENS

Connecticut

Columbia

Gazebo Gardens - Display Gardens
54 Hennequin Road, Columbia, CT 06237
Tel: (860) 228-0244

Internet Address:
http://www.members.aol.com/gazebog/
gazebens.htm

Hamden

Broken Arrow Nurseries
13 Broken Arrow Road, Hamden,
CT 06518
Tel: (203) 288-1026
Fax: (203) 287-1035

Internet Address:
http://www.brokenarrownursery.com

Litchfield

White Flower Farm - Display Gardens
19 Esther's Road (off Route 63), Litchfield,
CT 06759
Tel: (800) 503-9624
Internet Address:
http://www.whiteflowerfarm.com/

Monroe

Twombly Nursery
163 Barn Hill Road (off Route 110), Monroe, CT 06468

Tel: (203) 261-2133
Fax: (203) 261-9230
Internet Address:
http://www.twomblynursery.com

North Coventry

Caprilands Herb Farm
534 Silver Street, North Coventry, CT
06238
Tel: (860) 742-7244
Fax: (860) 742-7806

Internet Address:
http://www.caprilands.com

Thomaston

Cricket Hill Garden - Display Garden
670 Walnut Hill Road, Thomaston,
CT 06787
Tel: (860) 283-1042

Internet Address:
http://www.treepeony.com/

Illinois

Altamont

Alwerdt's Gardens
Route 128, 1 mile south of Route I-70,
Altamont, IL 62411
Tel: (618) 483-5798

Internet Address:
http://www.altamontil.net/alwerdt.htm

Decatur
Mari-Mann Herb Farm - Display Garden
St. Louis Bridge Road (north end),
    Decatur, IL 62521-9404
Tel: (217) 429-1404

Paris
Barkley Farms Nurseries - Display Beds
11200 East 1300th Road, Paris, IL 61944
Tel: (217) 463-7003
Fax: (217) 466-4040
Internet Address:
    http://www.barkelyfarms.com

Princeton
Hornbaker Gardens
22937 1140 North Avenue, Princeton,
    IL 61356
Tel: (815) 659-3282
Fax: (815) 659-3159
Internet Address:
    http://www.hornbakergardens.com

Indiana
Brazil
Dogwood Farms - Display Gardens
500 South 1000 East (between Routes 720
    S and 325 S), Brazil, IN 47834
Tel: (765) 344-0103
Fax: (765) 344-0133
Internet Address:
    http://www.hostagarden.com

Hartford City
Carolee's Herb Farm and Garden
3305 South County Road 100 West,
    Hartford City, IN 47348
Tel: (765) 348-3162
Internet Address:
    http://www.caroleesherbfarm.com

Shipshewana
Greenfield Herb Garden
310 Harrison St., Shipshewana, IN 46565
Tel: (800) 831-0504

Maine
Albion
Johnny's Selected Seeds - Trial Gardens
184 Foss Hill Road, Albion, ME 04910

Tel: (207) 437-9294
Internet Address:
    http://www.johnnyseeds.com

Sumner
Hedgehog Hill Farm
54 Hedgehog Hill Road, Sumner,
    ME 04292
Tel: (207) 388-2341
Internet Address:
    http://hedgehoghillfarm.com

Maryland
Buckeystown
Lilypons Water Gardens
6800 Lilypons Road, Buckeystown,
    MD 21717
Tel: (800) 999-5459
Fax: (301) 879-5459
Internet Address:
    http://www.lilypons.com

Middletown
Surreybrooke - Display Gardens
8537 Hollow Road, Middletown,
    MD 21769
Tel: (301) 371-7466
Internet Address:
    http://www.surreybrooke.com/

Michigan
Holland
Veldheer Tulip Garden
12755 Quincy Street, Holland, MI 49424
Tel: (616) 399-1900

Suttons Bay
Busha's Brae Herb Farm
2540 N. Setterbo Road (off State
    Route 22), Suttons Bay, MI 49682
Tel: (231) 271-6284
Internet Address:
    http://www.greatlakesherbs.com/bushas/

New Hampshire
Mason
Pickity Place
248 Nutting Hill Road, Mason,
    NH 03048
Tel: (603) 878-1151

Internet Address:
http://www.pickityplace.com/

New Jersey

Port Murray
Well-Sweep Herb Farm - Display Garden
205 Mt. Bethel Road, Port Murray, NJ 07865
Tel: (908) 852-5390
Internet Address:
http://www.wellsweep.com

North Carolina

Chapel Hill
Niche Gardens
1111 Dawson Road, Chapel Hill, NC 27516
Tel: (919) 967-0078
Fax: (919) 967-4026
Internet Address:
http://www.nichegdn.com/

Durham
Witherspoon Rose Culture - Display Gardens
3312 Watkins Road, Durham, NC 27707
Tel: (919) 489-4446
Fax: (919) 490-0623
Internet Address:
http://www.witherspoonrose.com/

Kings Mountain
Iron Gate Gardens - Display Gardens
2271 County Line Road (Route 216) (between Kings Mountain and Cherryville), Kings Mountain, NC 28086
Tel: (704) 435-6187
Fax: (704) 435-4367
Internet Address:
http://www.irongategardens.com

Raleigh
Plant Delights Nursery - Juniper Level Botanical Gardens
9241 Sauls Road (between Panther Branch and Willow Springs), Raleigh, NC 27603
Tel: (919) 772-4794
Fax: (919) 662-0370
Internet Address:
http://www.plantdelights.com/

Ohio

Bellville
Wade and Gatton Nursery
1288 Gatton Rocks Road (just off Route 97), Bellville, OH 44813
Tel: (419) 883-3191
Internet Address: http://www.pal-metto.com/hosta/wade/wade.html

Mount Pleasant
The Gardens at Sunnyside - Display Gardens
24 Union Street, Mount Pleasant, OH 43939
Tel: (740) 769-7675
Fax: (801) 838-0402
Internet Address:
http://www.gardensatsunnyside.com

Newark
Wilson's Garden Center - Display Garden
10923 Lambs Lane, Newark, OH 43055
Tel: (877) 389-6295
Fax: (740) 763-2874
Internet Address:
http://www.great-gardeners.com

Pennsylvania

Meadowbrook
Meadowbrook Farm
1633 Washington Lane (adjacent to commercial nursery), Meadowbrook, PA 19046
Tel: (215) 887-5900

South Carolina

Blythewood
Singing Oaks Garden - Display Garden
1019 Abell Road, Blythewood, SC 29016
Tel: (803) 786-1351

Georgetown
Brown's Ferry Gardens - Display Gardens
13515 Brown's Ferry Road, Georgetown, SC 29440
Tel: (803) 546-3559
Fax: (803) 546-0318
Internet Address:
http://www.brownsferrygardens.com/

Roycroft Daylily Nursery -
Display Gardens
942 White Hall Avenue, Georgetown,
SC 29440
Tel: (843) 527-1533
Fax: (843) 546-2281
Internet Address:
http://roycroftdaylilies.com/map.cfm

Greenwood
Park Seed Company - Gardens
1 Parkton Avenue, Greenwood, SC 29647
Tel: (800) 213-0076
Internet Address:
http://www.parkseed.com

Vermont
Bristol
Rocky Dale Gardens - Display Gardens
806 Rocky Dale Road (Route 116), Bristol,
VT 05443
Tel: (802) 453-2782
Fax: (802) 453-2462
Internet Address:
http://www.rockydalegardens.com

Granville
Little Siberia Perennials - Display Gardens
966 Maston Hill Road (off Route 100),
Granville, VT 05747
Tel: (802) 767-3391
Internet Address:
http://www.littlesiberia.com

Manchester
Equinox Valley Nursery - Display Gardens
Route 7A, Manchester, VT 05254
Tel: (802) 362-2610
Fax: (802) 362-2652

Internet Address:
http://www.equinoxvalleynursery.com

South Newfane
Olallie Daylily Gardens
129 Augur Hole Road, South Newfane,
VT 05351
Tel: (802) 348-6614
Fax: (802) 348-9881
Internet Address:
http://www.daylilygarden.com

Virginia
Fisherville
André Viette Farm and Nursery -
Display Gardens
Long Meadow Road (Route 608),
Fisherville, VA 22939
Tel: (543) 943-2315
Fax: (543) 943-0782
Internet Address:
http://www.viette.com

Gainesville
Nicholls Gardens - Display Garden
4724 Angus Drive, Gainesville,
VA 20155-1217
Tel: (800) 575-5538
Internet Address:
http://www.nichollsgardens.com

Raphine
Buffalo Springs Herb Farm -
Display Garden
7 Kennedy-Wade's Mill Loop, Raphine,
VA 24472
Tel: (540) 348-1083
Internet Address:
http://www.buffaloherbs.com/

INDEX

Hay, John, National Wildlife Refuge—The Fells (Newbury, NH), 206
Hayes Arboretum (Richmond, IN), 118
Heathcote Botanical Gardens, Inc. (Fort Pierce, FL), 53
Helen Avalynne Tawes Garden (Annapolis, MD), 145
Henry C. Bowen House-Roseland Cottage (Woodstock, CT), 30
Henry Clay Estate—Ashland—Gardens (Lexington, KY), 127
Henry Ford Estate: Fair Lane—Gardens (Dearborn, MI), 185
Henry Foundation for Botanical Research (Gladwyne, PA), 336
Henry S. Chatfield Memorial Garden—Warinanco Park (Roselle, NJ), 226
Henry Schmieder Arboretum—Delaware Valley College (Doylestown, PA), 333
Henry Timrod Park—City of Florence (Florence, SC), 365
Hepler, Jesse, Lilac Arboretum—University of New Hampshire (Durham, NH), 205
herb gardens, 2, 3, 4, 5, 6, 7, 8, 9, 10, 11, 15, 16, 17, 18, 20, 23, 24, 28, 34, 37, 40, 45, 53, 54, 55, 57, 58, 59, 61, 62, 66, 72, 73, 80, 82, 83, 91, 93, 100, 101, 106, 111, 112, 125, 126, 128, 129, 134, 137, 140, 150, 151, 161, 166, 167, 169, 170, 173, 175, 179, 182, 184, 187, 188, 192, 193, 199, 201, 204, 205, 212, 213, 216, 217, 218, 219, 222, 226, 227, 230, 235, 241, 242, 243, 246, 247, 252, 253, 254, 255, 256, 261, 263, 264, 270, 273, 274, 276, 283, 284, 286, 293, 295, 296, 299, 301, 306, 310, 311, 312, 315, 316, 317, 318, 319, 320, 323, 325, 326, 329, 333, 334, 337, 339, 341, 345, 346, 361, 365, 369, 372, 375, 376, 377, 382, 386, 388, 389, 391, 393, 394, 400, 402, 404, 405, 407, 408, 409, 410, 415, 420, 421, 422, 423, 424, 425, 427
Herb Society of America—Headquarters Demonstration Garden (Kirtland, OH), 318
Hereford Lighthouse Gardens (North Wildwood, NJ), 222
Hermitage: Home of Andrew Jackson—Gardens (Hermitage, TN), 373
Hershey Gardens (Hershey, PA), 337
Hezekiah Alexander Homesite—Garden—Charlotte Museum of History (Charlotte, NC), 284

Hidden Lake Gardens—Michigan State University (Tipton, MI), 195
Highland Park and Lamberton Conservatory—Monroe County Arboretum (Rochester, NY), 270
Highlands Historic Mansion and Garden (Fort Washington, PA), 336
Highstead Arboretum (Redding, CT), 23
Hildene—Gardens (Manchester, VT), 380
Hill, Chance, 125
Hill-Stead Museum (Farmington, CT), 16
Hills and Dales Estate (LaGrange, GA), 79
Hillsdale College—Slayton Arboretum (Hillsdale, MI), 190
Hilltop Garden and Nature Center—Indiana University (Bloomington, IN), 111
Hillwood Museum and Gardens (Washington, DC), 41
Historic Bok Sanctuary (Lake Wales, FL), 56
Historic Fallsington, Inc. (Fallsington, PA), 335
Historic London Town and Gardens (Edgewater, MD), 149
Historic Oliver Gardens and Copshaholm House Museum (South Bend, IN), 119
Historic Prattville and Gardens (Prattville, AL), 9
Historic Rosedale Plantation—Gardens (Charlotte, NC), 284
Historic Spanish Point/Gulf Coast Heritage Association, Inc. (Osprey, FL), 60
Historical Society of Talbot County Gardens (Easton, MD), 148
Hixon House—Gardens (La Crosse, WI), 424
HMA (Huntington, WV), 414
Hobhouse, Penelope, 188
Hofstra University Arboretum (Hempstead, NY), 244
Holden Arboretum (Kirtland, OH), 318
Holmdel Arboretum (Freehold, NJ), 214
Hopkins, Alden, 389, 390, 393, 395, 405, 409
Horticulture Center (Philadelphia, PA), 343
HSV (Pittsfield, MA), 170
Hubbard Park—City of Meriden (Meriden, CT), 19
Humes, John P., Japanese Stroll Garden (Mill Neck, NY), 250
hummingbird gardens. *See* butterfly/hummingbird gardens